Flying Solo

A Survival Guide for the Solo and Small Firm Lawyer

Fourth Edition

Editor
K. William Gibson

Contributing Editors
Reid F. Trautz
Joel P. Bennett
Larry Bodine
Joan R. Bullock
Diane M. Ellis
Storm M. Evans
Dennis Kennedy
Neal A. Kennedy
Carol A. Seelig
Jerry R. Sullenberger

ABA LawPracticeManagementSection
MARKETING • MANAGEMENT • TECHNOLOGY • FINANCE

Commitment to Quality: The Law Practice Management Section is committed to quality in our publications. Our authors are experienced practitioners in their fields. Prior to publication, the contents of all our books are rigorously reviewed by experts to ensure the highest quality product and presentation. Because we are committed to serving our readers' needs, we welcome your feedback on how we can improve future editions of this book.

Cover design by Kelly Book, ABA Publishing.

ABA Model Rules of Professional Conduct reprinted from Model Rules of Professional Conduct, 2004 Edition, *published by the Center for Professional Responsibility, American Bar Association, 2004. Reprinted with permission. Copies of ABA* Model Rules of Professional Conduct 2004 *are available from Service Center, American Bar Association, 321 N. Clark Street, Chicago, IL 60610, 1-800-285-2221.*

Nothing contained in this book is to be considered as the rendering of legal advice for specific cases, and readers are responsible for obtaining such advice from their own legal counsel. This book and any forms and agreements herein are intended for educational and informational purposes only.

The products and services mentioned in this publication are under or may be under trademark or service mark protection. Product and service names and terms are used throughout only in an editorial fashion, to the benefit of the product manufacturer or service provider, with no intention of infringement. Use of a product or service name or term in this publication should not be regarded as affecting the validity of any trademark or service mark.

The Law Practice Management Section of the American Bar Association offers an educational program for lawyers in practice. Books and other materials are published in furtherance of that program. Authors and editors of publications may express their own legal interpretations and opinions, which are not necessarily those of either the American Bar Association or the Law Practice Management Section unless adopted pursuant to the bylaws of the Association. The opinions expressed do not reflect in any way a position of the Section or the American Bar Association.

Printed in the United States of America.

Library of Congress Cataloging-in-Publication Data
Flying Solo: A Survival Guide for the Solo and Small Firm Lawyer, Fourth Edition. K. William Gibson, Editor. Library of Congress Cataloging-in-Publication Data is on file.

ISBN 1-59031-480-8

09 08 07 06 05   5 4 3 2 1

Discounts are available for books ordered in bulk. Special consideration is given to state bars, CLE programs, and other bar-related organizations. Inquire at Book Publishing, American Bar Association, 321 N. Clark Street, Chicago, Illinois 60610.

Contents

Acknowledgments

Credit for the success of the three earlier editions of this book belongs to the writers who were generous enough to share their wisdom, insight, advice, and even their warnings to aspiring sole practitioners. Likewise, credit for the success of this Fourth Edition of *Flying Solo* belongs to the forty-plus lawyers, legal administrators, legal consultants, law professors, and others who dropped what they were doing to answer the call when we asked them to distill their years of experience in law practice management into a few pages of easy-to-read prose.

Some of the authors in the book are new to *Flying Solo*, while others have written for some or all of the previous editions. To the authors who reprised their chapters from *Flying Solo* 1e, 2e, or 3e, we offer our special thanks because of your willingness to take what was good and make it better, fresher, and more helpful to your audience. To the authors who came new to the *Flying Solo* experience, we are grateful as well. Your combined contributions make this book an essential part of any solo practitioner's library.

The Contributing Editors were responsible for making sure that deadlines were met, standards were observed, and copy was accurate. Our special thanks goes out to Neal Kennedy, Joan Bullock, Carol Seelig, Jerry Sullenberger, Diane Ellis, Storm Evans, Dennis Kennedy, Larry Bodine, and Joel Bennett for doing such a great job. I want to extend a special thank you to Professor Gary Munneke, former LPM Section Chair, for contributing two excellent chapters and also for helping to insure that we were giving correct and appropriate advice in several areas.

Thanks, as well, to Tim Johnson and Neal Cox of LPM Publishing for their enormous contributions.

Reid Trautz, Chair of the Law Practice Management Section Publishing Board and Director of the District of Columbia Bar Lawyer Practice Assistance

Program, provided oversight and supervision and smoothed out a few wrinkles (and wrinkled feathers) along the way. We couldn't have done it without his leadership.

If too many cooks do indeed "spoil the broth," as the old saying goes, Beverly Loder of LPM Publishing proved herself to be the Master Chef. This was a project with more than a few cooks, yet the resulting soup turned out to be delicious. Bev always knew how to get things done and how to get things done right. Her good judgment and calm temperament were especially welcome as the project came to a hurried close and everything had to get finished at the same time. Thanks, Bev.

Finally, my thanks to my wife, Mary, for all her kind support and for not saying too much when the dining table was covered with paper for what must have seemed like months at a time. It was the only way I could think of to keep track of all 57 chapters.

—Bill Gibson, Editor

Pre-Flight Manual

I wouldn't think of getting in my plane and taxiing to the runway without doing my pre-flight planning. Before I start the engine on my Cessna, I always spend time thinking about where I want to go, which route to take, how long it will take to get there, and how much fuel I'll need to arrive safely. And, I always check the weather because it may be clear and sunny at the airport, but rainy and windy at my destination.

It is no different when you are planning to open a new solo law practice or to expand an existing practice. The amount of planning that you do before you open the doors and take on your first case is critical. It's as simple as this: The more planning you do, the more prepared you will be.

In this first part of *Flying Solo*, the authors consider a wide range of issues, beginning with the personal considerations involved in working for yourself and leaving your existing firm, for those of you already practicing. You'll also learn about the importance of creating a business plan up front. Subsequent chapters offer advice on selecting the type of practice that best suits your skills, abilities, and lifestyle. If you are thinking of specializing, Part I will help you make that all-important decision.

No amount of pre-flight planning will guarantee that you won't encounter a little turbulence from time to time, whether in the air or in your solo practice, but it will prepare you to deal with any situation that comes up during your flight.

Is Solo Practice for You?

Are You Cut Out for Solo Practice?

1

K. William Gibson

Nearly twenty years ago my then-law partner had just left our two-person firm to take a political job with our city's newly elected mayor. My partner and I had been practicing together for five years when he decided to leave. After two weeks on his new job, he called me to say that he had come into the office that morning to find a paycheck in his desk drawer. "I just showed up every day for the last two weeks and they gave me money. What a concept!" he exclaimed. We discussed how different that was from the way it worked in our small law office, where just "showing up" didn't guarantee that you would get paid. Life in the small law office is very different than life elsewhere and getting a regular paycheck is just one of the differences.

After I hung up from that phone call, I was envious for a few brief minutes, but then I realized that whether I got a regular paycheck every two weeks or had to fight for every draw, I wouldn't trade places with my former partner in his new job, or with any lawyer who worked for a regular paycheck in law firm, government, or business. I realized that I liked practicing law in a small office, and that getting regular paychecks was a secondary consideration. What's more, the paychecks did start coming regularly, and after that happened I never had a second thought about choosing to become a solo.

In the twenty-five years that I have been a lawyer, I have mostly practiced alone or with a single partner. I have been a solo this time for about five years. I am now working mostly as an arbitrator and mediator in personal injury litigation. In that line of work, I meet a lot of lawyers, both plaintiff and defense. They come from big firms—usually the defense lawyers—as well as from small firms—usually the plaintiffs' lawyers. I know a number of small firm lawyers (and even solos) who do insurance defense, but the largest plaintiff's firm in my state has fewer than a dozen lawyers.

It's easy to generalize, but I think that both my small-firm and large-firm colleagues would agree that life is different when you are out there on your own, regardless of what kind of law you practice. Small-firm lawyers, including solos, have a lot in common. Lawyers who work in larger firms have a lot in common. What these lawyers all have in common is not the kind of law that they practice, but the way they practice law. What they have in common is the way that their practices get managed. What they have in common is a similar level of support in running their offices. From a solo's perspective, it appears that large firms have an abundance of management resources, while solos have a scarcity of resources. With a little creativity and flexibility, however, an enterprising sole practitioner can turn what looks like a negative into something positive.

An example of the differences between large and small firms would be in the ways that a large-firm lawyer and a sole practitioner handle a lawsuit. If you were to watch two experienced lawyers—one a solo and the other from a large firm—try a case against each other, you probably could not tell which was which. Both would know the law and each would be proficient at putting on a persuasive and effective case. The difference between the two would, instead, be in what was going on behind the scenes, outside of the courtroom.

Both lawyers would prepare documents for the judge—everything from trial memoranda to jury instructions to motions for a directed verdict—but in the case of the big-firm lawyer, those documents would probably be coordinated and prepared by a supporting staff of legal secretaries, paralegals, and junior lawyers working as many hours as needed to get the job done. Those documents probably would be prepared well in advance of the deadline for submitting them to the court. In the case of the equally skilled solo, there may be only one person back at the office to work on those documents, and that person may not be able to handle everything that the lawyer needs. (For some solos, there may not be anyone back at the office.) That means, in all likelihood, that the sole practitioner would create his or her own trial documents—some may actually create and print the documents from start to finish, while others might have the luxury of instructing someone back at the office on how to do it. But, in either case, the solo's way of getting the documents done would be far different from—and more personally laborious than—what the large-firm adversary would have to do to generate the same documents.

This difference between large firms and small firms holds true for everything—from interviewing and subpoenaing witnesses to preparing trial graphics and scheduling experts. And as far as the sole practitioner getting everything done well in advance of deadlines… let's just say that it is far less likely to happen than in the large firm. Most solos spend their careers scrambling to meet deadlines

So, why would a lawyer choose to work where he has to do everything himself? Why would a lawyer not want to join a large law firm, where there are people whose job it is to do the clerical and financial work so that the lawyer can focus upon practicing law? Why would a lawyer prefer to be isolated in a small office when she could enjoy the support and collegiality of a larger group?

The answer may have as much to do with personality and temperament as with anything else. The answer may be that some people choose to forego the amenities and conveniences of a large organization simply because they do not want to work in a large organization. It may be because they prefer the independence that goes with working alone or as part of a very small group. For the solo lawyer, that independence involves being able to chart one's course without having to seek the advice or consent of superiors, peers, or subordinates. It may be as simple as needing to be in charge.

Independence may have to do with being able to come and go as one pleases without being accountable to a boss. The solo who leaves work early to coach soccer, to go for a run, or even to go home and take a nap must answer only to himself or herself. All of this independence and lack of day-to-day accountability means that a successful solo will need to develop good work habits and a strong work ethic.

The good news is that the smart solo can have the best of everything, in my opinion. He or she can have independence and freedom and still make a good living. The key is to recognize that you are walking alone on a tightrope and that you need to have a safety net to keep you from getting hurt when you slip or fall. Your safety net can take the form of dedicated employees, trusted colleagues, and a concerned spouse. Your safety net can include routines, systems, policies, and procedures. Your safety net can include a self-evaluation of your strengths and weaknesses. It can be something as simple as not getting overextended with litigation that will take all your limited resources for an extended period of time.

If you are to be successful, you will need to learn to delegate. You will need to develop good time management skills. You will need to learn when to ask for help in getting your work done.

The truth is that if you plan to practice alone for the next twenty-five years, as I have done for the past twenty-five years, you will need to make sure that things go right more often than they go wrong

Learning to practice law as a solo involves skills that need to be learned. No one is born with these skills and few law schools teach them. This book has good advice from successful professionals who have either learned to practice law as a solo or who have taught those skills to sole practitioners.

Life After the Law Firm: Personal Considerations in Going Solo

2

Diana M. Savit

An oft-repeated cliché admonishes us that no one ever died saying "I wish I'd spent more time at the office." In the long run, we tend to reflect most proudly, happily, or wistfully on what we do in our "off" hours with our friends and relatives, rather than on the many hours spent sifting through boxes of financial or medical records in pursuit of an advantage for a client—professionally beneficial though that may be. Your challenge as a solo is not to sacrifice those "real life" rewards and experiences for what can be an all-consuming work obligation. It isn't easy, but it can be done.

The decision to go solo involves much more than an assessment of your lawyering skills and your talent for developing business, although any analysis of life as a solo practitioner must begin there. Practicing law on your own forces you to become more self-reliant than in any other practice arrangement, and can limit your availability to others. Contemplating the solo experience requires consideration of the perhaps unanticipated ways in which your choice of business organization can affect your life in the "real world."

A solo practitioner is not only a lawyer, but also the sole proprietor of a small business. The solo wears many hats: administrator, rainmaker, workhorse, and chief financial officer, to name a few. Each of these can be a full-time job in itself, and a crisis in one area inevitably robs you of time to tend to equally important tasks in another. Add to that the need for a personal life—particularly if that personal life involves the unpredictable needs, joys, and crises of a family—and, well, that's a lot on anyone's plate.

It can all be balanced, but it requires sacrifices and self-awareness. First, recognize that law practice in general—and solo practice in particular—will, if you let it, occupy all of your waking hours (and a good many of your somnolent ones as well). Ultimately, allowing any one activity to displace everything else to which you could devote your time makes for neither a very satisfying existence nor a particularly good lawyer. So, make time for other things. This leads, however, to a second realization: Carving out a life outside the office can mean that your practice may not meet one commonly held definition of success—larger financial rewards may be sacrificed to the intangible pleasures and obligations of life. If you make sure to take annual vacations, attend your children's school plays and sporting events, exercise daily, socialize with friends, perform volunteer work or bar service, enjoy some cultural outings, and even spend time with your spouse or significant other, that time will not be devoted to billing or collecting fees. Therefore, your practice will not earn its theoretical maximum income. Does it need to? If you have no life, what will you spend all that money on?

On the other hand, solo practice inevitably includes canceled appointments and missed opportunities in your personal life. If a client needs a temporary restraining order, you must forego your box seats at the opera that night while you stay late in the office drafting papers because there is no one else to do the work for you. Every day off means that no one is minding the store, so you will think long and hard before taking a vacation of any length or traveling to inaccessible locales. You will find yourself showing up late for children's birthday parties and dinners with friends, or carrying a file folder of work with you to PTA meetings. The lack of depth in your office which forces you to cover every matter, large or small, by yourself, can be draining. No matter how much you may wish it were otherwise, each day has only twenty-four hours, each week only seven days, and only so much can be accomplished within those limits, especially if you want to maintain some semblance of sanity.

Another consideration in going the solo route is financial: Are you your own or your family's sole support? It is one thing to give up the high income available in the largest corporate mega-firms in favor of a more modest existence as your own boss; it is entirely another to embark on an enterprise that could cause you to lose the roof over your head. If you have a bad week, month, or year does it merely create a remote chance that your kids may have to give up attending a fancy summer camp this year, or does it mean that buying groceries next week is no longer a given?

Conversely, if you are in a two-career family your household may depend less desperately on your income, but then there may be no one to pick up the slack when you are too overwhelmed by work responsibilities to run household errands. If, for example, you lack the time to shop for a new car, don't count on the other breadwinner being able to do it, either.

The financial pressure associated with solo practice does not suit everyone's temperament. When you are a solo, you are responsible for generating not only your own income, but also that of your support staff. Your employees get paid first, as do the vendors with whom you do business, the government, and everyone else with a claim on your income. You take what's left. The absence of other revenue producers means there is no one to help you smooth out the peaks and valleys of your income stream. Can you shoulder this responsibility without panicking?

Finally, look carefully at your personal existence.

◆ Are you the only child of an aging parent who lives in another state? Your need to travel frequently on short notice to attend to this parent's needs may preclude practicing in a situation where you cannot easily drop your work in someone else's lap while you attend to a personal emergency.

◆ Do you or a member of your immediate family have a chronic health problem that can cause you to miss days of work at a time, or to work substantially reduced hours? Putting yourself in a situation where you will not be covered during these times may not be the wisest move.

◆ Do you expect to take maternity or paternity leave in the near future? Do you have a special-needs child? Are you deeply committed to religious practices or a charitable calling that require long or frequent absences from work? Do you aspire to a high office in the bar or a comparable organization? The solo life may not be for you. These other spheres have a higher priority for you and consume large chunks of your time. Perhaps you should be in a work situation where you can more readily absent yourself from the workplace to attend to issues not directly related to the practice of law.

Nevertheless, you can be a solo practitioner and still have a meaningful and fulfilling life outside the office. The keys are planning, organization, backups, resources, technology, and realism. You need them in both your personal life and the professional sphere.

Some of the following suggestions for maintaining a life apart from the law firm might be useful for anyone trying to keep multiple balls in the air—

even nonlawyers—but they are essential to the solo practitioner who wants to avoid sacrificing everything else to the law firm.

Planning is absolutely critical. Carve out time for important activities as far in advance as possible:

◆ Obtain as complete a school calendar as possible for each of your children as early as possible in the year and immediately block off "can't-miss" dates, such as parent/teacher conferences. Record these on your home and business calendars and treat them precisely as you would a trial date: When the judge asks "Are you available that day, Counsel?" the answer is "no." Update your calendars regularly as you learn the dates for performances, athletic events, meetings, and so forth.

◆ Do the same with respect to birthdays, anniversaries, family functions, and holidays.

◆ If there is something you enjoy doing, commit to it well in advance and invest some money in it. Buy season tickets. Place a substantial deposit on your dream vacation. Resist the temptation to schedule work-related activities during these times. The financial commitment will create incentive to follow through on your plans.

◆ Be equally serious about work obligations that cannot be canceled. Once a trial date is set, record it properly on your home calendar so that you don't inadvertently book an overlapping vacation.

◆ Don't overload yourself at work. Don't commit to inconsistent or incompatible schedules in competing cases, or you will find yourself sleeping at the office all week while you simultaneously attempt to get ready for one trial and prepare to file a dispositive motion in another case on the second day of that trial.

◆ Take care of yourself. Stay healthy, get appropriate medical care, exercise regularly. As a solo, you must minimize the risk that illness or injury will interfere with your work.

Organization overlaps with planning. A good filing system and a faithfully maintained and updated docket help make sure that you are in the right place at the right time with the right materials. An always-handy list of the critical telephone numbers in your life allows you to deal quickly and efficiently with emergencies.

You need backups in all spheres of your life. If you have to be out of the office, make sure that someone who will understand what he or she is reading and is competent to respond to whatever cannot await your return checks your mail and monitors your telephone calls and faxes. Join a network of solos (many bar associations sponsor regular meetings of solo and small firm practitioners to swap ideas) and find someone who will cover your practice for you when you're not there, whether deliberately or unexpectedly. If you have organized properly, these friends will be able to work with your records and files almost as efficiently as if you were there yourself. Offer to reciprocate for these indispensable stalwarts when they have to take time off from their jobs.

Backups are, if anything, more essential in the personal domain. If you have young children, pay whatever it takes to secure reliable and competent childcare. Don't skimp—these are your precious children. And I absolutely guarantee that the chance that a child will wake up on the morning of an important hearing with a 103-degree fever is directly proportional to the difficulty you will have in finding someone to stay home with that child on short notice.

Make friends with your neighbors. If you can't stay home one day, maybe a neighbor will be willing to wait for the plumber at your house, receive a furniture delivery for you, or drive you to work when your car breaks down despite your best planning.

Make friends with your parents' neighbors. There is no substitute for a child's presence during an elderly parent's severe crisis, but knowing that friendly eyes and ears are watching out for problems that you are not there to see will give you peace of mind, and may cut down on the number and frequency of emergency trips.

Assemble a stable of competent professionals to handle predictable emergencies, such as home repair, computer meltdowns, and known medical conditions. You will avoid spending fruitless hours searching for help on short notice, and a cordial past relationship may vault you to the top of the waiting list for service when you need assistance in a hurry.

Even if you choose not to affiliate with other lawyers to practice, make use of available resources. Start with good staff—a secretary, office administrator, executive assistant, and/or paralegal—who can stay on top of work and understands it well enough to handle crises and other unexpected matters for you in your absence. You'll feel a lot better taking a day or more off if you know that the papers that come in during your absence are filtering through capable hands, even if all that is done is to call a client or opposing counsel to say that you will respond on your return.

When your workload becomes overwhelming, consider hiring law clerks or temporary lawyers instead of killing yourself trying to do everything. While you put out fires and deal with the business aspects of your practice, temporary help can be sitting in an empty office dutifully plowing through a big box of documents that you never will get to if you wait for a day in which you can expect to have five continuous uninterrupted hours.

That solo/small firm practitioners network you joined to find friends who will cover for you in emergencies can also provide sympathetic listeners who will allow you to hash out your ideas (the absence of this resource being one of the great deficits of solo practice), as well as a ready pool of lawyers who specialize in areas other than your own whose brains you can pick when a problem arises that is outside of your area. Instead of spending the weekend in the library trying to figure out an obscure tax question that may have serious implications for a settlement you're negotiating, call a tax lawyer you know, get the answer in twenty minutes, and spend the weekend with your family. (You'll return the favor when the tax lawyer needs a quick explanation of a thorny civil procedure problem.)

Don't be afraid to use resources to make your life easier on the home front. The service economy is booming; one can find purveyors of just about every imaginable function, from personal shoppers to dog walkers to people who will stand in line to pick up your dry cleaning. Use them to keep your life on track when office responsibilities are overwhelming but you can't get away to tend to pressing "real life" concerns.

Technology may be the single most important key to keeping a solo practitioner's life in balance. Home computers and fax machines, laptops, cell phones, and the ease of e-mail access make it possible to work almost anywhere. Set up a home office with a computer, fax, and Internet access and you can work almost as efficiently at home as in your downtown office—a tremendous boon when you have to stay home for personal reasons or as an alternative to working late at the office and missing the kids' bedtimes.

Technology also allows you to get away from the office more readily. A vacation with a computer in which you don't leave your hotel room in the morning without first checking for faxes and e-mail messages, followed by a daily call in to your office's voice mail for the messages left there, with a final stop at the voice mail of your office staff or temporarily hired lawyer to give instructions on how to handle whatever has come up may not sound like much of a vacation—until you consider that unless you do all of this, a vacation of more than a few days may be out of the question if you are at risk of being unable to cope with the work that accumulates when you are gone longer.

Many years ago I had the misfortune to be served with a motion for a temporary restraining order on the Friday afternoon before I was scheduled to leave town for a week-long vacation with my family. Worse yet, the judge not only set the hearing on the motion for the following Thursday, he also allowed the moving party to take several depositions before then, and really did not want to hear about how my one precious week at the beach would be ruined. Fortunately, a colleague who was working with me on the case was able to pick it up and handle it, but only with a lot of guidance from me. We packed a fax machine and left for vacation. Each morning, while the rest of my family swam and dug for seashells, I sat in our rented condominium reading drafts of pleadings and discussing strategy by telephone. Afterward, I was excused for the day and had my afternoons and evenings to myself. It was far from the most pleasant vacation I have ever taken, but it beat staying home all week while my husband and children went to the beach without me, which would have been the only alternative.

I have also argued a discovery motion from a pay telephone on the New Jersey Turnpike, en route to a family celebration, and faxed to my office a pleading written on the airplane on my way to a bar association meeting thousands of miles from home. These are far from optimal conditions for these activities, but the effective use of technology makes it possible to take the office with you when your only other choice is never to leave your desk chair.

The tremendous advantage of technology, of course, is also its disadvantage—its ready availability. Once you set up your home office and it is sitting there ready to go, it is hard to resist your computer's siren song to sit down at 11 p.m. and tweak your client's trust documents just a little bit more. If you like feeling that you are in charge and on top of everything that is going on in your business—and enjoying that feeling is one of the reasons to become a solo—the temptation to check your voice mail hourly and to have all your mail faxed to you while you ostensibly are on vacation may be overwhelming. You may find your cell phone going off right in the middle of your son's piano recital, just as he is successfully pounding out that piece he worked on all year.

This leads us to the final key to maintaining your family and personal life as a solo—realism. Be realistic about your goals and about what you can accomplish in furtherance of those goals. Life is a series of trade-offs; as a solo practitioner you trade free time and the practice amenities that are available only in large-scale operations for professional independence. This will take a toll on your personal life. Solo practitioners generally are not well represented among those parents who are available to chaperone class trips or serve as Scout leaders. If you want to become president of a major bar association, be aware that lawyers holding those offices often do little billable work during their years of service, and essentially are supported by their colleagues in hope of a return to their firms. If you are a solo, who will carry you while you serve the community?

Is your marriage or other relationship one that will tolerate missed dinners and social events sacrificed to office emergencies? Is a six-month trip around the world your personal idea of heaven? Recognize that bearing the burden of running a business—especially a professional services operation, where you have a high ethical duty to your clients—will always be a front and center presence in your mind. Can you tolerate that?

These issues are not unique to solo practitioners. A lawyer in a firm with a 2,000-hour-per-year billing requirement also has little time for family and friends. A lawyer involved in a six-month-long lawsuit—even if but one member of a large team—probably has an ugly mass of unread papers building up on her desk. Any lawyer in management, whether as a partner, in-house counsel, or organizational supervisor, worries about paying bills, meeting the payroll, and getting quality work done on time. The difference for the solo is that you have all of these concerns, all the time, and that, for the most part, you face them alone. For some lawyers, this is exhilarating, challenging, and liberating. For others, it is their worst nightmare. Know thyself.

Another Perspective:
Lessons from the Rearview Mirror

Edna R.S. Alvarez

Having closed my solo practice after approximately twenty-five years, it occurred to me that a "retrospective" piece might be of use to someone considering entering the "solo highway of life." If I knew then what I know today, here are the questions I would have asked.

Question 1: Should I Be a Solo?

Being a sole practitioner requires a high energy level, an entrepreneurial spirit, and a risk-taking disposition.

- *High Energy Level*: A solo is responsible for all aspects of the practice—site selection, client development and maintenance, equipment acquisition, personnel, and finances. You must be excellent at juggling, prioritizing, and delegating. Doing all these tasks competently, especially while having an outside life, requires a high energy level.
- *Entrepreneurial Spirit*: A solo must be a person who (1) craves creating a new structure that reflects the solo's unique persona, rather than working within a preexisting "corporate" structure, (2) has a vision and wants to see that vision become a reality, and (3) is willing to put enormous personal resources into converting the vision into reality.
- *Risk-Taking Disposition*: In a solo practice, there are no third-party safety nets. As a solo, you must have the personal constitution to be able, metaphorically at least, to fly all alone, while surrounded by constant risks (personnel, technological, client, and financial) as well as the potential for tremendous rewards.

Question 2: What Is a "Practice Blueprint"?

Before embarking upon the "details" of a practice (such as location, equipment, personnel, and finances), you need a "practice blueprint," which must be committed to paper. This blueprint—or road map—should specify where you want your practice to be in five years and should include the following: start-up budget, substantive area(s) of law to be undertaken, size of practice, annual income, and quality of life. The resolution of these issues creates the framework for dealing with the specifics involved in establishing and operating your solo practice.

Significantly, it will be essential to revisit your "practice blueprint" as you continue your trip on the solo highway. You will change and your practice context will change over time. You will not want to get stuck operating with an outdated blueprint or road map.

Question 3: Where Should I Locate My Office?

The first issue is whether you will have an "at-home" office or an "outside-of-home" office. On that afternoon, decades ago, when I pulled the telephone and file into the bathroom and closed the door on my then two-year-old child so I could speak with an inheritance tax referee, and my daughter wailed and pounded on the door, I realized that type of at-home "office" was not for me.

It always amazes me how little attention many practitioners give to the issue of site selection. Obviously, you should not just fling yourself into the first space that comes to your attention. Your office must be affordable, make you feel comfortable, and be accessible to and comfortable for your clients. The space you select must fit your blueprint. Write it out: "I am selecting this space because. . . ." Your "because" phrase should refer to your budget, substantive practice area, size of practice, annual income, and quality of life.

For example, I selected my office site based upon the fact that I was going to have an estate planning practice comprising high-wealth clients, and upon the fact that I had two very young children. Although I live in Los Angeles where driving/commuting is a way of life, I did not want to be a commuter. I ended up in an office building three blocks from my house, in a "full office suite" complex of marble and fresh flowers—perfect. But if I had been going into a personal injury, an immigration, or a workers' compensation practice, I would have looked for space with an entirely different ambiance.

Question 4: What/Where/How of Equipment/ Supplies/Furnishings?

In my experience, the best gauge of what you will need in the way of equipment and supplies is other practitioners in your geographic area who have practices similar to yours. Fellow women practitioners who had recently begun to practice were enormously helpful to me in creating a complete rundown of necessities and sources for equipment and supplies. Furnishings, on the other hand, were a great collection from individual firm liquidations and "tony" office-furnishing stores. Through bar activities, you will meet practitioners who can be helpful to you in your efforts to establish the parameters of your needs and the sources to fulfill those needs.

Question 5: How Do I Deal with the Issue of Personnel?

There are five major components to the personnel issue: number and salary of staff, resources for staff acquisition, hiring procedures, training, and retaining.

In my experience, the issue of personnel was the most difficult issue I faced as a sole practitioner. Not having that highly competent person working for (with) you in the first place is just as disastrous as losing that person once he or she has become an integral part of your office.

I began with a part-time secretary—a teacher at a secretarial school who had been a legal secretary in Minnesota, and who is now the administrator of a major law firm. Ultimately, I had five people on staff, plus the "full-suite" receptionist. The key is to find alternative sources for staff (such as college campuses), rather than competing with the large firms. You need to have a clear checklist of required skills and personal characteristics established before the first interview. You need to anticipate putting an enormous amount of time into training, and you should create a procedure manual as you go so the next new staff member can use it. And constantly remember how expensive and disruptive it is to replace staff. In addition to hiring and training well, you should—through benefits on every level—make sure your staff feels that their lives at your office are irreplaceable.

Question 6: How Should I "Market" My Practice?

Marketing is really very simple. There are only two rules: First, remember that everything you do is "marketing"—whether you are engaging in "personal" activities (such as picking up the dry cleaning or standing in the grocery checkout line) or "business/practice" activities (such as hiring a caring, polite receptionist, standing to greet your clients, or sending a clearly stated bill), it all has to do with projecting your image as a competent, caring lawyer. Second, in your nonpractice time, do what you enjoy, and the clients will follow. I thoroughly enjoyed lecturing, writing, speaking, being active politically, and serving on bar committees and boards. Having an excellent meal with a prospective client or client source was never a chore, nor was sharing with enthusiasm the nature of my practice with those who inquired. On the other hand, if someone told me to play soccer as a marketing tool or to join a mountaineering club as a marketing tool, it would be a disaster. As William Shakespeare said, "To thine own self be true, and it shall follow, as night the day, that to no man can thou be false."

Now, if you do everything poorly other than practicing in your substantive field, and/or there is nothing you enjoy doing other than practicing in your substantive field, join a firm and leave the major marketing to someone else.

Question 7: What Are the Principal Financial Issues?

It would be inappropriate not to mention finances. It is essential to establish an adequate level of funding of your practice and to accept only those cases that you can afford to handle. To ignore finances is a disaster. Yet, many practitioners follow the "till" method—that is, if there is enough in the bank account to pay the bills, then the financial aspect of the practice has been addressed. Wrong! The solo must be aware of and conform to the state bar rules relating to finances (such as rules on unconscionable billing, trust accounts, commingling personal and client assets, and wrongful retention of client funds). Adequate insurance must be kept in effect. Proper books and records must be maintained. Taxes must be paid in a timely fashion. The solo ignores finances at the solo's own peril.

Question 8: How Do I Maintain My Professional Competence?

You must create provisions for continued professional competence by doing the following:

- Attending and/or teaching continuing education programs on a regular basis
- Subscribing to and reading journals in your field of practice
- Belonging to and being active in bar organizations, and participating on bar committees relating to your practice field
- Making arrangements to have necessary research materials available to you
- Creating work-product systems and models
- Belonging to appropriate study groups
- Establishing relations with other lawyers whom you can call upon for assistance with practice problems

Question 9: Where Can I Obtain Additional Information?

Assuming you still feel there is no practice environment for you other than in the solo arena, I recommend two great sources. First, the ABA Law Practice Management Section has incredibly useful materials for the sole practitioner, including many full-length texts, as well as articles in the Section's *Law Practice* magazine. Find and study these materials, and life in the solo lane will be much, much better for you. Second, colleagues, be active in your bar associations, meet fellow lawyers, and learn from them.

And so—that ends my look through the rearview mirror. It is time for you to decide whether to hop on the solo highway. If you make the leap, I hope you enjoy the journey as much as I did!

Creating a Business Plan

3

Gary A. Munneke
Carol A. Seelig

Why Have a Business Plan?

Sole practitioners often ask why they need a business plan to run a practice with only one lawyer. You may be wondering the same thing.

There are several reasons for having a business plan, but the main reasons are to create a blueprint for setting up your practice, to provide documentation needed to obtain loans or secure other financial resources, and to give yourself a clear idea of what you want the focus of your practice to be. Every firm—large and small—should think strategically about its goals and objectives, and solos are no exception to the rule. Going through the process of developing a business plan requires a great deal of strategic thinking on your part.

The contents of a plan can differ dramatically, depending upon the extent of experience in a law firm environment. If you are right out of law school, you need a very detailed plan, whereas if you have some experience and bring an existing caseload from another firm, you may need only a broad-brush outline of what you want to do. The level of your experience and your practice situation also determine the kind of business plan you need. For example, lawyers who plan to obtain commercial financing for their practices need to focus more on numbers and financial projections; lawyers who do not need to impress a lending institution may want to focus on marketing issues to establish themselves in a competitive marketplace.

For the purpose of this chapter, we assume you have spent some time in a law firm environment or have been on your own long enough to have gained some knowledge of the issues involved in running a law firm, including trust accounting, payroll, marketing, case management, and billing. If you are a solo who started on a wing and a prayer, you may now want to put everything in order to assure continued viability and growth. If you are a law firm expatriate, you probably had other people handle many of the management responsibilities that you will now have to handle yourself.

Whatever your situation, it is important to remember that a business plan should be geared to your particular needs. The plan should be a tool to help you get where you want to go, and not some mechanical model to follow rigidly. The term "business plan" acknowledges that you are running a business—a legal service delivery business—and that you have an organized way of arranging the parts of the business to achieve a goal: success in the practice of law.

Business Form

A threshold question for any aspiring sole practitioner is whether to operate as a sole proprietor, as a single-member professional limited liability company (LLC), or as a professional corporation (PC). Although the majority of solos are sole proprietors, there are valid liability and tax reasons for considering alternative forms of business.

Because lawyers may be sued by their clients and third parties for malpractice and other torts, they face the risk of financial loss in excess of the liability limits on their insurance policies. When a lawyer operates as a sole proprietorship, her personal and business assets are indistinguishable; this means personal funds may be subject to business liabilities, and vice versa. Thus, the advantage of the sole proprietorship is not limited liability, but rather, simplicity—you do not have to take any formal steps to create a sole proprietorship.

By creating a limited liability company or corporation, you might be able to shield your personal assets from some forms of potential liability, such as a slip-and-fall incident in your reception area. In many states, however, you may not be able to limit your personal liability for excess malpractice judgments, because liability for professional error passes through to personal assets. In any event, because the corporate form limits liability to the extent of the owner's investment in the company, we recommend the LLC or PC as the preferred form of doing business. You should consult the law of your jurisdiction for the specific rules on liability, the availability of alternative business forms (such as LLC and PC), and other rules governing the practice of law. New York, for example, does not allow lawyers to operate in a corporate form.

Many law firms today are organized as limited liability partnerships (LLPs). If you plan to practice as a solo, however, the partnership form will not work, because by definition a partnership includes two or more persons. Additionally, because Rule 5.4 of the Model Rules of Professional Conduct—in effect in one form or another in every jurisdiction except Washington, D.C.—strictly prohibits lawyers from forming partnerships with nonlawyers if any of the activities involves the practice of law, your partner must be another lawyer. Thus, you are not allowed to include a nonlawyer spouse, a nonlawyer professional, or a silent investor as a partner in a law firm LLP. (See Appendix B, page 605).

Solos who share office space with other solos must also be careful to avoid the appearance that they operate as a law firm, because many jurisdictions recognize the doctrine of implied partnership or partnership by estoppel. If you are not careful, you may find yourself being sued for professional malpractice for the errors of a lawyer whose only connection to your practice is that you share the same address.

Once you have made a decision about what business form is best for you, the next step is to develop the business plan itself. Every business plan addresses similar components: (1) an overview or big picture, (2) marketing, (3) resources, and (4) finances. The amount of detail allocated to each of these components depends upon the reason for the business plan. If the plan is being submitted to obtain a loan, then it should persuade the lender that you have strong financial stability, as well as a viable explanation for growth and dealing with competition. In addition, you must explain how you intend to use the proceeds of a loan or line of credit. If, on the other hand, you are preparing a plan to help get yourself organized, then you do not need to use the same persuasive approach required to impress a lender. Nevertheless, your analysis and attention to detail can have a major bearing on the decisions you make and can help you avoid potential pitfalls. When you commit your ideas to paper and think about possible problem areas, you are more likely to identify solutions in advance. A personal business plan addresses the area of law you have selected and why it appeals to you; it may state your values, such as interest in balancing professional and personal life, and articulate your annual profit expectations.

The Business Plan

Overview of the Plan

The overview of your business plan should remind you why you are doing what you are doing, especially on those days when you feel particularly frustrated or overwhelmed. The overview is a big-picture statement of what you want to accomplish in your solo practice. It also helps you determine whether you need to change what you are doing, as the reasons why a particular area of the law appealed to you initially may have changed. It gives you a baseline for comparing where you were when you started with where you are after a period of time. As you and your practice change, your interests, motivations, and approaches may change as well. The overview should be short and sweet; if you write more than a page, you are looking at the trees and not the forest.

Marketing Plan

The marketing plan should follow the overview. You should address this topic first, because if you have no clients, you have no practice. It is particularly important to identify your potential clients, as well as where and how you expect to find them. It is always better to think of a solution to a problem *before* it arises, so you have the solution readily available when you may be upset and not as able to think clearly.

In addition, this part of the plan should offer alternative strategies for developing your client base, in case the initial ones do not work or your long-term goal is to shift the focus of your practice. For example, if you just left the public defender's office to open your own private practice, people are likely to still think of you as a criminal defense lawyer, even though you ultimately hope to get out of criminal law in favor of a plaintiff-side personal injury practice. It might be necessary for you to take more criminal cases in the early years of your practice, as you build your personal injury practice for the future.

A marketing plan describes who your clients will be (the market), why these clients will want to use you as their lawyer, how you will make yourself known to them, and how you will deal with competition in the marketplace.

You must first decide to be something—it is always easier to market to a "niche" than it is to market yourself as a generalist. Generalists have gone the way of the family doctor. Today, everyone wants a specialist. Does everyone need a specialist? No, but this doesn't mean they don't want one. A niche has two components: a specific clientele and specific services for the clientele. For example, you might identify an audience of older people who need a discrete set of services that have come to be called "elder law," or you might as a motorcycle aficionado want to provide services to other bikers for legal problems they have on the road.

You might decide to specialize in more than one area. Some areas of practice seem to go well together. For example, if you want to represent individuals, rather than businesses, you could combine several areas that affect the lives of individuals, such as family law, personal injury, bankruptcy, and wills and estates. If you decide to represent businesses, you could combine real estate transactions, pension planning, and employment law. Of course, if you are eventually able to generate enough business in any one area of practice, you might want to limit your practice to that area and either refer the other areas to colleagues or associate with other lawyers who specialize in those areas.

Geography is important. You could focus on marketing your services to residents and businesses in a particular, small geographic area that you plan to serve. This way, everyone who needs that type of legal support or who lives in that specific geographic area can know you. Keep in mind that the size of your city or town affects your ability to specialize. In New York City, for example, there are probably enough people living in one city block to support a real estate lawyer, a trust and estates lawyer, and a personal injury lawyer. In smaller cities, there may not be enough legal work to sustain narrow specialty practices, and out of necessity lawyers may handle a variety of cases.

Part of your decision about developing a niche practice depends upon the competition in your community. If some areas of practice are not being handled by anyone, or if they are not being handled well by existing practitioners, you will have an easier time entering that area of practice. If other practitioners own your desired field, however, you must evaluate whether you want to go head-to-head with them, carve out a segment of the practice area that you can claim as your own, or consider some other area of law.

You must do research to determine whether the market is big enough to support you and your competitors. It might be or it might not be. If you want to go into real estate law, speak to real estate brokers and lenders who work in your area. Read local news and research demographic information on the number of building permits, property transfers, and other facts. In other words, do some field research and make informed decisions. There is good and bad news about market size. The good news is that the larger the size of the potential market, the greater the potential to find clients who need your services. The bad news is that it is more difficult to locate these clients. In a smaller market, there may be fewer clients, but they are easier to find and reach.

Once you identify your potential market and determine it will support another practitioner, you must obtain clients. Many lawyers have trouble doing this, although the basic principle is simple: the marketing methods you adopt should flow from the market niche you have targeted. There is no one-size-fits-all approach to getting clients, but the better you know your market, the easier it will be to reach it.

If you are bringing a book of clients with you from another practice, your challenge may be letting them know where you are so they can find you. Many jurisdictions limit the ways that lawyers leaving a practice may solicit their clients from the former practice. Partnership agreements may specify how and when departing partners can contact clients. Conversely, departing associates are not subject to such restrictions, and most states ethically prohibit covenants-not-to-compete for lawyers.

Many start-up solo practices rely heavily on referrals to reach new clients. Once you decide upon your niche market, identify one or two categories of people who have contact with the niche market. Then meet those people who can refer business to you. This way, you spend your time getting to know someone who can continually refer business to you, as opposed to working on getting a single client.

Examples of referral sources are bankers, financial analysts, real estate brokers, accountants, contractors, funeral directors, nursing home administrators, and insurance agents. If you think about which referral sources are most likely to come in contact with potential clients who will need your services, then it becomes easier to target which referral sources to develop. For example, now that many people preplan funerals, a relationship with a funeral director can be a good source for an estate planning lawyer and possibly a real estate lawyer. Architects can be a good referral source to contractors, and vice versa. Your referrals may even come from lawyers already practicing in your field, who have overflow work they cannot handle. Remember, however, that ethical rules prohibit giving anything of value to a lawyer for recommending the lawyer's services; therefore, avoid gratuities that could be construed as quid pro quo.

In short, your marketing plan should outline who your clients are and how you plan to get them. For a variety of reasons, many lawyers are uncomfortable with marketing, or are not very good at it. It is often easier to come up with ideas than to implement a marketing plan. By drafting a marketing plan as part of an overall business plan, you will make the implementation phase easier. In the end, to maximize the time you devote to marketing, your marketing efforts should reach your client base as efficiently and effectively as possible.

Resources Plan

The third part of a business plan identifies the resources you have and the ones you may need. You should address three specific types of resources: human resources (support staff, including backup lawyers), physical resources (office, equipment, and furniture), and information resources (knowledge base you must access to do your work).

- ◆ *Human Resources*: When you are creating this part of your plan, do the research necessary to locate the human resources you might need on a moment's notice. If you are swamped with work, where can you find a temp lawyer in whom you have confidence to use in an emergency? You should find a similar source for paralegal and other administrative support. In a different vein, what if you want to go on vacation? Do you have an arrangement with another lawyer in town who can speak to your clients in an emergency or appear in court on your behalf if something unexpected occurs? It's not a vacation if you are tied to your phone and your e-mail messages.

◆ *Physical Resources*: Machines are also resources. What equipment do you need to do your work? Who is going to fix your computer or the network when it goes down? If you have someone identified, you can call that person immediately to solve your problem sooner rather than later. It is helpful to have someone who is familiar with your computer arrangements, your e-mail accounts, your telephone system, and other machines you use to do your work. If the person already knows your systems, it will be far easier for him to identify and fix your problems.

◆ *Information Resources*: Information resources include client files, contacts, and records, as well as books, forms, databases, and public records relevant to your practice. How will you access this information—manually or electronically? How will you transfer vital records from your former practice to your new one? How will you conduct legal research? How will you manage the information that inevitably will flow through your office?

When you put the people, the physical assets, and the information together, you have a law practice. Whether your solo practice is just you or includes a number of support staff, and whether you operate out of your home, shared space, or your own building, and whether you are paperless or papered, most of the expenses associated with your practice are associated with these resources, and what you pay in overhead will not appear in your pocket as profit. The resources plan, therefore, is critical to the overall business plan, and worthy of your careful attention.

Financial Plan

Finally, you need a financial plan. If you write down the amount of money you want to make each month and keep that figure in mind, the likelihood of achieving that goal is increased. You will focus on getting money in the door each month, which requires an efficient and effective billing system. More generally, your business plan should include four financial statements: a start-up analysis, a pro forma profit-and-loss statement, a statement of assets and liabilities, and a cash-flow analysis:

◆ *Start-up Analysis*: If you are just starting your practice, you must determine how much money you have available (including personal funds and outside financing), the expenses you will incur *before* you open your doors for business, and the amount of operating cash you will have on hand when you actually open your doors. If you simply start spending money, you are likely to get into financial trouble right out of the gate; by analyzing your start-up finances, you can adjust your plans to avoid disaster.

♦ *Pro Forma Profit-and-Loss Statement (P&L)*: For non-CPAs, this is your budget. The P&L typically covers anticipated expenses and revenues for a period of one year. Because your second year of practice should be more stable than the first, you may want to prepare two-year projections. After you have been practicing, you will be able to compare your projected P&L with actual performance, and adjust your next budget accordingly. As a rule, lawyers who open new practices overestimate income and underestimate expenses; for planning purposes, you should estimate expenses liberally and income conservatively.

♦ *Statement of Assets and Liabilities*: The statement of assets and liabilities is also known as the balance sheet, statement of net worth, or equity. In the early years of your practice, this information may be less important (unless you need to borrow money), in part because you have few assets. Over time, however, you might want to know the value of your business to sell it, to borrow, or to form a partnership with another lawyer.

♦ *Cash-Flow Analysis*: Simply put, cash flow represents the money in your operating account, which fluctuates with deposits and withdrawals. You must maintain enough cash in the account to pay your bills, no matter how much money you have tied up in capitalized assets. When a law firm opens its doors, it is likely to be cash poor, and income flow may take months or longer to develop. Part of the cash-flow analysis includes a plan for assuring sufficient cash to make it through the start-up period.

You also need a contingency plan for how you are going to address a cash-flow shortage in any particular month. If you plan for this possibility, it is more likely you will have a workable solution and won't create unnecessary stress for yourself. Your plan could include having three months of monthly operating costs saved, or maintaining a line of credit with a local bank. Though you may not have this money saved today, if you have this as a plan, you can set aside a rainy-day fund over time.

Another chapter in this book discusses making sure you get paid for your work. You are better off playing golf with a potential client than doing work for an existing one who won't pay you. You must also allocate a certain amount of time to implementing your marketing plan, to keep the pipeline flowing. If you don't spend time finding new matters, preferably from existing clients, or referrals by existing clients, you will find yourself "caught up" on work one day—an event you don't want to happen.

Once you have written your plan and have been following it for three to six months, it is time to step back and see what is and isn't working. If you aren't getting your bills out and you constantly have a cash-flow problem, learn why this is happening and create a plan to prevent it. If you don't have enough work, look at your marketing plan. Have you spent time marketing? Has one approach worked better than another? Do you have a new insight for a niche to pursue or new referral sources?

Conclusion

A good business plan is an organic document, not a static one. You should have it readily available on your computer and change it whenever needed. As you continue to practice, you will find that your plan becomes increasingly refined, and that you have fewer problems in your practice and perhaps some extra time. Just remember that if you aren't following your plan, you must ask yourself why—is the plan unrealistic, or are you not interested in doing what needs to be done? People's interests change and it's possible that yours will. If so, you will need to create a new plan or change the existing plan to meet your current interests. You will find that a plan helps you identify and reach your goals. (For additional information on this topic, see *The Lawyer's Guide to Creating a Business Plan: A Software Package* (ABA, 2005).)

Leaving a Firm: Guidelines for a Smoother Transition

4

Dennis Kennedy

For the vast majority of those entering solo practice, starting a solo law firm means leaving a current law firm. In some cases, leaving a law firm can be a painful process, while in other cases, it can be painless; but, in most cases, there are significant hurdles to making a successful departure.

This chapter takes an in-depth look at what is involved in making an amicable exit from your current law firm and a happy move to your new solo practice. The chapter covers both practical and ethical considerations in your transition, gives you some tips and checklists of important questions, and addresses some of the psychological and other issues you are likely to face. The reality of leaving can be quite different from what you might have imagined, and good preparation and flexibility are necessary components of a successful exit strategy.

Making Your Decision

Far too often, lawyers who plan to leave their firms imagine a far rosier picture than what they find, in terms of their visions of future solo practice and the easy departure they expect to make from their current firms.

Your present firm may see your departure as a betrayal of trust and even friendships, engendering ill feelings that you never would have expected. News of your departure could easily throw the smoothly running law firm into chaos and create more disruption than you ever dreamed. There is an old military proverb that says, "A plan never survives first contact with the enemy." The transition plan you carefully developed in your own mind will never remain intact after you first float it by your colleagues. What you think is reasonable and logical may well be seen as insulting and overreaching. The warm, collegial atmosphere you took for granted may vanish in a puff of smoke.

You should remember that in large firms, lawyers leave on a regular basis and there may be procedures already in place that you must follow. Those procedures might involve a leisurely transition period when you and your soon-to-be former colleagues sort out the details of your departure in a friendly and cordial manner. Unfortunately, in other firms, those procedures might involve your being escorted out of the office after you announce your intention to depart, with a promise that your personal items will be boxed and shipped to you. The "escort out" approach is much more common than many lawyers expect. Assuming you will have a few weeks to get ready to leave may be a big mistake on your part. It might be impossible or impractical to learn in advance which way it will go. You may be able to make discreet inquiries about what happened in the past when others left the firm.

To avoid the embarrassment and inconvenience of an unscheduled and unceremonious departure, it is vital that you take all steps necessary to make your decision to go solo and your transition plan as solid, complete, and realistic as possible. The better you prepare, the better your departure and transition will be.

When You Are Ready to Make a Decision, Take Steps to Make It Quickly

Many lawyers think, dream, and even plot about leaving their firms and going solo for years. Others ponder such a move only as an emotional response to something unpleasant that happens at their firms. In both cases, the decision making is likely to be hazy, impulsive, or even irrational. Even when lawyers dedicate their efforts to making the move, they often do so in environments where full caseloads and distractions of daily life prevent them from giving the move their full attention.

It is important to realize that making the move from a firm to a solo practice is enormously distracting. Your work and your work relationships are likely to suffer. The longer it takes you to make your decision and to make your move, the more conflicted you will become about your current situation and the harder it will be to continue doing your work. It is natural to prepare ourselves to leave an existing situation by highlighting the negative factors, which helps give us reasons to leave and the courage to make our decision to leave. Unfortunately, as we dwell on the reasons we want or need to leave, we risk becoming negative and our relationships may suffer. The best transition happens when we focus on the positive aspects of the transition. By remaining positive, we reduce the chances of "burning bridges" as we leave.

The best approach, therefore, is to minimize the time period in which you make your decision and announce your departure. You can take your time gathering information, talking to people outside your firm, and conducting research, but when it comes time to sit down and make a decision, clear the decks and concentrate. I suggest taking a week of vacation and putting yourself mentally and physically in a place where you can think clearly and make a sound decision. If that means driving aimlessly on country roads, hiking in a park, or relaxing on the beach, do whatever it takes. If it means talking with family or friends, get them involved in the discussion. You will make it harder on yourself and those around you if you simply continue to work and pretend that nothing out of the ordinary is occurring. If you remain distracted and take a long time to make a decision because you are unfocused and distracted, your decision will reflect that lack of focus and distraction.

Do Your Homework

There is a lot to learn when you are planning to establish a solo practice. You can't cut corners or fail to do your research.

The best way to learn what to expect when leaving your firm and starting your own practice is by talking with other lawyers who have done the same thing. They will often tell you things you would never have considered. Their transitions may have gone smoothly or they may have been disastrous, but you can learn from them in either case. In addition, you can consult resources available from the American Bar Association, including books and magazine articles. Also, to avoid embarrassment and a possible legal battle with your firm, be sure to study the applicable ethical rules and any relevant case law. It is better to be prepared than to be sorry.

Consider Using Consultants, Coaches, and Advisors

In my transition to a solo practice, I used not one, but two career coaches. One coach helped me with the "big picture" issues and the other assisted with putting together the practical plan, outlining the steps involved, and keeping me on task and on target. Their advice did not come cheap, but it was money well spent and definitely saved me money in the long run. Many career counselors, coaches, and other advisors offer services by telephone or even e-mail messaging, so you can get help no matter where you live or work.

Study Your Market

One of the best questions someone asked me when I planned to go solo was, "Can you tell me where your first check from a client will come from?"

Lawyers often spend a lot of time on marketing, but far too little time on the market. What is your target market? Your marketing methods make sense only if you put them in front of the right market. Your target market might change substantially when you leave a firm. If you take the time to study your market and make sure it exists, your confidence and likelihood of success will both increase.

Know Why

I believe it is essential that moving to a solo practice be movement *toward* something you want to do, and not just movement *away from* something you do not want to do.

By the time you decide to go out on your own, you should be able to offer a plain and concise explanation about what you will be doing. You get bonus points if you can tell people about your "unique selling proposition" or "primary customer value," but the key point is to be able to make a short statement of what you are doing and why.

In my case, I wanted to provide services to businesses entering important technology contracts without getting the legal help they needed. Because my friends and colleagues thought I would be representing only technology companies, it was essential that I explain clearly what I planned to do. I decided to describe my new practice as providing "consumer protection law for businesses entering important technology agreements." When I told people that, they understood what I had in mind and reacted positively.

Timing Your Announcement

Deciding when to announce that you are leaving takes a lot of thought and consideration. You might also find that it is a moving target. Events can accelerate or postpone your announcement. Trust me—you will likely find yourself on a roller-coaster ride no matter how well you plan.

If you are in a large firm, you must take into account the speed and tenacity of the firm's gossip mill. Nothing moves faster in law firms than rumors. Unfortunately, unfounded rumors move just as quickly as well-founded rumors. If there are already suspicions about your likely departure, everything you do will be interpreted as further proof of your imminent departure. News of something that you accidentally left on the printer will circle your firm like wildfire. By the way, people will believe whatever they choose to believe. A certain percentage of your colleagues will believe you were fired, no matter the evidence to the contrary. Do not waste your energy trying to change minds.

As a general matter, your departure announcement should come as quickly as possible after you make your final decision to leave. You take the risk of being escorted out the door and not having a paycheck for as long as you planned, but prolonging the announcement of your decision can be painful and unproductive. Once you decide to leave, you begin to engage in a daily pattern of small lies. Everyone has his or her own threshold of discomfort. You will be faced with accepting long-term projects, important cases, or other matters that require you to lie to someone because you know you will not be around.

I recommend keeping your decision as secret as possible in the period before you make it final. At that point, it is best to disclose your decision to the people you trust most at the firm. Doing so reduces the risk of the abrupt departure, and it should help pave the way for a smoother transition. On the other hand, be prepared for the possibility that the day you announce will be your last day in the office.

Minimize the Length of Your Exit

Determining how long to stay at your firm can raise some thorny issues. Though it is flattering when firm members ask you to stay a while longer or until a particular case is concluded, the fact is that staying around knocks you off your path to a solo practice, diverts your energy, and limits your options. It can be tempting to stay a little longer to make some extra money, but you should have already put away enough money to finance your new practice.

Based upon what I have seen, the longer you stick around, the more likely something will go wrong. Why is that? Because once you announce you are leaving, you are no longer seen as a part of the team.

If you decide to stay awhile after announcing your departure, make sure you do not overstay your welcome. Better yet, make arrangements for a quick departure and transition. It will help you and it will help your firm get accustomed to your absence. Living in the twilight world of "having given notice but still in the office" all but guarantees that you will not give adequate attention to either your old practice or your contemplated new one.

I recommend that you consider a "delegate and get out" approach. Move your projects quickly to someone else. Move to your new office as soon as possible and ask your colleagues to call you there, if necessary. The exceptions to this rule are for cases you will continue to handle with the expectation of payment, and work of clients you take with you. Keep in mind that both exceptions are more complicated and more likely to cause ruffled feathers and bad feelings than you might ever expect, as discussed below.

Issues That You Must Get Clearly Resolved

There are probably hundreds of transition issues involved in the departure of a lawyer from a law firm. Some are handled directly and specifically while others, frankly, are never adequately addressed and, instead, gradually fade away. Be sure you identify and address the matters that are most important to you. The following list illustrates some of the issues that a departing lawyer should not take for granted.

Insurance Matters

Health insurance is a huge issue these days. Your only option might be to make the COBRA election on your existing health insurance coverage. Do not blow the chance to make the appropriate election because of an administrative mistake. Make sure you follow the process closely. Similarly, you might have rights to continue life insurance or disability coverage that might not be available to you as a solo. Do not miss the opportunity. It makes good sense to get your insurance agent, accountant, or financial planner into the mix to evaluate your options and shepherd you through the process. You must also understand any issues or gaps in legal malpractice coverage.

Other Benefits

If you have retirement or other benefits with your firm, you might have the ability to move them or make other elections or changes. It could take a year or more for your new practice to earn enough for you to contribute to retirement again. Therefore, you should consider available options, especially the ability to move assets so you have better investment opportunities.

Message Forwarding

Forwarding of calls and messages is a simple matter that often leads to bad blood and harsh words. Some firms instruct receptionists to say only that "X doesn't work here anymore" and give no forwarding number when someone calls for the departing lawyer. Many firms delete a departing lawyer as a user on the firm's network, which results in the "bouncing" of e-mail messages sent to the lawyer's former e-mail address.

These can be tricky issues, of course, but you should address them promptly and make contingency plans for whatever decision is made. The e-mail issue is important today, especially if you receive notices, client communications, and other time-sensitive information by e-mail message. You probably cannot get all the e-mail address changes made in time to avoid "missing" some e-mail messages. Because it takes little effort to forward your e-mail messages either to you or another lawyer in the firm who can screen them for important material, the cutoff of an e-mail address will raise tempers. The best approach is to agree upon a reasonable procedure to deal with these issues.

Equipment

"What do you mean *your* [insert laptop computer, cell phone, or other item here]? It belongs to the firm." You might find yourself in a conversation like that. I have seen departing lawyers become furious about the cancellation of a cell phone account (especially if they learn of it only when trying to make a call). There might be other equipment, supplies, furniture, plants, and the like that become the subjects of disputes.

You can never know what to expect. If items belong to you, take them home before you make your announcement. If someone is packing your office for you, he or she will probably decide issues in favor of the firm. Be assured, however, that no matter how sincere your anger and sense of entitlement, people will only laugh at you if they hear you are fighting over a rubber-tree plant.

User Name, Passwords, Keys, and the Like

The quick deletion of your user name and password can terminate your e-mail account prematurely and have other negative effects. There is a flip side of this issue, however. As long as your user name and password are active, someone using them can log on as you and take documents or cause damage. To remove you from the suspect list in case of an intrusion, theft, or other security matter, generally you should eliminate your rights to log in to the computer system, physically enter the office, or otherwise gain access to firm materials.

Intellectual Property

In the good old days, a lawyer leaving a firm took work product, forms, and other materials. No one gave much thought to this common practice. Today, however, lawyers create articles, presentations, videos, forms, software applications, Web pages, databases, knowledge management tools, and other pieces of intellectual property. Firms also realize the value of firm forms, brief banks, handbooks, and the like.

It is increasingly common for intellectual property issues to arise when a lawyer leaves a firm. Many lawyers take the approach that ownership issues apply only to associates (who are employees) and not partners. This assumption may not be the best one to make, especially when you plan to license or otherwise profit from materials created while at your former firm. A good number of law firms have added intellectual property clauses to their partnership agreements in recent years, and the consequences of those provisions might surprise you. If you have specific uses planned for materials, be sure to address and document the intellectual property issues.

Money

If you have a beer or two with any lawyer who has left a law firm, you will eventually hear about a money issue that still sticks in the lawyer's craw. In part, this is because money issues often are quite complicated. In part, it's because we all see justice and fairness in different ways. In part, it's just because money is involved.

If the money matters to you, you must nail down and document these issues in a writing signed by the parties. As a practical matter, if you do not have the money in hand when you leave, your odds of ever receiving it diminish greatly. In my opinion, it is better to settle for a current cash payment based upon some likelihood of what you would receive over time than to wait and see what happens. Take the money now and never bother to find out how much it might have been. Move on.

Others might prefer to put time and effort into calculating and following up on later payments. That might be the right choice for you. Keep in mind, however, that the more effort you expend on it over time, the more energy you take from building your practice. Decide whether you are willing to sue if necessary. Then answer what you will do if you are not prepared to sue.

Taking Clients

Who gets your clients? This is the hot-button issue (but I didn't have to tell you that). It is a world of surprises, where many things are not what they first appear. I discuss it in more detail below.

The Five Biggest Surprises About Leaving a Firm

Even if you do all the recommended research and planning for your move to a solo practice, I guarantee that the following five things will still surprise you.

The Amount of "Adminis-trivia"

Forms. Procedures. Elections. Sign this, please. Where does all the paperwork come from?

Formality of Colleagues

A friend of mine once told me that when a lawyer hears someone is leaving the firm, the first reaction is one of survival: "X is leaving! How does that affect me? What is X working on for me or my clients? Do I depend on X for work?" Once the lawyer assesses the potential damage and determines there is no negative impact upon himself personally, then, in his mind, the departing lawyer is already gone. I told my friend that he had a cold view of the legal profession, but I am almost to the point of agreeing with him.

You will be surprised by how quickly collegiality is replaced with a distanced formality and professionalism by your formerly friendly partners. It is nothing personal—just part of the coping mechanism.

Your Invisibility

The invisibility phenomenon is shocking no matter how many times you see it, and even more disconcerting when it happens to you. In the period between your announcement of your departure and when you actually leave, you may feel you have become invisible. You might be talking with a colleague and see another person approach that colleague and interrupt. It will appear as though this person does not even see you while he talks to your colleague. When finished, he will walk away without even acknowledging your presence. It is unsettling when it first happens, but when the cleaning people start doing the same thing, you know you have stayed too long.

Doubling of Your Workload with Half the Time

In some ways, this factor is the opposite of invisibility. Once you announce your departure, all the lawyers for whom you are doing work crank up the pressure and deadlines to ensure you get their work done. At the same time, other lawyers believe you are doing nothing at all, and they begin dropping by your office whenever they feel like taking breaks. Add to that your own desire to work on the details of opening your new office, and you will soon wonder why you are coming into the office earlier than ever and leaving later than ever and not making any progress on your work.

How Hard Your Firm Works to Keep Your Clients

One essential exercise to do before making your final decision about going solo is to develop a "worst-case scenario." To me, that means working out the numbers for what will happen if you have zero income for a year, or at least six months. Too many solos start with the expectation that some of their existing clients will come with them and give them enough work to allow them to buy vacation homes in a few months. Unfortunately, they often find that the "slam dunk" clients stayed with the former law firm or do not have the work they expected.

Do not fool yourself. The firm you are leaving will work very hard at keeping "your" clients. The firm might cut prices, give special attention, or make any number of efforts to keep the business. Your clients will likely hear a lot about the benefits of using a firm rather than a solo. Less likely, perhaps, but not out of the question, is the possibility that your clients will learn about your shortcomings or not hear about your abilities in the best light. While this "courting" is occurring, you will be so busy tying up loose ends that the clients may well make decisions before you can make your best pitch.

Taking Clients With You—Expectation Versus Reality

I do not know any lawyer who has left a firm who has not been surprised by (1) the clients the lawyer expected to follow who did not, and (2) the clients the lawyer expected not to follow who did. The ethical rules I discuss below play an important part in this phenomenon, but there are many other factors discussed in this chapter that can play a part.

Let me count the surprises you can find:

1. The client you thought loved you and your work actually hates you and your work, or actually loves the paralegal or associate who is staying with your former firm.
2. Your client contact does not have the authority to take the work from your former firm.
3. Your client contact is limited to an approved list of firms.
4. The client's choices include not only you and your former firm, but also other firms and moving the work in-house.
5. Your client requires technology or other infrastructure that you can no longer provide.
6. You misread or misinterpreted what you hoped were positive signals from your client.
7. Your former firm makes your client a better deal than you can.
8. You walk into a conflict of interest that you did not see coming.
9. Unbeknownst to you, your former firm blackens your reputation in conversations with the client.
10. Add your favorite story here.

Because you cannot "lock down" a client before your departure and the choice always remains with the client, you cannot be certain that any client will move its work to your new practice. Because the ethical rules also put obligations on both you and your former firm to contact the client, your former firm will always have an opportunity to try to keep the client. Making assumptions about clients leaving with you can be dangerous for your bank account.

The Rules of Departure—Clients and Other Issues

This section focuses upon the ethics rules that apply to leaving a law firm. First, however, is a discussion of the "applicable law" on this issue. There are five components of the "law" or "rules" on law firm departures. Three of the five will not surprise you. The other two might.

First, of course, are the applicable ethics rules and any cases or opinions interpreting them. Second, and increasingly important, are any applicable partnership agreements and/or employment agreements, which can specifically cover departure issues. Third are the cases or standards relating to the "fiduciary" obligations that lawyers in a firm have to each other; these may come into play in certain settings, especially when the first two sources mentioned do not cover the issue at hand. Fourth are local standards and practices that have evolved over the years in your geographic area. Though not set in stone, these practices might keep a firm from suing a departing lawyer or taking certain approaches to handling contingency-fee arrangements. Fifth are rules of etiquette and courtesy. "Don't burn bridges," or, "Gentlemen don't tell secrets," are examples of these rules. If the situation gets heated enough, these rules go out the window quickly, but they often function in the normal setting.

Considering each of these areas of "law" is important because they provide a range of options and approaches. If nothing else, taking them into account should keep you from blowing your cool and threatening to sue, when both you and your former firm know you will not back up the threat, and, in the process, lose what you could have easily obtained by agreement.

Because the second through fifth factors I listed vary by location and situation, let us focus upon factor number one—the ethical rules.

Ethical Rules and Guidance

It is extremely important to remember that the rules, decisions, and interpretations in your jurisdiction may differ from the general points discussed below, and that to reach your own conclusions, you must review the materials applicable to you.

Lawyers have been leaving law firms and moving to other law firms or starting new firms for many, many years. You might think the applicable rules and procedures would be (1) easy to find and (2) quite clear and well settled. If that is what you think, you will be surprised. The guidance on this matter varies widely from state to state, and applying the rules in any given situation can be a difficult exercise. There is no specific rule with a title like, "Actions Permitted When Leaving a Firm." In fact, the opinions and decisions seem to find relevant guidance from the "penumbra" of the rules of professional responsibility.

The ethical analysis always focuses upon the right of a client to choose and discharge his or her own lawyer, the limitations on a firm's right to restrict a departing lawyer's ability to practice law, and the limitations on direct contact with prospective clients. Generally, Model Rules 1.4 (requiring lawyers to provide enough information to permit clients to make informed decisions), 5.6 (prohibiting covenants not to compete), 1.16 (covering withdrawal from representation), 7.1 (mandating truthful communications to prospective clients), and 7.3 (dealing with solicitation of clients) will govern contacts with clients for lawyers leaving a firm. (See Appendix B, page 605). Because the Rules may vary from state to state, the conclusions drawn from this analysis may be different depending on the jurisdiction and the question involved. For example, a state might treat a departing associate differently from a departing partner, even if the associate is considered the "responsible" lawyer.

Let me attempt to summarize the general approach. A departing lawyer probably cannot solicit an existing firm client before her departure from the firm. Both the departing lawyer and the law firm have a responsibility to notify the client of the departure of the lawyer and the client's right to choose his own lawyer. The recommended practice is to have the firm and the departing lawyer send the client a joint letter that gives this notice. Both the departing lawyer and the firm must respect the decision of the client and, at a minimum, not hinder the orderly transfer of work and files. The firm may not by agreement restrict the departing lawyer's ability to practice law. After the departing lawyer leaves the firm, she can directly solicit the former client under the applicable solicitation rules. As a practical matter, before entering a representation agreement, the departing lawyer should have a copy of the client's discharge letter to the law firm.

As suggested, you will find a large number of nuances from state to state. Perhaps more significant, as most lawyers observe, these procedures are often honored in the breach. In many departures, the movement of clients with the departing lawyer proceeds as if planned in advance. Many departing lawyers have received some signal from one or more key clients about their intentions. In some cases, a client may have told a lawyer that if the lawyer ever leaves, the client will follow.

Law firms typically prefer making the first contact with the client about the departure, rather than using a joint letter. Firms typically want to approve the letter sent by the departing lawyer. Some opinions indicate that the information provided by or about the departing lawyer can be quite limited.

It is no secret that the transition of files can turn into a bitter battleground. Both lawyers and law firms can cook up many legitimate reasons to delay the process. Technological advances, ironically, seem to have created more reasons for delay rather than ways to speed the process. Lawyers' unreasonable actions in creating delays in the transfer of files are possible subjects of civil law suits and even disciplinary proceedings if there is harm to the client.

The area in which you find the most predictability is the general prohibition on restrictive noncompete provisions. Although it is not possible to get accurate statistics on the use of noncompete provisions in law firm partnership agreements, anecdotal evidence suggests they are not commonly used. However, though restrictive provisions might be thrown out in court, they give a firm leverage in settling with a departing lawyer who does not plan to test the provision in court.

Where does all this leave you as the departing lawyer? Typically with more questions than answers. You will not find certainty and a clear set of procedures. You should start with the general principles found in ABA Formal Opinion 99-414, the headnote of which states as follows:

Formal Opinion 99-414
Ethical Obligations When a Lawyer Changes Firms
A lawyer's ethical obligations upon withdrawal from one firm to join another derive from the concepts that clients' interests must be protected and that each client has the right to choose the departing lawyer or the firm, or another lawyer to represent him. The departing lawyer and the responsible members of her firm who remain must take reasonable measures to assure that the withdrawal is accomplished without material adverse effect on the interests of clients with active matters upon which the lawyer currently is working. The departing lawyer and responsible members of the law firm who remain have an ethical obligation to assure that prompt notice is given to clients on whose active matters she currently is working. The departing lawyer and responsible members of the law firm who remain also have ethical obligations to protect client information, files, and other client property. The departing lawyer is prohibited by ethical rules, and may be prohibited by other law, from making in-person contact prior to her departure with clients with whom she has no family or client-lawyer relationship. After she has left the firm, she may contact any firm client by letter.

Next, look at the applicable rules, comments, and opinions in your state. Check for any applicable court decisions. Then ask other lawyers about local practices and what has happened with other lawyers leaving your firm.

As you might expect, the most important factors in this process will be your courtesy, consideration, preparation, and good personal relationships, not specific rules and case law. Obviously, if there is no likelihood you will take a major client or case, the process should be an easy one. Otherwise, keep the focus upon serving the client, make reasonable requests, be willing to compromise on minor issues, and keep the process civil and on track.

Conclusion: Ten Tips for Leaving a Law Firm for a Solo Practice

1. Think long-term and keep the big picture (getting your new practice off the ground) in mind. You can win the war without needing to win every battle.
2. Assume nothing, especially about keeping clients.
3. Make a quick decision and a quick exit, and try to leave a gap of at least two weeks before you launch into your solo practice.
4. Consider David Scott's Rule of Threes: When starting a business, everything—and that means everything—takes three times longer, costs three time more, and is three times harder than you expected.
5. Today's technology options, especially with low prices and leasing, give you a platform on which to practice law at a high level almost immediately.
6. Remember that you will wear all the hats in your new firm. If the wastebasket has to be emptied, look in the mirror. If the computer must be fixed, look in the mirror. You will also be doing all the legal work.
7. When making your decision, do some financial-scenario planning. A best-case scenario might make you feel good, but taking a close look at a worst-case scenario is essential, if only to test your commitment.
8. Once you announce your decision to your firm, go public and tell everyone you can.
9. Know the ethical rules and applicable law, but remember that the key is to make a good exit, not the perfect exit. Expect to get less than you feel you deserve, be pleasantly surprised if you do better, and forget about it and move on to your new venture.
10. If one of your reasons for going solo does not have to do with having more freedom, go back to the drawing board.

A Checklist for Stunt Pilots*

5

M. Joe Crosthwait, Jr.

Lawyers are like stunt pilots. To be successful, we must amuse the crowds and defy death. This is particularly true for the general practice and solo and small-firm lawyer. Our flips, hammerheads, barrel rolls, dives, stalls, and inverted tailspins are what we call the practice of law.

All good pilots need a checklist. As the pilots in this group know, you live and die by the checklist. Here is one for takeoff.

The Checklist

- ◆ Have a good attitude.
- ◆ "Know thyself and to thine own self be true."
- ◆ Establish good client rapport.
- ◆ Provide "value-added" service.
- ◆ Develop excellent phone manners.
- ◆ Use e-mail systems.
- ◆ Keep an accurate and timely calendaring system.
- ◆ Manage your money and your cash flow.
- ◆ Be careful who you represent.
- ◆ Use written engagement letters.
- ◆ Bill frequently and accurately.

*An earlier version of this chapter appeared in *The Oklahoma Bar Journal*, November 16, 1996. Reprinted with permission.

- Hire the best people you can find, and keep them.
- Constantly improve yourself.
- Master technology.
- Know the source of your clients.
- Get involved.

Have a Good Attitude

Being a lawyer is a lifestyle. Even when you are not being one, you still are in the eyes of others. Everything you say and do, whether in your professional or personal capacity, reflects not only upon you, but also upon our profession and the justice system. A reputation that took years to establish can be destroyed virtually instantaneously. But seek balance and don't take yourself too seriously. Remember that if you are what you do, then when you don't, you aren't. When disagreeing is necessary, don't be disagreeable. Live each day as though it would be the focus of your obituary.

"Know Thyself and to Thine Own Self Be True"

Try to understand what it is you want out of life and the practice of law. If being a stunt pilot isn't what you want to do, do something else. Life is too short to spend it doing something you don't enjoy. Understand your abilities and limitations. Get and stay physically fit. Exercise and take care of the only real form of transportation you will ever have.

Establish Good Client Rapport

Apply the Golden Rule. Project the fundamentals of good interpersonal relationships—common courtesy, ordinary respect, empathy, trust, confidence, loyalty, comfort, clear communication, and businesslike conduct. Establish equality with your clients. When clients meet you for the first time, they may not know how and why you are qualified to assist them. Self-disclosure not only answers that question, but also engenders good relationships with clients. Would you have you as a lawyer?

Provide "Value-Added" Service

Project effort through effort. Be prompt, thorough, and prepared. Provide copies of everything to your clients. Give them regular updates. If you are working on their cases on weekends or at night, call them if you need to and let them know what you are doing and when you are doing it. Whenever you accept a new matter, immediately make a comprehensive memo to the file regarding the facts and initial impressions about the legal issues involved, witnesses, strategies, and related issues. Develop a game plan to see the matter through to its conclusion. Establish and continuously review good systems and checklists. Above all, delegate and have clear lines of authority and responsibility for you and your staff, but always recognize where ultimate responsibility lies. Make client representation a team effort with you as the captain. Put the client to work assisting you in getting information or whatever may be done that is within the client's abilities. Remember that clients come to you with situations, not cases. Let them know you sincerely care about them and their situations.

Develop Excellent Phone Manners

At the first meeting with a new client, let your client know how you handle phone calls. Explain that most of the time, you are on the phone, with a client, or in court. Assure the client that you or someone for you, as may be appropriate, will call back as soon as possible. Establish the legal assistant or staff person assigned to the matter as the client's first contact. Schedule phone calls when possible. Use conference calling. When you are meeting with a client, do not take calls or allow interruptions. Don't have your secretary get someone on the phone for you. Don't use a speakerphone unless absolutely necessary.

Use E-mail Systems

A few years ago, lawyers debated about whether to communicate with clients and other lawyers through e-mail systems. That debate is over, and e-mail systems won! Clients, lawyers, claims adjusters, and judges expect that they can send you e-mail messages and get prompt replies. One result of this instant communication is that everyone seems to be suffering from "e-mail overload." One way to minimize the stress of too much e-mail communication is to establish policies and procedures in your office. You should, for example, acknowledge receipt of an e-mail message and let the sender know when to expect a substantive response.

E-mail systems can be used for much more than correspondence. Increasingly, state and federal courts are either allowing or requiring filings to be done via e-mail communication. Check with your court's Web site to see what the rules are.

Keep an Accurate and Timely Calendaring System

Develop good docketing habits and systems. As Ronald Reagan said, "Good habits are hard to break." A computer-based system, frequently once backed up, is a highly reliable and effective system. I have no idea how we functioned before we converted. Commit absolutely nothing to memory. A good calendaring system, and adherence to it, is the first step to good time and risk management.

Manage Your Money and Your Cash Flow

Get and keep good credit. Don't spend money you do not have. Establish a realistic budget and make it work. Always pay your taxes—on time! Most small businesses fail and many lawyers get into ethical difficulties by not managing money and taxes properly. Unless you are highly skilled in financial management, get a good CPA and do whatever you must do to learn how to understand and implement good money management. Save and invest for rainy days, as well as for the future, and know the difference. Don't spend your savings or investments, except on those things for which you saved and invested.

Be Careful Who You Represent

If you have an opportunity to represent someone you don't like and don't care to learn to like, or who you sense does not like you and probably never will, do everyone a favor and pass. First impressions generally speak volumes about the future of a relationship. Trust your gut feelings.

Have Written Engagement Letters

Always have a clear understanding with clients regarding the matters for which they are hiring you and the fees they will be charged. Remember that when clients come to see you, they expect you to discuss the fees and costs. Most also expect to, and should, pay a retainer fee. That way they know they have a lawyer and you know you have a client. Don't underestimate the fees. Establish a reasonable expectation in the client about the financial ramifications of the undertaking, and put it in writing. The only case in which you will ordinarily have a fee dispute is one that is not in writing.

Bill Frequently and Accurately

A bill tells a client how and when a fee was incurred, and informs the client when to pay it. Be sure that all billing is strictly consistent with the fee agreement. Insist that clients abide by their financial obligations unless there is good reason not to. Promptly resolve any billing disputes.

Hire the Best People You Can Find, and Keep Them

Master the art and magic of delegation by clearly equating authority with responsibility and accountability. Recognize your employees' crucial role in a successful law practice: "A Lawyer's Staff Is His (Her) Strength." It's almost biblical. Have frequent office meetings to review cases, discuss management issues, and simply to "relate." Pay your employees well and, as part of your overall financial plan, establish profit sharing or another deferred-compensation plan. Provide opportunities for continuing education for the entire staff and insist upon their availing themselves. Develop methods to measure productivity of all lawyers and staff members. Most computer billing programs provide four productivity reports for all staff, whether or not their particular services are a component of billing. This can be incredibly enlightening information. Remember that we all do, or at least should, have a life outside the office. A happy, well-rounded employee is a priceless asset.

Constantly Improve Yourself

Learn—and not just the law. Read. Have hobbies. Keep those anapses and synapses in contact. Expand your horizons. Develop new skills. Above all, "Follow your Bliss," as Joseph Campbell would say. Remember to be who you are and not what you are.

Master Technology

Make a planned, organized, and continuous effort to learn the technology available to lawyers. Allocate adequate time and money for equipment, software, and training for you and your staff. The dramatic changes in the way technology affects the rendition of legal services have only just begun.

Know the Source of Your Clients

Find out how a client found out about you. If the client had a lawyer before you, find out why the client is no longer with that lawyer. It ought to tell you what not to do, and it might tell you whom not to represent. Always acknowledge referrals with at least a thank-you note or a personal phone call. Once you have represented a client, be sure to let the client know the other fields in which you practice. How often have you heard, "I would have come back to you, but I didn't know you did that kind of stuff."

Get Involved

Be active in professional associations. Too often we don't meet other lawyers except in hostile territory. This is especially true for solo and small-firm practitioners. The organized bar does good things for lawyers and for society. It's fun. The networking is invaluable, professionally and personally.

Have a nice flight!

What Kind of Practice?

Why Should You Specialize?

6

Gary A. Munneke

One of the first things any sole practitioner must address is whether to specialize in a particular field of law. Historically, and especially in small-town practice, solos have felt they needed to become general practitioners. The idea of a becoming a "womb-to-tomb" lawyer—one who handles all the client's legal needs from the moment of conception until the client's will is pro-bated—carries with it a certain appeal. In the past, lawyers often viewed themselves as family lawyers, and law firms often han-dled the legal needs of their clients over several generations. In today's practice environment, however, a number of factors make general practice a less-than-appealing approach to solo practice.

The term "specialization" has a checkered past. Tradition-ally, upon being licensed to practice law, lawyers were presumed to be qualified to provide services to clients in any substantive legal field. Specialization was viewed as a form of attracting new clients, which was prohibited under ethical standards until 1977, when the U.S. Supreme Court held in *Bates v. State Bar of Arizona* that a blanket prohibition of lawyer advertising was unconstitu-tional. In 1990, the Court, in *Peel v. Attorney Registration and Disciplinary Committee*, held that the bar could not categorically pre-vent lawyers from making communications about their specialties. Currently, Rule 7.4 of the Model Rules of Professional Conduct states as follows:

> A lawyer may communicate the fact that the lawyer does or does not practice in particular fields of law. . . . A lawyer shall not state or imply that a lawyer is certified as a specialist in a particular field of law, unless: (1) the lawyer has been certified as a specialist by an organization that has been approved by an appropriate state authority or that has been accredited by the American Bar Association; and (2) the name of the certifying organization is clearly identified in the communication.

Paragraph [1] of the Comments to Rule 7.4 goes on to say the following:

> A lawyer is generally permitted to state that the lawyer is a "specialist," practices a "specialty," or "specializes in" particular fields, but such communications are subject to the "false and misleading" standard applied in Rule 7.1 to communications concerning a lawyer's services.

However, because state versions of Model Rule 7.4 vary considerably, lawyers who intend to limit their fields of practice should consult the ethics rules in the state(s) where they are licensed, before marketing themselves as specialists. (See Appendix B, page 637 for the complete Model Rule 7.4 and Comments).

Trends in Law Practice

The reality of practicing law in the United States today is that individuals and law firms cannot do everything; they must choose to handle some legal work and decline or refer other work. As society has become more diverse, the law has become more complex. As more lawyers have chosen to concentrate their practice areas, the threshold of competence has increased in many fields. As clients have grown more sophisticated, they have increasingly sought lawyers with greater expertise in the areas of the clients' legal problems over lawyers with general legal knowledge of the law. Generalists simply cannot compete with specialists. It might be useful to examine these trends more fully.

As Society Becomes More Diverse, the Law Becomes More Complex

There is considerable anecdotal evidence that the number of practice areas has increased dramatically since World War II, as whole areas of practice—such as environmental law, computer law, historic preservation law, animal rights law, and countless other new fields—have arisen from previously unheard-of social problems. Other practice areas that were once obscure backwaters of legal practice have mushroomed; these include professional liability law, product liability law, entertainment and sports law, immigration law, and patent law. The internationalization of commercial markets has complicated even the most basic business transactions. Increased government regulation in some areas and deregulation in other areas have made the law more confusing to clients and practitioners alike. Simply in terms of pure volume, no lawyer is capable of learning or keeping up with all the constantly evolving fields of law.

As More Lawyers Choose to Concentrate, the Threshold of Competence Increases

At the same time, clients have become increasingly critical of their lawyers, second-guess their lawyers' professional judgment, and sue their lawyers when they are not satisfied with the results of legal representation. The incidence of legal malpractice has increased, a phenomenon that is statistically demonstrable. Legal malpractice carriers are placing greater pressure on lawyers to limit the number of fields of practice in which they will take cases. Think of it this way: If Lawyer A, a general practitioner, handles one immigration case each year, she will lack the experience of Lawyer B, who limits her practice to immigration law and handles several hundred cases per year. If Lawyer A does work in twenty substantive areas over the course of a year, she will handle, at most, a few cases in each area annually—far fewer than specialists in those areas. In short, the threshold for competent practice has been elevated, both by the greater expertise of specialists and by the greater risk of liability for those lacking such expertise.

As Clients Grow More Sophisticated, They Increasingly Seek Lawyers with Greater Expertise

One of the outgrowths of lawyer advertising is that information about lawyers and the law has become more accessible since 1977. Information about legal services and the law is available not only through lawyer marketing, but also through books, software, news media, the Internet, and referral services. It is often said that lawyers' clients, like doctors' patients, want to control their own cases, and neither are willing to accept paternalistic treatment by professional service providers. On the one hand, legal clients might be more willing to criticize and sue their lawyers, but they are also more likely to do their homework before selecting their lawyers. Modern clients conduct research to find the best lawyers to serve their needs, and the best lawyers are often the specialists.

A corollary of this concept is that it costs less to market to a small, targeted audience than to an unfocused, general audience. The generalist has to reach the public with an offer to do legal work, whereas the specialist needs only to reach the small group of people who have problems in the area of expertise of the specialist. The experience of the magazine industry is illustrative: national general-circulation magazines such as *Look*, *Life*, and *Saturday Evening Post* have disappeared, while specialty periodicals such as *People*, *Popular Mechanics*, and *Wine Spectator* have thrived. In the legal industry, lawyers who sell specialized services are much better positioned to reach their audiences than lawyers who do not.

Generalists Cannot Compete with Specialists

Specialists can assure quality by implementing substantive practice systems that utilize routine procedures for handling similar cases. Just as production lines in other industries can produce more items with fewer mistakes (cars, watches, or almost anything else), legal production lines can improve efficiency and quality as well. To be most effective, these systems require volume, so the generalist who handles one or two cases in an area each year can hardly be said to have a system. Assuming a practice system improves efficiency, the specialist can use this competitive advantage in one of three ways: to improve profitability by taking less time to do the same work as a less-efficient lawyer, where both charge the going rate; to reduce fees by undercutting the price of less-efficient competitors; or to reduce the number of hours the specialist must devote to legal work, providing more time for family and personal interests. In short, the competitive advantage offered by specialization makes it worthwhile for most lawyers to choose to limit their practice concentrations.

Should a Solo Specialize?

The question solos must ask is whether this advice applies to them. Should sole practitioners try to limit their fields of practice, or is specialization reserved for lawyers in larger organizations? Can solos generate enough business to maintain profitability if they do not take whatever legal work they can get their hands on? More specifically, can small-town solos specialize, given the limited population they are likely to serve in nonmetropolitan settings?

The answers to these questions are not simple. The general proposition that specialists make more money than generalists applies as much to solos as it does to other lawyers. So, for solos, particularly small-town solos, the critical issue is whether they can find enough legal work to pay the bills and earn a living. To assess this question, it is important to understand the relationship between price and volume.

In his classic work on law firm planning, consultant Bill Cobb describes the situation with a graph that illustrates the relationship between the amount of work available and the rates lawyers can charge for such work. The more generic the work, the more lawyers are available to handle it, and the less practitioners can charge for their services. For more specialized work, there is less available work and a smaller group of lawyers qualified to perform it, and those lawyers can charge more for their services. In theory, a lawyer who provides truly unique services that even a small number of people need would operate in a price-insensitive environment.

Applying Cobb's principles, Lawyer A providing generic services might be able to charge $100 per hour for his services, while Lawyer B providing specialized services can charge $300 per hour for his services. It is easy to see how the specialist can earn three times as much as the generalist, but it might not be as apparent that the specialist need serve only one-third the number of clients to earn the same amount as the generalist. In this sense, the specialist in a small town does not have to generate as many clients to stay afloat, even though the number of cases available may be fewer. Given the other efficiencies of marketing and delivery, the small-town solo can effectively concentrate her practice.

Lawyers seeking to specialize may find there are more competitors for better-paying specialty work. It is axiomatic that lawyers generally seek to provide more high-end services to more high-end clients over time; no one ever says, "My goal in practice is to be a bottom-feeder who takes all the cases that no one else wants." The trend is for lawyers to enhance their client mix over time. This means that a less-experienced lawyer first starting her practice may take cases that she would not take after her practice is established, or that legal work that is profitable when one is new to the practice may not look so good after practicing for a number of years.

Solos seeking to specialize today have many advantages that lawyers in earlier times did not. "E-lawyering," or providing legal information and services online, is one of the most dramatic changes. From informational Web sites to referral networks to interactive services, lawyers with the technological acumen to harness the Internet are no longer limited to the geographic boundaries of the town or county where they practice. Mass media also allow lawyers to extend the reach of their communications to clients they previously could not access, allowing them to deliver services to a much broader geographical circle.

In 2002, the ABA amended Model Rule 5.5 to permit lawyers to engage in authorized multijurisdictional practice (MJP) outside the state(s) where they are licensed, provided (1) there is some relationship between the multijurisdictional work and their home state practice, (2) they do not hold themselves out as being licensed in a state where they are not, and (3) they do not establish a permanent presence in such state. (See Appendix B, page 605). Although individual states have been slow to adopt this MJP rule, most lawyers have cases that take them beyond their home jurisdictions. Specialists are well served by more liberal MJP rules, because they have greater flexibility in serving their core client base than they would in a geographically rigid system.

Solos can also participate in referral networks, both to attract clients in their areas of specialty and to refer cases they are not equipped to handle. In the latter situation, lawyers can reduce the risk of liability if they do not take cases outside their fields of expertise. A referral network allows a lawyer to maintain some relationship to the client, while avoiding undertaking legal work outside the lawyer's knowledge base. Model Rule 1.5(e) allows lawyers who are not in the same firm to share legal fees, provided "(1) the division is in proportion to the services performed by each lawyer or each lawyer assumes joint responsibility for the representation; (2) the client agrees to the arrangement, including the share each lawyer will receive, and the agreement is confirmed in writing; and (3) the total fee is reasonable." Referral networks can include bar-sponsored referral systems, commercial networks, or affiliated groups of lawyers. Lawyer affiliations can be especially appealing to solos, giving them the scope of services of a larger law firm while maintaining the autonomy and other benefits of a solo practice.

For those lawyers who still favor the concept of serving the general needs of a clientele without engaging in a true specialty practice, the thought of serving as a referral hub may be appealing. Using as an example the primary-care physician who handles patients' basic needs but refers patients to specialists as necessary, the notion of a primary-care lawyer might work as well. Small-town lawyers and lawyers associated with a unique cultural, ethnic, or religious group, or some other affinity connection, might find a way to create a specialty in primary legal services, thereby creating a new kind of general practitioner.

Whatever solo lawyers decide to do about specializing should not be a matter of serendipity. Instead of waiting for something to happen, or for their law practices to evolve into something, solos should make reasoned and researched decisions about how to build their practices. Often lawyers become specialists by default: after handling a couple cases in some area—maybe an area the lawyer does not even like—the lawyer becomes known as "the lawyer who handles X." The better approach is for lawyers to look at their personal skills, interests, contacts, and opportunities, and then work to build the concentrated, high-quality practices they want. This is not something that will happen overnight; but, without some kind of long-range plan, practice specialization is not likely to happen at all.

A Solo Can Represent Big Business

7

Mark A. Robertson

Introduction

Can a sole practitioner represent big businesses? The answer is yes—an emphatic *YES!* No magic formulas or special credentials are required to represent large businesses (or any business, for that matter); lawyers need only keep in mind some simple points as they develop their practices and earn their livings. Above everything else, you should remember that with very few exceptions, *businesses (big or small) hire lawyers—not law firms—to represent them*. Just like an individual who comes to see you about a will, divorce, or property dispute, a business will seek the lawyer who it believes will represent it properly in its legal needs.

As a small-firm practitioner, I have enjoyed representing big and small businesses and individuals for their corporate legal needs and personal planning for nearly thirty years. I preface the rest of my remarks by noting that I have not always practiced in a small-firm environment. When I first went to work as a clerk in law school and later as a newbie lawyer, I worked for a firm that specialized primarily in litigation and had only three lawyers. Though it later grew to include more than thirty lawyers, even as a small law firm it represented the third-largest bank in Oklahoma City, several Fortune 500 companies, and a number of individuals who owned significant business interests throughout the United States. I changed law firms and went to a ten-lawyer firm that grew to forty-two lawyers, and then left for a higher quality of life with a smaller firm. In all three firms, I found that with the exception of some institutional businesses, clients hired the *lawyer* and *not the firm*, and when a lawyer left—to go to another firm or out on his or her own—the client went with the lawyer if he or she was capable of continuing to do the client's work.

That said, there are some activities that are important for any business-oriented practice, but are critical if you want to represent "big" business: developing core competencies, becoming actively involved in bar activities, establishing a client development program, and planning practice development.

Core Competencies

It should go without saying (but I'll say it anyway) that a lawyer trying to represent businesses should develop core competencies in areas in which businesses require representation.

If you plan to represent businesses in litigation matters, then you must demonstrate your abilities in that area. The first firm for which I worked specialized in "nuclear event" litigation—the variety that involved "bet the company" matters, multimillion-dollar exposure, or company survival. As a result of significant and successful trial experience, the partners were adept at this type of work and were good at telling people about it. Their satisfied clients were also good at telling people about it.

If you plan to be a transactional lawyer, then you must develop skills in areas such as negotiating and closing transactions, forming businesses, taking companies public, negotiating complex documents, and understanding the tax consequences of transactions or events. My second firm had lawyers with significant skills in these areas. Those skills increased with every successful transaction, and the lawyers had years of experience. Special training or degrees may be required, depending upon the area of practice (for example, an LLM in taxation or intensive continuing legal education in securities or mergers and acquisitions). The more transactions you complete successfully, the more your clients (and potential clients on the other side of transactions) are impressed with the quality of the representation. This results in more work from new, and sometimes larger, clients.

What expertise do you have to offer big businesses? Though a good utility infielder who can handle routine matters may be valuable, most larger businesses have that type of staff in-house. You should consider developing a core competency in a specialty that the prospective client does not or cannot handle in-house.

Competency comes with experience and, for that reason, I cannot give you any "tips" for helping you become more competent. You must practice and study your way to competency. One thing is certain, however—you must know the area of law you practice, and know it well, to represent businesses.

Active Bar Involvement

The second most important thing you need to represent big businesses is connection to individuals in those businesses who distribute work to outside counsel. For big companies, that usually means the inside general counsel. How and where can you meet the general counsel or in-house counsel? Go where they are—become active in the same bar association activities or entities in which they are active. Though other marketing activities can also increase your exposure to inside lawyers, active bar involvement is the most important, for two reasons: (1) it helps you improve your core competencies, and (2) you meet many lawyers from around the country. This second point is important because lawyers will refer work to other lawyers they know or have met before they will pull out *Martindale-Hubbell* or some other directory to find lawyers in your geographic area when they need them.

The American Bar Association has several substantive law sections that meet the test. The Section of Business Law is home to most business law issues and lawyers. It has committees on virtually every type of business transaction that most businesses and their lawyers address on a day-to-day basis. The committees include inside and outside corporate lawyers, as well as legal scholars—they offer a great territory to learn and schmooze at the same time. There are niche sections and forums with a strong business orientation, such as antitrust, franchising, and construction. The Law Practice Management Section and the General Practice, Solo, and Small Firm Section are both fertile areas to learn and network with lawyers from throughout the United States (as well as other countries) for education and business development. Most state and local bar associations also have sections and committees with a business emphasis (although the number of participants and the geographic diversity is far more limited than that of ABA sections and committees).

Client Development Program

Before a business-client development program can be implemented effectively, a lawyer must engage in some research and strategic analysis—identifying individual strengths, weaknesses, assets, systems, and perceptions in the community.

The first step is to conduct an internal survey of yourself and your staff—focusing on self-image, perceived strengths and weaknesses, core competencies, billing practices, and current and targeted practice areas. This information can be gathered with simple lists and, when compiled, will assist you in defining how you see yourself as a lawyer, what your strengths are, what you have to offer clients, and what resources are currently available.

The second step is to learn about clients—who they are, where they are from, what businesses they are in, and what legal services they receive from you and from other law firms. Most of this information can be pulled from records you already have. The rest can be obtained through a simple client questionnaire or survey. This step should be replicated for target clients—those big businesses you want to represent.

What information you want to compile on client and prospective client profiles is up to you. A typical profile should include not only basic information such as names, addresses, telephone numbers, industry classifications (SIC numbers or your own coding system), and billing and payment history, but also (1) the banks, accounting firms, and other law firms the client or prospective client uses, (2) the practice areas in which it seeks legal guidance, (3) the number of employees it has, and (4) financial information regarding its business. Developing a simple client profile is not a difficult task—staff members can compile much of the information. A simple database can be established on a personal computer or word processor, or manually on a form using a simple filing and cross-reference system.

One of the best, least-expensive, and least-used resources for external research on prospective clients is the public library. The reference desk materials and various business directories found in most public libraries (such as Dunn & Bradstreet's *Million Dollar Directory*, Moody's *Industrial and OTC Manuals*, and Standard & Poor's *Register of Corporations*) offer a wealth of information on companies and industries. In addition, commercial sources of information published for other groups might be useful. (For example, ask your accountant if your area is covered by any directories used to target prospects.)

The local or state chamber of commerce can also be a resource for information on the community and the industries and companies that are members. Area or state economic development agencies or departments often have industry information and public filings on companies using economic development assistance, and information on companies whose securities are publicly traded is readily available from the Securities and Exchange Commission or the state securities department.

In addition, numerous online databases can be used to locate information on individuals, companies, and industries. The ABA Law Practice Management Section has a terrific publication on Internet research, *The Lawyer's Guide to Fact Finding on the Internet*, Second Edition, by Carole A. Levitt and Mark E. Rosch (ABA, 2004), which has a chapter on company research.

Once you gather the necessary information, the process of identifying prospective clients is not difficult. You can also identify potential referral sources from this information. Analyzing information on existing or prospective clients is no different than thoroughly researching a legal issue for a brief, hearing, or trial. Knowing enough about a client's business and industry to be conversant with the client or prospective client is important in establishing and maintaining credibility and a comfortable relationship with someone who is deciding whether to select or retain you.

Practice Development

Big-Business Marketing Plan

The big-business marketing plan for an individual lawyer includes the same basic components as any other marketing plan: a position or aspirational statement, goals, objectives, policies, strategies, and a tactical plan to achieve the goals and objectives. The plan is a useful tool to focus and organize the individual's practice, highlight needed changes, attract new clients, and facilitate good client relations.

A big-business marketing plan might be as simple as setting a goal to represent the town's cement plant in all its corporate legal needs. After setting your goals and objectives, your marketing plan will include the specific strategies, tasks, and time lines necessary to achieve those goals and objectives.

Technology

Technology is the great equalizer—solos and small firms are more nimble in their use and acquisition of technology, both hardware and software. The cost for a large law firm to change word-processing systems, for example, is staggering compared with the cost for a solo or small firm. I have found that most large law firms are two to three years behind the technology-savvy small firms and, from my viewpoint, the gap is widening. Advantage: small firms and solos.

Small firms can leverage technology to gain a competitive advantage over large firms—both in the courtroom and in attracting clients. With an inexpensive scanner, a sole practitioner can produce the same volume of discovery as a large firm, simply by scanning the two hundred pages of interrogatories just received from the big firm, and then turning them into a word-processing document by running OCR software. The solo can then use the global search-and-replace function to change names in the interrogatories, add his own questions, and ship the document back to the other side in an hour or so! An extreme example, perhaps, but I think you get my point.

Large businesses may expect the sole practitioner or small firm to purchase and install technology that is compatible with that of the company. A solo must be prepared to do what the big business wants. This may mean having a Web site with secure access for document sharing (sounds complicated and expensive, but it is not), having e-mail capabilities, and having the same applications for billing, accounting, and word processing.

Growing Your Own

Most big businesses started as a dream in someone's head, and then became small businesses before ever becoming big. Once you have your systems and organization in place, the easiest way to represent a big business is to start with a new or small business and help it grow. Some of the largest clients I now have are those I helped when they were much smaller or just getting started. Many businesses stick with the lawyers with whom they started.

When we are first engaged by a business to do some legal work, our initial interview and the follow-up fee agreement begin laying the foundation for representing the business for all its legal needs. We tell the client that it should look to our firm as its outside general counsel and bring all its personal and business legal issues to us—*even if we don't do that kind of law!* Why? Because, as we tell them, we know which lawyers are competent to handle their affairs far better than they do—that is part of our job as their counsel. This is what we tell them:

> Our firm would like to serve as your legal counsel. With this position comes the responsibility to advise and counsel you on matters we are competent to handle and, if requested, to assist you in obtaining suitable representation from outside lawyers in areas we cannot handle for you. We look at ourselves as an asset to our clients by providing timely, accurate legal services that are affordable to both the client and the firm. We are pleased that you have selected our firm to represent you. We look forward to serving you and will use our best efforts on your behalf.

As the small business grows bigger, it will continue to call upon you, because you exhibited core competency in the areas in which it hired you to help, and you helped find other lawyers in the areas in which you could not help. You have become the business's outside general counsel.

Building a Network of Outside Lawyers

As a sole practitioner, you must understand your limitations and have resources established for referrals of items that lie outside your core competency. The big advantage of a large law firm is that it has many specialties under one roof and the ability to develop several niche specialty areas, along with the financial resources to continue paying for the beer and the beans while a new specialty is being developed. A solo or small firm may not have those financial resources, but it can develop a network of other solo and small firms that have the expertise required for nearly every legal matter that a client might have. Your relationships with other lawyers—which enable you to hire them on a contract or of-counsel basis, or to give them work outright—are important.

Developing Referral Sources Inside the Business

Who hands out the legal work at the target businesses? Identify those persons and get to know them. It may be the in-house lawyer at some companies, but it also may be the president, the chief financial officer, or some other officer or employee of the business. From your earlier research, you should know who this person is.

To meet the targeted individual, you might begin by identifying someone else you both know. Ask that person for an introduction, or take them both to lunch. If you don't have any common acquaintances, then a letter of introduction or a brief telephone call with some useful information might help. If you have developed an expertise in an area of law that is relevant to the company's industry, then it might be appropriate to send some of your publications or to write something addressing a problem that the business or industry is having. Cold-calling is often awkward and feels "unprofessional," but it might be the only way to establish a relationship.

Developing Referral Sources Outside the Business

Referral sources for a law practice are not always other lawyers. Many successful practices are built upon referrals from other professionals, such as bankers, accountants, insurance sales people, and investment advisors. It is important to develop relationships with these other professionals and to ask them for referrals of their larger customers and clients.

One inexpensive way to market your practice to prospective business clients is to join with a bank, an accounting firm, or an insurance company and cohost a seminar on business structures, planning, or other business issues. Put other professionals on your mailing list and your calling list for breakfast and lunch meetings. Referrals or endorsements from other professionals who already represent a big business are worth their weight in gold. Remember to thank those referral sources—several times.

Joining Trade Associations

Many of your current clients are probably members of various trade associations. Joining those trade associations yourself will not only generate goodwill and a better understanding of your clients' businesses, it can also help you develop additional legal work from those businesses, as well as from other members of the association whom you meet (or, better yet, who are referred to you by your member client). Demonstrating a genuine interest in the issues that concern members of a trade association and developing an expertise in a particular industry are important tools for developing clients within that industry.

Being a lawyer in a trade association also opens the opportunity for being a lawyer *for* the trade association, or at least for writing legal articles in the association's publications. When you publish as a lawyer in a trade association magazine or newsletter, your "expert factor" goes up geometrically. Reprints from such publications are also important marketing pieces to send to clients and potential clients who might not be members of the association.

Offering to Be Local Counsel

If you are outside a metropolitan area, market yourself to larger firms with big clients to be their local counsel. Representing one large business as local counsel often leads to other matters through referral from satisfied in-house or outside counsel. This relationship can be developed through bar activities and old school ties.

Personal Representation Leading to Business Representation

You can begin developing corporate legal business through representing the individuals who own or run the businesses. Remember, if a client is satisfied with your work in one matter, he is likely to hire you for the next matter, even if it is unrelated to the matter you last handled. As long as you have the core competency (or have a referral source with such competency), then requesting and accepting new work will lead to cementing the lawyer-client relationship.

As an example, many executives and owners need estate planning, which can be leveraged into additional corporate legal work. You could identify key executives in a target business and obtain an introduction from a common friend or business associate. Only about one-third of people in this country have wills, so there is a good chance that the key executives in the company have inadequate or nonexistent estate planning. Once you demonstrate your core competency in this area and satisfy a client, it becomes much easier to ask for the corporate work, particularly if you can demonstrate skills in that area as well. Estate planning often leads naturally to corporate work, through matters such as deferred compensation or buy-sell and shareholder agreements.

Making Your Resources Look Bigger

You can look bigger than you are if you present yourself properly. There are a number of simple yet effective steps you can take to present a professional picture of your practice that conveys a "larger look" to your clients and prospective clients:

◆ *Firm Name and Letterhead*: If you practice in a firm with other lawyers, your firm name is an important marketing tool. The firm letterhead should include the firm name and address, and the name of only the lawyer sending the letter (with a direct-dial phone number). A person who sees a letter from Able & Baker, with only your name and direct-dial number printed on the side, does not know whether you are one of two or two hundred lawyers. Modern word-processing systems and printers can produce this letterhead on demand, eliminating the need to have it done by an outside printing or engraving company.

◆ *Answering the Telephone*: How many big law firms answer their telephones with "Law firm"? None! How many other businesses answer their telephones with "Bookstore" rather than "Barnes & Noble," or "Doctor's office" rather than "Dr. Smith's office"? None. Businesses spend hundreds of millions of dollars every year trying to get the public to recognize their names. Most solo and small-firm lawyers seem to do the exact opposite by telling callers they are no different from the other 3,500 lawyers in the telephone book. Your name is a valuable asset—don't throw it away by having your telephone answered as if you are indistinguishable from every other lawyer in town.

◆ *Contract Lawyers*: With proper networking, you can offer the services of a larger firm by using contract lawyers for certain projects. (This also allows you to avoid the overhead and supervision that often accompany associates.)

◆ *Business Cards*: Have your business cards professionally done. Unlike letterhead, the business cards you can print from your own computer look like a do-it-yourself job. Have all the information on the card that a client needs, such as your e-mail address, URL (if you have one), fax number, and direct telephone number.

These steps should not be taken to deceive clients and prospective clients, but to demonstrate that whatever your size, you can present yourself professionally. You don't want to scream that you are small by acting small—you want to convey that size doesn't matter.

Using School Ties

Staying in touch with law school classmates should help with developing a networking relationship with fellow lawyers who have gone into corporate in-house practice. Many classmates work outside your geographic and specialty areas and some have gone in-house with major corporations. They should be a good source of business clients if they know where you are and what kind of clients you are looking to attract. Add school chums to your mailing list and send them the same article reprints, newsletters, and marketing material you send clients and prospective clients. They already know you and should be a good referral source of new business.

Learning "Business Speak"

Read the books and magazines that business clients read. Be prepared to discuss the critical business issues that clients, prospective clients, and their industries face. You must be able to "talk their language" to represent them.

I subscribe to more business magazines and purchase more business books than law books and publications. Why? Because that is what my clients and prospective clients read, and I need to be conversant in trends and issues that interest them. I clip articles every week and mail, fax, and e-mail them to clients and prospective clients. It keeps me in touch and often generates calls from the recipients. It tells them I care about their businesses and understand issues that are important to them.

The Solo Estate Planning Practice

8

Daniel B. Evans

An estate planning practice is often well-suited to the solo environment. Unlike complex litigation or large business transactions, estate planning does not require teams of lawyers addressing a variety of different legal and factual issues. A single lawyer can usually handle everything that needs to be done and the individual client won't care whether the lawyer has the size and prestige of a large firm. And because the practice addresses individual clients, marketing can be done on the budget of a sole practitioner—there is no need for large-scale, expensive marketing programs designed to attract large corporate and business clients.

A solo estate planning practice can create both opportunities and problems, some of which are described below.

Practice Limitations and Focus

When lawyers work together, whether in a small firm or a larger firm, they can combine their different experiences and abilities to serve the clients' needs. Without partners or associates to draw upon, a sole practitioner is limited by his or her own experience and expertise. That means a sole practitioner may need to limit her practice to a greater extent than lawyers practicing in a group, because the solo cannot seek help and advice from someone "down the hall."

One advantage of being a sole practitioner is having greater freedom to make practice decisions, without first obtaining approval from a management committee or worrying about how decisions will be received by firm partners. Another benefit is that because a solo generally has a more narrowly defined practice, it is easier and less expensive to market the solo's services to potential clients. Prospective clients are primarily interested in whether the solo has the expertise to help the client with an estate planning problem.

Following are some different ways of defining—and focusing—an estate planning practice:

◆ *By Age*: Elderly clients' needs differ from those of younger clients. Developing expertise and skills oriented to specific age groups, and marketing to those groups, can be an effective practice plan.

◆ *By Occupation*: Clients in the same occupation or profession frequently have similar estate planning problems. Speaking to business or professional groups about estate planning problems common to the group can be an excellent way of getting public exposure and developing client contacts.

◆ *By Income or Net Worth*: Some estate planning techniques are more suited to high-income or high-worth individuals, while others are more suited to people of more moderate means. Most lawyers would like to represent the wealthiest clients, but it might also make sense to develop legal expertise of interest to the less-than-very wealthy.

◆ *By Type of Assets*: Life insurance, retirement benefits, annuities, closely held businesses, real estate partnerships, art collections, and lottery winnings are all examples of assets that may require special estate planning knowledge and serve as the basis of a focused practice.

◆ *By Technique*: It's also possible to pick a particular type of estate planning technique (such as revocable trusts or "dynasty trusts") and use it as a practice focus and marketing advantage.

Technology

One reason why an estate planning practice is practical for solos is that there are a number of computer software programs that can provide both efficiency and "instant expertise." The software not only allows quick generation of most of the documents a lawyer needs for the practice, it also often has built-in substantive rules. That can help a lawyer avoid making the kinds of mistakes that would be caught by partners or associates in a law firm.

A complete description of the kinds of software available for estate planners is beyond the scope of this chapter, but additional information can be found in *Wills, Trusts, and Technology: An Estate Lawyer's Guide to Automation*, Second Edition, by Daniel B. Evans, which is published by the ABA.

Tax-Planning Software

Because of the complexity of estate tax planning, the lawyer must confirm the tax benefits of proposed estate planning techniques with each client and make sure clients understand both the benefits and risks of those proposals. Careful lawyers provide tax projections to their clients to illustrate the consequences of each estate planning recommendation. Some lawyers prepare these illustrations using spreadsheet programs, but there are also a number of specialized software programs on the market for these kinds of projections and explanations.

Ideally, a program allows the lawyer to enter a few critical numbers, choose the appropriate estate planning recommendations, and then generate the appropriate illustrations. Unfortunately, it's often not that simple, and the lawyer needs to spend some time confirming that the software is demonstrating the information about the right estate plan. Even though they are not foolproof, however, these programs represent a valuable tool for lawyers looking to provide clients with high-quality service when they don't have a team of associates or extensive law firm resources to call upon for assistance.

Document-Drafting Software

As part of the estate planning process, lawyers usually draft wills, trusts, and other kinds of documents to carry out clients' estate plans, and many lawyers use document-drafting software to automate the process. Document-drafting software can create documents in less time than it takes a lawyer to do so manually, and the software helps eliminate (or at least reduce) spelling and substantive errors. As a result, the quality of the documents is better and it is easier to customize documents to suit the needs of clients, even when they change their minds about what they want.

Some lawyers find that they can use their word-processing software's "merge" and "macro" features to create an acceptable system that prepares documents by filling in names and other information. Many other lawyers use special software programs to insert names and other information into forms, as well as to select alternate clauses or phrases to put into documents. Other lawyers buy will and trust forms that have already been automated and avoid having to go to that trouble.

Staff

Many books, articles, and seminars tell lawyers to "leverage" their time through the effective use of staff. Sole practitioners often have paralegals and other staff, but an effective estate planning solo should keep the number of employees to a minimum to save on personnel costs.

The proper use of computers can drastically reduce the need for clerical staff, or even paralegals. Because document-drafting software of the kind described above can prepare first drafts of wills, trusts, powers of attorney, contracts, and form letters that are 80 to 90 percent complete, the documents usually need only minimal revision and customization before they are ready for the client to review and approve. Lawyers need only basic word-processing skills to review and complete the final drafts without the assistance of clerical staff.

For lawyers who don't like to type, speech-recognition technology now makes it possible for a lawyer to dictate to a computer and prepare letters or more complicated documents.

By learning basic word-processing skills and using computers to prepare estate planning calculations, illustrations, and documents, lawyers can drastically reduce the need for legal staff. Some sole practitioners may find that a secretary or paralegal isn't needed at all, except to perform file maintenance and other administrative tasks, such as timekeeping, billing, and bookkeeping.

It may be advantageous for a solo to hire independent contractors as needed. Contractors can either work on-site or at different locations, depending upon the nature of the work they are doing.

Home Offices

For those who want to get away from downtown areas or more formal business offices, a solo estate planning practice is often well-suited for a home office. That depends, in part, upon the kind of clients the lawyer in the home office is trying to attract.

Some clients like the idea of dealing with a lawyer who works out of his home, perhaps because they think the lawyer will be more affordable or more convenient than a downtown lawyer in a big office building. They may also like the idea of dealing with a lawyer who works in such a relaxed environment. On the other hand, other clients, such as executives or business owners, may not be comfortable dealing with a single lawyer in a home office.

Younger clients may not be as wedded to the common notions of what a lawyer is supposed to look like, and what kind of office a lawyer is supposed to have, and therefore may be more willing to try a lawyer with a different way of practicing. At the same time, older clients may be more interested in a good personal relationship with their lawyer than in the trappings of an office, and be more interested in working with a lawyer they trust, regardless of the office arrangements.

A suburban location may be an advantage in attracting suburban residents, but a disadvantage in attracting urban residents and businesses.

Taking all those factors into account, an estates practice may be well-suited to a home office because it is often directed to older suburban residents, and typically does not require a large staff or a number of associates. Furthermore, most of the work is either meeting with clients (which can be done at their homes) or "office" work such as document drafting, tax return preparation, and accounting work. It is rarely necessary to spend much time in court, or to meet with opposing lawyers, witnesses, or other third parties.

Isolation

A solo estate practice can be one of the loneliest practices, and working alone at home can make it even more lonely. While litigators frequently meet with opposing counsel (in or out of court), and business lawyers and real estate lawyers often negotiate with lawyers representing other parties, estate planners spend most of their time either meeting with clients or preparing documents or calculations for clients.

An estate planner in a solo practice needs to make efforts to get out of the office (or out of the house) and meet other professionals. Bar association committees offer one good way to stay abreast of what is going on in the legal community, and continuing legal education programs also provide occasional "reality checks" to make sure that techniques and forms are up to snuff.

For those who like electronic communications, a medium for collegiality may be found in e-mail lists and other forms of online discussions. For example, the ABA-PTL list (**listserv@mail.abanet.org**), sponsored by the ABA Real Property, Probate and Trust Law Section, provides probate and trust law practitioners with a forum in which they can ask questions, share practice developments, and get different perspectives on problems from fellow lawyers. Instead of wandering down the hall and walking into your partner's office to ask whether what you are doing makes sense or whether you have considered all the issues, you can distribute an e-mail message to the list and get feedback from other practitioners.

The Life of a Family Law Lawyer

9

James A. Calloway

Some say that being a family law lawyer is a calling rather than a career decision. They may be right. It isn't easy work and it's not for everyone. A common observation I hear from colleagues is, "I could never do that kind of practice." Everyone who handles these cases knows the importance of the work to everyone involved, and the critical nature of the lawyer's role.

Family lawyers deal with important issues every day. Nothing is more important to us than our families. Nothing is more important than trying to protect children from dangerous or abusive situations. Nothing is more important than making certain that everyone from a splintered family has adequate resources for food and shelter.

The practice of family law can be intense. It can also be rewarding. But it will never be boring. A career in family law will likely be remarkably different from many other legal careers. And, you can make a decent living in the practice if you do it right.

Family law practitioners deal with people under enormous stress, and they must make sure that clients' stress doesn't become their stress. Almost all divorce clients are on intensely emotional roller coasters, and they often try to take their lawyers along for the ride. They won't understand how you can stay so calm and detached when their lives are in chaos. You cannot practice this type of law without learning to cope with intense and emotional outpourings. You must be sympathetic and supportive, but also avoid being so overwhelmed by everyone's emotions that you lose your objectivity. Your clients need support, but the most important thing they need is your objective judgments and advice. What's more, lawyers who get caught up in a client's drama risk getting into trouble.

Be prepared. The family lawyer's office differs from the typical lawyer's office. Clients cry more often than they do in other lawyers' offices. Boxes of tissues should be purchased in bulk quantities and strategically placed around the office. (If being around others crying makes you uncomfortable or nervous, you are in the wrong line of work.) Unlike when they deal with other lawyers, clients often bring children to their appointments with family lawyers. Children's toys and books must be readily available. Staff members should be prepared to occupy a client's children for a few minutes so the client can be free to discuss matters that should not be discussed in front of children.

Communications with Your Client

Giving advice to clients while they are coping with turbulent emotions is a challenge. Strong emotions cloud and impede rational judgment. Communications under these circumstances are difficult.

Stock your office with brochures, booklets, and pamphlets to distribute to clients, family members, and witnesses, as appropriate. The client will likely be receiving advice from a number of sources, such as neighbors, friends, family members, and "veterans" of divorce. Much of this information will be erroneous.

It is important to reinforce your advice with written materials, even if these materials are broad and generic. The well-prepared family lawyer has several "canned" sets of written materials to give clients at the conclusion of office consultations. Some of these may be reprints of other materials when permission has been granted to redistribute. Most of the material should be original content written by the lawyer and bearing the lawyer's byline. Use titles that spark clients' interest, such as, "How to Minimize the Effect of Divorce on Your Children," or "Ten Common Myths about Divorce Court." Note the importance of giving these handouts to the client at the conclusion of the conference. If they are distributed at the beginning of a consultation, they may become yet another distraction.

One of the most challenging things about family law practice is getting your client to consider your advice as being better than the advice she gets from her friends and family. You may actually have to persuade your client that you know more about divorce litigation strategy than her hairdresser or her favorite uncle. Having written materials will help make you seem like the expert.

It is also a good idea to send letters to the client at key stages in the proceedings. For example, when a deposition is scheduled, send the client a letter explaining what is involved in a deposition. A letter should not take the place of one-on-one discussions, but it can be used to reinforce the advice and other information you give the client.

Put It in Writing

Effective use of form letters, templates, macros, and other document-assembly techniques can allow you to improve communications greatly with your client, while at the same time streamline your operations. For example, if you always want your client to bring certain documents to a deposition or hearing, include that reminder in the "form letter" along with other information, such as the hearing date and location.

Most advice that you give one client also applies to every client and should be included in your form correspondence. Examples might include the following: "Don't initiate a conversation in the hall with your estranged spouse unless your spouse approaches you first." Or, "Don't ever discuss what I tell you with your spouse." Or, "Don't tell what we plan to do in court." Or, "It is fine and appropriate to discuss your children's activities, their needs, and scheduling of visitation directly with your spouse, but never negotiate a final agreement without checking with me."

Clients who are under stress sometimes do not hear what you are saying, even though they nod in agreement and seem to understand. For that reason, you must tell your clients what you want them to hear and then question them to confirm that they understood. Some people learn better from visual or written materials than from oral discussions. If you put your advice and instructions on paper, your client can read and reread everything at his leisure, perhaps when he is feeling less stressed or emotional. Another advantage of giving advice in writing is that it reduces the chance of a misunderstanding between you and your client, and provides documentation in the event a dispute arises between you and your client.

Urban lawyers should consider providing clients a map to the courthouse and directions/suggestions for parking. This helps relieve their stress on the day of the first court appearance. In my private practice, our maps also included the firm name, address, phone, and practice areas. Some clients probably kept the maps longer than they kept our business cards.

Developing a Network of Contacts

One of the initial discoveries of a family law lawyer with a new practice is that she has many clients with needs she cannot meet. It is important for the lawyer to develop a network of contacts to provide services to clients. These include counselors, therapists, and support groups. Certainly, some therapists may serve as expert witnesses to buttress your case, but oftentimes a distraught client needs someone with whom she can discuss problems and stress, even when there is no anticipation of testimony. A good family lawyer takes the time to meet and interview mental health workers before referring clients to them. The benefit of this is twofold. Not only will you be in a better position to make positive referrals—knowing something about both your clients' and the therapists' personalities—but the therapists and other professionals may serve as sources of referrals for your practice.

Your staff should also be trained to deal with panicked calls from clients in fear of violence. The local battered-women's shelter and other resources should be well-known to your staff, as should local phone numbers for law enforcement. Other social service agencies should be known and the services that may be available cataloged.

Family lawyers must also maintain professional contacts with private investigators, accounting expert witnesses, process servers, appraisers, and a number of others who can assist the lawyer with their expertise.

Marketing

Lawyers in certain types of practices sometimes develop so many regular clients who need their services that they accept no new clients. For example, a business lawyer may develop an entirely successful career based primarily on three major clients. But family lawyers have few clients with regular, ongoing legal matters or numerous different engagements over a long period of time. Therefore, new client development should always be on a family lawyer's mind.

The various methods of marketing used, both direct and indirect, largely depend upon the lawyer's point of view and client base sought. Traditional advertising, such as a Yellow Pages ad, brings a certain amount of new business. Word-of-mouth and referrals are likely to be the primary method of obtaining new clients. Some lawyers involve themselves in society and community affairs, such as charity fund-raisers, in hopes of becoming a familiar face who is later retained by a party in a more complex and potentially lucrative divorce. Other lawyers are more comfortable being involved with bar association committees and activities. Your efforts at marketing and promoting your name will likely be an ongoing part of your life, at least during the early years of building your practice.

Giving speeches in the community is also a time-honored method of making a name well-known. Many family lawyers do not limit themselves to marriage dissolution, but also handle family law matters such as adoption, juvenile law, or guardianship. These subjects often lend themselves to speeches at civic clubs and community organizations. A family lawyer might serve on the fundraising committee for a new juvenile center or a battered-spouse shelter. Making presentations at continuing legal education programs is a good way of becoming known as an expert among peers. Moreover, lawyers themselves sometimes need the services of a family law practitioner.

Getting Paid

Almost every family lawyer will, at some point in his or her career, decide to handle a case when there is almost no hope of getting paid any reasonable fee. Pro bono public service is an honored tradition of the legal profession. We should consider ourselves fortunate to live in this great country and have professional licenses granted by the state. Helping others is the reason why many of us got into the legal profession in the first place.

Unfortunately, the typical family lawyer sees dozens of deserving people who need more legal services than they can afford. The family lawyer must realize that to maintain a law practice to help others, the practice must be successful as a business. Our first obligation is to our families, our dependents, and, yes, even our creditors. This is especially true for the sole practitioner who has no "safety net" of other lawyers to rely upon during times of low income. Therefore, before the new family lawyer becomes concerned with a duty to provide pro bono services, she should make sure the law business appears to be cash-flowing each month and savings are available to make it through lean times. Many new lawyers take court-appointed cases at a lower-than-market rate to gain experience and exposure in the community. This is certainly appropriate, and provides some income at the same time.

If you feel strongly about doing pro bono work, consider joining a referral panel with your local legal aid organization and agree to take a set number of cases per year. That way, there will have been some advance screening to determine if the client is truly needy, and you will be able to focus on others as potential paying clients. You may even refer some clients who cannot afford your services to a legal aid organization yourself.

Many family lawyers report trouble with getting paid for the services they provide, and many write off large amounts of accounts receivable each year. The subject of getting paid for legal work generally could encompass an entire book. It is even more difficult in family law cases, where there are such negative emotions. In many divorce cases, one of the parties does not want the divorce, and it is particularly difficult to get someone to pay for something that he or she does not want. In other situations, the client may demand that the lawyer look to the opposing party for fees. Following is a thumbnail sketch of steps you can take to assist you in getting paid for your services:

- ◆ Do a good job of deciding which clients to represent and which cases to take. Know the warning signs of "bad" clients and do not take them.
- ◆ Discuss fees frankly and openly at initial client conferences.

- Get substantial retainer fees in advance to serve as security for payment.
- Have clear, written, attorney-client fee agreements.
- Have clear, detailed, and understandable bills and time charge descriptions.
- Send bills to clients at least monthly.
- Promptly follow up by telephone and/or letter when clients fail to pay as agreed.
- For clients who do not keep their financial commitments to you, file motions to withdraw when this can be done without prejudicing the case.

Often it is difficult for lawyers to be closely involved with their clients' personal and intimate problems and then "abandon" them over financial considerations. That is why it is so important for both the lawyer and the client to be absolutely clear about fees and payments in the initial interview. Certainly there can be some flexibility in arranging partial payments and payment plans, but the simple fact is that the client has agreed to pay you for your services and should honor that agreement.

A special problem that occurs with some frequency in family law cases is when a client's relative—often a parent—pays the legal fees. Generally, when that is the situation, it is not long before the lawyer receives a call from the payor, who wishes to discuss the case. If the lawyer declines, the next sentence usually is, "I'm the one who is paying you." Instead of being placed in a difficult situation, handle this potential problem in advance. Have both the client and the payor sign a brief statement acknowledging that even though a third party is paying for the legal services, the client will make decisions about the matter, and, due to attorney-client privilege issues, the lawyer will discuss the case only with the client and not the third-party payor. This is often easier said than done.

Many times a parent will accompany the client to the initial interview, particularly when the client is young or financially dependent. This is not always objectionable, but must be handled carefully, as the presence of a third party often impairs the attorney-client privilege for that conversation.

The Truth, the Whole Truth, and Nothing but the Truth

Practicing family law soon shakes your belief in the general truthfulness of people. It is often amazing how two people who lived in the same household and underwent the same experiences can have totally different statements about things.

It may be hard to grasp that when your clients do not tell you the truth, that does not necessarily mean they are lying. Memory is filtered through experiences and prejudices. Everyone recalls things from his or her point of view. Therefore, you should take everything your clients say with the proverbial grain of salt.

Understand that when your client tells you of the horrible and awful treatment she received at the hands of her spouse during this ten-year marriage, she may be summarizing her recent reflections on the last ten years as much as she is actually recalling specific events. Some exaggeration is to be expected in the initial client interview process. This is not to say, of course, that no one suffers abuse during marriages. They do. Representing someone whose very perception of her self-worth has been shaped by years of denigration and threats is a difficult task. A person with this experience often is barely capable of independent thought and action, and clearly needs professional help to recover fully.

Listening to your clients is an important skill. Lawyers tend to want to interrupt at every point that might need clarification. Make a note to do that later and let your clients keep talking. They may have some difficult and personal issues and once they get started, it is best to let them continue. (There is an exception to this rule for certain parties who seem to believe that you cannot represent them until they have recounted every day of their marriages.)

A client may tearfully tell of the day when the spouse was late in picking up the children after school and they had to wait in the cold for over an hour. The powerful image of scared children alone, waiting and wondering what happened for such a long time, may be significant evidence in a custody dispute. But do not be shocked if, in fact, the delay was only ten minutes, the children spent the time visiting with their friends, and the only reason they recall the day at all is because of the horrible fight that took place at their home that night over the issue.

Just because your client's account differs from everyone else's does not mean that the client is intentionally lying. The children might be trying to protect the other spouse, or perhaps everyone is simply telling his or her version of "the truth" as recalled. This gives you a chance to discuss how important it is to be calm and accurate. You can also use this situation to give your client insight into how court proceedings work. ("Just think if we had told the judge it was over an hour, and then the children said it was only a few minutes. That could make the judge think you were not being truthful about the rest of your testimony.") You can make the point that while you don't disbelieve the client, the trier of fact will be influenced by all the witnesses.

In addition to dealing with clients who have flawed recollection, you will, of course, encounter clients (and other witnesses) who are lying, pure and simple. Some of these people may be trying to gain some advantage by lying. Some may be trying to cover up embarrassing episodes that have little relevance to the divorce case. Others may be hiding or misrepresenting important and relevant information. When the facts keep shifting, it certainly makes for interesting trial preparation.

Before the first court hearing, have a talk with your client about truthfulness and exaggeration. Remind the client how the loss of credibility on even a minor fact can affect the entire case. Caution her not to guess if she does not know an answer or understand a question. In many ways, this is no different than preparing a client or witness for any type of testimony.

Dealing with inconsistent statements of witnesses may be more nuanced in family law than in other legal situations. In a criminal trial, the defense lawyer discrediting the witness who accused the defendant is critical, direct, and aggressive. A lengthy point-by-point dissection of a grandmother who has generally testified that she thinks her son is a better parent, however, will likely be unappreciated by the trial judge and affect the grandmother's relations with your client for a long time. There will be times when you must ask very hurtful questions, but that does not mean you should ask them every time you can.

Success in a Family Law Matter

A successful conclusion to a contested family law matter is sometimes difficult to discern. There is no guilty or not-guilty verdict. The court's ruling may not reflect the relief that either party sought. The litigants have to live with the ruling long after the case is officially closed. Sometimes a settlement provides more workable solutions than a court ruling because the parties have agreed, however grudgingly, to the arrangement. This is one of the primary reasons why so many contested marriage dissolution cases eventually settle. Even the family law judge would likely state that child custody arrangements worked out by the parties are generally in the best interest of all concerned. Of course, many cases cannot be settled, and a few should not be settled. Determining which is which is the challenging part.

So Why Practice Family Law?

Because it is interesting. There is never a dull moment. Because your work has real impact on real people. Because you get to influence children's lives. Because you will get good courtroom experience. Because people need dedicated and energetic family lawyers. Because you may, every now and then, actually get to make a bad situation better.

Flying Solo in Employment Law | 10

Mindy G. Farber

Introduction

Being an employment lawyer is like being a divorce lawyer, in that you must deal with parties who are very emotionally involved in their cases. Plaintiffs may be stinging from being fired or passed over for promotions, and defendants (usually employers) may be offended, insulted, and feeling unappreciated by plaintiffs. The parties' emotions frequently lead them into protracted litigation to prove they are "right." When a client is in that frame of mind, it may be difficult to get the client to consider a reasonable settlement.

So why practice employment law? Because it is fascinating, complex, and intellectually challenging, and involves issues of profound societal importance.

Employment law is a relatively new field. Until recently, it was merely one aspect of labor law. Now employment law is one of the fastest growing fields nationally. Legislative changes enacted in the past decade have resulted in a dramatic increase in litigation. Federal laws such as the Pregnancy Discrimination Act, the Family and Medical Leave Act, the Americans with Disabilities Act, the Older Workers Benefits Protection Act, the Civil Rights Act of 1964 (Title VII), and the Age Discrimination in Employment Act have expanded the rights of workers. State laws and regulations of a similar nature have had a substantial effect, as well.

Practicing employment law is not easy. There is a lot to read, memorize, and digest. There are hoops to jump through and traps to avoid. Missing a deadline or filing a claim without jumping though one or more hoops in proper sequence can have disastrous results. Nevertheless, even though it isn't an easy way to make a living, you can live well and provide valuable help to people and businesses in their times of need.

Educating Yourself

So where to begin? First, you must learn the law, or at least learn where to find the law. Employment law includes a number of subareas:

◆ Employment discrimination
◆ Business formation and business dissolution
◆ Employment contracts and covenants not to compete
◆ Wage and hour issues
◆ Employment handbooks

If you intend to learn the law and keep up with the changes, you must read a lot and engage in other learning activities. The following are "must-read" publications and "must-do" activities for employment lawyers:

◆ *Employment Discrimination Coordinator (BNA)*: This publication gives overviews of cases and settlements from all over the United States, as well as other information.
◆ *Lawyers Weekly* (**www.lawyersweekly.com**): This inexpensive periodical is aimed at solos and presents overviews of state case law.
◆ *The Labor Lawyer*: You will get this valuable journal when you join the ABA Section of Labor and Employment Law. Syracuse University publishes the journal in conjunction with the ABA.
◆ *Attend Continuing Legal Education (CLE) Programs*: Attend as many CLE programs as you can. The ABA regularly presents employment law programs, particularly within the Section of Labor and Employment Law. CLE programs are also produced by state and local bar associations and by private companies such as Lorman, based in Eau Claire, Wisconsin.
◆ *Ask for Advice*: Experienced employment lawyers are usually willing to take the time to offer advice and answer your questions. Meet for coffee or lunch if you want in-depth conversations, or call on the phone or send e-mail messages if you have specific questions or needs.
◆ *Be a Joiner!*: Join the ABA. Join the labor and employment law sections or committees of your state and local bar associations. Join NELA, the National Employment Lawyers Association. You can get valuable in-

formation from the publications of all these groups and make valuable contacts, as well.

◆ *Use Online Legal Resources*: Westlaw and Lexis maintain extensive information on employment law, including decisional law, treatises, and supplemental guidelines and handbooks prepared by federal agencies.

Other resources, mostly free, are also available online. Through the Internet, the Equal Employment Opportunity Commission (EEOC) and the National Labor Relations Board (NLRB) provide extensive and helpful information regarding practice before these agencies. Other private and government Web sites (such as **www.lawmen.com**, **www.findlaw.com**, and **www.gpoaccess.gov**) contain relevant and useful information on employment law issues. In addition, the U.S. Department of Labor (**www.dol.gov**) and the U.S. Office of Personnel Management (**www.opm.gov**) sites contain extensive information regarding the specific laws those agencies administer. Academic Web sites are good sources for up-to-date information on the ever-changing landscape of employment law.

Because U.S. Supreme Court decisions are the final word in employment cases, it is essential that you stay abreast of them, but it is the case law from your federal circuit that usually controls the outcome of your litigation. Federal and state decisions are available from the pay services and for free directly from the federal courts or from a variety of other Web sites. Cornell University's Web site (**http://supct.law.cornell.edu:8080/supct**) is a good place to check on a regular basis. Other law school sites contain law review articles analyzing recent decisions, as well as information about trends in employment law.

Marketing

Even if you believe you have become an expert in this field, your opinion means nothing unless you can convince other people that you are an expert, too. Making people believe you are an expert means becoming a mastermind in perception building. Of course, winning cases that become well publicized in your community helps convince people that you are an expert. But, as a sole practitioner, you do not have that much time to wait, so you need to jump-start your reputation and make your mark quickly. You do this by becoming your own public relations person. I believe the key to spreading the word about your expertise is writing and speaking.

Writing

Fortunately, there are probably a thousand periodicals that would like articles on a variety of employment law topics. You should be the person to write them. Write an article at least once a month for local trade associations, chambers of commerce, state bar newsletters, and professional organizations. Write the articles unsolicited and send them in confidently. Write about timely topics. Give the articles catchy titles that will appeal to your audience. Try to write for periodicals that deal with contemporary issues and are distributed to local audiences. It is amazing how many people will stop you in elevators, restaurants, and other public places to tell you how much they enjoyed your column and to suggest topics for the future. Clearly, this kind of recognition is what you need. It might take two or three years before your articles lead to steady recognition and client referrals, but this is okay. Never stop writing, and use your writing to advance your name. If you write an article and it is published, send a news clipping to your local or state bar association newsletter, noting that you have just been published. This is more publicity for you, which may even lead to an interview with you, the practitioner.

There is no doubt that provocative employment matters sell newspapers in today's society. Sexual harassment and other civil rights issues are high in reader interest. Send press releases to your local papers discussing the significance of your provocative cases. You never know what a local reporter will find interesting.

Once you get an interesting article written, reprint it and send it to your clients, prospective clients, and everyone else on your mailing list as a way to publicize why the recipients need you as their employment lawyer. Tell local reporters who write about employment matters that you are always available to provide quotes. Write letters to the editor about any articles that are employment related.

The goal is to become the local media darling in your area of the law. Although you may not get an immediate response, the newspapers' readers may clip the articles and remember your name when it comes time to refer cases or bring their own cases in the future.

If you have an article appearing in a journal or you are giving a speech out of town, be sure to send out a press release. Local newspapers and other periodicals like to publish success stories about local residents and will usually be happy to print these releases.

Speaking

It is equally important to volunteer your time as a speaker. Sign up for your local or state bar association speaker's bureau. Join your CLE committees and volunteer to speak at the programs. If all else fails, sponsor your own seminar.

Whenever you can, invite a respected authority in your field—but not a competitor—to join you in the talk. Invite the head of the local human relations commission, an administrative judge, or an elected official or other expert in local civil rights laws. I guarantee that you will get an audience. Then, after you speak somewhere, be sure to send a clipping to the local and state bar associations, stating that you have spoken somewhere. It is usually that simple.

Volunteering, Leading, Advertising, and Other Ways to Attract Business

Volunteer to mediate in employment law matters for the local human relations commission, the U.S. Equal Employment Opportunity Commission, or your local court. In short, look for any opportunity possible to promote your name in local enforcement agencies that deal with employment law. Concentrate on employment law, and do not dilute your practice by accepting other kinds of cases, such family law, bankruptcy, or personal injury cases.

One marketing strategy is to focus upon whatever industry dominates in your geographic area. Identify the major employers in your community, including federal, state, and local government agencies, as well as colleges and universities. If, for example, you work in the metropolitan Washington, D.C. area, you could consider becoming an expert in federal sector law. You could then advertise that fact in local newspapers and publications directed to government workers. If you are located in a high-tech community, you can advertise with the local high-tech council or send mailings to its member organizations.

You should join organizations not only to meet other lawyers and gain information about employment law, but also to promote your practice. When joining an organization as part of your marketing program, there are two basic rules to follow: (1) join only those organizations in which you have a real interest, and (2) plan to become a leader, not just a member, to achieve visibility. Most people start by serving on committees, boards, and task forces. Doing a good job with your assignments is essential for developing a good reputation. To enhance your reputation and get referrals, consider running for the executive board of the organization, whether it is a bar association, a civic group, the local Rotary Club, or the local ACLU chapter. If you decide to take this step, be certain that you have the time it takes to do a good job. If you are stretched too thin with work or personal commitments, it may be better to remain a committee member and limit your responsibilities in the organization.

Don't be reluctant to join organizations that have a lot of lawyer members, even if they are other employment lawyers. The more lawyers you know, the more potential referral sources you have. Employment lawyers often have conflicts and need to refer cases to someone else. If they know you and your reputation is good, they will think of you first.

Another good marketing tool is your bar association's lawyer referral service. It is usually a low-cost (or even free) way to let the legal community know that you specialize in employment law, and it might also be a way to get some good cases.

Become familiar with your local or state human relations commission. Commissions are often in need of lawyers to serve on local commissions or advisory panels. Such service may not generate a lot of referrals, but it will help you get to know the commission staff, including the investigators and compliance officers.

You can also enhance your reputation in the community by becoming a mentor for other lawyers who are just starting an employment law practice. You can agree to take an occasional pro bono case or volunteer to provide limited pro bono legal advice through a service or nonprofit organization such as a local commission for women. Those you help will appreciate and remember your generosity.

Internet marketing is essential. Start today to develop a Web site that tells the world that you are experienced in employment law. Don't hesitate to give examples of your accomplishments. Be free with information. Consider publishing an electronic newsletter on some important aspect of employment law. Invite questions. People will write to you.

If you are just starting your employment law practice, be sure to send announcements to state and local bar associations and to specialty bar groups. When someone refers a client to you, don't forget to send a thank-you card or a small gift.

Consider putting part of your marketing budget into Yellow Pages advertising. Yellow Pages advertising can be effective, but it is expensive and involves annual contracts that usually cannot be cancelled. Many lawyers now find that Internet advertising is much more cost-effective than Yellow Pages advertising, but remember that there are still people who prefer to "let their fingers do the walking." As a test, you may want to try a small, boxed ad that describes your expertise in employment law. It should succinctly give all the reasons why a potential client should pick *you*. Be sure to give your Web site and e-mail address. Set a nominal consultation fee, and when prospective clients call in response to your Yellow Pages ad, tell them about the consultation fee and get their credit card numbers when they make appointments. Try to avoid giving legal advice—particularly free advice—on the telephone.

Martindale-Hubbell and its online lawyer-locator service, **www.lawyers .com**, is another source of referrals. It is expensive, but worth the price.

Your office location and practice setting can be an effective marketing tool. If you practice employment law in a building or in a suite of offices with lawyers who do not handle employment law cases, you should take them to lunch, give them your card, offer them brochures, and do whatever else you need to do so they think of you when they need an employment lawyer.

Your office should reflect the fact that you are an expert in employment law. Diplomas, as well as certificates from organizations such as human relations commissions, women's commissions, and arbitration associations, should be displayed prominently in your office or waiting area. Handouts of articles you've written should also be strategically placed in your waiting area.

The professional contacts you make in the course of handling your cases can serve as a marketing tool. If you handle disability or sexual harassment cases, you will deal with a variety of medical experts. Physicians, psychiatrists, and physical therapists can be vital sources of client referrals. The same applies to other experts, such as certified public accountants, vocational rehabilitation specialists, and economists. In addition to providing referrals, these experts can also be available for informal discussions if you have questions about difficult cases.

Selecting Cases and Clients

Be discriminating in the types of cases you accept and the clients you represent. Selecting the right clients and the right cases is critical to building a good practice. There are many things you can do to help yourself.

First, beware of potential clients who ask you if you are "aggressive." Resist clients who have filed many lawsuits in the past. Shun people who tell you that you are their third or fourth lawyer, unless they have really good explanations. Stay away from clients who talk about their principles and their unwillingness to compromise their values, especially if they want you to take their cases on a contingent-fee basis. Cast a dubious eye on clients who defer to their spouses. Be wary of clients who balk at signing retainer agreements or who do not want to pay retainers.

Managing Your Cases and Workload

If you have done everything necessary to bring clients through the door, then you should experience a bounty of work and all the challenges of the legal issues your clients bring. Knowing you have the work is an exhilarating experience. Yet, exactly how do you manage it? Never panic. Always be resourceful.

Securing Retainer Agreements

Before you consider the client yours, make sure the client has signed a retainer agreement. In most jurisdictions, unless the client agrees in writing that he or she wants to retain you, you might have trouble convincing a court (such as in a suit for collection of fees) that you actually represented the client. A retainer agreement should spell this out clearly. Your local bar association will provide guidance on specific provisions that should be in the retainer agreement.

Try to have a retainer agreement for each of the client's different matters, particularly in the case of employee representations. This may seem cumbersome, but it helps when the client tries to insist you (1) were not to do a particular kind of work, (2) were not skilled in a particular kind of work, or (3) had no authority to do a particular kind of work.

The flip side of the coin is that if you handle several matters for the same client, particularly an employer, you are becoming the basic outside counsel in employment. If the client is paying the monthly bills on time, you might not need a separate retainer agreement for each matter. Your retainer agreement, however, should state that you are representing the client in an employment matter and, if possible, specify the type of matter (such as wrongful discharge, sex discrimination, or race discrimination). The agreement should also specify your hourly rate and billing practices. If you are working on a contingency basis, you should certainly have a contingency agreement; if you are working on an hourly basis, make sure you spell out the rates of associates, paralegals, and any administrative assistants, in addition to your own rate.

A retainer agreement should also indicate that you cannot guarantee a particular legal result and that your fees are not predicated upon a particular outcome. This is especially important when representing employees, because there are very few black-and-white cases and the likelihood of prevailing is much more dubious than in the past.

When you represent an employee, it is important that the retainer agreement explain that subsequent retainers may be required as the case progresses. You should also state that if there is a settlement in the case, any unpaid attorney's fees will be taken out of the settlement proceeds. Then there can be no argument when a settlement check arrives that the client should get the whole amount and pay you later—often weeks or months later when the work is already completed and you are no longer important to the client. When you represent an employer, you should, of course, get paid on a monthly basis.

The retainer agreement should include at least some of the following language to protect you in the event your client refuses to pay your bill:

♦ The initial retainer (that is, the initial money paid to the lawyer to initiate the case) may not necessarily cover the entire legal bill.

♦ The lawyer cannot guarantee a particular legal result, and the fees are not dependent upon the outcome of the matter.

♦ The lawyer will send bills monthly for work performed to date, at the hourly rates specified in the agreement.

♦ The initial retainer will be applied to the monthly billings.

♦ Once the retainer is expended, the firm reserves the right to ask for additional funds—a second retainer—to secure payment of future fees.

♦ Any fee dispute will be filed with the appropriate state court, and not with a fee arbitration committee. (Check with your malpractice carrier or state professional liability fund for the best way to handle fee disputes.)

Be as open, honest, and direct as you can in the initial interview with the client. Point out that while many employment cases settle, there are many that do not, and you cannot predict whether your client's case will settle. Discuss the financial aspects of the case, including both attorney's fees and litigation expenses. Talk to your client about hourly billing, flat-rate billing, and contingent fees, and explain why you use the method you do. Avoid contingent fees because of the risk of not getting paid and because you want to ensure the client has a stake in the matter. You can help shape your client's expectations by giving an estimate of how long the action will take and how much it will cost to take the case to trial.

Initiating the Case

Whether you represent an employee or employer in a dispute, once your client has signed the retainer agreement, ask for copies of all relevant documents, such as good and bad performance evaluations, letters of reference, records of promotions and salary increases, employee handbooks, employment contracts, and prior lawsuits or complaints.

Organizing an employment law file is really no different from organizing any other type of file. Documents must be indexed and organized; future tasks must be identified, assigned, and checked off when completed; and future appointments and events must be calendared, whether manually or with calendaring/case management software. In addition to organizing documents, you should organize the correspondence, forms, and pleadings associated with employment cases. These forms can be as simple as word-processing documents or as elaborate as custom templates to be used with a case management program. You can develop your own forms or get ideas from CLE materials or legal books and periodicals.

Resolving the Case

Try for early resolution. Employment principles are very dear, but very expensive in the long run. I would advise that you try to settle cases as early as you can, *no matter which side you represent*. If you represent employers, make it a practice to talk to your clients about the business aspects of settlement versus trial. If you represent employees, make it a practice to send a demand letter to the other side before you file suit to see what kind of response it generates. Let your client read the demand letter before it goes out, so the client feels he or she is part of the process. Having your client read the letter will also help ensure that you have all the facts and allegations listed correctly. Always take a measured approach to litigation, and don't ever let your clients push you into acting hastily.

Also, never let clients push you into making unreasonable demands. Don't let an unreasonable client turn you into an unreasonable lawyer. Your reputation will surely suffer, and your relationships with opposing counsel will suffer, as well.

One Final Tip

Every time work piles up on your desk and you find yourself not getting your work done (or your time billed), use the opportunity to review your situation and decide whether it is time to hire an associate or a paralegal, and perhaps time to stop flying solo.

The Solo Personal Injury Lawyer

11

K. William Gibson

My Introduction to PI Cases

I started practicing law on January 1, 1980. My practice included a small office, a law partner, and a manual typewriter. We didn't get our first secretary until a few months later. We got our first computer in 1984. My partner and I handled criminal defense, collections, domestic relations, bankruptcy, and everything else. We represented plaintiffs and we represented defendants. We represented friends and we represented family.

We saw ourselves as trial lawyers, but we never really had any big victories in those early days. Sometimes we tried the wrong cases and wondered why we lost. Other times we tried good cases, but didn't do as well as we had expected. Occasionally, we got good verdicts and felt like we had things figured out. Mostly, though, we tried drunk-driving cases. We so wanted to become personal injury lawyers that when someone asked us to take a PI case, we usually said yes, even if it wasn't such a good case.

For a while, I had three law partners. Unfortunately, we couldn't agree upon what we wanted to do. We couldn't even agree whether to advertise in the Yellow Pages. We took out a Yellow Pages ad only after I threatened to do it on my own if they wouldn't do it with me.

Eventually, my law partners went their own ways and I became a solo. Our longtime secretary quit—probably because she knew I couldn't afford her salary. I hired my sister to take her place. She did-n't have any experience, but she worked for less money. I kept the firm's of-fice space and eventually became a landlord for other lawyers. I also got stuck with the bill for the new Yellow Pages ad.

I knew that I really liked personal injury litigation, so I started focusing upon building and managing a personal injury practice. I quit taking every-thing else. After my small ad in the Portland, Oregon, Yellow Pages appeared, the phone started to ring. I rented a small office from a lawyer friend in a grow-ing suburb about twenty minutes away, keeping my main office in the city. I had no staff in the suburban office, but it was a great place to meet those clients who wouldn't drive downtown just to meet with a lawyer. Next, I took out an ad in the Yellow Pages for that suburb so people wouldn't have to go to the larger metropolitan telephone book.

To my amazement, the phone started to ring at the new location. People called me to help them with their injury claims. Fortunately, the call volume was low enough that I could personally meet with everyone and didn't have to add staff. I had seen other plaintiffs' lawyers get killed by their overhead ex-penses, so I vowed not to overextend myself by adding staff too soon. I still wasn't trying a lot of cases, but I was settling enough of them, either directly with the insurance company or with the aid of a mediator. Arbitration was just becoming popular, and many of the cases I couldn't settle went to arbitration rather than trial.

The phone kept ringing. Within two years of starting my personal injury practice, I was bringing in enough fees that my wife quit threatening to get a second job. (I think she really thought that *I* should get a second job, even though she never said so.) I continued to do everything I could to keep my overhead low. My sister was now my legal assistant and was doing a pretty good job, and I still wasn't paying her as much as our former secretary made.

I knew technology could help keep my overhead down. I had a computer on my desk and created my own letters and pleadings. We didn't have a com-puter network, so I saved my documents on a floppy disk and gave them to my legal assistant for printing. Our systems weren't sophisticated, but they kept us out of trouble. I had no idea how much technology would change over the next few years and how much it would change the way we practice law. Online legal research, the Internet, e-mail systems—none of it was a reality in the mid-1980s.

I also kept overhead down by renting my extra office space to other lawyers. I wouldn't recommend being a landlord to lawyers unless you enjoy negotiating with your tenants about everything under the sun. My tenants were all fine people and good lawyers, but they drove me crazy. Lawyers can sometimes be a little difficult to deal with. Thankfully, my stint as a landlord didn't last too long.

After twenty-two years of practice, and after fifteen years of doing nothing but PI, I am struck by how the personal injury business has changed. With the increased cost of litigation and the increased use of mandatory arbitration, PI lawyers aren't trying many cases. More and more cases go through mediation or informal settlement conferences. Many courts now require pretrial settlement conferences with a judge—something that was unheard of even a decade ago.

Sometimes new lawyers tell me they want to become personal injury lawyers, but don't have any cases and don't have any money to advertise for cases. I tell them that I faced the same situation not that long ago. *Starting* a practice takes money and a lot of effort. *Building* a practice takes money and even more effort, as well as a great deal of patience. It's not going to happen overnight, but it will happen if you want it badly enough.

It's About the Money

During my twenty-two years of practice, I have periodically run short of money and have wondered if my efforts were going to pay off. Patience was often in short supply. But I always knew how much I wanted to make it work and, because I didn't want to go to work for anyone else, I knew I had to make it work.

Starting a personal injury practice is not for the fainthearted. It differs from starting most other types of law practice. The difference is money. In other types of law practice, the lawyer takes a case, often gets a retainer to cover future fees, does the client's work, and then sends a bill for the time spent and gets paid. In a personal injury practice, the lawyer takes a case, then spends his or her own time and money getting the case ready for settlement or trial, and hopefully gets paid in a year or two if everything goes well. Of course, lawyers who bill hourly have money problems, too, such as accounts receivable, but their problems with money don't compare with those faced by PI lawyers. Personal injury lawyers who are on contingency don't necessarily get paid for all the time they spend on a case, but if they don't spend enough time, they may not get paid at all.

That is because in a personal injury practice, all cases require a lot of work and big cases require the most work. Everyone dreams about getting "the big case," only to be shocked to learn how much time and money it requires. Many big cases turn out badly because the plaintiff's lawyer doesn't spend enough *money* to hire the doctors, the engineers, the accident reconstructionists, and the other experts needed to analyze the facts and testify in court. Often that is simply because the lawyer doesn't have the money to invest in the case. Many big cases also turn out badly because the plaintiff's lawyer doesn't spend enough *time* to prepare the cases properly. Often that happens because the lawyer is busy handling other cases, perhaps those that will generate fees right away, to pay the rent and keep the doors open.

One difficulty with starting a personal injury practice is that having a lot of cases can present a problem—the more cases you have, the more people you need to help work on them. Those people must be paid every month, whether you settled any cases or not. You must come up with the money to pay them. If it takes two years for the average case to get resolved, you must be prepared to meet two years of payroll expenses without settling a case. Are you prepared to do that? How will you come up with that much money? Are you prepared to borrow money? Invest your own money? Sell your house?

If you plan to build a personal injury practice, you need to face these financial realities. But don't worry; once you survive the first couple years and generate some cash flow, it becomes a lot easier. Unfortunately, many aspiring plaintiffs' lawyers have not had enough capital to make it through those first couple years and are now doing something else for a living. (See other chapters in this book on money issues and financing your practice.)

Self-Analysis

Given the enormous financial and personal risks involved, you should analyze your personality and your tolerance for risk before undertaking this venture. Not everyone is cut out for it.

But that is not to say that all personal injury lawyers come from the same mold. On the contrary, they come in all personality types. They have different interests and aptitudes, and different strengths and weaknesses. Some thrive on courtroom activity, while others prefer to stay out of courtrooms and would rather settle cases. Which do you prefer? Some PI lawyers thrive on high-stakes litigation and are willing to mortgage a home to finance a good case. Others don't have that high a tolerance for risk. How much would you be willing to risk on a case? High-stakes cases mean long hours at the office, including nights and weekends, for months at a time. Many lawyers aren't willing or able to put in that amount of time or to work under that much pressure.

But it is quite possible to be a successful personal injury lawyer without handling high-risk, expensive cases. Many lawyers have satisfying careers handling more routine matters and go to court only once or twice a year. And, with the increasing popularity of alternative dispute resolution, including mediation and arbitration, lawyers are trying fewer personal injury cases than in the past.

You will be much happier and more successful by starting a practice that suits your own strengths and weaknesses. And there are alternatives to starting your own practice. If you want to become a malpractice lawyer or handle other high-stakes cases, but you can't afford to take the financial risk, you should consider taking a job with a lawyer or firm that handles those cases. That could teach you how to handle those cases, and give you opportunities to work on different types of cases and perhaps even try cases. Many lawyers have taken that route before going solo.

So, why start a personal injury practice? If it's because you think it offers the greatest opportunity to get rich, you will be disappointed. You may ultimately get rich, but you would be more likely to achieve the same or greater wealth by investing your time and money in any number of other ventures not connected with the practice of law. Even though the ranks of plaintiffs' lawyers include a number of high-profile, high-income lawyers, thousands more lawyers across the country toil in obscurity and make unremarkable incomes.

Yet, nowhere in the practice of law is there more opportunity to help those who are truly in need, who have been wronged through no fault of their own, and who are not going to get any relief without a lawyer who is willing to fight for their rights. Nowhere in the practice of law is there more of a David-versus-Goliath scenario than a working man or woman or retired person or child doing battle with a gigantic insurance company or corporation.

Any lawyer who has taken the case of a deserving client through the legal system all the way to trial, and who has ridden out the waves of delay, obfuscation, and occasional deception, knows there is no better feeling in the world than putting up with all that abuse from the other side and finally having your cause validated by a jury. When that happens, your client is convinced that you are the best lawyer on the planet, the opposing lawyers must concede that you might possibly know what you are doing, and you gain a measure of confidence and self-assurance that will keep you in the game for a while longer.

You will be able to enjoy those moments only occasionally, and then only if you have managed your practice wisely.

Lawyers who fail to build a successful personal injury practice often point to poor case selection, mismanagement of personnel, and poor use of time and money. No lawyer starts a practice intending to fail, but many start a practice doomed to failure because the practice is not built upon a sound foundation. The cornerstones of that sound foundation are these:

- ◆ Commitment to working hard to make your practice succeed
- ◆ Ability to manage your time, money, and people
- ◆ Adequate capital
- ◆ Desire to do the right thing for your clients

If those cornerstones are in place, success will follow.

*Serving an Aging Population—Elder Law** 12

Jay G Foonberg

Sooner or later you are going to have some senior clients. America is graying, and elder law is possibly the fastest-growing area of law practice and is likely to continue as such for decades to come. By the year 2010, 65 percent of the U.S. workforce will be fifty-five to sixty years of age, and 30 percent will be over sixty-five, up from 20 percent in 2004.

One of the warmest and best feelings you can have as a new lawyer is helping a senior. Helping people old enough to be your grandparents will make you feel good about having chosen law as a profession. In your early years, you may occasionally do a simple will or a health-care directive, or draft a trust document. As time passes and your practice grows, you may get involved with conservatorships, probate, taxes, and the myriad areas involved in elder law.

If you can prepare for some of the concerns listed in this chapter, it will be easier for you and easier for the client.

As we slow down and as we get older, it takes us longer to run a mile or climb a flight of stairs or remember a face or a name. Some seniors require just a bit more time to walk to your office. Some speak more slowly. Some require more time to understand a question fully and give a full answer.

I am not an audiologist, a gerontologist, a kinesiologist, or any other "ologist." These are my suggestions based upon my years of practice and suggestions from seniors themselves and senior organizations. As always, health-care professionals have the best advice and should be consulted.

Representing senior citizens does not have to be difficult. Just remember the three Ps of working with seniors: Patience, Patience, Patience.

1. *Age*: There is no magic number for defining when someone is a senior. Historically, sixty-five was a magic number, but with increased longevity, many people are physically and mentally fit well into their nineties. Don't be obsessed with numerical age as standing for anything.

2. *Your Office—Help the Client*: Meet your client in the reception area and introduce yourself. If the client is carrying documents or packages, offer to carry them. If the client is wearing an overcoat, offer to help remove it.

3. *Lead, But Let the Client Set the Pace*: Ask the client to please follow you to your office. Be prepared to walk slowly, especially if the client is using a cane or a walker. The client may become confused if you suddenly disappear from sight and the client is in new surroundings.

4. *Borrow a Wheelchair*: Practice going from the entrance of your building to the lobby or elevator and then to the suite door of your office while pushing an empty wheelchair. If you followed the advice in this book, you made sure the doorways in your office accommodate a wheelchair. Although your building may comply with access building codes, your interior office doors may not need to be in compliance and the building might be exempted from compliance for various reasons. If your client cannot get to your office from the street in a wheelchair, have a "Plan B" to meet the client elsewhere.

5. *Thick Carpets*: If the client is in a wheelchair, ask the client if he or she wants you to push the chair, especially if there are carpets to be navigated. Some clients will appreciate the help, some will appreciate the offer and decline the help, and some may resent your offer. Nonetheless, it is still best to offer to push the wheelchair.

6. *Chairs*: You should have at least one straight-back wooden or hard-cushioned chair with arms for the client to use if necessary. You really should have two, in the event you interview a couple. Keep them someplace other than your office until you need them.

7. *Getting Home*: Ask the senior how he or she plans to get home. You need to be aware of pick-up times if the client is being picked up, or time deadlines if public transportation is used.

8. *Communicating with Hearing-Impaired Clients*: It is estimated that more than one-fourth of all adult Americans have some hearing loss.

Hearing impairment is no longer the exclusive domain of seniors. Earphones and high-volume music have taken their toll on young people. Many people with impaired hearing will turn their heads slightly when talking to you. They are favoring their "better ear." The person may even cup his or her hand behind an ear to better hear.

9. *Hearing Aids*: Do not assume that hearing aids make everything normal. They often are almost useless. Anticipate that the presence of hearing aids indicates a need for communication assistance.

10. *Get the Client's Attention*: Get the client's attention by stating the client's name or touching the client, if appropriate. When you want the client to listen to what you are asking or explaining, get the client's attention first. Instead of saying, "What happened?" say, "John," and pause. Be sure John is looking at you and then say, "What happened?" If appropriate, touch the person's hand or arm to get his attention, or make a hand gesture or raise a finger.

11. *Remain Calm*: Don't get frustrated or upset. This simply makes any situation worse.

12. *Remember the Three Ps*: Again, remember the three Ps of working with seniors: Patience, Patience, Patience.

13. *Keep Your Mouth Empty*: Don't smoke, chew gum, or eat anything while talking. The listener may partially read lips or depend upon facial gestures.

14. *Get Close*: Face the listener as closely as is reasonable. Look up and speak up. Keep eye contact.

15. *Speak to the Client*: Talk to the client, not about the client or around the client. If there is a child, spouse, or third party present, don't make the mistake of directing questions or comments to the third party if the proper person to be addressed is the client.

16. *Remember Not to Say, "Forget It"*: Do not ever say, "Forget it." A frustrated lawyer may at some point want to give up and say, "Forget it," and move on to another question or area if not understood by the hearing-impaired person. This may anger that person. If you want to move to a different topic, do so without saying, "Forget it," as this communicates both frustration and anger on your part.

17. *Don't Get Frustrated*: Inability to communicate can frustrate both you and the client. When you are frustrated, you may become more impatient, or even angry, and do less than your best work.

18. *Quiet the Office*: Get rid of background noises if you can. If your office has a control to eliminate the office music system (it should), then be sure the background music is off.

19. *Use Graphics*: Use charts, diagrams, and visual aids. I find that seniors love it when I go to a whiteboard and use colored marking pens

to illustrate the flow of money or numbers or the steps in the case. Write key words, phrases, or questions on the whiteboard or on your notepad. Use erasable slates, used by children and scuba divers. Many a senior has said to me, "You are the first person to explain things to me," when, in fact, other lawyers had explained things to the senior, who could not hear or understand what the lawyer was saying. The graphs make things understandable.

20. *Have Lots of Paper and Colored Pens, Pencils, and Markers*: Either you or your client may want to write questions or answers. Inability to communicate orally can stress both the lawyer and the client, causing lack of confidence on the part of both. Having alternative communication methods can help calm the situation.

21. *Use Technology*: Consider purchasing a mechanical device for the client to use. A simple voice amplifier in a giant room might be adequate and not cost much.

22. *Slow the Pace of Questions*: Do not ask rapid-fire questions unless you are getting rapid-fire answers. The hearing-impaired person might need time to organize thoughts or remember something before answering.

23. *Use Your Computer Monitor*: Use a word processor and flat-screen monitor, if feasible. You might be able to type your questions on a word-processing monitor for the hearing-impaired person. Stand-alone flat screens can be turned so the hearing-impaired person can see your typed questions or comments. You can also print out your questions as a record of your interview. If you don't have a monitor that can be turned, give the client a chair where you can both see the monitor, but remember not to face the monitor when speaking.

24. *Speak Slowly*: Speak slowly, with exaggerated lip movements. Ask your client, in a slow voice with exaggerated lip movements, "Is it easier for you if I speak slowly?" If the person responds yes, then do so. Some seniors want more time to be sure they fully understand what you are saying.

25. *Ask the Client What You Can Do*: Ask the client what, if anything, you can do to make it easier to communicate. The client may have a specific suggestion, such as speaking to her left ear, or not covering your mouth, or touching her hand to get her attention.

26. *Look Up, Look At, and Maintain Eye Contact*: If you believe the client may have a hearing impairment, look directly at the client when talking. Never cover your mouth with your hands or turn your head down or away or speak from behind the client. The client may be reading your lips and looking for facial gestures to help understand what you are saying.

27. *Sign Language*: The use of sign language or sign language interpreters is beyond the scope of this chapter.

28. *Don't Scream*: Do not yell, shout, or talk more loudly than you usually speak unless the client asks you to do so. The hearing-impaired person may be able to hear you but not understand you. Yelling will not change that, and can even make the situation worse because of the distortion of speech caused by the shouting. Hearing loss is often a matter of loss in specific ranges. A client might be able to understand the lower-range voices of men but not the midrange or upper ranges of women. Shouting may have the unintended effect of decreasing understandability.

29. *Accents*: If English is not your first language or the first language of the client, understand that accents or lack of English vocabulary can worsen a communication problem. Use simple words, if possible, and use gestures.

30. *Lack of Hearing Is Not Lack of Intelligence*: Do not assume senility or mental deficiency when a senior has a hearing problem. One British hospital patient put a sign over his head reading, "I'm Deaf, Not Daft."

31. *Some Seniors Need More Time*: As we get older, we need more time to run a mile, more time to focus our eyes, more time to remember a fact, more time to absorb and understand a question, and more time to give an answer. Understand that a hearing-impaired person may need even more time to answer a question or add to the conversation. The person may have heard bits of your communication, with only some words or sounds being familiar. The person must match what she heard with what she saw in your facial expressions and put your question or comment in the context of the subject matter being discussed. All this must be done before the person can respond.

32. *If You Ask a Question, Wait for the Answer*: Give the hearing-impaired person time to respond to your question. He might be trying to put together the bits and pieces of your question he could recognize before answering. Remember the keys to good communication: Look up! Speak up! Look to! Speak to!

33. *Watch for Concealment*: Be aware of hearing-impairment concealment. Unfortunately, there are many reasons why people conceal hearing loss. It has been said that they are victims of their vanity. The underlying causes are complex, and an appropriate discussion is beyond the scope of this book. A few of the general reasons include the following:

❑ The wearing of a hearing aid is considered by some to be an admission of aging and mortality.

❏ Some people fear they will be treated poorly by those who discriminate against the elderly.

❏ Hearing aids often require adjustment, and some people are embarrassed to remove a hearing aid, adjust it, and return it to the ear.

❏ Some people are concerned that hearing aids will interfere with their hairdos, and vice versa.

❏ There may be a sense of frustration at comparing hearing aids with eyeglasses. Eyeglasses immediately convert poor vision to excellent vision. Hearing aids rarely restore hearing to original ability, and often make only slight differences in hearing ability.

If you suspect concealment, simply ask the senior again if you can do anything to be sure your questions are understood. Turning a head to have the "better ear" closer to you, or giving an answer that is not responsive to the question, are signs of a hearing problem, as is cupping a hand behind the ear to direct the shell of the ear toward you.

34. *Repeat the Question*: Ask if the person understands the question as often as necessary, especially for key matters. Remember that not understanding a question is a sign of hearing deficiency, not mental deficiency or incompetence.

35. *Make Sure You Are Understood*: Ask if the client wants you to repeat or rephrase what you just asked. Hearing the same question a second time gives a hearing-impaired person the opportunity to recognize a word that was not recognizable the first time. Other times, if you are going to repeat a question or comment, just repeat it as though you had not previously asked the question or made the comment. Repetition may make what you said understandable. It is not necessary to say, "I'm going to repeat the question." The listener will know you are repeating the question. Your announcing the repetition of the question will simply highlight your possible frustration.

36. *Work with Your Client*: Communicating with a hearing-impaired person requires work on the part of the lawyer and assistance on the part of the client. It is a rewarding feeling when you know you have successfully communicated with a hearing-impaired person and are helping him or her.

37. *Avoid Back Lighting*: Be sure your face is well lit, so the hearing-impaired person can see your lip movements and facial gestures. Do not stand or sit with your head in front of a light, sunlight, or a window, as the senior needs to see your lips and face.

38. *Choose Optimal Times for Client Meetings*: Schedule seniors for morning appointments. They often are more alert, and you also may be

more alert. When you are tired, you do a poor job of being patient and you may violate many of the rules of communication. From time to time, rephrase what you just covered to be sure you and the senior understand each other. Cover three, four, or five points each time you rephrase and review. Remember that the process of rephrasing may itself aid additional communication problems.

39. *Loneliness*: It is a sad fact that some seniors are lonely and eager to talk to anyone who will listen to them. They may "over answer" questions because they are happy to have someone listening to them. You may find it helpful to say something like, "That is really interesting. I hope that someday we will have the time for you to tell me more. You should consider writing it down for others to read. Right now, we have to finish our work together or we may run out of time." Or you may wish to say, "Ms. Jones, your stories are fascinating and I could listen all day, but I have to base my fees on the amount of time required. If you are willing and able to pay me to listen, I'll be glad to charge you, but I'm sure you have better uses for your money." Believe it or not, some seniors are so lonely they will pay you your hourly rate just to listen to them. I leave it to your conscience what you should do if you have a large number of senior clients who simply want someone to talk to. You should consider hiring a "listener."

40. *Mental Impairment and Lack of Competence*: Neither law school nor practice qualifies you to distinguish among conditions such as simple forgetfulness, slight dementia, advanced dementia, early Alzheimer's, advanced Alzheimer's, or any classification of mental impairment.

41. *Sample Interview Questions*: I personally devised a series of questions that I have used over the years to rule out competence problems. When I find what appears to me to be a possible competence problem, I suggest to the client that I would like a letter from his or her doctor stating that in the doctor's opinion, the person is competent to make a will or make a gift or execute a health-care directive or whatever the proposed work involves. I explain to the senior that this is in the senior's best interest, to prevent a fight where someone claims the senior might not be competent. Without that letter, I simply refuse to do the work. I would rather lose a client and a fee than find myself as a defendant or witness in litigation, when I will not be paid for my time.

When asking these questions, it is preferable that the client be alone with you. If a third person—such as a spouse, child, or caregiver—comes to the meeting, explain that the presence of the third party might impair attorney-client privilege and the third party really should leave the room. If it is not possible to exclude the third party, be careful to note whether the client was able to answer the questions or whether the third party was providing the answers. If the third person gives the answer, try to note whether the client did or did not repeat the information as being accurate or in some manner independently state the information as covered.

A sample line of questions (which I use in will interviews and other situations) includes the following. You may wish to change them to fit the needs of the legal matter involved.

- ❑ What is your full name?
- ❑ What is the name on your birth certificate?
- ❑ When and where were you born?
- ❑ What is your telephone number?
- ❑ What is your Social Security number?
- ❑ Did you serve in the armed forces? If so, what was your serial number? In what branch did you serve? When and where were you discharged?
- ❑ Are your parents living or dead? If they are dead, when and where did they die?
- ❑ What is (was) your mother's name, including her maiden name?
- ❑ What is (was) your father's name?
- ❑ Do you have any living brothers and/or sisters? If so, what are their names and approximate ages, and where do they live?
- ❑ Do you have any deceased brothers or sisters? If so, when and where did they die?
- ❑ Do you have any living children?
- ❑ Do you have any deceased children? If so, when and where did they die?
- ❑ Do you have any grandchildren? If so, where do they live?

The preceding questions are designed to put the client at ease. The following questions are the more serious ones.

- ❑ Do you know who I am?
- ❑ Do you know what I do?
- ❑ Do you know where you are?
- ❑ Do you know why you are here?
- ❑ Tell me what you hope to accomplish today.
- ❑ What are your principal assets? (If the person is there for a will)
- ❑ Tell me the assets of the trust. (If the person is there for an amendment of a trust or to create a trust)

Indicate in your notes whether the senior answered from memory, looked at a document, depended upon a third person to get an answer, or didn't have an answer.

42. *The Folstein Mini-Mental Status Test (MMSE)*: You probably are not competent to administer a Folstein Mini Test, but you should be aware of what it is. The Folstein Mini-Mental Status Examination (often called the MMSE) is used by health-care professionals and others concerned with determining various aspects of competency to screen for possible cognitive dysfunction. It is commonly used with hospitalized or medically ill patients. You should not try to administer it or to interpret the results, but you should know what it is, as you may see references to it. The tested person may be asked questions in some or all of the following areas:

❑ Orientation—identifying year, season, date, day, month, state, county, town, hospital, floor, address
❑ Registration—reciting three consecutive objects (ball, flag, tree)
❑ Calculation—counting and subtracting backward by 7s (93-86-79-72-65)
❑ Attention—spelling the word "world" backward
❑ Recall—after a five-minute delay, naming the three objects in the registration above
❑ Language—following instructions such as these: Name two objects (book and pencil). Pick up this book with your right hand and put it on the floor. Close your eyes. Write a sentence. Copy a simple design (circle, triangle, square).
❑ Level of Consciousness—alert, drowsy, stuporous, comatose

For each part of the test, points are assigned, added, and interpreted by the test giver.

43. *Videotaping or Audiotaping the Interview*: Videotaping and/or audiotaping interviews can be a double-edged sword. Although it can help confirm information and communications, your decision to tape can be interpreted as an acknowledgment by you that taping was necessary. Some lawyers routinely videotape interviews of all clients over the age of seventy or seventy-five, which can lead to accusations of age discrimination and the incurring of unnecessary expenses. I suggest the best solution might simply be to discuss the subject of taping with the client; ask the client if he or she wants to be taped to lessen the possibility of a will contest.

44. *Vision*: As we pass thirty years of age, our visual acuity decreases. We may need glasses to read at a relatively early age. Several things

are simultaneously happening to our eyes, which can affect our ability to read. We might need more light, more contrast, and/or large-type letters to read documents, even while wearing glasses. Consider doing the following:

❑ Type your letters and documents in boldface and/or larger type (size 16 font).

❑ Have a large rectangular magnifying glass available for the client to read documents while in your office.

❑ Be sure your professional cards and stationery contain your telephone number in large, boldface numbers.

❑ Avoid darkened rooms.

❑ If projection is required, try to avoid darkening the room.

45. *Ethics*: Representing seniors sometimes presents ethical problems. You have to be most careful to determine that you are doing what the senior wants, rather than what a third party says the senior wants. In general, you must be especially careful when there is more than one person in the room with you. You must ask yourself who the client is, and why the other person is present. The presence of third parties can put you in the middle of a malpractice suit. This is especially true if the third party will benefit from what you are being asked to do. In some cases, you will simply have to decline representing the senior. You are better off losing a fee than being in the middle of a civil lawsuit and a bar complaint.

Regardless of how many years you have practiced law, you will feel good about helping seniors.

Other Niche Practices to Consider 13

William D. Henslee

Specializing in a substantive area of law can allow you to develop a successful and personally rewarding practice. Rather than chasing any case that comes in the door, you can turn away cases that are not in your area of expertise. Turning away business can be very empowering. As a specialist, you can affiliate with other specialists who need your expertise for a particular transaction or who are willing to join you in servicing a client with diverse needs.

Use your imagination and develop a niche practice in an area of law that intrigues and challenges you. When choosing a specialty area, make sure it is not so specialized that you won't be able to attract enough clients to stay in business. In addition, make sure it is an area of law that interests you—it makes no sense to do otherwise. If the practice doesn't make you want to jump out of bed and go to work, find an area of law that will do that for you.

The ABA Law Practice Management Section and the ABA General Practice, Solo and Small Firm Section provide books and continuing legal education (CLE) programs to help you establish and manage your solo practice and to focus your practice in a specific substantive area of law. Marketing your specialty is covered in other chapters of this book. The discussion of specialty areas below is not designed to be exclusive, nor are the specialty areas discussed in any particular order.

111

Tax

A specialized tax practice may be ideal for you if you have a background in tax. If you are a certified public accountant (CPA) with a law degree, or a former Internal Revenue Service employee, you have the requisite background to attract clients and develop a tax practice. An undergraduate degree in accounting should also allow you to specialize in a tax practice. With expertise in the area, you should be able to accept referrals from CPAs and other tax preparers, as well as practitioners who need to affiliate with tax experts to help complete deals. You may have other opportunities for affiliation by making your services available to other specialists whose clients might need tax advice. The ABA Section of Taxation is an excellent resource for getting established and for keeping up with changes in the law.

Business Law

If you have a tax background, you might prefer to establish a business law practice. By specializing in business organization and corporate governance issues, you can take your clients from start-up to Fortune 500 status (although your role will evolve if the company becomes that successful). A business planning practice complements a tax practice and the combined areas should allow you to cultivate a diverse client base. The ABA Business Law Section is a very large section with excellent CLE programs and other resources.

Wealth Management

A wealth management and estate planning practice may be a logical extension of your tax and business practice, or you may want to specialize in the area without the business practice. Tax planning is an integral part of wealth management and estate planning; if you do not have a tax background, you should associate with someone who can provide that component of the practice. The ABA Section of Real Property, Probate and Trust Law can provide you with helpful information on the specialty area.

Criminal Defense

Criminal defense is a logical specialty area for former prosecutors and public defenders. Familiarity with the criminal court system, judges, and prosecutors should make you a logical choice for defendants in need of counsel. Referrals from prosecutors, judges, and bail bondsmen should help get you started. Referrals from former clients will multiply as word of your success spreads. The ABA Criminal Justice Section would be helpful in providing information on careers in the area.

In some states, courts assign death penalty appeals to practitioners who have developed expertise in the area and who are willing to work for court-specified fees. Check with your state bar or state supreme court to learn how to become qualified to handle death penalty cases and to become one of the lawyers on the list for case assignments by the court.

Entertainment

Sole practitioners, as well as large law firms, practice in the entertainment specialty area. To establish an entertainment law practice, solos need to specialize in film, television, music, theater, art, or book publishing. Each area has its own vocabulary and its own group of players. Though the most prominent practitioners are located in New York and Los Angeles, you can develop a healthy specialty practice no matter where you are located. The ABA Forum on the Entertainment and Sports Industries is an excellent source of information on the substantive areas of law included in an entertainment law practice. The ABA Career Series book entitled *Entertainment Law Careers* is a helpful resource on entertainment career choices.

Every state has a film commission that needs lawyers with industry expertise to handle the local requirements of the studios that choose to shoot pictures in that state. To serve as local counsel for a production company or studio, you must be aware of local labor laws, tax laws, permit requirements, and insurance requirements. Your local and state film commissions should be excellent resources for information on the film business in your state.

Television programs shot on location require the same type of representation as film productions. Television programs are usually shot on sound-stages, with location shooting reserved to establish a show's locale. Depending upon the particular show and episode, the program may require several days of location shooting. State and local film commissions also work on enticing television programs to the state. Your film commission should be able to provide you with information on the television business in your state.

Every city has a local music scene with musicians who need to protect their original music. Bands need to know how to structure their groups as businesses, split income and expenses, divide songwriting income, avoid liability while on tour and while playing at shows, and plan for future success.

Musicians also need to know how to secure rights to use music written and recorded by other bands. Venue owners need advice on complying with copyright laws, as well as local noise ordinances and liquor laws.

Local theater groups need to know how to secure rights to the material they want to perform, how to structure venue agreements, and how to comply with the Actors' Equity Association's requirements for local productions. Artists need advice on protecting their copyrights and retaining rights after the sale of a particular piece.

Many states have a "Lawyers for the Arts" group that needs volunteer lawyers to advise clients. Volunteer work is a good way to develop expertise in entertainment as you transition your practice. In addition, by serving as a volunteer, you might be able to develop a client base. Who knows, one of the clients who comes in for some free legal advice might become the next popular sensation; with any luck, you will be hired to advise the client as he or she becomes successful.

Sports

Sports agents work as solos or in small firms. To be a sports agent, you must be certified by the players association of the sport in which you represent clients, and you must register with the states in which you recruit athletes. The most difficult part of representing athletes is client development. If you know a player who will let you negotiate his or her contract, you are well on your way to becoming an agent. If you don't know any players who will let you negotiate their contracts, you are going to have an extremely difficult time cultivating clients. Also, remember that the Model Rules of Professional Conduct do not allow you to solicit clients in the same manner as nonlawyer agents. Before you abandon your other practice, make sure you have the client base to support you and your family. The players associations regulate the percentage of a player's income that you can receive from the player's team salary, so do the math before you decide to be an agent. Only a few select agents in each sport are successful enough to dedicate their entire practices to sports representation. Before you commit to sports representation as a career, make sure you are comfortable with your recruitment practices as they relate to your state bar's rules on professional conduct, and make sure you can earn a living doing it.

Real Estate

Developers, retail businesses, and home buyers need specialized legal advice when purchasing land, building structures, and selling land and structures to future owners and occupiers. Developers need advice on zoning ordinances, building codes, construction laws, insurance requirements, and union rules (in some states). Retail business owners need advice on commercial leases, insurance requirements, and employment laws at the federal, state, and local levels. Home buyers need advice on real estate contracts and deeds. There are many sources of clients for someone interested in real estate transactions and land use planning.

Disability

The Americans with Disabilities Act prohibits schools, businesses, and public facilities from discriminating against individuals based upon an individual's physical or mental disability, and creates causes of action for those individuals. Special education students and students entitled to individual education plans (IEPs) often need advocates to ensure their educational needs are met and their rights protected. Lawyers with expertise in laws governing special education and IEPs provide a valuable service to parents and their children. A specialization in the disability and special education areas must include familiarity with federal and state statutes and regulations.

Social Security

Social Security Administration (SSA) cases are regulated by the SSA. Advocates do not have to be lawyers. Practitioners are limited to statutory fees, paid from the amounts recovered from the SSA. There are very few lawyers with expertise in this area. This practice area fits within the scope of practices dedicated to ADA cases, workers' compensation cases, and/or special education cases.

Franchise

Both franchisors and franchisees need representation in their transactions. The franchise law specialty area has a base of clients with good business ideas (franchisors) and with enough financial resources to enter franchise agreements with major chains (franchisees). In addition reviewing specialized contracts, each party to a transaction must understand the value of—and limitations on—the use of intellectual property, as well as the product or service being franchised. A franchisee needs advice on establishing a retail outlet and all the other issues that flow from the establishment of a new business. This practice area fits nicely within a business planning practice.

Bankruptcy

Bankruptcy filings seem to fluctuate with the economy. When the economy is strong, there are fewer bankruptcies. When the economy is suffering, many businesses need bankruptcy protection to either liquidate their assets or reorganize so they can continue to grow within the constraints and protections afforded by federal bankruptcy law. Protection for creditors is sometimes necessary for a business to reestablish itself and become a healthy company. A bankruptcy practice could be a self-contained specialty or be combined with a business planning and/or tax practice.

Immigration

An immigration law practice can be established in any growing city or in any city with a substantial immigrant population. As people from around the world relocate to the United States, they need advice on their legal status.

Arbitration and Mediation

The trend toward alternative dispute resolution has created a need for arbitrators and mediators. Arbitrators and mediators need specialty training and certification, but once the process is complete, the potential for business grows. Some states have court-ordered arbitration and/or mediation. Most labor unions have arbitration clauses in their contracts with management. Many private parties have inserted arbitration or mediation clauses in their contracts. Family disputes are being referred to mediation. This is a growing area that can provide an alternative to the daily requirements of a standard law practice.

Specialization

Specialization may be the key to a personally rewarding career as a sole practitioner. If you don't specialize, you will find it difficult to keep up with developments in the law, in areas that may not even interest you, as you endlessly chase cases simply to pay the bills. If you are not invested in the substantive areas of law that your clients need, you may be in danger of committing malpractice. By specializing in an area that both interests and challenges you, you will enjoy both the work and the benefits of being a sole practitioner. (See also Chapter 6, "Why Should You Specialize?")

Selected Resources
for Part I

from the ABA Law Practice
Management Section

How to Build and Manage an Employment Law Practice, by Mindy
Farber, 1997.

How to Build and Manage an Entertainment Law Practice, by
Gary Greenberg, 2001.

How to Build and Manage an Estates Practice, by Daniel B. Evans,
co-published with the ABA Real Property, Probate, and Trust
Law Section, 1999.

How to Build and Manage a Personal Injury Practice, by K.
William Gibson, 1997.

How to Build and Manage an Environmental Law Practice, by Stu-
art L. Somach, co-published with the ABA Section of Environment, Energy, and Resources, 2000.

How to Start and Build a Law Practice, Fifth Edition, by Jay G
Foonberg, 2004.

Law Practice, bimonthly publication of the ABA Law Practice
Management Section.

*The Lawyer's Guide to Creating a Business Plan: A Step-by-Step
Software Package,* by Linda Pinson, 2005.

*The Lawyer's Guide to Strategic Planning: Defining, Setting, and
Achieving Your Firm's Goals, by* Thomas C. Grella, and Michael
L. Hudkins, 2004.

Financial Manual

Like other small business owners, solo lawyers are responsible for running a profitable business. If they do not show a profit, they go out of business. Many aspiring solos have thrown in the towel and taken a "real" job after failing to turn a profit. If those lawyers had read Part II, they might be running a successful and growing solo practice today instead of working for someone else.

Part II starts with the basics—"The Financial Nuts and Bolts" that you do not learn in law school. Everything you need to know is covered, from understanding how capitalization works to securing a loan to insuring your investment.

In addition, you'll learn innovative and time-tested methods for setting fees, keeping time, billing your clients, and getting paid. You won't veer off course if you follow the invaluable advice from this group of seasoned solos and respected practice management advisors.

The Financial Nuts and Bolts

Financial Overview

14

Carol A. Seelig

Many lawyers dream of running their own practices and being their own bosses. Many think that opening a law practice is somehow different from opening a dry-cleaning business or a bakery, or becoming a general contractor to build houses. Even though a lawyer offers a professional service—albeit one that requires years of training—the lawyer is still opening a business. And just as every business needs start-up capital, a lawyer needs money to fund start-up costs and to pay for ongoing expenses.

A solo law practice has three principal sources of funding: (1) money that the sole practitioner can personally invest, (2) funds that can be borrowed from family, friends, or banks, and (3) revenue from work for clients. Graduating from law school and passing the bar exam may give someone the right to open a law practice, but it doesn't provide the means to do so.

The only way for a lawyer to determine the capital requirements for starting a law practice is to prepare a business plan. The business plan should include one-time costs (start-up expenses such as office equipment and computer hardware and software), as well as ongoing operating costs (such as rent, office supplies, and salaries). The problem for lawyers who are just starting is that both start-up expenses and the first month's operating expenses must be paid long before the first fee check arrives. Even someone starting a practice with a few financially solvent clients and hourly fee-based cases will have to cover expenses for a couple months. Someone starting with only contingent-fee-based cases may have to cover expenses for six months to a year before collecting a fee. Likewise, if someone is starting with no clients, then it will be an equally long time before any revenue is produced.

The difference between your success and failure as a solo may well be in having access to capital that will carry you through this initial period when you need funds for start-up expenses as well as ongoing operating expenses. Although there are many sources of capital, they may not all be available to you.

If you are just out of law school, you may not have any money, or any property to sell to raise money. In fact, you may have no money and a lot of debt from student loans. Worse yet, you may have no money, a lot of debt, and not qualify for a loan from a bank or other financial institution. If that is the case, and if you are lucky enough, you may be able to turn to family and friends to borrow the money you need to start your practice. This is something most people want to avoid because there are so many emotional issues associated with borrowing from family and friends. Will you be putting those relationships at risk if you add an economic component to the mix? How soon will these people expect to be repaid? Will this put extra pressure on you to find the funds to repay these loans? How will you feel if you can't meet the payment schedule?

Even if you decide not to seek loans from friends and family, there are still interpersonal issues involved in starting a practice. If you have a spouse or significant other, that person must be willing to risk the family's financial future to support your new business venture. Your new practice might obligate your partner to get an outside job just to cover your family's day-to-day living expenses and obligations, such as car payments and student loan payments. Even if your partner is as committed to the new venture as you are, it can still create a high level of stress. The financial pressure could affect your performance on the job or put a strain on your relationship with your partner.

If you are going to ask your family and friends to make sacrifices by lending you money, or if you are going to ask your partner to make sacrifices by helping you start a law practice, you must first be sure that all the sacrifice is worthwhile. Many lawyers who enjoy practicing law do not enjoy the day-to-day duties of running a law practice. You should know—before you ask everyone around you to make sacrifices—whether you really want to run your own practice. The big question is this: Are you committed? Once you are truly committed, it can be amazing what resources will become available to you.

If you are starting on a shoestring, your main task will be to keep expenses as low as possible until the cash starts to flow. You must be creative. If you find that you don't have enough cash to fund your initial plan, look to see if there are noncash methods of obtaining the same results. Though you may have to pay for the phone, it's possible that a friend has an extra space in her office that you can use for free. You may already own some of the equipment and software that you need. Also, remember that when you start, you don't need the best available. You only need something that is functional. So, instead of buying printed stationery, create stationery on your computer; instead of using high-quality envelopes, buy the least-expensive envelopes available; and instead of incurring high costs for deliveries and express mailing, send as many documents as possible by e-mail messaging.

If you read the chapters in this book that address capital, cash-flow issues, and obtaining loans, you will have an understanding of the financial aspects of your practice. The chapters that discuss setting your fees, using alternative billing arrangements, and collecting fees will help you evaluate the amount of revenue you might expect from your practice during its first six to twelve months.

As the old saying goes, where there is a will, there is a way. This doesn't mean that everyone can start a business today, but it does mean that everyone who wants to be a sole practitioner can begin planning and taking steps that will permit him or her to achieve that goal.

The Capital and Capitalization of the Solo Law Practice

15

James J. Orlow

A law firm's assets and resources are its "capital." This includes both financial and physical assets, as well as certain intangibles such as reputation. In the instance of a sole practitioner, there may be a real or apparent merger of the capital of the practice and the assets and resources of the lawyer personally. Many of the resources are a function of finances; a better office may cost more rent. If the cash flow is uneven, cash or credit capital may be needed for slack periods. A new practice must acquire furniture and equipment, and, to develop a reputation for service, may take cases that do not pay well; the uncompensated time and expense of such cases are an investment in the practice and a form of intangible capital.

Capitalization of a solo law practice is functionally the same as for any other size law firm, even the largest. Capitalization is proportional to the size and nature of the practice. It is smaller for a sole practitioner than a larger firm. However, unless the solo lawyer is attentive, it is disproportionately unlikely that anyone else will do anything about an orderly capital program. Moreover, inattention to capital can easily become the source of significant—though preventable—problems for a solo law practice. The recognition of the need for capital, and a realistic plan for its acquisition and use, are critical.

Capital Needs

Every law practice, even a solo law practice, needs and uses capital. Financial capital consists of funds used in the current period but not earned in the current period. Commonly, capital is needed for leasehold improvements, equipment and facilities, carrying accounts receivable and work in process, staff training, and cash reserves for routine operating expenses and periods of low cash receipts. New and reorganized practices also need funding for start-up periods, before sufficient and regular cash flow is established. The amount of capital needed depends upon the following:

- ◆ the type of practice
- ◆ the style of practice
- ◆ the way that funds are used
- ◆ the acquisition of facilities (the decision to make or buy, buy alone or share, buy now or buy later, or buy or rent)
- ◆ the practice's stage of life
- ◆ the cost of doing business

The dictionary meanings of "capital" vary slightly. One dictionary defines it as the money needed to carry on business. Another defines it as possessions that bring in income. A third relates it to financial resources. All are accurate. Capital includes the assets of the practice, both financial and nonfinancial. The capital assets of a practice are its funds, furniture, fixtures, leases and equipment, unbilled and unpaid work, and goodwill for future work (client relationships, client files, and general reputation). The most overlooked capital resources in a law practice are the capabilities of the lawyer and staff. All nonfinancial assets reflect the investment of time, effort, and money in the expectation of future income. Whatever the need or solution, the premise of this chapter is that a thoughtful plan, pursued seriously, will sooner lead to a better night's sleep than to the unease of vague and careening financial worries. Now, the details.

It is inevitable that a law practice, large or small, will require a capital investment to pay for current operations as well as acquisitions. The size of the practice affects the amount of capital, but not the need for capital. Realization of the income from professional fees may be weeks, months, or years after the productive time and money has been spent. Some of these investment values show on a balance sheet; some don't. This is even more true if the firm is accounting on a cash basis rather than on an accrual basis. However, all these values are reflected in the net income, net profit, and net cash flow for the period and for later periods. A distinctive aspect of capital is that it is a class of accounts for current-period operations and future operations.

Capital needs are predictable to a greater degree than may seem possible at first assessment. Predicting capital needs depends upon establishing a reliable budget and then performing at or near predicted levels. Budgeting includes not only the control of expenses, but also the predictability of income. Income budgeting relates to being engaged for enough work per period, completing enough work per period, and being paid for enough work during the period to meet goals. You need capital to cover those periods when there is either no income or less income than required for expenses of that period.

An example of a successful practice with potential capital problems is that of a sole practitioner with a few large cases in litigation. Each case represents a major portion of the expected total income. Earning of the fee may be contingent upon the outcome achieved. Achieving the result will be delayed by the normal pace of litigation, even if the result is substantially assured. During the preparation and trial phases of each case, the office must operate, staff must be paid, and the needs of the lawyer and his or her family must be met. Ideally, the fee from a prior case arrives and some of the fees from other prior cases have been saved for the slack period. In the current period, the receipt of deferred income from a previously completed case is a form of capital. The financial strength of a practice is this stream of income from work previously completed. It pays for current work in process. Current work completed continues the flow of income in future periods. Work in process is the principal capital in a law practice; it represents the professional form of "sweat equity."

The same is true for professional fees billed but uncollected. Even when a client pays promptly, it is likely that the billing will be paid in the next calendar month; that is, in a later period. When there is a longer delay in payment, the extent to which there are other accounts providing cash flow is a major capital strength in a law practice, as in any other entity. Should these income sources slacken in their flow, however, additional working capital may be needed. A practice dominated by a few major cases is more likely to have an uneven cash flow than a practice with a regular and relatively constant level of work, billing, and receipts. The differences dictate the capital requirements and the ways of achieving them.

Other capital needs involve the acquisition and use of facilities and equipment, bought and paid for in an earlier period but used over a longer period. This includes leasehold improvements, furniture, fixtures, and the increasingly more sophisticated electronic equipment now common for law practices. The techniques available for managing the costs of this type of capital are similar. These items can be bought outright from current earnings or from funds invested directly. They can be bought from funds borrowed from a bank or similar lender, to be repaid as an equipment loan. They can be leased (in the purest sense); that is, rented for the short run. A more standard mode of capital equipment acquisition is the lease-purchase. This is effectively a loan from a financial institution, usually at a higher rate of interest than a standard bank loan. It may be helpful when a standard loan is not available, or available but insufficient. Leasehold improvements, renovations, and decoration of office spaces over the amount provided at the landlord's expense can also be "financed" as part of the lease transaction. The charges for the improvements may be paid as part of the monthly rent over the period of the lease, sometimes without a charge for interest.

Capital used for training and motivation of the lawyer and staff is the most productive investment, as trained and motivated people are the most important part of the practice. This includes general training, specific instruction, and continuing general education, as well as continuing professional education. Little or none of this is directly billable to a client. Nor can the income in a current period be expected to realize the values or recover the costs of training. The values will appear in later periods as:

- a calm and professional staff
- an office operating with "the right stuff"
- the absence of fear of the knowable
- flexibility during periods of higher caseloads
- recognition for improved job skills so employees can qualify for promotion
- lower employee absence and turnover rates
- client recognition for the quality, tone, and style of operation

Training funds are often seen as the least important in amount and visibility, and there is strong pressure to cut this expense in slack times. However, that is exactly when training least interferes with getting work done. Successful capital management requires continued and practical investment in the lawyer and the staff.

Capital Resources

Once you have considered the amounts and time value of funding, your next questions involve where you get it and whether it is available to you. Capital can take the economic forms of cash, credit, physical assets, intangibles, savings, forbearance, and use or "opportunity costs." For the sole practitioner, the amount of capital needed may provide a significant degree of flexibility. Without partners to consult, decision making is less complex, but not less difficult. Just because the amount may be smaller does not mean it is proportionately smaller. Just because the decision may appear to be simpler does not mean that the process is easier for a solo, who has too many things to do in the first instance. Financial capital may be derived from the following:

- cash contributions
- forbearance of income
- deferred acquisition of capital assets
- retained earnings (savings)
- depreciation saved rather than disbursed
- disciplined budgeting practices
- loans and lines of credit
- revised fee practices
- revised billing practices

Direct cash investment as equity or loan is a clear enough source of capital. So, too, is forbearance of income. Forbearance can take a variety of forms, from a deliberate underdistribution of a fixed proportion or amount per period to the omission of payment for a particular date or period. In some firms, large and small, partners underdraw. The undistributed earnings fund serves as cash capital for the payment of operating expenses. The late distribution of part of the income creates a funded source of capital during the period that the cash is not drawn.

Forbearance also is a characteristic of the decision to defer acquisition of certain furniture and equipment, or the decision to get used items rather than new ones. In such decisions, the capital needed is provided, in part, by reduction or deferral of the cost of the item. The ability to sustain the decision is measured by the ability to defer the more expensive alternative. However, the loss of use is a noncash economic cost.

The development of savings as a source of capital is subject to personal trade-offs between the need for capital and the need for income. As discussed more fully below, the gap may be filled with bank financing.

An income-tax-driven source of savings for capital is in the treatment of cash income sheltered by depreciation. The tax deduction allowed for depreciation of assets involved in the practice is an expense that does not result in a cash disbursement in the current period. It is a charge against income as a proportion of the cost of an asset placed in service in prior periods as well as the current period. When there is a deduction for assets purchased in the prior period, the equal amount of income earned in the present period is said to be "sheltered" from income tax. This amount can be retained for capital purposes because it results from the use of capital assets that require replacement in a later period. The act of actually saving, rather than spending, the money is no less difficult because the fund was generated through tax consequences.

Disciplined budgeting is sometimes overlooked as a source of capital. Budgeting, in this sense, is the disciplined coupling of cash management with the timing of capital requirement. This does not mean being cheap or crying poor. It means setting realistic standards and holding to them. It also means revising the plan if conditions change. Tight budgeting provides enough support for lawyer and staff training. It also provides enough support for practice development. For instance, a choice to rent rather than buy at a particular time may have cash and noncash effects. The overall cost of rental payments may be higher over the period of the lease than the cost of purchase. Invariably, the cost of a true lease is high enough that this is not an effective alternative except for short periods or select situations. However, in shorter periods, the rental payment is a smaller monthly operating expense. The decision to purchase calls for an investment of cash or credit in the present period. Higher operating expenses may be the required cost of too little available capital in the current period.

Although this analysis appears to focus upon the purchase of "things," it is equally applicable to employee salaries and expenses. For example, in the shorter period, there may not be funding available for a full-time, salaried secretary (or additional secretary). Services can be obtained from secretarial services or temporary agencies. The unit cost of this service is greater than for a full-time employee. When a full-time secretary is not needed, and when the flow of income does not fund the required full-time salary and benefits, "rental" may be preferred over purchase. Though this may reduce the short-term cash outflow, short-term hires or employment agency personnel may result in an increase in per-unit output expenses and a decrease in capital requirements. With the increased use of "contract" lawyers and "project" employees, the cost and risk of this alternative may have been reduced.

Another way to spare expenses is to avoid overstocking supplies. Suppliers can ordinarily provide supplies on an as-needed basis. Though this item of expense is quite small compared with other categories of costs, there is no reason not to utilize the "just in time" supply systems now available.

Capital budgeting provides for sources of cash and credit. Some lawyers would rather not borrow for their practices because it might appear to announce that they are not doing well enough financially. Realistically, practice development, relocation, or major technological equipment might require a loan or financing through a lease-purchase, although it might be difficult to arrange this if there is no credit history. Appropriate capital planning includes creating a loan for the ultimate purpose of establishing a credit history for the law practice, even if the immediate stated purpose of the loan is the purchase of new furniture or a copy machine.

The control of work in progress and billing is critical, for they have an impact on capital needs as much as on income. To the degree that the income is realized sooner rather than well after the work is done, there is a decreased need for capital to fund operations for the interim. The same effect on capital requirements to fund current operating expenses is even more obvious with the control and collection of accounts receivable. There are many discussions of the effect on income of monitoring work and billing, particularly the imperative of keeping accurate accounts of actual work to be billed before it becomes a vague memory. The practice of maintaining adequate income decreases the pressure for operating capital.

The capital needs of a practice can be significantly changed by the way that fees and client disbursement costs are charged and the way that bills are sent and collected. The most dramatic version of reducing the need for operating capital is the fee arrangement that provides for full or substantial prepayment of the fee. When this can be arranged, it is as applicable to fees charged on the basis of time as it is to fees charged as a flat prepayment, as is common in a criminal defense practice. The unearned fee and deposit for costs are held in escrow until billed and then transferred within a short time of a periodic statement, under the terms of the agreement with the client. Some lawyers have an arrangement specifying that when an escrow fund falls below an agreed-upon amount, the client will make a further payment to escrow. Though my own practice does not permit this type of fee agreement readily, my agreements with clients require the prepayment of case-related disbursements, which can be substantial. This type of arrangement provides a greater reduction of capital needed than would be the situation if case costs had to be billed and carried as accounts receivable. (See Chapter 19, which discusses billing practices, as well as Chapter 20, which discusses cash flow, as both directly affect capital needs.)

Whether to charge interest depends upon the agreement with the client and applicable truth-in-lending laws. Though originally thought to be "too commercial," accepting payments with credit or debit cards—when acceptable to clients—is useful for increasing cash flow and decreasing needs for operating capital. A useful source of information on the requirements for credit card and debit card procedures is a banking office at the commercial bank where you have an account. The ABA has established a credit card banking program as a member benefit. The program includes VISA, MasterCard, and American Express Card remittances, all at competitive discount rates, and operates under the title "Professional Payment Services" by U.S. Bankcard Center, Nashville, Tennessee (800-727-1143 or 615-254-1539).

Capital Management

The heart of capital management is in planning and budgeting. Planning deals with the physical category (the "what"), and budgeting is the financial aspect of the plan (the "how much"). Planning involves daily operations as well as longer-term requirements. The operating budget concerns the periodic (monthly/quarterly/annual) operations, with usual expense and disbursement categories, such as the following:

- salaries and benefits
- rent and utilities
- telephone and other communications
- liability insurance
- library and research facilities
- professional dues
- lawyer and staff training
- repayment of loans and equipment leases
- disbursements for case-related costs
- marketing costs
- payments to the lawyer
- retirement funding
- funding for future projects

The usual income items are as follows:

- fees earned and collected
- case costs reimbursed
- interest earned on reserves

The Way That Funds Are Used

Determination of the capital required is a function of a capital budget. Settling upon a reasonable amount to borrow (as much as the ability to repay) limits the availability and acceptability of a loan as a capital source. This reflects the trade-off between debt repayment and practitioner income. However, limiting the investment to the amount that can be afforded in the short run may have a substantial noneconomic cost. The retention of strong client relationships may require offices at a certain site. It might be more prudent to secure a smaller office (at less rent) and furnish and equip it properly (through a loan or lease-purchase) with funds from the rent-not-spent, than to get a larger office that is inadequately furnished and equipped. This is an example of the "way that funds are used" category mentioned earlier in this chapter under the Capital Needs section.

Another "way that funds are used" is in the timing of acquisitions of equipment. When the telecopier (fax) was first introduced, I was duly fascinated, but skeptical of its actual utility. A rental was arranged—not as a demonstration, but as a true lease—for thirty days. At the end of the period, I returned the equipment and ended the lease; the telecopier had been used only twice. Acquisition then, by purchase or lease, would have been premature. It would have been an ineffective use of funds.

The Type of Practice

An example of how the "type of practice" reflects differing capital needs is the way in which certain long-term client matters are financed. In certain personal injury cases, the plaintiff's counsel is paid only on success. Defense counsel is paid at intervals during the period, with the amount determined more by effort than result. The plaintiff's lawyer relies more upon interim funding—such as sweat equity, forbearance, and loans—than the defendant's lawyer. Similarly, in estate practice, work is done well in advance of the audit and approval of the account, including counsel fees. The security of the earned fees may justify borrowing. However, unless this resolution is actually in place, there is an adverse effect on the cash flow of the practice and of the lawyer.

The Style of Practice

The "style of practice" category differs subtly from the "type of practice" or "way that funds are used" categories. For instance, in certain commercial practices, there may be little problem in charging interest on overdue billing. The clients may be accustomed to this type of billing from other suppliers. However, some lawyers feel that charges for professional services should not appear to be the same as for other commercial suppliers; hence, no specified interest charge. This does not mean that those lawyers finance accounts without charge. The cost of financing work in process and accounts receivable is part of overhead costs. It is part of the fee charged to all clients, those who pay slowly as well as those who pay promptly. The charge is simply not stated as a separate item for delay in payment.

"Style of practice" also includes the capital and operating expense when a lawyer wishes to have an oversized office, special facilities, or excess staffing. The costs may or may not be wasted. The particular "extravagance" might be the only effective way to accomplish a needed part of the practice. However, it has its cost, whatever the actual value may be. The cost may be reflected in capital for facilities or for expenses paid for staff in one period, but not recovered as income until another period.

The Acquisition of Facilities

The acquisition of facilities is the activity most often contemplated as requiring capital, particularly when a new office is opened. This involves a series of decisions on the equipment for a given office, at a given time, and in a specific place. There is no standard answer. These decisions involve alternative choices and the scaling of priorities during a brief period, and are made in incremental terms, rather than as a package. The touchstone is not in restricting purchases and acquisitions solely for the sake of reducing cost, but rather, in making disciplined, realistic, and effective decisions given your cash flow and the amount of debt you can repay each month. This requires a well-developed and realistic concept of the organization to be staffed, equipped, and housed as a basis for determining the physical offices to be organized and equipped. In this way, the decisions as a whole can be reasonable in relation to the work to be done, and the whole effort can be coherent.

The choices for equipment decisions are to "make or buy," "buy now or buy later," and "buy or rent." "Make or buy" means the decision about whether to perform the function in-house or buy it from a supplier in a finished or partly finished form. For instance, I might prefer to buy or lease a larger photocopy machine, but may instead buy or lease the smaller size and send the occasional larger copying jobs to an outside duplicating service.

Capital considerations often dominate a decision about whether to "buy alone or share." An example of sharing is pooling the use of staff facilities and equipment rather than having exclusive use. Pooled use is more efficient, because rarely are all facilities, equipment, and staff needed by one lawyer, full-time, every day. If they are available concurrently with another lawyer who shares the costs, both lawyers save in cost and in capital. Another form of sharing is subletting, whereby the user pays the owner a fee to use the equipment, facilities, or staff. This cost is usually less than outside service purchase. It, too, saves both lawyers, as it contributes to the owner's income and allows the user to avoid investing in the equipment.

Capital considerations also apply to the "buy now or buy later" decision. A lawyer might buy a smaller copying machine or computer now, fully intending to buy the larger size at a later, specific time or event. These decisions include not only the specific equipment but also the related furniture, the space for its use, and the staff with the skills and training necessary for operation at a high level of performance.

In the decision to "buy or rent," the question is not about access to the equipment and facilities, but how to pay for it. "Buy" might include payment from current income, payment from existing capital sources, or payment from capital sources created for the purchase. "Rent" might include a true lease, a lease-purchase, or a loan arrangement for the purchase of the equipment in which the purchase money is "rented." Rental property for lawyers has recently begun to include not only the basic space, but also services and facilities such as a central library, duplication services, and other ancillary equipment on an "as-used" basis. When the decisions are well-matched with the needs of a particular practice, the investments produce good work, goodwill, and professional satisfaction. When they fail, there are both financial costs of the disbursement and additional costs of alternatives and opportunities not taken.

The Practice's Stage of Life

A law practice's stage of establishment also controls the need for capital. In a solo practice, this might parallel the professional maturation of the practitioner. This may also account for the situation of a practitioner newly embarked in solo practice after practice elsewhere. However, a sole practitioner who starts later may bring sources of income that the younger practitioner might not have available.

The style of the practice and the style of the sole practitioner are also limited by the way the practice of law is conducted in the particular location. If the area is conservative, then a too-fancy office setting might be counter-productive, even if the setting enhances the lawyer's own productivity. When a particular clientele is somewhat insecure personally, too spare a setting might appear to be "down at the heels" and not sufficiently reinforcing of the clients' need for proof of the lawyer's ability to perform, even before the matter is begun. In every locale there are specific expectations of what the offices should look like.

Working Capital

A specific capital requirement is for operating funds—that is, the cash for the costs of a period. This recognizes that even though there may be fee prepayments or retainers and deposits for expected disbursements in many, if not most, cases, the work and costs come first and the payment follows. The amount of working capital should also include the lawyer's draw or salary, unless the lawyer is prepared to do without income from the law practice if cash runs low. Working capital projections must also account for the normal ebb and flow of income. For instance, when the practice is heavily tied to the lawyer's personal presence, ebbs may be expected for the period following a vacation.

A frequent question relates to the amount that should be budgeted for working capital. Accountants with whom I have worked have advised that I set aside a fund of between one and two months of disbursements as an operating reserve or working capital. In my experience, the usual amount set aside was (and is) between half a month and one month of expected disbursements as a reserve, depending upon the stage of the economic cycle—I anticipate that clients will pay more slowly in a down period and there will be a greater need for capital to finance accounts receivable. Each practice develops its own parameters of operating cash needed.

In a solo practice, the capital need is directly linked to the lawyer's personal assets and needs, particularly for operating capital. The lawyer may prefer to invest less in the practice's account and defer an occasional draw, rather than investing the money in the practice and then draw as if earned, when it is only the return of previous after-tax income that had been put back into the practice. In the multilawyer firm, the expectation is that the lows in income flow will not affect all lawyers at the same time; such an expectation may be faulty. The basis upon which I have managed working capital for some years has included reliance upon underdraw as a source of working capital. This practice has become sufficiently broadscale to get the nickname "haircut," referring to cutting or shaving the available draw.

A specific technique of capital management is the need in certain situations to anticipate future capital requirements with savings. For instance, if the office lease is about to expire and relocation is planned, it may be prudent to start saving some of the expected costs of renovations and reequipping the new site in advance.

As Machiavelli might have stated, "Into every reign a little life must fall." The rainy-day reserve is for times when the ups and downs of income are mostly downs and downs. The rainy-day reserve is a fund saved and set aside in addition to operating capital. For the sole practitioner, a particularly stormy period is any period of illness and recuperation that lasts longer than that due to a bad cold. For the sole practitioner, this reserve can be in the form of personal savings and investment. It need not be in the practice accounts directly. However, it must be planned and funded. It should provide for added money for operating the office, as well as for income for the lawyer. When it is needed, it is needed; when it is not needed, it is a potential enhancement to the retirement fund.

Another economic effect that creates demand for capital and for capital planning is the state of the business cycle. The need for more capital to finance anticipated slower payments by clients was noted above. More significant is the effect of the state of the economy on a law practice itself, because of the economy's effect on clients. Current economic circumstances in some parts of the country have shifted substantial work from acquisitions, real estate, and other transaction-driven employment to litigation, particularly bankruptcy and contract disputes. This generates the need for a lawyer to reposition himself or herself with other clients who need legal services. There may be a lag in income during the time needed for repositioning. There may also be direct costs for the time and expense for staff and lawyer retraining and office library enhancement. Even when repositioning of a practice is successful, there is a delay between engagements for new matters and payment of the fees earned. There may be an even longer period for fees earned in the completion of litigation.

A final capital use is related to planned growth of the practice. By growth, I do not mean the development of the practice from solo to partnership or some other arrangement with other lawyers. The concept of planned growth applies equally to multilawyer organizations, but the perspective here is limited to planned growth within the context of a sole practitioner's practice. Growth in this sense is the provision of additional equipment, facilities, staff, and time for development of the practice into additional areas. For instance, if there were a commercial collection part of a practice, it may be useful to buy computer-driven case management and substantive law practice software, as well as the accompanying hardware. This requires funds for lawyer training, designated operator staff, backup staff, and space. It also requires certain cash capital and time for training to install and start operations. This takes money before it produces money. Once installed, however, the same capability not only enhances the practice of commercial collection cases, it also has the potential for applications in other areas of practice. Any practice will grow, in size and strength, with the appropriate use of capital to pay for worthwhile capability in advance of that capability paying for itself.

Capital Accounting

The two principal accounting instruments for the estimation and control of capital are the cash-flow analysis and the capital budget. The flow of cash through the practice is a major determinant of the need for capital. A detailed discussion of these techniques is more appropriate for an accounting text or in consultation with your accountant. The principles are simple, but the process for each analysis requires detail and sophistication.

A balance sheet and, to a slightly lesser degree, a profit-and-loss statement are snapshots of the enterprise. The balance sheet provides necessary information for management by counting the "beans" at a specific time. Cash-basis accounting omits certain nutritious assets that reflect unrealized or potential values—such as work in process, goodwill, and reputation—which add real value to professional practice. In cash-basis accounting, the profit-and-loss statement is a snapshot of a particular crop year for "beans," from seed through growth, harvest, and sale. It is neither an analytic nor a dynamic analysis. Accrual-basis accounting attempts to match the expenses for a period to the income for the period. When it succeeds, accrual accounting is analytic. However, it states revenues in terms of sales. This can overstate income and increase the income tax liability imposed to the degree that it includes "write-downs" and uncollectible fees as earned in a period, notwithstanding the reserve for these items as an expense. Because most professional practices, including law practices, appear to use cash-basis accounting, it is assumed as the accounting basis for the balance of this discussion, unless noted.

The analysis of cash flow is a dynamic, as well as an analytic, technique. It identifies amounts and the times that funds are required. When coupled with the analysis of the application of funds, it identifies the sources and uses of the funds. Projection of the cash flow assembles and compares the projection of the income and disbursements expected for the period.

The projection of these amounts can be based upon a variety of methods. The choice is based upon the confidence the lawyer has in the method for the particular item projected. One basis of projection is the "indicator" or "index." This applies to the projection of income if the practice is linked to a particular segment of the economy. A falling economy can be an "indicator" of the decline in real estate practice and the increase in bankruptcies. Projection of staff salaries and related expenses can be estimated based upon the "index" of the increase in wages and benefits in the general economy or in similar service industries. Another standard method is reliance upon historical experience. This may or may not be reliable for the prediction of income. Client relationships may be quite strong. However, relationship alone is not a reliable premise for the projection of clients' actual future needs. Experience is a useful basis for the projection of expenses and disbursements that have been contracted, such as rent and insurance, and those that are highly competitive, such as supplies and telephone and delivery services. A more usual basis is professional intuition or "guesstimation." Professional intuition can be used to its full advantage as long as there are regular revisions to correct errors.

Capital budgeting can account for, and discipline the planning for, the predicted amounts and the times when funds will be needed. The budget should also address the sources of financial capital, including investments, loans, and leases. The initial projection required is of the availability of cash. It includes a minimum amount for working cash (capital) and seeks to identify the seasonal, cyclical, and professional effects that would change this minimum. Examples of estimated cash receipts and disbursements are presented in simplified form in Tables 1 and 2. They omit the consideration of income taxes and depreciation and do not specifically identify interest costs as a disbursement or as an opportunity cost. The numbers used may not relate to a particular circumstance; they are intended only to illustrate the process.

In Table 3, the assumed availability and demand for cash are balanced. However, if the extraordinary expenses of April came before a surplus of retained earnings had been built up, there would have been a need for capital greater than the $10,000 starting balance. Similarly, if the starting working capital had been significantly less, this budget could not have worked. Most notable is that the lawyer intends to draw $9,000 per month, or $108,000 per year, in a practice that plans to gross a little over $250,000 per year. The ratio (43.2 percent) is not that favorable, and the degree to which this represents an underdraw may also indicate problems of operation other than potential cash-flow problems.

Suppose there were significant changes in certain items. For instance, suppose that the lawyer in Table 4 was involved in a protracted trial during much of March, that the trial adjourned in April because of the judge's prior trial commitments, that the case settled in April, and that settlement was not funded until June. The fee for the work was $20,000, paid from the settlement. The resulting cash flow is illustrated in Table 3.

The circumstances suggested are real enough. They produce a higher income for the period. They also require $11,000 more in capital and for a longer time. In the first cash analysis, the cash deficit might be financed by deferring draw and slowing the payment of certain routine expenses by one month. In the second, these means alone do not produce the needed funding.

TABLE 1 Estimated Cash Receipts

Anticipated new billable work (000 omitted)	Jan. 20	Feb. 18	Mar. 20	Apr. 22	May 20	June 22	Total 122
Retainers and consultations	5	4.5	5	5.5	5	5.5	30.5
5 percent of the current month's new billing	1	.9	1	1.1	1	1.1	6.1
40 percent of prior month's new billing	7.2	8	7.2	8	8.8	8	47.2
25 percent of second prior month's new billing	5	4.5	5	4.5	5	5.5	29.5
Receipts from slow-pay billing							
—over sixty days	1	1	1	1	1	1	6
—long-term regular payment	1	1	1	1	1	1	6
Cash collections	20.2	19.9	20.2	21.1	21.8	22.1	125.3

TABLE 2 Anticipated Cash Expenses and Disbursements

(000 omitted)	Jan.	Feb.	Mar.	Apr.	May	June	Total
Fixed costs and expenses	8	8	8	8	8	8	48
Expenses that are uneven							
Repayment of loans	1	1	1	1	1	1	6
Draw	9	9	9	9	9	9	54
Total disbursements	18	18	18	18	18	18	108

TABLE 3 Cash Flow Analysis I

	Jan.	Feb.	Mar.	Apr.	May	June	Total
Beginning balance	10	11.2	13.1	15.3	15.4	14.2	10
Cash collections	20.2	19.9	20.2	21.1	21.8	22.1	125.3
Available cash	30.2	31.1	33.3	36.4	37.2	36.3	135.3
Disbursements	19	18	18	24	20	20	119
Indicated balance	11.2	13.1	15.3	12.4	17.2	16.3	16.3
Minimum required cash disbursements (not including draw)	10	9	9	15	11	11	10
Excess or (deficit)	1.2	4.1	6.3	(2.6)	6.2	5.3	6.3
Borrowing/forbearance of draw				3			
Repayment/extra draw					(3)		
Ending balance	11.2	13.1	15.3	15.4	14.2	16.3	16.3

TABLE 4 Cash Flow Analysis II

	Jan.	Feb.	Mar.	Apr.	May	June	Total
Beginning balance	10	11.2	13.1	10.6	15.7	13.7	10
Collections	20.2	19.9	15.5	15.1	18	42.1	130.8
Available cash	30.2	31.1	28.6	25.7	33.7	55.8	140.8
Disbursements	19	18	18	24	20	20	119
Indicated balance	11.2	13.1	15.3	12.4	17.2	16.3	16.3
Minimum required cash disbursements (not including draw)	10	9	9	15	11	11	10
Excess or (deficit)	1.2	4.1	1.6	(13.3)	2.7	24.8	11.8
Borrowing/forbearance of draw				14			
Repayment/extra draw						(14)	
Ending balance	11.2	13.1	10.6	15.7	13.7	21.8	21.8

In budgeting ongoing capital for a law practice, calculations are customarily done for periods of years, because disbursements for costs used within the current year are expenses rather than capital investments. Capital budgeting also includes the effect of depreciation, the costs of money (interest and discounts), the effect of taxes, and the salvage values of any major equipment taken out of service and sold, traded, or donated to charity. The items to be budgeted for a going law firm or law practice also include the following:

◆ increases (or decreases) in working capital in anticipation of the practice's growth (or shrinkage)
◆ funds for future acquisition of major equipment or major redecoration
◆ funds for anticipated relocation
◆ increases or decreases in the rainy-day reserve
◆ repayment of loans and lease purchases

Budgeting includes the timing, source, and cost of the funds and the mode of repayment. Last are the effects of depreciation and taxes.

Budgeting capital for continuing operations is separate and apart from the capitalization of a new practice or a relocated practice. A new practice normally needs everything and may not yet have its first paying client. A relocated or reorganized practice has certain furniture, equipment, and facilities. More to the point, it already has an established client base on which to build. The practice should produce income during the first month, if not from the first day. The need to provide capital as a source of the first few months of salaries and rent is far less for a sole practitioner than a start-up operation.

Unlike cash-flow analysis, there is no example of capital budgeting; the mentality that focuses upon capital budgeting is the perspective of a capital-intensive enterprise. Although the capital involved in a law practice is not insignificant, law is labor intensive. The mind-set of lawyers centers on cash flow, not return on investment. Indeed, if the average lawyer were to consider the actual return on the capital invested in the practice, and if the cash value of that capital could be realized, then the lawyer might buy a good investment, close up shop, and go fishing.

Special Considerations on Ending a Solo Practice

To this point, the discussion has concerned the acquisition and use of capital, both financial and nonfinancial. We turn now to one of the singular problems of solo practice—the realization of these capital values in the event the practice ends. Practices end for a variety of reasons, including not only retirement, death, or disability, but also merger into partnership. Though the management of capital requires a dynamic analysis, realization of its value begins with active inventory (bean counting). Certain values are book or balance sheet items, and others are subject to appraisal (formal and informal) and guesstimation. Other values may not be subject to realization without the specific lawyer's active involvement, due to the personal identification of that lawyer with the asset or value.

One of the most elusive values is the value of a law practice as a going business. This includes the coherence of the operation, the capabilities and stability of the staff, the establishment of the office in a particular place, and the furniture and equipment in use rather than as used. Changing the business changes these values. Withdrawal of the sole practitioner is the most fundamental change. There is also an attrition factor in the collection of accounts receivable once the lawyer is no longer in active practice. When the lawyer will actively participate, as with semiretirement or partnership, this shrinkage is reduced.

The physical assets of the practice—such as its equipment, property, and leaseholds—are capable of appraisal, but their value is less as separate items than as an assembled operating unit. The same attrition applies to accounts receivable. Collecting an account when continuing an ongoing professional relationship is more reliable and productive than collecting a balance when closing a practice. The difficulty of the collection process when closing a practice is compounded by an interest in completion, which encourages accepting a lesser amount to be paid sooner rather than waiting a longer period for the full amount. Unbilled work in process is the most fragile. On the one hand, it represents current client needs, which a qualified successor practitioner might be welcomed to address. However, considerations of professional ethics place the selection of successor counsel in the clients' control. In these circumstances, and whether selected by clients actively or passively, the successor counsel becoming familiar with the details of pending matters represents a cost. To some degree, the value of the unbilled work in process is subject to the cost of educating the successor counsel.

One major capital value of a sole practitioner's law practice is goodwill. Goodwill exists in several forms:

- anticipated work for current clients, including work presently pending (open files)
- future work for current and past clients (closed files)
- future work for new clients (general reputation)

Although in some states it is now permissible to sell the professional goodwill of a lawyer, the sale is still barred in others. In states that prohibit transfer, the value of goodwill cannot be realized without a predeath arrangement for the transfer of the practice that is agreeable to the clients. The most common technique of ethical transfer of goodwill is by partnership (including a professional corporation).

Retirement and death planning are major issues for realization of capital values of a solo law practice. Full discussion of these issues is beyond the scope of this treatment of the subject. However, one aspect of death planning requires special mention—planning for the conduct of the practice during the short period immediately following death. To realize the values of the practice, there must be only minimal breaks in the continuity of office operation and service rendered by the staff. This calls for operating capital during a time when the assets of the practice and the practitioner may be in an estate administration, or otherwise not accessible for office operations and payroll. The need is answered by a minimally funded inter vivos trust, funded at death by a dedicated life insurance policy, for the purpose of managing the practice during a defined interim period. The trust might also act as agent for the estate administration (1) to be created, (2) to collect the practice's funds, prepaid expenses, and accounts, and (3) to secure the practice against unraveling until a suitable alternative arrangement can be found. This concept also protects the clients to the extent possible; though there is no ethical mandate to do so, there may be a sense of obligation when the relationships have spanned decades.

As you read this, the better alternative—prearrangement with a colleague—becomes convincing. A trustee simply cannot marshal the effort that a successor might. Because we do not schedule our deaths, nothing is arranged. The lawyer without an adequate estate plan (including a plan for the disposition of the values in the practice) is no different from the shoemaker's barefoot children. Making a prior arrangement is an idea more hallowed in the speaking than in the doing. Proper estate planning requires serious effort to achieve the road to preservation and realization of the capital of a sole practitioner. It is synonymous with effective practice planning and effective capital planning. The capital from years of work might be the sole practitioner's single largest asset at death. It is worth the serious effort required.

Which brings me to "counsel for counsel"—the need for a lawyer, particularly a solo, to have a detailed estate plan and written plan of operation for the law practice for the weeks following death. This serves to assure the staff and exonerate good-faith mistakes (which is preferred to doing nothing). As with the affairs of a client's business, the planning process calls for advice from the businessperson-client's lawyer, accountant, and banker—this is no less true when the business is (or was) a solo law practice.

Discussing a solo practice in financial terms—when it is such an intensely personal effort—risks commercializing and depersonalizing it. The risk must be taken. The failure to capitalize the effort and manage the capital effectively will limit the practice or, worse, destroy its very personal and professional potentials.

Bankers and Lawyers: The Odd Couple, or How to Get a Loan

16

Edward Poll

Law, as any other business, requires money to operate, and sometimes, money is in short supply. The reasons for that, and the kinds of money or cash that may be needed, can be many. Here are some examples:

- *Seed Money*: Seed money is the initial money needed to get you going in planning a new business. Consider it "earnest money"—the financial outlay that proves you're serious about this endeavor.
- *Start-up Capital*: Start-up capital is what pays for the initial equipment and initial expenses of getting the firm underway. This is the money that really gets the firm going, but barely. Buying on credit is also considered a form of start-up money.
- *Working Capital*: Working capital is money used to finance accounts receivable and operating expenses. These are the funds that keep you afloat until the cash flow from the business starts flowing in your direction.
- *Growth Capital*: Growth capital is money used for expanding sales, purchasing additional equipment, and adding new employees. Usually, growth is financed from the profits of the firm; sometimes, however, the profits are too narrow to finance growth, or the growth is too great to be handled by the existing level of profits.

The first question to consider is this: How much money do you need? The key word here is "need," not "want." Think only about what your firm needs to survive, not about how much you want to take out for personal needs.

Following are some factors that determine financial need:

- *Sales Volume*: The greater the billings, the greater the need for cash in the firm. Why? Because nationally, the average time between billing someone and receiving payment is approximately four-and-one-half months—this means that the greater the billings, the greater the amount of cash needed to hold you through this waiting period. Some firms actually limit their capital needs by limiting their billings. One way to do that is by raising prices; if a firm raises prices, the number of clients decreases.

- *Growth Rate*: Faster-growing firms require more money; in fact, they can be real "money eaters." When a firm increases its accounts receivable and workloads, it also increases its need for items such as personnel and office space. And whereas clients may take more than four months to pay a firm, the firm's staff, landlord, and outside vendors expect to be paid promptly. Growth must be managed carefully, or the entire "ship" may sink.

- *Gross Margin*: This is what's left after you subtract operating expenses from revenues. It reflects the degree of "profits" the firm generates that are distributed to the lawyers as salaries or draws. The lower the margin, the greater the need for additional outside funds. The larger the margin, the higher the profits and the smaller the requirement for additional outside funds.

- *Lead Times*: The longer it takes to get something accomplished (such as training an associate to handle more sophisticated matters), the more money is required.

- *Terms of Sale*: The more lenient the credit terms you extend clients, the more money you'll require to stay in business. The sooner you get paid, the sooner you can use your profits (revenue minus costs) to finance your own growth.

Firms may need additional capital for any number of other reasons. For example, a firm may need capital because it cannot collect its accounts receivable as quickly as anticipated. Or the firm may be growing more rapidly than anticipated, and additional cash is needed to pay new staff, to acquire equipment, or to lease additional office space. Or perhaps the firm needs to replace outdated equipment or facilities.

Whenever the cash needs of a firm exceed its own cash-generation ability, the firm must have a source from which to borrow the money. Of all the available loan sources, the least expensive is firm partners, who may be able to advance additional capital to the firm. But because solos or partners in a small firm do not normally have extra cash on hand, the firm will likely need to borrow the additional cash.

A firm should plan ahead for such a situation by establishing a good relationship with a bank. The following discussion includes tips, considerations, and important factors that can help in the acquisition of a bank loan.

Types of Loans

Some banks have established specific guidelines for loans to lawyers and law firms. Guidelines used by the typical banking institution are as follows:

- ◆ *Line of Credit, or Revolving Line of Credit*: The amount of the loan depends upon each bank's perception of the total loan package. Some banks limit a loan to three times the monthly expenses of the firm, excluding partner draws. In the case of a line of credit, the borrower may borrow and repay at will, up to the amount of the "line"; the bank usually prefers that the borrower be "clean" or out of debt for at least thirty to ninety days each year. The line of credit is then reviewed annually and extended, increased, or terminated, as circumstances warrant. In the case of a revolving line of credit, the borrower usually obtains a designated sum of money over a period of time; the revolving line of credit is then converted to a term loan and is repayable over a period of two, three, or five years.
- ◆ *Equipment Term Loan*: The term of the loan will normally be no more than the depreciable life of the equipment—usually three to five years. Some borrowers may be able to obtain loans for longer periods, but this is usually when the equipment being financed is expected to last longer than equipment typically acquired for use by a law firm.
- ◆ *Term Loan*: These loans can be for as long as seven to ten years for a large law firm, and three to five years for a smaller firm. Most involve leasehold improvements and furniture/equipment purchases. Frequently, the term loan is drawn down over a period of six to nine months; the payback period begins within three months of the final draw. The periodic payments may be structured as equal amounts until the loan is repaid in full, or they may provide for a balloon payment at the end of the term.

Selecting a Banker

Not every lawyer can properly represent every client. Similarly, not every bank is appropriate for every borrower. It is important for lawyer borrowers to know the prospective banker, the types of loans preferred, the type of customer base the bank seeks to build, the general pricing structure of the bank, and the flexibility of the bank in seeking new ways of helping the lawyer or firm with future plans.

Lawyers and law firms are generally attractive customers for banks desiring to grow. Banks believe, and rightly so, that good lawyers have the ability to stay employed and accumulate a substantial net worth. Lawyers, aside from being good customers themselves, tend to be opinion leaders in the business community and are viewed by banks as a rich source of referrals.

A lawyer should look for a bank that gives him or her the desired type of services and level of responsiveness. A bank can effectively handle not only the needs of the firm, but also the personal financial needs of individual lawyers.

Banks typically offer the following types of services for law firms:

- ◆ Credit arrangements to finance office relocation, leasehold improvements, capital expenditures, capital contributions, and other cash needs
- ◆ Online financial networks to facilitate cash management (for example, the opportunity to set minimum and maximum cash balances in the firm's general account, with "extra" funds being transferred daily to money markets and interest-bearing accounts, and cash advances being drawn from a line of credit in the event the general account falls below the minimum)
- ◆ Lawyers' investment accounts—also known as clients' trust accounts—that can simplify management of clients' funds, consolidate record keeping, and prepare year-end Internal Revenue Service reports
- ◆ Payroll administration, including tax reporting and record keeping
- ◆ Banking services for firm staff
- ◆ Short-term investment instruments, such as certificates of deposit, money market accounts, commercial paper, U.S. government agency repurchase agreements, and other portfolio options
- ◆ Pension plan administration

Banks offer the following types of services for individuals, both lawyers and staff members:

- ◆ Personal loans
- ◆ Home mortgages
- ◆ Interest-earning deposit accounts
- ◆ Discount brokerage
- ◆ Custody (trust) services
- ◆ Trust and estate services
- ◆ Personal financial planning

The foregoing list of services may not always be available at one bank. However, larger banks in metropolitan areas do offer all these services, and more. The selection of the firm's bank should center on the needs of the lawyer and the law firm.

Getting to Know the Banker

The borrowing process tends to go faster and smoother when your banker understands your business plan. You can expedite the loan process by meeting with your banker on a regular basis, and inviting him or her to your office to see that your business is well managed and that you have good controls in place.

Lawyers need to educate their bankers, and get to know them, as well. The banking relationship must be open and candid, and built on trust. Good bankers are creative people who find ways to assist good customers of the bank. Your banker can be most creative when he or she has a full understanding of your goals and circumstances. In time, your banker could prove to be a valuable source of information, advice, and possibly even new business.

Bankers require that borrowers understand their businesses. Following are four areas of concern that a banker may discuss with you. The better prepared you are to answer these kinds of questions, the more confident the banker will be in lending you money.

1. *Financials*: Can your business be characterized as a financial success? Why? How does your company compare financially with its competitors? Is your performance solid and consistent? Do you recognize financial shortcomings and understand their origins?
2. *Marketing*: Is your marketing approach effective? How do you measure this effectiveness? Do you understand the link between marketing and financial results? Do you manage your marketing resources efficiently?
3. *Management*: Is your firm well managed? Does it incorporate a good mix of management skills? Do the managers have quantitative and qualitative problem-solving capabilities? Describe any weaknesses.
4. *Product*: Does your product (providing legal services) provide any benefits beyond those of your competitors? Are perceived product benefits accounted for in your pricing? Do your staff members understand product differentiation? Does management know how to price the services, balancing market factors with costs?

Understanding the Bank's Loan Requirements— Do I Qualify for a Loan?

Beyond the points raised above, banks make loans based upon "The Four Cs": character, capacity, capital, and collateral. The average banker weights these factors in the decision-making process as follows: character—80 percent; collateral—15 percent; capacity and capital together—5 percent.

Character

The first question the bank asks is whether the ethics, business practices, and general reputation of the prospective customer/borrower is such that the bank is comfortable. Does the bank want to do business with this lawyer? Unless this threshold question is answered in the affirmative, there is no further discussion. The elements of character are honesty, integrity, and ability.

Capacity

The next question is whether the cash flow of the law firm justifies confidence that the loan-carrying costs (interest and related charges) and the principal amount of the loan will be repaid at the appointed time. A cash-flow statement (not just an income or revenue-and-expenses statement) must be submitted to the bank for its consideration.

Capital

The bank wants to know the purpose of the funds. Usually, borrowing money to meet payroll is a danger signal of more serious problems, except in a planned expansion of the law firm. In that case, the bank will want to see more information about the expansion.

If the loan proceeds will be used to help purchase an asset, the bank may want to know how much of the asset will be purchased by the law firm with its own assets. In other words, how much equity (or debt-to-equity ratio) will the law firm have in the asset? If the law firm has an adequate capital base in the investment, the bank is more comfortable in assisting the firm in the completion of the purchase.

Collateral

Loans to law firms may be either secured or unsecured. Unsecured loans are increasingly rare and are normally given only to the bank's best customers.

A bank may require collateral to provide it with security in case the law firm is unable to repay the loan. Depending upon the size of the loan and the financial condition of the law firm, the bank may ask for collateral in the form of real estate owned by the firm, equipment owned by the firm, or some other asset of substantial value owned by the firm.

The bank may ask for personal guarantees from the solo or firm partners, or it may ask the solo or partners to provide collateral in the firm of personal assets. Because partners in a law firm are jointly and severally liable for the firm's debts, if one partner has substantially greater personal assets than other partners, he or she may be at higher risk in the event the firm defaults on the loan, and may therefore be entitled to additional compensation in exchange for taking that risk.

Documents the Bank Wants to See

When entering a new banking relationship, you should prepare the following documents for presentation to the bank:

- Documents of governance (partnership agreement, LLC, LLP, or Articles of Incorporation)
- Fiscal year-end statements for the past two to five years, prepared by an accounting firm acceptable to the bank
- In-house quarterly statements for the period following the last year-end statement
- Aged accounts receivable schedule
- Cash-flow projection (sometimes considered an annual budget) for the next twenty-four months
- Personal financial statements of net worth of the principals
- Personal tax returns of the principals, for the past two to five years
- Law firm tax returns for the past two to five years

Additional documents—such as a business-interruption insurance policy, or disability and/or life insurance policies—may be required. These instruments may have to be assigned to the bank as additional collateral to secure the payment of a loan.

Additional Issues to Be Discussed with the Bank

In addition to presenting documents to the bank, be prepared to discuss the following issues, which help complete the picture concerning your law firm's viability and future growth prospects:

- *Financial Statements*: Are your statements prepared on an accrual or cash basis? Most statements are prepared on an accrual basis; be sure your banker understands the difference between the two. If the law firm's financial statements are prepared on a cash basis, be sure to submit schedules of liabilities (that is, accounts payable) and accounts receivable, neither of which will show on a cash-basis financial statement.
- *Capital Adequacy*: How much of the law firm's capital is permanent? What are the firm's pay-out and pay-in policies?

- *Hidden Assets*: Are there any hidden assets of the firm? Is there a lease that has increased significantly in value? Are there significant amounts of billable hours that have not yet been billed? Are there contingency cases that are ripe for settlement, or that promise to be winners in forthcoming trials?
- *Billing Practices*: What are your billing rates? How do these rates compare with those in the industry? How frequently are statements delivered to clients? What are the firm's aging, reserve, and write-off policies? How quickly are receivables collected (turnover rate)?
- *Litigation Risk*: Does the firm carry an errors-and-omissions insurance policy? What are the deductible and premium amounts?
- *Cost Controls*: What is the firm's gross profit margin? Are there any major cost-containment programs in effect? Are there any major cutbacks or expansions planned for the near future?
- *Partner Control*: Does any one partner or group of partners control a significant percentage of the firm's business? Does any one partner control the business decisions of the firm?
- *Client Base*: What type of client is attracted to the firm? Is the client relationship generally based upon transaction or relationship with the lawyer or law firm? Is the firm focused on one area of practice, or is it a diverse practice?
- *Management*: How is the firm governed?
- *Financial Strength*: What are the ratios of liquidity, leverage, and debt capacity? What are the profits per partner, and what is the revenue per lawyer?

Lawyers should think of banks as suppliers. Suppliers provide lawyers with the goods and services that allow the firm to deliver high-quality legal services. One of these suppliers, for most lawyers, should be the bank. Good banking relationships provide the necessary funds and services to allow a law firm to maintain itself and grow.

Insuring Your Investment and Managing Your Risk

17

Reid F. Trautz

Introduction

As lawyers, we take risks everyday. As lawyers who are also business owners, we take more and different risks. And as sole practitioners, the risks increase.

For example, we take risks when we accept a new client—often multiple risks. Each new client expects that we have the competence to resolve his or her legal matter, and further expects that we will expend the time needed to do so. When we accept a new client, or a new case for an existing client, we risk the consequences of failing to meet the client's expectations.

Each new client assumes that we do not have any conflicts of interest that will preclude us from fully representing his or her interests. We take a risk that we do not have a conflict of interest with an existing client. And we take a financial risk each time we take a new client or a new case—we risk not being compensated for our time and expenses. There are also ethical risks, including the risk of improperly handling client funds that come into our possession.

Some situations faced by sole practitioners have minimal risks, while other situations may have greater consequences. We often remain unaware of some risks until they unfold in front of us. Failure to recognize and deal with risks can lead to painful results, such as loss of clients, loss of money, loss of sleep, loss of reputation, or even loss of the right to practice law.

The key to risk management in a solo practice is to identify the common risks of practicing law and minimize their consequences. When we can manage the risks associated with the practice of law, we reduce the occurrence of financial and emotional losses, lower our levels of stress, increase efficiency and productivity in our practices, and improve the delivery of legal services to our clients.

Every lawyer—especially if practicing alone or in an office-sharing arrangement—needs to assess the risks associated with practicing law, and establish policies and procedures to manage those risks.

What Is Risk Management?

Risk management is the process of identifying and analyzing risk exposures, and then adopting specific and regularly enforced policies and procedures to minimize the possibility that identified activities will result in negative consequences.

What Are My Risks in Solo Practice?

Professional malpractice is the most common risk lawyers associate with private practice. Malpractice, or professional negligence, can result from either incompetence (such as not knowing applicable laws or procedures) or failure to have proper management practices in place. About half of all malpractice claims result from incompetence, while the other half are due to management problems.

Poor management can result in missing important deadlines or court dates. Missing a statute-of-limitations deadline results from inadequate calendaring procedures more often than from not knowing the statute-of-limitations date. The same applies to court hearings or trial dates. If you receive notice of a court hearing, but do not write it down, you will probably forget the date and miss the hearing. If you note the date in a couple different calendars and use an established reminder or tickler system, your chances of attending the hearing increase greatly.

The same applies to your files and record keeping. If you fail to keep organized client files, you might misplace important documents or evidence, which can cost your client the case, and cost you your relationship with the client.

There are financial risks involved in running a solo practice. The biggest risk is that you won't get paid for your work. That is why retainers are critical. When you take a client's case without getting the client to pay a full retainer, you are taking a financial risk that your client will not pay you for your services at a later date, after you have already done the work. That is a risk you should not take. Other financial risks involve signing leases that you may not be able to afford, or hiring employees that you may not be able to pay.

You also face a variety of ethical risks. To name just a few: the risk that conflicts of interest will cause you to lose clients; the risk that you can provide competent legal services in new areas of practice; or the risk that you can properly handle client funds through your trust account.

There are risks associated with being responsible for your client's property. If you fail to take proper care of important client documents or other property, you will be responsible if something should happen. A fire in your office or a nearby office could cause fire or water damage to client files and other important documents. Burglary and vandalism are rare, but may happen, and could result in the theft or destruction of important papers or other property. Computer problems—including hard-drive failures, computer viruses, or firewall intruders—could easily result in the loss of valuable client information, as well as the financial information you need to bill clients and run your practice.

Unfortunately, these are just a few of the common risks. Fortunately, though you cannot eliminate all risks, you can significantly reduce them with a little effort and self-discipline.

What Can I Do to Minimize My Risks?

The most common risk-management tool is insurance. And while insurance is absolutely necessary, it is the risk-management tool of last resort, meant to cover losses *after* the fact, not to avoid them in the first place.

The best way to minimize or avoid risks is to review your present practice, identify areas where you have risk, and then adopt ways to reduce or avoid the risks. Implementing risk-management procedures is less expensive and less time-consuming than dealing with problems after they happen.

Some of the most common and useful procedures for reducing risk include the following: (1) having a calendar/docketing system, preferably a redundant system involving both paper and computer-based calendars, (2) regularly checking for conflicts of interest before taking new cases or clients, and (3) having systems in place for client intake/selection, client communication, computer information storage and recovery, and document/file management.

How Do I Implement Risk-Management Procedures?

The best way to implement procedures is to incorporate them into the way you now practice. Do not try to reinvent the way you practice. Such a radical change is bound to fail. Instead, discard risky habits and procedures, and slowly replace them with new risk-management procedures. Start with an area of your practice you believe is your strongest—where you already have procedures in place to avoid risk, such as an appointment/calendar/docketing system—and ask yourself the following questions:

- What risks am I trying to avoid?
- What risks have I successfully avoided?
- What procedures do I have in place to avoid the risks?
- What specific steps are included in those procedures?
- What risks have I failed to avoid?

Now write the process or procedures you use to avoid the risk of missing an appointment, court appearance, or other important event in your practice. Do it step by step. For example, identify how each type of event is placed on the calendar, how it is entered, who has the primary responsibility for entering it, how it is checked for accuracy and mistakes, and how often each entry is rechecked for accuracy. Next, review the written procedures and identify weaknesses in the process. Add steps or actions to improve the accuracy and reliability of the process.

Once you have done this exercise for one area of risk, repeat it in another area of practice, perhaps one that has the highest risk or weakest systems and procedures. Repeat this process for every area of your practice, from trust accounting to backing up data on your computer network.

Next, establish a process whereby all systems and procedures are periodically reviewed to see how they are working. Get your staff members involved in the process. An effective risk-management system or procedure needs to be simple to use, easy to remember, and used and maintained regularly.

Although risk management may seem burdensome, it is important to keep in mind that if you expect to reap the rewards of solo practice, you must also be solely responsible for managing the risks and the financial and emotional consequences they may entail.

Common Risk-Management Systems and Procedures

Following is a discussion of some of the most common areas of risk management in a solo practice. Use the information and suggestions as a basis for developing procedures tailored to your own practice.

Client Intake/Selection

The riskiest period for a lawyer occurs between the first call from a potential client and the lawyer's acceptance or refusal of the representation. Before the end of the initial consultation, you must check for possible conflicts; determine if you have the time, competence, and resources to represent the client; convey to the potential client your interest in handling his or her legal business; and determine whether the client has the financial ability and desire to pay your fees. Make the following risk-management procedures part of a new-client intake checklist that you use for each new client file.

Check for Conflicts of Interest

When a potential client initiates contact with you, he or she must be screened to avoid putting you in conflict with an existing client. Relying solely upon your memory to screen conflicts can be dangerous. Even with a solo practice, it is not possible to remember all your clients over time. And, if you later join a firm, you need to have a written record of past clients. Create a centralized, written record of all your clients. A conflicts-checking system need not be complicated, but it must be effective.

Existing computer programs, such as case-management systems or time-and-billing systems, may contain the information you need to check for conflicts. It is possible to use a word-processing program to create a list of all past and present clients, and then search the list to identify any conflicts. It is important to search index cards or other noncomputerized lists, as well.

During the very first contact with each potential client, ask for the information that will help you determine whether you have a potential conflict. Be sure to ask the potential client if he or she has gone by any other names. A good practice is to search for conflicts before the initial client interview and before discussing anything of substance with your potential new client. Research any matches or similar names. The process need not take long, but, even if it does, do not skip this step. Also, even if you decide to decline the matter, be sure to add that potential client to your conflicts database.

Assess the Ethical and Malpractice Risks

During the next stage of the client-intake process, you need to assess the ethical and legal risks of representation so you can decide whether to accept the matter. Ask yourself the following questions, and remember—honest answers will provide the best results:

- ◆ Looking at my present workload, do I have adequate time to devote to this matter?
- ◆ Do I have the legal abilities and experience to handle this matter with the required level of competence?
- ◆ Do I have the financial resources to handle this matter?

If you answer no to any of these questions, consider whether you can find another lawyer with whom you can associate on the case, or, if not, whether you can refer the matter to someone who is better equipped to handle it. If you answer yes to all the questions, then continue through the client-intake process.

Assess the Financial Risks

You should also assess whether you can accept the financial risks associated with taking this matter, just as the potential client will assess whether he or she can (and will) pay your fee. Whether the potential client is an individual or a business entity, look for signs suggesting an intent—or lack of intent—to honor the impending commitment to pay your fees. Discuss your fees directly. Did the potential client balk at your retainer? Did he or she forget a checkbook for the initial consult fee? Does he or she have a recognizable source of income from which to pay your fees? Is the potential client unreasonably angry with the opposing side, or fighting solely for "principle?" Does he or she owe fees to a prior lawyer in the matter? Are you the second, third, or even fifth lawyer? Did the potential client bring legal papers stuffed in a duffel bag? Does he or she have references, if a potential business client? If you are concerned about the answers to any of these questions, you may want to decline the matter.

One method that helps with getting paid is to open a merchant credit account so you can accept credit cards. This is commonly accepted practice today, and many clients view payment by credit card as a convenience.

Client Communication

Good communication forms the foundation of a successful attorney-client relationship. Good communication starts with the first contact with your office, which should give potential clients feelings of confidence and security that they will be well treated in your office. Reinforce that impression by making them comfortable when they come in for initial interviews. Let them know that you intend to provide frequent information about case status, and encourage them to be open and honest with you about all matters pertaining to your relationship.

Once you meet with the client and mutually agree to enter an attorney-client relationship, prepare a fee agreement containing the explicit terms of your relationship. If you decide not to enter that relationship, confirm the fact in writing by sending a letter immediately.

Many lawyers fail to send letters to prospective clients when they decide to decline representation. There have been instances when prospective clients waited until after expiration of the statute of limitations on their claims, and then made successful malpractice claims against lawyers who they claimed had promised to represent them. Protect yourself by sending *every* potential client either an engagement letter or a nonengagement letter. The latter can be a short, standardized form letter, tailored to the specifics of each situation. Do not take the time to evaluate the merits of the case, or do anything that might discourage the person from taking action. Do advise the person to seek legal help before deciding how to proceed. Be sure to thank the person for consulting you.

An engagement letter and fee agreement should specifically state what you agree to do and when you plan to do it. The letter and agreement should specify when you will begin work for the client. It should include all the details of the attorney-client relationship, and serve as a source of reference should a question arise between you and the client. The fee agreement should specify the client's financial obligation, and give you the right to withdraw if the client fails to pay as agreed or provide you with agreed-upon security for payment.

After you accept new clients, let them know what is happening with their matters. Don't ignore your clients. Return their telephone calls and e-mail messages, in a timely manner. Answer your clients' letters. Having a good communications system is a key component of a successful risk-management program.

Docket/Calendar Control

The most important risk-management system you have in your office is your docket/calendar control system. In fact, many malpractice insurers will not insure you if you do not have this system. Every docket/calendar control system should include a tickler or reminder system.

A docket/calendar control system helps you keep track of all the important dates in the life of your practice. Those dates include court proceedings, appointments of all kinds, continuing legal education seminars, holidays, due dates for discovery matters, limitation dates, trial preparation reminders, and so on. How well the system works depends upon how you set it up and how well you use it.

Basically, the docket/calendar system is a set of two calendars controlled by two separate people, who track events important to the firm and its clients, communicate regularly to ensure both calendars are accurate, and resolve all discrepancies promptly. One calendar is usually portable, to go with you out of the office; the other is stationary in the office, not subject to the risk of being lost. Either or both can be paper-based or computer-based systems.

Traditional paper-based calendars are quickly being replaced by computer-based systems. Case-management software available for lawyers today includes calendar programs that make it easier than ever to record upcoming events. The information can be securely stored and retrieved from multiple computers or locations, depending upon your computer network or Internet capabilities. Of course, as with traditional paper-calendar systems, the problem of human error still exists.

The key to a successful system is to have two sets of eyes and two brains frequently comparing and updating the calendars. Humans make scheduling errors, and juries tend not to forgive failures to enter statute-of-limitations dates on calendars. In the best of all possible worlds, as a lawyer and business owner, you will control the entries on one calendar and a staff person will control the other. Compare the two calendars on a weekly or bi-weekly basis. Read aloud—line by line—through one calendar while the other person follows on the other calendar. (Review at least the upcoming two months on the calendar.) Make sure you did not accidentally double-book time, record an event on the wrong day or time, or forget to add an event to both calendars. Best of all, if your computer-based calendar crashes or you lose your portable calendar, you have an accurate backup calendar that avoids almost certain disaster.

If you do not have a staff person to control one of the calendars, make entries in both yourself; when you enter an event on your portable calendar, enter it again on your office calendar as soon as possible. Then ask a spouse or another trustworthy sole practitioner to help compare calendars every week or two.

Tickler/Reminder System

A tickler system should run in conjunction with a docket/calendar system. It is a separate system to remind you of events that are scheduled to take place in the near future. A common system is to have an accordion file with thirty-one file folders numbered one through thirty-one. When you receive a letter or document for a court hearing, deposition, settlement conference, or similar important event, make a copy of the first page of the document and file it according to the day of the month. (Don't worry about separating by month.) Each Friday, pull the copies from the file folders numbered for each day of the following week. Review them and prepare for events of the following week. Pull these tickler notices two weeks in advance, if it makes you feel more comfortable. A computer-based tickler system is also easy and practical. Try scanning notices into your computer and storing them by date; retrieve them one or two weeks in advance.

Computer/Information Storage and Recovery

The goal of computer/information management is to avoid the loss of information on your computer. The loss of certain types of information—such as pleadings, research files, forms, and financial and billing data—may cause harm to your clients or your practice.

The main risk is a hard-disk crash that wipes out your computer. "Backing up" your information on a daily or weekly basis reduces the risk of loss. When you perform backup, you basically copy everything in your computer onto a hard disk or diskette outside your computer. Some solos remember to do this daily, but many rely upon timed backup utility programs to help copy data.

Finally, you should test whether you can successfully restore your computer data from your backup system to your hard drive. Periodically practicing these steps will help you learn and remember how to return the data to the hard drive.

A Primer on Legal Malpractice Insurance

Why Do I Need Professional Liability (Malpractice) Insurance?

You need insurance to protect yourself financially from a malpractice claim, but, more importantly, to protect your clients. Like automobile or homeowners insurance, malpractice insurance covers you when the unexpected happens. In the event of a malpractice claim against you, you should not have to worry about losing your assets. Malpractice coverage allows you to continue with the assets of your practice and your personal assets.

Having malpractice insurance is also part of your professionalism. If you make a mistake, it is up to you—as a lawyer and a businessperson—to make the client whole. Therefore, when setting your coverage limits, you should consider the highest reasonable claim a client could file against you.

It is important to note that under the ethics rules in most jurisdictions, a lawyer must remain personally liable to clients for his or her professional conduct. That liability cannot be limited by a retainer agreement (except in very limited circumstances), nor by forming a corporate or partnership entity. Insurance remains the only remedy to cover the financial costs of a successful malpractice claim.

What Do I Need to Know about Buying Malpractice Insurance?

Malpractice policies and prices differ among insurance companies. You need to know the various terms of art in a typical policy, the factors that affect the coverage, the factors that determine the premium you pay, and information about the insurance company issuing your policy. Finally, you need to know that the lowest premium quote you receive may not be the best insurance value. Knowing these differences can save you money and some unexpected surprises in the future.

What Are the Terms of Art I Need to Know?

A typical professional liability insurance policy is a claims-made policy with prior-acts coverage and an optional extended reporting endorsement. Let's try to define these terms in plain language.

◆ *Claims-Made Policy*: A claims-made policy covers you against any malpractice claims made against you and reported to your insurer during the time the policy is in effect, regardless of when the alleged act of malpractice occurred. If, for example, the policy started September 1 and a former client informs you of a claim on October 2, you are covered because the claim was made after the effective date of the policy. Simple? Not quite. Unless the malpractice act occurred after September 1, the policy must specifically include "prior-acts coverage" for coverage of any acts prior to the effective date of the policy.

For example, if you started practice on September 1, 2003, and your policy effective date is also that date, then all acts are covered. If you were in practice prior to the effective date of the policy, the policy may or may not cover those acts, even if first reported during the term of the policy.

◆ *Prior-Acts Coverage*: Prior-acts coverage is usually included in a malpractice policy, but it is important to check this because it can be written out of a policy to reduce the cost of the premium. It covers you for acts of malpractice you allegedly committed before your insurance policy was effective, for claims made during the policy period. For example, assume your new insurance policy took effect on September 1. On September 2, a client alleges you committed malpractice on August 30. If you have prior-claims coverage, the claim should be covered on your current insurance policy. If you do not have prior-acts coverage, the claim will not be covered, even though you have a claims-made insurance policy in effect.

If you decide to include prior-acts coverage, the longer the time period covered by the policy, the more it will cost. If you are comparing policies, make sure they have the same coverage. If you cannot afford full prior-acts coverage, you can often negotiate an earlier coverage date (called a retroactive date) to be a year or more prior to the actual beginning date of the policy you are purchasing. The policy will cover you for acts of malpractice occurring after the retroactive date, provided you had no prior knowledge of a potential claim.

◆ *Extended Reporting Endorsement*: The extended reporting endorsement (generally known as tail coverage) is optional coverage that extends the time you have to report a claim for an act occurring during the effective dates of the policy. This extra provision in the policy covers you for claims made after the policy terminates, for acts that occurred when the policy was in effect. This is especially important when you leave another firm and want to be covered by acts that occurred in your former firm. Be sure to discuss and resolve this with your former firm and its insurance company. It is also useful when leaving or retiring from the practice of law.

How Much Coverage Should I Have?

You should have the higher of the following: coverage to protect what you cannot financially afford to loose, or coverage to pay for the highest reasonable claim a client could bring for damages. Also, if you are leaving a firm to open a practice, ask to review the firm's malpractice policy to see what coverage follows you for acts that occurred while you were with your former firm. With this knowledge, you can more accurately assess your future malpractice insurance needs.

What should your minimum coverage be? That varies, but the ABA Standing Committee on Lawyers' Professional Liability recommends a minimum of $1 million in annual coverage. Many solos suggest a minimum of $500,000 in annual coverage. Remember, too, that although it is rare, you may have more than one claim of malpractice in a given year. Some policies have a total coverage amount, but limit the number of claims per year. For example, a $1 million policy may cover one claim per year up to $1 million, or two claims per year up to $500,000 each. There are numerous combinations of total coverage and claims, so it can pay to shop around.

What Information Do I Need to Know about a Prospective Insurance Company?

Not only are the terms of the policy important, the insurance company that writes the policy is also important. Insurance is usually sold through a broker, who represents one or more insurance companies. Following are some factors you should consider when selecting your insurance company:

- *Broker/Agent*: Professional liability insurance is generally sold through a broker. Is the broker knowledgeable and helpful? Does he or she want your business?
- *Security/Stability of the Insurer*: Is the company financially secure and reputable? In short, will it be around to pay a possible claim? Check with the insurance commission in your state or jurisdiction. Also, check the ratings issued by AM Best and Standard & Poor's.
- *Bar Association Endorsement*: Is the insurer endorsed by your bar association? Many bar associations review and screen insurers, and then endorse one they believe provides the best policies and service for its members.
- *Premium History*: Does the company have stable annual premiums? A "bargain" policy may turn out to be more costly if the rates increase significantly after the first year or two.

- *Claims Service*: Does the insurer have reputable claims service for policyholders? Does it have staff available to answer policy and claim questions in a timely and professional manner?
- *Value (Cost of Liability Limits)*: Is the premium reasonable in light of the total coverage offered? It can pay to compare the policies of two or three companies.

What Policy Differences Should I Understand?

There are differences among policies, often buried deep inside their verbiage. Following are the major ones:

- *Coverage Period*: This is the duration of coverage under the policy.
- *Extended Reporting Endorsement*: This is discussed in detail above; check the cost, availability, and duration of tail coverage after the end of the coverage period.
- *Defense and Settlement Requirements and Costs*: This involves whether the cost of paying lawyers to defend a malpractice claim is covered within your total policy limits (often called eroding limits), or paid in addition to the limits stated on the policy. For example, if you have a $500,000 per claim policy with eroding limits, the cost of defending the claim ($80,000) is subtracted from the limits, leaving $420,000 to pay any settlement or judgment. Policies with eroding limits are the most common, but check this on any policy you select.
- *Exclusions*: Many insurance policies have provisions that exclude certain acts or events, such as fraudulent and dishonest acts, claims arising out of separate business (nonlegal) entities, investment advice, and sexual harassment claims, just to name a few. Be sure to look for exclusions and read them carefully.
- *Settlement Control*: Some policies allow the insured to decide whether to offer to settle a malpractice claim, and for what amount. Others call for peer review. Still others limit the insurer's liability to the amount of the settlement rejected by the insured if the case goes to trial.
- *Definitions*: The definitions of the terms in the policy are very important. They are boring to read, but have a huge impact on the policy. Please read them and have the broker explain them to you.

Other policy differences you may want to consider before choosing your policy include the insurer's right to cancel the policy, the cost of adding an associate to the policy, and coverage during periods of disability.

How Much Does Malpractice Insurance Cost?

The cost of malpractice insurance varies and depends upon a number of factors, but it is often less than you think. The variables that affect the total cost of your policy include the following:

- *Jurisdiction*: Where you practice can have an impact upon the amount of your insurance premium. Insurance companies keep statistics on malpractice claims in each state to help them establish the cost of malpractice coverage.
- *Area of Practice/Types of Cases*: Some areas of practice, such as plaintiffs' personal injury, have higher rates of malpractice claims than others. Some areas of practice, such as securities transactions, have greater financial exposures associated with each case. Also, lawyers who tend to accept high-profile cases with significant legal or financial implications almost always pay higher premiums.
- *Policy Limits*: This is the total financial coverage of the policy. Generally, policies also contain "per occurrence" and annual payout amounts that limit how much the insurance company will cover per claim and/or each year.
- *Deductible*: The minimum deductible amount is often $1,000, and can go much higher. Many solos have $1,000, $5,000, or $10,000 deductibles. The higher the deductible, the lower the premium. The choice is yours, but you should make it according to your ability to pay the deductible if a claim arises.
- *Culture of Redundancy*: This refers to whether the lawyer or firm has redundant systems and safeguards to reduce the risks of practicing law. A redundant calendar system, as discussed above, is just one example of what insurers want to see.
- *Defense Costs*: As explained above, when the cost of paying the defense lawyer is included in the policy limits, the policy cost is lower, but you may need higher overall limits.
- *Coverage*: This specifies the different acts or services that are covered by the policy, and the time frame during which the policy will cover those acts. This includes prior-acts coverage.
- *Exclusions*: The acts and/or services *not* covered by the policy are the exclusions.
- *Insurance History*: This refers to your previous coverage history, and history of any claims, including unsuccessful claims.

Where Can I Get Malpractice Insurance?

Malpractice insurance is available from a number of sources. You can contact insurance agents you find through the Internet or Yellow Pages directory, or you can contact any agent that insures your home or business. Ask the agents if their companies carry professional liability insurance for lawyers. Remember, though, that you might save some research, time, and money if you contact your state bar association first.

Most state bars do not require lawyers to carry malpractice insurance, but many of them endorse a particular carrier. Usually, the bar association has done some of the legwork for you, finding the best overall coverage and rates for its members. (Coverage costs will still vary from lawyer to lawyer, so you may want to compare policies and rates with other carriers.) The bar-endorsed insurance companies are often easy to work with and responsive to bar member service requests. After all, if the bar receives too many complaints from members who use the bar-endorsed insurance program, it may decide to cancel the endorsement, causing the insurance company to lose a good source of business.

What Should I Do If I Think a Claim Will Be Made against Me?

As lawyers, we try to solve other people's problems. This is often our first reaction when we hear from a client (or the client's new lawyer) about a potential malpractice claim. We believe we can resolve it objectively and successfully, and we are often afraid to disclose our problems and mistakes to others. Unfortunately, this initial reaction is a dangerous one. Most insurance companies (and some state bar risk managers) can be extremely helpful in resolving potential claims before they reach the status of actual claims. The companies have lawyers and legal personnel who have experience in resolving these matters. Let them. Contact them early, and have them handle the situation.

Who Pays for Defending the Malpractice Claim?

The cost of defending a malpractice claim is usually paid by your insurance company after you have paid your deductible; however, some companies offer "first dollar" coverage to help resolve any potential claim before you pay the deductible. Defense costs are often paid within your coverage limits, meaning defense costs will reduce the money available under your policy limits to pay a claim or claims.

What Else Can I Do to Manage My Risks?

In addition to everything discussed thus far, there are other steps you can take that will help you manage your risks in the practice of law:

1. *Adopt a positive attitude, and never lose it.* Your attitude toward your work has a huge impact upon the quality and quantity of work produced by your office. Generally, if you and your staff have positive attitudes about your clients and your practice, you will have fewer problems that can lead to malpractice claims. For example, a secretary with an uncaring attitude might carelessly put a letter to a client in the wrong envelope—possibly addressed to opposing counsel. Obviously,

significant malpractice and ethics problems could result. If your attitude toward the practice of law sours significantly, you should re-assess your practice. What is causing the problem? Your selection of clients? The area of law you practice? Office or personal problems? Honestly address these issues to avoid a dangerous spiral into almost certain malpractice.

2. *Understand your ethics obligations.* Ethics complaints are more common than malpractice complaints. They are not covered by malpractice insurance, and can be costly to defend. And such charges can damage your reputation.

3. *Have a copy of your jurisdiction's legal ethics rules within reach.* Consult it before you open your own practice, and stay familiar with it. The rules will help you understand many things: What can you print on your letterhead? Can you have a Web site? What fees can you charge your clients? How do you handle client funds? These rules are available from your state bar or law society, with many now published on the Internet.

4. *Think twice before suing your client for a fee.* Studies show that clients file counterclaims for malpractice in about half of all fee-collection suits by their lawyers. Often, the amount of the fee the client owes is more than offset by the costs of the insurance deductible and the time defending the suit—even if the lawyer is represented by counsel. The collection suit is an indication of a breakdown in lawyer-client communication. Rather than ever allowing matters to disintegrate to this point, you should discuss your clients' financial obligations early and often during the course of representation. If a client falls behind in payments, this must be discussed openly and professionally, and any problems should be resolved. If payment is still not forthcoming, you should consider terminating the representation before the situation deteriorates further. If you terminate the representation before the client owes you too much money, you won't need to sue for unpaid fees.

5. *Consider other insurance coverage.* You may need additional insurance, depending upon your circumstances and personal risk tolerance. First, check your office lease (or homeowner/renter insurance policy) to see what coverage you have for your premises, office equipment, client files, and other valuable contents. What are your responsibilities in the event of a fire in your building? What happens if your computer or coffeepot has an electrical short and causes a fire? Are you financially prepared for the result? Are you willing to risk that it won't happen to you? Investigate the costs of insuring against these risks.

Second, consider how you will generate income to pay your expenses if you are injured or otherwise disabled. A disability or income-replacement policy will provide income if you cannot practice law. Many solos view this as important coverage.

You may also want to investigate insurance coverage for acts committed by your staff, such as theft of client funds.

The Importance of Professional Staff

Not every sole practitioner needs or can afford to hire a professional support staff, but keep in mind that choosing the right personnel can help you maintain the systems used to reduce the risks of solo practice. If you decide to hire one or more staff persons, keep the following ideas in mind.

No matter how experienced a person appears on a résumé, do your best to investigate that person's qualifications. Remember, if you hire the person and he or she makes a mistake, it is your responsibility. Carefully select your staff. Look for individuals who are conscientious, reliable, and discreet. Check references thoroughly.

After hiring, spend the time necessary to train your employee. Even if your new employee has law office experience, take time to remind him or her of the special ethical responsibilities of a law practice. Review your confidentiality rules. Explain your risk-management procedures, especially your docket/calendar and conflicts systems. Even when you feel comfortable handing over responsibility for office procedures, still remain involved. Too often, lawyers completely transfer responsibility to staff for calendars, trust funds, incoming fee payments, and personal finances, and later regret the total delegation of power. Keep a handle on your business, as well as your clients' business. Remember, it is your license on the line.

Although it can be expensive to hire staff persons, it is more expensive to hire the wrong staff persons. Spend a little more time and money if that is what it takes to get qualified employees. Finally, remember that retaining staff is usually cheaper than training new employees. Keep staff compensation on pace with the marketplace. If money is tight, try to reward staff members in creative ways; seek their input to find the right ideas.

Parting Thoughts

Solo practice is rewarding, but it is not without risks. Creating and using risk-management procedures takes time, but, in a short while, you will be in the habit of better managing your risk and your practice. Reducing the risks will reduce your stress and increase your satisfaction in the practice of law.

Other Sources of Risk Management Information

- ◆ Law practice management program of your state bar association or law society
- ◆ Risk Prevention Library of the ABA Standing Committee on Lawyers' Professional Liability: **www.abanet.org/legalservices/lpl/prevention library**
- ◆ Risk-reduction information and training from your malpractice insurer
- ◆ *The Essential Formbook: Comprehensive Management Tools for Lawyers, Volume IV: Disastery Planning and Recovery/Risk Management and Professional Liability Insurance*, by Gary A. Munneke and Anthony E. Davis (ABA, 2004).

Fees and Billing

The Value of Timekeeping: Time Is Money— Don't Lose Either

18

Theodore P. Orenstein

The results of economic surveys of lawyers consistently reflect that those who always keep contemporaneous time records have 25 to 40 percent higher income than those who do not. There are a number of reasons why this is the case. One is that lawyers who keep time records can effortlessly draft highly detailed, descriptive bills. Another is that lawyers who keep time know the true value of their services and are more likely to send bills that reflect all the time and effort put into a matter. A third is that lawyers who keep time are able to determine which types of cases are less profitable than others, and so are able to spend more time performing more profitable work. They can also better ascertain whether they are on target for meeting yearly income goals.

Drafting Detailed and Descriptive Bills

It is important to send detailed narrative bills telling clients exactly what you have done on their behalf. Clients who understand what you have done are more likely to pay you for your work. It is nearly impossible to draft a detailed narrative bill unless contemporaneous time records have been kept. Without time records, you must go through the file and reconstruct all the work you did and how long each task took. With a timekeeping

175

system, the hard work is done for you and no reconstruction is necessary. Timekeeping can be done manually, using paper time slips, or with a time-and-billing software program.

Timekeeping can be a relatively painless exercise, whether done manually or with a computer. You may have put off keeping time before now because you thought it was time-consuming. It is not. It takes only fifteen to forty-five seconds to complete a time slip. When you address your attention to a file, glance at a clock and note the time on the slip. Then write the date, your initials, and the client's name and file number. That takes about ten seconds.

After you complete your work on the file, finish the time slip by entering a description of what you did and how long it took. It is important to write this description clearly and concisely, using the wording you would use on a final narrative bill to describe for your client the legal service you have just performed. You may use abbreviations so long as the person inputting the information into the timekeeping program understands what they mean and can convert them into complete language, or the program automatically converts the abbreviations into the correct words. Use as much of the time sheet as is necessary for this complete description.

After completing the description, glance again at your watch or clock and note the time on the time slip. Then, compute the time elapsed and place it in the chargeable time portion of the time slip in tenths of an hour. Some programs will do this for you. That entire process probably took you another ten to thirty seconds. That's it!

When it's time to send bills to your client, anyone can type chronological and descriptive bills from your manual time slips, or print the bill automatically from your time-and-billing software. You then have a fully descriptive bill. You need only check the amount of the fee to ensure it is reasonable and proofread the bill before sending it out.

Of course, there are some types of cases in which it is not necessary to send itemized bills, such as contingent-fee cases and some fixed-fee cases. However, in the majority of fixed-fee cases, you should still send itemized bills, because it is important to let the client know exactly what you did to earn your fee. When your clients feel that you worked hard for them and they got their money's worth, they recommend you to others and call you again when the need arises. This is important, irrespective of the fee arrangement.

Determining Time and Effort Spent

By keeping track of your time, you will be able to determine precisely how much time and effort you expended. You may decide not to bill for all your time, but, even so, you will know how much of your time you gave away for free. On the other hand, if you do not keep accurate time records and are forced to go through the file and your calendar to reconstruct your time, you will not know exactly how much time you put into the case. You will have only an estimate. It MAY be a low estimate, because it is natural that we tend to forget much of what we have done. You will, therefore, not have all the information you need to fully explain all your time and effort to the client.

Determining Profitable Work

Another benefit of detailed timekeeping is that once you know how much time you spent working on a matter, and how much you collected from the client for that work, you can calculate your actual hourly rate. If you know only the number of hours billed, and not the number of hours worked, you do not get an accurate measure of your true hourly rate. By knowing how much you "realize" per hour of work on various cases and for various clients, you learn that certain matters or certain clients are less profitable than others. That knowledge can help you decide how you want to spend your time. You may decide to forego or refuse less profitable work, leaving you free to do more profitable work. It is important to perform this exercise on contingent-fee work as well.

Keeping accurate and detailed time records can also help solos increase their income. Many solos feel their income is not high enough to satisfy their needs. They work hard and put in long hours, and cannot understand why their income is so low. Accurate time records can help them determine this.

Once lawyers begin keeping accurate and contemporaneous time records, they often find that their billable hours are less than they thought, or less than they should be. They try to increase their billable time, but find they cannot substantially increase their billable hours. To increase billable hours, it is necessary to analyze how all your time is spent, including both billable and nonbillable time. Nonbillable time includes time spent on office management, employee supervision, bar association or other professional activities, personal time, marketing and client entertainment, and other activities for which you cannot bill clients. Once you determine exactly how your nonbillable time is spent, you can better evaluate whether to limit some portion of it. For example, you may learn that you spend much more time than you thought on bar association work, or office management. Perhaps you can refuse some of this work or delegate it, thereby increasing your billable hours and your income.

Establishing an Income Goal and Meeting It

You should establish a yearly income goal, before taxes. To that figure you should add the estimated overhead expense you expect to pay during the year to run the law practice. That is easy to estimate just by looking at Schedule C of last year's federal tax return. The total of those two amounts is the total gross receipts you must receive during the year in order to meet your income goal.

Then determine how much you must bill during a year in order to actually reach your income goal for that year. Do that by dividing the total dollar amount you recently billed for a year's work (or other representative period) by the total dollar amount you actually collected for that same billing period. Then multiply the total yearly gross receipts figure by that number to learn how much you must bill in a year in order to actually receive your income goal.

Once you have been keeping contemporaneous time records for three months or more (the longer the better – a full year is best), you can calculate your average billable hours per day by dividing the total billable hours you have worked (not necessarily billed) during that period by the total number of actual work days in that same period. Exclude weekend, holiday, and vacation days you do not work in order to determine your actual work days. Multiply your average billable hours per day by the number of your actual work days in your year to determine your yearly total of billable hours.

Then divide the total dollar amount you must bill in a year by your yearly total of billable hours to determine the hourly billing rate you must set in order to meet your goal of total money actually collected for that year. Of course, you must compare that hourly billing rate with the factors set forth in your state's ethics rules and the rates charged by other lawyers in your community to determine if it is reasonable and realistic.

After performing all of these exercises, you may discover that the hourly billing rate you need in order to live at the income level you want is unrealistically high. With the techniques described in this chapter, you can exercise control over your income. You can increase your billable hours per day, increase your average billable rate by focusing your time on more highly paid types of work or clients, and increase the proportion of your billed fees that are actually paid.

Keep a running total of the billable hours you have worked at the end of each day, and at the end of each day compare that total to the average daily billable hours amount upon which you based your yearly income goal. This will tell you whether you are falling behind your yearly goal and need to put in more billable hours to catch up. Because you have probably more than enough work waiting to be done, working longer hours or increasing the proportion of your day's work that is billable would help you catch up to your daily billable hour goal.

If you do not keep accurate and contemporaneous time records, it will be difficult—or impossible—to know at any given time whether you are on target toward your income goal for the year. You will suspect that you are working hard, but you will not know until months later if you are translating that work into income. By then, it will be too late.

Billing—By the Hour or by the Project

19

Paul McLaughlin

Although most sole practitioners would like to "just practice law," law is a professional services business in which you must make a living if you want to continue serving your clients. The economic environment in which lawyers now find themselves is characterized by increasing competition, price pressure, expensive and bewildering technological change, specialization, increasing costs, and increasingly sophisticated clients with demands for greater levels of service. In this environment, no aspect of practice management is more important than the topic of this chapter: how to establish what you charge for your services.

The ideal is for both the lawyer and the client to feel that the amount charged is appropriate for the work done. However, lawyers and clients take different factors into consideration. The lawyer wants to charge a fee that is ethical and profitable, and that reflects the results obtained for the client (and there may be tension among these goals); the client wants to pay a fee that is commensurate with the value received.

These days, clients reserve the right to define value in their terms. Your fee should be a measure of the value of intangibles such as effort, concern, honesty, ethics, and the demonstration of competence, not just success or failure. Setting the amount of your hourly rate or a total fee for a case is as much art as science. It depends upon many factors that are particular to your practice. It takes experience to develop the sound judgment needed to excel at this skill.

The Contextual Factors Involved in Setting Fees

When setting your fees, you should consider the following factors in the context of your practice: professional ethics codes, the marketplace, business considerations, the specific file or type of file, and the client. After reading about these factors, you should analyze them for your practice, shake them around a bit, and then use the newfound knowledge to set your fees, using the billing alternatives discussed in the next section.

Professional Ethics Codes

Professional ethics codes set forth the criteria you must apply so your fees are fair and reasonable. Rule 1.5(a) of the Model Rules of Professional Conduct provides as follows:

> A lawyer shall not make an agreement for, charge, or collect an unreasonable fee or an unreasonable amount for expenses. The factors to be considered in determining the reasonableness of a fee include the following:
>
> (1) the time and labor required, the novelty and difficulty of the questions involved, and the skill requisite to perform the legal service properly;
>
> (2) the likelihood, if apparent to the client, that the acceptance of the particular employment will preclude other employment by the lawyer;
>
> (3) the fee customarily charged in the locality for similar legal services;
>
> (4) the amount involved and the results obtained;
>
> (5) the time limitations imposed by the client or by the circumstances;
>
> (6) the nature and length of the professional relationship with the client;
>
> (7) the experience, reputation, and ability of the lawyer or lawyers performing the services; and
>
> (8) whether the fee is fixed or contingent.

Although professional codes represent laudable intentions and put some general limits on the fee-setting process, they may be of little help when you have to come up with a specific amount to charge on a particular file. (See also Appendix B, page 608 for the complete Model Rule 1.5 and Comments).

The Marketplace

The marketplace is the second contextual factor. What do your competitors charge for similar services? What do your clients expect to pay? If you stray too far from what the market expects, either up or down, your business may be adversely affected.

Unfortunately, there is little reliable information available to help sole practitioners find answers to these difficult factual questions. Economic surveys of lawyers' fees are usually not precise enough to be of much use, and most solos don't have the resources to conduct their own surveys. They could ask other lawyers, but most solos find this a difficult conversation to initiate. Nevertheless, the best way to get the information you need is to call acquaintances in other firms or local alumni from your law school and ask if they are willing to exchange information about rates and fees on a confidential basis. Do they have a preferred rate? Do they offer a range of rates or fees?

Business Considerations

Business considerations also have to be taken into account. The nobility of your calling as a lawyer does not exempt you from the fundamental rule of business: if you aren't profitable, you go broke. Lawyers who make poor business decisions go bankrupt all the time. Indeed, solos are particularly vulnerable to the dire effects of bad business decisions, because they often don't have the deep resources of larger firms.

Fees are your main source of revenue, so you must set your fees high enough to cover your costs and produce enough profit to keep you motivated. You don't have to make a profit on every file, and there may well be good business or professional reasons for taking a loss on a particular file, but you need to collect enough fees in each fiscal period to be profitable. Knowing how much it costs to run your business, pay yourself a living wage, and pay your tax obligations for a year will help you determine the minimum rates you can set.

On the other hand, you can't charge so much that you scare clients away. Fee setting is as much a marketing process as a financial one. You have to perform a difficult balancing act, and the success of your business depends upon finding the right equilibrium.

You should have annual and monthly targets for revenue and expenses, which you monitor carefully to ensure that your business remains viable. You should adjust your billing policies to meet your targets.

Specific File or Type of File

The specific file or type of file is another factor to consider. At some point, you must decide how much to charge for *these* services, on *this* file or *this* group of files. Are they routine matters that can be handled by any number of lawyers, or do they require particular brilliance or specialized expertise? Can you set a flat fee for a type of file that gives you a reasonable, average profit? If you are using fee arrangements such as hourly billing, contingency fees, and percentage fees, is your calculated fee reasonably commensurate with the value of your services to the client? As much as possible, you should try to set the fees in advance, but on files where you can't set the final fee until you know the outcome, you need to ask whether you got a predictable result, did better than expected, or got clobbered.

The Client

The client is the final factor. It goes without saying that you shouldn't gouge your clients, but a proper fee is not a fixed amount, it's a range, and you may want to take the client's characteristics into consideration when picking your spot within the range. For example, you might decide to give a break to a regular client who feeds you a lot of work or a new client you want the opportunity to impress (although you should be careful not to create an expectation of low fees that you don't intend to meet in the future). On the other hand, a particularly difficult, demanding, or stress-inducing client might be charged at the higher end of the range because of the extra burden he or she puts on you, your staff, and your resources.

Some lawyers use high quotes as a means of discouraging clients they do not want to represent. Sometimes, the clients retain them anyway, but they are often difficult clients to manage because they know they are paying a premium. At the same time, the lawyer finds it hard to maintain the necessary level of self-motivation because he or she didn't want the client in the first place. You will be better off if you simply tell these clients you will not act for them.

Billing Alternatives

As a solo lawyer, you will use one or more of several different billing arrangements to bill your clients for your services. Billing for a file can be done on an hourly basis, a contingency basis, or a flat-fee basis. There are many considerations associated with making this choice. Chapter 21 includes a detailed analysis of various billing alternatives, which will help you make these decisions.

Nickels and Dimes

What do you include in your fees? Do you "unbundle" photocopying, fax charges, word processing, and other indirect charges and other recoveries of office expenses, and charge them separately from your fees? Or do you "bundle" them into your fees?

There are two schools of thought on this issue. The "unbundlers" say that fees are for legal work, while these other charges are a legitimate recovery of costs expended to do the work. They say that charging for them is fairer than including them in the fees, because some matters require more copies or faxes or word processing than others, and charging for them allocates the costs to the clients for whom they were incurred. They also point out that these charges represent a significant revenue stream, and that they would have to raise their rates—whether hourly, contingency, or flat fee—to cover the loss of revenue they would experience if they stopped charging for the costs separately.

The "bundlers" say that such "nickel-and-dime" charges should be viewed as normal costs of doing business in the twenty-first century, and that they irritate clients, are costly to track and bill, and make it more difficult to discuss fees at the beginning of a file because they are so unpredictable. They also say that clients are not particularly interested in whether these costs are allocated fairly among a law firm's clients by usage, as long as the total amount of the bill is fair and reasonable; the clients, they say, prefer certainty and simplicity. Some "bundlers" absorb the costs of doing business (such as postage, faxes, copying, and long-distance phone charges) within their hourly rates or contingency or flat fees. Others charge a one-time flat fee at the beginning of the matter for customary costs, thus avoiding the "nickel and diming" that clients dislike. It is easier to bundle when you use flat-fee billing. You can analyze your experience over a period of time to determine the average number of copies, faxes, and similar items on typical transactions and include them in the flat price.

The ability to pass on these internal costs to clients is easier than it used to be, due to computerized accounting systems and electronic interfaces with fax machines, photocopiers, and telephones. However, just because technology is available, it does not follow that it should always be used to do everything it can do. Technology should serve the practice of law, not vice versa.

In particular, you should be careful not to let your billing practices needlessly annoy your clients. You do no favor to yourself or your profession if you seem so intent on recovering every penny that you lose perspective on the total amount the client is being asked to pay. Does it really make sense to charge an extra $3.25 for photocopies on an account for $2,500 in fees? If you do so, it may look like you lack good business judgment.

Your resolution of this issue depends upon whether you are wearing your financial or your marketing hat when you make your decision. If you are thinking as a marketer, you will find unbundling shortsighted.

Discussing Fees with Clients

The fee discussion with the client is an integral part of the fee-setting process. Too many lawyers avoid this discussion. Don't be like the lawyers who dislike talking about money and are so keen to get on with the work that they don't take the time to find out if the client considers it to be important enough to justify what it will cost.

Your clients want to know what it will cost to solve their legal problems. However, they may be timid about introducing the topic, so it is up to you to take the initiative, preferably at the first interview. (If you are not sure what you want to charge at the first interview, and there are no imminent deadlines, there is nothing wrong with saying, "I want to give some thought to the fees I should charge you for this matter. If you will come back next Monday, I will go over the issue of fees in detail with you at that time. In the meantime, I won't do anything that will cost you any money.")

Using a retainer agreement is an excellent method for introducing this topic. A retainer agreement accomplishes several purposes. First, it describes the scope of the work you are undertaking on the client's behalf. A client who reads what you need to do will have a greater sense of the complexity of the file. Second, a retainer agreement describes how you will bill for the matter—on an hourly, a contingent, or a flat-fee basis—and when you will bill and how you expect to be paid. Third, it addresses what is required for you to start work on the matter, as well as the consequences of the client's delinquency in paying bills. This business approach is appreciated by clients, and gives them a better understanding of the billing process and your expectations of them as clients. Many jurisdictions now require lawyers to use a retainer agreement before representing any client. This is a good business practice, and should be followed even if your state doesn't require it at this time. See *The Essential Formbook, Vol. II* (ABA, 2005) for examples of retainer agreements.

Try to develop a "routine" for introducing the topic. For example, you could say, "I guess you're wondering how much this is going to cost you. Well, . . ." and then outline the basis for your charges. The discussion of the scope of the file, as well as your fees, should be frank, candid, and comprehensive. It should take as long as necessary to ensure that the client's concerns are addressed in full. Do not imply, "I'm sorry this is going to cost you so much, but. . . ." If your fees are reasonable, there is no need to apologize.

Remember that your clients are often under considerable stress when they are in your office. Your explanation of fees and disbursements may be a model of clarity, but it may go in one ear and out the other. This is another good reason for using a retainer agreement. The client takes the retainer agreement home, and has an opportunity to evaluate it and confirm an intention to go forward on the terms set forth in the agreement. It is a good practice to require the client to sign and date the retainer letter and return it along with the initial retainer (or fee advance). The retainer agreement is a legal contract between you and your client. Both parties should operate within the parameters set forth in the agreement. If the client hesitates to pay a retainer, this is often a sign that it will be difficult to collect your fees from this client. Clients who understand and accept the fee arrangements are much more willing to abide by them than those who do not.

The issues that should be covered in your fee discussion and confirmed in the retainer agreement include the following:

- *Scope of Services*: Specify the services you will render and, if it will help your client understand the limits of your relationship, detail the services you will not undertake. For example, if the client retains you for an uncontested domestic relations case, be certain to define "uncontested," explaining that the fee applies only if you do not have to negotiate custody, access, support, or property division.
- *Preconditions on Services*: If applicable, clearly state that you will not commence the representation until the client performs a future act, such as paying a retainer fee, providing money for filing fees, or providing crucial background information.
- *Basis upon Which Fees Will Be Charged*: Carefully explain legal terms with which clients may not be familiar, such as contingent fee, costs, retainer fee, or flat fee. For example, if a contingency fee is used, explain what the percentage fee means in terms of dollars.
- *Costs*: Be sure the client understands that he or she will be responsible for costs, regardless of the outcome.
- *Uncertainties*: If an hourly fee is used, you should try, to the best of your ability, to estimate the number of hours the matter will take, and periodically update the client.
- *Payment Terms*: State specifically when the client is expected to pay.

Managing Pro Bono Matters

The fact that a client does not have sufficient funds to retain you on your normal terms is not your fault. Although you have an obligation to do your share of pro bono work, you are not responsible for every client who needs legal services, and you are not morally or ethically bound to represent every client who comes to you, although you may be ethically bound to continue representing a client once you have started. Declining the matter may mean you have less work, but it also means faster response times to your other clients, a more effective staff, more time to devote to the management of your office, less stress, more money, and a happier family. Here is some good advice:

> Considerations of whether the client can afford the retainer should not focus on the client's spare cash or expendable savings. If the matter brought to you by the client is not important enough to the client to cause him or her to borrow the retainer or to liquidate assets, perhaps the client should think twice about undertaking the matter.

> . . . If a sacrifice must be made in order to pursue the matter, it should be the client's sacrifice, not yours.

Do not be fooled by the feeling that you do not want to lose the client's business. *That business has no value to you if you are not paid for it. Do not look for an opportunity to lose money.* (Theodore P. Orenstein, "Practical Billing Techniques," *Legal Economics*, July/Aug. 1985, emphasis added).

When a new client cannot afford to retain you, you may decide that the client's matter is of sufficient interest or importance that you are willing to accept it as a charity or learning experience. That may be a sound moral and business decision, provided the client receives competent legal services and you keep the amount of pro bono work under control.

So, how do you get better control of your pro bono work? Try using the pro bono list and the pro bono screen—simple management tools for controlling the inadvertent intake of nonpaying work.

The Pro Bono List

The pro bono list works like this:

- Decide how many pro bono files you wish to carry. (This is the "pro bono target," which is usually between five and ten files.)
- Write the numbers from one to your pro bono target on a sheet of paper.
- Beside the numbers, write the names of the pro bono files you currently have, if any. (If you have more files on your list than openings, you cannot take any new pro bono work until the number of files is reduced to your target number.)
- Put the list on your desk where it is readily accessible.
- From now on, you do not open any new pro bono files or allow any existing files to convert to pro bono status unless there is an opening on your list.

When you interview a prospective client who does not have enough money to pay for the legal work required, or discover that an existing client cannot afford the work needed to finish an ongoing matter, you can explain that, like most lawyers, you carry a certain number of files for free or at reduced fees, but you presently have no openings on your list and, therefore, are not in a position to help or continue to help. You must give your client reasonable notice of your decision to terminate a representation; you should address your client's ability to pay in a timely fashion, or you may not have any choice but to continue.

The Pro Bono Screen

The pro bono screen is used to select clients when there is an opening on the pro bono list. If you have an opening on your list, you shouldn't necessarily give it to the next person who comes through the door who can't afford to pay for the legal work needed. Once you agree to work on a pro bono matter, you must apply the same level of competence and timeliness that you apply to any other matter. You have to consider how to keep yourself committed if you don't have the motivation of getting paid. What other factors can you count on to sustain your enthusiasm? Here are some additional screening questions you can use to avoid accepting pro bono files that will turn into dog files:

- Do you like the client?
- Is the client reasonable?
- Will the fact that the client is not constrained by the obligation to pay for your services result in unreasonable demands?
- Does the client have anything invested in the file?
- What are the client's motives for pursuing the matter?
- Is the file interesting to you? Is it challenging enough to keep your interest, but not so challenging as to demoralize you? Is it a worthy cause? Does it pique your moral indignation? Does it stir your blood?
- Are you competent to do the work? Do you have the resources required to do a competent job, including lawyer time, staff time, and cash for disbursements? Can you get the work done efficiently, without it having an adverse impact on your other clients?
- Can the client make a partial contribution to fees, or at least cover the disbursements? Are there other sources of funding you or your client can tap?
- Is this a unique matter, or will it open the doors to other paying work?

Remember, few things are more depressing and wasteful than spending time and energy responding to a complaint or an insurance claim against you that arises from a pro bono matter, when you thought you were doing someone a favor. Keep yourself out of this situation by taking control of deciding who will be the objects of your charity.

Adjusting Expectations

Fee setting does not end when you get the client's signature on the retainer letter. Throughout any representation, your client continually weighs the value of your work against the prices you charge. It is incumbent upon you, both as a professional and a businessperson, to remain constantly sensitive to your clients' perceptions of the relationship between value and price.

Of course, legal matters follow many unpredictable pathways. Even when you do an excellent job setting a fee, events may overtake your estimate. The worst thing you can do in this situation is to ignore it. You and your client have agreed upon certain expectations; if the assumptions that underlie your agreement change, it is up to you to initiate further discussions with the client to change the fee agreement. You may well find that the client was pressed to the limit by your original arrangement, and is simply not interested in pursuing the matter if it is going to be more expensive than originally thought. It is important to give the client the opportunity to withdraw before you create a bill your client is not willing or able to pay.

The Effect of Delay on the Fee-Setting Process

For many lawyers, the end of the legal work on a matter signals the beginning of the really hard work—getting paid. Other more interesting, challenging, and urgent matters grab the lawyer's attention. Before long, two or three months pass and the bill still hasn't gone out. The lawyer is embarrassed and, because of the delay, feels hesitant to charge full value for the work done. By the time the discounted account goes out, the client has forgotten the wonderful result the lawyer achieved. Moreover, the client is annoyed at having been subjected to months of stewing about how much the final account will be. The client is liable to treat paying the account with the same degree of diligence as the lawyer did in sending the bill—so, six or ten months after the work was done, the lawyer is sweating bullets trying to extract the money from a now un-grateful client.

A policy that helps alleviate final billing problems is to set a time limit for final billings—say, a week after the legal work is done on a matter—and dele-gate the responsibility for doing the preparatory work and meeting the dead-line to staff members. For example, a secretary or bookkeeper can be trained to prepare a draft bill, saving you valuable dictation time and, more to the point, getting the account moved quickly toward completion. The person to whom you delegate this responsibility should also have the authority to de-mand your time to review and finalize the account within the preestablished time frame. It will be frustrating for the person operating the system if the lawyer's part of the work is not performed diligently. See Chapter 22 for a more detailed discussion on how to collect your fees.

Conclusion

We end where we began, with the reminder that your fees should reflect an agreement between you and your client about the value of your work. Ideally, your clients will be satisfied that they have paid a reasonable fee for the serv-ices you provided, and you will feel that you have been appropriately and pro-fessionally compensated for your work. Remember, too, that setting fees is as much art as science.

Keeping Your Pockets Full: The Fine Art of Cash Flow

20

Edward Poll

Brad M. Waters was angry. He just received a notice from the state bar. A doctor involved in a case that was settled had filed a complaint with the bar, claiming that Waters had not sent him his check. Yes, it was true, but he was planning to do it as soon as he could get around to it. He was busy.

Very busy. He was the sole lawyer in his seven-person private practice. Here he was, grossing over $700,000 annually from his small law firm, but he never seemed to have enough time. And he could never figure out where the money was, nor why his pile of accounts receivable never seemed to get smaller. "Why," he thought, "am I getting so bogged down? I just want to do what I do best—practice law." Although the name is fictitious, the scenario is not. The doctor's complaint against Waters is merely the symptom of a much larger problem.

By far, the most common complaints—in excess of 39 percent, according to one state bar disciplinary board—concern lawyers' performance (mostly "failure to perform, delay, abandonment, lack of communications, or failure to communicate"). And the main reason that small firms or sole practitioners get into trouble—with the state bar or with their own cash flow—is an inability to run the business of the practice efficiently. And if lawyers can't take care of themselves, they obviously aren't going to do a very good job taking care of their clients.

In consulting with lawyers, I find they have two problems. First, they are egocentric and therefore require the control of situations to remain in their hands. Second, they have grown up with cash and therefore believe they know how to handle it. That is, they believe they know how to manage cash as well as, if not better than, anyone else in their offices. Couple this with the fact that all lawyers are busy seeking to take care of their primary task, advocating their clients' interests, and it becomes clear that management of cash, if not the whole office, takes a secondary position. And that attitude leads to trouble.

Improving Cash Flow

How can you improve the flow of cash? Several suggestions follow.

Write a Business Plan

If you already have a business plan, review and update it. It is imperative that you know what your goals are. If you do, the road to achieving them often becomes self-evident.

To delineate your goals clearly, you must have a business plan. The creation of a business plan is an important step to your future growth. It sets the path for attainment of your objectives. This is similar to developing the route for travel from Los Angeles to Chicago by looking at alternative routes on a map. Few of us can just get in the car and travel to locations never before visited. We need to be guided by looking at a map. That is the business plan. It doesn't have to be ornate, published in a fancy binder, and so on. But it does have to be logical, consistent, and well designed. See *Attorney & Law Firm Guide to the Business of Law, Second Edition* (ABA, 2002) for additional guidance on developing a business plan.

Develop a Cash-Flow Statement

The cash-flow statement is sometimes called a cash-flow budget, a statement of cash, or a forecast. Whichever name makes you most comfortable, you need to concern yourself with this document at least weekly, if not daily. It is the single-most important tool for the success of any business activity. This financial statement should be the third segment of your business plan, the first segment being a statement of your goals and the second segment being your marketing plan. See *Attorney & Law Firm Guide to the Business of Law, Second Edition* (ABA, 2002) for more details.

Reduce Variable Expenses

Many expense items, such as rent and insurance premiums, cannot be controlled or reduced once they are established. However, some variable items can be reduced, such as library expenditures (you can share a library or use the county law library), dues and subscriptions, and, to a more limited extent (especially for sole practitioners), payroll. Savings in these three areas alone can be substantial. Further, if you know when to anticipate low and high cash-flow periods, you can postpone or advance equipment purchases.

Transfer Client Disbursements

Disbursements on behalf of clients, such as filing fees and expert-witness fees, should be paid by the client directly to the third party.

Increase the Size of Retainers

Most of the time, a client comes to a lawyer because of a specific recommendation by a friend or colleague. The client is concerned about the cost of the legal services, but not so price-sensitive that a modest increase in the size of the retainer will chase the client away. The larger the retainer, the larger the portion of the retainer that can be made nonrefundable (subject to applicable ethical restrictions). Thus, your immediate cash flow increases. (Note: The nonrefundable portion is a "true retainer" that can be deposited in your general account; this is the portion paid to keep you from talking to the adversary and being engaged by the adversary. The balance of the "retainer" relates to prebilling and must be placed in your client trust account; this affects cash flow only tangentially.)

Consider Flat-Fee Billing

In flat-fee billing, the entire amount of the fee can be deposited in the general account upon receipt. A variation of this method is progress or structured billing, which occurs upon the completion of designated tasks.

Change Your Billing Cycle

Bill one-fourth of the alphabet each week. That way, you will receive money from clients on a regular basis—probably weekly, rather than only once per month.

Send Statements Before the First of the Month

If you remain on a monthly billing cycle, be sure your clients receive your statements on or before the first day of the following month. To do this, your billing cycle must end on or about the twenty-fifth of the month. The theory is that most people pay their bills on or about the first of the month. If a statement reaches the client after this time, it is normally placed in the pile of bills to be paid in the following cycle. That means as much as a seventy-five-day delay in payment of your statement: the first thirty-day period is for your performance of the work, the second thirty-day period is for the missed payment cycle of the client, and the remaining fifteen-day period is for the length of time it takes the client to write the check and the post office to deliver the check to you. If the client delays payment even further, the time extends beyond seventy-five days. Thus, anything you can do to shorten the cycle will be that much better for you.

Send Statements After a Particularly Beneficial Event

Soon after you win a motion in court, or draft an important contract with which your client is pleased, or close the negotiation on a deal that favors your client, send a billing of services rendered to date. At this time, the client sits on the peak of the "client satisfaction curve," the time of least resistance for payment of fees (see graph on next page). Invariably, at any later time, the client will have forgotten how important you were in the process of the result, and may wonder why the bill is so high. Once the client is in that state of mind, the statement for services will sit, unpaid until some future date.

"Age" Your Accounts Receivable Once a Week

This is an important piece of information in the management of your practice: Do not ignore clients who do not pay in accordance with their agreements. Time passes quickly when you are busily engaged in practicing law, advocating your clients' interests. You tend to forget that one client owes you money while you are working on other clients' matters. Forgetting or ignoring late-paying clients results in forgetting or ignoring the accounts receivable. This, in turn, results in failing to collect the accounts receivable. It is important to correspond with clients frequently. Sending regular weekly reminders that money is owed to you allows you to pursue collection more successfully. For clients who recently submitted payments, the regular communication gives you the opportunity to thank those clients. These courtesies go a long way toward maintaining good client relations.

Stop Work for Delinquent Clients

Be sure your engagement agreement discusses the consequences to the client if the client fails to honor his or her agreement to make timely payments. (See the ABA publication, *Collecting Your Fee: Getting Paid from Intake to Invoice*, for further discussion.) If, based upon the aging information from your periodic accounts-receivable analysis, you are aware that a client is delinquent in the payment of fees, stop further work for that client. Go to the beach, spend more time with your family, expand your marketing efforts for new clients. But under no circumstances should you do any further work for that client. Before stopping work, however, be sure the client knows that you will do no further work until payment is made. If the matter involves litigation, make the appropriate motion to be relieved. Not only will you most likely get paid, you will also see a better attitude in your client toward your efforts on his or her be-

The Client's Curve of Gratitude

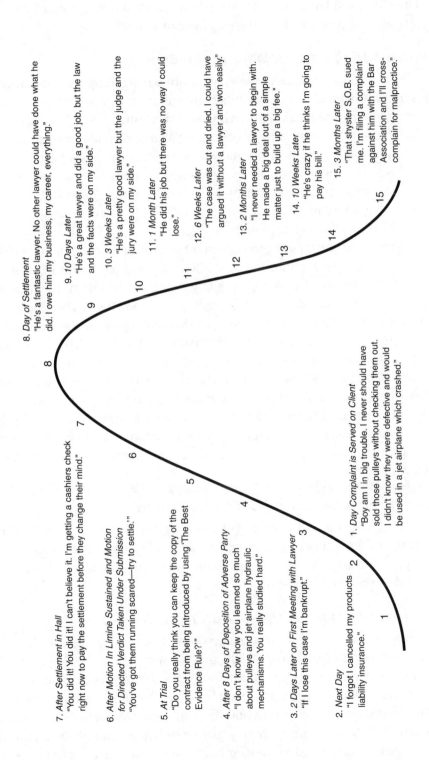

7. *After Settlement in Hall*
"You did it! You did it! I can't believe it. I'm getting a cashiers check right now to pay the settlement before they change their mind."

6. *After Motion In Limine Sustained and Motion for Directed Verdict Taken Under Submission*
"You've got them running scared—try to settle.'"

5. *At Trial*
"Do you really think you can keep the copy of the contract from being introduced by using 'The Best Evidence Rule?'"

4. *After 8 Days of Deposition of Adverse Party*
"I don't know how you learned so much about pulleys and jet airplane hydraulic mechanisms. You really studied hard."

3. *2 Days Later on First Meeting with Lawyer*
"If I lose this case I'm bankrupt."

2. *Next Day*
"I forgot I cancelled my products liability insurance."

1. *Day Complaint is Served on Client*
"Boy am I in big trouble. I never should have sold those pulleys without checking them out. I didn't know they were defective and would be used in a jet airplane which crashed."

8. *Day of Settlement*
"He's a fantastic lawyer. No other lawyer could have done what he did. I owe him my business, my career, everything."

9. *10 Days Later*
"He's a great lawyer and did a good job, but the law and the facts were on my side."

10. *3 Weeks Later*
"He's a pretty good lawyer but the judge and the jury were on my side."

11. *1 Month Later*
"He did his job but there was no way I could lose."

12. *6 Weeks Later*
"The case was cut and dried. I could have argued it without a lawyer and won easily."

13. *2 Months Later*
"I never needed a lawyer to begin with. He made a big deal out of a simple matter just to build up a big fee."

14. *10 Weeks Later*
"He's crazy if he thinks I'm going to pay his bill."

15. *3 Months Later*
"That shyster S.O.B. sued me. I'm filing a complaint against him with the Bar Association and I'll cross-complain for malpractice."

© 1975, 1976, 1984, 1991, 1999, 2004 by Jay G Foonberg

half. The client will know that you are serious, and that you protect your own interests as stringently as the interests of your client.

Maintain a High Daily Balance in the Bank

Most banks today calculate the average daily balance in your bank account. This is one of the most significant bits of information with which a bank works in analyzing a loan request. Thus, you should maintain as high a balance as possible. This can be done either by keeping a large sum of money in the bank or by keeping limited funds in the account for a longer period of time. You can keep funds in the account longer by depositing revenue immediately upon receipt and spreading the payment of bills throughout the month. Do not pay your bills all at one time; this causes an exaggerated dip in your account balance rather than allowing an even flow of funds.

The first rule of cash-flow management is this: Do not accumulate checks for deposit at the end of the week. While the check is sitting in your desk drawer, too many catastrophic events might occur. The client might become angry, for whatever reason, and stop payment on the check. The check might reach your client's bank at a time when the account is overdrawn, causing the check to be returned to you marked "insufficient funds." The client might have been named as a defendant in a lawsuit for which attachment procedures are available, and the client's bank account might have been attached and "marked" for a sum that is large enough to cause the presentation of the check you are holding to be rejected. In each of these cases, and many others that you can conjure, had the check been deposited immediately upon receipt, it probably would have cleared the client's bank account and been credited to your account.

Maintain Personal Control of Check Writing

Be sure that you sign all checks. Do not delegate this authority. You must know the present status of your business at all times. You must know who is getting paid and why. Anything less opens you to the risk of fraud, embezzlement, and possible disbarment.

Establish an Account with an "Automatic Sweep"

Banks can provide an "automatic sweep" on a daily basis. Establish a minimum amount of money, such as $2,500, to remain in your general account. The exact sum depends upon the total amount of checks you write and deposit each month. You can instruct the bank to segregate all funds in excess of this amount at the end of each day and "sweep"—or transfer—those "excess" funds into an interest-bearing money-market account until needed. Likewise, the bank can be instructed to transfer funds automatically back to the general account from the money-market account should the balance go below the established minimum amount. The better approach, however, is to ask the bank to call you on any day during which the balance of your account goes below the minimum amount established by you. This latter approach, as contrasted with the automatic sweep into the money-market account, forces the one responsible for these activities to know, rather than guess, the status of the cash balance at any given moment.

Conclusion

Some lawyers believe that they are not in a business—that they specifically chose the practice of law instead. However, the practice of law *is* a business. Unless you recognize that as a fact, you may do things that violate ethical and professional rules and destroy your ability to earn a reasonable fee for your efforts. Remember, you may delegate authority, but you cannot delegate responsibility. You are responsible for the effective and efficient operation of your office. Cash-flow efficiency procedures will help you do this, and, at the same time, improve the delivery of your legal services.

Alternative Billing Methods 21

James A. Calloway
Mark A. Robertson

The majority of lawyers in the United States practice in a solo or small-firm setting. These lawyers often face different challenges concerning pricing for their services. Yet, in many ways, a smaller-size practice—with its lack of bureaucracy and certain institutional traditions—allows lawyers to move more nimbly in adopting changes. For many of these practices, the analysis of pricing requires considerations not present in the larger law firm, while some of the factors important in the larger firm are either minimized or nonexistent.

Solo and small-firm lawyers are not homogeneous. Many small firms operate in the same manner as larger law firms and serve similar clients. This is particularly true for small firms that originally existed as practice groups of larger firms. When lawyers who spent their early years practicing in large-firm settings move to smaller-firm settings, they tend to continue practicing in the same way they always did.

But for many solo and small-firm lawyers, there is a significant difference between their practices and those of their large-firm brethren. This difference relates to who or what might be a typical client. Generally speaking, larger law firms spend most of their efforts representing businesses, and the bigger the business clients are, the better. This is not to say that law firms of all sizes do not represent individuals. But generally, corporate clients constitute the bedrock of a larger firm's clientele.

Many sole practitioners and small-firm lawyers spend a larger portion, if not all, of their time representing individual consumers of legal services and the local "mom-and-pop" businesses. Some of these lawyers consider themselves to be general practitioners, while others have highly specialized or limited practices focusing on areas such as consumer bankruptcy, criminal defense, or family law.

There are significant differences between these typical small-firm clients and major corporate clients. The smaller-business owner often has more in common with a consumer when making any type of purchasing decision than a large corporate client engaging in business-to-business negotiations with a large law firm. Small-town lawyers, suburban lawyers, and those in other practice settings who represent mainly consumers have some history of the use of flat fees, contingent fees, and various methods other than the billable hour. For easy reference and lack of a better term, we shall refer to these lawyers collectively as Main Street lawyers.

Hourly billing is an objective method of determining the cost of delivery of legal services and for many years has served as the benchmark for determining the price and value of the legal services. But for the clients, or potential clients, of the Main Street lawyer, the billable hour may seem more like a blank check payable to the lawyer than a reliable method of determining a fee.

The value of legal services is sometimes an elusive concept. We are all aware of situations when a single, informed telephone call might be worth hundreds or thousands of dollars. Determining value to the clients and establishing realistic alternative billing policies is no easy task for the Main Street lawyer.

The Value Curve

Consultant William C. Cobb is the managing partner of WCCI Inc. (William Cobb Consultants), based in Houston, Texas. He created the Cobb Value Curve as a way of graphically representing the value of legal services. You can review his online article, *The Ten Toxic Assumptions of the Legal Profession*, which includes an explanation of the Cobb Value Curve, at **www.cobb-consulting.com/doctoxic.htm**.

Generally, Cobb's ideas are based upon the notion that the pricing of legal work is directly related to the value that the purchaser perceives it to be. At one end of the spectrum are the "nuclear events," where cost is no object. For a consumer, this might be a criminal charge or a disabling injury. In one instance a flat fee might be more appropriate than an hourly rate, and in another instance, a contingent fee might be the best choice. In both instances, the consumer wants and needs the best he or she can afford. On the other end of the spectrum are those matters that legal consumers, both individuals and small businesses, believe anyone can do. In fact, they may believe that a lawyer is not really necessary. If a consumer believes that what he or she wants done is in this category—let's call it "Boilerplate Work"—the consumer will either go to the Web and purchase a form, or engage the least expensive person in town to do the work.

Projects that may fit in this category are house closings, wills, and the proverbial "simple contract that just needs to be looked over." If the consumer makes a decision based upon price only, then more experienced lawyers may lose an opportunity if they quote only their hourly rates. Experienced lawyers work more efficiently and use less time to produce the work product, be it a document or research. It takes newer lawyers longer, so they charge lower rates. An uneducated consumer will assume it costs more to have a will done by a lawyer who charges $175 an hour than by a new lawyer who charges only $90 an hour. The uneducated consumer believes it will take both lawyers the same amount of time to do the work, because the document is already on the computer; so, if the choice is based strictly on price, the more experienced lawyer will lose.

For this reason, it makes sense to set a flat fee for certain work that we acknowledge the legal consumer believes is "Boilerplate Work." If the experienced lawyer can do it faster than the inexperienced lawyer, then it is likely that each can charge the same flat fee for the project. By taking this approach, you won't lose the person who calls and asks either, "What is your hourly rate?" or, "How much does it cost to get X done?"

Even though you may have developed much expertise over time, you may not get paid for it by the legal consumer who makes a decision based only upon price. This is where educating the consumer is important. You can tell a prospective client that you charge $X to do plain-vanilla, simple wills, but you can further explain that your experience has taught you certain issues that must be addressed when creating wills. If you can show the potential client that his or her will isn't plain vanilla, then that person may be willing to pay for your expertise. You could share the disastrous results that can occur when someone who thinks he needs only a simple will goes to an inexperienced lawyer who doesn't ask for enough details and information. Your objective is to educate, not scare, the potential client, who will hopefully understand why a lawyer with the right experience is the right choice. You could even accept the work at a flat rate, with a written agreement outlining the facts that make the will simple, and explaining that if other or different facts emerge, the will is no longer plain vanilla. Using an engagement letter in this way gives the client what the client wants, while protecting you and the client if the matter becomes more complicated.

Another type of legal consumer makes decisions based upon the perceived status of the lawyer. Certain lawyers are recognized as preeminent within the legal community, and perhaps within the broader community as well. For example, in a community with only one or two banks, many people know which lawyer represents the bank and attends its board meetings. Similarly, although there may be many competent family practice lawyers in a community, there seem to be a few who usually represent the community's most wealthy or influential citizens when they experience divorces or other legal problems. Other examples abound, from the second generation of lawyers representing the second or third generation of local business owners, to the affluent citizen who wants the best of everything, including the "best" lawyer in town. If you want to attract this type of legal consumer, who primarily values perceptions of reputation or expertise, it is important that you gain name recognition in your community.

With the exception of certain well-known areas, such as bankruptcy and personal injury practice, Main Street lawyers have traditionally avoided advertising and other marketing efforts targeted at the public. (Advertising is problematic in some ways; the ABA Law Practice Management Section has published several books on marketing that you might find helpful in this regard.) Developing a reputation and becoming known as the best and most educated in a certain area of the law, even a narrow one, is a positive approach with positive results. For example, though perhaps a lawyer cannot become renowned in all aspects of criminal law, the lawyer could become an expert in administrative drivers' license suspensions or vehicle forfeitures. It might surprise you how readily other lawyers and clients seek services and advice in a narrow area. Although such a narrow subspecialty might not be a source of extensive income, it does place the lawyer in a market niche where the price sensitivity of the consumers is not so strong. This provides the opening for a greater premium, at least on these matters.

Another type of legal consumer is one faced with a legal issue that can have life-altering implications. It could be a messy divorce, a custody battle, a driving-while-intoxicated charge, or a major contract for a small business. In these situations, the consumer wants the "best," but may have limited resources. How do you handle this category of consumer? Let's look at a lawyer group that often represents clients with problems of this magnitude and, generally speaking, comprises those most free from dependence upon hourly billing—the criminal defense bar. For most individuals, a serious criminal charge is a life-changing event. Certainly the prospect of destruction of reputation, imprisonment, or the ultimate penalty—death—is exceedingly serious. The prospect of a criminal trial is so filled with tension, conflict, and drama that countless movies, television shows, and novels have been placed in this setting. These cases involve large stakes, and not just any lawyer will do. Members of the public generally understand that not all lawyers go to court and not all litigators handle criminal matters. So how have members of the criminal defense bar charged for their services?

Generally speaking, attorneys' fees for criminal defense lawyers are not based upon hourly rates. Instead, these fees are usually determined according to one of the so-called alternative billing methods—either a flat fee for the entire defense, or a separate fee for reaching clear landmarks (for example, one fee for a grand jury proceeding, another for a preliminary hearing, and another for the jury trial). In most instances, these fees are payable in advance. White-collar criminal defense cases are sometimes contracted on an hourly basis, but not often. Several factors have led to the use of a flat fee (or similar alternative billing method) in these cases, with assurance of payment being one. If a defense is unsuccessful, it may be difficult to obtain payment. Mailing billing statements to a prison cell is likely to be unsuccessful. There is an obligation among defense counsel to explore all avenues of defense, and therefore this should not be a situation in which the client and lawyer can make joint business decisions about the scope of the representation. Typically, for a truly life-changing problem, a client will find a way to pay you what you ask, if the client is confident you are the perfect lawyer to handle the problem.

Handling Clients and Billing

In consumer-oriented practices, lawyers deal with a greater percentage of relatively unsophisticated clients. This does not imply that these clients are in any way graceless or ignorant. But they are often inexperienced in dealing with lawyers. Whether a matter concerns adoption or arrest, a will or a workers' compensation claim, the simple fact is that a consumer client may have had no prior experience with the legal subject matter and no prior need for a lawyer.

There can be no give-and-take discussion about various alternative billing methods when the client has little or no understanding of the process. There is little common ground for negotiation, and the fee is often presented to the client as a take-it-or-leave-it proposition. For consumer legal services, fees are often based upon market forces and lawyer experience, rather than negotiation with prospective clients. In fact, many Main Street lawyers have a long tradition of refusing to negotiate their fees. This is understandable, particularly with hourly rates: a lawyer charges a set fee per hour, and it seems unfair to charge a lower rate to one client just because that client pleads for one. Also, many offices have been organized to compute at one rate, and instituting various billing rates would increase administrative complexity in preparing bills.

Of course, most of us understand that Main Street lawyers might sometimes charge a discount rate, but generally that rate is reserved for business clients who have a regular volume of matters to be handled and who always pay their bills. Sometimes clients receive a "professional discount" if they are likely to refer clients to the lawyer in the future. In general, if there has been a discounted rate, it has been for "wholesale" or preferred customers, while the client coming in off the street with an initial need for a lawyer on a single matter would be considered a "retail" customer.

There are ample ethical rules and community standards that proscribe a fairly narrow range for an acceptable fee or rate. Unsophisticated clients are those who might most appreciate the simplicity and clarity of many fixed-fee arrangements.

Suppose a potential client makes an appointment with the lawyer about a relatively straightforward probate proceeding. The Main Street lawyer discusses handling the matter and discloses his or her billing rate. For many consumer clients, a statement of the lawyer's hourly rate—the cost per hour—is not sufficient information. Almost immediately, the next question is, "How many hours will it take?" or, "What will the total cost be?" This is when lawyers often give a most unsatisfactory answer: "It depends."

It is not surprising that this can be a source of frustration for the potential client. After all, most consumer purchasing experiences do not proceed like this. Throughout retail stores, price tags and signs abound. There, the price is stated in advance. Imagine buying a refrigerator after being told that the final price will be set only after you agree to make the purchase! Even a car dealer will make a firm offer. In fact, the Main Street lawyer has a fairly accurate mental understanding of what an average fee for this matter will total. But the estimate communicated to the client is often couched in broad terms, with many disclaimers. The lawyer cannot give an exact quote when the number of total hours to be expended is unknown to the lawyer, as well as the client.

Although some may view this reluctance as an attempt to conceal something from the consumer, in reality, the lawyer is exercising time-tested judgment. The experienced lawyer knows that if an average fee is mentioned, the client will focus on that number as "the fee." If the lawyer quotes an estimate of $2,000, the lawyer will view a final total billing of $2,165 to be right on target. But too many clients would respond with, "No, wait, you said $2,000." So the lawyer learns to express the estimate as a range, with plenty of room at the top end of the range to ensure that the total fee will almost certainly be less than the highest number mentioned. In this example, the lawyer, if pressed, would quote a range from a low of $2,000 to a high of $4,000 or $5,000.

Imagine how much more consumer-friendly and nonthreatening this transaction would be if the lawyer simply said, "This probate case can all be yours for the low price of $2,450." We are all consumers. We understand the attraction of simplicity. We understand the value of limiting the risk of a charge being much higher than anticipated. It is disingenuous to deny that we would prefer the certainty of the fixed fee if we were the client.

"Wait," many lawyers would cry, "there are many variables, and many contingencies." The extent of legal services required is often outside the lawyer's control. The lawyer understands that an unreasonable opposing counsel, a procrastinating opposing party, or a recalcitrant judge can increase the workload by several orders of magnitude. The lawyer does not want to bear that risk, and the hourly rate serves that purpose very well. Whether it is a necessary party who cannot be located for service of process or an unanticipated and complicated factual situation, if the matter becomes more burdensome, the lawyer invests more time, and the lawyer should be paid more. But the lawyer *does* know the variables—far better than the client. In many ways, lawyers do not want to get pinned down. Lawyers know they will treat a client fairly, but they also want to make sure they are not treated unfairly by working many extra hours without additional compensation.

In fact, though, in a matter involving contingencies that might dramatically change the work involved, the fee arrangement need not be based upon only one flat fee. The fee agreement may cover numerous contingencies: if event A happens, one fee will be charged; if B happens, then another fee. The most important thing is for the unsophisticated client to understand and comprehend fees quoted in this manner, without referring to an hourly billing rate. The client no longer must ask, "How many hours will it take?"

Where the sophisticated and experienced business client may need a jointly developed plan based upon the experiences of both the client and the lawyer, the consumer client needs information, explanation, and less uncertainty about the future. Written materials for the client to take home and review are extremely useful in these situations.

For many consumer cases, so-called alternative pricing is quite naturally a part of the case plan. Consumer clients usually need their matters handled by one lawyer from beginning to end. They need understanding and reassurance. They need certainty and as much information as possible about the uncharted waters ahead. Hourly billing may be simple for the lawyer, but a consumer will appreciate the clarity and certainty of a fixed fee—even if that certainty is embodied in a road map with a dozen possible total fees, depending upon future variables.

Pricing Structure as the Basis of an Office System

The pricing structure, when properly communicated to the client, can provide the basis of the attorney-client agreement and the case plan. The less familiarity the client has with the situation, the more detailed the disclosure should be.

In a probate case example, the consumer may indicate she will likely hire the Main Street lawyer and asks about the fees. In response, the lawyer produces not an intimidating document entitled "Attorney-Client Fee Agreement," but one called "Case Plan." This document appears in the form of a timeline, and may be more graphically designed than the standard legal document. The lawyer explains the anticipated chain of events—drafting and filing documents, sending notices, and so on. The document clearly notes the fees at each stage of the proceeding. The document or set of documents may also include many typical provisions and disclaimers. Much of this form can be preprinted, but because the client decides certain variables (such as sales of property within the probate), the form has blanks that are completed during the interview.

Of course, there may be unknowns and unknowables, in which case the lawyer makes a good-faith estimate *in writing*. Yet, the end result is a complete document detailing the entire course of the legal matter, the anticipated timing of events, a likely date of conclusion, an estimated fee, and the probable maximum fee.

Some lawyers object to attaching any estimate to an unpredictable fee. They may also disagree with giving clients time lines for completion of tasks, no matter how general. After all, probate cases sometimes drag on. But the message to the client should be that they do not "drag on" in *this* lawyer's office. The beauty of a case plan is that it is constructed to interlock with the lawyer's office procedures. The case plan provides a road map for the lawyer's staff, detailing tasks and anticipated time lines. The law firm's system provides not only for the drafting of required documents, but also for important standardized client communications. Instead of receiving two-sentence transmittal letters, the client receives detailed status reports accompanying file-stamped copies, which refer to events outlined in the case plan. If contingencies occur and trigger a fee increase, the system generates a thoughtful explanation and discussion of what has transpired, to accompany the request for additional fees. The client has a reference guide throughout the matter to judge the lawyer's performance against predictions.

With this approach, the Main Street lawyer is highly motivated to improve, embellish, and streamline the system. Compared with other clients, the Main Street lawyer's clients receive superior, regular, and more detailed communications, because the lawyer has judged that a few "extra" letters are less expensive to the firm than receiving numerous "extra" telephone calls from the client.

And what of the estimate of the unknowable fee, when the fee was underestimated due to an event that has now improbably occurred? Will the lawyer be judged by his or her own candor? ("Yes, I stated probably no more $2,000, and the charges are now $3,500. But, . . .") This is yet another aspect of the system that the lawyer should design and prepare in advance. When it becomes evident that an estimated charge may be exceeded, a letter of explanation can be sent to the client immediately, not when the final fees are requested. ("Please be advised that A and B have occurred, and the scope of work is beyond what we initially discussed. Accordingly, the costs will exceed our original estimate. You may contact me at no additional charge if you wish to discuss this.") This is not to say there will never be a time when a consumer manages to use a fee estimate against a lawyer, even if only for a bargaining position to compromise the final fee. But the system functions to create understanding, predictability, and trust. A client is then predisposed to view a contingency as something that happened in his or her particular case, and not as the lawyer simply deciding to charge more.

Conclusion

For the Main Street lawyer representing mainly consumer clients, the decision to embrace alterative billing is not as simple as changing from hourly fees to flat or fixed fees. Rather, it involves a potentially painful examination of office procedures, use of staff, and use of technology. It involves an understanding of consumer attitudes, even when the lawyer believes such attitudes are incorrect and unjustified. It often involves changing the lawyer's mind-set from a case-by-case approach to a system of processes focused on efficiency. The result should not be a "cookie-cutter" or "assembly line" style of practice, but rather, a system where the lawyer has more time available for face-to-face client consultation and counseling.

In many ways, the search for the completely efficient, productive office system is like the quest for the Holy Grail. Improvements and refinements can—and should—continue. But the promise is not illusory. This quest can lead to an office where the clients are more informed and more certain about the fees they will pay, where more information about the progress of a matter flows regularly to the client, where the client is given realistic goals and expectations by which to measure the lawyer's delivery of services, where the lawyer is more confident that matters are being handled efficiently, and where the lawyer is rewarded for efficiency by increased profitability.

The journey may not be easy, but the rewards will be substantial.

The Solo's Guide to Collecting Fees

22

Linda J. Ravdin

Next to bringing in business, collecting fees is probably the management issue of greatest concern to the solo lawyer. This chapter presents a series of steps to enhance fee collections. A realization rate of 100 percent is a worthy goal that few of us achieve. However, a good system of setting and collecting fees will significantly increase realizations, and will do so for a modest investment of lawyer and staff time. The last step is a lawsuit against the client. Lawsuits are the least effective method of collecting fees, and should be avoided most of the time.

Client Selection

The starting point in any system of enhancing fee collections is careful selection of clients and cases. In the first telephone call and in the first consultation with the potential new client, the lawyer should "size up" the client, based upon his or her ability and willingness to pay the fees that will be charged for the work the client is asking the lawyer to do. Take a few minutes to speak on the phone with potential new clients or invest time to train a staff person to conduct an initial screening. That person should understand your criteria for accepting clients and, more importantly, your criteria for rejecting clients. The most important thing you can do at this point is to eliminate those who are obviously wrong for you, so that you can concentrate on landing the good clients and doing their work.

Develop a set of questions for the first phone call that will allow you to identify potential "problem clients" quickly, or that will give problem clients the opportunity to reveal themselves as clients you want to avoid. Look and listen for the danger signs in the first phone call and at the initial consultation:

- The client whose first question is, "How much do you charge?" Certainly the client is entitled to this information, but the client who wants to know that before asking you anything else might be trouble.
- The client who has switched lawyers several times. This client may have unreasonable expectations.
- The client who, when you say you charge $300 per hour, tells you the lawyer down the street will do the job for $250 per hour. Why is he telling you this? Why doesn't he hire the lawyer down the street?
- The client who, in the initial phone call, insists upon telling you her whole story or who insists upon getting legal advice before agreeing to come in for an appointment. This person may be looking for something for nothing.
- The client who balks at paying a consultation fee or fee advance. This person may be looking for something for nothing.
- The client who is switching lawyers, owes the other lawyer money, and does not want to pay. This may or may not be justified, but it warrants caution.
- The client who appears overly demanding but evinces insufficient willingness to pay for the privilege.
- The client who shows up in your office with her documents in a shopping bag in no particular order and wants you or your staff to sort them out.
- The client who shows up for an initial consultation without any of the documents you requested and does not have a good excuse.
- The client who refuses to provide the documents you requested because he has decided you don't really need them to answer his questions, but insists upon getting an answer anyway.
- The client who puts the blame for all his problems on everyone but himself. Someday you will be to blame for all his problems.
- The client whose anger is all out of proportion to the wrong committed.
- The client whose primary motivation is revenge.
- The client who wants a miracle.
- The client who is not prepared to listen to a realistic appraisal of his prospects.

- The client who insists upon trying to pin you down to a prediction of the outcome or cost in a situation where such predictions cannot be made.
- The client who, when given a prediction of the cost of handling a complicated matter, responds, "Let's keep it simple. You lawyers always want to solve problems that don't exist." A variation on this is the client who wants you to do half the job for half the price.
- The client who will never be satisfied, no matter how good a job you do.
- The client who says, "It's not the money. It's the principle of the thing." The implication is that the client is willing to pay whatever it costs to pursue the principle. But when all is said and done, few clients are willing to pay fees that are out of line with the financial stakes. Beware of people who say they are.
- The client who hired the cheapest lawyer in town who messed up her case, and now the client cannot afford to pay you to clean up the mess.
- The client who hired a lawyer who promised him the moon, took all his money, and didn't deliver, and now the client wants you to handle the appeal for free.
- The client you simply do not like. Give yourself permission not to represent someone you find irritating or whose personality clashes with yours, especially if the matter is one where you must work closely together. If you do not like the client, he will sense it, and will come to resent you as you will come to resent him. The next thing you know, the client will not want to pay the bill.

A complete discussion of client selection is beyond the scope of this chapter. Suffice it to say, selecting out those individuals who are likely to be troublemakers when it comes to paying bills eliminates a significant percentage of uncollectible fees. Lawyers are taught to make judgments based upon concrete facts. In deciding who should be accepted as clients, lawyers need to pay more attention to their instincts. Sometimes it's not possible to articulate why you have a bad feeling about a particular person after the first meeting or phone call, but the uneasy feeling persists. Act on it! Do not take the client.

Some lawyers, especially those new in practice, will say they cannot afford to be so selective, and that with time on their hands they might as well take a chance. I say, even lawyers new in practice should be picky about whom they represent. As Jay Foonberg says, "It's better not to do the work and not get paid than to do the work and not get paid." The time you spend working for free could be better spent marketing yourself to the kinds of clients you want to have.

Case Selection

Equally important is the careful selection of cases. Even when the client is the right kind of client, the matter should be one the lawyer can handle competently and efficiently. Stick to your expertise. If you are attempting to develop a new area of expertise, either take matters with lower stakes until you gain some experience or associate with a more experienced lawyer until you develop sufficient competence. Recognize that in handling matters where you have not yet developed full competence, you are likely to put in more time than is warranted. You will then have to write off some of the bill or risk the client balking at paying the full amount. Make the investment in learning more so you develop a higher level of expertise, but don't treat the "excess" charges as a collection problem. Both for ethical reasons and good client relations, it is better to write off some of the charges than to wait for the client to get angry.

Setting Fees: Ethics and Practicalities

Setting fees often seems like a fine art. Deciding upon the hourly rate requires the lawyer to consider the requirements of state rules of ethics, as well as more practical factors such as the cost of doing business, a reasonable income for the lawyer, and what lawyers in that practice specialty with similar experience charge. Rule 1.5 of the Model Rules of Professional Conduct requires a lawyer's fee to be reasonable and establishes a nonexclusive list of criteria for judging reasonableness, as presented on page 180, or in more detail in the Appendix B, page 605.

These criteria really address the total fee charged for the matter, rather than the hourly rate. A lawyer with an unusually high hourly rate who works unusually efficiently may charge a total fee that is more reasonable than a lawyer with a low hourly rate who works slowly. The reasonableness of a given fee in a particular matter is usually determined when a dispute arises, by looking back after the work is done. How do you know what's reasonable? No formula answers that question. Consequently, the judgment—which, in the event of a fee dispute, is made by a third party, such as a judge, jury, or arbitrator—will be somewhat arbitrary. How can you reduce the chance that someone exercising twenty-twenty hindsight will deem your fee unreasonable?

As discussed above, evaluate the stakes before taking the case and try to avoid cases where the stakes are too low for the fees you must charge to make a profit. Reevaluate the stakes as the matter continues and you get new information. Strive to keep the fees in line. Tell the client what he or she can do to reduce the time that you or your staff would otherwise have to spend on the matter; for example, have the client organize documents for discovery. In low-stakes cases, consider limiting the representation to discrete components of the matter—such as preparation of documents—and letting the client handle other components pro se. (See Forrest S. Mosten's book, *Unbundling Legal Services*, published in 2000 by the ABA.) Document what you did and why you did it. To the extent your fees are the result of the conduct of the opposing party, the opposing client, or your own client, document that in your bills. Keep the client informed with copies of all relevant correspondence and pleadings. Give the client opportunities to make informed decisions about the conduct of the representation that affects the fees incurred. Document in writing the information used in making the decision and the client's reasons for the conclusion reached. Get bills out promptly so the client has current information on the status of the matter and the fees incurred to date.

Discussing Fees in the First Telephone Call

Whatever basis for your charges you choose, you must firmly and confidently communicate information about fees to potential clients. If you charge by the hour, tell any potential client your hourly rate during the initial phone call. Some potential clients will be looking for lower hourly rates. If so, they will go elsewhere without wasting your time. Some will not balk at your hourly rate, but it will be evident to you after a short discussion that the cost of your services will be out of proportion to what is at stake or what the potential client is prepared to spend. Conducting a preliminary screening with a prospective client before offering to make an appointment can help you eliminate many who are not right for you and conserve your time for good prospects.

Ordinarily, you should not attempt to set a fee advance during the first telephone call, because you do not have sufficient information to make this determination. However, if you sense from the conversation that the prospective client may not be able to afford you, consider telling him that the fee advance will not be less than a specified amount. If he is not prepared to pay that amount, you can save him from paying you for an initial consultation only to find out he cannot afford you, and you can save yourself some valuable time that could be used to land a client who can afford you.

Charge for Initial Consultations

Charge for initial consultations and expect payment at the time of the consultation. Tell potential clients during the first phone conversation that they are under no obligation to hire you to do anything beyond the consultation, that you charge for the consultation at your regular hourly rate, and that the only obligation they have is to pay for the consultation at the conclusion of the first meeting. Suggest to prospective clients things they can do to save time at the first consultation, such as gathering relevant documents and preparing narratives of the facts. The good prospective client will appreciate your willingness to save her money. The one who balks at paying for the first consultation or will not do the homework assignment is a potential troublemaker.

Fee Advances

Get an adequate fee advance. What is "adequate" depends upon the complexity of the matter, time constraints, whether you will need leave of court to withdraw from the matter in the event of nonpayment, and other factors.

Set a range of standard fee advances for certain types of matters. These are internal guidelines—not to be publicized to clients. You can and should set a higher fee advance if the matter warrants. You should almost never set a lower one. Remember, there was a reason you set these standard fee advances to begin with, and it was probably based upon your experience (or the experience of other lawyers) that these were reasonable minimums given the amount of work required for the type of matter. Use your internal standards to discipline yourself to look a potential client in the eye and say, "My fee advance is $5,000 for matters of this type."

Some clients do not have sufficient funds on hand to pay fee advances, especially if their legal problems were unanticipated. It is entirely appropriate for the lawyer to suggest sources of funds. For example, many people can obtain loans from their credit unions. Some have IRAs or retirement plans they can tap. Others can borrow from family members. There are also credit cards, bank lines of credit, or home equity loans. Sometimes a security interest in a vehicle or a second trust on real estate to secure your fee is appropriate.

As a general practice, the lawyer should require the full fee advance up front. In some cases, however, it is appropriate to discuss alternate arrangements that meet your requirements, especially if they are suggested by the client and are reasonable. For example, imagine you ask for a $5,000 fee advance for negotiating a marital property settlement agreement. The client says she came prepared to give you $2,500, because she had spoken to friends and expected it would be at least that much. She goes on to say she is impressed with your approach to resolving her case and she is prepared to borrow another $2,500 from her credit union. She wants to know if you will take $2,500 now and the balance in thirty days. The answer should be yes, because this client demonstrated a commitment to pay your fees and recognized that it is her responsibility to figure out how she is going to do it.

In short, work with clients to make it possible for them to have you if they really want you. The client who sincerely wants to hire you and is not looking for a free ride will recognize that your requirements are reasonable and customary. At the same time, you must always be sensitive to the financial sacrifice many clients must make to come up with a substantial fee advance to hire a lawyer.

Dealing With Potential Fee Problems

Early Discussions About Fees

Many potential collection problems can be averted by having frank discussions with clients at the outset. Often clients ask the right questions to prompt such discussions; when they do not, the lawyer must initiate the discussions. Many people have little experience dealing with lawyers and do not understand lawyers' expectations. Part of your job is to educate them about your expectations. Most people will try to live up to your expectations if they know what they are.

Some people, for example, may think it is customary for lawyers to provide financing by accepting monthly payments of fixed amounts or by waiting until matters are concluded to collect, even when the fees are not contingent upon the outcome. Of course, if you like lending money to clients through these mechanisms, then by all means tell the client. If you do not, you must let the client know that.

Most people can be helped to understand why you cannot fund their legal matters. You can explain that you try to do a good job for every client, that you do not take more matters than you can handle properly, that if you did not get paid adequately for your services you would be forced to accept more than you can handle, and that you are not willing to do that. You can also explain that you are a sole practitioner and, while that means every case gets your personal attention, it also means you are not in a position to extend credit to clients. Some clients do not understand this until you explain it to them. After you explain it, the client has a chance to react appropriately by either developing a plan to pay your fee advance or by going elsewhere.

Credit cards can be an important weapon in the solo lawyer's arsenal. Almost everyone has one or more credit cards. With the ready availability of credit, few clients should have excuses for not paying required fee advances or keeping accounts current. Someone without credit cards or available credit lines may not be someone you want as a client. Offering payment by credit card makes it possible to incorporate into your initial fee discussions with potential clients the message that you do not finance litigation, that you expect clients to keep their accounts current, and that if they need to borrow to do so, they can borrow from a credit company, but not from you. Here's a little speech you may wish to give in response to the client who asks if he is expected to pay his bill every month, inquires about monthly payment schedules, or indirectly hints that he may not understand your expectations about fees:

> We are not in the business of lending money. All we do is practice law. We do accept credit cards. We make that service available to people who wish to use it or who find it more convenient for financing their legal fees. Visa, MasterCard, and American Express are in the business of lending money. So that's an option you have to pay your monthly bills. We do expect you to keep your account current. If you need to borrow to finance your fees, you must use a credit card or borrow elsewhere. Then you can work out the payment schedule with that entity. We are simply unable to extend credit. I hope you understand that.

If having the client make monthly payments is acceptable to you, then use such arrangements, but establish the terms in the beginning and get them in writing. Follow up with the client to make sure she honors the payment terms. Also, your agreement should permit you to require the client to increase the monthly payment if the level of attention required is greater than anticipated.

Turn away people who can't meet your terms. If you established a fee advance that reasonably anticipates the amount of work you need to do, and the client cannot or will not pay it, decline the representation. If appropriate under the circumstances, give the client a referral to someone who might be more affordable.

Be wary of the potential client who, when told the amount of your fee advance, launches into a lament about how broke he is, rejects all your suggestions about other sources of funding, and is bereft of any ideas of his own. After all, what message is the client sending when he says he does not want to cash in an IRA and pay the penalty, does not want to use his credit card and pay the high interest rate, or does not feel he can ask his parents? Why does this person feel unable to go to his parents for a loan but can ask you, a total stranger, for one? Why does this person feel entitled to an interest-free loan from you, but not from MasterCard? This person may be looking for something for nothing. If the client is very belligerent and demanding, that usually means big trouble, and it's time to end the conversation. This is someone you do not want as a client under any circumstances.

Applying the Fee Advance—The Evergreen Retainer

Many lawyers apply the fee advance to the initial bills until the advance is depleted, and only then start billing the client for fees that exceed the advance.

This means several months may go by during which you send bills, but the client is not asked to pay you anything because you are still working off the advance. The client may get lulled into thinking her financial obligation to you has already been met, or may not make adequate provisions for paying the bills once the fee advance is depleted. By the time she gets the first bill asking for money, she hasn't read the engagement agreement in months. She may have forgotten that the agreement requires her to pay the bills after the fee advance is used. It may be sixty or ninety days beyond that point before it becomes clear you have a "problem payer" on your hands and, by that time, the client may owe you a substantial amount and it may be too late to withdraw.

A better approach is to use an evergreen retainer, whereby the fee advance is a deposit you draw against as you earn fees or incur costs. The client is required to replenish it as it is used. This allows you to assess, sooner rather than later, whether there are going to be problems with payment. Often these problems can be resolved at an early stage in the representation. Sometimes all it takes is establishing your expectations and making the client understand that you really do expect him to replenish the deposit. You could arrange a payment schedule that allows the client to get caught up. Other times, it may be appropriate to agree to suspend work until the client is able to catch up. It is much easier to resolve such problems early in the representation, when the amount the client owes is modest. At that point, if the client does not make satisfactory arrangements for payment, you can get out with little or no loss.

Engagement Agreements: Provisions to Aid in Collection of Fees

The importance of having the fee agreement in writing cannot be overstated. It shows the client that you mean business and that you operate in a professional manner. It helps avoid later disputes. It is powerful evidence in response to the client who says, "She told me the total fee would be $2,000," when the engagement agreement says you will bill at your hourly rate for all time spent on the matter against a fee advance of $2,000. Some jurisdictions' rules of ethics require a writing, such as a fee schedule, though a formal, written agreement may not be required. Quite apart from ethics requirements, courts are likely to construe a dispute about the terms of an oral fee agreement against the lawyer. Therefore, it is wise to have one in every case.

At a minimum, every fee agreement should contain the following elements:

- Description of the matter sufficient to limit the scope to that which the lawyer agreed to handle
- Applicable hourly rates, or other basis or rate of the fee
- Amount of the fee advance and whether you will bill against it

- How the fee advance will be handled (whether it will apply to the initial billings, the last bill, or some of each)
- Whether the client is required to replenish the fee advance
- Your intent to refund unearned portions of the fee advance
- The intervals at which you will bill
- Requirement that bills are payable on receipt
- Exclusion of costs from your hourly rate or the flat fee
- Your intent to bill the client for certain costs (such as postage, photocopying, and messenger fees), and your expectation that the client will advance other costs (such as filing fees, expert-witness fees, and court reporter fees) before they are incurred
- Statement of any intent to charge a minimum billing increment (Some state ethics rules or opinions require that you state any such intention in your agreement. See, for example, D.C. Bar Legal Ethics Committee Opinion 103, which stated that minimum billing increments for phone calls and letters were not unethical if provided for in the engagement agreement.)
- Statement of your inability to guarantee the outcome and, unless you charge a flat fee, your inability to guarantee the total fee amount

Other provisions that can be useful in enhancing collection efforts include the following:

- You have the right to require an additional fee advance under various circumstances; for example, if suit must be filed before a settlement is reached, if after initial investigation or review the matter appears more complex than anticipated, or if at any time you conclude that the level of attention required by the matter is greater than anticipated.
- The client can be required to pay an additional fee advance thirty days before trial in a predetermined amount or in an amount to be determined at that time.
- The agreement is limited to the matter described; if additional services are desired, an additional fee advance may be required.
- In agreements for flat fees, work in excess of the tasks provided in a detailed description will be charged.
- You have the right to withdraw if the client fails to pay fees as agreed.
- If a collection action is necessary, the client will pay attorneys' fees.
- Fee disputes will be resolved by mandatory arbitration. (Check your state's ethics rules and ethics committee opinions regarding such provisions. In some jurisdictions, lawyers are required to arbitrate. For example, see D.C. Bar Legal Ethics Committee Opinion 218, and D.C. Bar Rule XIII.)

◆ Interest will be charged on overdue accounts. (Again, check local rules of ethics and ethics opinions. If you intend to charge interest, determine whether you are required to make disclosures under the federal Truth-in-Lending Act.)

Maintaining Detailed Records and Preparing Descriptive Bills

The most basic component of any system designed to maximize fee collections is maintaining good records of the work done and time spent doing that work. You must make contemporaneous, accurate, and detailed time records. Use a time-and-billing program that includes a timer feature. Do not record at the end of the day, week, or month by attempting to remember what you were doing. Your time records will be inaccurate, most likely not capturing all your work. Moreover, in a fee dispute, contemporaneous time records are inherently more credible than those reconstructed later.

The detail with which the work is described is equally important. A full and detailed description—of the work done, the reason for the work, or the purpose of the phone call or meeting—communicates value that, in turn, encourages the client to pay the bill. If there is a later fee dispute, detailed descriptions are inherently more credible than cryptic, two-word descriptions. Compare the following pairs of detailed and cryptic descriptions:

Sample 1:
Legal research to review case law on various theories of invalidity of premarital agreements, including fraud, duress, undue influence, failure to make full disclosure, substantial change in circumstances, and unconscionability; evaluate related issues, such as burden of proof, circumstances under which burden shifts to proponent of agreement; prepare preliminary memorandum summarizing findings, applying case law to facts of our case, identifying additional factual issues to explore with client; prepare first draft of complaint for divorce seeking determination of invalidity of agreement.

7.0 hours	$2,100

versus

Legal research; draft complaint. 7.0 hours $2,100

Sample 2:
Phone conference with client to discuss her views on adequacy of settlement offer, likelihood of getting better result at trial, cost to go to trial, risks of trial, possible difficulties in collection, potential for appeal, delays during appeal process, and advise client good chance

cost of trial will exceed incremental benefit; draft letter to client recapitulating facts, issues in dispute, analysis of issues, strengths and weaknesses of our case, advice re our settlement position.

3.0 hours $750

versus

Phone conference with client; letter to client.

3.0 hours $750

The larger the amount of time charged in a single block, the more detailed the description should be. With a time-and-billing program, the amount of time the lawyer must spend recording a detailed description is tiny, and the small investment has such a big payoff that it's well worth the effort. There will be fewer occasions to discuss the bill with the client because virtually everything the client wants to know is there. Compare, for example, the ten minutes you might spend explaining why you spent four hours in the library with the thirty seconds you would spend recording it in a time-and-billing program. And it's likely you will not be able to charge the client for the ten minutes you spent explaining your bill without infuriating the client.

Whether you are charging by the hour or otherwise, you should keep track of all the time you spend on client matters. By going back later and reviewing the time spent, you can determine whether you should increase your required fee advance or flat-fee charge. Moreover, if there is a dispute about the fee in a flat-fee case, it will be essential that you have documented your time.

In addition to documenting your time, you should document the work you do for the client. Maintain organized files. Keep detailed, contemporaneous, accurate records of oral communications in chronological order. Your files should track your time records and vice versa. Be able to document the work your bills and time records say you did. Keep the client informed by sending copies of all correspondence, court filings, and other documents generated in the representation. A client who is kept informed of everything happening in a matter is more likely to be willing to pay the bills as they come due.

Billing Procedures That Enhance Collection

Most clients being charged on an hourly basis should be billed once per month. It is extremely important that bills go out regularly and that they go out promptly after the close of the billing cycle. With a time-and-billing program, if the lawyer records his own time as he goes along, the bills can go out the same day the billing cycle ends. This means the client knows exactly what has been done on a current basis. By getting bills out promptly, you send a message that it matters to you that you get paid promptly. It should be self-evident that you cannot get paid until you bill for your work. Moreover, if your bills are current and the client is unhappy with the bill or the quality of the work, she has an opportunity to stop you before you do a lot more work on the matter.

Designate a particular day every month for bills to be prepared. Someone other than the lawyer should be responsible for preparing the bills. This could be a secretary, office manager, bookkeeper, or part-time college student. The person doing the task must give it undivided attention on the designated billing day or days. Getting the bills out in a timely fashion should be the number-one priority for this person, who should be insulated from other distractions. The lawyer will always have a higher priority than getting bills out: getting current client work done. That is why the lawyer should delegate this important task. The lawyer's involvement should be limited to reviewing the draft bills before they go out, making any necessary corrections to the descriptions or adjustments to the fee. If a good time-recording system is in place, the lawyer's time investment in reviewing bills should be minimal.

What to Do After the Bill Goes Out

Once bills go out, you should see that many clients pay promptly—*if* you followed good practices in selecting clients, setting fee advances, recording your time, and preparing your bills. The key to the system is to act early to establish with the client your expectation that bills be paid promptly. By acting early, you also identify possible "problem payers" while there is still time to get out of the representation. Later, how you handle clients who do *not* pay promptly can make the difference between a successful practice and one that teeters on the edge.

At the conclusion of each billing cycle you should receive a list of all accounts receivable. A good time-and-billing program allows you to generate such a list easily. The list should include the name of every client, with work and home phone numbers, the last billing date, the last payment received, the amount of the last bill, and how much of the outstanding bill has been due for thirty, sixty, ninety, and one-hundred-twenty days. Review the list and note everyone who has not made a payment in the last thirty days. Of those, determine who should receive a personal phone call. There may be some with accounts over thirty days who do not need to be called immediately, such as a client with a good payment history who occasionally pays late, or someone who has recently mentioned to you that he is about to send a check. All new clients without established payment histories should be included in the list of those to be called, as should all existing clients who routinely need reminding to pay their bills.

The lawyer must make a decision about who should make such calls—the lawyer or someone else. I strongly recommend that the lawyer not be the one to make the phone calls. First, as discussed above, the lawyer always has a higher priority than calling clients to remind them about overdue bills. Second, lawyers often find it distasteful to make such calls and tend to put them off. That defeats the whole purpose of early intervention. It allows clients who may already have been lulled into thinking they do not have to pay any more bills after paying the fee advance to continue to be lulled. Third, often by the time the lawyer gets around to calling the client, she has become angry about the client's seeming lack of appreciation for all the hard work she has done. That makes it difficult to strike the right manner and tone of voice with the client.

The person assigned to make the calls must be someone who understands the importance of the task. She must understand that you want to collect your fees, but that you also want to maintain a good relationship with the client. Therefore, in the conversation with the client, the caller must be gracious and polite, yet firm. The caller must be just as warm and friendly to the client as she would be to the same client in greeting him and offering him coffee in the office. A dialogue with the client might go something like this:

> **Collection Manager:** Hello, Ms./Mr. Client, I am calling from Linda Ravdin's office regarding your account. How are you today?
> **Client:** I'm fine. How are you?
> **Collection Manager:** I'm doing well, thanks. We haven't received your payment this month and I am calling to find out when we can expect it. If you want to use a credit card, we accept MasterCard and Visa.
> **Client:** I must have forgotten to send the check in. I'll put it in the mail to you today. Oh, you accept MasterCard and Visa? I'll charge it. Let me give you my number.

Sometimes the client is not forthcoming about whether or when payment will be made:

> **Collection Manager:** Hello, Ms./Mr. Client, I am calling from Linda Ravdin's office regarding your account. How are you today?
> **Client:** I'm fine. How are you?
> **Collection Manager:** I'm very well, thank you. We haven't received your payment this month and I am calling to find out when we can expect it. If you want to use a credit card, we accept MasterCard and Visa.
> **Client:** I can't tell you when I will be able to pay.

At this point, the collection manager may terminate the conversation and turn the problem over to you, become more insistent, or suggest a payment schedule, depending upon your instructions. The most appropriate choice depends upon several factors, such as the amount the client owes, the client's payment history, and whether you are in the middle of a representation with significant fees yet to be incurred, or are nearing the end. If arranging a payment schedule is deemed appropriate, the collection manager should attempt to obtain a commitment from the client first, and only if she is unable to do so should she turn it over to you:

> **Collection Manager:** I am authorized to work with you on arranging a payment schedule to meet your obligation, but I do need your cooperation.
>
> **Client:** Well, I get paid on Friday. I can send $500 then.
>
> **Collection Manager:** Fine. However, given the size of your bill, we will need you to make monthly payments of $1,000.
>
> **Client:** That's more than I can pay.
>
> **Collection Manager:** Give me an amount that you can pay every month. I am willing to be flexible.
>
> **Client:** I can pay $700 monthly.
>
> **Collection Manager:** Fine. So our understanding is that you will send a payment of $700 this Friday, and make monthly payments of $700 after that on the first of each month. Correct?
>
> **Client:** That's right.
>
> **Collection Manager:** Great. Thank you for working with me. I'll be sending you a letter confirming what we agreed.

In the event the collection manager is unsuccessful at getting a commitment from the client to pay the bill, you must step in and insist that the client address the problem. The dialogue might go like this:

> **You:** Joan, we have a lot that must be done on your case in the next few months, but you haven't paid your bill for the work I've already done. What are you going to do about that?
>
> **Client:** I know I owe you a lot of money. I'll pay you as soon as I can.
>
> **You:** I know you've been under a lot of financial pressure because of the dispute with your former business partner. But I hope you appreciate that I cannot carry you indefinitely. I'm happy to discuss payment arrangements with you. But you have to tell me specifically what you intend to do about the bill. We need to discuss that now. It can't wait any longer. Do you want to charge your bill to Visa or MasterCard?
>
> **Client:** Can I charge half of it now and authorize you to charge the other half in two weeks?

You: Sure. That would be fine. I appreciate that. I hope I can count on you to keep your account current going forward.

The crucial component of this conversation is that the client must be made to state her position regarding the bill: either she's going to pay it or she's not. It is not enough to tell the client you hope she will pay the bill and have the client say okay. There must be a commitment about when or, better yet, an authorization to charge the outstanding bill to the client's credit card. Most people will, if confronted, tell you whether they are going to pay. If the client is not going to pay in full, there must be some alternative satisfactory arrangement or the representation should be terminated.

Follow up the Follow-Up

In most instances, the phone call from your collection manager will result in receipt of payment. Sometimes this process must be repeated over several billing cycles. More often than not, however, the follow-up calls become unnecessary once the client gets the idea that you are serious about your fee agreement's provision that bills are payable on receipt. Sometimes the reason for nonpayment is that clients are busy professionals who are not good at keeping up with personal obligations. Those people would likely pay eventually anyway, but why wait until they get around to it while your cash flow suffers? Most will appreciate the reminder.

What happens if the client promises to pay by a certain date and does not? He gets another phone call a few days after the date the check was expected. The dialogue might go something like this:

Collection Manager: Hello, Ms./Mr. Client. I am calling from Linda Ravdin's office. We spoke last week regarding payment on your account. At that time you told me you were mailing a check that day. We haven't received that payment. Perhaps you forgot to mail it? Did you want to go ahead and charge the bill on MasterCard or Visa?

Client: Yes, it did slip my mind. I just put it in the mail today. I'm sorry. I usually pay my bills on time and don't need telephone calls to remind me to do so.

What happens if the client indicates that he is having financial difficulty or some other problem, and did not expect the bill to be so large, but does not dispute the amount due? In appropriate cases, have the collection manager arrange a payment schedule with the client. You must determine when you will permit installment payments, and whether you will allow them to stretch over long periods of time or will require that the account be brought current within a month or two or before doing any more work. The collection manager should become familiar with your general philosophy on such matters. She should generally know whether a $250 per month payment is acceptable for an outstanding bill of $2,000, or whether you think $500 per month is the minimum reasonable amount. In some cases, particularly when the amount due is relatively small, let the collection manager work it out with the client on her own authority. In others, she will have to discuss the proposed schedule with you and then get back to the client with your response. The collection manager should have the client propose the payment schedule. Often the client will propose an amount higher than you would have been willing to accept. The dialogue might go like this:

> **Collection Manager:** Hello, Ms./Mr. Client. I am calling from Linda Ravdin's office regarding your account. We have not received your payment and the account is overdue. We do accept MasterCard and Visa, if you want to use your credit card for payment.
>
> **Client:** Yes, I know that I have not made payments as I should. But I am not able to make payment in full right now. I had some unexpected expenses and I'm struggling to get caught up on my bills. Is it possible for me to work out a payment schedule?
>
> **Collection Manager:** I am authorized to work out a payment schedule with you. What would you propose?
>
> **Client:** Can I make payments of $1,000 per month?
>
> **Collection Manager:** That would be fine. Thanks. I appreciate that.

As long as the client acts in good faith, a reasonable proposal should be accepted. On the other hand, if the client proposes to pay an amount far below what you consider reasonable, without an adequate excuse, it might be time to consider terminating the representation or suspending work for a period of time. If you terminate the representation, you may not collect any of the amount due. On the other hand, it is usually better to cut your losses early than to keep working and have an even larger uncollectible account.

What if the client responds angrily to the collection manager's telephone call? Many lawyers hesitate to have someone make these reminder calls, and some are especially hesitant to have such calls made as early as thirty days after bills go out, because they are afraid clients will get angry. This thinking is misguided. If a client gets angry at a reminder call, consider yourself fortunate to have discovered early in the representation that you made a mistake when you took the client. If you discover your mistake early, you still have a chance to correct your mistake by getting out of the matter before your losses become too big. Most people are embarrassed to receive calls from service providers reminding them to pay overdue bills. Therefore, most people respond by paying the current bill and being more faithful about paying future bills because they want to avoid further embarrassment. People who do not have the decency to be embarrassed, and people who become angry at being asked nicely to pay for services they have already received, are people who think they are entitled to something for nothing. You do not want these people as clients.

Think about which is worse: (1) having a client get angry when someone calls to ask for payment of a $2,000 bill, so you withdraw and the client stiffs you for the $2,000, or (2) not reminding the client to pay the bill, not making the client angry, and getting stiffed for $20,000 in six months?

What If the Client Complains?

What does the collection manager do if the client complains about the amount of the bill or the quality of the representation? The lawyer must then take over. However, if up to this point you have done everything right, there will be few such instances requiring your personal attention.

If the client has a complaint about the bill, be willing to discuss the bill and explain it. If you do not send detailed bills, offer the client a copy of the original time records if that is responsive to the client's concern (such as when a client says he does not understand why the bill is so high). If you record your time using a time-and-billing program and you provide detailed descriptions of what you did, you should rarely have to explain the time charges on a bill, because everything the client needs to know is already there.

Resolve the problem with the client. Sometimes the client has a point, after all. Perhaps you inadvertently charged for something you should not have. Even if you do not agree with the client, sometimes it's better to knock off something that really irritated the client than have the client feel you have been unfair. But tell the client that's why you're doing it and get a quid pro quo: "I'll be happy to reduce your bill by $500 on the condition that you pay me the balance of what you owe me immediately." Be sure to reach some resolution with the client about the complaint—don't allow it to remain in limbo. Agree upon how much the client owes, or how much the client will pay in settlement of the outstanding bill. Make the client tell you when you can expect to get paid.

Insist that the client state clearly whether he is satisfied or dissatisfied with the representation. Sometimes the dispute is simply about the amount of the bill and the client thinks you are doing a great job. These disputes can easily be settled. Sometimes the real reason for the dispute is that the client is unhappy about the quality of the representation. Often, when the lawyer is having difficulty getting the client to agree to a resolution of what appears to be a fee dispute, it is because the client is unwilling to say the real problem is dissatisfaction with the quality of representation. You may have to probe to get the client to admit it. When you get the sense the client may be dissatisfied, ask bluntly, "Are you not paying the bill because you are dissatisfied with the quality of the services?" You may not like the answer, but you need to find out, and there's no other way to do it.

If the real reason the client has not paid is dissatisfaction with the quality of services, you must withdraw from the representation. The client must understand he cannot have it both ways; he cannot continue to accept your services, yet use dissatisfaction with those services as an excuse not to pay. Once again, this may be an opportunity for the lawyer to cut her losses. If you get out of the matter at this point, you may not collect anything more from the client, but you will save yourself from the additional uncollectible fees down the road and you will reduce the chances of needing to defend a malpractice case.

Terminating the Representation

If efforts to collect outstanding fees and resolve fee disputes amicably have failed, withdraw from the representation or make the client fire you. If you have entered an appearance in a case and the tribunal's rules require leave to withdraw, you must seek such leave. (See Rule 1.16 of the Model Rules of Professional Conduct.) As discussed above, early identification of clients who will not meet their commitments allows for early enough withdrawal that, in most cases, the client and other parties will not be prejudiced by your withdrawal. If the client fires you, have the client put it in writing and sign a consent to your withdrawal, if leave of the tribunal is required.

When leave of the tribunal is not required, you may simply withdraw by terminating the representation. Note that Model Rule 1.16 permits the lawyer to withdraw if the client fails to meet an obligation to the lawyer in connection with fees, even if withdrawal would prejudice the client. To withdraw, you must do more than just stop working on the client's case. According to Model Rule 1.16(d), you must notify the client, take steps to avoid any prejudice to the client, and return to the client any papers and property the client is entitled to receive.

Fee Collection Following Termination of Representation

When the client still owes money at the conclusion of the representation, efforts to collect should continue. Of course, at this point, the lawyer has less leverage and may have no choice but to accept monthly payments over a period of time. But the procedures for telephoning regularly can still be effective. Whether there is an express agreement that the client will pay on a payment schedule, or the client has simply been making partial payments, the client should receive a reminder each month in which a payment is not received within thirty days of the last payment. Make a deal with the client. For example, say a client owes you $10,000 and has been making payments of $500 per month. Offer to accept $8,000 in full settlement, provided the client pays you in full within ten days. For the client with the wherewithal to borrow the money or use a credit card, this is a great deal. It's a great deal for the lawyer, as well: $8,000 today is a lot more fun to have than $500 per month spread over twenty months, and there is no risk of the client's bankruptcy or re-ordering of priorities. There is sometimes another bonus to an arrangement like this. When the representation has been long and the client has already paid you a lot of money, the client will likely appreciate your willingness to knock something off the bill when you do not have to, in recognition of the client's faithful performance of her obligations in the past.

Attorneys' Liens

In limited circumstances, it is possible to impose an attorney's lien. There are two types of liens: the retaining lien and the charging lien.

At common law, a retaining lien is a possessory lien on files, client documents, money, and property to secure fees due the lawyer for any matter, not only the matter for which documents or property are retained. Check your state's statutes, ethics rules, and opinions, as the common-law rules have been altered in many states. In any event, the lien is only as good as the client's need for what the lawyer is withholding. Pleadings can always be reconstructed from the court file. Moreover, if you have been keeping the client informed (as required by Rule 1.4 of the Model Rules of Professional Conduct; see Appendix B, page 605) by giving him copies of all significant work product and correspondence, and have returned to the client all original documents after making photocopies for yourself, there may not be much to withhold. Nevertheless, there may be the occasional case where an attorney's lien will be available and effective.

The charging lien is a lien on the proceeds or result of a representation. It is limited to charges rendered for the particular action. A charging lien must be enforced through a court action. To create a charging lien, the lawyer must have an express agreement with the client entitling the lawyer to collect the fee from the proceeds. (See *Elam v. Monarch Life Insurance Co.*, 918 F.2d 201 (D.C. Cir. 1991).)

When All Else Fails

Hire your own lawyer. Have your lawyer write a demand letter—some clients who refuse to respond to your letters will respond to a letter from another lawyer. Have your lawyer call the client—some clients who won't talk to you will talk to your lawyer. Settle with the client for whatever you can get for the least amount of additional effort on your part.

When all nice efforts to collect have failed, the lawyer is on the verge of having to earn her fee twice—once for doing the work and once again for the time spent trying to collect. Therefore, know when to quit and cut your losses. In many cases, the time to quit is when the lawyer's personal efforts and the efforts of the lawyer's staff have failed, or, if a lawyer has been hired, after that lawyer's informal efforts have failed.

Fee Arbitration

If your fee agreement requires fee arbitration, or if the client insists upon it in accordance with a local bar rule, you will be required to go through arbitration to collect your fee. Even if arbitration is not required, you could propose it to the client. Many clients accept such proposals because arbitration is less threatening than being involved in court proceedings, and it is private.

There are a number of advantages to fee arbitration. Probably the number-one advantage is that the client cannot use a malpractice counterclaim as a defensive maneuver, because you do not have to agree to arbitrate malpractice claims unless a local rule or your fee agreement requires it. Thus, the client will need to hire a lawyer and file a separate malpractice action if he is serious about his claims. By contrast, many clients are unrepresented in fee arbitrations and spare themselves the cost of hiring counsel. An arbitration proceeding will likely resolve the fee dispute much faster than would be the case if suit were filed, and the expense will be smaller, as well. There are no significant disadvantages to fee arbitration. It is far preferable to seeking fees through a lawsuit.

Suing the Client

Suing the client for the fees due is sometimes effective, but you should proceed with caution. This should always be considered a last resort. Some clients who ignore every other effort respond when they get served with process, and they then agree to settlement terms.

You should not represent yourself, but should hire counsel, preferably on a contingent-fee basis. There are several reasons for this. First, at this point, you should have an objective person evaluate the merits of your case and your possible malpractice exposure. Second, even though you will pay a significant percentage—between 25 and 40 percent—of whatever you get to your lawyer, it will be worth it. Think of it this way: your outstanding $20,000 bill is now worth nothing. You hire a lawyer and settle for fifty cents on the dollar and pay your lawyer one-third. It did not cost you anything but the filing fee. Your lawyer made an account worth nothing into $6,666.

Some suits produce counterclaims. Don't sue if you're vulnerable. You know better than anyone what mistakes you made in representing the client. If they are mistakes that should never see the light of day, do not sue. Even if you didn't make any mistakes, if the client is crazy, or the amount is small, think twice before suing. It probably will not be worth it even if you win, because the investment of your time in pursuing the case will take you away from current paying clients and marketing efforts to develop new ones.

Conclusion

A good strategy for maximizing fee collections begins before the client comes in the door. Careful selection of cases and clients to eliminate troublemakers reduces one of the biggest sources of nonpayment. Establishing expectations early in the relationship with all new clients reduces the other significant source of problems. Doing so makes it possible to take fewer clients and do a better job for each one.

Selected Resources
for Part II
from the ABA Law Practice
Management Section

The ABA Guide to Lawyer Trust Accounts, by Jay G Foonberg, 1996.

Billing Innovations: New Win-Win Ways to End Hourly Billing, by Richard C. Reed, 1996.

Collecting Your Fee: Getting Paid from Intake to Invoice, by Edward Poll, 2002.

Compensation Plans for Law Firms, Fourth Edition, edited by James D. Cotterman, Altman Weil, Inc., 2004.

The Essential Formbook: Comprehensive Management Tools for Lawyers, Volume I: Partnership and Organizational Agreements/ Client Intake and Fee Agreements, by Gary A. Munneke and Anthony E. Davis, 2003.

The Essential Formbook: Comprehensive Management Tools for Lawyers, Volume II: Human Resources/Fees, Billing, and Collection, by Gary A. Munneke and Anthony E. Davis, 2005.

The Essential Formbook: Comprehensive Management Tools for Lawyers, Volume III: Calendar, Docket, and File Management/Law Firm Financial Analysis, by Gary A. Munneke and Anthony E. Davis, 2003.

The Essential Formbook: Comprehensive Management Tools for Lawyers, Volume IV: Disaster Planning and Recovery/Risk Management and Professional Liability Insurance, by Gary A. Munneke and Anthony E. Davis, 2004.

How to Draft Bills Clients Rush to Pay, Second Edition, by J. Harris Morgan and Jay G Foonberg, 2003.

How to Start and Build a Law Practice, Fifth Edition, by Jay G Foonberg, 2004.

Law Practice, bimonthly publication of the ABA Law Practice Management Section.

The Lawyer's Guide to Creating a Business Plan: A Step-by-Step Software Package, by Linda Pinson, 2005.

The Lawyer's Guide to Increasing Revenue: Unlocking the Profit Potential in Your Firm, by Arthur G. Green, 2005.

The Lawyer's Guide to Strategic Planning: Defining, Setting, and Achieving Your Firm's Goals, by Thomas C. Grella, and Michael L. Hudkins, 2004.

Results-Oriented Financial Management: A Step-by-Step Guide to Law Firm Profitability, Second Edition, by John G. Iezzi, 2003.

Unbundling Legal Services: A Guide to Delivering Legal Services a la Carte, by Forrest S. Mosten, *2000.*

Winning Alternatives to the Billable Hour: Strategies that Work, Second Edition, edited by James A. Calloway and Mark A. Robertson, 2002.

Operations Manual

Pilots spend a lot of time understanding systems and procedures. My flight instructor used to say that systems and procedures are there so that you don't have to think about every situation that comes up during the flight. Instead, you simply rely on the system or procedure that applies to a particular situation. It's the same with a law office.

Part III explains how to set up systems and procedures and how to select and train your employees to learn those systems and follow the procedures. One important aspect of running an office is ensuring that all ethical rules are followed. The chapters ahead tell you just what you need to do.

What's more, Part III contains sound advice on how and where to set up your office, whether you plan to share space with other solos or work out of your home. And once you decide on the location, you'll find comprehensive instruction on how to design your law office. You'll want to keep this manual in the cockpit, close at hand.

Office Space and Location

Leasing and Subleasing Space 23

J. R. Phelps
RJon Robins

As you are no doubt aware, the three most important things to consider in connection with real estate are location, location, and location. However true this axiom may be, it fails to address the fourth, fifth, and sixth most important things to consider with real estate, especially with leasing professional office space. This chapter addresses location considerations, and also space planning, what to look for (so you look like you know what you are doing), and lease terms. The chapter also provides a step-by-step action plan you can follow to be sure you don't miss anything.

Location

There is an old saying that you should "fish where the fish are." When deciding where to locate your office, think about your clients' convenience. Unless you have a heavy-duty litigation practice where you must be at the beck and call of the court, an office next to the courthouse is probably unnecessary. Instead, consider a location that would be more convenient to your target client base. Identify your target market and ask prospective building managers or leasing agents to provide demographic information. If they can't, use that as a negotiating point and consult with your local cable-television stations, newspapers, board of realtors, chamber of commerce, or economic development council. These organizations make it their business to know where the fish are.

Marketing and Business Development Components of Selecting a Location

The area demographics you may want to consider include age distribution, employment, education level, income level, sources of income, ratios of residential-to-commercial properties and owner-occupied-to-rental properties, percentage of single-family and multifamily units, home values, and value trends. Each of these items affects how well your new law firm will do in a given area. Be sure your intended practice area is likely to be in demand by people who live and work nearby.

Accessibility

Does the office space comply with the Americans with Disabilities Act (ADA)? Is it near public transportation? Will mobility-impaired clients have to enter the building through an ADA-compliant but second-class entrance at the rear of the building? Even a few steps or a broken sidewalk can be a huge barrier to an elderly or wheelchair-bound client who has trouble negotiating stairs but is otherwise fully independent. Remember: If prospective clients cannot get to you easily, it's going to be difficult for you to serve their needs.

Parking

A grandmother of one of the authors preferred doing all her business in suburban strip malls where she could dock her Cadillac across three parking spots. At one time or another, nearly everyone has used parking convenience and expense as the determining factor in deciding where to go. Be sure your prospective office has safe, convenient, and affordable parking. Is the parking lot secure and well lit? Employees of law firms often work late hours, and a firm may be liable if it fails to ensure the safety of its employees.

Visit the parking lot at different times of the day to see how crowded it will be during your intended business hours. Don't take false comfort in overflow private parking lots, as these may be developed into office buildings with tenants and visitors who will compete with your staff and clients for spots.

Will the landlord provide reserved parking for existing and future employees as the firm expands? Many leases tie the number of assigned parking spots to the number of leased square feet. Consider the impact on clients and staff when they must pay for parking. This factor alone may have a chilling effect on potential employees who will have to pay for the privilege of coming to work for you.

Prestige

Not everyone can claim a prestigious address as home. Consider how important it is to your ego and your clients to have the "right" address. Be honest with yourself, because you may easily spend more waking hours in your law office than you spend at home.

Amount of Space Needed

One of the first questions to ask regarding space is, "How much?" Consider how much space you need today and how much you hope to need in the future. As a general rule of thumb, 600 square feet per lawyer provides enough space for the lawyer, secretarial support, active case files, and a portion of the conference, library, and reception areas.

Be aware that most commercial landlords expect tenants to pay for a portion of building maintenance. Your lease may be for "net" or "gross" space; not to be confused with "net rent" and "triple net rent," which are lease price terms discussed later in this chapter. Net space refers to actual "usable space" while gross space includes your pro-rata share of common areas, such as hallways, stairwells, and mechanical equipment rooms.

If you have trouble keeping the terms straight, just remember how grossly unfair you feel it is that you must pay for the landlord's inefficient use of common areas, such as an oversized mechanical room. Expect to see a "load factor" of somewhere between 8 percent and 12 percent—the difference between net and gross space.

Space Planning

Space planning encompasses a wide range of concerns, from interior design—which is largely a matter of personal taste—to the placement of walls and doors. If you are going to err with interior design, err on the side of conservative. Depending upon the length of your lease, the landlord might agree to perform "build-out" for you or provide a build-out allowance. Landlords of commercial office space regularly maintain crews to renovate and modify the interior spaces of their facilities. Often, they can modify your space at much lower costs than you would incur through independent contractors.

If you decide to have the landlord build out your space, be sure to specify the quality of materials in the contract. Any vagueness will likely be interpreted by the landlord to mean "cheap." Attach actual carpet and paint samples to avoid later misunderstandings.

Be sure the space can be configured to your needs. You don't want to be in the middle of a build-out when it is discovered that a structural column runs right through the middle of your planned conference room.

While you are planning the processes, procedures, and policies of your law practice, there are many things you can do to affect lease expenses. Though another chapter covers these subjects in more depth, just one example illustrates the point. A well-conceived file management system can save a lot of money. For example, a four-drawer vertical file cabinet requires 5.5 square feet, compared with a lateral, which requires 9.0 square feet. By far, the most space-efficient filing system is an open-shelf system, which requires only 3.25 square feet and can be fairly inexpensive to create if you are handy or know a carpenter who can help you. It may seem like a minor consideration to quibble about on-site filing systems, but the savings can really add up, especially when combined with an off-site storage policy. There's simply no good reason to pay prime office rent to store dead files when perfectly adequate off-site storage is available at a fraction of the cost.

What to Look For (So You Look Like You Know What You're Doing)

For many of you, this will be the first time you have leased commercial office space. Although you may have studied real estate and contracts in law school, by now it should be clear that law school courses don't always offer practical advice about how to fly solo.

Steven Foonberg, a commercial real estate broker in Beverly Hills, California, who has experience with the unique needs and concerns of new lawyers, offers this advice: "Even though lawyers are generally good negotiators, it sometimes makes good strategic sense to hire a professional commercial real estate broker to represent you in the lease negotiations. An informed and experienced intermediary who is familiar with your local market can often negotiate a better deal for a tenant than the tenant can for himself or herself."

Factors to Investigate and Consider

In no particular order, the following factors should be investigated and considered before committing to a lease.

Management Quality

The standards to which a building is currently maintained should give you some idea about the quality of management to be expected if you become a tenant. This is not the time to be shy. Visit other tenants and ask whether they are satisfied. Incidentally, if you do move in, this could be the start of a valuable networking effort.

Security

What are the policies for after-hours access to the building? There are few things more frustrating than hearing the exit-only door click shut behind you on a Friday evening, just as you remember an important file on your desk inside. Though you want to be able to come and go as you please, it's no comfort to know the building (or parking lot) is easily accessible to anyone who cares to wander in. Does the building have security cameras? Are they monitored or just taped?

Emergencies

What procedures does the building management have for dealing with emergencies such as power outages and bomb threats, as well as fire-related emergencies?

Stairwells and Life Safety Facilities

Are stairways well lit and easily accessible? Be sure you know where they lead, as well as the number of doors between your office and the emergency exit so you can count your way in the dark. Ideally, stairwells should be pressurized to prevent escape routes from being blocked by smoke.

Heating, Ventilation, Air Conditioning (HVAC), and Elevator Equipment

How old is the equipment, and how well maintained? You don't want any unscheduled days off because the building's equipment fails. Modern buildings are built airtight to maximize energy efficiency. If the artificial-temperature-control equipment takes a day off, your office will too. In addition, many leases have an escalation clause based partly on energy costs. An inefficient building costs tenants more money. Finally, be sure your office space can be cooled or heated as appropriate on weekends and holidays, if you need it to be. Be aware that landlords often charge overtime for these services after "normal" business hours. Hourly fees for these services can be high. Also, be sure to learn whether the landlord is capable of delivering overtime HVAC suite by suite, or only floor by floor.

Lease Terms

Once negotiations begin, the perfect space may no longer look as attractive. Lease terms, while perhaps not first, second, or third in importance, surely finish a close fourth and are worthy of your careful consideration. In keeping with the theme of the book, this chapter focuses on issues of importance to the sole practitioner or small firm. Remember that lawyers working for the landlords draw commercial leases and favor the landlords heavily, especially in the "boilerplate."

You should be aware of the following terms and concepts, as you will be trying to negotiate them in or out of your lease. They can be classified into two categories: those that allow you to reduce or eliminate liability, and those designed to allow you to grow. Your level of success in your negotiations depends largely upon your rental market. Nonetheless, you should try to negotiate the most favorable lease you can.

It's important to remember that once you commit to a long-term lease, your most valuable leverage point (ability to walk away) is gone. The time to negotiate your exit or expansion strategy is *before* you commit to a lease. Before you commit to a long-term lease with "space to grow into," consider that the economy and legal industry are inherently cyclical. If you are reading this chapter during a boom time, take our advice: don't overcommit. If you are reading this chapter during a bust time, take our advice: plan for future growth. If you just don't know, be conservative.

As you read the next section, remember not to get too caught up in all the terminology. You should rely upon the operative terms in the lease, not these "terms of art," which can, and often do, mean different things to different people at different times and in different markets.

Fixed Rent, Gross Rent, Net Rent, and Triple Net Rent

Fixed rent is common in residential real estate. The tenant pays a fixed rate, which may or may not include basic utilities. Landlords typically include allowances for annual rent increases, based upon factors such as inflation.

There are two types of commercial leases commonly available: "gross" or "net." In a gross-rent lease, the tenant pays a fixed amount and the landlord covers all other building expenses, such as real estate and property taxes, trash removal, and maintenance. A net-rent lease includes a base rent amount and some or all of the expenses of operating the building. A triple-net-rent lease means the tenant pays all building operating costs.

Full-Service Growth

A hybrid, full-service growth lease combines elements of fixed, net, and triple-net arrangements. Typically, a fixed-rent price will be established, called the "base-year rent." Each year, the base rent remains the same but tenants pay their pro-rata share of building operating expenses. In other words, building expenses pass directly through to tenants. As advised by commercial real estate broker Steven Foonberg, "Be sure to investigate what your prospective landlord considers to be a direct pass-through expense. Expenses such as advertising, legal, and accounting should not be in this category, but sometimes are. Don't accept a base-year figure unless it's calculated on at least a 90 percent occupancy rate, or you could find yourself making a disproportionately high building maintenance contribution."

Common-Area Maintenance and Real Estate Taxes

Landlords often pass the expense of common-area maintenance and real estate taxes (CAM/RET) to tenants. Be sure you know ahead of time how your share will be calculated. Will it be based upon percentage of occupancy or percentage of space? Be sure to know exactly what categories your prospective landlord includes in tenant CAM/RET invoices. CAM/RET should not include legal, accounting, or advertising expenses. Ask about the landlord's annual efforts to protest property tax assessments. Ask to see invoices for the past year or two, so you know what to expect. Find out when you will be invoiced for these expenses, and be sure to reflect the estimated expenses in your cash-flow budget.

Exit Strategies

Landlord Liens

The time to get your landlord to agree to subordinate any statutory landlord liens is before you sign the lease. It may be advantageous if the landlord subordinates its lien to lessors of equipment and/or any finance companies with an interest in your equipment. In the event these companies must repossess their equipment or collateral, it's better if you can avoid the added expense of their legal fees spent fighting an uncooperative landlord whose statutory lien may supersede the lessor/lender's interest. While you are at it, get the landlord to agree to a collateral assignment of the lease. After you read this chapter, you'll probably have a lease with some attractive terms. In the event you want to assign it to someone else, like a lender as part of a work-out, a prenegotiated collateral-assignment provision can prove useful.

Sublease and Assignment

As the term implies, these lease provisions allow a tenant to sublet the space or, if you are a really good negotiator, assign the lease altogether. Generally, you can expect the landlord to reserve the right to approve or disapprove a potential subtenant or assignee. Be sure to include language that limits the landlord's discretion so approval is not "unreasonably withheld, conditioned, or delayed." Be sure that any rights you have under the lease are transferable to the subtenant or assignee. Expansion rights can be attractive to a potential subtenant or assignee, and having them might make it easier to relieve you of the lease payment obligation.

Space Reduction

Sometimes referred to as a give-back option, this provision allows you to give back a predetermined amount of space to the landlord at specified times during the lease term. Expect the landlord to want to specify which areas and how much space you can give back. Also expect to pay some penalty for exercising this valuable option.

Lease Termination

This provision gives you the right to terminate the lease before the scheduled expiration date. Expect to pay a penalty to exercise this option. Negotiate the length of time required for any termination notice. If you are unable to obtain an unrestricted termination option, consider asking for the right to terminate under the following scenarios:

- Landlord unable to provide adequate expansion space
- Merger or acquisition
- Loss or cancellation of major client
- Death or disability of rainmaker
- Firm ceases doing business in the city

Options

Hold Option

Some landlords may be willing to set aside predetermined units of space for your possible future expansion. The amount of space you rent and the length of your lease affects how much space the landlord is willing to set aside, and for how long. Two years is usually the outer limit. At the end of the hold period, the tenant has the option, but not the obligation, to exercise the option and lease the additional space.

Take-Back Option

A take-back option functions in much the same way as the hold option, except that the landlord is free to rent the designated space to another tenant until your option date arrives. At that point, if you exercise your option, the landlord must take the space back from the interim tenant—hence the name of this option or agreement. Plan on the landlord asking for as much as twelve months' notice. Be sure to notify your space planner of your ability to exercise this option, as office layout and even choice of materials may be affected.

Hold/Take-Back Option

This is a combination of the two approaches discussed above. The number of hybrids and combinations is infinite, limited only by your creativity and the landlord's willingness to indulge. A hold/take-back option generally describes a situation in which the landlord holds space vacant and you, as the beneficiary of the agreement, pay a reduced rate for the beneficial option. A hold agreement may be the easiest to obtain, as the landlord probably knows that certain space will be available at a predetermined date as other tenants' leases expire.

Expansion Option

Expansion options are the most difficult for landlords to accommodate. They require the landlord to make space available to you at particular points in time. The landlord may have the option of what space to provide; this differs from the hold and/or take-back approaches discussed above, which generally specify the exact space affected. You should still expect the landlord to ask for up to twelve months' notice, and you may even have to be prepared to move your entire office for the landlord to accommodate your expansion needs.

Special Considerations for the Solo Just Out of Law School

For the sole practitioner just out of law school, there are some special considerations. You probably don't have any steady clients yet. You may or may not have sufficient personal credit to qualify for leasing a suite of offices. Most importantly, you may not be sure whether you want to commit to a long-term office. Lucrative employment opportunities are sure to present themselves once you get out there and start networking. Student loans may be eating a large portion of your disposable income, and you probably don't yet have a need for a large library or even much staff.

Office Suites

The option of renting space from a professional center may be appealing. Shared law office suites for lawyers were pioneered by Paul Fegen in California. His company, Attorneys Office Management Inc., rents thousands of law office suites around the country. Visit the Web site at **www.fegen.com** to see some options for office suite rentals. Then look in a telephone directory under the "Offices" or "Real Estate" headings.

A law firm is a place where people expect a certain level of decorum and professionalism. Be sure your neighbors are involved in businesses that recognize similar standards. An incompatible neighbor can really hurt your practice. Compatible neighbors, on the other hand, can refer business, and provide valuable sounding boards and social opportunities. After all, deciding to "go it alone" as a sole practitioner can sometimes be a lonely proposition.

To combine the benefits of being your own boss and having the social outlets offered in a large-firm environment, consider renting space from an established firm. Just like you, large firms must consider taking more space than they currently need to provide for future expansion. With a bit of research and the assistance of an experienced commercial real estate broker, a sole practitioner might be able to find surplus premium office space within an existing firm. Benefits of doing this include use of a receptionist, a conference room, and office equipment on a cost-per-use basis. If you can be flexible and creative, you might find a great deal. Think about taking interior space with no windows. Decorate with curtains, and no one will know. (One of the authors used to meet all his clients in the landlord's conference room.)

Home Office

Another chapter in this book covers home offices in detail. For purposes of this discussion, consider the option of combining a commercial office lease with a home office, which can work well for solo lawyers. An issue that frequently arises is where to meet clients. Consider three approaches:

1. *Go to them.* Many clients will appreciate the convenience. Another chapter in this book addresses the computer equipment needed to outfit yourself as a "road warrior." Computer technology has advanced enough and prices have decreased sufficiently to make this a viable option, and the trend will likely continue.

2. *Meet on neutral ground.* Almost every courthouse and public library has private space available where you can meet clients. If you do meet a client in a public space, take care to protect your attorney-client relationship. Most jurisdictions hold lawyers to a "reasonableness" standard. Clients tend to hold their lawyers to a higher standard when it comes to protecting their confidences. Be sure to take all discarded notes with you for disposal back at your office. Invest the time now to "scout out" your spot. Make sure passersby cannot hear your conversations from the spot. Remember, it's a lot easier to explain to a bar grievance committee that you thought a room was soundproof than to try to explain why you thought no one else was in the stairwell.

3. *Use a "virtual" office at another firm.* At one time or another, most law firms have loaned conference rooms or vacant offices to visiting lawyers. Call around to find a firm with whom you can formalize this relationship. The firm may charge you on a per-use basis for the space and/or equipment. It might take some legwork, but you might find a firm willing to accommodate you in hopes that you will refer business to its lawyers. If you have a particular area of expertise, you might even get some business from the host firm, as long as you agree to

meet the client in the firm's office. (Be sure to see the previous paragraph's discussion on confidentiality in public areas.)

How to Do It: A Step-by-Step Plan

If you adhere to the following steps, you are likely to be satisfied with the result of your efforts to find an office space that suits your needs:

- ◆ Plan ahead
- ◆ Identify your target market
- ◆ Set growth goals
- ◆ Calculate present and future square-footage needs
- ◆ Plan the features of your space
- ◆ Shop around
- ◆ Compare your options and negotiate
- ◆ Sign the lease
- ◆ Schedule your move-in
- ◆ Send announcements and forward mail
- ◆ Audit your lease and invoices

Each of these steps is addressed in more detail below.

Plan Ahead

The amount of time needed to locate space depends upon the firm's size, the complexity of its needs, and the effectiveness of its forward planning. A month is surely too short; a year may not be enough. Give yourself sufficient time to refine your plans. Dedicate a notebook to your search for office space and address each consideration listed above. Keep track of important dates, such as when you need to give notice to your current landlord, clients, and the telephone-directory company (so you are sure to be listed in the upcoming book).

Identify Your Target Market

Who are your target clients? What are their demographics? Where do they work and live? Don't bother to look at space until you are armed with this critical information.

Set Growth Goals

Where do you want to be next year? How about the year after that? Consider where you want your law firm to take you during each of the next five years. How much money do you realistically want to earn? How many hours do you need to work to reach your income goal? Can you leverage your time with staff? If so, how many staff members do you need, and what qualifications must they have? What equipment will you need to accommodate your future staff? Will your office be wired for a network? How much office space will you need to grow your firm, and at what intervals?

Calculate Present and Future Square-Footage Needs

As discussed earlier, 600 square feet per lawyer is the rule of thumb, but advances in the size of computers and media storage devices may reduce this figure over time. In any case, be sure your calculations provide space for files, computer servers, telephone service equipment, and office supplies.

Plan the Features of Your Space

Visit a few different law offices and decide what features you like and dislike. An experienced space planner can really make a difference. Though it may be too early to retain a space planner, it's not too early to talk with a few of them and play with your own sketches. While you are at it, look around for furniture. Don't dismiss the option of renting or leasing used office furniture.

Shop Around

By this time, you should know the demographics of your office, how much space you need, and some basics about the structure and amenities you'll require, as well as plans for future space. It's time to shop around. Be prepared to see at least three spaces: one at the high end, one at the low end, and one in the middle. Each will expose you to features you might not have otherwise considered. Take a camera, tape measure, and sketchpad to each potential office space. Take pictures of the front and back of the building, the parking areas, and, of course, the space itself. Sketch its location within the building and take measurements. This will save you a lot of headaches when you get to the next step involving comparison.

Compare Your Options and Negotiate

By this time, you should have decided whether to use a professional broker. When negotiating with a landlord, it's best if you appear to have other options available. The best way to appear as though you have other options is to really have them. Negotiate with more than one landlord at a time, and be prepared to take the best deal offered. Don't forget to look at the terms, not just the price.

Sign the Lease

Before you get to this step, you may have to complete a credit application, and may even need a cosigner or guarantor. This step is going to be scary, and there's no way around it. Take comfort in the fact that you have approached this important decision in a logical manner, designed to ensure you have considered all relevant factors. Be prepared for "lessee's remorse." Similar to "buyer's remorse," its symptoms include excitement, panic, and late-night contract rereads, followed by morning dread.

Schedule Your Move-In

Take care of the computer and telephone systems first. Of course, it will be easier if you can tell the installers where the furniture will be, for proper outlet and telephone jack placement. You'll save money if the network and telephone installers don't have to work around furniture, filing cabinets, and accumulated moving junk.

Send Announcements and Forward Mail

Send announcements to former and existing clients to let them know you have settled in. (At the end of the planning stage, you should have sent them announcements explaining that you were planning a move.) Consider hosting a small reception to show off your new digs.

Audit Your Lease and Invoices

Once you are settled in your new space, attention naturally turns to the actual practice of law. After all, that's why you went through the trouble of leasing space in the first place, right? But wait, there are still some things left to address that can have significant impact upon your law practice's profitability.

Commercial landlords have been known to invoice tenants for more than their pro-rata shares of building expenses. Tenants have discovered services delivered to neighbors included on their invoices. It's not unheard-of for non-negotiated landlord expenses to find their way onto CAM invoices. This is such a widespread problem that an industry has developed to audit leases and occupancy-related invoices. Typically, these auditors have commercial real estate backgrounds. The good ones work on contingency. There are many things you can do to save yourself the trouble and expense of hiring an audit service. Read your lease and make a checklist of expenses for which you are responsible. Compare your invoice with the checklist. Landlords often have slightly different deals negotiated with each tenant, and may not be able to customize their invoices for everyone. Insist upon seeing back-up documents, including the actual bills for items such as electricity, signage, property tax, and janitorial services. Make sure the amount on the invoice matches your correct pro-rata percentage according to the lease.

The Essentials of Office Sharing and Executive Suites

24

Nancy Byerly Jones

Introduction

Office sharing offers many advantages to lawyers and continues to grow in popularity. Much of the credit belongs to soaring rental and purchase costs, as well as to the decrease in suitable space in many localities. Also, many lawyers with healthy incomes prefer office sharing to more conventional setups, as it provides an instant network of lawyers or other professionals (such as accountants or insurance agents). Office sharing provides a "family" of familiar faces each day—something many solos find they miss when going it alone. On the other hand, office sharing has its share of hidden time bombs for lawyers who fail to do their homework before entering such arrangements and for those who refuse to take common-sense precautions while sharing space.

This chapter focuses on smart "must-dos" for office sharing, and on ways to avoid (or defuse) potential time bombs. It is not meant to be all-inclusive; rather, it serves as a starting point and as food for thought. It applies to those who are considering sharing space, as well as to those who already share space and need to conduct a "health check" of their current situations. Finally, this chapter briefly discusses the executive-suite option—sometimes called the instant office—that falls within the office-sharing family. Although traditional office sharing and executive-suite options are two different concepts, they both require that similar safeguards be taken to protect lawyers from the potential hazards of sharing space with folks who are not members or employees of their firms.

You May Want to Consider Office Sharing If . . .

◆ You are on a tight budget.
◆ You are financially stable and healthy and want to be a solo, but not at the cost of sacrificing the chance to be around and network with other lawyers and professionals.
◆ It provides you access to certain equipment or amenities you could not otherwise have (such as a receptionist, a secretary, conference rooms, a more sophisticated telephone system, voice mail, fax and copy machines, a popular and convenient location, and/or traditional or online libraries).
◆ You have unused space that could be rented to bring in additional income.
◆ You want to "test-drive" working around certain folks to determine whether you want to eventually form a firm together.
◆ You need more time to develop your practice before establishing a permanent office home.
◆ It just feels right!

Short "Hot List" of Must-Dos

◆ Have a written office-sharing agreement.
◆ Inform and educate clients.
◆ Avoid partnership-like actions or appearances.
◆ Protect client confidentiality at all times.
◆ Be respectful of others' property and space.

The Written Agreement

This is definitely not the fun part of forming an office-sharing arrangement, but it is an essential element. As with partnership agreements, the office-sharing contract should cover every possible scenario, in addition to the more traditional terms like rent and shared costs. If a potential office mate balks at or makes fun of your efforts to have a written agreement, it should be the only signal you need to run—not walk—from involvement with that person.

As lawyers, we would never advise our clients to enter contractual relationships without documents that clearly and thoroughly set forth all the terms. Why would we demand less for ourselves? We humans can disagree and hit stalemates with one another from time to time, in spite of the best efforts and intentions. It is only wishful thinkers who believe that a shake of the hands is all that's needed. Wouldn't it be nice if our world worked that way? The truth, however, is that it doesn't, and we are fooling ourselves if we think we are unique and that common-sense documentation rules don't apply to us.

Checklist of Agreement Terms (Not Intended as All-Inclusive!)

♦ A strict prohibition against any lawyer representing the shared office as a partnership in any manner—impliedly or otherwise

♦ A requirement that all lawyers carry professional-liability insurance—preferably with the same insurer, the same deductible amount, and the same limits—and that all insurers are appropriately notified of the office-sharing arrangement

♦ A requirement that all parties send to all clients engagement letters that include clear statements regarding the status of their legal entity (that is, sole proprietorship, and not in partnership with others), and that all clients acknowledge their receipt and acknowledgment of their engagement letters by signing and returning duplicate copies to the responsible lawyer

♦ An agreement not to take adversarial positions in a case unless in strict compliance with your jurisdiction's applicable ethical rules and opinions

♦ A statement of the necessity to protect client confidentiality at all times, and a requirement that each lawyer provide an appropriate number of locked file cabinets, install office door locks, and take other similar measures to ensure the confidential safekeeping of client files and property

♦ A clear understanding of what, if any, office equipment is to be shared, who is to provide the equipment, who is responsible for its repair and maintenance, and how the other lawyers will be charged for use of the equipment

♦ A clear understanding of the sharing, if any, of office personnel and all related issues (for example, the establishment of work priorities, the payment of all relevant salaries, a no-nonsense prohibition against any form of sexual harassment, payments for continuing education courses and the like, and the rules and procedures for hiring, training, supervising, and, if necessary, firing office personnel)

♦ An agreement to take full responsibility for informing and training all personal staff members, including temporary help, about how to respond properly to clients' and others' questions so they never give the impression that the lawyers are a partnership

♦ A detailed outline of all financial responsibilities of each individual lawyer and of the group collectively, and of the ramifications if payments are not made on time or as otherwise agreed (for example, interest charge or eviction)

- A plan for sharing traditional and online libraries, conference rooms, and the like (for example, a procedure for reserving conference rooms, and how scheduling conflicts are to be handled)
- A clear understanding of responsibilities regarding day-to-day office maintenance and cleanup
- An acknowledgment that as with all other successful, worthwhile relationships (personal and professional) proper attention, monitoring, and needed adjustments must be given to the office-sharing situation; a further acknowledgment that if problems are ignored for too long, or if relationships are neglected or taken for granted, then relations will deteriorate and potentially cause harm to the lawyers, their practices, their staff members, and their clients
- A mechanism for breaking "ties" when there are only two lawyers or when an equal number of the participants hold opposite opinions when trying to reach decisions that must be jointly made
- An acknowledgment that if the participating lawyers make client referrals to one another (perhaps because cases are outside one's area of expertise, or one has a heavy caseload), there is an inherent risk that the referral will result in some clients liking the other lawyer so well that they decide to retain him or her for all future legal work
- An agreement regarding how to handle matters if the foregoing situation occurs (for example, the other lawyer refuses to accept new legal matters from the client after the close of the referred case, or the referring lawyer agrees to accept the client's choice graciously and without any resentment)
- Provisions clearly stating the duration of the agreement, as well as renewal options, if any
- An agreement about what, if any, input each party will have in selecting future new office mates
- The terms for handling dissolution of the office-sharing arrangement (for example, the amount of advance written notice required by each party to the agreement, the manner of dividing or compensating for shared equipment, a decision about whether the departing office mate or the landlord/owner has responsibility for finding a substitute tenant, and the decision about whether to use mandatory mediation or arbitration when agreement cannot be reached on certain issues)

Informing and Educating Clients

All clients should be informed at their initial consultation—whether in person or by phone—that the lawyer is not in partnership, or any other kind of law firm relationship, with the other lawyers in the office. Likewise, engagement letters should include a clear statement regarding the legal structure of the lawyer's practice setting (that is, sole proprietorship). Clients should be reminded not to leave confidential materials or messages with anyone but their own lawyer and others who work for their lawyer. These types of reminders should be repeated often to remind clients of their shared responsibility in helping protect their confidential information.

Whenever two or more lawyers in the office work on a case together, their clients' permission should be received before any work is commenced on the case. Additionally, all clients should be clearly informed in writing of how the responsibilities for the case will be divided between or among the lawyers. Clients should be instructed to make separate payments to the individual lawyers as itemized for them on their statements. It is also important to check the requirements and prohibitions of any other applicable ethical rules in your jurisdiction regarding joint representation by associated counsel.

Clients should be informed immediately when their lawyer moves to a different office and should be given the new phone and fax numbers, mailing address, street address, and directions to the new location. If the lawyer has moved into another office-sharing situation, another letter should be sent to all clients informing them that this new relationship is not a partnership (see above) and explaining all confidentiality safeguards they should take.

Avoiding the Appearance of a Partnership

Ethical and common-sense precautions should be taken to ensure that the public is not misled into thinking the lawyers are a partnership or any other form of a corporate or similar entity. There are some lawyers who don't mind giving the impression that they are in partnership with their office-sharing peers. They perhaps are just sloppy when it comes to preventive practices. Or, they may think it gives them more prestige or gives outsiders the impression that they are part of a larger firm. Such tactics, however, can backfire on lawyers in many ways, including being named as a defendant in a malpractice action because of the negligence of their alleged "partner." The bottom line: A lawyer should never do anything that tends to indicate that a partnership exists—and any lawyer who does shouldn't be surprised when those same habits and actions are used by a good plaintiff's lawyer to prove a partnership existed and, therefore, so does joint-and-several liability!

Some of the precautions to be taken include the following:

- ◆ Outdoor signs that clearly delineate separate lawyer offices (for example, one sign for lawyer John Doe—"Law Office of John Doe, Attorney at Law"—and another sign for the office-sharing lawyer, Jane Smith—"Law Office of Jane Smith, Attorney at Law")

- Organization of interior space to emphasize separate offices
- Separate telephone lines, answered not as, "Law Offices," but as, "Law Office of John Doe"
- Separate filing systems not accessible to anyone but the responsible lawyer and his or her staff
- Colored-coded files, if sharing staff, to minimize erroneous filings and confidentiality problems
- Proper training and supervision of staff to ensure they do not say or do things that imply a partnership exists
- Rules that prevent entering closed doors without knocking first, and other rules that minimize the appearance of inadequate safeguards to protect confidentiality in the presence of clients and other visitors (for example, overheard discussion between lawyers regarding their cases)
- Separate mail and fax reception procedures, and precautionary measures regarding shared copier or fax machines to protect client confidentiality
- Client engagement agreements that inform clients of the solo status of their lawyer
- An office-sharing agreement signed by all parties, acknowledging and agreeing to the terms of the arrangement, including how each lawyer will take steps to ensure the group is not perceived as a partnership

Executive Suites

The renting of an executive suite (often called the instant office) is an ideal arrangement for many lawyers, such as those working out of their homes primarily, traveling lawyers who need temporary space, or lawyers considering opening a branch office in the area after a trial period. Executive suites can be found in all major cities, and in many smaller communities as well.

Most office-sharing professionals must be responsible for furnishing, equipping, and staffing their offices. Executive suites, on the other hand, do not require large capital investments and often come completely equipped, furnished, and staffed. In addition, some executive-suite operations have an impressive array of amenities for their tenants, such as discounted car rental and hotel rates, courier services, language interpreters, insurance options, Web site design and monitoring services, publication services, and videoconferencing.

In addition to the suggestions discussed above, some other questions to ask when considering an executive-suite and/or office-sharing arrangement include the following:

- What kind of turnover rate does the group have with staff members?
- Who supervises and trains the staff?
- Does the receptionist answer the phone and greet outsiders in a professional and courteous manner?
- How soundproof are the offices and conference areas?
- What do prior tenants say about the facility, its owners and occupants, and other matters? (Get references.)
- Does the Better Business Bureau have any former or pending complaints against the service provider?
- What kind of security is offered, both for tenants and for valuables left overnight?
- Is the parking adequate, safe, and close by?
- What kind of impression will the facilities and outside grounds make on clients?
- Is there adequate handicap access both into and within the building?
- What type of external signage is available, if any?
- How are complaints and repairs handled in terms of responsiveness and timeliness?

Conclusion

Renting an executive suite offers many advantages, including financial savings, overall convenience, and no setup worries. Likewise, office sharing helps keep expenses down, as well as giving a lawyer the option of outfitting and decorating his or her personal office space (within, of course, the limits of any terms of the office-sharing agreement).

Both arrangements open many options for lawyers, but, like anything else, it is critical to do your homework before obligating yourself to either situation. If time permits, you would be wise to conduct a thorough investigation of all possible options in addition to office sharing or renting an executive suite (such as creating a home office, or purchasing an office condominium). Besides giving thoughtful consideration to these and other issues discussed in this chapter, it is perhaps even more important to ask yourself the following questions:

- How flexible am I?
- Am I really good at sharing?
- Do I function well within a group, or do groups frustrate and annoy me?
- Will I want to "hog" any shared staff members or equipment?
- Do I handle conflict situations in a positive and constructive manner, or do I tend to brood over things without searching for or initiating a productive resolution?

- Am I willing to practice "safe" office sharing, or will I sport a "Don't bother me with that stuff" attitude when it comes to creating and signing an office-sharing agreement, reviewing any applicable ethics rules and opinions, or taking the necessary extra steps to ensure client confidentiality is protected?
- Given my manner and all my personal and office habits—the good, the bad, and the ugly—would I be a good office-sharing candidate? Why?

If you decide that office sharing is the best option for you and your office, then do all your homework, dot all the "i"s and cross all the "t"s, and enjoy the experience. With the right preparation and attitude, it can be one of the most enjoyable experiences in your professional career. Office sharing brings with it the chance to create mutually beneficial, loyal, and supportive networks, the opportunity to learn from others, and the financial savings that result when sharing expenses. Done right, office sharing offers all these benefits while allowing sole practitioners to maintain the independence they so highly value.

Designing Your Law Office

25

Jon S. Schultz
Suzette S. Schultz

Introduction

The design of your office could seem like the least of your worries as you establish your practice. But viewing your office as a marketing tool and as something that can make you more profitable, the extra thought you give it in this early stage will reward you for as long as you stay there.

Solo-practice spaces vary widely. Some lawyers have highly elegant and technologically advanced offices, while others avoid standard offices and make house calls, keep records in closets at home, and use laptop computers. It is a daunting task to cover such a wide range in a single chapter; after giving it some thought, we have decided to accomplish it in the following way.

We will share some thoughts on how to find and work with the best design professionals. But that is only a starting point, because most solo budgets will never have a nickel for the best designer in town. Nevertheless, we ask you to bear with us briefly, because careful use of a good law firm designer can save plenty of money in building costs, square-footage requirements, operating costs, and your own billable time. As we progress through the chapter and discuss how to work with the professionals, we will show you why they do some things and how you can take advantage of some of their techniques. Making use of whatever level of professional support you can afford (including none), you can get more for your money by using these same techniques. In any case, the chapter will help you get the most out of your investment.

Even if you have little concern for aesthetics, you can be sure that others will. Your business plan needs an abiding concern for the effect of aesthetics on client attitudes and the attitudes of others who can help you generate clients through referrals or other means. Perhaps even more important, your office and its contents are one of the front-end costs likely to send you searching for start-up financing. Though efficiency and cost control have become the primary watchwords for law office design, we must add the idea of service to the client, which creates even more design plan issues. For example, clients increasingly require advanced technological capabilities of their lawyers, and this affects the office plan. As another example, solo lawyers increasingly split time among multiple workplaces, such as home offices and one or more shared offices or conference facilities that are more convenient for their clientele. The types of issues that are important to a prospective lender are the ones that provide our starting point.

Your Space Plan as Part of Your Business Plan

Like any other business, yours needs a written business plan, and a major part of your business plan is the home for your practice. You can get help in establishing your planning budget by talking with design professionals, and the same people can help you determine whether your construction budget is realistic. Contractors and prospective landlords can also help with initial estimates for the construction budget. Because your office space is typically your second-biggest expense, it would be a serious mistake to shortchange this opportunity to boost your marketing, your efficiency, and your bottom line. Though you have plenty of people to satisfy with your planning efforts (such as lenders and guarantors, building inspectors, code inspectors, subdivision committees, safety and environmental regulators, utility companies, the post office, and your spouse), your own satisfaction is what counts. The plan must help your practice prosper and serve the needs of your clients. Give your review the rigor it deserves.

The Contents of a Plan

Planning implies thinking before doing. For projects ranging from simple room renovations to multistory, high-rise law offices, the planning effort produces two products: (1) drawings or graphic representations, and (2) specifications (a list of requirements for construction). A plan and its specifications provide the information necessary for someone to estimate construction and furnishing costs with acceptable accuracy. The plan has a continuing life, as it becomes the document by which the project must be constructed and, for future maintenance, repairs, and construction, it provides a record of what is behind those walls.

Planning begins with asking questions about what your practice needs and what you would consider purchasing. The programming phase produces the data you need to shop for your office space. In this phase, checklists and interviews are used to help the space planner learn which features are important, what activities will take place in the space, and which of those activities must be adjacent to others. The investigation explores room capacity and mechanical requirements, as well as priorities for convenience, status, privacy, and support facilities.

Armed with an analysis of the data collected from these exercises, a space planner can compile a design program. The program may look like a collection of one-page briefs on each of the necessary rooms and spaces, showing the requirements for square footage, adjacency, electricity, heating, air conditioning, lighting, equipment, and storage, as well as other factors such as security, privacy, and accessibility that affect the drawings and specifications. The program guides the designer with the job of preparing alternative designs and specifications to fit an available space or new location. At the very least, you should write your requirements for each of these features as you consider each room. The following checklist should help you think about spaces and features for the design program:

- Number and size of lawyer offices
- Number and size of paralegal offices
- Number and size of secretarial stations
- Space for office administrator or other support staff
- Conference room seating, facilities, and amenities
- Reception area seating—number of seats and receptionist station
- Project workrooms (case or war rooms)
- Administrative area (service center)
  - spaces for copying, incoming and outgoing mail, fax
  - expressage
  - printing and scanning
  - binding
  - deliveries and runners
  - office supplies and storage
- Filing
  - centralized or decentralized
- Library and office bookshelves, library work areas
- Technology
  - file server
  - telephone system
  - security system

- ◆ audiovisual equipment
- ◆ audio teleconferencing
- ◆ video teleconferencing
- ◆ technology support staff
- ◆ Accounting
  - ◆ in-house or outsourced
- ◆ Storage
  - ◆ coats
  - ◆ exhibits
  - ◆ evidence
- ◆ Food service
  - ◆ no sink
  - ◆ sink with cold water
  - ◆ sink with hot and cold water (requires hot-water heater)
  - ◆ under-counter refrigerator
  - ◆ under-counter refrigerator with freezer
  - ◆ under-counter refrigerator with freezer and ice maker
  - ◆ full-size refrigerator with freezer and ice maker
  - ◆ microwave
  - ◆ under-counter ice maker
  - ◆ coffeemaker
  - ◆ dishwasher
  - ◆ water-purification system
  - ◆ water cooler, bottled water
  - ◆ water cooler, direct plumbed
  - ◆ toaster
  - ◆ toaster oven
  - ◆ vending machines—beverages
  - ◆ vending machines—snacks
  - ◆ space for table and chairs in coffee area
  - ◆ space for canned drinks
  - ◆ space for bottled water

Involving a Space-Planning Professional

Will you be working with a design professional? Here are a few reasons why you might consider it. In many cases, design professionals can save you the cost of their fees by freeing your own billable time. Some landlords have designers or architectural firms that can assist you. One word of caution about using a landlord's design professional: he or she is there to do only one job for you. Because the design professional looks to the landlord for more work, he or she will try to please the landlord before trying to please you. You can also bring your own independent designer and negotiate to have the landlord pay all or part of the fees. It may be money well spent to use a little cash from your own pocket to accomplish this. Your designer can also coordinate with the contractors working in your space to save you valuable billing time.

Hiring a design professional can be much like hiring a lawyer, an accountant, or other professional. You need up-front talk about fees. There are plenty of competent people available. Just the same, you will save time and design costs if you find someone who has designed other law firm offices. Check the designer's references and ask to see comparable law firms the designer has done.

You will have the opportunity to work with architects, interior designers, or interior decorators. Most law firm renovation involves the services of either an architect or an interior designer. Architects are licensed to design building structural systems as well as interior components, while interior designers limit their services to the design and construction of the space within the building envelope. For commercial buildings that house law offices, both architects and interior designers sometimes retain structural engineers (for advice on the building's structural integrity and floor loading), mechanical engineers (for help with the design and specification of heating, air conditioning, and plumbing systems), and electrical engineers (for the specification of electrical systems). Architectural firms often have interior designers on their staffs, and many interior design firms employ architects. Architects, designers, and interior decorators all provide consulting on the aesthetics of a space—such as fabrics, finishes, accessories, and furniture—but the practice of interior decorators is limited to these areas. Many interior decorators are affiliated with furniture stores or other vendors. Typical billing arrangements for architects and interior designers are hourly rates or fixed fees. Commissions on recommended items often augment interior decorators' fees. The net cost of decorators' services may not be evident, because furniture and decorative materials often have multiple discount pricing tiers.

Finding a design professional is much like finding a lawyer, with the delightful exception that a law office stands as tangible evidence of the quality of the designer's product. Look at plenty of law offices. The more law offices you see, the better idea you will have of the capabilities of various design practitioners. Lawyers and other people who work in their offices are seldom secretive about who designed their offices. They may be quick to point out good and bad features. If you find an office you like, consider interviewing its designer. National professional associations such as the American Institute of Architects (AIA) and the American Society for Interior Design (ASID) and their local counterparts maintain listings on Web sites, and this may yield some candidates. You will avoid much frustration if you can find a designer who has design experience with other law firm projects. This will shorten the designer's learning curve and let you learn from your designer. Unless you want your office to look like Aunt Minnie's parlor . . .

Design professionals divide their work into two kinds: commercial and residential. Some do both, but the kind you want for your law office is commercial. In addition to the commercial design practitioner's professional background in dealing with regulatory matters like Americans with Disability Act (ADA) provisions and commercial building codes, the design product is likely to be more responsive to your professional needs. And, as tempting as it is to do your own design work, do not forget that professional designers will save your personal time, which can be put to better use as billable time.

The Focus of Your Practice Reflected in Your Plan

Beyond the budgeting aspects of your office, your business plan should reflect your choice of the home for your practice. And beyond the bare respectability that makes an office appear professional, your office design should target the areas that support your clients' expectations of their legal counsel. From the all-important reception area, where clients sit and soak up information about you and your firm before they meet with you, to the conference space and your office, take care to make the spaces reflect your plan in a most professional way.

What image do you aim to create? The focus of your practice should have a profound effect on your planning. Do not be tied to trite images of a law firm or lawyers' offices with traditional furniture in dark wood tones with wild-duck prints on the walls. Most of the larger, successful firms do not portray that style in their designs and furnishings. Think outside the box. Some firms prefer a fresher image that appeals to a younger generation. Your approach to technology may be used to advantage, but keep in mind that the state of the art changes quickly, and you need to avoid showcasing anything that might seem outmoded.

Who are your clients? They need to be comfortable with the professionals whose advice and representation determine their own success or failure. High-technology corporate clients might appreciate a clean, modern look that shows off your savvy and active style of lawyering, while estate planning clients might desire an atmosphere of personal support and confidentiality. A general practice should have good-quality furnishings in public areas and a look of uncluttered competence. While your office may reflect your personality and provide indicia of your stability, your qualifications, and perhaps your outside interests, keep in mind the variety of people who come into a solo law office for advice and services. Accordingly, we hope you will analyze your potential clientele carefully before you include your taxidermist in your office planning.

Who will refer clients to you? The same issues apply, and you will not have the opportunity to know when someone did *not* feel comfortable referring a client to you.

The real estate watchwords—location, location, location—certainly apply in the sense of convenience for clients, but a solo lawyer can also provide the advantage of flexibility by having meetings at clients' offices or other convenient locations. Continued rapid development of handheld communication technology and wireless networks will increasingly give mobile lawyers the ability to work conveniently in multiple places. Consider the possible combinations—ranging from a home office from which a lawyer makes house calls to multiple shared-office suites, obtained through borrowing, leasing, or temporarily renting "on call." Larger firms are increasingly adopting "hoteling" office arrangements, whereby office space is shared by lawyers from the firm's other locations when they are in town. It may be possible to arrange to borrow space from larger firms.

The location of your office should depend upon the demographics of your practice. Do you want to be near your clients? Do you want to go to them, or do you want them to come to you? Do you want to be close to a courthouse? Do you want to be downtown? Do you want to be in the suburbs? It's all a function of where you see your practice. In most places, downtown space is more expensive than suburban space, but this is not true for every city.

For prestige and quality factors, office buildings in some areas are categorized as Class A, B, or C. Classification follows no uniform system, but is derived from a combination of physical aspects of the building and its location. Class A buildings are generally the best buildings in a given area. They are well located, with excellent access, and have the best tenants, building materials, and management. In most cities, a Class A building will be one of the best high-rise buildings, though high-rise buildings can be classified as Class A, B, or C. Rental rates follow the A, B, and C classification as well.

Finding and Securing an Office Space

Home offices to high-rise buildings—all can house a solo practice. Your office may be your second-largest cost item, but it can also be a capital expenditure and an investment in the future of your firm. The most basic decisions about your office require you to determine how you want to allocate your time and money. If you are not overwhelmed with work, you might be able to afford the time necessary to build your office or to buy and renovate an older structure. In any case, you should avoid underestimating the time these ventures require. When you lease office space, you have the luxury of avoiding tax, security, and day-to-day maintenance issues, as well as the time commitment for managing a building. You do *not* avoid the cost of those things, but you gain predictability of some major operational expenses.

Finding and securing an office space takes longer than most realize. Our advice is to start early—a minimum of six months before you expect to occupy the space, but preferably longer. If you have an existing lease, you should start looking for new space at least a year before the lease expires.

If you are thinking about leasing or renting office space, you generally have two ways to go about it. You can do the legwork yourself, or you can engage a broker. The landlord, not the tenant, pays the broker's fees. Brokers typically get 4.5 percent of every dime that you pay over the life of the lease. They know their areas, and they can advise you about current rental rates.

You should always have alternative office spaces from which to choose. Never negotiate with only one landlord. You should have at least three options, so that you can leverage one against the other in negotiations.

You will find that most landlords have diagrams or floor plans of available space. If not, feel free to take a tape measure and a notebook and sketch the dimensions. You may also find a camera or video recorder helpful in remembering some of the details; when you look at multiple spaces, they tend to run together.

Most landlords will offer a free "test fit" before signing a lease. This gives you an opportunity to compare buildings. You provide your project requirements and the landlord has a design professional do a quick plan to see how the space would lay out under your program. If the landlord does not provide this service, you can try doing it on your own. Later in this chapter, we provide some plans and diagrams of typical layouts that you might find helpful.

Lease Arrangements and Negotiations

You may not be familiar with leasing terms such as rentable square footage and usable square footage. Usable square footage is the actual square footage of the space; if you are a full-floor tenant, this includes the square footage in areas such as the restrooms and mechanical rooms. Usable square footage is generally considered to be anything that is not a vertical penetration, such as a fire stair, a mechanical shaft, or an elevator shaft.

Rentable square footage is greater than usable square footage because it includes an add-on factor. The add-on factor differs with every building, depending upon the efficiency of the building. Rentable square footage includes your pro-rata share of common areas, such as elevator lobbies and corridors if you are located on a multitenant floor. The typical add-on can be anywhere from 10 percent to 25 percent.

Rental rates may incorporate your build-out cost. One way this is achieved is to roll construction costs into the cost of rent, which could substantially raise the amount of rent if it were prorated over the life of the lease. You can also negotiate to have a certain portion of the build-out incorporated into the lease (and, therefore, the rent), or, for example, you can negotiate and agree that the landlord will pay for everything up to $30 per square foot, and you will pay for everything above $30 per square foot.

Look at the space you are considering, and determine the absolute minimum renovation or modification you can live with. Remember that renovations affect your rental rate and the length of your lease. The renovations are also important matters for negotiation before the lease is signed.

The document containing your agreement with the landlord about building improvements, renovation, and physical conditions that you receive in exchange for your lease payments is called a work letter. Work letter negotiation is a major part of larger construction contracts. Many office buildings establish a standard set of improvements, providing a rather Spartan build-out that is generally not suitable for public areas of law offices. Negotiation of terms for the lease and work letter often begin from the standard improvements, which might include the following:

- ◆ Build-out costs for items above the ceiling—including standard light fixtures, ceiling grid and tiles, sprinklers, and mechanical work—paid by the landlord
- ◆ Longer hours, perhaps 7:00 a.m. to 7:00 p.m. and Saturdays, for air conditioning
- ◆ Free power and HVAC (heating and air conditioning) during the build-out
- ◆ Free use of the freight elevator and loading dock
- ◆ Contiguous expansion space for your offices
- ◆ Guarantee of a maintained interior temperature range during specific extreme temperatures in hot or cold weather
- ◆ ADA-compliant building, from the parking lot to your office front door, provided by the landlord
- ◆ Sound and heat insulation for all walls, with walls between tenants to go to the structure above the ceiling
- ◆ Refurbishment (typically new paint and carpet) provided by the landlord if you renew the lease
- ◆ Janitorial services five days a week
- ◆ Signage style and location
- ◆ No landlord fee on build-out costs
- ◆ Determination of who pays for utilities

Negotiate your lease to provide flexibility for the future of your practice. If your practice is successful, your needs will be quite different than if business is less than you planned. Moving is usually more costly, disruptive, and inconvenient than you think it will be, so consider negotiating optional extensions to your lease.

External Requirements and Limitations

Your project will be subject to zoning and deed restrictions, building codes, and your landlord's requirements. Zoning ordinances may include historic zoning, which in some cases can create financial incentives for the renovation of distinctive buildings. Minimum parking requirements must be considered. As you check your municipal codes and ordinances, you may be referred to a specific edition of the new international building codes from the International Code Council. Widespread recent adoption of these codes has produced significant changes as they replace other standard building codes that have been in place for decades. For all except the most minimal work (like painting and carpeting) on your space, building permits are required in most cities and towns. Permits and inspections are required for most of the regulated trades as well.

Insurance carriers impose important limitations on the use of space. For example, owners of buildings that are insured as residential space may not be able or willing to insure part of the building as office space. Other insurance policy limitations may set requirements on alteration, occupancy, or use of buildings because of their location in areas prone to floods, earthquakes, or storms.

Your landlord's requirements and limitations for use of the space will be spelled out in the lease you negotiate and in the work letter. The limitations will relate to a broad range of construction themes, such as occupancy, availability of the building to your contractors, utilities, insurance and indemnity, signage, cooperation among contractors and subcontractors, and cooperation and consent of the landlord.

Reusing Space

Whenever you contemplate moving your offices into a building, you consider whether your budget allows you to (1) gut and rebuild the space, (2) modify the existing space to support your needs, or (3) use the space without modification.

Demolition and rebuilding of office space is costly because unseen conditions from prior work often cause delays and changes in the job. Asbestos abatement and quirks in building mechanical systems are notorious examples. However, rebuilding is frequently the only way to make the available space look right and serve the needs of your office.

A solo law office is not a very big job for most contractors, and most of the bigger and more prestigious contractors are not willing to bid on smaller jobs. And because you may not appear to be a prospect for repeat business, your office may be considerably less important to the contractor than it is to you. Select your general contractor carefully, and make sure the contractor has enough available time, personnel, and resources to get your job done right and on schedule. The horror stories you have heard about subcontractors who don't show up for work are probably true; your contractor must have a good list of extra subcontractors to call upon when this sort of thing happens.

The working drawings that accompany every building project are not only for the contractor. They provide an important opportunity for you to keep on top of the project at all stages. To prevent the designers of your project from taking it in a wrong direction before the plans are completed, ask your designer for a 50 percent review set. Review the plans carefully, looking for changes that can be made before other work is done. Also review the plans carefully when they are 100 percent complete.

In most cases, you need to have a mechanical, electrical, and plumbing (MEP) engineering firm provide drawings and specifications to receive a building permit. The same thing can be done in a less expensive way if the MEP subcontractors have licensed engineers on staff who can do the drawings. However, the absence of a system of checks and balances can cause a conflict of interest; for example, this might occur if only one electrician does the building and designing, or one mechanical engineer does the designing and his crew does the building. An independent engineer is likely to design the correct way and not try to cut corners.

Minor Modifications: How Many Lawyers Does It Take to Change a Light Fixture?

Minor modifications can provide an effective and economical treatment for many spaces. Minor modifications are the ones a do-it-yourselfer can do with a bit of instruction from the home-building store or from the wide selection of available books and Internet sites. Painting, changing the flooring, refinishing the floor, and changing light fixtures, door hardware, and window treatments are all simple things that most of us can do with a review of safety procedures and some advice on materials.

We have a few discouraging words about the prospects for doing minor construction yourself. Most lawyers rent the space their practice occupies. Renting and leasing infuse the strong interest of a landlord into the life of your law practice. In addition to the limitations of a lease's general tenancy terms, the landlord must limit the tenant's activities to protect itself against liability claims. Whether the landlord's insurance carrier requires it or the landlord simply wants to avoid potential liability, most leases do not permit the tenant to perform the construction necessary to turn a space into a law office. Do-it-yourself law office construction is the exception, rather than the rule. After all, what landlord wants to risk having work done by somebody who might damage the building and endanger other tenants?

Of course, there are exceptions, and smaller commercial properties and residential conversions are more likely to have fewer limitations in the leases. Among the many advantages of owning your own building is the flexibility it affords for building your office using a sensibly planned combination of your own work and that of specialists in the building trades. In any case, you should protect yourself with appropriate insurance coverage. If you build an office in the home you own, be aware of any zoning and building regulations, homeowner association rules, and subdivision architectural committee requirements.

Many easy-to-find Internet sites provide instructions for specific renovation tasks. A standard source for finding materials, equipment, and fixtures for your building projects is **www.sweets.com**.

Using the space "as is" can be an economical solution to your needs. To get the most advantage from paying for little or no renovation, be sure you do not take too much space. Touch-ups and extra cleaning for floors and walls are good investments. Keep your clients' first impressions in mind. The entrance to your space should be as attractive as you can make it, and that includes door hardware and finish, signage, and lighting.

Advice on Spaces and Layouts

The generally accepted standard space requirements for lawyers' offices have been shrinking over the past two decades. More lawyers are meeting with clients and opposing counsel in conference rooms, not their offices. The average-sized partner and associate offices are 15' x 15' and 10' x 15', respectively, assuming the building is built on a 5' module or grid. This module measurement is the distance between the perimeter window mullions. Why, you ask? In some cases, partitions that demise offices must terminate at window mullions, so partners have three mullions and associates have two.

Most large office buildings are designed with a heating and air-conditioning zone that extends approximately fifteen feet from the window wall of the building, providing the fifteen-foot depth of offices. Fifteen feet is also a dimension that works well with most furniture layouts, so the trend in larger law firms extends readily to others. In large and small firms, paralegal offices are typically determined by resultant space after lawyer offices are designed.

Ever since we started using personal computers heavily, the traditional combination of a desk and a credenza has become less efficient. For most lawyers, a "C"-shaped workspace is probably the most user-friendly and flexible arrangement, especially for using a notebook or personal computer. Fortunately, computer machinery has become more compact.

Secretarial stations typically have two to three work surfaces in "L" or "C" configurations. They should have storage space for files, binders, reference books, and other small items. A typical station has two-box file pedestals and space for a shared printer and paper storage. Somewhere in the office's service center, you should consider having a typewriter station for completing hard-copy forms. A typical secretarial station covers about sixty to seventy square feet.

For a sole practitioner—who of necessity is the management committee, head of the litigation section, and inside counsel to the firm—clutter happens. For this reason and others, we recommend a conference room for meetings with clients and other lawyers. A conference room can be kept presentable more easily than your office. A well-furnished, small conference room can double as a library or an overflow waiting area, and it allows you to reduce space requirements for your office. A useful variation is to separate the office from the conference room with double doors so the two can be combined for large meetings. Be sure to have plenty of clearance for chairs around the conference table; five feet from the edge of the table to the wall is standard practice.

A solo practice or a very small firm is a microcosm of a large firm in its needs for support activities. This includes an area for administrative items such as copying, faxing, scanning, mail deliveries, and expressage. Carefully consider your coffee service area and related facilities. Most offices can get by with the minimum of bottled water, a small refrigerator, and a microwave oven, as these do not require plumbing. Plumbing for commercial buildings is expensive. A small coffee bar adds a minimum of approximately $10,000 to costs for the space.

Other support areas include filing areas and library facilities. Filing needs vary widely from one office to the next. Though formal library spaces have shrunk to zero in many law offices, bookshelves and administrative functions for handling printed information should remain part of your planning.

We have a top-ten list of mistakes often made in planning, but the following six really stand out:

1. Taking more space than needed. (Your lease negotiations should include options for expanding your office into contiguous space within the building.)
2. Not taking advantage of vertical space. (Consider all the underutilized wall space and use it to store files, books, and notebooks. Space is expensive.)
3. Forgetting to plan for storage areas.

4. Not negotiating for contiguous expansion options.
5. Not negotiating to have the thermostat installed in your offices rather than in a neighbor's office.
6. Not negotiating for some less-expensive space in the building, such as the basement, for storage of inactive files.

Furniture: New, Used, Refurbished, Rented

Furniture is readily available in new, used, or refurbished condition, and can also be rented. Your design professional should know about sources for each.

For new furniture, never pay the full "list" price. You should expect to get it for about 70 percent of the catalog list price. Most office furniture dealers will not show you price lists; your job is to shop around and compare price and quality. In furniture stores, however, you should expect to pay the full sticker price.

For the start-up firm, the most economical route is to purchase good-quality, used office furniture. The used-furniture market is saturated, due to high turnover in the corporate community in the last decade. It pays to shop around. Larger cities have the best sources, and there's always eBay. Refurbished furniture can provide a wonderful result for the money, especially if you can select high-quality, classic pieces from good manufacturers. Avoid residential furniture. Your conference room should not look like a dining room.

Rental furniture can be expensive, but if that's your only alternative, try negotiating price and terms with the supplier. Before negotiating, you need a realistic plan of how long a rental term is required. This affects the monthly charge drastically. Also consider the lease-to-purchase option. Be aware that rental furniture is usually not the best, or even medium-grade, quality.

The Move

Moving into your first solo office can be your easiest move ever, but when you already have clients and pending matters and need to make a smooth transition from one office to another, you need a good plan.

Develop a list of all items to be moved to the new space. Determine with your new and existing landlords when freight elevators and freight docks can be reserved or scheduled. If these are not applicable, determine when and how the moving van(s) can gain access to the existing space and the new space. The "how" and "when" can greatly affect the cost of the move. When interviewing movers, be sure to show them the loading dock or point where they can stage their trucks, and tell them the situation with freight elevators or stairs. Make them responsible for determining which of their trucks will fit into the loading docks at both the existing building and the new space.

In an intrastate move, movers work on an estimated hourly basis. They will also come and estimate weights of all items to be moved. Carefully compare these estimates. Have the movers provide with their estimates a preliminary schedule of the sequencing of items to be moved.

Movers must also provide adequate means of vertical and horizontal protection to both existing and new facilities. Before they remove items from the existing space, walk through the space and mutually agree upon areas of existing damage. Do the same at the new space. The movers must be held responsible for damage to the existing space, new space, and items moved, as well as their path of travel from their trucks to the intended space. This means one-quarter-inch Masonite board on the floors when required by the landlord or you. Also, vertical protection is needed at all points of entry, corners, doorframes, and other sensitive architectural or furniture features. Determine who will move the electronic and technological equipment. Also, confirm who will guarantee that the equipment will function properly after the move.

Work closely with utility companies and your computer advisors to ensure a seamless transition from your former office to the new one. Library books need to be moved and reinstalled in sequential order, although, in practice, this need is rarely met.

To make your transition as painless as possible, work with the moving company and develop a detailed plan for the move. For example, using the floor plan of the new space, identify offices, secretarial spaces, storage areas, file cabinets, libraries, and other areas, and assign simple designators to each space. Offices are labeled or numbered on the floor plan. Correspondingly label the actual physical space: for example, for Office A on the floor plan, tape a large "A" on the actual doorjamb. Furniture, pictures, plants, boxes, and other items destined for Office A also receive large labels, such as 1-A, 2-A, and so on. Your premove inventory may identify 1-A as a potted ficus tree, but the movers only need to know that 1-A goes into the office labeled "A." You can further refine the outcome of the move by making a sketch of where furniture, plants, and other items are to be placed in Office A. The less you have to reposition major elements after the movers leave the premises, the better.

The Process Checklist

Putting it all together, the following checklist offers our suggestions for coordinating planning, construction, and quality control.

1. Write your business plan.
2. Determine the technology to be used, as this affects the amount of space you need:
   - copier(s)
   - personal computers (including laptops and docking stations)

- printer(s)
- scanner and fax
- file server
- telephone system
- UPS systems for uninterrupted power supply
- Internet service provider
- network
- security system
- after-hours or independent heating and air-conditioning systems

3. Write a program for space requirements:
   - number and size of lawyer offices
   - number and size of paralegal offices
   - number and size of secretarial stations
   - conference room seating, facilities, and amenities
   - reception area seating—number of seats and receptionist station
   - project workrooms
   - administrative area (service center)
     - copy, mail, and fax; receiving and outgoing
     - expressage
     - printing and scanning
     - binding
     - deliveries and runners
   - filing—centralized or decentralized
   - accounting—in-house or outsourced
   - coffee area
   - storage
   - library
   - technology needs

4. Find space options (hopefully, you will have three).
5. Negotiate with prospective buildings.
6. Get landlords to do free "test fits" to see which building works best and is most efficient.
7. Negotiate lease with selected building.
8. Have final plans prepared.
9. Review drawings; making changes now will be much less expensive than after construction starts.
10. Get multiple bids.
11. Award contracts; receive construction schedule from contractor and begin construction.
12. Coordinate owner-provided items; be sure voice and data cabling are pulled at appropriate time *during* construction.

13. Start shopping for furniture. (Actually, this can occur much earlier, in case you find a color scheme you like that can influence the carpet and wall-color selections. Take preliminary space plans with you, so you know the furniture will fit the space.)

14. Schedule weekly meetings with contractor and landlord to review work, progress, and construction schedule; make them demonstrate each week that they are on schedule.

15. Establish delivery dates and times with any vendors delivering or installing owner-furnished items, such as the following:
    - telephone system
    - computer-related equipment
    - furniture
    - copiers and fax machines
    - movers
    - signage

    These items are typically delivered after construction is complete. However, delivery times must be established far in advance. Also, check with the landlord to see if freight elevators must be reserved.

16. Conduct walk-through with punch list. (When construction is complete and the space has had its final cleaning, walk through it with the contractor and discuss the items on your punch list. This is a written list that documents any items that were not satisfactorily done and need to be corrected, such as lack of paint coverage, damaged ceiling tiles, or marred walls, doors, or frames. Document items room by room. The contractor should repair these items before you move in. If time does not permit this, allow the contractor to do it afterward. You can negotiate coverage of move-in damage at no extra cost.)

17. Plan for the move in detail:
    - Inventory your existing furniture and label what goes to the new space and what stays.
    - Using the new floor plan, label all new spaces.
    - Label furniture, accessories, and boxes with destination labels that correspond to the new space identifiers you've temporarily put in place.
    - Explain the plan to the movers before they begin.
    - Have a few people in the new space to oversee and help the movers place items in the correct locations.

Setting Up an Efficient Home Office* 26

Diane L. Drain

The master in the art of living draws no sharp distinction between his labor and his leisure, his mind and his body, his work and his play, his education and his recreation.

He hardly knows which.

He simply pursues his vision of excellence through whatever he is doing and leaves others to determine whether he is working or playing.

To himself, he is always doing both.

Michael Scott Karpovich

In 1990, I began to reevaluate the basic principles I was using in practicing law. During that evaluation period, I realized that I had adopted a style of practice I did not respect. I also came to the recognition that I had long ago abandoned my family and community. I worked long hours for clients I never met, mass-produced documents for land developers I did not respect, and was responsible for multimillion-dollar construction projects I never saw. I was responsible for overseeing other lawyers and staff members—people I really did not know. I did not know much about their personal lives, nor did I know whether they liked their work. Firm rules strictly prohibited mingling with staff and other lawyers not on the same floor or not in the same department. The firm's method of billing for services (the billable hour) created so much in-house competition that the office atmosphere was similar to a series of small, warring camps, rather than a large unified body focused upon producing the best legal work for the firm's clients. I talked to others from my law school class and found that most were having similar problems; the size of the firm did not seem to matter. Therefore, I was left with the realization that these problems had invaded the mind-set of most of the legal community, not just my small part of the world.

What was the answer? The best one for me was to open my own practice, where I could control more of my practice style. That was a very expensive and scary prospect. I had several practical issues to address: Where would I get the money to finance this new practice? Would I be a solo or join others to form a small firm? Would my large corporate clients come with me? Would they believe that a solo/small-firm lawyer could provide the type of service they had come to expect? The supervising agent for my main corporate client summed it up when she said, "Diane, we send the work to you, not your firm. We do not care where you practice. We just care that the quality you have always given us continues." That response finalized my decision to go solo.

My family changed at the same time I was reanalyzing my practice style. I had just married a wonderful man with three very confused and angry young girls. The new members of my home were not accustomed to having a mother who worked outside the house, much less one who literally lived at her firm. If this marriage was to be a success, and if I was to help these children through the most difficult time in their young lives, I would have to reprioritize my life. How could the needs of a family and a demanding profession—two very different worlds—be given equal time when it appeared they were in direct conflict with each other? After a great deal of soul-searching, my new husband and I decided we could handle the challenge. My husband's profession was industrial blue-collar, so there were no options for him; on the other hand, I owned my profession and therefore I had options. The only answer was to move my work to our home, which would then remove the physical barriers I had accepted for so many years. This breaking of the physical barriers is the key to a successful blending of family and profession. It allowed me to become a valuable force in both worlds.

What are the challenges of a home-based office? When I first decided to set up an office in my home, I did so very quietly. Why, you ask? Because I was not sure whether my clients and peers would respect a lawyer who practiced out of her home. Was I ever wrong! From the first day my office opened, I realized I was able to provide more efficient and cheaper service for all my clients. Those clients referred other clients, who referred other clients, and so on and so on. No one cared whether I was housed in an elaborate, marble-be-decked castle. My clients wanted to be able to communicate with me, be involved in the management of their cases, know the status of their files, and feel their money was being well spent. My elderly clients had really disliked driving downtown to meet with me. I was able to provide options to meet all these needs, and many more.

Originally, my move to a home-based office was intended to be tempo-rary—until my family situation stabilized, which I believed would take up to two years. Again, that was in 1990. The family situation stabilized long ago, and my client base has grown to be strong and consistent. I have discovered that I adore being a lawyer, and my career has skyrocketed. Each year has been more financially, professionally, and emotionally rewarding. Losing the physical barriers added hours to each day: no commuting or waiting for doc-uments from the word-processing department. Despite the challenges, I have never regretted making the move.

I refer to my office as one that is "on-site" or "in conjunction" with my home. By that, I mean my office is a full-time, completely self-sustained law of-fice that just happens to be connected to my home. I have never looked at my practice as a part-time job. However, the suggestions in this chapter fit any alternative style, including part-time practice. Issues regarding the business of practicing law and making decisions about technology and client relation-ships apply equally to home offices and traditional offices. This chapter is unique because it discusses the philosophical issues related to blending the practice of law with a home and family, along with offering some very practi-cal tips for surviving the transition.

This chapter is designed to help you analyze whether a home office is a practical solution for you and your situation. What you are considering is sim-ilar to merging several different companies: your profession, your clients, your family, your extended family, your neighbors, your community, and your personal goals and needs. Any corporate lawyer will tell you that the merger of multiple companies is not an easy task and can be accomplished success-fully only with a great deal of advance planning.

Is an Office in or Near Your Home Possible?

According to *Link Resources*, 37 million people work at home. Of that number, 10 million work full-time at home. The average age of these workers is 41.2 years, with an income of $58,400; 54 percent are male and 46 percent female. Workers with postgraduate degrees total 34 percent. AT&T employs approximately 35,000 telecommuters, and IBM estimates a savings of approximately $35 million in overhead costs as a result of its telecommuting program.

Understand Your Goals

In deciding whether you want to change your current situation, you must first clearly understand your own goals. These goals may be best defined by recalling some of your past dreams that depicted your future. First, define the following four terms: success, respect, security, and responsibility. Put these definitions in writing and make sure to use your own interpretations, not those of your family or friends. Next, analyze the long-term needs of yourself, your family, and your business relations. The following questions may help you define your goals and analyze the style of practice that best suits you. For this exercise to be most helpful, please be completely honest.

1. Break your definition of success into specific terms. Draw a pie chart using these terms: money, power, reputation, family relationships, community involvement, or something else. Place each term in a separate area, making the size of each area proportionate to its importance. How does each item rate in relationship to the way you are currently living?

2. What are your specific needs for time, money, emotional commitment to family, and work?

3. What are the specific needs of your family for time, money, and emotional commitment?

4. How do you picture your future? Examine the next five, ten, twenty, thirty, and fifty years. Create a picture in your mind of your surroundings and your involvement in your family, profession, and community. Build upon that picture so that each successive time period adds additional pieces of the puzzle until the ultimate picture is complete. (Hint: It is usually easier to first visualize one of the later periods and then work backwards.)

5. Determine what you need to accomplish each year to create the picture you have for these various stages in your life. Never reject an option just because it does not fit one of your other goals. Some of the wildest ideas can become the mainstay of your future life. Also, be willing to reanalyze your long-term goals to determine whether you have changed your ultimate picture. Do not be so flexible that your goals have no chance of becoming reality.

6. If one of your goals is to open your own office, then answer these additional questions:
    ◆ Are you able to motivate yourself? Where are your deficiencies in being your own boss? Is it possible to supplement those deficien-

cies with other resources? (For example, you can hire a bookkeeper if you cannot or will not balance your checkbook or bill your clients on a timely basis.)

- How much staff assistance do you and your area of practice require?
- How much peer interaction do you and your area of practice require?
- How will your clients view a move to a solo office?
- What resources do you and your clients deem necessary? Which of those resources are merely luxuries and could be supplemented with alternative resources? Can you afford to purchase the resources that you and your clients deem necessary?
- Do you believe you can produce high-quality work on your own?
- Do you need the environmental stress inherent in the traditional law firm environment (the adrenaline rush from all the hustle and bustle)?
- Are you capable of handling a multitude of tasks at one time?
- Are you challenged by, and do you take pride in, multitasking?
- Are you willing to compromise billable time for management time? (Most solos will tell you that they spend at least half their time managing their practices.)
- Are you willing and able to keep up with technology, including taking the time to learn how to use equipment in which you have invested?

Look closely at your answers to determine whether a solo practice—in your home or downtown—is the best option for you.

Special Issues Related to On-site Offices

An on-site or home-based office can be either an extension to a traditional downtown office or your only office. In addition to the issues discussed above, consider the following:

- *Your Family Situation*: Will your family tolerate your invasion of their privacy? What are their expectations of a normal home?
- *The Geographic Location*: Will your new office be convenient for your clients? How far is it from the courts or other necessary services?
- *The Physical Layout*: Is your home, with its existing floor plan, practical for an office, or will you need to remodel, add on, or move? What can you afford?
- *The Balance of Work and Home*: Will you be able to balance the invasion of work into your home, and vice versa? Do you have the ability to separate each mentally, so that you have a home and not a bed within your office?

◆ *Security and Privacy*: Issues of security and privacy are often over-looked in setting up an on-site office. Determine what you can do to provide you, your family, your clients, and your clients' information with a secure and private environment.

◆ *Zoning*: Check the zoning restrictions for your property before invest-ing in a new office. Most of the older CC&Rs limit or prohibit busi-nesses in the home that will "substantially increase traffic" in the neighborhood. Some of the newer residential developments have ab-solute prohibitions on any home-based offices. In the future, as home-based businesses become the norm, there will be increased demand that these limitations be relaxed or eliminated. For now, be sure you are fully informed about the restrictions, and be willing to make nec-essary changes.

Establishing Your Home-Based Office

The considerations in setting up a small office in conjunction with your home are the same as those for setting up a multiple-lawyer firm, except that you are the sole decision maker. You must determine all requirements for equipment, files, and staff. Your choices will be influenced by the physical size of your of-fice, monetary constraints, clients' requirements, and/or the particular de-mands controlled by your type of practice. The following issues relate specif-ically to an on-site office.

Office Requirements

Your office must be a separate room dedicated solely to office equipment, furniture, and files. Not only will this satisfy IRS requirements, it will also as-sist you in practicing more efficiently and creating a professional image.

Design a layout for your desk and other work surfaces that satisfies your needs based upon the available space. Take into consideration equipment that needs to be easily accessible, the necessary file space, and whether you are your own secretary. In addition, you need at least two client chairs (as-suming you will be seeing clients in your on-site office).

To ensure privacy, it is essential to have a door that separates your of-fice from the rest of the house. The only exception to this requirement would be if you are the only occupant of your home and do not have pets. If you have a family, remember that your family members have the right to a normal home environment. The separation between the two "worlds"—office and home—will help give them that normal environment.

The perception of a home conflicts with the current perception of the typical office environment. Giggling children, barking dogs, and washing ma-chines are part of a normal home, but are not acceptable sounds for an office.

These sounds will disturb your meetings with clients and inhibit your ability to work efficiently. Most importantly, these distractions reduce the professional image you wish to create.

You have an obligation to protect and secure client confidentiality. This includes protecting client files from the peeping eyes of others. Your office is not a place for personal visitors or children at play. It is essential that you educate each member of your family to honor the confidences of your work and respect your clients' information and documents. Receive personal visitors in your home, not in your office. Meet with your clients in your office, not in your home.

In addition to a security alarm system on both the house and office, and to enhance the security of my office, I built a lattice patio as part of the entrance to the office. This adds a wonderful atrium and provides me a conference room in a lovely garden setting. The patio adds privacy to the entry of the office and limits visibility from the street. Curious passersby cannot see into the office, nor can they see the expensive electronic equipment.

Adequate file storage is a necessary evil. If storage in your home is limited, then rent space in a convenient, air-conditioned facility. The rent payment will be an additional overhead cost, but it is usually inexpensive. As technology becomes more reasonably priced, you will be able to convert all files to computer images through scanning. (See Chapter 34, "Adobe Acrobat for E-Filing and More"). Storage can then be on small disks, which will eliminate most storage problems.

Clients

Your choice of location or style of practice may be dictated in large part by your current or prospective clients. Many of my clients are large, commercial, out-of-state lenders. Historically, I met these clients at their local offices, or we limited our meetings to telephone calls, e-mail messages, and/or fax messages. For these clients, an on-site office was extremely convenient. In fact, most of them have come to prefer it because they can make arrangements for me to be available during hours that a traditional law office is closed. In a profession where clients are spread throughout the world, this flexible work schedule is very appealing to clients who work in different time zones.

The majority of my individual clients are professionals or referrals from other professionals. These people are typically self-employed and many have their own home-based offices. They enjoy the low-stress environment offered by my on-site office. I can pull computer court dockets, make necessary copies, and direct my runner/process server, all while my client is in the office to help with the instructions. Evening and weekend hours are easily arranged. The client's travel time is greatly reduced, with little or no traffic or parking problems.

Client Management

It is very important to lay the ground rules for your on-site office. It is not permissible for clients to "drop by." Explain to them that each client has assigned times for meetings, thereby assuring that their meetings are uninterrupted. Place a pickup and delivery box outside the entrance to your office and invite your clients to use it at any time. Explain that the office phone is answered only during normal business hours, but that the fax machine is left on twenty-four hours a day. Let your clients know that in special situations you can be available during nonbusiness hours.

Equipment

In addition to the normal computer and electronic equipment required for every small office, a few other items are specific to an on-site office.

There are as many different choices for telephones as there are long-distance providers. It is advisable to stay with a manufacturer that has a good reputation. At a minimum, you should have a two- or three-line phone with speaker, hold, conferencing, mute, caller-identification, and do-not-disturb features.

One line must be dedicated as your main office line. This number should be listed as a business line and included in the Yellow Pages directory under your specific area of practice. There will be an additional charge for this business line, but it is worth the few extra dollars to have a presence in the business section of the telephone book. Make sure you have a caller-identification feature on this line. Include voice messaging, or some similar service, which will answer all incoming calls after a predetermined number of rings, or if the line is busy. Do not use the call-waiting feature on your office line—it is far too distracting for you and your callers, and does not give the professional image you want to project. Establish a habit of turning off the ringer on the phone during nonbusiness hours, unless you have made special arrangements to receive late or weekend calls.

The second phone line should be used for the Internet connection and fax/modem, and as a second outgoing line. This separate line will permit you to leave the fax machine on twenty-four hours a day, seven days a week, and permits clients, worldwide, to fax at their leisure and not be limited by the hours of your office. Of course, e-mail messaging has replaced this form of communication for many clients.

Use a third line as your home line. Do not give this phone number to any of your clients. All incoming and outgoing personal calls should be restricted to the home line, and not be placed on your business lines. You may decide that you do not want your personal phone number included in the personal section of the telephone book. That is an individual choice. I retained my maiden name, and therefore can list our home number under my married name and still retain privacy.

Depending upon your preference, you may decide to use a speaker-phone. Personally, I find speakerphones objectionable and I believe that most clients mirror my opinion. If you are too busy to pick up the phone to talk directly to your clients, then your clients may decide to find another lawyer who has more time or is willing to treat them with more respect. Also some older clients have a difficult time understanding someone using a speakerphone, as the echo distorts the voice. The use of a speakerphone can also create issues related to confidentiality.

To reduce your chiropractic bills, invest in an ear-loop attachment as a replacement for the handset. This device is extremely helpful in eliminating the stiff neck suffered while holding the phone between your chin and shoulder. It also frees your hands to type or write comfortably. The person on the other end of the phone can rarely tell whether you are using an ear-loop attachment or the regular handset.

Check into using an answering service that takes your calls if your line is busy or the call is not picked up within three rings. Other options include the use of voice mail or a physical answering machine. Many phones have built-in answering machines, or you can use your computer as an answering machine. I have elected to use my telephone provider's voice-mail system. I leave a message to the caller any day that I am going to be out of the office for more than a couple hours. The message relates a basic overview of my day's activities. My standard voice-mail message includes a reference to my Web site for additional information in my area of practice—bankruptcy.

Make sure to wire your entire home for access to these three lines and networking for all computers. It is less expensive and disruptive to do the entire house at once then to do it separately. Originally, we wired only my office. Later, as computers became an integral part of our personal and professional lives, we realized that all the computers needed to be connected. This permitted us to piggyback onto my office Internet connection. As children grew up and left home, we remodeled the office, taking more space. It would have been simpler had we wired all the rooms at the beginning. Warnings: (1) have a very good firewall, (2) train everyone in your family about use of virus and e-mail protection, and (3) most importantly, have your office computer data electronically locked so that no one but you or your staff can access the data.

Staff: Employees and Contract Labor

Even if you work from an on-site office, you will still find it necessary to consider hiring employees or outside labor.

Factors to consider regarding the hiring of employees include the following: (1) the training and supervision necessary for these employees to be self-sufficient and profitable, (2) whether you have the space to accommodate them, (3) whether they can work full-time or part-time from their homes, and (4) whether part-time employees will accommodate your needs. Your imagination is the only limit to the possibilities. Do not forget the additional legal obligations you have as an employer, such as covering payroll taxes and providing a safe work environment.

Contract lawyers, research assistants, legal assistants, and secretaries can be used on a one-time or ongoing basis, depending upon your needs. Be very careful whom you allow to gain access to your computer via modem.

Even if you decide not to hire office staff, you should contract with a delivery and process-servicing company. Learn to consolidate deliveries and other errands by using your delivery service.

Other Considerations

There are three basic matters related to the operation of any small office: mail, libraries, and supplies. In addition to establishing office policies regarding each of these matters, you must also address the unique issues for the on-site office.

Mail

Do not use your home address on your correspondence or business cards. This will make privacy and security more difficult.

One option for an address other than your on-site office address is to rent "virtual" space from an existing law firm and use its address for your mail and deliveries. This rental may not include any physical use of the offices, or it may be expanded to hourly use of the conference room and a per-use charge for the copier, the fax machine, and other equipment. Some offices even offer reception services so that you can forward your phone calls when you are out of your office.

Library

The Internet has become a very popular place for research. Some state statutes are now online and can be used for no charge. Cornell University Law School has a site that provides access to U.S. Supreme Court cases and the federal code (**www.law.cornell.edu**). There are hundreds of other sites for free research. The best free legal Web site is **www.findlaw.com**. Make sure to sign up for the free daily updates and weekly specific case law updates.

Office Management

Additional office management policies you need to establish include the handling of mail, docketing, file maintenance, timekeeping, and accounting. Each of these items could be an entire chapter of its own, and some are covered in other chapters of this book. Several helpful books are listed in the resources section at the end of Part III. Also check with your local bar association to see if it offers an office management assistance program or service. In Arizona, ours is called LOMAP. It audits law offices, offers suggestions on management and trust fund changes, and offers training on certain software.

Final Thoughts

To bring honor, pride, civility, and community purpose back into my life and my profession, I took the steps discussed in this chapter. They worked for me and can work for you. If you dream of having control over your daily life, and of including your family as part of your day, then an on-site office may be the answer to your dreams. I guarantee your clients will appreciate the lower hourly rate, the more timely response, and the ease of accessing their lawyer without maneuvering through several layers of staff.

Remember—image is everything. As long as you believe that you are a professional, as long as you look, act, and talk like a professional, then you are a professional. Trust yourself.

Personnel Issues

Staff: Selection, Management, Motivation, and Delegation

27

Susan G. Manch
Marcia Pennington Shannon

Creating a productive and satisfying work environment for you and your staff begins with selecting the right staff members and then employing management skills that promote challenge, learning, teamwork, and motivation. Few things are more devastating to a sole practitioner than to go through the time-consuming and expensive processes of selecting and training staff members and then have them leave because of the lawyer's lack of essential management skills. A practice can come to a complete standstill while the lawyer hires and trains someone new. To avoid wasting a substantial investment of time and money, the lawyer must spend the requisite time in the hiring process and then follow through with appropriate training *and* support of staff members. Careful planning before placing the first advertisement for a new staff member can pay great dividends in the growing success of a practice. This chapter discusses selecting and retaining staff, as well as honing essential management skills that contribute to an effective team environment.

Selecting the Right Candidate

Defining the Best Candidate

Before placing advertisements or interviewing candidates, determine the specific skills, experiences, and attributes you seek in your new staff member. Begin by creating a detailed job description. The description should include every task and responsibility you expect this staff person to fulfill. From this detailed description, extract the criteria you will use in selecting candidates. Consider the following:

◆ What set of skills/qualities/experiences does the position require? What are the baseline requirements needed to do the job? These criteria are the easiest to determine when reviewing résumés and interviewing candidates.

◆ Why would an individual be attracted to and successful in your firm? These criteria suggest that a particular candidate will want the job and be successful in the position. Specific interest in your practice and attraction to the type of work required are examples of these factors.

◆ Who would be a good fit for your firm? These criteria are the personal characteristics that allow the individual to integrate successfully into the culture of your practice and feel a sense of belonging. Examples include maturity, self-confidence, good judgment, sense of humor, and effectiveness under pressure.

By defining the criteria you will use to select an individual, you do not leave the process to chance. These criteria will help you make the best match between your needs and personality and those of the candidates. Taking the time to determine these criteria is essential for creating an efficient hiring process that greatly reduces the chance of making costly hiring mistakes.

Evaluating the Résumé

Proper screening can be the most productive means of ensuring an efficient recruitment process. There is no greater waste of time than scheduling and conducting interviews with applicants who do not meet the baseline requirements for the position. Identifying well-qualified candidates to participate in the interview process is the key to maximizing the value of time invested in the recruiting process.

The key to successful résumé screening is knowing the key elements of your search. The average résumé gets about a twenty-second "read" before a decision is made about whether to move forward. Deciding in advance what criteria will be applied in the review and screening process allows you to scan for specific selectors, and, upon finding them, choose the most qualified candidates from among the résumés received.

Developing the Interview Plan

Good planning prevents poor performance. To have a productive interview, you must have an interview plan. Most of us are incapable of reading a résumé and conducting a thoughtful interview at the same time. Creating an interview plan allows you to maintain consistency in the process and capture the information necessary to make a successful hiring decision.

Interview Segments

The interview itself is divided into several parts, each with its own purpose and importance. As you plan for and conduct the interviews, consider how you will approach each of these segments:

- *Introduction and Agenda*: The first minute or so of each interview should include an introduction and brief overview of what you hope to accomplish in the time allotted.
- *Rapport Building*: Spend a few minutes on questions or comments that help "break the ice" by introducing a topic that is unrelated to the candidate's qualifications or experience. Rapport building at the beginning of an interview is important because it allows you to put the candidate at ease. Reducing tension improves the overall quality of the candidate's responses and sets the stage for a comfortable and relaxed interview.
- *Information Gathering*: The information-gathering phase of the interview is the core and should be apportioned the majority of time. In an initial or screening interview, you should look for information on the candidate that cannot be determined from a simple reading of the résumé. Remember, the main goal of a screening interview is just that—screening out candidates who are not appropriate for the position. Be sure to leave adequate time for the candidate's questions, as well.
- *Closing, and Outlining Next Steps*: In this phase—the closing of the interview—inform the candidate of the next steps in the process. You might want to tell the candidate how you are approaching the selection process, what to expect next, and your timetable, if you have one.

Effective Questioning Techniques

Creating effective questions is essential to a successful interviewing process. At this stage, you already have clearly defined selection criteria and candidates' resumes. You need only put these together to come up with the right questions.

Open-ended questions—those that elicit more than a yes or no answer—force the candidate to provide thoughtful responses. They allow the candidate to give more detailed answers, filling in information not readily accessible by reviewing the résumé. Examples of open-ended questions include the following:

- What led to your decision to look for a new job?
- How would you describe your ideal work environment?
- What was your most interesting assignment?

◆ Give me an example of a difficult situation and how you handled it.
◆ What is your least favorite part of your work?

Checking References

You have interviewed candidates and narrowed it down to your top two or three choices. Checking references is the next step in the recruitment process; though very important, it is often neglected. Concentrate on speaking with current or past supervisors. Proceed with caution if the candidate gives you only "personal" references with whom to speak. If the candidate is presently employed, then to protect confidentiality, do not speak with anyone from the candidate's present place of employment unless you receive permission from the candidate to do so. The candidate should still be able to provide you with other individuals who are well aware of his or her working abilities.

Do your best to speak directly to an individual's references. This gives you the opportunity to ask questions that are relevant to the position you are filling. Include open-ended questions that elicit more introspection on the part of the reference. Effective questions include the following:

◆ What are the candidate's strengths?
◆ What are the candidate's areas in need of further development?
◆ How does the candidate interact with individuals in authority? With colleagues?
◆ How does the candidate handle stressful situations?

Be sure to include more specific questions that relate to the position itself. Examples include the following:

◆ What opportunities has the individual had to interact with clients? How would you describe those interactions?
◆ Have you observed the individual handling a variety of tasks at once? How would you describe the person's ability to multitask?

Most candidates have positive references, but occasionally you will hear something negative or even neutral about an individual. Obviously, you should speak with more than one reference to see if there is a pattern. If there is, the candidate should probably be dropped from consideration. Do not hesitate to ask for more references if you have any concerns. A mistake that many potential employers make is to either not check for references or not heed what is being said (or not said!) in reference checks. This can be a very costly error.

Making the Offer

As you formulate your offer, determine the elements of the initial offer and decide which among them are negotiable and which are not. Elements of an offer include the following:

- *Salary*: Have in mind a range of what you are willing and able to pay.
- *Benefits*: Some form of health, disability, and life insurance is often in-cluded in an offer package. Additional benefits might include sick leave, family leave, paid parking, and contribution toward a retirement plan. If possible, try to identify the dollar value of each benefit. Some-times an attractive benefit package can offset a lower salary offer by giving the candidate assistance in an area of key importance to him or her.
- *Vacation*: Offering two weeks (ten days) of paid vacation time is typi-cal, but some employers have found that candidates have a positive view of expanding vacation time in place of a higher salary. Being able to balance work and personal life is a factor that candidates rank high in identifying the characteristics most valued in an employer.

Motivating and Retaining Staff

Be a Good Boss

The number-one way to motivate and retain staff is to be a good boss! As-sessing your own managerial behaviors is an excellent first step.

Following are some attributes of motivated employees:

- They want to come to work
- They care about how they do their jobs
- They understand how they fit into the firm's work
- They continue to achieve by learning new skills and accepting more responsibility
- They contribute positively to the firm's culture and reputation

According to authors Beverly Kaye and Sharon Jordan-Evans in their book, *Love 'Em or Lose 'Em: Getting Good People to Stay* (Berrett-Koehler, 1999), the most frequent reasons people stay in their jobs are the following:

1. Career growth—learning and development
2. Exciting and challenging work
3. Meaningful work
4. Great people
5. Being part of a team
6. Good boss
7. Recognition for work well done
8. Fun on the job
9. Autonomy—sense of control over work
10. Flexibility—work hours, dress code

11. Fair pay and benefits
12. Inspiring leadership
13. Pride in the organization

Notice that pay and benefits are number 11! Having a good boss is much more of a contributing factor to keeping good people. Clearly, as you look at this list, you can see that as a supervisor, there is much you can do to motivate your employees. Time invested in learning what motivates each of your staff members, and then putting into practice the elements that contribute to their motivators, is time well spent. Meet with each staff member to communicate his or her value to the organization and to ask if there is anything you can do to increase the individual's job satisfaction and motivation. Ask questions such as the following:

- What motivates you on your job?
- What do you like about your job?
- What keeps you here?
- What would make you happier?
- What might lure you away?

In addition to asking your employees what they want, employ motivating managerial behaviors. The three most effective are communication, soliciting employees' ideas and input, and seeking opportunities to praise.

Communicate with Employees and Seek Their Input

Communication is about giving your staff members the information they need to do their jobs. A weekly staff meeting can be an excellent conduit for communicating important information to your employees. Review the week's schedule, noting particular periods that may cause added demands. For example, depositions, due dates for briefs, or staff vacation days can cause increased stress in the firm. If the staff members know about these things ahead of time, they, as a team, can plan for the situation. This is also an excellent time to institute the second motivating behavior—asking for ideas and input. Make it a practice to encourage individuals to make suggestions, raise issues or conflicts, and identify problems and possible solutions.

Communicating information and soliciting input from employees should, of course, continue outside the staff meetings. Effective communication is used to describe expectations and accountabilities, delegate work, resolve conflicts, evaluate performance, and advise individuals. Two-way communication sends the message that your staff is an integral part of your firm.

Seek Opportunities to Praise

Most of us want to know that our efforts are recognized and appreciated. Many have left positions due to feeling "unappreciated." Authentic praise is a wonderfully effective motivator, and it sows loyalty and long-term satisfaction in your employees. Becoming aware of opportunities to praise can be one of your best motivational techniques.

Create Other Motivators

Other suggestions for motivating and retaining staff include the following:

- Be respectful and promote an environment where respect is the rule. Lack of respect from lawyers is the most common complaint from legal support staff. Start the day with a "good morning," and follow with "please" and "thank you" whenever called for.
- Provide adequate training so employees are comfortable with their work. Training allows them to be successful and develop skills. It can be provided through continuing legal education programs, seminars in substantive practice areas, computer training, and membership in professional organizations.
- Combine sick leave and vacation leave to create annual leave. This permits employees to make decisions about how to use days off in ways that best meet their needs.
- Provide tuition reimbursement for courses that apply to employees' jobs, with the condition that reimbursement depends upon a passing grade and is paid six months after successful completion of the course.
- Allow employees to choose the form of their bonuses. You establish the amount and let them decide how it will be paid—in cash, travel, gift certificates, time off, or schooling, to name a few ideas.
- Introduce your secretary/assistant to clients.
- Institute flexible hours.
- Create job-sharing positions for those who can work only part-time.
- Present an award/certificate/plaque of recognition or a small gift or memento to recognize extra efforts.
- Take staff members to lunch occasionally.
- Institute "bring your pet to work" day if your office space allows for it.
- Allow individuals to take their birthdays off.
- Hold team parties that include families.
- Ask about and discuss personal passions and interests. If possible, allow some of those passions or interests to be exhibited at work. Examples include a "green thumb" employee who creates an indoor garden for the office, an art-minded individual who displays his art or helps select office artwork, and a music enthusiast who finds quarterly concerts for the office staff and guests to attend.
- Ask about and discuss long-term career goals with individual staff members. Look for ways to help them with those goals.

Honing Essential Management Skills

Although creating a motivating environment is very important, honing essential management skills is central to maintaining an effective team. Delegation and feedback are particularly valuable management skills.

Delegation

Delegation is a beneficial tool, not only for time management purposes, but also as a training device for your staff. Delegation uses time and human resources effectively. It saves supervisors from performing routine tasks, and increases responsibility for staff members who wish to develop skills. Delegating to others allows those individuals to learn new skills, face new challenges, and contribute more substantially to your practice. These are all key ingredients for a happy and productive workplace.

Begin the delegation process by making a list of your current projects and activities. Assess your list. Which activities must you keep entirely on your own plate? Which can you hand to someone else? Looking at the activities you can delegate, categorize them into two types:

1. Activities that are routine and repetitive in nature (Though these may require some skill or training, they can usually be learned quickly by someone else. Many administrative tasks fall into this category.)
2. Activities that require a specific kind of skill (You need to assess the experience of the person to whom you delegate these activities, which provide professional development opportunities.)

For each project to be assigned, consider the individuals on your staff. Does a specific individual have the skills and training necessary to accomplish this assignment? Knowing the strengths, weaknesses, and working styles of your staff plays an important role in delegating. Without this knowledge, you will never feel comfortable delegating tasks. Also, the chance of delegating an inappropriate task to an individual is much greater.

The biggest pitfall in delegation is lack of communication between the one assigning the project and the one doing the work. If you don't properly describe the assignment and expectations, and give complete information, resources, and advice, you doom the assignment to failure. The more information you give up front, the fewer questions the person will need to ask during the assignment. Nevertheless, communication must continue throughout the assignment. Depending upon the complexity of the tasks involved and the delegate's experience, regularly scheduled check-ins may be necessary.

In summary, the "must dos" of delegation include the following:

- Clearly define the task and the desired outcome, including expectations and timetables. Put the assignment in writing to prevent any misunderstandings.
- Be sure your timetable is realistic. Emergencies do occur, but make sure you don't create them by making unreasonable promises to clients.
- Delegate the authority necessary to accomplish the task.
- As a training tool, delegate slightly more than you think the person is capable of handling, but do not set up failure. This communicates your confidence in the staff member.
- Empower employees to come up with their own ideas and solutions.
- Don't micromanage. That's not delegating. You're doubling your work and the individual will learn little from the experience.
- Resist the temptation to solve a problem.
- Expect mistakes. We all make them. Help your staff members learn from them.
- Never take a project back.
- Be available for questions and advice. The project will be completed faster, with fewer errors, and the person will benefit from your knowledge.
- Don't forget praising!

Feedback

Feedback is a powerful tool for enhancing relationships, teaching those you supervise how to be more effective, promoting your expectations, reinforcing desired actions, pointing out developmental needs and ways to improve them, giving recognition, and showing appreciation. Feedback lets your staff members know how they are doing compared with what is expected. Feedback can be both reinforcing and corrective. Delivered effectively, feedback is an essential ingredient in creating a motivating work environment.

Certain criteria transform feedback from meaningless to invaluable:

1. *The feedback must be given soon after the action involved, to enhance the connection between the action and your response to it.* Employees often learn of poor performance only at annual reviews, months after assignments are completed. Giving feedback that is far removed from a particular situation is meaningless. Not only are the specifics already forgotten, the individual has no chance of correcting something that occurred months ago.

2. *The feedback must state the specific action to which you are responding.* This may sound obvious, but it pays to make sure you and the other individual are really on the same page.

3. *The feedback must be detailed enough to have meaning.* This may involve both negative and positive comments. Compliment the behaviors that are positive so they are reinforced. If something was done incorrectly, give a detailed description of the mistake. This feedback helps the individual learn and develop. If it's necessary to give constructive feedback, you can promote the employee's continued motivation by remembering to use the "sandwich" method—two compliments "sandwich" the criticism. Start with a sincere compliment. Give suggestions for correcting the problem. Close with another sincere compliment.

Corrective feedback helps put the employee back on track. It says that a change is required for future success. The individual must understand and accept what you say, and be able to do something about it. Develop an improvement plan and follow up afterwards. Feedback of this kind should never be solely negative or mean-spirited, or given only in a negative context. Following are some ways to minimize the chance that a person will become defensive in response to constructive or corrective feedback:

- Plan ahead regarding the specific comments you want to deliver and your goals for the feedback.
- When delivering the feedback, be as specific as possible about the assignment, action, or behavior to which you refer.
- Begin and end with a positive comment about the person's performance.
- Give specific examples of the action or behavior you want changed.
- Provide illustrations of the specific changes to be made.
- Discuss the specific steps that will help the person make the needed changes, and explore alternatives.
- Be sensitive.

As a reinforcing tool, feedback offers recognition and praise. All of us want to be appreciated for our contributions. Look for opportunities to praise—it is quite motivating!

People often say they do not have enough time to give effective feedback. But the few minutes needed to plan and deliver it pay off in many different ways, including enhanced staff effectiveness and productivity, greater job satisfaction, and increased motivation. Most importantly, your staff will want to stay!

Ethical Responsibilities of— and to—Your Staff 28

Lynda C. Shely

This chapter outlines key training areas for law firm personnel that will help ensure everyone in the firm understands the ethical duties owed to clients. Two fundamental points are necessary to establish your staff as a professional team:

1. Delegate, but don't abdicate responsibility to supervise.
2. Remember that your firm's integrity is based upon the actions of *everyone* in the firm.

Everything You Know About Clients Must Be Kept Confidential

Every law firm, no matter the size, should memorialize the ethical responsibilities of nonlawyer employees in a handbook, a manual, or an office memo. And the very first concept in that Law Firm Staff Ethics Manual should be about maintaining the confidentiality of *all* the information pertaining to firm clients. Even seasoned litigation paralegals may misunderstand the concept of confidentiality, and mistakenly believe that it is the same thing as attorney-client privilege. Explain that these are different concepts, and that the firm must keep as confidential all information about clients—even their names, addresses, and exciting legal matters. Remind staff (and lawyers!) that they cannot chat about exciting cases with their friends from other firms at lunch, or with their spouses, or even with other employees of the firm when they are in public places such as elevators, courtroom hallways, and restaurants. Lawyers are responsible for assuring that support staff adhere to ethical standards, such as confidentiality (Rule 1.6) by virtue of the Model Rules of Professional Conduct Rule 5.3. (See Appendix B, page 605.)

Initial Client Intake

Rule 1.18 of the Model Rules of Professional Conduct requires that lawyers treat the information they receive from certain prospective clients as confidential. Practically speaking, this means that initial consultations with such prospective clients should be logged into the firm's database for conflict purposes. Yes, this means that people with whom you have just an initial consultation may need to be treated as clients, for ethics purposes.

To avoid unintentionally creating an attorney-client relationship with a prospective client, train receptionists, paralegals, and anyone else who has contact with new clients to (1) limit the amount of information they receive when performing an initial conflict check, and (2) explain to the prospective client that an attorney-client relationship has not been established by the intake process. Gather only the information necessary to do a thorough conflict-of-interest check.

Communicating with Clients—and Lawyers

One of the most common reasons for discipline charges against lawyers is failure to return phone calls. A lawyer doesn't even have a chance to return calls promptly if the lawyer doesn't know they exist or the staff has not alerted callers that the lawyer is out of the office for the day or week. Confirm that everyone in the office knows you have an ethical duty to communicate promptly with clients, and that your duty requires that messages be efficiently transmitted to you. Create a system for alerting you to new messages, and either return them that day or assign a staff member to make the contact. Your staff also can be a crucial communication link with clients by knowing your schedule; that way, they can explain to callers when you will be available to return calls.

Conflicts of Interest

Support staff must avoid conflicts of interest, just as lawyers must. Staff members can also bring conflicts with them, if they are hired from other firms. Establish a system whereby new staff members must list the names of spouses and family members, and, if hired from another firm, the names of the clients for whom they worked. This allows you to screen such persons immediately from any matters on which they may have conflicts. Notations must be made in the paper files and document software to alert everyone about screened staff members. Also, have your staff members regularly update their personnel listings in the conflict database.

Money Supervision

Accounting functions can be delegated, but should never be abdicated. Never have one staff person doing all the deposits, accounting entries, and monthly reconciliations. At a minimum, (1) have someone else (or you) do the monthly reconciliation of the law firm trust account, (2) receive the monthly bank statement unopened, and review it for clearing of sequential checks and unusual amounts that you do not recall authorizing, (3) read what you sign, and ensure there is proper documentation to support every withdrawal from the trust account, and (4) ensure there is a sequentially numbered cash receipt book that you review. Do not let anyone except an equity owner in the law firm have signature authority on the trust account. Have some type of safe on the premises to store cash and checks that are received late in the day and will need to be deposited the next day.

Unauthorized Practice

Nonlawyers cannot give legal advice, negotiate legal rights for clients, or represent clients in tribunals (except as specifically permitted by statute or court rule). Establish clear guidelines for staff members on how to transmit legal advice from you to clients, while refraining from answering clients' questions for advice from them (such as when a client asks a staff person, "What *should* I do?"). Specify that you must review pleadings and correspondence that provide legal advice. If you authorize staff to negotiate certain matters within very explicit parameters, make sure those parameters are followed and that the paralegal/legal assistant explains to whomever is on the other side that he or she is transmitting the offers from you. Failing to supervise staff and permitting them to engage in unauthorized practice of law will result in discipline, which really isn't fun. . . . (See Appendix B, page 605.)

Professionalism/Decorum

Encourage all your staff members to look, act, and be professional. Your firm's reputation is based upon the actions of *everyone*—from the receptionist to you.

The Unavoidable Details of Employing Staff

29

Gisela B. Bradley

What Kind of Help Do I Need?

Due to the fluctuating demands on a solo law practice caused by varying workloads, expansion into other practice areas, personal work schedules, or any number of other factors, every lawyer—at some point in his or her career—thinks about hiring additional staff to ease the daily responsibilities of serving the client in the most efficient and cost-effective way. The decision to expand the practice in this way should be followed by a careful analysis of the type of help that would bring the most relief to the lawyer and add service to the clients.

In years past, law firms hired support staff to "work for the lawyer." Secretaries were assigned to specific lawyers, and receptionists were trained to carry out the lawyers' work while answering the phone and greeting clients. Paralegals were given assignments by the lawyers and told to handle specific aspects of cases, often not knowing the key issues of the cases overall. This philosophy has changed somewhat, due to the movement of firms toward client-oriented service environments. Firms now look at staffing the office as a means to serving the clients better as a team. This means that more emphasis must be placed on skills beyond the traditional job skills, such as typing, drafting, filing, accounting, and research.

This chapter begins by looking at the legal requirements of becoming an employer, and then discusses a methodology for performing a needs analysis for proper staffing. The material presented here is meant for discussion purposes and is not meant to be an exhaustive study of the subject. For a thorough analysis of this topic, you are encouraged to seek individual advice from a human resource professional and/or management consultant.

So You Want to Be an Employer?

Before you hire anyone and become an employer, you may—depending upon the requirements of your state—be required to do the following:

1. Obtain an employer's federal identification number from the Internal Revenue Service (IRS)
2. Obtain workers' compensation insurance
3. Establish an account for unemployment insurance payments

Obtaining an Employer's Federal Identification Number

You may want to become familiar with the following: Circular E, Employers Tax Guide (IRS Publication 15), and IRS Form SS-4, which is the application form for your employer identification number (EIN), along with instructions for this form. The IRS has many helpful resources accessible at **www.irs.gov**, from where you can also e-mail any questions you may have.

Once you establish your EIN, the IRS will keep you current with important information, such as changes in requirements, due dates for tax reporting, and necessary forms.

Obtaining Workers' Compensation Insurance

Generally, most firms obtain their workers' compensation insurance from the same carriers that provide their general liability and property insurance. Insurance companies generally report the existence of this type of insurance to the state.

Establishing an Unemployment Insurance Account

This account is usually established with assistance from your payroll company. The payroll company remits this money on your behalf to the applicable state agency. This requirement or procedure is the one most likely to vary from state to state. In most states, the state government Web site has information about doing business in the state, which can be a helpful guide. Your accountant can also be of great assistance.

Now that you are set up to be an employer on the federal and state levels, we can proceed with the steps of finding you the help you need.

It Is Time to Get More Help!

If you have noticed any of the following symptoms, then *it may be time to get more help*:

1. In your service to your client:
    - You do not have enough time to do quite as much research as you would like to do on a particular issue.
    - You do not complete a task as quickly as you need to.
    - You cannot accept any more new cases or clients because you are overloaded as it is.
2. In your internal office organization (assuming you already have some staff members or temporary help):
    - Your secretary is working overtime consistently.
    - Your bookkeeper does not give you the management reports on a timely basis.
    - Your file clerk consistently has a backlog of filing to do.
    - Your paralegal is not as thorough as he or she needs to be.
3. In your personal life:
    - Your children are always asleep when you leave the house in the morning and when you return home at night.
    - Your spouse misses that fun-loving person you used to be.
    - You have not taken a vacation in three years.

If you realize that any of these symptoms is a regular occurrence, do not rush to hire the neighbor who just lost his job, the cousin who would be so loyal, or the friend to whom you owe a favor! Any of these individuals may be the best suited for what you need, but look first at what you really need to enhance your practice and the service to your client.

This requires a needs analysis. You must establish (1) the type of tasks that, if done by someone else, would give you enough time to do what you need to do, and (2) the type of skills that would enhance your client services and that are not currently available. This type of needs analysis can be done only with a complete time study. I suggest you use your timekeeping software for this analysis, establishing categories for additional activities you may not currently track, such as billing, filing, handling personnel issues, taking care of office supplies, community activities, continuing legal education activities, marketing, training on equipment and software, and answering the phone.

Start the study on the first day of a month and require *everyone* in the firm to record *everything* they do. "Everyone" means no exceptions! At the end of the month, you can use the timekeeping software to obtain a report by individual, or you can total each person's daily sheets by activity. The results should give you information that answers the following questions:

- How much time are you spending on nonclient-related issues that someone less expensive could be doing for you? Multiply that amount of time by your billing rate and see what it costs you to perform these tasks yourself.

- Are there redundancies in the systems that should be eliminated? For example, are the secretary and the paralegal performing filing tasks when a less expensive, part-time student could do this and free those individuals to do what they need to do?

- Are entire steps of the process missing? Are things falling through the cracks?

- Are there just not enough hours in the day to accomplish the work that has been accepted? For example, did you record a high number of hours on a project and still not get everything done in the expected amount of time?

This type of analysis will help you determine where the help is needed and what kind of help would be most beneficial to the overall efficiency and effectiveness of your practice. You will know if you need more legal support and can then decide to look for the right level of expansion. For example, would a law clerk with research capability be the answer, or a paralegal with drafting skills, or an associate with brief-writing abilities? Or should you look for a partner? If your office is lacking in clerical/administrative support, the time study will reflect the shortage in these areas as well. Ask yourself: What would help me serve my clients better, and what would make my life a little easier?

If you already have staff members and are simply trying to determine if it is time to create additional positions, this study can be instrumental in evaluating the type of new positions that would make your existing team more complete.

The important thing in hiring is developing a legal team and not adding more stress by unplanned hiring, which often results in costly, high turnover rates and fails to give you the desired results.

Office Systems and Procedures

Creating Practice Management Systems and Procedures | **30**

Reid F. Trautz

The practice of law is a profession, but your law practice is a business.

Every business needs a set of systems and procedures to accomplish the work that must be done. Common systems in law practices include those for time and billing, to track expenses and bill clients for services, and those for calendars and docketing, to ensure that lawyers are organized, are on time, and do not miss important events.

These systems, if properly implemented, improve the efficiency of your practice, improve your legal services to your clients, help you avoid problems that can lead to malpractice and disciplinary complaints, and reduce the stress in the day-to-day practice of law. Creating these systems does not have to be a complicated process. Actually, a simple system that works is better than a complicated one. The hard part is having the discipline to stick with your system until it is so well integrated into the way you do business that you cannot work without it!

The most common types of law office systems are discussed below. The procedures outlined are to help you get started—use them to develop your own systems. Put your systems and procedures in writing, describing them step by step. Do this so you will remember them, but also so you will have a resource for employees to use when they learn how your systems work. The ABA Law Practice Management Section publishes a helpful tool entitled, *Law Office Procedures Manual for Solos and Small Firms*, Third Edition (ABA, 2005). This workbook can help you memorialize the procedures for your office.

Client Communication Systems

Attorney-Client Relationship

Effective and regular communication is the foundation of positive and profitable relationships with your clients. To build relationships and avoid problems, communicate with your clients throughout your representation. Follow these guidelines:

1. *Listen to your client.* Learn the client's initial goals for the relationship and put them in writing. Provide realistic advice and guidance. Continue to listen to the client's goals and expectations throughout the relationship. If the goals or expectations change, note these in writing to the client.

2. *Provide a written fee agreement.* This is the foundation of your lawyer-client relationship. The written fee agreement should encompass the scope of the representation, the basis for the fee, the timing of your services, and any other issues negotiated.

3. *Write a nonengagement letter when you decline representation.* If you decline to represent a prospective client, write a letter to confirm your "nonengagement," so the "client" doesn't wrongfully claim later that you were his or her lawyer.

4. *Write a disengagement letter when representation ends.* A disengagement letter should be sent with a final bill. An order of withdrawal may also still be necessary.

5. *Schedule periodic, face-to-face meetings with your client.* Use these meetings to build your relationship with your client, especially if the circumstances of the case or the expectations of your client change.

6. *Recognize special communication problems with "difficult" clients.* Learn to identify problem clients who may need more direct communications. These clients include lawyer shoppers, clients who are reluctant to pay retainers or who seek reduced retainers, vengeful clients, and clients who have unreasonable expectations. Do not be afraid to terminate a client appropriately if the problems persist, for you may be the client's next defendant.

Telephone Communications

The telephone is an important communication tool, and managing your calls is critical. Many clients choose sole practitioners and small firms because they want quick access to their lawyers. Following are a few guidelines to keep clients happy (and remember, a happy client is a paying client):

1. *Handle incoming calls professionally and appropriately.* Your receptionist is the "Manager of First Impressions." The way your receptionist welcomes and handles clients by telephone (and in person) sets the tone for how clients view your firm. Poor skills and attention result in fewer clients. If you are unavailable to talk to clients, your receptionist must take clear and accurate messages and leave the clients confident that their messages will get to you. If you have an answering service or machine, make sure that the outgoing message is clear and the system works properly; test it from time to time. If you retrieve your own messages, write them on individual message slips so you have a record of each call. Use message slips on colored paper to make them easier to find on your desk or in your briefcase.

2. *Use each telephone message slip as a prompt to return the call.* When returning the call, take notes of the conversation with your client; if you do not get through to the client on the first attempt, make a note of the date and time on the slip. If your client complains that you did not call back, you will have a record of your good-faith attempt(s).

3. *Respond to all telephone calls within twenty-four hours.* If at all possible, respond the same day. If you cannot respond, assign a responsible staff member to call and take a detailed message.

4. *If possible, set aside blocks of time each day to return telephone calls from clients.* Prompt return calls are appreciated by clients and will help build your relationships with them.

Written Communications

Frequent and thorough written communications with clients offer another way of building and strengthening lawyer-client relationships. Suggestions for written communications include the following:

1. *Send copies of documents and materials to the client.* Give your client a constant reminder of your progress by sending copies of most, if not all, written materials in the matter. Send a copy of all pleadings and motions, along with a brief note of explanation and a reminder to call you with any questions. Also send copies of correspondence to and from opposing counsel in the same manner. If you are billing hourly, be sure to log this time. If you are billing on a flat-fee basis, be sure to include this service in your quoted fee.

2. *Give your client a file for written communications.* Give your client a legal file folder when he or she signs the written fee agreement. Put the client's copy of the written fee agreement in the file, and instruct

your client to keep all written communications, pleadings, and bills in the file for future reference.

3. *Use bills to communicate.* Monthly bills can be an excellent form of communication with your client. The bill should project your efforts on behalf of the client. Use detailed and descriptive terms that inform the client of your activities. Avoid short descriptions such as "Services Rendered" or "Research." A bill that projects effort and value is more likely to get paid!

4. *Create a standard cover letter for the client.* If you make a form cover letter for each client, you can generate a letter quickly to any client. Include the client address block, greeting, and salutation, and preformat the form letter for your letterhead. Store it in your computer for easy retrieval the next time you need to send the client a letter. This will keep your costs low by increasing your productivity.

Docket/Calendar Control System

A proper docket/calendar control system must have at least two separate calendars: both paper based, or one paper based and one computer based. Following are guidelines for ensuring a useful and accurate system:

1. *Two individuals must keep calendars.* The key to a successful docket/calendar control system is to have two sets of eyes and two brains frequently comparing and updating the calendars. You can control the entries on one calendar and a staff person can control the other. (If you are a sole practitioner without employees, consider sharing the task with a convenient, noncompeting colleague.) Together, compare the two calendars on a weekly or biweekly basis, making sure you have not forgotten to add an event to both calendars, accidentally double-booked time, or recorded an event on the wrong day or time. Immediately resolve any discrepancies. This system helps correct inevitable human errors in scheduling, and also provides an accurate backup calendar if the other calendar is lost or destroyed.

2. *Train staff on using the system.* Staff should be adequately trained to schedule calendar events properly, and should understand the paramount importance of an accurate calendar.

3. *Place events on the calendars according to the system.* When a new event is scheduled—such as a client meeting, deposition, closing, or discovery due date—the date and time of the event should be placed

on both calendars. Develop a form that is circulated to all calendars in your firm or practice group.

One person should be charged with receiving all incoming mail, faxes, and hand deliveries. Each incoming document should be date/time stamped and reviewed to see if it is a docket/calendar item. The item should be placed on one calendar immediately. The document should then be forwarded to the lawyer who will manage the calendaring for the second independent calendar. If the event is set by telephone or in person, the person scheduling the event should give the details to the person in charge of the second calendar.

If the calendar item is court related (such as a notice of hearing or discovery date), then the person receiving the document should make a copy for the tickler file. (See the next section for details on creating a tickler system.)

4. *Perform cross-checks.* The system must be cross-checked periodically—preferably weekly. Each Friday, a weekly calendar for the following week, showing all events for all lawyers in the firm or practice group, should be distributed to each lawyer and appropriate staff. At that time, the tickler file (see below) should be cross-checked against the items on the calendar. Thereafter, the two calendars should be compared for the following week. At least once per month, the two calendars should be compared for a four- to six-month time period.

5. *Plan for emergency situations.* In case of illness or emergency, each lawyer should have a backup lawyer to handle court dates and certain other matters on the calendar. If you are a sole practitioner, find a compatible colleague who can monitor your cases. Seek permission from your clients to have another lawyer handle any emergencies while you are away. Be sure to check for conflicts in advance and resolve them.

Reminder/Tickler System

A reminder/tickler system is a way to remind you of upcoming events or deadlines. It is separate from your calendar, and works as an independent system to make sure you never miss an important event or deadline. The tickler system can be part of a case management program on your computer, or it can be a paper-based manual system you create yourself. The best one is whichever one works for you. Following are some helpful suggestions:

1. *For a manual system, use a file with thirty-one subparts.* Create a file or use an accordion file with at least thirty-one subparts, numbered one to thirty-one. Make a copy of each document with dated events—such as motions, notices, hearings, discovery dates, letters to opposing

counsel for which you are awaiting response, and deposition notices—and place it in the file according to the date of the month on
the document. The date of the event should also be entered on your
calendar system. You or a staff member should regularly check the
tickler file at least several days or a week in advance. (It is fine to file
documents for different months in the same folder.)

2. *Check your existing software for tickler systems.* Computer-based calendaring programs and personal information managers (PIMs) usually
   include some form of tickler system. Any of these software programs
   can be helpful if used consistently.

3. *Conduct reviews of the system.* Because no system is foolproof, you
   should plan a physical review of each of your files at least six times
   per year. This often results in catching events you missed, and may
   even generate new ideas or tactics in a matter.

Conflicts Checking System

Each firm should have a written policy on conflicts and how to check for client
conflicts. The policy should include a process for maintaining a conflicts filing
system, a procedure for checking conflicts before a prospective client is interviewed, and a procedure for checking conflicts before hiring new lawyers
or staff. You may find the following suggestions helpful:

1. *An alphabetical file card system that includes all clients and opposing
   clients may be adequate for some practices.* List the type of legal service performed next to the client name. Also note the date the file was
   opened, the date it was closed, and the lawyers in your office assigned
   to the matter. If you do corporate work, include additional information
   about officers, directors, subsidiaries and parent companies, principal owners, and other professionals serving the entity. You must also
   keep track of prospective clients you interview, but who do not engage your services.

2. *Keeping your conflicts file on a computer can be very effective if the information is kept up-to-date and is well organized.* Many lawyers use
   their case management or time-and-billing programs to enter all
   clients, even clients not retaining the firm. The program can then be
   searched to check for conflicts. One way to establish an inexpensive,
   computer-based conflict system is to create a WordPerfect or Word
   document that includes the names of all potential conflicts. You can
   then search that document for possible conflicts by using the
   "search" function in the word-processing program.

The more complex the matters you handle, the more sophisticated and thorough your conflicts system should be. You can delegate this task, but you should not abdicate responsibility.

File Management System

After calendaring, a file system creates the greatest opportunity for sloppy management. Sloppy files lead to sloppy cases. Sloppy cases lead to disgruntled clients. Disgruntled clients lead to—well, we don't need to go there! Effective file management includes a system for filing each client file, and filing each paper document in each file. An organized file allows you to work more efficiently, and shows the client your level of commitment to the matter. Consider the following guidelines:

1. *For good file control, develop an easy system and stick to it.* Start with centralized storage of all files; alphabetical storage of files in a file cabinet will do. (Some lawyers swear by a numerical filing system that avoids rearranging file drawers when new clients arrive. It requires you to memorize the file number for each client.) Even if you are a sole practitioner without administrative help, file the files correctly each time. Do not leave files on your desk unless you are working on the file. Each file should have the client name displayed on the file tab. Avoid file labels that include detailed client information; when you take the file to court or other public places, confidential information may be visible for all to see.

2. *For good file organization, create a filing system for each file, based upon your particular practice area.* Use files that have at least four inside surfaces with prongs to attach documents. Keep each file organized the same way, so that you know where each type of document is in each file. For example, file all documents related to your attorney-client relationship inside the front cover. Place all correspondence on one surface, and all pleadings on another. Use the additional surfaces for discovery forms, evidentiary documents, and reports.

3. *Use a thorough system for closing and storing client files.* At the end of each matter, review your client's file for materials that can be returned to the client. Make copies of case law, briefs, and memos that may be useful for your "forms file." If you agree to keep the client file, be sure to maintain the file in a safe, secure location for future reference. Let your client know you will keep the file in storage for a minimum of five years. (See D.C. Legal Ethics Opinion 283.) Though it is true that your client is more likely to return to your services knowing that you have

a complete history and file, the point is that you have a responsibility to maintain the file properly.

Form/Document/Evidence Management and Retrieval System

Creating a process to recover pleadings, briefs, and memos from case files will save you time and effort the next time you encounter a similar case or factual issue. The basic idea is to save helpful documents you created or copied so you do not have to re-create the documents from scratch. Also, you must develop a way to ensure the proper safekeeping of client documents, evidence, and other materials. Try using the following procedures:

1. *Organize ways to recover useful documents from files.* After preparing a pleading or brief, store the document in a "forms" directory of your word-processing program for later access and use. The same issue may arise in a later case, and you will already have the basis for a new pleading or brief. At the end of each matter, search the physical file for documents from all counsel in the case, which may be used for pleadings or briefs in later cases. Copies of published cases should also be recycled from client files for use in later cases.

2. *Use separate file drawers to archive these documents.* In one drawer, file the pleadings, briefs, and memos alphabetically in folders labeled by subject area. In another drawer, file copies of published cases alphabetically in folders by case name. Even if you keep only the leading cases in your practice area, reusing the copies of these cases in the future will save time, money, and trees.

3. *You are responsible for the proper storage and safekeeping of your client's materials.* Important client documents and evidence should be protected from theft, fire, or other physical damage. Most lawyers do not have space or resources to house everything in fireproof file cabinets, but there are some things that may be worth the additional investment. For example, a "one-of-a-kind" piece of evidence in your possession should probably be kept in a fireproof safe. Evidentiary photos can be stored separately from the negatives; store the negatives off-site in a secure and confidential location, such as a safe-deposit box.

Timekeeping and Billing Systems

An efficient timekeeping system captures more billable time. An efficient billing system helps you collect your fees for the time billed. Following are some procedures for establishing both:

1. *Keep a time sheet on hand at all times.* The time sheet can be a preprinted form or a "pop-up" timer on your computer. Decide what type of time-capturing device is best for you, and stick to it.

2. *When you finish a task for a client, log your time immediately.* Studies are unanimous: The sooner you log your time after completing the task, the greater your financial return on the time billed. If you wait to log the time, you are likely to forget to bill it. And if you do remember later, you will often forget the actual amount of time spent on the task, and log less time so you do not risk overcharging the client.

3. *Update your billing system regularly.* Periodically throughout the month, transfer your time sheets into your billing system. This way, at the end of the month, all time logged is ready to be billed.

4. *Use a regular, standard procedure for billing clients.* The primary goal of billing is to turn your legal services into financial compensation. Send monthly bills to every client for whom you did work that month, and to any client who still owes you money.

   The secondary goal of billing is to communicate with the client. A properly drafted bill informs the client of the progress in the case. Even if you didn't do any work that month for an active client, getting your name and telephone number before the client keeps you in your client's mind.

   Print your bills (on firm letterhead) and mail them on the same day each month. Clients will expect to receive a bill about the same time each month. Time your bills to reach your clients at the point in the month when they are most likely to have funds to pay.

5. *Discuss expenses with your client.* Be sure to do this on a regular basis. Reach an understanding about discretionary expenses, such as large-volume copying and overnight-delivery charges.

6. *Consider establishing a credit card merchant account so you can accept client payments by credit card.* You can do this through the financial institution that handles your other banking needs. The cost is usually less than $400 for the credit card scanner and printer, plus approximately 3 percent of each transaction. It is an inexpensive way to increase your collections.

7. *If a bill is going to be unusually large, call the client to discuss it.* Do not feel guilty and reduce the bill. Make sure the client understands the value of your work, and your efforts to provide value to the client.

Periodic Reevaluation

Every law practice system and procedure should be reviewed periodically, for two important purposes: to see whether each system is being used as intended, and to evaluate whether the system is working as intended. If you and your staff are not using a system or procedure the way it was meant to be used, it will be impossible to evaluate the system fairly. At the same time, your evaluation may reveal that the reason the system is not being used is because of problems with the system or procedure. Once you know what the real problem is, you can look for a solution.

Make time to get away from your office every few months to review all the systems and procedures used in your practice. Treat these occasions as "firm retreats" and set the dates and times well in advance so nothing gets scheduled at the same time. If you can, go somewhere relaxing. Be sure to include your staff, if you have a staff. If you are a solo working without any support staff, consider bringing in someone from outside your office to help you with the review. Most state and local bar organizations offer some help in this area.

File Retention and Document Management

31

Terri Olson

Gentle Reader: Who says there's a right way and a wrong way of doing things?
Miss Manners: Miss Manners does. You want to make something of it?

Miss Manners' Guide to
Excruciatingly Correct Behavior

Why Organize?

Bring up the subject of filing in a law office, and almost everyone agrees that a well-maintained file cabinet or file room should be a high priority. Yet, as a consultant who regularly visits firms of all sizes and descriptions, I have seen that practice and theory in this area are very far apart indeed. Most law firms have poorly organized files. Some can't even find the files to see whether they're organized or not.

Why is this important enough to merit a chapter on the subject? Obviously, there are malpractice issues involved here. If you can't locate your files or the papers within them, you can't get work done for your clients in a timely or accurate fashion. Many malpractice claims and bar complaints arise over situations such as the following:

◆ A lawyer missed a deadline because he placed the file (which he was using to remind himself of the work that needed doing) in the trunk of his car and forgot about it.

◆ A lawyer lost an important client document that was supposed to be in the file on which she was working. Although the file could be located, the document was nowhere to be found.

◆ A firm placed an order relating to one case in another file and sent the wrong client a copy of the order, violating client confidentiality and embarrassing the firm.

◆ When work on a file was completed, the paralegal put the file in the closed-file storage room. No request for final billing was made, so no one in the firm noticed that $3,000 of client funds remained in trust.

◆ One year after a case was concluded, the client claimed the lawyer lied to her. The file, which could have verified one position or the other, was nowhere to be found, although other closed files of the same age were in the file room.

In most firms, these situations don't result in the worst-case scenarios described above. At the last moment, someone finds the missing document, calls opposing counsel, or somehow manages to pull the fat out of the fire. But the cost in lost lawyer time and money, extra secretarial work, and weakened attorney-client relationships is staggering.

The chief argument I get from staff is that organizing files "takes too much time." With dictation to type, phones to answer, and depositions to schedule, no one wants to sit down and make labels for tab dividers or log incoming documents into a file. I maintain that the time spent in these tasks is minimal and much more than amply made up by the amount of time *not* spent hunting for files or papers within files.

Also, procedures can be put into place to minimize the disruption and amount of time these organizational activities require. Ideally, if the materials needed—such as file labels, tab dividers, folders, client information sheets, and fee agreements—are readily at hand, setting up a new file should not take more than five to ten minutes of staff time (not including time needed to perform other tasks that may be required by the lawyer when a file is created, such as entering information in a billing system or sending a letter to an insurance agency). Returning documents to an already organized file should take less than a minute, including the time to "check in" or log documents.

Obviously, many law office systems affect filing, and not all are within the scope of this chapter. Conscientious law firms certainly should examine their procedures in areas such as these:

◆ Mail and fax handling: How are mail and fax transmissions opened, logged, sorted, routed, and placed in the file?

- Computerized litigation support: Is the firm taking advantage of the many computer programs available to log, summarize, annotate, and organize documents in litigation?
- Billing: How much time is spent going through files looking for expense or time records before billing? How many files are not placed in closed-file storage because final billing has not been completed?

Devising a Plan

Though I am adamant that there are good and bad ways to set up and administer files, I don't feel there is one best way for all law firms. Many factors—including, but not limited to, the size of the firm, the types of matters handled, and the personalities of the lawyers and staff—must be considered when making the best choice for your firm.

So does this mean that because it's a judgment call, anything goes? Not quite. It is true that your files may look different from those in the firm across the street, but certain basic concepts apply everywhere, and you need to consider them. Far too few firms devote any time or energy to these issues, and that's why law firm files look the way they do.

The central issues concerning file retention and document management are these:

- Location—where active files, closed files, and administrative files should be kept
- Processing—what happens to files when they're opened, closed, or put up for the day
- Tracking—how firms keep track of what's in the files and where the files are
- Organization—what the inside of the file should look like, and why

Within these areas, there's a lot of "wiggle room" for individual preferences or needs dictated by the size or type of file. Organizationally challenged law firms may find that a simple piece of paper in the front of a file that lists all documents in it is the best they'll be able to achieve, and represents a significant improvement over how things were in the past. Other firms may Bates stamp each document and enter the number in a document management program. But both kinds of firms are attempting, within reasonable limits suggested by their sizes and philosophies, to impose order on chaos—and that's what needs to be done.

Critical to the success of your organizational attempts are consistency and responsibility. Somebody within your firm—your secretary, your receptionist, or even you, if you don't have any staff assistance—must be clearly assigned the duties necessary to maintaining order. You must also clearly indicate what these duties are, and how they should be carried out.

You must not subvert your efforts by changing your policies at whim or allowing constant exceptions to the rules. If you determine that incoming documents must be logged into files, don't amend that rule to say, "except when I'm busy, and then I'll just toss them in." If you institute a checkout procedure for your files, don't apply the footnote, "except when I really need the file right this minute." And you must never reprimand staff for doing what you told them to do, even if you find yourself inconvenienced by your own policies.

Determining Who Does What

File management is not a single task; it is a system of interrelated tasks that combine to create an organized office. To determine who does what in your filing system, you must first break the process of file management into its component parts:

- Preparing files (organizing, setting tabs or dividers, placing form documents in blank files)
- Opening files
- Closing files
- Destroying files
- Logging file contents
- Putting documents in files
- Getting files out
- Putting files away

Not all of these functions must, of course, be handled by the same person. In fact, there are good reasons to have different persons responsible for various aspects of the filing system. Some procedures can be carried out by someone sitting at a desk; others require getting up and moving around. Some can be interrupted without serious consequences; others require concentration to complete without error. Some require a good amount of legal experience; others can be performed by any conscientious employee who follows directions well.

For some of you, the size of your firm dictates the personnel responsible for filing tasks. If you are all there is, then you will do the filing. If your support staff consists of a single secretary, then your secretary will do the filing. But if you are lucky enough or large enough to have a variety of support staff positions, I suggest you use experience, physical placement, and time available to help you determine who is responsible for each step. The following discussion of positions may help get you started.

Receptionist

Without a doubt, receptionists are underutilized in small firms, where there may not be enough foot traffic or telephone calls to keep them busy. One way to keep receptionists occupied during down time is to involve them in filing tasks that do not require getting up and moving to the file cabinets. Receptionists are also good choices for filing tasks that do not require intense concentration, as they are frequently interrupted. Consider having the receptionist perform the following tasks:

◆ Preparing files: type internal file labels (such as exhibits and correspondence), blank fee agreements, and client information sheets so extra copies will be on hand when files need to be opened

◆ Opening files: physically create the file label, place documents in the file, and open the file on whatever case management and/or billing programs the firm has (Access to the billing software can easily be limited to simple data entry; the receptionist will not be able to pull up everyone's salaries.)

◆ Closing files: pull duplicates from files, check for outstanding trust or accounts receivable balances, and close the file in your case management or billing software—*if* the receptionist has experience and can be trusted to exercise good judgment (If your receptionists tend to be inexperienced—which is, unfortunately, frequently the case in a position with such high turnover—you may wish to leave these tasks to an experienced secretary.)

Secretary

A secretary is a good choice for filing tasks that either require some experience and judgment or cannot be done by someone remaining seated. If you have a file clerk, the file clerk can handle the latter tasks. Secretarial filing tasks might include the following:

◆ Pull documents that need to be reviewed (if your policy is to separate documents from the file as a whole).

◆ Use the firm's tickler system to determine which files need to be worked on that day, pull those files, and place them on the lawyer's desk.

◆ Put incoming documents in the appropriate files.

◆ Copy documents or files as requested.

◆ Close files: pull duplicates from files, check for outstanding trust or accounts receivable balances, archive word-processing documents, and close the files in case management or billing software.

File Clerk or File/Copy Clerk

If your firm has a file clerk, then first of all, good for you! Too few firms do. Now put that person to work doing all the tasks that do not require legal judgment and also require the person to be in motion—copying documents and placing them in the appropriate files. Although the job description sounds simple, even a small firm with fewer than one hundred files in litigation can keep a clerk busy copying and filing for two to three hours a day.

Lawyer

Unless you have no staff at all, your involvement in filing should be kept to an absolute minimum. As the saying goes, "Work should be performed by the lowest-compensated person capable of performing the task." So unless your secretaries make lawyers' salaries, it is they, and not you, who should handle the filing.

This may seem like a rather obvious point; few lawyers would argue that they should be elbow-deep in a file cabinet for a good portion of the day. But what actually happens in many law firms (as opposed to what is supposed to happen) is that the lawyer opens a file, begins looking for a document, and absentmindedly begins organizing the documents chronologically in an effort to find the paper. Or, upon discovering that a case everyone thought would settle is now going to trial, a lawyer may sit down and begin, almost without conscious thought, to sort documents into what will become a trial notebook. If you do that, you are well on the way to becoming the office file clerk.

The good news is that usually these things happen because there is no system in place for organizing and logging documents as the file is created and worked. So, if you follow the advice given in these pages for developing a system for having your files organized from "Day One," you will not need to scramble to prepare a file for trial.

Developing Written Procedures

Once you have decided what you are going to do about your files, and who will be responsible for them, you must commit your system to writing. This is the only way to make sure it gets done the right way, the same way, every time.

Like other oral traditions, instructions that are not written tend to get corrupted over time. You will also have to repeat your instructions to each new staff person you bring onboard. And you will have no easy way of ensuring your instructions are being followed. On the other hand, a written checklist can be signed off on, initialed, or otherwise marked to indicate compliance.

Two sets of written instructions are involved in this process:

1. *Job Description*: You must write who is responsible for filing duties, and what those duties are. If your receptionist will open files and the secretary close them, put this information in both their job descriptions. You do not need to write the full instructions for how these tasks are to be carried out in the staff job descriptions, although you can. What is more commonly used for this purpose is a procedural manual.

2. *Procedural Manual*: This is a book outlining the specific procedures approved by your firm as the right way to open a file, close a file, answer the telephone, sort the mail, and the like. A procedure can be simply a description of how the task is to be performed, or it can be a checklist that describes how a task is to be performed, with a place where staff can check off and date each step as it's completed. I prefer the latter, although sole practitioners with a single secretary might consider it overkill. (For a step-by-step guide to creating a procedures manual, see *Law Office Procedures Manual for Solos and Small Firms*, Third Edition (ABA, 2005))

If You Are Your Own Secretary

After reading the above, some of you may be saying, "This is all well and good if you have a secretary, but my law firm consists of *me*!" If you are a "true solo," without any staff, does this mean you cannot have a file management system in your firm? Of course not. It is true that implementing a consistent system is, in some ways, harder for the solo operating alone. But it can—and more importantly, should—be done. The trick is in mimicking the way the system would work in a larger firm.

Write the procedures. It may seem silly to create a written list of procedures for opening or closing a file when you are the only one doing the work. But it's necessary for two reasons: (1) the written list will help you organize your time and remember what you have and haven't done, and (2) at some point you will probably have clerical assistance, and it will be far easier to transfer the responsibilities to another if these tasks have been codified in some fashion.

Organize your time. Instead of handling the filing chores as time permits and the spirit moves, assign specific blocks of time (your "clerical" time) to opening files, organizing papers within files, and so on. You will find that you get more work done in less time when you focus on one process, and, again, it makes handing the work off in the future easier.

Computerized File Management

In today's climate of ubiquitous technology, what does it mean to suggest implementing computerized file management? A host of related but distinct applications may come to mind, including bar coding, file tracking, litigation support systems, Bates-stamping systems, and deposition and other document indexing, storage, and retrieval. Obviously, a complete discussion of all this is beyond the scope of this book, let alone this chapter, but we can hit a few points to ponder:

1. *Expense*: One little-considered "gotcha" of systems designed to manage documents or files is their frequent dependence upon expensive hardware. How do your documents get into the system? With the high-speed scanner with document feeder. How do you track the files going in and out of the file room? With the bar-code reader. What's the best way to distribute the twenty-five annotated copies of the deposition? With the multifunction, networked printer/copier. These hardware purchases can really mount up. Then there's the cost of training, maintenance, and upgrades. For any purchase you consider, be sure to ask these questions: What is the total price for everything necessary to implement the system as it's described? What are the annual maintenance and upkeep costs? How much training is recommended for optimal use?

2. *Portability*: Even in this day and age, higher-end systems for document tracking or hardware-dependent applications, such as bar-coding systems, may be proprietary and not easily transferable from one system to another. Ironically, some firms may view this as a plus, if they don't want departing associates to be able to copy five years' worth of research with a click of the "send to" button.

3. *Ease of Use*: In a solo's office, it's unlikely that staff will be dedicated to one particular task, such as scanning and indexing incoming documents or checking files back into the file room. While we always want our computer systems to be easy to use, it's imperative that in a small practice—where one person may go from the scanner to the bar-coding "wand" to the case management and document-tracking program in a matter of minutes—all these systems be intuitive in everyday use.

For more information on computerized file management and on many other topics as well, solos are encouraged to contact their state or local bars' practice management assistance programs.

Selected Resources
for Part III

from the ABA Law Practice
Management Section

The Complete Guide to Designing Your Law Office, by Jon S. Schultz and Suzette S. Schultz, 2005.

Easy Self-Audits for the Busy Law Office, by Nancy Byerly Jones, 1999.

The Essential Formbook: Comprehensive Management Tools for Lawyers, Volume III: Calendar, Docket, and File Management/ Law Firm Financial Analysis, by Gary A. Munneke and Anthony E. Davis, 2003.

The Essential Formbook: Comprehensive Management Tools for Lawyers, Volume IV: Disaster Planning and Recovery/Risk Management and Professional Liability Insurance, by Gary A. Munneke and Anthony E. Davis, 2004.

How to Start and Build a Law Practice, Fifth Edition, by Jay G Foonberg, 2004.

Keeping Good Lawyers: Best Practices to Create Career Satisfaction, by M. Diane Vogt and Lori-Ann Rickard, 2000.

Law Office Procedures Manual for Solos and Small Firms, Third Edition, by Demetrios Dimitriou, 2005.

Law Practice, bimonthly publication of the ABA Law Practice Management Section.

Paralegals, Profitability, and the Future of Your Law Office, by Arthur G. Greene and Therese A. Cannon, 2003.

Recruiting Lawyers: How to Hire the Best Talent, by Marcia Pennington Shannon and Susan G. Manch, 2000.

Technology Manual

Solos can look and act "bigger" than they are by leveraging technology. Some solos even use innovative technology to compete with larger firms for large clients.

Part IV covers the vital information that every solo should know about computers and other law office equipment, along with chapters on software tools, e-mail and Internet use, security, and more. In addition, you'll find advice on training options for your staff and when and how to bring in a computer consultant.

Just as the latest aviation technology helps make flying an airplane easier, legal technology will ensure that your solo practice hums along at top speed, resulting in a more-efficient, productive practice and happier, more-satisfied clients.

How to Assess Your Technology Needs **32**

David J. Bilinsky

Introduction

It has been four years since I first wrote this chapter. Much has changed in legal technology over this time, and yet the principles underlying the acquisition of legal technology have stayed relatively the same. Certainly, technology has become completely integrated into the practice of law—as a practice management advisor, I find it extremely rare these days to come across a lawyer using a manual accounting system or working without an e-mail system. Lawyers have migrated to case management software, evidence analysis and case strategy software, document management systems, and personal digital assistants (PDAs).

While seemingly yesterday we were dealing with issues such as data backup methods, the impact of the Internet, and the need to institute firewalls and antivirus software, today's technology has created a whole new set of issues with which lawyers must grapple: wireless network (in)security, Adobe Acrobat and scanners, privacy legislation implications, viruses, worms, spyware and malware, password security, instant messaging, extranets, the theft of office computers containing confidential data, and the like. It is understandable that lawyers sometimes say, "I just want to get back to practicing law!" However, once the magic technological bottle is opened, there is no going back and storing the genie on the shelf.

Accordingly, we all must acquire the management skills needed to implement legal technology into our offices, for the benefit of our clients and ourselves. Indeed, despite the daily headlines regarding the problems with technology, the benefits far outweigh any drawbacks. (Just try to wrestle Amicus Attorney or Time Matters from a dedicated user!)

The Steps in Assessing and Meeting Your Needs

Let's explore the steps needed to ensure that you get maximum benefit from your technology dollars, and that your systems meet your needs, are robust and secure, and allow you to migrate smoothly into newer technology as your needs change and systems evolve.

First: Consider How Your Type of Practice Relates to Your Technological Needs

What type of legal services do you render, and how does that drive your office technological needs? A solo criminal lawyer can function perfectly well with a cell phone, a PDA, some basic word-processing support, and back-of-fice accounting support for rendering invoices and keeping track of retainers in the trust account. Conversely, a solo transaction lawyer can make use of a good document precedent or document generation system (integrated into the word-processing system) that allows for quick production of a core of standard documents, a document management system, and integrated time and billing with general and trust accounting. A solo litigator can benefit from a case management system, evidence analysis software, scanners for digital-izing evidence, and trial strategy or electronic litigation notebook software. Of course, all can benefit from online legal research, Internet access, e-mail systems, PDAs, cell phones, photocopiers, and good telephone systems.

From an analysis of your legal services should come an analysis of your needs, your business flows, and your projected growth. Your business needs should drive your technological planning. To lawyers who ask, "Should I get Windows XP Pro or Home Edition?," my answer is, "What are your needs in terms of networking, software, and mobility? Features of certain operating systems clearly outweigh others, given what you need to do and the software you need to run. Your present and future needs should determine which operating system is most effective for you." As a simple rule, you should buy more technological capacity than you currently need (that is, avoid being constrained by future growth), without spending money on features that bear little relation to what you do.

Lawyers' needs generally go beyond document production, office management, and accounting support. As a solo, marketing activities should consume a goodly portion of your time and resources; after all, you need to draw in the high-paying clients for whom you will render services! These days, effective marketing can and does take place via technology. You must plan your marketing activities and determine how they can best be assisted with technology. For example, you could build an e-mail list of clients and send them monthly electronic newsletters. A high-quality, electronic newsletter is inexpensive to produce, adds value to existing clients, and assists in recruiting new clients, due to the ease with which it can be retransmitted from present clients to potential clients.

Sit down and think about the business goals of your practice—what you need to do to make your office run efficiently and effectively in terms of end results—and consider how that is related to your technological needs.

Second: Determine What Equipment You Already Have, and What You Can Obtain for Low Cost

What technology or equipment do you already have? What can you obtain for low or no cost? There are many ways to secure items without necessarily paying full retail cost. Used-furniture stores, office bankruptcy sales, and bailiffs can be great sources of serviceable equipment. (Back in the days of typewriters, I once acquired a wonderful IBM Selectric typewriter in this way.) Desks, chairs, lamps, fax machines, telephone systems, filing cabinets, computers, scanners, photocopiers, and the like can all be acquired in this way. Put your money into the mission-critical systems that you need; look for ways to economize on the rest.

Third: Consider Where You Want to Go

Where do you want to go? Present needs may not reflect real change and efficiencies that can be achieved by rethinking, reworking, and upgrading your system workflows and your technological investment. For example, by integrating your case management and accounting systems (for example, integrating Time Matters, Amicus Attorney, or PracticeMaster with PCLaw, Tabs III, or Juris), you can avoid paying staff to key in your billable time entries, as these systems track your billable time and post it directly into your accounting system.

As another example, having the ability to update your Web site quickly can be a great marketing tool. Many solos and small firms put great effort into their Web sites, which can pay huge dividends in practice growth. (See **www.visalaw.com** and **www.bcfamilylaw.ca** as two examples of very successful, award-winning, small-firm Web sites.)

Scanning and imaging is another emerging law firm technology. David Masters, a solo lawyer in Colorado, has had great success in implementing Adobe Acrobat's PDF document format into his litigation practice. Taking your office in a paperless direction holds great promise for reducing the time needed to search for and retrieve documents, as well as for more effective advocacy.

Document assembly programs (such as Hot Docs and GhostFill) allow for the automation of standard, repetitive documents. When lawyers combine these programs with alternative billing methods, they can achieve billing rates that are multiples of their nominal hourly billing rates.

Accordingly, you should look not only at how you run your present practice, you should also think about how you can implement new systems that will allow you to become more effective and efficient, and reach out to new clients.

Fourth: Think About Your Replacement Timetable

What is your replacement timetable? You should purchase a "Cadillac" only if the return on your investment justifies such an expense. If the "Cadillac" will be replaced in five years or so, perhaps a different model would deliver a better cost/benefit ratio.

When acquiring any piece of equipment, look at the total cost of ownership (TCO). For example, an ink-jet printer has a low initial cost, but the cost of the ink soon eclipses the initial purchase price. A laser printer's cost can be several times that of an ink-jet, but the subsequent costs per page are relatively low. If you use an ink-jet printer only sporadically, the high costs per page probably do not matter. By pricing out the lifetime of the equipment and the expected throughput of the equipment, you can determine your unit costs for the technology (such as the total costs per page for your printer).

Furthermore, you should always reflect upon the useful lifetimes for computer hardware and achieving the "sweet spot" falling somewhere between initial cost, performance, and TCO. Look at your essential software, your desired or additional software, and how often you will need to upgrade these. Both software and hardware require replacement and maintenance. Build this into your planning.

Plan your replacement timetable by ranking your most critical technology to your least. Schedule regular replacement of your critical equipment to ensure you do not face an unexpected expense when a necessary piece of technology fails due to outlasting its reasonable lifetime.

Fifth: Budget and Plan

Budget, budget, budget. Plan, plan, plan. Pencils were made with erasers to allow mistakes to be corrected easily. However, expenditures are hard to erase. There are many considerations—from telephone systems to photocopiers/scanners to staplers and desks to paper and printers. Write all your possible needs on paper by running through a typical day, from start to finish. Separate your "wants" from your "needs."

Then plan your floor space and layout. Pay particular attention to existing electrical outlets (they will be a big constraint on where you can place equipment) and networking jacks. Decide what needs you have—for power, networking jacks, telephone jacks, and the like. Plan the layout of the office and envisage work flows. What needs adjusting? Where will you store the photocopier? Paper? Where will the telephone system be installed?

Build an initial budget for setup and technological purchases, as well as for your cash flow and expenditures over the next year. Build in unrecoverable receivables as well as unexpected expenses. Try to ensure that your technological expenditures can be curtailed or eliminated if forecasted cash flows do not materialize as expected. Certainly build in training time and costs to make maximum use of your equipment.

Take your replacement timetable and price out the ballpark costs over your replacement cycle. Now build those costs into your office budget—if necessary by amortizing the costs over the equipment's lifetime—and establish a contribution fund to replace the equipment over time.

Sixth: Prioritize

Prioritize your purchases based upon your available funds, your needs, and your projected growth. Again, separate "needs" from "wants." Look at your essential systems and the frills. By prioritizing your purchases, you can help sort through your essential business needs and distinguish them from the frills.

Seventh: Don't Forget Training

I know many lawyers who use just a fraction of the technology they have already purchased—yet they always look for new things to buy. For example, spreadsheet programs such as Excel or QuattroPro can do many of the tasks of an expensive database program such as Access. They can maintain client lists, and be used for budgeting by building statements of adjustments and the like. The best news is that they are included in most standard office suites, so you do not pay anything extra for this technology. As another example, WordPerfect 12 can convert documents into PDF format, without you purchasing the expensive Adobe Acrobat Writer. (The reader, which is free on the Internet, cannot create PDF documents.)

By implementing training on the software you already have, you can realize more benefit from your existing technological expenditures and hopefully use ingenuity to avoid further expenses. Training can bring out features you already paid for but may not realize are sitting there waiting to be used.

Eighth: Don't Forget the People Side

In my humble opinion, one of the downsides of working with technology is that we rely upon it to be there, 24/7. Unfortunately, I believe this "always on" aspect of technology causes us to look at staff members the same way—and this is dehumanizing. Notwithstanding a wonderful technological setup, working with technology still requires us to work with people and, as a result, we need to focus upon a major aspect of technology—the human side. Support staff will be needed to install, run, maintain, and use your technology. There are real human issues and considerations in this area for you to think about.

Ninth: Ensure Your Security

You are forced to consider security, privacy, and intrusion issues. Desktops, laptops, and PDAs are being stolen in distressing numbers. When you are a solo and a stolen computer contains all your accounting data and electronic files, not to mention your bring-forward and limitation date systems, you have a major ethical, liability, and logistical problem on your hands. You need to consider a system that secures your data, even if your laptop develops legs. Your office systems also need to be redundant and secure in the event of a component's failure, either through age or malicious act. Furthermore, the Internet is becoming a pool of viruses, worms, Trojan horses, browser hijackers, spyware, and other malicious applications. Your security system must be robust and secure enough to protect your data and your client's confidences.

Beyond Word Processing— Using the Rest of Your Office Suite

33

Daniel Pinnington

Introduction

Word-processing software is the foundation application in every law office, large or small. Microsoft Word and Corel WordPerfect are the two most widely used products and can be installed as "stand-alone applications" or as part of a "suite" of programs, including presentation software, spreadsheets, database programs, e-mail systems, and contact managers. Unfortunately, in many law offices, programs other than the word-processing applications are not being used to their maximum potential, if they are used at all.

What Is an Office Suite?

An office suite is a bundled set of software programs from the same company. Most basic suites include a word processor, a spreadsheet, and a presentation program. Some suites include a database program, an e-mail client, a personal information manager, a graphics application suite, and/or Web-authoring tools. Suites with more components cost more to purchase.

One key advantage of office suites is that all the programs within a given suite can interact with each other so that the user can move data, graphics, images, and other information seamlessly between programs. Another advantage is that each program within a suite will have a similar user interface—similar toolbars, menus, and options—so that time spent learning one program will transfer to the rest of the suite.

Word-Processing Software

The backbone of every office suite is the word-processing application. Until a few years ago, the legal profession was "standardized" on WordPerfect. That was certainly true during the DOS era, and even continued after the introduction of Microsoft Windows in the early 1990s. WordPerfect still has its devoted followers in law offices, but Microsoft Word has solidified its place as the market leader, in part because of the popularity of other members of the office suite—particularly Microsoft Excel and Microsoft PowerPoint.

This chapter will not delve into the nuances of word-processing programs, except to say that it is increasingly rare for law offices to adopt one brand of word-processing application and another brand of spreadsheet or presentation product.

Presentation Software

The most widely used presentation software is Microsoft PowerPoint. In fact, the term PowerPoint has become synonymous with presentation software. The version in Corel's WordPerfect suite is called simply Presentations. Apple has recently released a presentation program for Mac OSX called Keynote. Adobe Acrobat Pro now contains features that make it an attractive alternative to PowerPoint.

PowerPoint and other presentation programs are used to create and give presentations, from the basic "slide show" to ones containing sound, movies, and other sophisticated tools. Presentation software can also be used to create and automate traditional overhead transparencies, which can be printed on color laser printers for maximum effect and a truly professional look.

Presentation software is increasingly being used by lawyers in many practical and useful ways, from the courtroom or other tribunals to proceedings such as negotiations, mediations, and arbitrations. Presentation software also has great potential for client marketing purposes, either formally at seminars or informally in one-on-one settings. Lawyers and their marketing staff can create and communicate focused marketing messages to clients about the services and expertise the firm offers. Clients can easily be provided copies of presentations by e-mail message, CD, or DVD.

For more information on learning how, when, and why to create eye-catching computer presentations that are heard, understood, and retained, see *Persuasive Computer Presentations: The Essential Guide for Lawyers*, by Ann E. Brenden and John H. Goodhue, published by the ABA.

Spreadsheets

Spreadsheet programs top the list of *underused* software tools. Spreadsheets have the potential for helping virtually every lawyer become more productive. What's more, most lawyers already have a spreadsheet program installed—Excel if you use Microsoft Office, or Quattro Pro if you use WordPerfect Office.

Spreadsheets allow you to organize and manipulate numerical data or other information in many different ways. A spreadsheet is simply a rectangular table (or grid) of information. This information is often numerical or financial data, but it can also be dates or other textual information. Information in a spreadsheet is displayed in rows and columns. The intersection of a row and column is called a cell. Data or information within one or more cells can be manipulated and organized in many different ways, including in numerical calculations, and can be searched, sorted, or filtered to specified criteria. You can also create mathematical formulas within a cell that perform calculations based upon the values in other cells.

Spreadsheets allow you to change the appearance and formatting of information within them, including the size, color, and formatting of text or data within cells. Spreadsheets have extensive graphing capabilities. With just a few clicks on your mouse, you can transform a simple chart of numbers into a nicely formatted color graph in any one of hundreds of different formats. Most spreadsheets also have the ability to automate calculations or perform other manipulations of data with a scripting or programming language of some type.

Spreadsheets are very effective for doing financial calculations, including budgeting, tracking annual billings or hours, preparing financial statements on matrimonial or business matters, preparing asset summaries on estate matters, calculating total damages on litigation matters (including prejudgment and postjudgment interest), and calculating structured settlements.

The incredible power of spreadsheets comes from their ability to perform instant recalculations on dozens—or even hundreds—of related figures when one figure involved in a calculation is changed. For example, consider a spreadsheet that calculates damages on a complex and lengthy personal injury matter. It could include figures under several categories of damages (such as loss of income, medical expenses, pain and suffering, legal fees, and disbursements), and complex prejudgment interest calculations with interest rates that vary monthly over several years. Such a spreadsheet could be very useful for settlement purposes.

If settlement discussions occur over several months, the total damages can increase if further expenses are incurred, if damages amounts are amended, and if prejudgment interest accrues. There could easily be fifty or more figures that would need to be added to determine total damages and interest, and some of these figures could involve complex calculations on their own (prejudgment interest, in particular). If this were done by hand, even with the help of a calculator, it would be very time consuming to recalculate the damages if one or more figures involved were changed or if new amounts were added. On the other hand, if these calculations were done on a spreadsheet, you could amend existing amounts or add new figures in a few seconds, and the spreadsheet would do all necessary recalculations in the blink of an eye. Spreadsheet software also allows you to print a nicely formatted paper copy of the calculation, complete with headings or other information.

Spreadsheets aren't just for number crunching. They can also be used to sort and organize textual information. For example, in the litigation context, consider a listing of documents relevant to discovery. Each document in the list could have several pieces of descriptive information, including a Bates number, the date of the document, a brief description of the document, the name of the author of the document, an indication of the type of document (e-mail message, letter, contract), an indication of whether the document is privileged, an indication of whether the document was produced already, an indication of whether the document helps or hurts your position, and so on.

You could, of course, create this list in a Word or WordPerfect document, but it would be far better to create the list in a spreadsheet. Why? Simply because within a spreadsheet you could easily and instantly search, sort, or filter the list in many different ways that could help you better handle the matter.

Entering information in a spreadsheet is easy. If you already have it in a word-processing document, you can cut and paste it into a spreadsheet. If it is not in a word-processing document, you simply type it in, filling in the rows and columns of the spreadsheet. Each document would appear on a separate row. Each of the different pieces of descriptive information would appear in the same vertical column. Within the spreadsheet you could easily sort the documents by date, see all the documents to or from a particular individual, see only privileged documents, and so on. A spreadsheet makes it easy to print a paper copy of the full list of documents or a filtered subset (everything but privileged documents, for example), formatted exactly how you want, with all or some of your various descriptive pieces of information. Note also that you could easily cut and paste the list of your documents from a spreadsheet into your word processor.

Lawyers in every area of law have dozens, if not hundreds, of different ways in which they can use spreadsheets. An excellent guide to using spreadsheets in a law office is John Tredennick's book, *Lawyer's Guide to Spreadsheets*.

Databases

Database programs allow you to gather, organize, and manipulate information. In many ways, they are more powerful versions of spreadsheets. Once information is captured in a database, it can be manipulated or searched in a variety of ways. In addition, you can create paper or electronic reports that sort, total, and summarize the data in the database in a manner that is most appropriate to your needs.

Your firm probably already has one or more database programs. The most common example of a database in the law firm environment is a computerized accounting program system, which keeps track of legal fees, disbursements, and trust entries. The various practice management software products are also databases.

Though there are hundreds of specialized off-the-shelf database programs available for use in law offices, some lawyers may want to build databases for custom and specific needs. For instance, you may specialize in a particular area of law and have a number of different standard documents that you repeatedly generate. Perhaps there is no software program available that creates these documents or meets your needs. With a database, you can create a custom software program that collects and organizes the information relevant to the matters your office handles, and it will automate production of the documents you must create for handling those matters.

The most popular generic database management system in law firms is Microsoft Access. Larger law firms implement more powerful database technology, such as Microsoft SQL Server or Oracle.

Databases allow you the luxury of using and manipulating matter or firm-related information exactly how you want, often far more quickly and efficiently than you could otherwise do the work. However, implementing a custom database can be time consuming and expensive, and it requires staff with specialized expertise.

E-mail Clients and Contact Management Software

Some suites include contact management software, which is sometimes called personal information manager (PIM), and/or e-mail clients. In law offices, the most widely used e-mail client and PIM is Microsoft Outlook.

A PIM is a program that usually contains a book of names, addresses, and telephone numbers of contacts, a detailed calendar of events, and a "to do" list. It sometimes has the ability to record the time spent on various activities. A PIM serves as an electronic calendar and a telephone book.

Two PIMs commonly used in law offices are Microsoft Outlook and Novell Groupwise. A PIM can be a very useful time management tool for lawyers. Most PIMs can exchange data with personal digital assistants (PDAs) such as Palm Powered™ devices, which makes it very easy to take your calendar, contacts, and other information outside the office.

An e-mail client is a program that can send and receive e-mail messages. Microsoft Outlook has both a PIM and an e-mail client, and is part of the Microsoft Office suite. Although used mainly as an e-mail application, Outlook also provides calendar, task, and contact management. When used with Microsoft Exchange Server, it allows you to share calendar, contact, and task information with multiple people.

Web-Publishing Software

Most law firms now maintain Web sites for their clients and prospective clients. Many have also developed internal Web sites (intranets) that are used only within the firm, and private Web sites for external clients (extranets).

Web pages are created in a standard format called HyperText Markup Language (HTML). Creating HTML documents used to require specialized Web-publishing tools. Most word processors now permit a user to open an HTML document, edit the document, and save it back to HTML (both Word and WordPerfect support this). This means that it is relatively easy for a law firm to develop and publish its own Web materials.

Advanced users tend to use other products that have more advanced features for creating Web pages. Microsoft FrontPage (included in some versions of the Microsoft Office suite), Adobe GoLive, and Macromedia Dreamweaver are examples of these.

The Different Office Suites

Microsoft Office

The Standard Edition includes Word 2003, Excel 2003, Outlook 2003, and PowerPoint 2003, plus a collection of utilities, templates, and clip art. Like the latest versions of most programs and suites, Office 2003 has a handful of features mainly targeted at collaboration and data sharing. It makes greater use of Extensible Markup Language (XML), and includes a feature called information rights management (IRM), which authenticates users and allows you to specify who is permitted to read, edit, or distribute documents. Generally, these features are of interest to large business and enterprise users; for most, there may not be enough new features in this version to warrant upgrading from Office 2000 or Office XP.

Word is the most widely used word processor, both inside and outside the legal profession. It is a powerful and full-featured word processor, and allows you to create any document required in a law office. Word 2003 hasn't changed much from its previous incarnations. Most of the changes revolve around supporting new Office 2003 features, such as collaboration, XML, and IRM. It also has a new reading layout view, which divides the display into one or two screens or columns of text, much like the facing pages of a book. Protect Documents is another new feature, which lets you define the formatting styles that others can use for markup purposes. You can select areas of a document that are frozen or protected from edits or allow only certain people to edit certain areas.

Excel is the spreadsheet by which all others are judged. When it comes to crunching numbers or data, there is very little you can't do with Excel. Excel 2003 includes a few enhancements, including a list tool that allows you to identify a column of data as a dynamic list. Excel also supports Smart Tags. These allow you to link to external data.

PowerPoint is the most widely used presentation software. All recent versions have many features that allow you to prepare and present professional-looking presentations and handouts. Animation support has been beefed up in the latest version, PowerPoint 2003. You can define paths for objects to move along, and move multiple objects at the same time. You can now play video files in full-screen mode, and place video playback controls within a slideshow for easier control during a presentation. Another new feature, Package For CD, makes it easy to gather all the linked files necessary to run a presentation and copy them to CDs for distribution to others. With these new features, PowerPoint can do many of the things that the specialized trial presentation packages can do.

Outlook is the e-mail client included in the Microsoft Office suite. It is one of the most widely used e-mail programs, in both law offices and other business environments. Don't confuse the full version of Outlook with the more basic Outlook Express. Outlook Express is distributed for free with most Microsoft products, and can be used only for sending and receiving e-mail messages. The full version of Outlook includes e-mail capability, plus contact management, calendaring, and task management functionality. Many law offices using the full version use the contact management and calendaring features of Outlook. Outlook can be used as a stand-alone application, but can also operate in conjunction with Microsoft Exchange Server to provide enhanced functions for multiple users in an organization, such as shared mailboxes and calendars and meeting time allocations.

Corel WordPerfect Office

Corel's WordPerfect Office 12—its latest version—is designed to appeal to WordPerfect loyalists looking for smoother integration with the Microsoft Office environment. The Standard Edition includes WordPerfect, Quattro Pro, Presentations, an address book, and some other utilities. Many of the improvements in this version help it more seamlessly exchange data with Microsoft products. It also provides for an easy transition for anyone switching from Microsoft Office by allowing work in an interface that closely resembles the corresponding Microsoft programs. But while the back-and-forth compatibility is better than in previous versions, there will likely be problems with heavily formatted files.

Past and present WordPerfect users rave about the reveal codes feature, which is still part of the current version of WordPerfect. This feature allows simultaneous viewing and editing of both text and formatting in an easy and intuitive way. Word has no equivalent feature (although a third-party product can give you similar functionality—CrossEyes from Levit & James Inc., **www.levitjames.com**). A special legal interface mode has some law-office-specific tools for pleadings and other legal formats.

In terms of features and functionality, Quattro Pro is virtually on par with Excel. Presentations is a more basic presentation program than PowerPoint. Corel no longer upgrades the Paradox database, but still includes it in WordPerfect Office 12 Professional.

Those using earlier versions of WordPerfect who haven't experienced problems sharing documents with Microsoft Office users won't find much reason to upgrade to WordPerfect Office 12. But those who want to remain with WordPerfect and who need a suite that is more compatible with Microsoft Office should consider doing so.

OpenOffice

OpenOffice (**www.openoffice.org**) is a multiplatform office-productivity suite created as open-source software by interested members of the public. The source code that runs the software is in the public domain, and the suite is available to download for free. Yes, it is *free*.

OpenOffice 1.0 includes the key desktop applications that the other basic suites have, including a word processor (Writer), a spreadsheet (Calc), and a presentation program (Impress). It includes a drawing program (Draw), but not a database application. It also does not include an e-mail client, but will directly connect with external e-mail software. The OpenOffice suite will do pretty much everything you need to do in a law office. The user interfaces and feature sets of the various programs in the OpenOffice suite are as sophisticated as those of the other major office suites. OpenOffices native file format is XML, although it also works almost transparently with a variety of other file formats, including those of Microsoft Office, and HTML. It will view

PDF files and runs natively on almost every modern operating system, except Mac OS X.

Writer is at the heart of the suite and is a sophisticated word-processing and document layout program. It has all the key features the other major suites have, including special formatting for legal documents, autocorrect, indexing and linking, a versions system, the ability to work collaboratively, form-letter management, and database integration.

Calc is a powerful spreadsheet program with a comprehensive range of advanced functions, including cross-tabulation, summaries, natural-language formulas, templates with built-in functions, scenarios, and charting tools to visualize data in two or three dimensions. Calc can connect to most database programs.

Impress allows you to create effective and professional multimedia presentations. It includes templates, auto layout, two- and three-dimensional clip art, special-effects animation, and various other features necessary to prepare presentations and handouts. With Draw you can enhance your Impress presentations with your own diagrams or graphics. Draw will import and export graphics to and from all common formats.

Which Is the Best Suite for Your Office?

Picking the best suite for your office involves considering a number of factors. First of all, find out if there is a suite already installed on your computer. In all likelihood, there is. This option costs you nothing, at least for the software. Remember that you need to spend some time and money on training to learn these programs.

Next, don't assume you have to upgrade to the latest and greatest version of whatever suite you are using. When learning to use new software, you usually work with more basic features, and the programs in older suites may perfectly meet your needs, at least initially. Also, many of the applications in newer versions of various suites have virtually the same core functionality, adding only Web and collaboration functionality, which may not be essential or even necessary for you.

When it comes to price, Microsoft Office 2003 is the most expensive suite. It is available in different configurations. The different editions include different components. Most solos should consider the Small Business Edition.

WordPerfect Office 12 is somewhat cheaper than Microsoft Office, and is also available in different configurations. These include the Family Pack with light editions of WordPerfect and Quattro Pro, the Standard edition, and the Professional (license only) edition.

If you want to buy a new suite, or want to upgrade your existing suite, the best time to do this is when you buy a new computer. You won't beat the price you can get on a new suite or an upgrade when you are purchasing a new system. If you have previous versions of a suite, make sure you take advantage of upgrade pricing, which is always cheaper than the full price. Note that volume discounts may be available for as few as five users.

If you are on an extremely tight budget, and don't expect to be exchanging documents with clients regularly, OpenOffice is an alternative worth considering. It doesn't have an e-mail client or a database program, but it has a decent word processor, spreadsheet, and presentation program, and you can't beat its price: free!

For the sake of compatibility with the rest of the world, likely including all or most of your clients, Microsoft Office is probably the best choice. This is especially true if you expect to be regularly exchanging documents in their native formats with your clients. Documents do not always convert nicely when switched back and forth from one suite to another. Conversion problems will frustrate you and your clients, and can be avoided if you both use the same suite. However, though the compatibility of Microsoft Office is an important benefit, there are other factors to consider.

If you are still happily using it, the Corel WordPerfect Office suite may already be on your computer, and could make sense for you. Also, you and your staff will already be familiar with how the components within this suite operate. This is a bonus, and if compatibility with clients is not an issue, stay with it. Note that Presentations does not have the range of features that PowerPoint does. Also, Quattro Pro hasn't been updated since version 10, and Paradox, the database application, is not included in the Standard version of this suite.

If you're buying your first office suite and want to keep things as simple as possible, Microsoft Office 2003 Standard Edition is probably your best bet. However, take a close look at the Small Business Edition, which is well worth the extra money. The Standard Edition includes the three main applications (Word, Excel, and PowerPoint) that are the most widely used and considered by many to be the best in their respective classes. Office 2003 also includes Microsoft Outlook, which many law offices already use for their e-mail programs. Note that the Corel and OpenOffice suites do not include an e-mail client. If you have older computers in your office, note that Microsoft Office 2003 runs only under Windows 2000 or XP.

Making the Most of the Other Applications in Your Office Suite

The vast majority of people make use of only a small fraction of the functions and abilities of the software on their computers. This is equally true for all programs, including those people use every day, like word processors.

Making sure you and your staff make maximum use of all the technology available will transfer more dollars to your bottom line. Following are some things you can do to improve the computer skills of everyone in the firm:

1. *Training*: When it comes to competent use of any program, there is absolutely nothing more important than training. To get the most out of any software program, you must spend some time formally educating the people who will be using it. Remember that people have different learning styles. Some need to be taught in a formal and structured way, such as a classroom setting. Some prefer self-paced learning, which can be accomplished with books. Another option for self-learners is videotape or CD-based instruction.

2. *Take Baby Steps*: When you do sit down to try to increase your skills in a program, don't try to tackle too much at once. (And don't make your staff do so, either!) In conjunction with proper training, tackle one new program at a time, and, if you can, try to master one new feature or function at a time.

3. *Take the Tour*: Get a tour of any new application from someone who already knows it, and, ideally, who also knows what you need to do with it. That person will be able to walk you through the features and functions that will be the most helpful to you. Although you won't remember everything the person shows you, you will likely remember enough to be able to explore, find, and try things on your own.

Summary

Make and take the time to learn to use the other software programs in the office suite installed with your word processor. It is well worth your time to understand what these other programs can do, and to explore how they can be used in your office. Regardless of whether you want to be able to make more professional and compelling presentations, or access and manipulate data and information about your files, or practice using spreadsheets or databases, these other programs are powerful tools that can make your practice more productive and profitable. Remember, to make the most of these tools, it is essential to set aside the day-to-day pressures of work and make time for some formal training. Also, work to overcome any reluctance by you or your firm to spend money and time on this training. In the end, your efforts to learn and use the other programs in your office suite will be richly rewarded.

Adobe Acrobat for E-Filing and More | 34

David L. Masters

Introduction

Consider for a moment what it would be like to be able to find documents at your desk without rummaging through file cabinets or boxes. Think of all the paper you put in files because someday you may need it, only to never see it again. Consider the unpleasant process of closing those files and moving them to storage. Recall the times you've gone to storage to retrieve a single piece of paper. Now consider keeping all those documents in electronic format, readily available if needed, and then closing files by dragging them from an active work directory to an archive directory. Electronic filing (e-filing) in your office makes this possible.

Paper takes space, weighs a lot, becomes misplaced or even lost, and is just plain cumbersome. Your client brings you three banker boxes of documents. You spend hours sifting and organizing the documents into folders, which are, in turn, organized in various redwells. You spend hours rummaging through the folders and redwells, knowing that "one" document can be found in there—somewhere. On the day of trial, you pull out the trusted dolly, load your boxes of redwells, and head to court. The redwells are splitting at the seams, beginning to fray and tear. Then opposing counsel makes mention of that "one" special document. Your fingers race through the pages, folders, and redwells. There is an easier way: e-filing in the office means all your documents can be available in the courtroom or anywhere you can take a laptop computer.

Law Office Information Systems

Lawyers and law firms process information. We receive information from clients and other sources, we add information gained from research and experience, and we deliver information. The information that lawyers process and deliver takes many forms—it may be a pleading, an oral presentation to a court, an opinion letter, or a contract. No matter its form, in the end, it is all information that must be processed and delivered.

Most of the information that comes into law offices arrives in the form of paper documents. For that matter, most of the information output from law offices (work product) goes out as some form of document. Taking a very simple and abstract view of the typical law office, there are three primary systems involved in handling the documents that contain the information we work with daily:

1. a generation system,
2. a copying or replication system, and
3. a retention or filing system.

The document generation system includes not only computers and printers, but also fax machines, couriers, and the daily mail. The latter generate as many incoming documents as the internal systems. All these documents contain information lawyers need to analyze, store, and retrieve. When documents come into the typical law office, the information system can be depicted as in Figure 34-1.

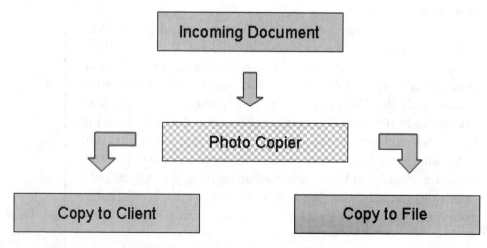

Figure 34-1: Incoming Document

When the law firm generates an outgoing document for delivery to a third party, the information schematic looks like that in Figure 34-2.

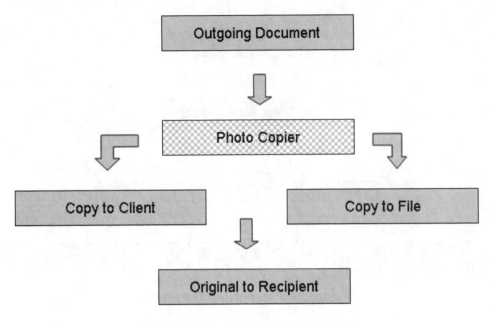

Figure 34-2: Outgoing Document

In addition to the basic scenarios for incoming and outgoing documents, consider the special case of litigation documents. When documents come in during litigation, whether from the client or an opposing party, they are typically preserved as a clean set, which is then photocopied and Bates numbered. The Bates-numbered set is then copied to create a file set, a working set, and sets for distribution to other parties. That's a lot of paper, a lot of copies, a lot of toner, and a lot of time. When dealing with litigation documents, the typical law office information system copies, numbers, and replicates the documents as depicted in Figure 34-3.

Basic Concepts and Terminology

To understand the e-filing concepts described in this chapter, familiarity with a few basic concepts and terms is necessary.

First, the e-filing concepts described here relate mostly to the use of Adobe Acrobat. Acrobat 6.0 comes in three varieties: Reader, Standard, and Professional. Reader is free. With it, anyone can open, display, search, and print documents in Portable Document Format (PDF). Reader does not allow you to add bookmarks, notes, links, or most of the other features that make Acrobat a valuable tool in the law office. Acrobat Standard and Professional

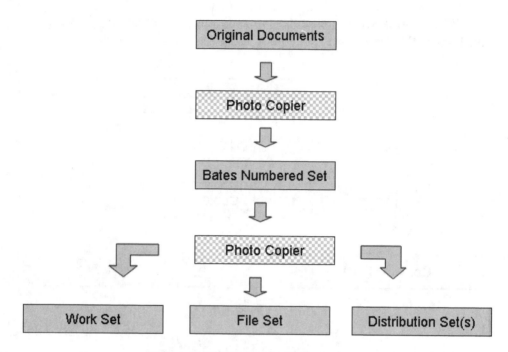

Figure 34-3: Litigation Documents

are the "full" versions of the program, and are the applications for working with PDF documents.

Next, not all PDF documents are created equally. There are image-only PDFs and image-on-text files. Understanding the fundamental difference between image-only and image-on-text files is absolutely critical. Regardless of whether you work with image-only or image-on-text files, the image remains an exact duplicate of the original paper-based document. Image-only PDFs are just that—images only, just digital photocopies of paper documents. Think of image-only PDF files as pages in a notebook: you can look at the pages, but you cannot search the notebook without reading each page. Even though image-only files cannot be searched, they are still more useful than a notebook full of paper pages. Image-on-text files have an exact image of the hard copy, with text behind the image. Image-on-text files are created by printing an existing computer file to PDF (word-processing and spreadsheet files are good examples), or by running a PDF image-only file through an optical character recognition (OCR) application. Acrobat 6.0 has the built-in ability to perform OCR on PDF documents. Acrobat calls this function Paper Capture. Image-on-text PDF files are the Holy Grail of legal document management. When paper documents are scanned to other image formats (such as TIFF or JPEG), only a digital image of the paper exists. If characters from that image are converted to text, the conversion process inevitably changes the appearance of the text in the image file. Not so with PDF files. The image remains an exact duplicate of the original while the interpreted text exists independently behind, or a layer below, the image. The text file behind or below the image can be searched. Depending upon the quality of the paper documents scanned, thousands of pages can now be captured as exact copies and made searchable through the use of OCR applications. Beware, however, as there are limits and caveats with OCR technology.

Why PDF and Why Acrobat?

There are many reasons why you should consider Acrobat and PDF if you are thinking about moving from paper-based files to e-filing digital records. Acrobat provides good image-acquisition capabilities, the ability to perform OCR on the images while retaining an exact image of the scanned pages, and easy sharing with other users. State courts that have adopted the LexisNexis File & Serve system for the electronic filing of documents have settled upon PDF as the standard. The federal Case Management/Electronic Case Files program (CM/ECF) relies upon PDF. If the courts are using PDF, then it should be a good standard for law offices to apply.

In addition to using Acrobat for creating PDF files by acquiring images with a scanner or printing image-on-text PDF files from native applications, you can use it to make the PDF files truly useful. For example, you can add bookmarks and sticky notes to image-only files as well as image-on-text files. Pages can be copied, removed, rotated, and cropped. If the files have a text background, you can highlight, underline, and strike through the text. PDF files with background text (image-on-text) can be searched; image-only files cannot be searched, but information contained in the document summary or in attached notes will be included in indexes of document collections. PDF files can be bookmarked to create a table of contents linked to exact points within the document.

COMMON PAPER AND PDF FILE TASKS

Paper File or Notebook	PDF File
Remove and discard page(s)	Delete page(s)—Ctrl+Shift+D
Remove, copy, replace page(s)	Extract page(s)—6.0 Alt+D-P-E; 7.0 Alt+D-X
Number page(s)	Add headers and footers—Alt+D-H
Reorder pages	Drag and drop page(s) on pages navigation tab
Bates number page(s)	StampPDF, IntelliPDF Bates Pro (third-party plug-ins)
Highlight text	Commenting tools (highlighter)

Annotate (add notes)	Commenting tools (sticky notes and free text)
Copy entire file	Save as (with new file name) or Ctrl+C (in Windows Explorer)
Create table of contents	Bookmark—Ctrl+B
Browse through file	Page up/page down keys, or next page/previous page buttons
Go to specific page	Go to page—Ctrl+Shift+N

Basic Digital Document Management

Figures 34-1, 34-2, and 34-3 show the course of paper documents (incoming, outgoing, and litigation) as they pass through the typical law office copying or replication system. In most offices, a photocopier acts as the copying or replication system. In the paperless office, a scanner replaces the photocopier. Incoming documents pass through the scanner, rather than a photocopier, producing digital copies that are stored electronically. See Figure 34-4. Outgoing documents, rather than being scanned or photocopied, are retained in their original digital format and printed (converted) to PDF. See Figure 34-5. Litigation documents are scanned and replicated as electronic files without taking up valuable floor space.

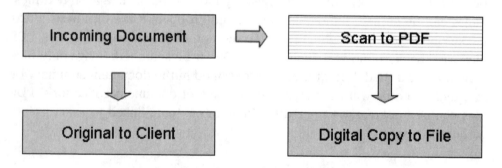

Figure 34-4: Incoming Document Scan

The Digital Filing System—Folders

What system do you use now to find a given piece of paper? It may sound something like this: Every client matter has a file, and somewhere you have an index of all those files. So, if you want to find the Smith file and can't remember where in the filing system it resides, you go to the index, find the file identifier (that is, a file number), and then locate the file. Now, you knew the doc-

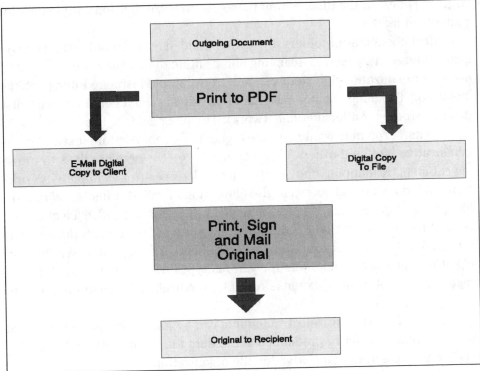

Figure 34-5: Outgoing Document Print PDF

ument you wanted was in the Smith file, but what if the Smith file contains 5,000 or 10,000 pages? At this point, the paper filing system starts to break down. How many subfolders are you willing to create, and how do you keep track of them? Unless you have an absolutely huge number of files, or a medium number of really huge files, then the paper file system can be replicated, refined, and expanded in the digital world.

To e-file PDF documents in your office, you need follow only a few simple rules:

- ◆ *Rule Number One*: Scan all incoming documents to PDF.
- ◆ *Rule Number Two*: Print (convert) all items of outgoing work product to PDF.
- ◆ *Rule Number Three*: Store digital images of all incoming paper and outgoing work product in logical folders.

It may help to think of the digital filing system in terms of a physical filing system. The digital file room consists of electronic filing cabinets filled with folders that contain everything found in traditional paper files. Think of a shared hard-disk drive as the file room, and the cabinets within the room as large divisions on the disk. Within those cabinet-size divisions are folders for each client matter.

Most client matter folders are further divided into subfolders to aid in organization. As high tech as scanning and printing to PDF may sound, the storage and organizational system can adhere to an old-fashioned filing cabinet metaphor. The filing cabinet exists in virtual space (on a computer hard-disk drive shared over a local area network). The filing cabinet has a name, such as "Clients." (You may want separate digital filing cabinets for closed files, administrative files, and others.) Each computer on the network links to the filing cabinets by mapping one or more network drives (for example, X:\Work). Now each desktop has access to the filing cabinet called "Clients." Within the filing cabinet are folders, one for each client (X:\Clients\Smith). If a client has several matters, then that client folder has a subfolder for each distinct matter (X:\Work\Smith\Corporation and X:\Clients\Smith\Wills). Within each client matter folder are folders for various types of documents, such as correspondence, pleadings, expense receipts, research, privileged matters, and so on.

A simple system for electronic filing can be implemented and standardized by creating a set of predefined subfolders for client matters. Figure 34-6 shows a simple system for litigation file organization.

The main folder bears the name "Litigation," meaning that this folder contains the file structure for new litigation matters. The folder below Litigation in the left pane contains a set of empty "month" folders (for example, 01 Jan, 02 Feb, and 03 Mar—the numbers and leading zeros are used to make the list sort properly). The subfolders in the new-matter folders are empty; when opening a new litigation file, you simply highlight the Litigation folder, select all (Control-A), copy, and then paste this file structure onto the folder created for the new matter. Now, every litigation matter has the same organizational structure, at least to start with. As you can see, this file structure provides more detail than what you have been using in the paper world, and, of course, you can add all the subfolders you want and simply drag-and-drop the contents from one folder to another. File reorganization could not be much easier. Create predefined folder sets for the types of matters you commonly handle (such as estate planning, estate administration, transactions, and so on).

The Digital Filing System—Dual Folders

To maintain a digital file that looks like a paper file, consider using dual folders for correspondence and pleadings. One folder contains the native application files (Word or WordPerfect), the other the PDF versions. For example, correspondence files created with WordPerfect are stored in a subfolder named "CorresWPD." All correspondence files in PDF format are stored in a

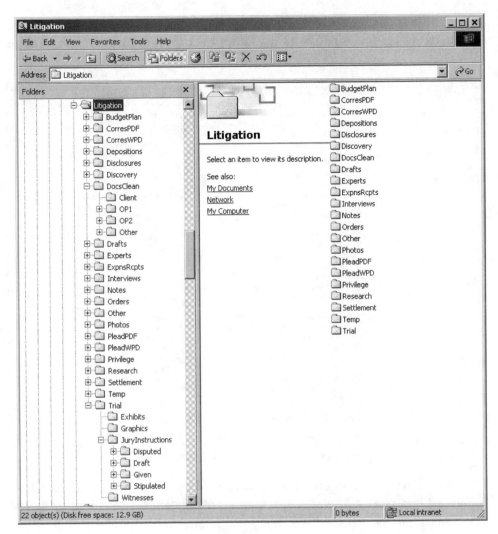

Figure 34-6: Litigation Folder Set

subfolder called "CorresPDF." A similar dual-folder system can be created and maintained for pleadings.

There are two reasons for maintaining dual folders. First, keeping the original work product in its native format allows for easy reuse. Second, the PDF folder acts like a familiar paper file, containing all the incoming and outgoing correspondence or pleadings, as the case may be.

The Digital Filing System—File Naming

The files within the folders are named following another simple convention. The first part of the name always contains the date of the document in reverse year/month/day order, followed by a few descriptive terms (for example, X:\Clients\Smith\PleadPDF\020327 Complaint). As simple as this may sound, using the document date as the first part of the file name is hugely important; it causes all the documents within a folder to sort chronologically. See Figure 34-7.

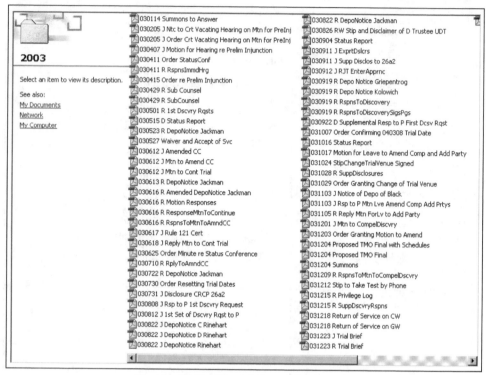

Figure 34-7: Date-Sorted Pleadings

If you are willing to adopt more rules and impose further regimentation on your filing system, then consider standardizing another element or two of file names. For correspondence files, you might find it helpful to follow the date with the initials of the author, followed by the initials of the primary recipient, followed by the short description (see below). For pleadings, you might find it useful to follow the date with the initials of the authoring (filing) party. Decide at the outset of litigation what letters will be used to identify each party. Adding these elements to file names will provide valuable identifying information at a glance.

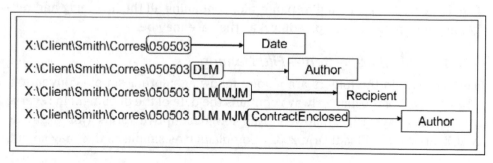

The Digital Filing System—An Example

Implementation of Rule Number One (scan all incoming documents to PDF) can be accomplished quite easily. The mail (such as correspondence, pleadings, and bills) goes to a staff person who scans each piece, stores the image to the appropriate client or administrative folder, and then distributes the paper to the proper recipient within the office (lawyer, paralegal, bookkeeper) for action. For example, when a pleading arrives from opposing counsel, it goes through the scanner, and then goes to the proper recipient within the office. A letter is written to the client, discussing and forwarding the pleading. In accordance with the procedure, paper comes in, goes through the scanner, and then goes out to the client. In some cases, with the right client, you can simply send an e-mail message and attach a digital copy; the original pleading then goes to the recycle bin or shredder.

Working with PDF Files

"Working with PDF Files" could cover a broad range of subjects. "Working with" could include indexing, searching, annotating, and a host of other tasks beyond the scope of this chapter. That said, if you have read this far and are thinking about e-filing documents in your office, then you deserve an introduction to working with PDF files.

Think of working with PDF files as working with a notebook full of paper documents. You add, remove, and delete pages. You can do this and more with PDF files. You can quickly build an electronic table of contents using bookmarks, and you can use the more advanced feature of links to provide instant navigation. You can build a link from virtually any point within a PDF document to lots of other types of digital information, not just other PDF files. You can control how your PDF document will "look" when you or someone else opens it, including how the pages will be numbered; that is, what your notebook will look like. At the same time, you can add identifying features so your notebook can be found. Some of the ways you can work with PDF files are so similar to the paper world that pointing out the obvious would serve little purpose.

Adding Pages

Say you have a PDF document, whether one or one thousand pages, and you want to add one or more pages. New pages can be inserted at any point in the PDF document. You need only decide whether the page or pages will be added before or after the insertion point. For example, in a ten-page document, you want to add three new pages between current pages seven and eight. You open the existing document and turn to page seven, and then you insert the new pages after the insertion point; if you were at page eight, the insertion would be "before." The pages to be added, or inserted, can be single- or multiple-page PDF documents. To add pages:

- ◆ 6.0 Menu (Add Pages): Document > Pages > Insert
- ◆ 7.0 Menu (Add Pages): Document > Insert Pages
- ◆ Keystroke (Add Pages): Shift > Ctrl > I

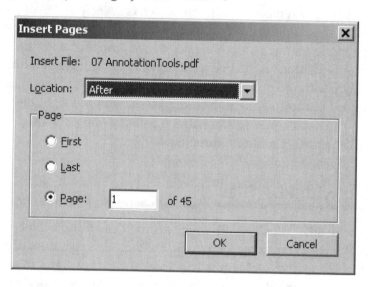

Extracting Pages

Extracting pages means taking pages out of a PDF document and saving them as a separate document. They may continue to exist as a separate document or may be inserted into another document or documents. To extract pages:

- ◆ 6.0 Menu (Extract Pages): Document > Pages > Extract
- ◆ 7.0 Menu (Extract Pages): Document > Extract Pages
- ◆ 6.0 Keystroke (Extract Pages): Alt+D-P-E
- ◆ 7.0 Keystroke (Extract Pages): Alt+D-X

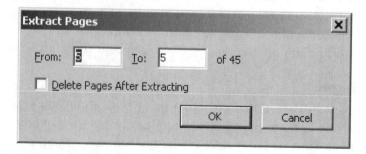

Deleting Pages

Deleting pages means taking the pages out of the current PDF document and throwing them away. No, they do not go to the recycle bin, so you can retrieve them if you change your mind. This is like taking pages out of a notebook and running them through the shredder—they are gone for good (so use with caution). This procedure is handy for ripping out blank pages. To delete pages:

- 6.0 Menu (Delete Pages): Document > Pages > Delete
- 7.0 Menu (Delete Pages): Document > Delete Pages
- Keystroke (Delete Pages): Ctrl+Shift+D

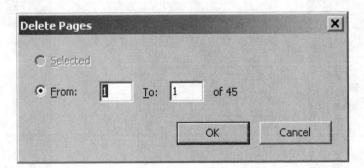

Cropping Pages

Sometimes the information on a page can be enhanced by removing extraneous material from the edges. (You know, those black borders from the photocopy process.) This procedure is also useful when someone scans in a bunch of pages to legal size when they should have been letter size. If you use Acrobat indisplay mode, **Crop Pages** can be used to curve out a portion of a document so that it can be displayed following a full-page display to create an effective zoom effect. (See figures 34-8 and 34-9.)

To crop pages:

- 6.0 Menu (Crop Pages): Document > Pages > Crop
- 7.0 Menu (Crop Pages): Document > Crop Pages
- Keystroke (Crop Pages): Shift+Ctrl+T

Once the menu or keyboard commands have been issued, a dialog box appears, allowing the user to set the parameters for cropping. The current page, all pages, or a range of pages can be cropped. You can also crop pages by selecting the cropping tool from the Advanced Editing toolbar. After the tool has been selected, use your pointing device to select the area of the image to be retained (drag to draw a box inside the area you want to crop), and then double click inside the box and the crop pages dialog box will appear.

Rotating Pages

Now this is something you cannot do in your paper notebook, or at least not with as good a result. It can be particularly useful when working with scanned

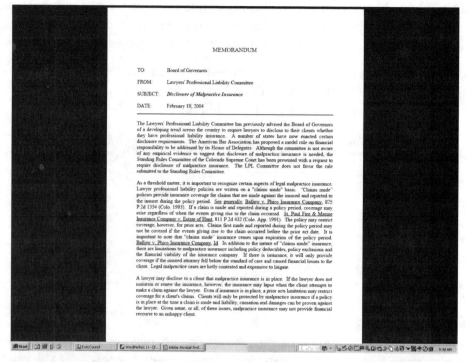

Figure 34-8

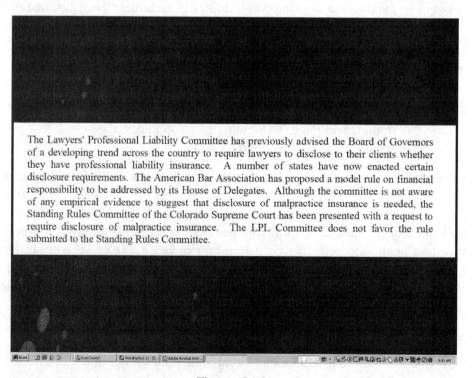

The Lawyers' Professional Liability Committee has previously advised the Board of Governors of a developing trend across the country to require lawyers to disclose to their clients whether they have professional liability insurance. A number of states have now enacted certain disclosure requirements. The American Bar Association has proposed a model rule on financial responsibility to be addressed by its House of Delegates. Although the committee is not aware of any empirical evidence to suggest that disclosure of malpractice insurance is needed, the Standing Rules Committee of the Colorado Supreme Court has been presented with a request to require disclosure of malpractice insurance. The LPL Committee does not favor the rule submitted to the Standing Rules Committee.

Figure 34-9

documents. By virtue of mechanics, all documents go through the scanner in portrait orientation, regardless of how the information on the physical page was set. After documents have been scanned, pages can be rotated to correct the orientation. (The software that ships with some scanners will automatically orient pages.) Rotating pages comes in handy when someone scans in the page top down. To rotate single or multiple pages:

- 6.0 Menu (Rotate Pages): Document > Pages > Rotate
- 7.0 Menu (Rotate Pages): Document > Rotate Pages
- Keystroke (Rotate Pages): Ctrl+Shift+R

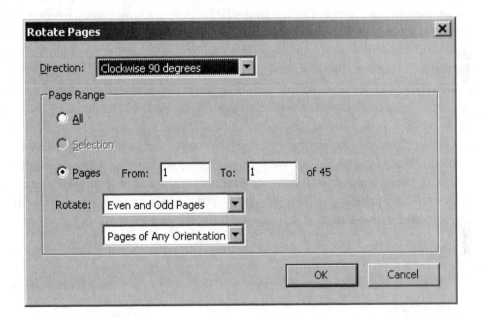

Once the menu or keyboard commands have been issued, a dialog box appears, allowing the user to set the parameters for rotating pages, including the direction and amount of rotation (clockwise 90 degrees, counterclockwise 90 degrees, or 180 degrees). The current page, all pages, or a range of pages can be rotated. Note: Rotate "View" is different; this function rotates the view for the entire document and cannot be saved.

Rearranging Page Order

You've added, extracted, deleted, cropped, and rotated pages—great! But now you want page five to come before page three. Use the thumbnail view to drag and drop pages to reorder them. This is handy for small documents; the larger the document, the less practical it is. To rearrange pages using thumbnails:

- Select the Pages tab on the Navigation pane
- Left click on the desired page and while holding down the left button, drag the page to the desired location; multiple pages can be selected by holding down the Ctrl key while clicking on the desired pages
- As you move the page or pages by dragging, a vertical bar appears between the thumbnails displayed in the Pages window; when the desired destination has been reached, simply release the left button on the mouse (pointer)

Document Summary

Think of PDF document summaries as card-catalog entries. Having card-catalog entries for image-only PDF documents can make a world of difference in locating them using the search function in Windows Explorer. Remember, image-only PDFs are just that—images only. Without document summaries, the location of a given image-only PDF document can be determined only by knowing its file name. Searching for the file by name can be narrowed down a bit by using other criteria, such as date ranges and file type. But, in the end, finding image-only files by file name comes down to a manual search, much like rifling through a box of paper looking for a particular document. The manual search can be avoided by using Document Summary, which harnesses the power of the computer to locate specific information. Information contained in Document Summary will be found by Windows Explorer searches of files and folders "containing text." To create a document summary:

- Menu (Document Summary): File > Document Properties [select Description in left pane]
- Keystroke (Document Summary): Ctrl+D [select Description in left pane]

Once the menu or keystroke commands have been issued, the Document Properties dialog box appears. The Document Properties dialog box looks different between versions 6.0 and 7.0. In version 6.0, document property categories (Advanced, Custom, Description, Fonts, Initial View and Security) are selected in the left pane. See Figure 34-10. When Description has been selected in the left pane, information about the document may be entered in any of the four fields (Title, Author, Subject and Keywords).

In version 7.0, the Document Properties dialog box uses "tabs" across the top rather than the left pane to access the document property categories (Description, Security, Fonts, Initial View, Custom and Advanced). See Figure 34-11. When the Description tab has been selected, information about the document may be entered in any of the four fields (Title, Author, Subject and Keywords). More information about the document can be added by clicking on the Additional Metadata button.

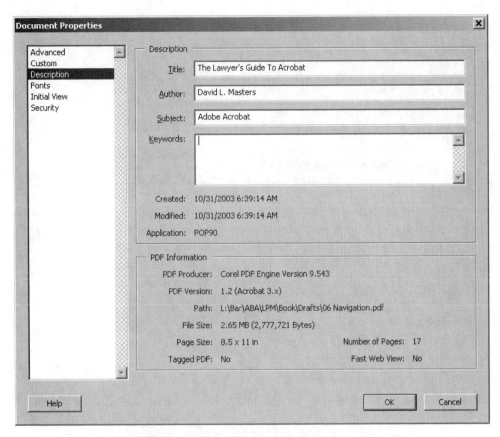

Figure 34-10: Document Summary

Conclusion

By following a few simple rules, any office can switch from paper to electronic filing:

1. Scan all incoming documents to PDF.
2. Print all outgoing work product to PDF.
3. Create a virtual filing cabinet with folders for each client matter.
4. Segregate document types within the client matter folders into appropriate subfolders.
5. Use the document date (yymmdd) as the first part of the file name to produce chronological ordering.

Finally, know that when your documents are stored electronically, they can be copied, backed up, replicated, and stored in multiple locations.

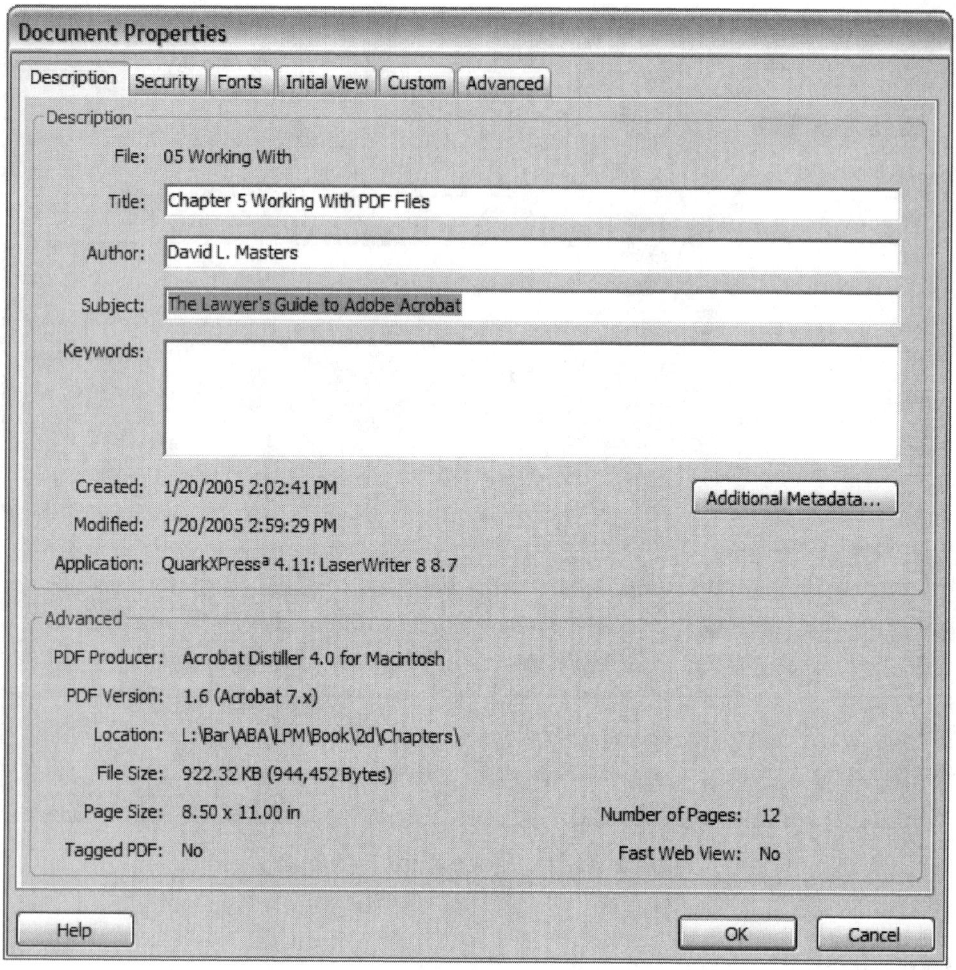

Figure 34-11: Document Description

Hold the Phone!

35

Barry L. Brickner

Discussions of legal technology have revolved around the use of computers in the law office. Further, talk of law office communications has centered around e-mail messaging and the Internet. Although these are very important subjects, the technological survival of the law office does not depend upon being online. I think we should look back a few years and concentrate on one of the technological wonders that has greatly simplified the practice of law. I am talking about the telephone. You may get caught in the debate over how much you should computerize the office or if it's time to upgrade or buy a laptop and go mobile, but the one thing you never debate is whether you should get a phone. You already have one or you are not practicing law.

First Things First

The first thing any lawyer does when setting up a practice is to order a phone. A great portion of legal business is conducted on the phone. Before you order your cards or order the stationery (if you do not generate it—and why don't you?), you get a phone number. What good are the cards without the number? How are you going to build that practice without that number? How are your clients going to contact you without a phone? Not to mention what would happen to that poor fax machine if you did not have a phone line. Over the past several years, I have changed my address, but I have been able to keep the same phone number. My clients may not know where my office is, but they know how to get in touch with me. My identity is intact. I am, therefore I dial.

From the very beginning, the use of the phone has been intertwined with the law. As everyone knows, Alexander Graham Bell's first words on the phone were, "Watson, come here, I need you." The next words could have been, "Don't trip over the cord on your way—I can't afford the lawsuit." Bringing the concept forward to today, some courts believe that legal technology means having a telephone pretrial conference. Forget about your fancy computers and your e-mail accounts. When did you ever hear a judge ask you to set up a chat line or listserve on the Internet so that all the lawyers involved in the case could communicate jointly with the court? Come to think of it, that's not a bad idea . . . but don't hold your breath. For many lawyers, the telephone *is* legal technology.

Telephone

Depending upon your financial situation, phone systems can be the stripped-down variety or can come with every bell and whistle known to humankind. The simplest systems are the older mechanical systems that allow incoming calls to trunk over to an empty line and allow you to place a call on hold. Though this type of system may seem automatic to the user, there are switches and other mechanical devices that allow the system to work. Speakerphones and speed-dialing apparatus can be added to these basic systems. The only time you will see an old mechanical system is if you move into an office with an existing phone system.

The newer electronic systems allow for more versatility. Instead of having mechanical switches perform functions such as trunking and placing calls on hold, everything is done electronically. With electronic systems, you can have trunk hunt lines, call holding, conference calling, speed dialing, redialing, and a speakerphone all built into the phone on your desk. Electronic systems allow for features such as music or message on hold, timing phone calls, caller identification (caller ID), and interoffice call forwarding. Some electronic phones come with digital displays that show the number called, plus date and time, not to mention caller history. Both systems allow for a local line for interoffice calling and the ability to interface with a computer modem. Expansion is easier with electronic systems, as is maintenance. Many of the additional features for an electronic system are modular and can be added later at less expense than is possible with a mechanical system.

The basic difference between the mechanical and electronic systems is the way the system "brain" or central processor operates. One uses mechanical contact switches and the other uses electronic switches. In earlier systems, the phone lines would come in from the outside and were connected to the system "brain," which was connected to the phones. In all phone systems the "brain" is the most expensive part. In both mechanical and the more sophisticated electronic systems, the "brain" is located on the premises and is a component of the phone system. With the smaller electronic systems, such as two-line systems, the function performed by the "brain" component is at the phone company and not on-site. You pay for the phones that have the functionality built in and get the "brain" component as part of your phone service from your local carrier. Another advantage to the small electronic system is that it is easier and cheaper to move. When you do not have to deal with buying, installing, and moving the "brain," you can save a great deal of money. If you are on a low budget, you may be able to pick up a used mechanical system cheaply, but the parts that make these dinosaurs work might be hard to find. In other words, if it breaks, how are you going to fix it? The purchase of a newer, electronic phone system is the better investment. No matter which system you get, you should start with a minimum of two lines for your telephone system. Depending upon your budget, one of the lines can double for fax machine and modem purposes. However, a third line for a fax machine and modem is recommended.

There is a new electronic phone system currently on the market called the computer phone or Internet phone. It is based upon Voice over Internet Protocol (VoIP) and it works in conjunction with your computer system. VoIP was first introduced as a way to make long-distance calls over the Internet to avoid long-distance charges. It is now becoming popular due to the communications concepts of interoperability and convergence. VoIP allows for the transmission of voice, data, and video over the same connection. The convergence of these technologies is now available and will become the dominant form of communication in the future. However, the systems that deliver VoIP are on the pricey side now, which is something to think about if you are on a limited budget. Also, these systems are more susceptible to failure during power outages than other phone systems.

Instant Document Distribution

Sometimes talking to a client is not enough and delivery of a document in a day or two is just not acceptable. Fax machines fill that gap. There's nothing like reaching out and touching someone with a document. A fax machine is a type of photocopy machine with an attitude. Fax machines combine the ability to copy a document with the ability to send the copy, line by line, to a receiving machine over the telephone lines with a built-in modem. The price of fax machines is feature-driven—the more features, the higher the price. The types of features available on fax machines include phone number memory, automatic redial, fax messages printed on the top of the transmitted pages, polling, automatic document feed, plain-paper feed, transmission confirmation, a log of outgoing calls, a timer to send faxes at nonpeak hours, a stamper to verify that a document was transmitted, the ability to buffer transmissions in case the fax machine runs out of paper, and a phone handset that allows you to use the fax machine as a phone.

Fax machines come in four basic varieties. The first two are stand-alone machines and are differentiated by the type of paper used: thermal transfer onto heat-sensitive paper or plain paper. The paper on thermal fax machines comes on a roll. The plain-paper fax machines work like laser printers and print on precut bond paper. The plain-paper fax machines also come in three basic varieties: the toner type, the ink-jet type, and the ones that use a film transfer process. Some of these machines are capable of doubling as a copy machine. The quality is much better with plain-paper fax machines, but at a higher cost. The third type uses your computer as a fax machine. The fourth is a hybrid of the fax machine and is a multipurpose fax/printer/scanner/copier. The multipurpose machines replace the traditional printer for a computer. A majority of these fax combos use ink-jet printer technology, but also come in the toner engine variety.

Although the legibility of a transmitted document is important, the quality of the copy is not necessarily the main reason for purchasing a fax machine. The purpose of the fax machine is to send and receive documents quickly. There are two major drawbacks to having a fax machine. The first is the loss of one of the greatest excuses of all time: "I mailed the document the other day; didn't you get it yet?" The second is that your mistakes now get out of the office at the speed of light. Therefore, be sure the document is correct and that the number you dial is truly the intended recipient.

When purchasing a fax machine, a major consideration should be the price per copy. Though toner cartridges are more expensive than ink cartridges, the price per copy is much less and you do not have to change the toner cartridges as often. Further, the quality is much better with toner fax machines than ink-jet machines. The thermal paper fax machines are disappearing.

Fax machines are so widely accepted in the practice of law that some courts will accept documents filed with the court by fax machine. Some courts are accepting faxed signatures and service of some documents by fax machine. Because receiving fax machines automatically date stamp, the court knows when you sent your documents.

When You Are Away from Your Desk

With your phone and fax systems in place, you are ready to practice law. You can now converse with clients, negotiate big contracts and settlements, and order pizzas, all without leaving your office. However, you may not always be in your office, and some clients may not understand that you might go home before midnight. You may not have a full-time secretary, voice mail, or an answering service to take messages during the day. Your clients have the right to be informed, and you must maintain the lines of communication. Several devices have been developed to allow you to keep in contact with your clients, even when you are not in your office. On occasion, you may have the urge to hide, but if you fail to return calls from your clients, you will never have to worry about hiding again.

Answering Machine

The simplest way to maintain the lines of communication is to use a phone answering machine. Clients will generally leave recorded messages, as long as you call them back within a reasonable period of time. Most answering machines easily attach to your phone, while some are built right into the phone system. You may wish to consider two-line machines so that both phone lines are covered. The smaller units give a recorded message and request that a message be left at the sound of the beep. Some answering machines allow for more than one outgoing message, and automatically place the day and time of the call at the end of the message. Time-and-date stamping on the recorded message is most helpful in avoiding the claim that "I called you at eight in the morning and you didn't get back to me until three in the afternoon." Most systems allow you to call your own answering machine and retrieve your messages from a remote telephone by entering a private code from a touch-tone phone.

Voice Mail

As is the case with most automated equipment, the phone answering machine has a super-deluxe version called voice mail. Only those still living in caves have been spared from dealing with these behemoths. Voice mail comes in three basic formats: a recorded-voice menu system, an operator-assisted system, and a system through the phone company. The first has an automated voice that informs the caller of the available options and instructs which numbers on the phone will activate each option. With luck, at the end of the button pushing, you will find a real, live person. If not, you can always leave a recorded message. The second system starts off with a real, live person—the receptionist—and ends up with either the person you are seeking or a recording of that person asking you to leave a recorded message. The third system is similar to an answering machine, but the messages are stored by the phone company.

If you are willing to leave your computer turned on all the time, a multi-function computer board including modem, fax, and voice mail may be the wise choice. For a solo, the computer board solution may work the same as an answering machine. The computer has the added ability to store and redial phone numbers. However, for most small offices, an answering machine is simpler and generally adequate.

The major complaint about voice mail systems is that they are frustrating and impersonal. With an answering machine, you listen to a short message, and you leave a response. With an outside voice mail service, the caller goes through a series of menus and still ends up leaving a recorded message. The worst part of dealing with these systems is that the person you are trying to contact might actually be there, but if that person is not at the proper station, no one answers the phone, and the caller gets the recorded message. Clients might accept this type of treatment from large firms, but they may find the same type of treatment intolerable when dealing with sole practitioners. Clients expect prompt and personalized service. For some unknown reason, clients seem less threatened by answering machines. No matter which message retrieval system you use, if you do not return the call, the client will not return.

Voice mail through the phone company can activate even when all your lines are in use. Instead of getting a busy signal, the client is given the opportunity to leave a message. This makes the voice mail service superior to a stand-alone answering machine. There is a monthly service charge for the voice mail service, as opposed to a one-time purchase price for an answering machine. Another feature of voice mail through the phone company is linking the service with a pager. The client has the option of either leaving a message or actually paging you with either a voice or digital page, depending upon your paging equipment.

If your phone service has caller ID and your phone has a digital read-out, your phone can probably store the information on the last hundred callers. This is like having a digital answering machine. The caller might not leave a message or the phone might not even be answered, but you can still get a digital read-out of who called, unless the caller has a caller ID blocker. If I miss a call because I was on the other line or if the caller does not leave a message, I still have the ability to identify who called because of that feature.

When You Must Be Available: Pagers and Mobile Phones

There are two devices that yield the fastest responses when your clients absolutely must find you immediately. They are the personal pager (beeper) and the mobile phone. The personal pager, which is worn somewhere on the body, notifies you when you are wanted. The user is informed of a page by a loud beep or by a vibration that is silent but felt by the wearer. You can choose to either scare everybody around you or suffer silently with something akin to electroshock therapy. The pager displays the number to call on a viewer or may even play a short voice message. Some store several numbers in memory. The services you can get from personal pagers continue to increase to keep pace with mobile phones. You can get news and sports information, stock tickers, text messaging, and even e-mail capabilities. Much of this same information is available with mobile phone services, but a personal pager gives you a little more choice of whether you want to call someone back.

Pagers are popular with lawyers but not with judges, who find them disruptive. Some judges post warnings to lawyers to curb their pagers or suffer consequences. One unlucky local lawyer spent a week in jail for not turning his off after being warned.

The cost of the service depends upon the area covered. You can choose between regional, state, or worldwide paging services.

Callers on the Move

The current trend in telephone communications is to go wireless. Mobile phones have taken over the market. Where I live, the phone market has grown so rapidly that I am on my third area code in four years. Between home phones, business phones, fax machines, dedicated modem lines, pagers, and mobile phones, society is rapidly running out of numbers. I have so many numbers of my own, that I am having difficulty remembering them all. Fortunately, I do not tend to call myself.

When purchasing a mobile phone, you should check the features. Cell phones have many of the same features that their desk-bound brethren have. Features like redial and speed dial or memory dial are standard, plus call waiting, caller identification, voice mail, and conference calling, but there are other factors specific to the portable breed:

- Battery life is always important. Does the phone use standard batteries or are they rechargeable? The longer the life, the more talk time between recharges.
- Perhaps you want another power source. Can you use an adapter to plug the phone into your car lighter or utility port?
- Size may make a difference to you. Some phones clip on your belt, fit in a shirt pocket, or fold into a neat little square. Will the phone fit into your purse or briefcase, or doesn't that make a difference?
- For some, the most important question is whether the phone comes free with service. Many cell phones do, but if you want the fancy gizmos, you pay extra.
- Check for additional features, such as news, sports, stock tickers, and fax or e-mail capabilities.

Mobile phone features combine pagers with telephones; that is, they are helpful for those of us who do not mind being found, but who do not necessarily want to communicate with the person looking for us. If you do not want to be found even on your portable phone, or if it is off, your voice mail service can take a message.

For the ultra-geeks among us, there is the ability to link with a laptop modem so you can go online anywhere, anytime. Nowhere to run, nowhere to hide. Though some cell phone services allow you to receive e-mail messages on the phone itself, this is not quite the same as going online on your computer. Parts of the country have been outfitted for a wireless rapid download online service—a wireless service specifically for mobile computers. You have to check your region to see if this service is available.

Some management types are already thinking that because this service costs extra, the client should pay a premium to talk to you on your cell phone. There are a few lawyers who spell out in their retainer agreements the amount of additional charges that will be levied if the client feels the need to contact the lawyer on the cell phone. Remember, whether you make the call or receive it, the cell phone's owner is charged for the call. The phone companies really clean up when both the sender and the receiver are on cell phones. This is one instance where you should check out the features of your cellular service. Some services do not charge for the first minute of an incoming call. Other services give you a "call pack" for members in a group or family, with "free" calls amongst the group. Nextel has an intercom service for members of a group, with direct connect to all members of the group.

Antenna on the Rise

Originally there were only two cell phone companies licensed by the Federal Communications Commission (FCC) per state. This was because the bandwidth for cell phones was very narrow. For a cellular company to get coverage, it places antennae throughout the areas it services. Each antenna represents a cell. The linking of the different cells allows for continuous coverage. As you travel through a series of cells, the equipment automatically hands off your call from cell to cell, so that you have an uninterrupted conversation.

Cellular companies are always looking for more sites for their antennae, for two reasons: (1) so they can have complete coverage in an area, and (2) so they can meet the demand for usage. If you have ever experienced the drop in service called a "dead zone," which causes the user to break up or lose the call, it is caused by a lack of coverage in the area. When your call cannot be handed off to the next antenna, the connection is broken or "dropped"; thus the term, "dropped call." Didn't you ever wonder where that term came from? Even though a cellular company may have a cell in the area, if it has too many users trying to access the cell at the same time, some of the users will be shut out until the next opening is available. For those of you who have never been treated to the "system busy" response on your phone, consider yourself lucky. Of course, if you did not get the "system busy" response, you would not need the redial feature as much.

Owing to the consumer acceptance of cellular service, the FCC opened a new band for wireless phone service. The government sold the new band for $13 billion. This new band accommodates another five or six licenses. The government gets more money, the consumer gets more service and competition, and our cities get more antennae. Oddly, the newcomers do not wish to be called cell companies. They use the term "P.C.S.," for personal communication service. The P.C.S. bandwidth is at a higher frequency, which results in more cells for similar coverage.

The early cell systems were all analog. The next generation was digital, which gave the user clearer reception. The newest format is called Global System for Mobile communications (GSM), which is an improvement over the old digital systems. The GSM system is akin to the system used in Europe, but the two systems are not completely compatible. The mobile phone carriers are converting their systems to the GSM format. Because most of the carriers are changing over, the consumer can purchase a phone with GSM alone, GSM and digital, or GSM, digital, and the ability to work in parts of Europe. GSM currently exists in most major markets and along most major transportation corridors. Digital has coverage over most of the United States. Eventually, GSM will have the same coverage as the digital and the digital will be dropped. Always check the coverage of the area where you make most of your calls to determine which carrier to use. Your phone may have all the features in the world, but if you cannot connect to your carrier, what good are they?

Cellular Service Shopping

What should you look for when buying into one program or another? The price of the service is always first. Another consideration is coverage. Some providers have better coverage in certain areas than the others. While some providers are still looking for sites for their antennae so they can cover an area, the other providers are only looking to fill in dead spots and to increase capacity. If you travel outside the area where you live, make sure the service will travel with you. Always make sure the service you choose will get you the coverage you want.

Verizon Wireless and Cingular are the current names for the original cell phone companies. Nextel, which works on a different type of system and offers the walkie-talkie feature, has also been around for a long time. The newer, but well-established, companies are AT&T Wireless, T-Mobile, and Sprint. The number of providers is limited not only by the cost of establishing the networks, but also by the availability of usable spectrum that is licensed by the

FCC. Mergers and name changes are not uncommon in the industry, but the frequency of change has greatly reduced in the past few years. However, that did not stop Cingular from merging with AT&T Wireless, and Sprint and Nextel from announcing their merger.

The competition between mobile phone service providers or carriers has lowered the cost of the service. When selecting a carrier, you should look at the cost and the coverage. A very good rate might be masking limited coverage. Before committing to any carrier, make sure the carrier provides adequate coverage for your needs. If you request, the carrier will give you a map showing existing and future coverage areas. This information is important, as most carriers expect you to make a one- to three-year commitment to their services. If you travel extensively, check to see if the carrier has roaming charges. This extra charge might be enough to send you to a carrier that caters more to calling patterns and does not have additional charges for being out of town.

Cellular services usually sell per-minute packages. The more minutes per month you purchase, the cheaper the per-minute rate. You should try to estimate your usage and purchase a package that best suits your usage patterns. Most of the carriers are going to anywhere/anytime packages. You get charged the same to call across the street as across the country. These anywhere/anytime minutes are a bargain, and the rates that are available for cellular services are actually cheaper than using landlines for long-distance calls. What is part of your per-minute area rate on your cell service could be a toll call on your regular phone service. Some cell packages even give unlimited or extended airtime after hours and on weekends or during nonpeak calling times. I often use my cell phone more on weekends than I do my regular phone, because of the unlimited calls in my plan. Another feature to consider is rollover minutes: if you do not use all your minutes in a month, the remaining minutes roll over to the next month.

I use a pager so I can be found, and I call back on my cell phone. I keep my cell phone turned off to prolong battery life and to keep from annoying other people. I use my cell phone for mostly emergency situations, such as responding to my secretary when she wants me to pick up lunch. I have seen some sole practitioners who use cell phones as their main source of communications. They are walking offices. Everything is in their briefcases and their clients contact them on their cell phones. I have also seen some practitioners who forward all office calls to their cell phones when they leave the office. This avoids answering machines. I once returned a call to a lawyer and got him on his cell phone halfway across the country. In the future, your phone number will not identify a specific location such as your home or office, but a mobile location where you are.

The government removed the providers' stranglehold on their users by making phone numbers portable. If you change your provider, you can take your number with you. The only caveat about being available anywhere is the problem of your phone ringing while you are in court. Most judges have unpleasant ways of dealing with lawyers whose phones ring during court proceedings. To avoid unpleasant consequences, and as a matter of common courtesy, you can turn your phone off and rely upon voice mail, or put the phone on vibrate while you are in court.

The leader in the no-place-to-hide, you-can-find-me-anywhere department is the Blackberry device. It is a multiband/multijurisdictional e-mail device that you can also use as a phone. You can get e-mail messages anywhere there are transmission towers. The only drawback is typing on that itty-bitty keyboard. Now your spam can follow you around the world.

Land Phone Service Shopping

All the great rate deals are not only with cellular services. With the ever-increasing number of long-distance carriers and increased competition in local carriers, you should do some price comparisons before you pick a carrier. I am sure that I am not the only one in the world who gets a least one call a week asking me to change phone companies. I always listen to the rate being quoted and then I start asking questions.

Once I am told the per-minute rate, this is the first question I ask: "Is there a monthly charge to get that rate?" Some phone companies give you a great per-minute charge quote, but fail to mention that the rate is predicated upon you paying some amount per month, per line. When that is factored in, the per-minute rate could go up drastically. When confronted with the per-line rate, some carriers will waive it, especially if you tell them you are not paying one now. One thing I learned when dealing with phone companies is that they will not tell you if they have a lower rate plan than the one you are currently using. If you don't ask, you don't get. This is a sorry state of affairs when a loyal customer is literally charged more for phone service than a new customer, who has just been wooed away from another carrier with the promise of lower rates. If you do change carriers, see if the new carrier will cover the transfer costs that the old carrier will charge you for transferring service (they usually will).

Here is the next question I ask: "Is this per-minute billing or incremental billing?" Incremental billing can save you a tidy sum. Some carriers charge by the minute. A sixty-one-second call is charged as two minutes on your bill. Companies that bill incrementally charge by units of one to six seconds. You pay for what you use.

Sometimes state-to-state long-distance calls are much cheaper than intrastate or Inter-Lata calls. Inter-Lata refers to local toll calls or zone calls not within your local call area. I am always amazed that my local carrier would charge me more than twice the per-minute rate to call across town than I would pay my long-distance carrier to call outside my state. I negotiated a flat rate for all toll calls in my state. I am now charged the same rate if I call from my office to my home, which is eight miles away, as I am charged to call five hundred miles away within my state. Because other companies were starting to get close to my carrier's rates, I just negotiated one flat rate for the whole country, including my state and my 800 service. The point is that you should shop around for the best rates and then negotiate for the best deal. I shy away from the bonus or cash-back plans because you have to jump through too many hoops to figure out your true rate.

When you are checking out phone rates, you should also check out the rates that the carriers are quoting for calling cards and 800 service. When I changed services a few years back, I asked for calling cards so that I could make long-distance calls from anywhere and charge the calls to my account. Because most of the calling-card calls were to my office, my sales representative suggested that I get 800 service as well as the calling cards. The per-minute rate for the 800 service is much cheaper than the calling-card rate. I followed his suggestion and now I can contact my office from anywhere in the United States at rates comparable to my regular long-distance rates. If the call is originated from a pay phone, I am charged thirty cents for using the pay phone plus the regular per-minute charges. I currently have no monthly fee for the 800 service and I am charged only for the calls that come in on the 800 number. The 800 number can be used as a marketing tool to attract new clients. The only problem with 800 service is that you are charged for people dialing the wrong number. As the number of wrong numbers and the cost for them is minimal, this has not dissuaded me from keeping the service. Even though I usually use my cell phone, the 800 number still comes in handy when my battery runs low, I forget to bring my cell phone, or I am in a dead zone.

I use the calling card for other calls that do not go back to my office. If you have concerns about the overuse of a calling card, you can purchase pre-paid calling cards for both long-distance service and for cellular service. Your usage is controlled by the fact that the service terminates when all your minutes are used. If you want to talk longer, you have to purchase more minutes. Self-limitation does have its drawbacks.

Reach Out from Anywhere

One of the most frequent complaints that clients have about their lawyers is that they cannot communicate with them. What with phone systems, cellular phones, fax machines, answering machines, voice mail, and pagers, your clients should be able to reach out and touch you wherever you are. I just hope you are not ticklish.

Leveraging the Net 36

Jerry Lawson

The Internet transforms industries, often in unexpected ways. The trucking industry is a good example. Truckers now waste less time in frantic, often fruitless, bouts of long-distance telephone calls, trying to find something they can haul to avoid returning home with an empty trailer. Truckers log onto private Internet sites called *intranets*, where information about loads needing transportation is readily available. The result? A more efficient trucking industry, one that in the long run will probably have fewer, but more highly paid, truckers.

Lawyers don't deal in freight, but they do deal in information and communication by the truckload. The Internet can assist lawyers in many ways:

- Helping a lawyer operate more efficiently, including reducing overhead.
- Bringing a lawyer's skills to the attention of potential new clients.
- Making a lawyer more attractive to clients by enabling new conveniences and a higher quality of service.

Along with benefits and advantages, the Internet also introduces many security risks.

Security Issues and Solutions

Viruses—"I Love You"

Many computer security threats take advantage of people's curiosity. The infamous "I Love You" virus spread as far and as fast as it did because people were understandably curious to find out who was sending them what looked like a love note. The result was devastating and completely avoidable. Countless variations have wreaked havoc throughout the business world. The key to most viruses and security scams is to get you to give out information that you normally would keep confidential. A healthy skepticism can go a long way toward avoiding viruses and other computer security scams.

Use Antivirus Software

Many businesses, including law offices, have had their operations shut down after being infected by a virus or other infestation. *Malware* is a generic term for programs such as viruses or worms and the dangers they spread via such techniques as *keystroke loggers*. Keystroke loggers infest your computer and then record everything you type (including passwords) and send that information on to a third party by e-mail.

Other programs, known as *remote access trojans*, look like legitimate remote access software, but, once installed on your computer, can be used by hackers to take control of your computer, including programs, data files, and personal information. The solution is relatively easy:

- ◆ *Antivirus Software.* Install good antivirus software and keep it updated. The leading brands of software include Norton and McAfee. Because new viruses are springing up regularly, make sure you get an antivirus program that alerts you to automatic updates via the Internet.
- ◆ *Firewalls.* Install one or more firewalls, monitor them, and keep them updated. Firewalls are screeners intended to let desired Internet traffic reach your computer, while keeping undesirable traffic away. Firewalls can be hardware (including a properly configured router) or software (such as Zone Alarm or Black Ice). Since they protect against different types of threats, it is best to use both hardware and software firewalls.
- ◆ Avoid opening suspicious attachments to e-mail programs, even from parties known to you.
- ◆ Avoid using computers in libraries or other public places to conduct sensitive commercial transactions online. Keystroke loggers can steal your log-on information.
- ◆ Consider switching from Microsoft Windows-based applications to less-vulnerable software running on Mac OS or Linux.

E-mail and Internet Security

Some security safeguards simply involve using common sense. For example, don't ever respond to an email from someone you don't know and don't ever click on a URL contained in an e-mail message from a stranger.

Don't send credit card or other personal information over the Internet unless you are absolutely sure that you are connected to a secure site. Some sites advertise themselves as being securely encrypted. The problem is that the hackers can cause phony Web sites to give out phony assurances of security. Make sure you know who you are dealing with.

If you are concerned about someone intercepting your e-mail communication, consider using encryption. A program called Pretty Good Privacy (PGP), **http://www.pgp.com**, is an excellent choice, both for purposes of ease of use and having a high level of security. It's my best recommendation if the type of law you practice or the type of clients you have leave you at heavy risk of a security attack.

Even lesser levels of encryption can still protect against some threats. For example, Microsoft Word has a feature that encrypts files so they require a password to read them. Even though security experts consider Word's encryption to be pitifully weak, the fact that you are using anything consistently will make you a less attractive target for would-be snoops.

In summary: Most lawyers will probably not need to encrypt most e-mail messages. Some lawyers, and some messages, are at greater risk than others, so avoid using e-mail for messages whose disclosure could cause harm to you or your clients if discovered. With some clients, or on some cases, it may be a good idea to encrypt all messages. While using a strong encryption program will give you a higher level of security, even weaker programs can provide some practical protection.

Unintended Dissemination

One of the biggest e-mail "security" vulnerabilities is unintended persistence or dissemination. It's so easy to send an e-mail message that comes back to haunt you.

Some widely publicized court cases involving damaging e-mail messages produced in litigation have resulted in various vendors selling services that purport to give senders more control over e-mail they send. They claim to allow senders to recall, modify, or set an expiration date for e-mail messages that have already been sent. These services might conceivably have some value, but they also have significant disadvantages. They add new inconveniences and are far from being foolproof. Even in the absence of a technical glitch, recipients could do a screen capture or take a photo of an incriminating e-mail with a digital camera, for example. If a human being can read it, he or she can copy it.

Perhaps worse, using these services could cause legal problems. The category that undertakes to tell you whether someone has read your e-mail could violate anti-spyware laws. Further, these products do not always prevent others from being able to determine that an e-mail was transmitted to or from a particular person at a particular time. The message that "disappeared" might have been innocuous, but it certainly won't sound that way after an opposing party has made the argument that you wouldn't be using such an unusual service unless you had been trying to hide something unsavory.

Metadata

Many computer data files such as word-processing files, spreadsheets, and others contain *metadata*, or data about data. This can create problems when sharing information over the Internet or by disk, since the metadata can contain a wide variety of information, including prior versions of the text, authors, subject, title, company, prior revisions, hidden text or cells, comments, and summaries. The results can range from embarrassment to legal liability. The metadata tools released by Microsoft and third-party vendors to deal with these problems have not been uniformly successful.

Web Bugs

Web bugs are small, usually invisible graphic files used for tracking documents. They contain a hypertext link to a tiny picture file on a Web server controlled by the snoop. When a bugged document is opened on a computer connected to the Internet, it attempts to retrieve that graphic from the Web server. The log file on the Web server records the graphic file name, date, time, your computer address, and domain name. You can detect Web bugs with Bugnosis, a free program from The Privacy Foundation: **www.bugnosis.org**. (See Chapter 38 for additional information on security issues.)

Getting Online

Every Internet user knows that bandwidth is the name of the game. Slow, modem-based dial-up connections are only used by people who do not have any other alternative.

The two leading contenders for high-speed home and small office connections are TV cable and Digital Subscriber Lines (DSL). Unfortunately, neither TV cable nor DSL is yet available everywhere. Satellite connections, land-based transmitters, and wireless broadband connections are alternatives. Getconnected.com (**http://www.getconnected.com**) tracks the availability of high-speed connections across the country.

Wireless networking (WiFi) is a method of connecting computers to networks, including the Internet. It adds new utility to laptops and even Portable Digital Assistants (PDAs). Businesses like Starbucks and Borders bookstores have arrangements with providers such as T-Mobile, but other coffee shops, malls, airports, and businesses increasingly offer free WiFi access. WiFi Free Spot, **http://www.wififreespot.com**, is a good place to learn about free "hot spots" around the country.

Jeff Beard at Law Tech Guru Blog has some tips on WiFi security. Go to **http://www.lawtechguru.com** and search the <u>Privacy & Security</u> section of the archives.

E-mail Efficiency

E-mail is the single most important Internet application for most lawyers, so it is essential to master the timesaving features of your e-mail software. Perhaps the biggest potential efficiency booster is learning how your favorite e-mail program uses filters to sort and otherwise process e-mail. E-mail "signature blocks" serve the same functions in e-mail that letterhead serves in paper mail. Having your e-mail software automatically add a signature block to outgoing messages is a convenience. Good e-mail software lets you have a default signature block, with the ability to choose from alternates when desired.

Modern e-mail and personal information manager (PIM) software give the option to use electronic equivalents of paper business cards, calendars, and invitations. The vCard standard makes it easy for a recipient using compatible software to add a new contact to their address book software. Similarly, the vCalendar standard makes it easy to add an appointment to electronic calendar software. The iCalendar standard goes further, simplifying the process of scheduling appointments where multiple parties are involved. All three standards are useful when dealing with clients or other lawyers who are reasonably sophisticated about technology such as personal digital assistants.

Some lawyers prefer Web-based e-mail services such as Hotmail (**http://www.hotmail.com**) or Yahoo Mail (**http://mail.yahoo.com**). These services have some good features, especially for lawyers who travel frequently, but they are not as well-suited to a high volume of e-mail as conventional e-mail is.

The biggest e-mail annoyance is unsolicited commercial e-mail, or spam. Federal regulation has had no perceptible effect; the volume of spam has actually increased since enactment of the CAN-SPAM Act of 2003.

Spam wastes time, but a bigger danger is that a critical e-mail message may get overlooked in all the clutter. Here are ways to reduce the amount of spam you receive:

◆ Avoid giving out your e-mail address unless absolutely necessary. Don't fill out Web-based registration forms or online surveys.
◆ Don't respond to spam messages or (unless you are certain the spam came from an otherwise reputable business) request to be removed from the spam list. Such responses merely confirm to the spammer that your address belongs to a human being who actually reads spam.

♦ Because automated "harvesting" software is one of the leading ways spammers find new victims, don't let your e-mail address appear on a Web page without a good reason, especially in an unprotected form. At present, you can get some protection by posting your e-mail address in a form calculated to fool the harvesting software. Instead of **jlawson @sololawyer.com**, you could spell it **jlawsonSTOPSPAM@sololawyer .com**. The idea is that a human being would be smart enough to re-move the letters STOPSPAM before trying to use the e-mail address. Al-ternatively, there are free sites that will produce an encrypted version of your e-mail address that is transparent to human readers of the page, but (at least for the time being) not readable by harvesting soft-ware. E-mail Riddler (**http://www.dynamicdrive.com/emailriddler**) is one version.

Spam screeners can help you handle the remaining spam. This can be a service provided by your Internet Service Provider, a service from a third-party vendor, software installed on a server run by your law practice, or soft-ware installed on your computer. This market is crowded. Spamnet, Qurb, and SpamAssassin all have fans, but because this is a rapidly changing environ-ment, I recommend researching resources like *PC Magazine* (**http://www .pcmag.com**) or *PC World* (**http://www.pcworld.com**) before you buy.

Other Communications Tools

No one under fifteen years old needs to have Instant Messaging (IM) explained to them. For the uninitiated, IM allows you to have your message drawn to the attention of the recipient right away, as long as the recipient is using compat-ible software. MSN Messenger and AOL Instant Messenger (AIM) are some of the more popular programs. Some lawyers who have made themselves avail-able in this manner report great client enthusiasm.

"Voice Over IP" refers to using Internet connections for voice phone calls. This technology has been around for years, but only recently has the quality and reliability of these services improved enough to make them a credible alternative to regular phone service. Some of them, like VoicePulse (**http://www.voicepulse.com**), and Vonage (**http://www.vonage.com**), plug into a broadband router and any standard phone.

"Chat" allows two or more parties to communicate in real time by typing in messages that are instantly visible to other chat participants. Being a good touch typist helps, as most people do not find voice recognition adequate for chat.

Conferencing software goes beyond chat to include a shared whiteboard (graphics or other computer screens displayed on one computer visible to other participants), voice communications, and even video displays. WebEx (**http://www.webex.com**), is one popular vendor.

Factual and Legal Research on the Web

Research, especially factual research, is one of the major ways to obtain a competitive advantage using the Internet. The amount of useful information on the Internet increases daily.

An excellent resource for online legal research is *The Lawyer's Guide to Fact Finding on the Internet*, Second Edition by Carole A. Levitt and Mark E. Rosch (American Bar Association, 2004).

Blogs: An Exciting New Type of Internet Presence

Weblogs, also known as blogs, are the hottest new thing on the Internet. The legal variety has been dubbed "blawg" by Denise Howell, who runs the "Bag and Baggage" blog. Veteran Internet lawyer and visionary Erik Heels, author of the first book on Internet legal research, has called blogs "the most important development since the Web itself." Why all the excitement?

Blogs have very low out-of-pocket cost, yet in some ways they are proving to be more effective than conventional Web sites. I regularly discuss the latest developments in lawyer blogs at **Netlawblog.com** (**http://www.netlaw blog.com**).

Web sites that track the coming and going of weblogs include **http://law-library.rutgers.edu/resources/lawblogs.html** and **http://www.blawg.org/**. (See also Chapter 48, "The Ins and Outs of Blogs.")

Recommendations

Take advantage of technology, especially the Internet, to reduce your overhead and provide a higher level of client service.

Here are a few of the many ways in which this can be done:

1. Learn to use free or inexpensive research sources on the Internet. Superior factual research can lead to winning cases more often. Online research may also let you reduce the money you spend on expensive online services or investigators. One San Francisco private investigations firm has already attributed a 40 percent reduction in revenue to former clients now using the Internet for much of their factual research.
2. Give clients the option to fill out intake forms at your Web site. This can reduce your expenses, as you no longer need to have your staff in-

terview the clients or decipher their handwriting. To maximize the efficiencies, look for Web site software that interfaces with your case management and document assembly software. This technique is known as "outsourcing to the customer." In addition to saving money, this can improve quality. The Direct Marketing Association reports that errors drop by 50 percent when customer orders are completed over the Internet, instead of by telephone. Finally, many clients prefer online forms, since this technique allows them to complete the form at the time that is most convenient for them, and in their home, where they are more likely to have ready access to their records, thus further improving the quality.

3. Use your Web site not just as a marketing tool, but as a way of providing clients with basic information at their convenience. This lets you devote more of your face to face meeting time to developing a rapport with the client and delivering high value customized advice that justifies a higher billing rate. As Internet pioneer Greg Siskind has noted, "An educated client is the best client."

Make yourself more attractive to clients by making yourself as convenient to do business with as possible.

In the Internet business, this is known as making yourself "sticky;" that is, make working with you so easy that clients are reluctant to leave you for someone else.

By now so many people have come to prefer e-mail to paper letters, faxes, and the telephone for most communications that using e-mail provides a lawyer little competitive advantage. However, e-mail is just the beginning. Use instant messaging, blogs (with RSS feeds), Web sites with your contact information, maps, lawyer biographies, and FAQs or articles on basic legal questions, online calendars, conferencing software, Extranet sites for particular clients, and whatever else your clients will find makes it more convenient to do business with you.

Use the Internet to develop a reputation as a top expert in one or more niche markets, and help you attract new clients with problems in those areas.

Look for narrow legal markets and focus on them, positioning yourself as a leading expert. As pointed out by another Internet pioneer, Lance Rose, "Brand names create geography on the Internet." Try to make yourself a brand name in one or more marketable legal specialties. On the Internet, reputation and "mindshare," or public awareness, have significant value.

Static Web sites are far from being the be-all and end-all of Internet marketing. Look for chances to build and profit from virtual communities. Use e-mail mailing lists, interactive Web-based discussion groups, or both to facilitate interactive communications with groups of people with common interests, and in the process develop or enhance your reputation as an expert.

Use technology, especially the Internet, to target the high end of the market.

At a CLE program a decade ago, when the Internet was still very new to lawyers, I suggested to a fellow panelist that he establish a Web site to market his practice. He was skeptical, pointing out that he was a solo lawyer whose practice included a lot of court-appointed criminal defense work, and that most of his target market did not use the Internet. The idea I gave him then is one that could be beneficially heeded by many lawyers today:

"Maybe you should be aiming for a higher class of criminal."

A Web site with the right focus could facilitate a move from a largely indigent client base into the more lucrative white-collar criminal defense market. Look for opportunities to reposition your own practice.

Greg Siskind uses his Web site for exactly this type of upscale approach. His Web site attracts so many prospective clients that it allows him to be selective. While he does more than his share of pro bono work, most of the paying clients he accepts are not members of the "huddled masses" class lyrically saluted on the Statue of Liberty, but well-educated clients with high earning capacity.

Look for new opportunities, either inside or outside the legal profession.

In many cases this will involve more entrepreneurial thinking than comes naturally to most lawyers.

Greg Siskind was not satisfied with developing just the highly successful **Visalaw.com** immigration law Web site. He also developed two subsidiary Web sites (**Visajobs.com** and **Visahomes.com**) focused on linking his employer clients with foreign nationals seeking positions in the United States. The sites generate revenue directly and also indirectly by making matches that result in the need for an immigration lawyer's services.

Be the change

Instead of passively waiting for changes to occur, and hoping you don't get hurt, why not take the initiative? If the changes are inevitable, why not help them come about, if you can benefit by doing so?

Instead of complaining that online document assembly services are taking your clients, why not position your practice as providing "unbundled" legal services to clients who have used online document assembly, or even partner with one or more such Web sites?

Lawyers who develop and deploy expert systems stand to make good money, displacing other lawyers in the process. If these changes are going to happen anyway, as appears likely, why not be one of the lawyers who develops, deploys, and makes money from such systems, instead of one of the lawyers who is displaced?

Would helping to bring about a restructuring of the legal profession be something to feel guilty about? Actually, it would make you a hero, according to people like Alan Greenspan and other leading policy makers and economists who speak favorably of the economic doctrine known as "creative destruction." The basic concept is that even though restructuring may be painful in the short run for those who are adversely affected, the increased efficiencies that result provide significant long-range benefits to the overall economy. They consider the restructuring of established industries in the face of new competition to be a sign of economic health, not weakness.

Solo lawyers, like the rest of the legal profession, face the prospect of technology-induced turbulence over the next decade and beyond. The lawyers who thrive will not be those who stubbornly try to cling to the old ways of doing business, but those who embrace the coming changes, using new technology, including the Internet, to provide a higher level of client service, benefit from the new efficiencies, and seize new opportunities.

E-mail Management 37

Dennis Kennedy

Internet usability expert Jakob Nielsen has said, "Whether people get 10, 100, or 1,000 e-mails a day, they all say that the number they get is 'overwhelming.'" Computer magazines run covers that trumpet, "Is E-mail Broken?" E-mail messaging is still valuable in many, many ways to solo lawyers. In fact, it would be nearly impossible to practice today without it. However, e-mail capability is no longer the wonderful tool it used to be; associated with it are many issues and burdens:

- ◆ *E-mail Messaging Is Just One Communications Tool*: E-mail messaging is a great tool for delivering information to someone quickly when you do not know if that person is available. Otherwise, a telephone call or instant messaging may be the better choice. For group discussions, e-mail messaging is much less useful than conference calls. You should use e-mail messaging only when it is the appropriate tool.
- ◆ *E-mail Messaging Creates Time Management Issues*: Your e-mail in-box is not a substitute for your "to do" list, but many people treat it that way. The sheer volume of e-mail messages may cause you to "lose" tasks you need to do. If you have to spend a lot of time sorting and responding to e-mail messages, you will not be spending that time on billable or otherwise important tasks.
- ◆ *E-mail Capability Creates Record-Keeping Issues*: What is the "file" today? Are e-mail messages and attachments integrated into client files? Are you confident that you can retrieve the "complete file"?

389

- *An E-mail Program Is an Important Marketing Tool*: It may be more important to have your own domain to use for your e-mail address than for a Web site. If you do not have an e-mail address such as you@your-firm.com, you undercut your credibility. You should know that you can simply purchase a domain name and have a host forward e-mail messages to your existing e-mail account. In addition, using "signatures" on your e-mail messages (name, contact information, and tag line) is one of the most effective free marketing tools you can use.

- *E-mail Messages Leave Your Control*: Once you send an e-mail message to someone, he or she can forward it and it might be seen by the whole world. All e-mail messages should be composed with this fact in mind.

- *E-mail Messaging Creates Security Issues*: The most common way to get viruses, spyware, and other "malicious code" is through e-mail messages.

- *An E-mail Account Is the Land of Spam*: A few recent statistics illustrate the dimensions of the spam problem. In recent months, as much as 70 percent of all Internet e-mail messages were unsolicited, commercial e-mail messages, or spam. Of the spam, an estimated 50 percent of messages contained viruses, spyware, or other "malware." The Federal Trade Commission recently backed away from creating a "Do Not Spam" list because it felt that such a list might benefit spammers more than e-mail users.

Experts are also beginning to believe that e-mail programs are being asked to do more things than originally intended. Remember the days when getting an e-mail message meant you were getting a short, informal, and usually helpful message? As we increasingly ask e-mail programs to serve as document managers, record retention policy tools, collaborative discussion and drafting tools, message thread managers, and security, confidentiality, and encryption tools (and even more), the humble e-mail tool begins to break down.

Seven Basic Goals of E-mail Program Management

There are at least seven goals of e-mail program management:

1. Control the overall volume of messages
2. Make the most important messages most accessible
3. Turn actionable messages into to-do items
4. Make messages findable
5. Minimize security and other dangers
6. Enhance your communications with others
7. Protect your client's interests and avoid malpractice

How many of these goals are you currently achieving? How many can you reasonably expect to achieve? How can you realistically attempt to achieve them? What are the consequences if you do not?

Protecting Your In-Box

Good e-mail management can be attained by carefully focusing upon the phrase, "protect your in-box." If you concentrate on the notion of protecting your in-box and make it your primary theme in guiding your e-mail management efforts, you will maximize your success.

Your in-box, ideally, should contain only actionable e-mails that have recently arrived. In fact, most of the time your in-box should be empty, nearly empty, or in the process of becoming empty. Here's the key concept: an in-box should be an in-box, not a message repository, not a to-do list substitute, not a research folder, and not a junk drawer. I once heard a lawyer admit to having over 29,000 messages in his in-box! Limit the amount of unnecessary messages coming into your in-box. Move "categorizable" messages out of your in-box and into appropriate folders, either manually or automatically.

The following practical, four-part approach to handling e-mail messages will help you put this theme into action. These steps concentrate your action on four key "pressure points" at which your efforts can have the greatest results. The approach does not focus upon spam—those unsolicited, commercial e-mail messages—though spam handling flows naturally out of the process. I would argue that placing too much focus upon spam results in some negative effects on your total e-mail management efforts.

By focusing upon these four pressure points, a modest amount of effort will give you 80 to 90 percent of the results you wish. You will get the best results if you address each of the four points, but you can achieve impressive results by working on only one, two, or three of the pressure points. The four pressure points are as follows:

1. Before e-mail messages are sent to you
2. When you send e-mail messages
3. When you receive e-mail messages
4. When you read and/or store e-mail messages

1. Before E-mail Messages Are Sent to You

People are often surprised by the high number of e-mail messages that arrive when they submit information online or provide their e-mail addresses on Web sites. The collection of e-mail addresses is big business, and your own actions contribute much to the amount of spam you receive.

The approach to follow is a simple one. First, make it easy for the people you want to send you e-mail messages to do so, and make it difficult for the people you don't want to send you e-mail messages. Second, adopt a "multiple e-mail address" approach and attempt to steer e-mail messages to the appropriate address.

Let's look at the second point first. One of the tried-and-true approaches to e-mail management has been to use at least two e-mail addresses. As a practical matter, you have a "work" e-mail address and a "home" e-mail address. Most people have a "yourname@yourbusiness.com" address at work and a "yourname@yourisp.com" that came with their Internet accounts at home. Another common approach, which I advise, is to have a third e-mail account through a free Internet e-mail service, such as Hotmail or Yahoo mail. Once you have these e-mail accounts established, go back and apply the first principle and make it easy for people to send e-mail messages to the appropriate address.

First, make it a priority to reserve the work e-mail address for business e-mail messages. This is the address you should use on your business card, on your firm's Web site, and for clients and potential clients. You may give it out in public, but try to do so only in the business context. Move nonbusiness e-mail messaging away from this account aggressively. For example, if you have a business associate who sends you jokes or attachments, simply say that your firm does not allow them and have the associate send this e-mail message to your home account. Business-related e-mail newsletters should also be sent to the "work" e-mail account. As a result, your work in-box should contain, for the most part, two things: business-related e-mail messages and spam.

Second, direct "personal" e-mail messages to your "home" address. Use this address for friends and family, hobbies and other interests, and other nonbusiness e-mail messaging. Ask business colleagues who use this address to direct business-related e-mail messages to your work account. As a result, your home in-box should contain, for the most part, two things: personal e-mail messages and spam.

Third, set up a Hotmail, Gmail, Yahoo, or other free e-mail account for online shopping and for those times you must supply an e-mail address when you have a concern that providing your e-mail address will lead to unsolicited e-mail messages. Use this account accordingly. This account will contain, for the most part, order acknowledgments, shipping information, other receipts, and spam.

Some people go as far as to set up one or more other accounts for e-mail list servers or discussion groups. I don't think it's necessary to go that far. Having two or three e-mail addresses will give you most of the benefits without adding the burden of checking multiple accounts.

If you use this approach, you will have in-boxes that are easy to "triage." You can determine quickly whether a message is a "keeper," and use your delete key to handle spam. Following are a few other useful tips for handling predelivery e-mail messages.

First, understand the notion of "opt-in" and "opt-out." Most of us prefer a policy in which we must opt in or explicitly choose to get newsletters and commercial e-mail messages. In other words, we must check a box or do something affirmative to get the e-mail message. In an opt-out system, you will see boxes prechecked for you. Understand what you are signing up for when you leave these boxes checked.

Second, pay attention to privacy policies and be wary of providing information when a privacy policy indicates that your e-mail address may be sold, rented, or given to third parties. In such cases, use the third e-mail address discussed above.

Third, consider carefully whether you should join high-volume e-mail lists. E-mail lists can be enormously valuable, but also can have traffic of hundreds of messages a day. Some lists may be configured to send you a single message that contains all the postings for that day. Joining any list should be done only after you have determined how you will manage the messages you will receive from the list.

Fourth, avoid replying to, unsubscribing from, or, if possible, even opening spam messages. Some studies indicate that 90 percent of spam comes from about two hundred companies in the unsolicited commercial e-mail business. Stay off their radar screens. Anything you do that shows that your e-mail address is "live" invites further spam.

Finally, some Internet service providers (ISPs) have started applying spam filters and antivirus checking before your e-mail message even reaches you. Taking advantage of this option, or moving to an ISP that has this option, can weed out the most obvious and offensive spam before it comes into your in-box.

2. When You Send E-mail Messages

Ironically, what you do when sending e-mail messages has a great impact upon your ability to manage the e-mail messages you receive. Some of your options are simple and straightforward. You should definitely use the standard features of your e-mail software. Save e-mail addresses in the "contacts" folder or address book so you don't have to retype e-mail addresses every time. Keep copies of sent e-mail automatically. Other options take just a little effort, but can really help you.

First, check whether you are e-mailing from the "right" e-mail address. Almost invariably, your recipient will simply reply to your e-mail message and the reply will come to the address from which you sent your message. If you send a business message from your home address, the reply will not make it to your work address, and you will lose some of the benefits you gained in addressing the first pressure point.

Second, use effective subject-matter lines. To me, the intentional sending of an e-mail message with a blank subject-matter line is unforgivable. It does not help the recipient or you to receive a "Re: [blank]" message or reply. Similarly, cryptic or overly simple subjects (such as "Agreement" or "For you") do not help much. Using a subject such as "My Materials for 2003 Missouri SAS-FIRM Conference Attached" helps me find the e-mail message later, helps my recipient manage his or her own in-box, and gives my message appropriate priority—a definite win-win. I also like the idea of adding the phrase "No Reply Necessary" to the subject line to help your recipient manage those types of e-mail messages.

Finally, use your head when deciding to forward or carbon copy e-mail messages. A huge number of messages do not need to be forwarded, and too many people routinely, but unnecessarily, "cc:" a whole list of people. Take a second to think about what you are doing before you send e-mail messages to multiple addressees. Don't add to the e-mail volume problem.

3. When You Receive E-mail Messages

At last we turn to what you do when you actually receive e-mail messages. This point is the one most commonly focused upon in e-mail management solutions, and is the object of spam software. On the "fourfold path," however, we have already seen that we can do much before we even get to this point. In fact, if we follow steps 1 and 2, we will have already reduced our volume of messages, and will have established a couple in-boxes where we can easily determine what mail is important and what is not.

It is also at this point where paths can diverge based upon personal preferences. I like to keep a very clean in-box that contains only those items that require response. Others like to move these types of messages to "action" folders or use chronological folders ("today," "yesterday"). There is no one best choice. You should do what works best for you.

People often have staggering numbers of e-mail messages in their in-boxes. Remember the person I previously mentioned who had 29,000 messages in his in-box! Almost any system at all will be better than that system!

Your first step in in-box management is commonly known as "triage." After I download my e-mail messages, I quickly go through them, delete what I don't need, and read what looks important to me. Deleting messages makes it easier to focus upon what is left, like separating the chaff from the wheat. Here's a very important point: You do not have to read or even open every e-mail message. In fact, it can be dangerous to open e-mail messages that contain viruses and, as I've mentioned, simply opening spam can lead to even more spam. A common technique uses a bit of code, generally known as a "Web bug," to let the sender know that you have opened an e-mail message. Web bugs and similar approaches tell the spammers that you have a "live" address, which means they keep you on the spam list. If you think a message is spam, delete it without opening it.

Your second step is to create folders within your in-box. I'm surprised by the number of people who do not know that you can create these folders. (That's part of the reason I suggest that if you plan to take one computer class this year, take a class on your e-mail software.) You can—and should—create a number of folders in your in-box. (In Outlook, for example, go to the File menu, then New, then Folders.) Again, you will get the best mileage by creating the folders that work best for you. I personally use fairly broad subject categories, such as Client, Speaking, Articles, Newsletters, and Contacts from Web. Once you read an e-mail message and determine that you want to keep it, move it out of the in-box and into the appropriate folder. With little initial effort, your in-box stays clean and you can find old messages relatively easily.

Even better, you can automate this process by using filters or rules, which should be your third step. Every e-mail program these days has these features. A rule is a simple if-then management tool that you can apply to your e-mail system. The simplest is the "move to folder" rule, which most people consider to be essential for managing membership in an e-mail list. When you use this type of rule, your system "looks" at an incoming message and, based upon the sender's address, keyword, or other factor, automatically routes it to a folder so that it never appears in your main in-box. As a result, your main in-box stays cleaner; you can perform triage easily on it and then turn to the various folders.

In Outlook, for example, under the Tools menu, you will find a Rules Wizard that walks you through the process of creating a rule. Even better, the Outlook Organize tool creates common rules with only a few mouse clicks, and gives you the choice of running the rule on your existing messages in your in-box, making it a great way to clear out and organize an overflowing in-box. The Organize tool and the Rules Wizard (or their equivalents in other e-mail software) also allow you to create rules to take care of standard spam and adult-oriented e-mail messages.

You can be as elaborate as you want with folders and rules, but I like to keep it pretty simple, on the theory that 20 percent of my effort will give me 80 percent of the results. Though some people use spam filters and other tools, for most of us, the four steps in this section will go a long way toward both handling received e-mail messages and dealing with spam. I personally am not an advocate of spam filters—they are not perfect, and I would rather delete a few spam messages than miss a message intended for me that contained a common word that triggered a spam detector.

4. When You Read and/or Store E-mail Messages

Much has been written lately about retention and deletion policies for e-mail systems. The issues are real and need to be addressed. For purposes of this chapter, I assume that you have developed appropriate policies, and I will concentrate on the e-mail management aspects at this fourth pressure point.

Although you might think this issue arises at the point of storage or filing, it actually arises when you read the message. Must you respond to the message? Today? Tomorrow? In due course? Does it require another action or forwarding to someone else? Do you need to keep it? Can it be deleted? I probably use a heavy finger on the delete key. Other people delete much more than I do, and many delete much less. The guy who had 29,000 e-mail messages in his in-box triggered several postings to an e-mail list, explaining the existence and location of the delete key.

I clear my in-box by either deleting or moving messages to a folder. Ideally, my in-box contains only messages that need replies or action by me. E-mail messages that don't need replies go the appropriate folder immediately. Once I reply, the original e-mail message goes to the appropriate folder. I also evaluate whether a rule could be created to send this type of message to a folder automatically, where I could deal with it separately, with like messages.

After that, it's a simple matter of file management. I tend to create subfolders semiannually or annually, depending upon size. For example, after June 30, 2005, I might move all the e-mail messages in my Client folder to a subfolder called "Jan to June, 2005" and keep only the newer messages in the actual Client folder. This approach makes folders a bit more manageable and easier to search.

I also use my Newsletter folder as an inexpensive knowledge management tool. I keep about six months of newsletters in the folder before I delete older messages. That way, if I run into situations where I think I saw something on a topic recently, I can do a quick search in that folder and generally find a reference.

E-mail programs also give you methods to archive and compress e-mail messages. Using these features from time to time will keep your e-mail system easier to manage.

Summing Up the Benefits

Although I am not sure I can solve all your e-mail management problems, this four-step approach will take you a long way toward getting a firm handle on your e-mail system and making your life easier. At its foundation is the idea of protecting your in-box, in a number of ways, so that what you see in your in-box is what is most important to you. There's no silver-bullet software solution to e-mail management, and I certainly do not recommend that you run out and get the latest spam tool. E-mail management is more a process—an evolutionary, personal process—than a search for a tool. The better you under-stand that concept and work thoughtfully on the process, the better your re-sults.

Seven Habits of Highly Effective E-mailers

It doesn't take too long before you realize that there's much more to using e-mail systems than meets the eye. Both internal office e-mail messages and ex-ternal e-mail messages can fill your in-box. In short order, you might find that the volume of e-mail messages you receive has become overwhelming.

Gradually, you will come to realize that you want to develop strategies so you can take greater advantage of the benefits e-mail messaging offers you. You'll want to become a "power" e-mail user. With a nod to Stephen Covey and his famous "seven habits of highly effective people," here are seven ways that you (and your firm) can become more effective e-mail users and use e-mail programs more effectively.

1. Cut Your Costs

Do not underestimate the cost-cutting benefits e-mail systems can bring to your firm. In certain settings, the cost savings can be enormous.

Using e-mail messages instead of long-distance phone calls can save money. Attaching draft documents to e-mail messages rather than sending them by express delivery saves money. Sending an e-mail message rather than playing phone tag can save time and money. Sending an e-mail message rather than sending a standard transmittal letter saves money, paper, and postage.

Look around your office for ways that an e-mail system can result in cost savings. Do you print, copy, and distribute a daily announcement sheet? Send it by e-mail message instead. Do you mail a client newsletter? Making an e-mail version available will save you printing and postage costs. Signing up for e-mail newsletters can get you information commonly copied and passed around in law firms. Sending the URL of an article by e-mail message saves the cost of copying and distributing the article.

2. Respond Responsively

Many users have full-time Internet e-mail connections and expect instant re-sponses. You need to keep that in mind.

Often, a one- or two-sentence response or a simple direction to a Web ad-dress is all that is required to respond to an e-mail message. The important thing is to be sure to respond in some fashion to e-mail messages you receive. Ignoring e-mail messages sends a very poor message about you, your firm, and, most commonly, your Web site.

3. Mind Your Netiquette

There are a surprising number of "rules of the road" that have grown up around e-mail messaging. Some are common sense, and all are directed at imposing a set of good manners or etiquette on e-mail usage. These rules are commonly known as "Netiquette." The "Miss Manners" resource on Netiquette is Virginia Shea's *Netiquette*, the core elements of which can be found at **www.albion.com/netiquette/corerules.html**.

It is surprisingly easy to make mistakes of form and manners when entering e-mail discussions. E-mail communication lies somewhere between the informal communication of a phone call and the more formal communication of a business letter. E-mail messages tend to be unedited first drafts that are removed from the context of vocal inflections and mannerisms. As a result, it's easy to misunderstand and be misunderstood. Some people are far more aggressive in their e-mail messages than they would be in person. The term "flaming" refers to conversations where anger and feelings get out of hand.

4. Select Subject Matters Sagaciously

Make good use of the subject-matter line of your e-mail message. Give a good, concise summary of what's in the message, which can help people assess the priority of your message and locate your message when needed later. Compare the subject line "Financials" with one that says "August 2004 Income and Expense Report (NEED COMMENTS BY FRIDAY)."

That's not to say that writing wry and humorous subject-matter lines can't be fun. It is, and it can be a bit of an art form for some. There is, however, an appropriate time and place for it.

Today's spam filters place a premium upon well-chosen subject lines. Lack of a subject, capitalization, or use of certain words can trigger spam filters and keep your message from making it to your intended recipient.

5. Sell with Signature Blocks

A wisely chosen signature block can help you market your firm. You've probably noticed signature blocks. Often you'll see a block of text immediately below the sender's name at the bottom of his or her message that includes title, company, address, phone and fax numbers, e-mail address, Web site address, and even quotes, slogans, graphics, or other matter. These are signature blocks.

Most e-mail programs allow you to create a signature block that is automatically inserted at the end of each message you send. You should create a signature block that contains the appropriate information about you and your firm. If you have a Web site, include the URL in your signature block. Here's a helpful tip: be sure to type the "http://" in front of your Web address (http://www.denniskennedy.com, rather than simply, www.denniskennedy.com). If you do so, many e-mail programs will let the reader click on the address and go directly to the Web site.

6. Reach for High-End Software

You can use a variety of e-mail programs. Some are free. Some are simple. All will get the basic job done. But the highly effective e-mailer wants more than that.

I recommend moving to the high-end e-mail packages and the newest versions. These include Microsoft Outlook/Exchange, Novell's Groupwise, Eudora Pro, Netscape (or Mozilla) Mail, and, in certain special cases, Lotus Notes. Macintosh OSX users will find Apple Mail to be an excellent choice.

What makes one e-mail program better than another? Control, management, flexibility, and power. You want the tools that can take your use of an e-mail system to the highest level. The big-time packages allow you to create rules and filters that sort and move your mail to folders upon arrival, view mail in ways that work for you, create mailing groups, and do countless other things for you. E-mail usage is a completely different experience with the high-end tools. As your volume of e-mail messages increases, you'll appreciate having the extra power.

7. Sharpen Your Saw

This habit is really one of Stephen Covey's seven habits. The notion here is to keep learning and to hone the tools that you have so they are ready to use when you need them. Because e-mail systems are so easy to use, many firms give little or no training on them. Many users are simply unaware of helpful features readily available in their programs. Becoming a highly effective e-mail user requires that you update your skills regularly, experiment with software features, and devote yourself to continuous learning and improvement.

E-mail use raises issues on a regular basis. You should keep informed about virus and security issues. Encryption is a growing and important issue. Monitor developments. A helpful book on the e-mail program you use or the occasional foray into Help screens can be especially rewarding and give you new ideas, techniques, and tools.

Conclusion

Great e-mailers are made, not born. It will take some time and effort, but the rewards are immeasurable. Adopt these seven habits and you will become a highly effective e-mailer.

Seven Rules for the New E-mail Era

1. You do not need to open, read, or reply to every e-mail message that you receive. In fact, you do not even need to see certain e-mail messages.

2. You are no longer obligated to reply instantly to every e-mail message, and there is no longer an expectation that you will do so, despite the hype you might hear. Explicitly discuss expectations about e-mail responses at the initiation of the relationship.

3. You must treat spam as a security issue, best addressed by managing behaviors. Risky behaviors will negate the benefits of even the best spam filters.

4. Keep your in-box empty or nearly empty most of the time. If you have this goal, all other aspects of e-mail management will fall into place.

5. Use e-mail programs for the purposes for which they were designed. E-mail messaging is not the best choice for multiparty discussions or certain other types of communications.

6. Do not waste time looking for the perfect solution, because it is not even in the realm of possibility. Good, solid solutions that can be implemented quickly are far superior to extended efforts to find "best" solutions.

7. You must be a leader in your firm and with your clients on e-mail practices. Security, encryption, and other best practices will not spring forth by magic.

Frequently Asked Questions About E-mail Messaging

1. *What disclaimer language should I use on my e-mail messages?* E-mail disclaimer language has evolved into those six paragraphs that everyone other than lawyers laughs about. They are automatically placed at the bottom of every e-mail message, even the ones you send to name the restaurant where you will meet someone for lunch. Assume that a question about confidentiality or privilege arises. The judge hears that you attach the same confidentiality label and disclaimer to the bottom of every single e-mail message (where it can't be seen until after you have read the whole message) and take no other steps. On the other hand, I conspicuously label only selected messages with the words "CONFIDENTIAL/ATTORNEY-CLIENT PRIVILEGE" at the top of the message and either encrypt or password-protect attachments to those messages. I like my chances better than your firm's chances.

2. *How big is the "metadata" issue in documents that I attach to e-mail messages?* Large law firms have already been publicly embarrassed because they failed to remove the metadata from Word and other documents. If you have neither the tools nor procedures in place for handling metadata, you have a train wreck waiting to happen.

3. *How can I be sure that I can find all the e-mail messages related to my case or client?* Because of the way e-mail systems have been used in the last few years, there is no assurance in many cases that any individual can have access to all the "documents" in the "file" (in the classic sense we had in the paper world), or even be certain that identification of the original or current versions can be accurately tracked. Worse yet, you can no longer be sure that the "complete file" can ever be accurately reconstituted. Yes, clients are increasingly concerned about this issue.

4. *What happens if someone thinks I sent an e-mail virus, but I do not think I did?* Because of the way e-mail viruses now work, the odds that it will appear that you sent a virus to someone outside the firm have increased greatly. Even worse, the odds that spyware is sending out information from your computer or your firm's network have increased dramatically even in the last six months. In many cases, nothing you can do as an individual will prevent this from happening.

5. *Should I take a class on my e-mail program?* Assuming that "everyone knows how to use e-mail programs" is a big mistake. Classes on e-mail programs may be the best technology investment you can make.

6. *What e-mail programs should I consider?* Firms that use old versions of e-mail programs, e-mail programs intended for the home or consumer market (such as Outlook Express), or, horrors, Internet e-mail programs such as Hotmail, are assuming an astonishing level of risk. Consider the following recommendations: If you live in the Microsoft world, use Outlook 2003 (the contacts, tasks, and other features more than justify the price). If you do not want to use Microsoft products, use Eudora or Mozilla's free Thunderbird e-mail program.

7. *Can I implement an e-mail management solution that will really work for a long time?* The volume of e-mail messaging will overrun even the best-planned system. Working on the volume side of the equations can help a lot, but looking for good solutions that you can easily work with is really your best hope.

Today's Top Tips for Reducing Spam

◆ Protect your in-box by using the techniques discussed in this chapter.
◆ Never reply to any spam message.
◆ Never click on anything in a spam message.
◆ Never even open a suspected spam message.
◆ Never open any e-mail attachment unless you are expecting it and it arrives in the format you expect.

- Install Windows updates, antivirus programs, firewalls, and spyware detectors; failing to do so is both dangerous and irresponsible.
- Move to heavy-duty e-mail programs and make fuller use of advanced features.
- After doing all the above, consider using a spam-filtering program.

A Roundup of Internet Resources on E-mail Systems

- *Everything E-mail*: a very helpful, one-stop resource on a wide variety of e-mail matters (**www.everythinge-mail.net/e-mail_resources.html**)
- *The Core Rules of Netiquette*: essential reading; excerpts from Virginia Shea's classic book, *Netiquette*, the "Miss Manners" guide to using e-mail programs (**www.albion.com/netiquette/corerules.html**)
- *Outlook Resources*: I use Microsoft Outlook for e-mail messaging (**www.microsoft.com/office/outlook/default.asp**)
- *Legalethics.com*: great Internet resources on all issues relating to legal ethics (**www.legalethics.com**)
- *Eudora*: learn about Eudora's e-mail software (**www.eudora.com**)
- *E-mail Etiquette Rules*: good information on how to use e-mail programs well (**www.emailreplies.com/**)
- *Managing E-mail with Outlook Rules*: good information on rules (**www.winplanet.com/winplanet/tutorials/1001/1/**)
- *Rules for E-mail Lists*: excellent article by Jim Calloway (**www.okbar.org/members/map/articles/web.htm**)
- *E-mail911.com Resources*: a good list of e-mail resources (**www.email911.com/resources/**)
- *E-mail Tips and Techniques*: another good set of resources (**www.ibiztips.com/email_archive.htm**)
- *Tips for Managing E-mail Systems*: written for senior citizens, and has some great tips (**www.seniortechcenter.org/info/articles.php?aid=156**)
- *Ten Most Important Rules of E-mail Netiquette*: as the title says (**www.email.about.com/cs/netiquettetips/tp/core_netiquette.htm**)
- *You've Got (Too Much) Mail*: excellent article in *PC Magazine* from early 2003, which covers software and a variety of issues (**www.pcmag.com/article2/0,4149,842567,00.asp**)

Computer Security for Solos

38

Dennis Kennedy

Recent studies indicate that an unprotected computer running a nonupdated version of Microsoft Windows will be attacked and compromised in no more than twenty minutes after connecting to the Internet. Unfortunately, these studies paint an accurate picture of the level of danger for anyone who connects to today's Internet.

For many years, solo lawyers and small firms, for the most part, got away with paying little or no attention to computer security issues. The common feeling was that small firms and solos flew so far below the radar of intruders, crackers, and other bad actors that there was little or no risk. Many lawyers also believed that they simply did not have anything valuable enough on their computers to make them targets. Until recently, lawyers treated viruses and security issues as completely separate concerns.

The Internet has become a much more dangerous place. Full-time, broadband Internet access has dramatically increased the opportunities bad actors have to attack your system. Even worse, software tools are readily available that allow nearly anyone to break into your computer, whether or not they know what they are doing. Many of today's viruses deliver a mixed payload that often includes a range of programs known as spyware, Trojan horses, and malware, any of which can create security problems.

Even the common assumptions that you are flying below the radar, are too small to matter, or have nothing of value to an intruder no longer apply. Attacks today are not made for innocent purposes or to show programming prowess. They often maliciously delete files and destroy data, and even make computers inoperable.

Worse yet, the availability of your computer alone is reason enough to make your system a target. Gaining control of your computer so it can be used for future purposes is reason enough to justify attacking you. Your computer can then be used to send spam, launch attacks on other systems, or store programs, tools, and other information for other purposes. Today's spyware and keystroke loggers make it ridiculously easy for your information—including passwords and credit card numbers—to be transmitted to third parties without your knowledge.

To the extent that your computer holds client data, you also expose your client's information to compromise and misuse. For example, lawyers practicing family law have reported disgruntled ex-spouses "hacking" into law office computers to find information or even stalk ex-spouses.

In today's computer world, attacks are often made automatically by software programs that can try to compromise thousands of computers in a single session. Your lack of attention to security makes you a likely source of viruses and other "malware" reproduction that can have a damaging effect on your system, the systems of people you know, and the Internet at large. Some have argued that using the Internet without adequate security precautions is irresponsible.

In this chapter, you will learn the basic steps that every computer user must take in today's Internet environment, as well as practical ways to adopt a reasonable approach to handling security issues. As a result, you will become a responsible computer user, make wise choices, and minimize your risks of failing to protect client confidentiality and your business and personal information.

Three Principles and One Analogy You Must Understand

Your approach to computer security must grow from a solid understanding of the following three principles:

1. As soon as you connect to the Internet, you are at serious risk.
2. Security is a process, rather than a destination. Unfortunately, complete security is growing more impossible as the "bad guys" get better and faster.
3. You will always face trade-offs between security and convenience/usability. The more secure your computer system, the less easy and convenient it is to use. Your approach to security involves making wise decisions about reasonable compromises.

Though your attitude must be realistic, it is important that you not be pessimistic. You can (and will) make substantial improvements in your security by making steady efforts. In fact, you can develop excellent, although not perfect, computer security for no cost whatsoever. By following the steps in this chapter, you put yourself in the top tier of security among all lawyers.

The best way to think about computer security is to think about how you keep your car secure from thieves: you discourage "opportunity criminals" and get them to pass by you. If a car thief is walking down a line of cars testing door handles, you want your car to be the one that is locked and has a little flashing red light on the stereo, so the thief passes your car as he looks for one with doors unlocked. However, you also understand that if professional thieves want a car exactly like yours, there's almost nothing you can do to stop them. This chapter will help you take the steps that will suggest to computer intruders that it is better to move along to easier targets.

Special Concerns about Living in a Microsoft World

Security experts have good reasons for the concerns they routinely voice about Microsoft Windows, Microsoft Office, and Microsoft Internet Explorer. The second Tuesday of each month has become known as the day on which Microsoft releases critical updates and patches to address security issues. The security issues arise both from holes left by Microsoft programmers and the incessant efforts made around the world to find new holes to exploit.

If you operate in the Microsoft world, and most of us do, you have special concerns and obligations. You must keep up with current developments and take recommended precautions.

Should you move away from Microsoft products? As I mentioned, you will always be balancing security and convenience. Non-Microsoft products have their own security issues. Because of the ubiquity of Windows and Microsoft Office, moving to non-Microsoft products can raise compatibility, availability, and training issues of various kinds. A decision to leave the Microsoft world requires careful consideration and should not be made on the basis of security reasons alone. In fact, you can walk into a worse security situation if you dump Microsoft and assume the non-Microsoft world is a safe and secure place, where you are free not to worry about, pay attention to, or take consistent steps to address security issues.

Three Recent Security Developments You Must Know

Three recent developments have greatly changed the face of computer security. If you understand these three factors, you will be able to make great strides in improving your security.

The first development is the targeting of publicly known security holes. From viruses to intrusions, today's computer attacks focus upon exploiting known security issues. The sad fact is that nearly every exploit today *takes advantage of a problem for which a security patch or update has already been available*. Some of the most damaging viruses or "worms" of 2004 used methods for which patches had been available for a year or more.

The second development is the "automation" of computer attacks. Readily available software allows for probing and compromise of computers attached to the Internet to be done on an unattended basis, simply by running computer programs. Password-breaking and antiencryption software is powerful enough to break down most protections in a relatively short period of time. For example, the so-called "dictionary" password crackers have made guessing passwords a quaint notion of the past.

The third development is the "professionalization" of computer attacks. Many people still believe that viruses and intrusions are carried out by teenage "hackers" joyriding on the Internet or trying to prove their programming abilities. The fact is that the writing of viruses and other malware (that is, software that has a malicious purpose, such as worms, Trojan horses, spyware, and the like) and breaking into computer systems increasingly involves international organized crime and terrorist groups. FBI cybercrime agents will tell you that some foreign groups control fleets of thousands of compromised computers from which they potentially can launch attacks of their choosing. You may one day find the authorities at your door investigating your computer's role in launching computer attacks, sending out massive amounts of spam, or storing stolen credit card information, child pornography, or terrorist plans, all without your knowledge.

A Reasonable Approach to Computer Security

People often throw up their hands about computer security. They focus upon the fact that you can never be completely secure, and use that as a rationale for taking no steps at all.

The simple fact is that we live in a world of imperfect security on an everyday basis. We have become comfortable with the idea of making reasonable compromises in many contexts. Our homes and offices all reflect our willingness to take security precautions and our assessment of the likely risks. I guarantee that the locks, burglar alarm systems, and other security tools you have chosen will not protect you from a squad of well-trained commandos with detailed plans to break into your office. However, you have made a reasonable assessment of the odds of that type of attack occurring, and your security efforts reflect your judgment of what you need to do to protect yourself from the most probable dangers.

Computer security, properly understood, is built upon a similar model. We each need to assess our dangers and take the steps we think are appropriate. I might go further than you are willing to go, much as your neighbor with the fancy burglar alarm system might appear to be a "security nut" to you. Our approaches will likely evolve over time, especially if we become the victims of crime. However, there are certain basic approaches, such as locking our doors, that we can all agree upon and implement.

The Three Pillars of Computer Security

You should become familiar with Microsoft's security page, at **www.microsoft .com/security/**. Microsoft offers some plain-language explanations of security issues, links to resources and updates, and solid advice for protecting your computer.

Microsoft and many others advocate a three-step, standard approach to computer security. Taking these three steps should be seen as the computer world's equivalent of locking your front door. If you do not take these three steps and your computer system is successfully attacked, you should expect to receive exactly the same amount of sympathy you would receive if something valuable was stolen from your office and you told people you never locked the office front door. In other words, these steps constitute the bare minimum effort you should make:

1. Update Microsoft Windows on a regular basis, installing all critical updates and security patches.
2. Install, run, and keep updated antivirus software.
3. Install, run, and keep updated firewall software.

Updating Windows

I also mean that, if you do not use Microsoft Windows, you should keep whatever operating system you use (including Macintosh OS or Linux) patched and up to date. However, I will focus upon Windows, because the vast majority of lawyers use Windows at home and in the office.

In 2005, my best advice is to run Windows XP, with Service Pack 2 installed, and with the option for automatic downloads and installation of critical updates turned on. In a law office setting, there are some arguments to use XP Pro over XP Home, but, as a general matter, either version of XP, if fully updated, will provide you with the best level of Windows security currently, as long as you keep patching.

If you are using Windows 2000, you must keep fully current on updates and patches. If you do so, you will have a reasonably good level of security, but whether you can reach the same level of security as XP users will be questionable. The reason is simple—all of Microsoft's best security people are focused on XP, not 2000, and the "date of death" for Windows 2000 will soon be approaching. If you are still running Windows ME, 98, or, good heavens, 95, many security experts will tell you that you cannot reach even a reasonable level of security. Your best security move is to go to Windows XP. Windows ME and the Windows 9x family have reached the end of their product lives, and support for these programs is scheduled to end in 2005.

In addition, you must keep current with updates and patches for any network operating software (such as Windows Server 2003, Windows Small Business Server, or Novell).

Windows updates can be taken care of either automatically or manually. You can—and should if you have never done so—go to **www.microsoft.com/ windows** (or the easier-to-remember **www.windows.com**) for information and instructions. In general, you go to the "Windows Update" page on the Microsoft site, and install a small application that checks your computer and informs you about the updates you lack. You may then download and install the updates, all of which can be done automatically and in the background while you do other work on your computer.

You can also set up your computer to check for, download, and install updates automatically. In Windows XP, click on the Start button and then open the Control Panel. Open the System option in the Control Panel. In the box that pops up, you will find a tab called "Automatic Updates." Select this tab and you will see your options for selecting the appropriate settings. The Help menu option will assist you in understanding the choices.

Using automatic updating is now the recommended approach. However, it is prudent to check the Windows Update page manually on a periodic basis as a precaution.

Antivirus Software

How many years have people been preaching to you about installing antivirus software? If you haven't yet done so, just do it now.

There is no one "best" antivirus program. You can buy a program, buy a subscription service, or use one of several free antivirus programs. Some people even use two or more antivirus programs on the same computer. The important point is that you install and use an antivirus program of some kind. Note that you will have to set up your antivirus software to scan your computer periodically, load on start-up, and monitor activity, including e-mail messaging. Settings are adjustable and you should make sure that the software is doing what you think it is doing and, most important, that it is, in fact, turned on and running.

Even more important, however, is keeping your antivirus program up to date. Most antivirus programs have an option to update the program and the virus definitions automatically. You want to choose that option. If there is a highly publicized virus making the rounds, it also makes good sense to check for updates manually rather than to wait for the next scheduled automatic update. The most common antivirus problem is when people install antivirus software but do not update it. In part, antivirus software companies bear some blame. Many people do not realize that the antivirus protection installed on many new computers is only a trial subscription that expires unless you activate and pay for a new subscription over the Internet.

Your antivirus program should provide a "console" or a pop-up screen that will tell you if you are set up to get automatic updates, and will list the dates on which your system was last scanned and your software was last updated. Weekly full scans are probably sufficient, but you must look into what is happening if you see "last updated" dates that are more than a few days old.

If you are infected by a virus or even suspect that you may be, go to your antivirus software company's Web site and follow the instructions you find there. (Note that some viruses now carry a payload that includes a small program that blocks your access to the Web sites of the antivirus companies.) In many cases, there will be a "disinfectant" program that you can download and run to clean your computer. Run this program, then reboot your computer and run the disinfectant again. In some cases, your settings will result in the infection returning when you reboot, which will require some more efforts on your part, none of which will be much fun.

Firewall Software

"Firewall" is a generic term that refers to hardware or software that blocks unwanted traffic on certain "ports" into your computer or network. Hardware firewalls typically are built into the routers and switches you may use in connection with a broadband connection to the Internet. Software firewalls accomplish the same things, but are programs rather than devices. In many cases, both types of firewalls are used simultaneously.

The class of firewall software known as "personal firewall software" is now considered an essential component of computer security. The good news is that one of the most common and widely praised personal firewall programs, ZoneAlarm (**www.zonealarm.com**), comes in a free version that should be sufficient for your purposes. With Service Pack 2, Windows XP now has a built-in software firewall that will be turned on by default and, while generally not considered to be as good as ZoneAlarm, will provide you with a reasonably good software firewall. Many people, including me, run both ZoneAlarm and the Windows XP firewall simultaneously. Unless you find conflicts or other problems, there is no downside to running both firewalls (and a hardware firewall too).

Firewall software blocks attempted intrusions into your computer and/or network. ZoneAlarm also monitors and seeks your approval for programs running on your computer to go out to the Internet. New users of ZoneAlarm (or any similar firewall program) are invariably surprised by three things: (1) the large number of attempted intrusions that occur, (2) how quickly and consistently the attempts take place, and (3) the large number of unfamiliar programs that ask for access to the Internet. Although a large number of standard programs and Windows processes go out to the Internet, a personal firewall program can help you identify and block spyware and other programs sending out information about your computer usage or other information from your computer.

More Practical Steps for Reaching a Reasonable Level of Protection

As I indicated, the three standard steps in the preceding section are the computer equivalent of locking the front door. Most of us are not content simply to lock the front door. Reasonable physical security involves a number of additional steps, depending upon our local crime rate, geographic location, the value of what we have at the location, and similar factors. The same approach applies in the computer world. In this section, you will find the computer equivalents of adding deadbolts, putting documents in lockboxes, adding burglar alarms, and other approaches that are reasonable escalations of your computer procedures. In other words, these are advisable efforts that make good sense in most situations.

Install, Use, and Update Spyware Detection Software

Today's viruses often have mixed payloads that include self-propagation tools (for example, the virus sends itself out by e-mail message to the people in your e-mail address book), spyware, and other malware. Spyware generally refers to software that collects information from you without your knowledge and sends it out, without your knowledge, to a third party. You may agree to the installation of spyware and the use of this information in a "click-through" license agreement that you didn't read, but many spyware programs are installed surreptitiously, with bad intentions and without your approval. Spyware may cause pop-up ads, collect information about your Internet surfing habits, or collect and send out passwords, credit card numbers, account numbers, and other valuable information.

Related to spyware are programs such as keystroke loggers and Trojan horses. Keystroke loggers track and report all your keystrokes, which can reveal passwords and other important information. Trojan horses are seemingly innocuous or hidden programs that create a trap door to your computer through which a third party can later enter easily, and often without leaving much of a trace. The dangers of these types of programs should be obvious, and often they are the worst part of a virus infection.

In 2004, it became generally accepted that spyware detection software was an important component of computer security that should be present on every computer system. Again, the good news is that the two most frequently recommended spyware detection programs, Spybot Search & Destroy (**www.spybot.info**) and Ad-Aware (**www.lavasoft.com**), are available for download for free. These programs search for known spyware programs (Spybot Search & Destroy, for example, searches for approximately 15,000 known spyware programs), let you delete the ones they find, and, in some cases, allow you to block the introduction of certain spyware programs.

Adding spyware protection is an easy and recommended step for you to take. Experts recommend running both of the free programs I mentioned, because their coverage may not precisely overlap. Like antivirus software, these programs must be updated on a regular basis.

Adjusting Browser Security Settings

Whether in the form of downloads, e-mail messaging, or simple Web browsing, use of the Internet is the most likely channel for security problems to arrive at your computer. Virus infection by disk sharing is far less common than it once was, because people are aware of the danger and because disks are rarely swapped anymore.

Let's use Internet Explorer as our example browser. Internet Explorer has gained a reputation recently as a security nightmare. It certainly is vital to keep current on Windows updates if you use Internet Explorer, because the biggest danger comes from using an unpatched version. Some experts have advocated a move from Internet Explorer to the Mozilla family of browsers (Mozilla, Netscape, or FireFox). However, leaving Internet Explorer completely is much trickier than people expect (it is the default browser in a number of applications), and the Mozilla browsers have experienced their own security problems.

You can make your Web browsing less dangerous by making some adjustments to the security settings of your browser. In Internet Explorer, click on the Options item on the Tools menu. One of the tabs in the box that pops up is called Security. You can select a higher level of security or you can customize your security settings. There is a similar process in the Mozilla browsers. You can easily find articles recommending appropriate changes to make in your settings, and it is not difficult to move to a custom approach.

If you change your security settings, however, you will quickly learn how increasing your level of security invariably reduces your level of convenience. Today's suggested high-security settings result in certain features of some Web sites not working, pop-up permission requests, and a variety of warnings that disrupt your normal Internet experience. As a result, most people back away from a high-security approach. With careful attention, however, you can use the custom settings to improve security while not significantly disturbing your Internet experience.

Update Applications and Install Patches

Any list of software applications with the most security issues will probably have Microsoft Outlook Express at the top and Microsoft Outlook right behind it. Symptomatic of today's world of computer security, the fixes for Outlook's most widely known problems have been available for several years and have been eliminated in the default settings for Outlook 2003. Outlook Express still makes security experts nervous.

Best security practices for your standard software applications involve two steps: updating to current versions and installing critical updates and patches.

It is an unfortunate fact of life that using old versions of software opens you to security problems. The business rationale for moving to Office 2003, for example, can be made on security reasons alone. Old versions also create security issues in non-Microsoft applications. Remember that most security problems result from exploits of known holes in commonly used programs. Many of these are a result of default settings, default passwords, and other problems in early versions of software that have been resolved in later versions of the software. If you run noncurrent versions of any software, you must check the software maker's Web site for information about known problems and the availability of patches and fixes. Be aware that for some programs, the only fix is to move to the newest version.

Installing patches and running critical updates for all your applications are highly recommended practices. Although Microsoft can be criticized for many things, it has—with Windows Update and the similar Office Update (accessible by way of **www.microsoft.com/office/** or the "Check for Updates" option under the Help menu of Microsoft Office programs)—made it easy for users to stay current and get the updates they need. The wide publicity that each Microsoft vulnerability receives also helps keep users on their toes and current. Unfortunately, that is not the case for most other programs. Users must make special efforts to learn about and obtain updates and patches. Generally, you must check the customer support areas of the Web sites of the programs you use.

I must emphasize that it is dangerous to assume that security problems and the need for updates and patches is only a Microsoft issue. In 2004, non-Microsoft operating systems (such as Mac OSX and Linux), browsers (such as Mozilla and FireFox), e-mail programs (such as Eudora), and standard applications (such as Adobe Acrobat) all suffered from security problems for which patches and updates had to be released. There is a lot of well-meaning misinformation on this topic. You have probably heard people say that moving to a Macintosh or using Eudora will eliminate security problems. That is flat-out wrong. It might reduce your exposure, but if you do not pay attention to the unique issues of the software you use, moving away from Microsoft may put you in a more vulnerable place.

It is also worth noting that the operating software for some hardware, especially routers, may have security problems that require the installation of software patches.

Granting Appropriate User Rights and Changing Default Settings

Anyone who gains access to your system will generally have only the user rights of the "user" under whose account the attacker gained access. In large networks, the granting of only limited rights to each user is a cornerstone of good security practice. Some programs, including network software and operating systems for network hardware, such as routers, come preset with default users, such as "guest" and "administrator," which have certain default rights and default passwords. The most dangerous accounts are those that have administrator rights. As a general rule, if a user has administrator rights, he or she can do anything on your computer or network. The goal of any intruder is to obtain administrator rights to your computer.

In Windows XP Professional, it is very easy to set up new users and grant the rights associated with each user (assuming, of course, that you have administrator rights, which, as the owner of the computer and purchaser of Windows XP, you will have). You can give a user administrator rights or limited rights. From your perspective, the major difference will be that a limited user cannot install new programs or change the settings of other users.

In general, avoid usernames like "Administrator" or "SuperUser" for accounts with administrative rights. That will make an intruder's job a little more difficult. You may also want to set up multiple user accounts for yourself that have only limited rights, and generally avoid using administrator-level accounts for general use of your computer. For example, I set up a limited-rights user account that I use when accessing the Internet through a wireless network in a restaurant, airport, or other public place. If someone were to "hack" into my notebook, he or she would not be able to install programs, access client or personal directories, and so on. If I used an administrator account, the intruder could do anything I could do, including many things that I probably do not know how to do that could create havoc.

In addition to limiting administrator user accounts and setting up multiple limited user accounts, you should be aware of administrator accounts that have been assigned default passwords. If you set up a wireless network in your home or office, the instructions for setting up your router will warn you about the default settings and strongly suggest that you change them. Any attack, automated or manual, will probably start by using the default passwords for default accounts.

Limiting the Damage from Intrusions

A standard consideration in all security practices is how well the security system is set up to respond to failure. If perfect security is impossible, and it is, then we must be concerned with minimizing the consequences of failure. Using limited-rights accounts is one example of good "failure practices."

Other good failure practices include encrypting or hiding key files, not giving obvious names to documents listing passwords, account numbers, or other valuable information, and similar efforts. In each case, you will notice that improving your security makes everyday usage less convenient.

Perhaps the easiest to do and most important of these efforts is to turn off the "allow print and file sharing" settings for each of your folders, other than one or two where you place files that you intend to be shared with others. You then manage the one or two shared folders to remove key documents when you no longer need to use or share them. In Windows XP, there are a number of methods for setting up your folders this way. Perhaps the easiest is to open My Computer or Windows Explorer, find a folder, right click on it, and then choose the Sharing and Security item. On the tab called Sharing in the pop-up box, you will be able to check and change the settings, and even make a folder private. As a result, an intruder may not be able to get to, or even see, the vast majority of your files.

Minimizing Failed Login Attempts

In certain network situations, you can set the number of permitted login failures before a user is locked out of the network. Choosing an appropriately low number will help prevent intrusions by those who use password-guessing techniques. The trick is to arrive at a number that will not lock *you* out when you inadvertently type in your password several times with the CAPS LOCK key on, or mistype your password too many times in a thirty-day period. This example illustrates the trade-offs involved in balancing increased security with potential inconvenience.

Special Concerns for Wireless Networks—Home or Office

The widespread introduction of wireless networking has brought many benefits, but also a new set of security risks. For the most part, the wireless router or switch you purchase to set up your network includes the basic security information you need. In general, you should change default passwords, set up the WEP or WPA encryption that may be available, change the network name (referred to as SSID) to something unattractive to potential intruders, turn off the SSID broadcast feature, and restrict access to computers on—and users of—your network. No wireless network will be secure if targeted by an expert with sufficient available time, but these few steps will help make your wireless network generally invisible and reasonably well protected, compared with the great majority of wide-open wireless networks existing today.

Guarding Against Theft

Theft of office computers is more common than you might think. In addition, thousands of notebook computers and personal digital assistants (PDAs) are stolen every year. You can also add to the list the loss or theft of USB "thumb drives," other removable hard drives and CDs, disks, and other storage media. You have to be very careful in public places—it is surprisingly easy to leave a restaurant remembering your doggie bag while forgetting thousands of dollars worth of computer equipment.

There are many different kinds of locks, alarms, tracking services, and other security devices and services. Depending upon your level of forgetfulness, where you travel, and other factors, one or more of them may be appropriate for you. Using an encryption program to encrypt important files on your hard drive and other storage devices is a wise, but infrequently used, option.

Handling the People Problems

Security experts complain that the most boring and overused cliché in computer security is that "a chain is only as strong as the weakest link." We are not yet so jaded that we cannot meaningfully use this truism.

Unfortunately, the weakest link is the "human factor," which, in a solo practice, will look a lot like you. Our inadequacies, lack of knowledge, lack of attention to detail, fatigue, and other factors contribute immensely to our security problems. You cannot combat all the potential security lapses you might cause, but there are a few big steps you can take.

Use Strong Passwords

Perhaps the most beneficial security step you can take is to start using what are known as "strong passwords." Generally speaking, strong passwords consist of strings of at least eight characters that include a combination of letters, numbers, and symbols (@, #, $), a mixture of upper-case and lower-case letters, and no recognizable words or names. A strong password should also not be your birthday, zip code, address, license plate number, or other common number. In addition, a strong password is one that is changed frequently.

Let's face it, few people use strong passwords. Some studies show that "password" is the most commonly used password. A large percentage of people use the name of a spouse, child, or pet as a password. Most people use passwords that are guessable, but guesswork has become irrelevant. Dictionary-based password-cracker programs will break most word-based or name-based passwords in seconds.

The stronger the password, the harder it is to remember. Any password constructed to meet the definition of a strong password will invariably require that you write it down, which is generally considered a bad idea, unless, of course, you die, in which case your survivors will be grateful that you did write it down.

Once again, you must make a reasonable decision about balancing security and convenience, ideally strengthening your current approach. A reminder: using the same password in every setting, especially if it is your bank account PIN number, is a poor practice. The difficulties we all experience with passwords are likely to lead us toward the use of fingerprint readers, random password-generation keys, and "biometric" devices as password substitutes in the near future.

Defeat Efforts at Phishing, Social Engineering, or Otherwise Getting You to Give Away the Jewels

Successful computer thieves have found that the easiest way to collect passwords, get access to computers and networks, and otherwise obtain valuable information is simply to ask for it. With astonishing frequency, people will reveal network user names and passwords, account numbers, and the like to strangers who ask for them, especially if there is a compelling story.

When I speak to audiences about computer security, I use a little exercise I learned from a computer security expert at a large corporation. I ask everyone in the audience to take out a pen and a piece of paper. Then I ask them to write down their network or other important passwords and to fold the paper up. I proceed to ask a series of questions about the types of passwords they might use (spouse's name? child's name? birth date?). Invariably, I am shocked by the amount of information that is revealed. By the way, I end the exercise by asking people how they plan to dispose of the pieces of paper that have their passwords written down, and making them promise they will never be as forthcoming about passwords ever again.

Maybe it isn't as obvious as it should be, but if it is a bad idea to write your password and keep it in your office, then it is crazy to write your password in a public setting. As a general rule, you should not give anyone any clues about the password you use or share it with anyone. If you inadvertently disclose your password to someone, or are in a situation where you need to give someone you trust your password to access a document or handle an "emergency," then change your password as quickly afterward as you can.

Similarly, no legitimate bank or other organization is going to ask you for account numbers, PIN numbers, passwords, and the like by e-mail message, no matter how much the e-mail message looks like an official message from the organization. Use of these fake e-mail messages is now known as phishing. Identity theft is a serious problem that can take years to recover from, and you do not want to do anything to make it easier for the "bad guys."

Treat Spam as a Security Problem

Everyone hates spam. We install filters and we pass laws. Still, the problem gets worse. One problem is that spammers make lots of money from spamming. Another is that a surprisingly large number of people open spam messages, reply to them, and even purchase the items "advertised" in them.

Don't be one of them. In 2004, studies indicated that perhaps 50 percent of spam messages contained viruses, spyware, or other malware. Many spam messages contain links to Web sites that download spyware, collect information from your computer, or exploit security holes.

Your best practice is to treat spam more as a security problem than an annoyance. I recommend deleting any suspected spam message without opening it. If you do open spam messages and are running nonupdated versions of Windows, Outlook, or Outlook Express, you may have inadvertently launched viruses or other executable files, none of which will be good for you. Do not respond to, unsubscribe from, or click on the links to any Web sites in a spam message. Finally, do not open any attachment to a spam message.

Be Smart about Opening E-mail Attachments

Today's viruses take advantage of social-engineering concepts. They have attractive or "normal" subject lines. They come to you as attachments without the ".exe" suffix that used to warn us of potential problems. They often do not overtly announce your infection. Most importantly, the preferred manner of propagation is for a virus to attach itself to e-mail messages it generates to send to everyone in your e-mail address book, all without your knowledge.

If you read one hundred articles about virus protection, they will all say to never open an e-mail attachment from someone you do not know. Unfortunately, given the current preferred method of propagating viruses, this rule neglects the gigantic danger you face from attachments to e-mail messages from people you know and trust.

As a result, the new rule you must know is this: *Never open an attachment from someone you do know, unless (1) you are expecting an e-mail message with an attachment from that person, (2) the attachment you receive is of the type and nature that you are expecting, and (3) you have called the person to verify he or she sent the attachment, if you have any question about that.*

Here's an example: You are expecting a Word attachment from a colleague. You receive an e-mail message with a somewhat unusual subject line and message and a ".pif" file attached that has a name unrelated to the document you are expecting. Do you open it without checking with your colleague? Your answer had better be no.

The attachment from someone you know may be at least as dangerous as attachments from people you do not know.

Avoid Bad Internet Neighborhoods

Computer security has many real-world analogies. As a general rule, you will be safer if you stay out of high-crime neighborhoods. The same rule applies for computer security. If you go to Web sites that offer illegal, highly questionable, or unsavory products or services, you historically have increased your risk of experiencing viruses, spyware, malware, and other security problems. Enough said.

Careful Use of Public Computers

Public computers are very convenient. This fact should make you concerned that the high level of convenience means a low level of security. If you have drawn this conclusion, you are correct and you are becoming a strong student of security. An evildoer might install keystroke-loggers or other tools on a public computer for later retrieval. You will also leave all kinds of tracks of your activities on a public computer unless you take affirmative steps to delete those tracks, such as changing browser settings, deleting history and temporary Internet files, and cleaning out the recycle bin. You need to be thoughtful about how you use a public computer, and avoid activities that require your credit card numbers or other passwords.

The Often Forgotten Aspect of Security—Backup

Good security practice means that we plan for failure. In most cases, a security breach requires that we clean up a hard drive and reinstall programs and data, or that we restore an earlier, clean version of our system. In both cases, the magic word is "backup."

Lawyers have heard for years that backup is vital. However, some estimates suggest that as many as two-thirds of small-firm lawyers and firms do no backup whatsoever. I'm not going to preach to you. The arguments are well known. You can make your own decision.

There are, however, three developments in backup for you to consider. First, the availability of high-capacity, portable USB or Firewire hard drives for under $100 have changed the backup environment in both affordability and ease of use, as compared with the old tape backup systems. Second, DVD writers have dropped below $100, making it possible to archive huge amounts of data on a single disk and store it off-site in a safe place. Third, Internet-based backup services are available that will automate and handle your standard backup for $10 to $20 per month. The bottom line: Any of these developments will result in backup that is infinitely better than having none at all, they are easy and affordable, and your excuses no longer hold any water.

Education and Training

There are many good resources on computer security and related issues. Try to acquaint yourself with a few of them. You want to be sure that you find current information, because the security environment is subject to frequent changes. The Microsoft Security page mentioned above should continue to be a good starting point. Otherwise, find material that is in plain language and not overly technical (a big danger in this area). Although I hesitate to recommend a specific resource, given how long after this chapter is written that you may be reading it, I will suggest Dan Appleman's *Always Use Protection: A Teen's Guide to Safe Computing*. It's written for an audience of teenagers and children, meaning that it might even work for lawyers. But seriously, it is a practical, common-sense approach that will teach you about risks and how to make good choices about computing practices and use of the Internet, which, not coincidentally, is the purpose of this chapter.

The Price of Security Is Vigilance

There is no question that maintaining a high level of security is very difficult and demanding work. It requires that you achieve a significant level of education about the issues and the procedures you need to adopt. It requires that you keep current with developments and changes. It probably requires you to spend more money on software updates and at a faster pace than you did in the past. It also requires that you make thoughtful decisions among a variety of options, each of which has its own set of problematic consequences.

Most important, it requires that you accept treating security as a process, and one without a final destination at which you will arrive. The alternative? An unprotected Windows computer attached to the Internet that will be attacked and compromised within ten to twenty minutes.

Unfortunately, in today's world, not making a decision about security is still making a choice, and a choice with potentially devastating consequences to you, your family, your clients, and your practice. You might adopt a cavalier attitude and be lucky. For a while. However, one day you might find yourself on the witness stand to defend yourself against the loss of your client's confidential and/or privileged information and hear yourself repeat over and over, "No, I did not take that basic step. No, I could have done more." It's a nightmare, but one that has more chance of becoming reality today than at any time ever before.

It's your decision to make. The tools and procedures are widely available, and you will notice that you can take great strides in improving security at little, or even no, out-of-pocket cost. Implementing good practices at the start of your new firm will be easier and provide greater benefits than doing so at a later point. Even a late start will be better than trying to lock the barn door after the cows are gone. You should notice that I'm not even asking you to take all the steps in this chapter, only some of the most important ones.

Well-known computer expert and author Fred Langa has said, "I think running an unpatched, unprotected PC is a form of negligence analogous to driving a car with bad brakes or broken headlights: You're going to get yourself into trouble, and also make things worse for everyone around you. Just as drivers who share the road must also share responsibility for safety, we all now share the same global network, and thus must regard computer security as a necessary social responsibility. To me, anyone unwilling to take simple security precautions is a major, active part of the problem."

Let's be more careful out there.

Technology Training Options

39

Storm Evans

Many solos make expensive investments in computer hardware, network equipment, and scanning and imaging systems without giving any thought to training the people who will be called upon to operate the systems and equipment. Likewise, many solos purchase complicated software packages without considering who will teach the users how to use the software. The result is that the solo and his or her employees are left on their own to figure things out. While they are figuring things out, they probably are not getting their work done and the entire office is falling behind. Solos who purchase software and hardware and carefully plan for implementation and training will avoid such unpleasant and costly circumstances.

The two main issues involved in planning for training—any kind of training—are as follows:

1. What type of training is appropriate and cost-effective?
2. How will employees be trained without adding to their workloads or requiring that they put in additional work hours?

Choosing the Appropriate Type of Training

It is usually true that using even the most basic computer hardware or software will require some amount of training. The training may be as simple as an orientation session or as complex as an ongoing weekly training regimen. Once you determine that training is important, your first task is to consider what kind of training is needed. If you plan to introduce new hardware and software at the same time, or if you plan a radical overhaul of your systems, it may be best to undertake comprehensive training that covers everything.

One-on-One Training

One-on-one training may involve either sending the employee (or the lawyer) off-site for intensive training or bringing a trainer to the law office. Compared with other types of training, one-on-one training is more expensive, but it is sometimes the best method of training for complex systems. Because effective training often depends upon the learning styles of the individual employee, and because some people learn best when someone works directly with them, one-on-one training is often the fastest, if not the least expensive, way to educate. The key to one-on-one training is for the trainer to have a high level of expertise with the subject being taught, as well as the ability to communicate with the student and the patience to anticipate and answer even the most basic questions.

Formal Classroom Training

Formal classroom training works well for most software packages. An industry has grown up around training for word-processing programs, spreadsheets, databases, case management programs, and the like. Such training classes have been in existence long enough that the training methodology has had time to mature. Most classroom trainers can respond to the needs of fast learners as well as students who need extra attention. A solo or his or her staff can save money by attending a class conducted by a private training company or by a community college.

Demonstrations

Demonstrations of new features may be sufficient training in some cases, such as minor upgrades to software or operating systems. For example, the differences between two versions of Microsoft Word or WordPerfect may not be significant enough to justify a term-long course at a community college, but are significant enough to warrant an afternoon in a conference room with a trainer. In some cases, a demonstration by a trainer, followed by individual tutorials at each employee's workstation, not only provides the necessary training, but can also reduce each employee's anxiety about the new product.

Follow-up Seminars

Formal training sessions can be followed up by lunch-hour seminars. Such seminars can help reinforce topics that might not be remembered from the initial training. Seminars can also serve as a way to introduce new features of software or hardware. Hour-long seminars provide an excellent way to get feedback from users and to continue to encourage consistency in the office. Seminars should always include opportunities for questions and answers, as well as something in writing for the participants to use as a reference source at later times.

On-Site Training

On-site training is valuable for both group and individual learning situations. On-site training can be planned in advance to accompany the introduction of new hardware and software, or it can be tailored to meet the needs of new employees and employees who have changed jobs and are now using equipment or software for the first time. In addition, on-site training can be as simple as providing someone with a brief overview of features that they have not yet used. On-site training should always provide students with the opportunity to practice the tools they will be using on the job, preferably with their own computers.

Do-It-Yourself Training

Some lawyers are good trainers and have the ability to train their employees. Others lack either the expertise or the skills necessary to train their employees effectively. Do-it-yourself training should not be undertaken lightly. In most cases, the lawyer will find that he or she is dollars ahead by hiring a qualified trainer or consultant.

Customizing Training

Whether training takes place on-site or off-site, in small groups or in one-on-one settings, it needs to be the result of a customized training plan. Training plans should look at the learning styles of the students to be trained, the complexity of the material, and the amount of time available for training.

Training Materials

All training programs should include written training materials. More sophisticated training programs also include CD- or DVD-based interactive training. Written materials can be as simple as checklists or as complicated as PowerPoint slides. Most hardware manufacturers and software publishers have valuable training information on their Web sites, which can be incorporated into training sessions. Some even offer online tutorials for new users.

Final Observations about Training

Some final observations about training:

1. Employees should be encouraged to "buy in" to the training program. "Mandatory" training of unwilling students never works.
2. The goal of training should be to make people want to come to training to solve their problems.
3. Training should be designed to meet a variety of needs.

When and How to Use Technology Consultants

40

Natalie R. Thornwell

Lawyers are often found saying that people sometimes don't know when to call a lawyer. Computer consultants, likewise, find themselves saying that lawyers sometimes don't know when to call a computer consultant. So when does the tech project or situation in your firm warrant help from a consultant? What can these consultants do that you can't? How much do they cost, anyway? Understanding the types of technology consultants available to law firms and the scope of their services can help you weather your next technology storm.

Types of Consultants

Technology consultants for law firms come in a variety of flavors, but you will generally find that they serve your concerns for network setup and hardware, or work with you on software implementation and training, or both. There are even consultants who can assist you with telephone systems and other communications hardware. However, most firms need help with setting up their computers and getting the software they need, not to mention someone who can fix their systems if there are problems.

Network consultants or systems integrators mainly work to ensure that your office network is running properly. They can sometimes even build workstation computers for your office, or administer your network remotely. Called the "computer person," this type of consultant is often certified in network administration on major operating systems and programming applications.

Certified consultants for software, on the other hand, are trained and directly certified as experts by software application vendors. Legal software certified consultants often make their livings by implementing the applications with which they are familiar in the offices of their law firm clients.

Web site or Web consultants are vendors who help you design, build, and perhaps maintain your firm's Web site. These consultants can offer canned Web pages or be available to develop and keep your site up to date. They might also be responsible for making sure your e-mail accounts are set up and administered properly.

Services of Technology Consultants

Computer personnel outside your firm can be experts at getting your office wired and getting your staff up to speed on the latest versions of essential software. What else do these consultants do? Here is a short list of the services you might expect from legal technology consultants:

- Analysis of your technology setup
- Assistance with your technology budgets and plans
- Conversion of data from other applications
- Uploading and maintenance of Web site information
- Installation and upgrading of hardware components
- Installation and upgrading of software
- Training of end users and administrators on proper use of software
- Customer service and technical assistance on software concerns
- Ongoing support for software and hardware issues

This is not an exhaustive listing of services that you might find being offered by legal technology consultants, but you should recognize both the breadth and importance of their role in the modern law office.

Cost of Consultants

Although most consultants' rates are similar to those charged by associates in law firms, you can find some reasonable fees if you simply shop around and/or barter for services. It is not at all uncommon to find lawyers who handle the incorporation of their computer person's computer business in exchange for setting up their own office systems. The trade of services can often help lower the typical hourly rates charged by the consultant.

In metropolitan areas, you can generally expect to pay more for consulting services than in other parts of the country. You should consider negotiating a deal as part of a long-term relationship with a consultant, which will allow you to lower your total. For instance, you might be able to get software installation and training from one consultant, and have that person work with another consultant to make sure the infrastructure for the technology and the hardware in your firm is working properly. This arrangement might get you a lower rate when the two other experts are working together. Regardless of your scheme, you should always remember to negotiate for the services that you are sure to need.

Contracts and Requests for Proposals

Written contracts are almost always needed when working with legal technology consultants. In only rare circumstances would it be adequate to operate on verbal agreements when it comes to your computer systems and office technology. A professional consultant will probably approach you with a written agreement in hand. Make sure you contract for what you need and do not sign up for a situation that could potentially leave you without service when you really need it. You might consider an ongoing contract for which you are regularly billed, versus one where you are allotted a certain amount of time or just a limited amount of service.

You should also make sure that consultants and those who might be working for them understand the need for confidentiality while working with your clients' sensitive data. It is a good idea to have consultants read and sign a confidentiality agreement before beginning work in your office. If necessary, check for insurance and bonding of the persons performing the work.

You will need to be involved with requests for proposals (RFPs) when working with—or looking to work with—legal technology consultants. When you are interested in having multiple vendors vie for your business, you can draft an RFP that outlines your needs and the expected services. The consultants then respond with their proposals and quotes to do the work for your law office. Review these responses carefully.

When drafting RFPs, be sure to remember the previous advice about negotiating for services. Although you need not directly indicate in the RFP that you are flexible in terms of paying or bartering for the services you seek, you might indicate that the terms for contracting for services are negotiable and may have some impact upon the decision regarding who will receive the bid for your law firm's technology work.

Compatibility Concerns

You may have the best consultant in your neck of the woods, but if you or members of your staff are not able to see eye to eye with this consultant on your needs or the manner in which your needs should be met, you will likely find yourself in an unhappy relationship. You should view hiring your computer person just the same as hiring someone for your office staff.

Is the consultant's personality compatible with those of others in the firm? Does the consultant's style of training and implementation match what you desire or might have envisioned for your technology situation? Can the consultant assist you in the long term or only for a short period? Can he or she produce good references that you can check for yourself? What experiences—good or bad—has the consultant had with other law firms, especially firms that practice in the same areas as you? Does the consultant have experience on the exact systems and software you have? What certifications does the consultant have, and how current are they? All these questions can help you determine if the consultant you are considering is appropriate for you and your firm.

Know Your Systems (or System Needs)

Although you may come to rely upon the word of your computer person, realize that in many instances he or she is acting from a sales standpoint. To avoid being sold or outfitted with something you don't need or paying too much for some technology product or service, you must know your hardware and software situation and your needs. It is also beneficial for you to understand the level of expertise you and your staff have with the software you use daily. This knowledge about you and your firm will help you get better technology solutions and service.

If you are a true novice regarding computers and what your office might require, then use some of the general computer technology magazines and Web sites to learn more about computers and how they work. The legal-specific technology periodicals and listservs are also good ways to find out more. Locally, look for continuing legal education programs and services related to legal technology; these can help you learn more about one of your most important practice tools.

Ultimately, your experiences with technology consultants will likely be similar to those you've had with your clients. And, as with clients, you should always look to develop the best relationship possible. Technology is a necessary tool for modern law practices; consequently, working with consultants is also probably necessary for your practice. To have the most beneficial experience, be wise in how you shop for and utilize consultants, and remain educated and flexible when it comes to technology in your law practice.

No More Books?
An Electronic Library
for Solos

41

Catherine Pennington Paunov

Only a few years ago, LexisNexis and Westlaw were the only games in town for online legal research. Today, the Internet has opened a world of both free and fee-based materials available to the solo and small law office. However, these materials vary widely in both quality and quantity, especially in comparison with the depth and searching capabilities of LexisNexis and Westlaw. So what are researchers to do? The answer, of course, is that it depends—upon the field, the jurisdiction, the need for currency, costs, and so on. The goal of this chapter is to make you aware of what is available, and how to stay current with what will be offered in the near future.

Essentially, there are three types of research services available on the Internet—subscription, pay-as-you-go, and free. Each of the three types of services has its pluses and minuses. Subscription and pay-as-you-go services are typically commercial operations run by companies such as West Publishing, LexisNexis, American Lawyer Media, and other well-respected concerns. The free services are academic or government-run entities. As with every rule, there are exceptions. Some companies do provide some searching at no cost, and some governmental agencies charge for access to their databases.

Subscription Services

The best-known subscription research databases are LexisNexis and Westlaw. Both services have existed for many years; LexisNexis celebrated its thirtieth anniversary in April of 2003. These extraordinary services are made up of literally thousands of databases covering U.S. federal and state laws. For example, West's federal materials include all reported cases, statutes, administrative rules and regulations, legislative histories, pleadings, motions, judgments, jury verdicts, court rules, bill tracking, briefs, and court dockets for all district courts, courts of appeal, bankruptcy courts, and the Court of Federal Claims. Although most state materials are not as exhaustive, those for larger states, such as New York, California, and Texas, are extensive in both depth and breadth.

In addition to U.S. law, Westlaw covers the United Kingdom, Australia, China, Hong Kong, Bermuda, the Cayman Islands, twenty countries in the Middle East and Africa, Argentina, Brazil, Chile, Venezuela, the European Union, and Canada. Many of these materials are simply brief summaries of recent legal developments in a particular country or region, but some, such as those for the United Kingdom and Canada, are similar in depth and breadth to U.S. law.

Supplementing the databases organized by jurisdiction are Westlaw's topical materials based upon subject matter, including intellectual property, administrative law, antitrust, and workers' compensation. Numerous secondary sources—such as law reviews, bar journals, treatises, form books, ALR, AmJur 2d, and similar law-related titles—are also available on Westlaw.

Users can check the status of cases and other materials by using West's citation research service, KeyCite. This allows users to trace the history of a case, statute, decision, or regulation to make sure it is still good law, retrieve all citing materials, and, with KeyCite Alert, be kept current on its status. Another invaluable service is WestCheck.com, which allows users to check all the cites in a brief or other document in a matter of a few minutes.

Naturally, access to such a wide range of materials is expensive. However, many medium and large firms have negotiated flat rates for access to all the materials. Although most solos and small-firm practitioners would likely find this range of materials unnecessary, a few doing extensive multijurisdictional litigation, for example, should consider this option, too. Smaller law offices may choose to subscribe to WestlawPRO, which allows them to select portions of the Westlaw database—for example, materials for California or a particular field of practice, such as bankruptcy. WestlawPRO customers can access other West databases, but they will incur additional charges, including a charge to print items.

Some of the most useful resources for lawyers who don't generally perform extensive legal research are the public records databases on Westlaw. These public records include aircraft and watercraft records, asset locators, and real property transactions for all fifty states and the District of Columbia. Practitioners of family law, probate, and personal injury litigation will find these resources invaluable.

Like Westlaw, LexisNexis also offers public records databases for all fifty states and the District of Columbia, but also adds extensive public records for the province of Ontario in Canada. LexisNexis claims it has over one billion such records in its database, including person and business locators (for both the United States and Canada), civil and criminal court filings, bankruptcy filings, and professional licenses.

Another strength of LexisNexis is its newspaper and periodical files with over 31,000 titles. And these are not just legal titles. They include wire services, most major newspapers in the United States and elsewhere, and trade and professional publications. Note that LexisNexis has thousands of foreign titles, too, but many are not available in translation. Those wishing to read last week's *Der Spiegel* had better be able to read German. This does not preclude one from reading German news in English, however. The German wire service, Deutsche Presse-Agentur, for example, is available in English, as are many foreign sources. These can be essential tools for tracking information on individuals and companies outside the United States and Canada. And because LexisNexis has maintained many of these databases for years, it is possible to find historical information. For example, LexisNexis's *Newsweek* file begins in January of 1975.

In addition to exhaustive American and Canadian legal databases, legal resources for other countries include Argentina, Australia, the British Commonwealth, China, the European Union, Hong Kong, India, Ireland, Malaysia, Mexico, New Zealand, Singapore, South Africa, and the United Kingdom and Northern Ireland. Note that some of these resources are simply current awareness services, while others, such as that for England, include statutes from 1267!

So why should solos or small law office practitioners be interested in these sources? Unlike large firms that are likely to have EU or UK legal materials on hand, solos may find it difficult to locate such materials in their local county libraries when foreign or international law questions come in the door. Questions on foreign law arise all too frequently out of family law, including child custody, jurisdiction in personal injury and airplane incidents, and estate planning and probate. One caveat: the Mexico and Argentina databases are extensive, but they are in Spanish.

As with Westlaw, LexisNexis's American and Canadian legal resources are exhaustive. And, like its competitor, LexisNexis allows the solo and small law office practitioner to subscribe to selected portions of a database by jurisdiction (state or federal), topic or practice area, secondary sources, news, business, and factual discovery/public records. LexisNexis provides citation checking through its Shepard's service. This service lists all history and subsequent citations to the cited case, and parallels the listings that have appeared in the Shepard's books for years. Users can also validate cases with analysis using another feature of Shepard's, as well as the AutoCite service. Both Westlaw and LexisNexis have features that permit the automatic verification of every citation from a document. For this feature alone, either of these services can pay for itself.

And speaking of paying, what does it cost to subscribe to these services? The answer, of course, is, it depends. For example, for a flat rate, a solo in Miami could get access to Florida materials on Westlaw. At the low end, the user would have access to primary materials, including case law and the digest, annotated statutes, and court rules. KeyCite is included with even this basic subscription. For additional sums, users can add U.S. district court decisions out of Florida and Georgia, decisions of the Eleventh Circuit Court of Appeals and the U.S. Supreme Court, U.S. Code Annotated, and various other federal titles. This subscription, Florida Essentials Plus, does not include the Federal Register or the Code of Federal Regulations. At the high end, WestlawPRO Plus users would also have access to the legislative services, the administrative code, and Attorneys General Opinions for Florida, as well as secondary sources such as law reviews, treatises, and several newspapers within the state.

As noted earlier, practitioners may be interested in access to materials by topic, rather than by jurisdiction. West offers such subscriptions for bankruptcy, commercial law, environmental law, taxation, insurance, and labor and employment. These, too, range in price, depending upon the number of databases and the number of records in each. Again, all these subscriptions include the use of KeyCite to verify citations.

A lawyer can purchase a Lexis/Nexis subscription covering a particular jurisdiction at a very affordable monthly rate through a state or local bar association. The monthly flat-rate program gives users access to selected case law, court rules, and legislative materials. It also includes access to Shepard's. Those also needing administrative materials, public records, Uniform Commercial Code filings, and secondary sources such as journals and law reviews will pay slightly more per month. LexisNexis, like Westlaw, offers specialized topical contracts covering twenty-seven different subject areas, including bankruptcy, criminal law, and taxation. These vary in price depending, again, upon the number of databases and the records in each. Need more? Consider an All Services contract.

Whether one chooses Westlaw or Lexis, note that contracts through a state or local bar association may reduce costs. Additionally, both companies do permit access to materials outside the contract for an additional charge.

For the lawyer looking for current awareness in his or her field, a subscription to American Lawyer Media's Law.com may be a useful tool. This daily service provides news, digests and full text of new case decisions, practice papers, and practice tools. Papers include analysis by well-known practitioners in the selected field. Tools include checklists, sample contracts, and other forms created by top experts. These databases are updated daily from sources including all of American Lawyer's publications, such as *American Lawyer, Corporate Counsel,* and *National Law Journal,* and regional publications such as *Legal Times, New York Law Journal,* and *Texas Lawyer.* Practitioners receive daily e-mail messages covering business, employment, intellectual property, litigation, or technology law. A free, thirty-day trial allows lawyers to see if the service meets their needs before committing to a year.

Some other online subscriptions now come "bundled" with membership in organizations or as part of hard-copy versions. However, many are moving to free access online, including many newspapers, law reviews, and the *ABA Journal.* See more below in the discussion of free services.

Pay-as-You-Go Services

For those solos who simply cannot rationalize a subscription commitment, pay-as-you-go services may be the answer when sources such as Westlaw and Lexis are needed. For example, Lexis/Nexis's service for the solo and small law office—LexisONE—allows access to a number of libraries on a daily or weekly basis. For ad hoc need, this may be the answer for many solos. Be warned, however, that compared with the monthly rate, these services can be expensive by the day or week. The public records libraries for each state include Uniform Commercial Code filings, property and corporate records, jury verdicts, the person locator, judgment and lien records, docket filings, and bankruptcy filings. Unless searching of these types of records is done infrequently, a monthly subscription makes economic sense.

Additionally, LexisONE subscribers can search the Lexis database for free, but are charged by credit card for each document retrieved. There is no charge to become a LexisONE subscriber, and, as noted below, subscribers are provided access to some free services. Similarly, Westlaw offers a credit card service that allows users to retrieve cases for a flat fee and KeyCite them for an additional charge. There is no additional charge for printing.

Some automated form-generation systems are also available for download. For example, users can download LexisNexis Automated California Judicial Council Forms for a flat fee. These forms run on HotDocs Player software, which can be downloaded for free. Increasingly, vendors will market downloading of form books and other such resources, due to the number of law offices with high-bandwidth Internet access today.

The two major subscription-based vendors have moved into the pay-as-you-go market specifically to meet the needs of solo and small-firm practitioners. Those choosing to use such services should avail themselves of free online and telephone assistance in formulating their searches. Good legal research online is different from a Yahoo or Google search, requiring the use of specific connectors, for example. Sorry, but that's just the way it is. Get help before making a costly mistake. And the help is there twenty-four hours a day, seven days a week. Westlaw can be reached at 800-WESTLAW and LexisNexis at 800-543-6862. (Canadians should dial 800-553-3685.) Both companies also provide online training, but rather than spending time relearning the system each time online research is required, use customer service.

Free Services

As noted at the beginning of this chapter, Westlaw and LexisNexis both provide free services. LexisONE allows free access to a few selected databases, including all U.S. Supreme Court decisions since 1790 and many federal and state court decisions for the last five years. The advantage to using this source instead of those offered by the courts themselves is the ease of searching. Even those not trained on Lexis or Westlaw will find the search box easy to use, and it does permit multijurisdiction searching. Users should check the coverage limitations, as many courts are not available through this service. In spite of these limitations, it is the place to go for recent case law research. The company is not being altruistic; it is using these free services to attract solo and small law office researchers who have, by and large, ignored LexisNexis and Westlaw, considering them too expensive. Searchers can access the pay-as-you-go service from the same page.

West's free service, Findlaw.com, is considered by many, including this writer, to be the best place to begin free legal research on the Internet. This well-organized series of Web pages provides links to services for the public, businesses, students, corporate counsel, and legal professionals. The section for the legal profession is divided into jurisdiction, field of law, research and reference, and legal careers and services. The latter provides paid listings of sources such as court reporters, experts, consultants, software, technologies, and online continuing legal education programming. One of its real strengths is the forms section. This includes state forms, as well as forms for each federal district court and circuit court.

So why wouldn't a lawyer use one of the free services instead of LexisNexis or Westlaw to access materials? There are two essential reasons—searching capabilities and limitations on what is available. Although Findlaw itself provides access to most court decisions for the last five years, earlier cases need to be searched on the state's own database, if available. And each state uses a different methodology for searching. Some require the user to know the docket number or the names of the parties. As of the time this chapter was prepared, most older state court decisions were not available from a free Web site. Also, unless a user knows the administrative code or state statute citation, it can be challenging to retrieve such documents from many sites established by a state or the state's university. However, if it exists, Findlaw will list it and provide a link.

Other useful Web sites providing free services include the following:

- FirstGov, a federal government Web site, provides links to all publicly accessible Web sites provided by federal agencies, the U.S. Congress, and the courts.
- The ABA's Legal Technology Resource Center provides links to a wide range of legal Web sites, including directories, law schools, and sites such as FirstGov and Findlaw. In addition, its monthly publication, *Sitetation*, highlights new or useful Web sites of interest to the legal community. This publication is free, and a subscription can be obtained on the Web site.
- Global Legal Information Network, operated by the Law Library of Congress, provides links to foreign law resources worldwide. Searches can be done by jurisdiction, subject, date, type of legal instrument, or a combination of these elements. Be aware that the subject searches are based on a "fixed" thesaurus. Only those terms in the thesaurus can be used. Summaries are in English. Access to the full text of documents is restricted to members of the Network, but some lawyers may qualify for associate membership status.
- Need law review articles? The Legal Information Institute is the place to go, not only to search for an article, but also to link to those law reviews that are now available online, in full text.
- Articles from other periodicals can be searched and read at the Gale Group's FindArticles service. This service provides access to more than five hundred periodicals, ranging from the *American Journal of Sports Medicine* to *Sunset* to *U.S. News and World Report*.

Whether the solo or small law office practitioner chooses to use free, pay-as-you-go, or paid subscription services, or all three, frequent use is essential. The more experienced the searcher, the more reliable the results for the client. And that is, above all else, the goal of any legal research.

Web Sites Mentioned in this Chapter

- American Bar Association: **www.abanet.org**
- American Lawyer Media: **www.law.com**

- Cornell University's Legal Information Institute: **www.law.cornell.edu**
- FindArticles: **www.findarticles.com**
- Findlaw: **www.findlaw.com**
- Federal government: **www.firstgov.gov**
- Global Legal Information Network: **www.loc.gov/law/glin**
- Internet Lawyer: **www.internetlawyer.com**
- LexisNexis: **www.lexis.com**
- LexisONE: **www.lexisone.com**
- Westlaw: **www.westlaw.com**

Selected Resources
for Part IV

from the ABA Law Practice Management Section

ABA Law Practice Management Section's *Online Library,* at **www.lawpractice.org/downloads**, provides access to forms and other documents available for immediate downloading.

How to Start and Build a Law Practice, Fifth Edition, by Jay G Foonberg, 2004.

Law Practice, bimonthly publication of the ABA Law Practice Management Section.

The Lawyer's Guide to Adobe® Acrobat®, Second Edition, by David L. Masters, 2005.

The Lawyer's Guide to Creating Persuasive Computer Presentations, Second Edition, by Ann E. Brenden and John D. Goodhue, 2005

The Lawyer's Guide to Extranets: Breaking Down Walls, Building Client Connections, by Douglas Simpson and Mark Tamminga, 2003

The Lawyer's Guide to Fact Finding on the Internet, Second Edition, by Carole A. Levitt and Mark E. Rosch, 2004

The Lawyer's Guide to Marketing on the Internet, Second Edition, by Gregory H. Siskind, Deborah McMurray, and Richard P. Klau, 2002

The Lawyer's Guide to Palm Powered™ Handhelds, by Margaret Spencer Dixon, 2004.

The Lawyer's Guide to Summation, by Tom O'Connor, 2004.

The Lawyer's Quick Guide to Microsoft® Word Versions 97/2000, by David Greenwald and Alan S. Adler, 1999.

Telecommuting for Lawyers, by Nicole Belson Goluboff, 1998

Wills, Trust, and Technology: An Estate Lawyer's Guide to Automation, Second Edition, by Daniel B. Evans, co-published with the Real Property, Probate, and Trust Law Section, 2004.

Marketing Manual

Every lawyer, especially newly minted solos, needs to bring in new clients and earn more work from existing clients. While you could consider flying over a football stadium towing a banner with your name and phone number, more conventional marketing techniques are probably a better idea.

Part V features chapters from some of the legal world's leading authorities on how to market your law practice and how to do it without spending a fortune.

Part V starts with a "Five-Minute" marketing course, then offers tips on everything from rainmaking for women lawyers to Yellow Pages advertising to marketing on the Internet and more. And, you'll not only learn how to market effectively, you'll learn how to do it ethically.

Read this Part. Get more clients. It's that simple.

Note: The ethical rules governing marketing legal services are incorporated in the Model Rules of Professional Conduct, Rules 7.1–7.5 (see Appendix B), and these rules apply to all the chapters in Part V. The applicable rules vary considerably from state to state, so check your local rules. See also William E. Hornsby's *Marketing and Legal Ethics*, Third Edition (ABA, 2000) for a more detailed discussion of this subject.

A Five-Minute Marketing Training Course*

42

Jay G Foonberg

The following list, intended to give you a five-minute course in good client relations, was developed during my thirty years of presenting more than five hundred programs for bar associations and private law firms in every state of the United States and several foreign countries. Add your own rules to the list.

- ◆ Always carry high-quality professional cards.
- ◆ Offer clients and other visitors coffee or soft drinks while they wait in your reception area.
- ◆ Be sure your reception area contains periodicals indicative of the kind of practice you want people to think you have.
- ◆ Be careful when you answer the question, "What kind of law do you practice?" Don't limit yourself or your firm.
- ◆ Send thank-you letters when someone refers you a client.
- ◆ Other lawyers and professionals can be good sources of referrals. Try to be active in your bar associations.
- ◆ Send thank-you letters to the witnesses who testify for your side.
- ◆ By telephone, e-mail message, or fax, return all phone calls yourself or be sure someone returns them for you.
- ◆ Send clients copies of all "correspondence in" and "correspondence out" relating to their matters.

*This piece is reprinted with permission from *Law Practice Management* (April 1990).

- Dress the way you would expect your lawyer to dress if you were a client paying a fee.
- Get as much cash up front as possible from new clients. This is known as Foonberg's Rule and is a modification of Lincoln's statement that when a client has paid cash up front, the client knows he has a lawyer and a lawyer knows he has a client.
- Be sure your fee agreement is in writing.
- Send your clients, and referrers of clients, Christmas cards or season's greetings cards.
- Remember that your invoices are a factor in your clients' opinions of you.
- Dump the "dogs"; get rid of the "bad news" cases and clients before they really give you problems.
- Learn how to convert acquaintances who seek "social consultations" at weddings and other such events into paying clients by being attentive, letting them know they may have serious problems, and suggesting they come into your office where you have the facilities to help them.
- Remind the staff in the firm that they may refer their friends' legal matters to the firm.
- Remember that availability or nonavailability is the single most important factor in your being selected or not being selected after you are recommended.
- Send a tax newsletter to clients in November, spelling out any new tax laws that might affect them. Be sure to remind them that cash-basis taxpayers can deduct legal fees only if they pay them before December 31.
- Send clients "no-activity" letters when their cases are inactive for ninety days or more.
- Always discuss fees and payment schedules at the first meeting.
- Remind the client that the firm has a good reputation in the community.
- Reassure clients that you have handled cases similar to theirs (if true). Clients don't like being used for educational purposes.
- Plan ahead and remind clients of the need for annual minutes of shareholders' or directors' meetings, lease renewals, judgment renewals, and so on.
- Show clients how your bills can be tax-deductible, if possible.
- Recognize and appreciate that clients have high anxiety levels when they go to see lawyers. Try to put them at ease.
- If you adjust a bill downward, be careful that the client doesn't think you were deliberately overcharging in the first place.

- Be sure that you, and not the clients, decide (before you do the work) which clients are going to get free legal work.
- When collecting fees, try to coincide clients' payments to you with the clients' receipt of money.
- Be firm and in control with clients when discussing their matters or fees. If you act wishy-washy or wimpy, your clients quickly will lose confidence in you, stop using you, and stop recommending you.
- Don't complain about how hard you're working.
- Have sample letters prepared to explain conflicts of interest and to obtain appropriate waivers of the conflicts and consents to representation.
- Use high-quality legal stationery, with your address clearly legible and copyable.
- Provide some firm, hard-back chairs in the reception area for disabled or elderly clients.
- Introduce your clients to your secretary and the paralegals and/or associates who will be working on their matters or will have contact with them.
- Have new clients come into the office to meet with you before giving them any legal advice or quoting fees.
- Be wary of clients who have lots of complaints about their former lawyers.
- Communicate to a new client that what the client tells you is normally covered by attorney-client privilege and that you won't discuss the client's personal affairs with other people.
- When an interview is over, stand up, walk to the door, and tell the client the interview is completed.
- After the interview or meeting, accompany the client to the reception area or elevator.
- When a matter is over, send a letter to the client telling him or her the matter is closed and expressing thanks for the opportunity to have been of service. In this manner, the client will understand that the matter is closed and you are not expected to do more work on the matter. Tell the client to request items from the file, because the file may be destroyed without further notice.
- When a case is lost, be simple, direct, and honest. Notify the client by phone or in person and follow up with a letter.
- When quoting settlements, be sure the client understands the difference between gross settlements and net settlements after fees, costs, and liens.
- When quoting fees, be sure to cover (in writing) the difference between fees and costs, and what the fees do and do not cover.

- When collecting fees, remember that people are more willing to pay for what they desperately need and don't have, than for what they used to need desperately and already have. Clients are more eager and willing to pay before the work is done than after the work has been done. They, and you, will feel better if you get the advance retainer check before you do the work.

- If, during a meeting with a client, you are interrupted by an emergency long-distance call or secretarial inquiry, be sure to say to the client in the office, "Don't worry, I won't charge you for the time I spent on that matter."

- Be sure to ask a client whether you should send correspondence to the home or the office, or whether the client prefers to pick up the correspondence (to keep information from getting into the wrong hands).

- Keep a photo of your children or family on your desk, facing you, to remind you of unpaid bills and your need to be sure that clients clearly understand from the beginning their financial obligations in the matter and that they can meet them.

- Potential clients will probably check your Web site before calling. Be sure your Web site is user-friendly and has telephone, fax, and e-mail contact information.

- Have someone telephone your office for you while you listen in and determine how the query is handled. See if the receptionist projects a helpful attitude or simply is functioning as a human answering machine. Remember, people can and do hang up and call other lawyers when they're not pleased with the way their calls are handled.

- Be sure you clear your voice mail messages at least twice a day and return all calls within two hours (if possible) or have someone return the calls for you.

- End every interview by saying, "Is there anything else you want to ask me or tell me? I don't want you leaving here with any unanswered questions."

- You have two ears and one mouth, not two mouths and one ear. You should listen to clients at least two-thirds of the time and not talk more than one-third of the time. Clients want to tell their stories, not listen to yours.

Successful Marketing for the Sole Practitioner

43

Thomas E. Kane

To be successful at marketing, several things must occur. First, you must have an understanding of the following:

1. Why solos are no different from lawyers in larger firms, in most cases
2. Basic marketing principles
3. The need for developing an action plan that includes the best marketing practices to take you to the next level of success

Dispelling the Myths

It is a myth that only lawyers in large firms can afford to market their services, that they are better at it, and that they are able to obtain work easier than sole practitioners and lawyers in small firms. It is also a myth that the most effective marketing is expensive. In larger firms, individual (versus institutional) marketing is still conducted by a lawyer on an individual basis, in most cases. Some group practices and client teams market collectively; however, as a general rule, lawyers in large firms still market, if at all, with a personal focus.

The reasons for this vary from firm to firm, but it usually comes down to a question of how the compensation system rewards marketing. Deciding who should get credit for bringing in a new client, when it is not clearly done by one lawyer, can be problematic. Accordingly, many lawyers do not market because they don't feel comfortable doing it and would prefer to rely upon a firm's "institutional" marketing efforts (again, if any) or simply the firm's name to bring in more work. Furthermore, many large-firm lawyers are still not convinced that their compensation system rewards efforts other than billable hours.

In any event, the most effective marketing is still done on a one-to-one basis. Moreover, in my opinion, the techniques that work best are not expensive. The legal services business is a very personal one. That is why the top-ten list of marketing activities discussed later in this chapter can work just as effectively in a small or solo firm as a large one. In fact, too many lawyers in larger firms still believe the work will show up on their desks because of the firm name. This creates enormous opportunities for sole practitioners.

Institutional Versus Individual Marketing

It may be true that small firms and sole practitioners cannot spend the amounts that larger firms do for institutional marketing, for items such as ads in national publications or significant contributions to local charitable events. However, in my experience, these are not the most effective forms of marketing anyway. Having been an in-house marketer for several large law firms, I can attest to the fact that the most effective marketing is what I call "individual" marketing.

The most effective marketing tools and techniques have nothing to do with dollars or firm size. Rather, the best marketing practices are those that are individual and personal. It is true that large firms spend big bucks on marketing, not all of it smartly, to be sure. Case in point: the $3 million television ad campaign by a large West Coast firm, the year before it went out of business. Roger McKenna, a marketing guru and frequent author and speaker, said at a law marketing conference that was all abuzz over the campaign, that the money would have been better spent if the firm had taken its top clients to Hawaii for a week. I'm not sure it would have saved the firm, but it sure would have saved a lot of money.

Basic Marketing Principles

To have a better understanding of how the top-ten best practices for sole practitioners fit into the overall concept of marketing, it may be worthwhile to discuss the basic elements of marketing. Of course, you should keep in mind that there are as many different definitions of marketing as there are business school professors.

In its simplest form, marketing can be defined as the process of determining:

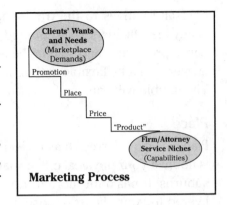

1. The clients' wants and needs (marketplace demands)
2. The firm's legal services capabilities (niches)
3. The steps, or Four Ps (Product, Price, Place, and Promotion), needed to bring the two together at a profit

Marketplace (Client) Needs

Obviously, you cannot sell a service that is not needed or wanted. If you are a tax lawyer, and the client is having employee issues, your services are not going to help very much, and you are not likely to be retained for that matter. So, it is important to know whether what you offer in legal services is needed by the client or client group. Moreover, you should learn the needs of clients before you spend time and resources trying to sell them something they do not want.

Firm Capabilities (Niches)

You must also be *capable* of offering the services that clients want or need. As a solo, you pretty much know what you are capable of doing. If you are providing services that you would prefer not to offer, then you must work at developing the niches that you are interested in offering to clients. Once you determine the legal services you can and want to offer, as well as what clients want, then you can use the Four Ps to try to obtain that work from those clients.

Product

This is where the "legal" side of legal services comes into play. Your product is preferably what you do best and enjoy doing most. Whether it is a transaction involving many documents or representation as a litigator, it is what your expertise is all about. The product is what you pull from your pool of capabilities to resolve the client's needs and give the client results. This is where you narrow your expertise and capabilities to an identified product the client needs to resolve his or her specific problem.

Price

You next determine the pricing structure you will place upon the product you offer. This is not simply your hourly rate anymore. Today, you may need to offer alternatives to the traditional fee structure. Clients may prefer contingency fees, fixed fees, discounted fees for a specified volume of work, results-based premiums, and so on. The legal profession is very competitive today, so lawyers must be flexible in their fee structures to meet the demands of clients. The nimble will win.

Place

Place is also referred to as delivery. It is the "service" side of legal services. It is not just your physical office space, and whether you are downtown or in the suburbs. It has a lot more to do with the quality of service and how it is delivered to your clients—those intangibles that often mean as much, or more, to clients than the actual product they receive. High-quality service delivery includes constant communication with clients, meeting deadlines, returning phone calls, seeking client feedback, and the lawyer *and* staff treating the client well. Think about that. Most clients didn't go to law school, so they cannot judge the quality of the legal product, but be assured that they can judge the quality of the service they receive. In a marketing sense, that can be devastating.

Promotion

Promotion is the marketing component most readily identified as "marketing" by many in the legal community who do not understand the broader discipline. This is the "sales" side of marketing. It includes all the recognized activities associated with marketing, such as conducting seminars, writing, speaking, entertaining, advertising, mailing, networking, and so forth. As you can see, however, it is just one aspect of the total process of marketing of legal services.

Best Practices for Success

The top-ten best practices for sole practitioners are set forth below. I have listed them according to what works in the short term, and then what can be effective over the longer term.

1. Visit Clients

The most effective, immediate way to obtain work now is to visit a client at his or her place of business. These visits are not for the purpose of discussing the matter on which you are currently working for the client. Rather, they are "off the clock" (a point you must make clear to the client), and for the purpose of relationship building. The stated reason for the visit is immaterial. It can be to view a new facility or renovations, it can be to meet someone with whom you have talked on the phone but never met, or for any reason that makes you feel comfortable. Although you may decide to take the client to lunch or dinner as part of your visit, keep in mind the importance of meeting for at least some of the time in the client's business space.

Ask the client about business issues encountered on a daily basis, or what keeps him or her awake at night. This is an opportunity to learn more about the client's business, industry, family, hobbies, and the like. This not only enhances your relationship, but also leads to immediate work in most cases. In my nearly two decades in marketing, and based upon my own experience as a practicing lawyer, this type of effort led to immediate business in more than 80 percent of cases. Don't be discouraged if it doesn't work every time. It will work often enough to produce immediate work, if you make the effort.

2. Obtain Client Feedback

Getting feedback from clients is extremely important, and there are three ways to do it. In decreasing order of effectiveness, they are in-person client interviews, telephone surveys, and written questionnaires. In-person interviews are the most effective because of the obvious value of face-to-face contact, but they are also the most expensive, due to the time it takes to conduct them.

Using any of the three methods is far better than doing nothing at all. If there is a problem in the attorney-client relationship, it is best to find out while the client is still using your services. Oftentimes clients do not complain to their lawyers; rather, they just don't use them on subsequent matters. In other words, they simply walk away. By getting feedback from clients, either at the end of matters or on an annual or other regular basis, the lawyer can uncover problems, dissatisfaction, or even minor irritations before they lead to lost clients.

3. Improve Communication and Responsiveness

Find ways to send information to clients and referral sources frequently. You can congratulate them, send them birthday cards, or forward news clippings. This is a good way to keep your name in front of people, so they will think of you when they—or others they know—need a lawyer. Moreover, you do not want clients to dread opening envelopes with your firm's return address because the only communication they get from you is monthly invoices. If they receive a variety of communications from you, they may not respond as negatively when your bills arrive.

Being responsive is also a very effective marketing tool, if done consistently. Lawyers are notorious for not meeting deadlines, or just barely doing so. Often these deadlines are self-imposed. It is not unusual for a lawyer to promise a client some type of work product by an unrealistic date. This practice usually arises from the lawyer's fear that if he or she doesn't tell the client the work will be done by that date, the client may not engage—or continue to engage—the lawyer. In the long run, however, it would be better if the lawyer was frank and realistic. From a marketing standpoint, it is better to give a realistic deadline and beat it by a day or two than to miss an unrealistic deadline. The former practice is unusual for lawyers, and will be extremely impressive to the client.

4. Arrange Speaking Engagements

Speaking is still a very effective tool of marketing. Extra credibility ensues when the lawyer speaks at a conference sponsored by an outside, respected organization. Of course, the topic should be timely and important to the audience. Any speech must be well prepared, rehearsed, and lively, and include interaction with the audience. Send follow-up information to the attendees. If a list of the names and addresses of the attendees is not available from the sponsoring organization, offer to send additional information to those who leave their business cards or write their information on a pad you have available.

5. Respond to RFPs

Responding to requests for proposals (RFPs) can be useful for marketing purposes. But be careful: you can waste thousands of dollars chasing the wrong work, failing to be responsive, or failing to use the client's format. In your proposal, forget the fluff (boilerplate) and demonstrate your expertise. It's best if you can meet with, or at least talk with, the person or group that will decide who is hired. The legitimate pretext to making a contact before submission is that you do not want to waste the client's time in submitting a proposal that does not respond to specific needs. I have seen RFPs that fail to address what the prospective client needs or seeks. So, call and ask additional questions to help you prepare a response that puts you ahead of the competition. Again, your proposal should talk about the client's issues—not how good you are. I would include what you would do for them, explaining in a generic sense that you have done similar things for other clients. If you haven't done similar work, you shouldn't be going after the the this work in the first place, unless you passed the bar exam only yesterday.

6. Entertain

Because we are in the "people" business, entertaining clients and referral sources is still an effective means of promoting your practice. Clients are people, too. For the sole practitioner, the entertainment can be more modest, and thus affordable. You don't need a skybox at the stadium to entertain a client or referral source effectively. Dinner and a decent seat can work just as well.

The important thing is to know the type of entertainment the person prefers. It could be sports, but it could also be the arts, or something that includes children. Ask your clients and referral sources about these things as you develop your relationships.

7. Network

I define this as simply finding someone to introduce you to someone else—preferably someone for whom you can provide legal services. Networking can take place at an organizational activity, but it need not be limited to that. Everyday encounters can lead to the exchange of business cards or the suggestion of a contact, which, if you follow up on, could lead to other desirable contacts that lead to business. Keep in mind that every person you meet can be someone to help expand your network of contacts. Enter each person in your contact list, and regularly review the list for opportunities for follow-up.

8. Maintain Media Contacts

Take your local reporter to lunch. Get to know the local media, whether they are involved in daily, business, or legal publications. Not only could they do stories about your firm or practice, they could also call upon you when they need a lawyer's perspective on a news item of current interest. If they know you and you have kept in touch regarding your areas of practice, they may remember to call you when they need to get some background information or a quote from a lawyer *not* involved in the specific matter at hand. (Because, as we all know, if it is your matter, there are likely to be confidentiality issues that will prevent you from discussing it.)

Additionally, don't hesitate to issue press releases on newsworthy matters about you or your practice. Of course, if it involves a client matter, make sure you have your client's permission to discuss it, even if you do not disclose proprietary or confidential information.

When you do these things, you may find that you are considered an expert because you have been cited or quoted in the paper or interviewed on radio and television.

9. Write

Whether you write an article or a book, authorship can also establish your reputation as an expert in a particular area of the law. Some small, local newspapers accept regular columns from lawyers on various legal topics. If you would like to do this, remember that you don't have to write every column yourself. You can get other noncompeting lawyers (who may also be in a position to refer work to you) to write some of them. In any event, wherever you get published—preferably where your intended audience will see and read it—make additional copies of the article and distribute them to clients and referral sources as an item of interest. (Be sure to check first with the publication, to avoid copyright issues.)

10. Join Organizations

The primary reason for joining organizations is to network. There is nothing wrong with joining a civic, cultural, or community organization because you believe in its mission and want to get involved. But if you are doing this for marketing purposes, then join only those organizations that interest you, and make sure you quickly become active in those organizations—lawyers who join but are not active will find the endeavor to be a waste of time. You should aim to become the president or chairperson, or to reach some other position of leadership. In addition to paying your dues, work for the organization in ways that help it reach its goals and objectives. The good will come back to you over the long term, many times over.

Write an Action Plan

Once you decide which of the best practices will work for you or most closely conform to your personality, it is then time to prepare a written plan that lists what you intend to do, when you intend to do it, and how much it will cost. If you do not write your plan, you will not become an effective marketer. You may do one or two things, when you feel like it or are "less busy," but your efforts will be infrequent at best, and nonexistent at worse. If you don't put your plan in writing, and revisit it at least quarterly, you will be cheating yourself. Following is a two-page plan that will at least get you started.

An oft-quoted saying from *Alice in Wonderland*, which actually is a paraphrase of a statement by the Cheshire cat, goes like this: "If you don't know where you are going, any path will take you there." This is just as true for legal marketing as anything else. If you do not decide what kind of practice you want and the type of clients you would like to have, and do not plan *how* you will accomplish your goals and *when*, then any or no activity will get you somewhere—you just may not like where that is.

Marketing Planning Form

Name: _____   **Date:** _____

Statement of Goal(s): *General Statement to reflect intended growth for the year:*

Objectives: *Measurable items that will reflect a contribution to firm's growth.* [For example, number of new matters/clients, $ in billings/collections; % increase. Choose one or more.]

/__/   Increase work in (specific type:_____) by ___%

/__/   Get _____ [number] new matters/clients (specify type: _____)

/__/   Collect $_____ in revenue

/__/   Obtain _____ [name] as new client

/__/   Get new matter from _____ [client]

Targets: *Persons toward whom marketing activities will be directed.*

Clients:	Referral Sources:	Prospects:
1.	1.	1.
_____	_____	_____
2.	2.	2.
_____	_____	_____
3.	3.	3.
_____	_____	_____
4.	4.	4.
_____	_____	_____

Action Plans: *What activity will be done and when.* [Fill in all those that apply.]

  1.   **Entertainment:**

/__/   I will entertain _____[name] at _____ [lunch, breakfast, dinner, civic, cultural, sporting event, golf, etc.] on _____[date].

  2.   **Client Visits:**

/__/   I will visit _____ [client name] at his/her place of business for a tour of the facility or to learn more about business on _____[date].

3.   Civic/Trade/Bar Organizations:

/__/   I will join and be active in _____
        [name of target organization(s)].

4.   Newsletters/Advisories/Law Alerts:

/__/   I will write an article on _____ [subject]
        by _____ [date] for _____ [name of publication].

5.   Seminars/Speeches:

/__/   I will speak on _____ [topic]
        before _____ [organization name] on _____ [date].

6.   Articles/Books/Manuals:

/__/   I will write an article for _____ [target
        publication name] on _____ [subject] by _____ [date].

7.   Send Information:

/__/   I will send information (e.g., case decision, newspaper clipping, etc.)
        starting on _____ [date] to the following on a quarterly basis:

Client _____   Referral source _____

Client _____   Referral source _____

Client _____   Referral source _____

8.   Press Releases:

/__/   I will submit information (e.g., upcoming speeches, election/appoint-
        ment to position, or other newsworthy info) to media via press re-
        lease on a quarterly basis.

9.   Proposals/Presentations:

/__/   I will make a proposal/presentation to _____ [client/prospect]
        for _____ [type of matter] by _____ [date].

**10.   Other Activities: (e.g., teach course, radio/TV appearances, net-
        working, etc.)**

/__/   Other [specify what activity and when it will be accomplished]:

        _____

        _____

        _____

Rainmaking for Women Lawyers

44

Gilda R. Turitz

A client of mine who was an Olympic athlete and successful entrepreneur described his goal for his energy bar product: to improve athletic performance 1 percent. I thought, why 1 percent? It was such a low goal. What was the point? But to my client, 1 percent was everything. It is one meter in a hundred-meter race, one mile in a century ride—the difference between winning and losing. That 1 percent was the edge in competitive athletics.

This 1 percent goal was not achieved overnight. My client simply did not know the meaning of the word "no." To him, "no" just meant "find another way to do it." This attitude resulted in my client's ultimate success in developing his product line, which dramatically increased the consuming athlete's ability to perform and therefore to compete at a higher level. His company soared from humble beginnings of selling energy bars from the back of his station wagon to being acquired for hundreds of millions of dollars.

Turning Leads into Clients

Women lawyers who want to be rainmakers would be well advised not to take "no" for an answer. It is vital for the aspiring woman rainmaker to have a vision of what she wants to accomplish and what margin of improvement she wants to see—or, in some cases, to become a rainmaker where that role has never before taken root. Setting and ultimately reaching a goal of improving business development performance by a measurable amount can have great effect on the bottom line.

When and whether to set a business development goal depends upon the individual lawyer's situation. Lawyers in private practice face issues of retaining and expanding their client base to varying degrees, depending upon seniority and situation. On one end of the spectrum are the younger lawyers in firms who generally do not need to concern themselves with rainmaking. Rather, they need to learn how to be excellent lawyers and satisfy the needs of their internal clients, the partners in the firm who refer them client work. These are the building blocks for young lawyers before they launch their own business development efforts. On the other end of the spectrum are sole practitioners or lawyers in small firms who constantly concern themselves with rainmaking because their practices cannot survive without successful client development.

Women lawyers who succeed at rainmaking work hard at it, and have the same attitude about "no" as my entrepreneur client did. Rainmaking is not just the result of being in the right place at the right time, although luck certainly can play a part in any rainmaker's success. Women who are intent upon building sustained practices manage their time well, develop plans that suit their visions of where they are going and who they want to be, and incorporate marketing into their professional activities as an essential matter, not a frill.

Successful women rainmakers proactively generate leads for new business and turn leads into clients. Women lawyers can exploit organizations of women professionals both in and outside law for networking, referrals, and mentoring that can create business. They also can take advantage of corporate initiatives to diversify representation and increase the amount of work sent to women lawyers of the total sent to outside counsel. Though women may have extra opportunities, some also experience challenges in rainmaking: lack of access to the "old boy network" and no ready equivalent, lack of client acceptance, and finding time for rainmaking while raising children or caring for elderly parents. Unfortunately, women lawyers still confront stereotypical barriers and discrimination—exhibited by clients and by firm members—that can impede their rainmaking efforts. Although it is beyond the scope of this chapter to deal with these impediments, the suggestions below for business development opportunities take into account the challenges women lawyers often face.

Principles of Success

Following are several principles that women can employ to succeed at rainmaking:

- Expanding business from an existing inventory of clients
- Developing a profile or niche practice to market
- Networking, matchmaking, and information brokering
- Staying in contact with clients and referral sources
- Exploiting opportunities unique to women lawyers
- Cooperatively marketing with others, or cross-selling
- Public speaking opportunities and client seminars
- Writing articles or books
- Making rainmaking a routine practice

Inventory Assessment

Anecdotally it has been said that the so-called 80-20 rule applies to rainmaking; that is, 80 percent of revenue comes from 20 percent of clients (or repeat referral sources). Most lawyers would be overlooking a tremendous rainmaking opportunity if they failed to mine that 20 percent of their client base to the maximum. After all, these are clients who already made the decision to retain the lawyer for certain types of engagements and presumably are satisfied with continuing to use the lawyer's services. These clients may have additional matters of a similar type or other matters within the lawyer's or firm's expertise that can be the source of additional business. Therefore, an inventory assessment is vital.

To mine additional work from existing clients, women lawyers should periodically do inventory assessments of those clients and the types of cases or transactions on which they work for those clients. Successful rainmakers take the time to learn as much about their clients as they can—their businesses and their personal concerns as well as their legal problems. They understand how these clients came to them in the first place (such as by referral from another person or agency, through a directory, an Internet search, or some other listing, or by client solicitation of lawyers to respond to a request for proposal or other bid process). They also understand which of these methods can be enhanced and exploited for additional business.

An inventory assessment should not be merely a snapshot of the present, but a review over a meaningful period of time. Looking at the last three years of new matters opened may show interesting trends or patterns as well as reveal client prospects that might otherwise be forgotten or overlooked. Such review also allows the lawyer to analyze the composition of her existing client base, allowing her to detect certain concentrations of industries (financial institutions, manufacturers), types of businesses (professional service firms, family-owned partnerships, small property owners), or types of individuals (high net worth, divorcing couples, entrepreneurs). Patterns may be seen from which additional obvious development opportunities can be launched. Moreover, such analysis may reveal where that 20 percent of clients who generate 80 percent of revenue comes from and whether such clients are likely to have continuing or additional legal needs to be satisfied.

A great benefit of this type of review is that it gives the lawyer the opportunity to make sure no client or referral source has become neglected. Rainmaking is as much about keeping the existing business as finding new business. Paying attention to those who are presently served or have been served in the recent past is vital to maintaining a client base. It also presents the most likely way to yield results with minimal effort.

Clients' Wants versus Clients' Needs

The inventory assessment looks at what work has already been done for clients, and possibly identifies new areas of client needs. Clients frequently tell their lawyers what they want, and many lawyers proceed to represent clients on that basis. Successful rainmakers do that, but also go beyond. They respond by listening carefully and probing to identify what their clients *need*, which may be very different, but which presents rainmaking opportunities. They offer practical and creative solutions to solve the clients' problems. A lawyer who demonstrates to a client that she can satisfy a need the client has not recognized builds client confidence and loyalty, enhances the likelihood that the client will turn to her in the future for counsel, and expands her business.

Many women lawyers have unique strengths in this area, which is highly dependent upon well-developed listening and communication skills. They should not hesitate to get to know the client's full situation as deeply as possible, to identify needs as well as to respond to expressed client desires.

Mining Additional Work from Existing Clients

On a practical level, there are several things women lawyers can do to expand work from existing clients.

♦ *Keep in frequent contact with clients.* Law is a relationship business. Nurturing the relationship is vital; to nurture, contact is critical. Clients are more likely to call the lawyer who keeps in touch with them than the one who does not.

♦ *Ask clients if there is anything they need help with in addition to whatever you are presently doing for them.* Even if the answer is, "Not now," you are reinforcing that you are capable and available to provide other services.

♦ *Visit your clients' places of business, even when it requires a special trip.* Clients enjoy showing their premises, explaining their businesses on-site, and introducing their key staff members. After all, most clients are in the business of selling products or services and have pride in what they offer to their markets. Visiting demonstrates the lawyer's commitment to the client and gives the lawyer an opportunity to meet more people in the business, connect names to faces, and possibly find new opportunities to provide legal services.

For example, I once visited a corporate client's office and noticed some marketing material with use of an interesting logo for a subsidiary. Discussion revealed that the company had not taken any steps to protect its intellectual property. I left with that assignment, and would not have had that opportunity without having visited.

♦ *At the conclusion of a matter, review "lessons learned" with the client.* This is particularly valuable after litigation over a challenged business practice where the lawyer has spent significant time in depositions learning intimate details of the way the client's staff handles problems with customers, employees, or vendors. A concluded matter may have arisen from some ambiguities in the client's standard form of contract or from a failure to have a writing at all. Concrete suggestions for improvement in the way the client conducts business may lead to a new assignment of rewriting a standard contract or manual, or reviewing certain client operations, such as an audit of leases or customer practices.

As an example, I defended a products liability case for a motor manufacturer in which an injured party claimed the machine had a design defect—it failed to have a guard and a sufficient warning in the repair manual. The company had never been sued in its one-hundred-year history, and the design and warning issues were the subject of extensive and expensive litigation, which ultimately was settled. I proposed and was retained to give management a thorough post-litigation review of suggestions for improvement in the process of product development to put to good use for the future, and, as a preventative measure, all that had been learned, but not fully appreciated, about potential risks of continuing to do business as usual. Clients generally are receptive to this type of value-added proposal, because they see it as a means of lowering future exposure.

Know What You Are Marketing—Create a Profile of Expertise and Niche Practice Areas

Building upon their inventories and identification of trends, women lawyers can create profiles to highlight their special skills or expertise and particular niche practice areas. Some women lawyers particularly capitalize on representing women who seek women as their advocates, and that can be the basis for development of a niche practice. This appears to hold true particularly regarding women seeking representation for discrimination and sexual harassment cases, medical malpractice, family law and domestic partnership dissolutions, and other representation where intimate personal details may be involved.

More broadly, though, lawyers can develop specific "sound bites" to describe their practices in concise and pithy ways. For instance, the general description "intellectual property lawyer" can be translated to more precise phrases such as software licensing expert, trade dress litigator, music copyright specialist, or biochemical patent prosecutor. To embellish a fairly generic practice area such as "commercial litigation," lawyers can be more specific, using terminology such as consumer rights advocacy, lender liability defense, ADA access claims prosecution, medical device liability litigation, shareholder rights enforcement, or unfair competition defense. Alternatively, the "sound bite" may focus upon the types of clients served, such as technology start-ups, commercial landlords, drug manufacturers, high-net-worth individuals, nonprofit corporations, venture capitalists, or software developers. To generate business, the lawyer must have a succinct description of the product she is selling. Such "sound bites" help the rainmaker identify to existing and potential clients what she has to offer.

Networking, Matchmaking, and Information Brokering

Most lawyers, and women lawyers are no exception, get business from referrals because—and this cannot be repeated often enough—law is a relationship business. The foundation of the relationship is trust between lawyer and client. Clients will return to lawyers again and again if they trust them and believe the lawyers have served them well.

How the clients came to the lawyer in the first place is the subject of the inventory assessment discussed above. But, in the end, almost every client comes from a referral of some sort—perhaps a self-referral after hearing of the lawyer's reputation, or a referral from a trusted advisor such as an accountant or a financial planner, or from another person in the industry or field of the client who may himself also be the lawyer's client, or from another lawyer.

Because referrals are vital to developing business, women lawyers must network extensively. Women have unique opportunities to network in professional organizations that serve women members, such as women's bar associations or committees within general bar associations (such as the ABA Law Practice Management Section's Women Rainmakers or the ABA Litigation Section's Women's Advocates Committee), and industry groups such as Financial Women of America, National Association of Women Business Owners, Women in Technology, and Women in Communications. Becoming active on those organizations' membership committees or other committees of interest is an effective way to meet many women professionals who may have their own legal needs or who can introduce women lawyers to those in their organizations who are responsible for hiring counsel. Recreational organizations where professional women congregate, such as Executive Women's Golf, also present networking opportunities and often have networking as an express part of their missions. Similarly, organizations such as the National Women's Political Caucus present opportunities to meet women who are potential clients or referral sources.

A caveat is important here. A woman lawyer should never join an organization merely to look for clients there. If the woman lawyer does not have a sincere interest and commitment to the organization, she will not develop the credibility or the contacts for its members to think of her as a person to whom they would want to refer business.

Matchmaking is also very important for relationship building. This is simply networking in another form—helping connect people together who may have common interests or goals who would not otherwise know of each other. The successful woman rainmaker is a master at this. She can identify potential service providers for her clients or others, and vice versa. Both are grateful and will have her at the top of their lists when they need help, and will be highly likely to refer others to her because she has successfully connected them and satisfied needs without any immediate return.

Information brokering is a technique for effective networking. By sending clients and referral sources information of interest to their particular needs—such as a new case or regulation that may affect their business practices or estate plans, or present a new opportunity for their operations—the rainmaker demonstrates that she is always thinking about them and their needs. This, in turn, keeps the rainmaker in the clients' and referral sources' consciousness. Information brokering does not have to be time consuming. With an e-mail message and a simple standard form letter or transmittal card, the rainmaker can achieve an excellent result with minimal effort.

Cross-Selling

Frequently lawyers find it difficult to market their own services, but are comfortable singing the praises of partners or colleagues. Women lawyers can take advantage of their good working relationships with other lawyers to introduce them to their clients when the clients have need for the other lawyers' expertise. A natural cross-selling opportunity arises, for example, in family law and estate planning. It is a natural lead-in when counseling a client who needs a prenuptial agreement or divorce to discuss whether he or she also needs to update an estate plan or prepare one if none has been done to date. If the lawyer does not have the expertise to do the estate plan herself, cross-selling the services of a colleague with that expertise, even if the client does not see that need as immediate, presents a rainmaking opportunity for that lawyer if the colleague is in the same firm, or a networking and referral opportunity if the colleague practices elsewhere.

Less obvious opportunities may arise in the litigation context. Business lawyers regularly refer clients to litigators when they have disputes that have escalated to the stage of implicit or overt threat of suit. They also can sell the services of litigators for preventative law issues on matters such as arbitration and mediation clauses, and jurisdiction and venue provisions, about which litigators have greater practical experience. Conversely, litigators may be able to cross-sell the services of corporate colleagues when they identify practices that could use improvement or ways in which the risk of liability may be reduced through reorganization or restructuring.

Women rainmakers will be particularly effective at developing relationships with other women lawyers to cross-sell their services to the increasing number of companies who have signed commitments to shatter the "glass ceiling" or to diversify their representation by outside counsel. Women in solo or small practices should particularly seek opportunities to partner with other women to present increased scope of services to corporate decision makers who retain counsel. Cross-selling is an excellent way to expand business for both existing and potential clients.

Speaking and Writing

A speaking engagement is a classic method of demonstrating knowledge and expertise in a particular area of law. Writing an article is another way to be recognized as having expertise in a particular area of law. Women lawyers can capitalize on rainmaking opportunities by actively seeking speaking engagements and publication opportunities on topics that are within their niche practice areas and by recycling the same general subject matter for different groups.

Women lawyers can maximize client opportunities from public speaking and writing by being selective about their content and audiences. They must analyze whether the subject matter is sophisticated enough that lawyer members of the audience will view them as lawyers to whom to make referrals, or whether the subject matter serves only an education function that is unlikely to generate leads or referrals. The latter may be a legitimate service to the bar, but it is not likely to satisfy a marketing goal. If the target audience is a client group, such as real estate brokers or financial advisors being updated by the lawyer on current trends or ways to avoid being sued, the likelihood of leads or referrals increases.

Although speaking and writing are critical tools for many rainmakers, women lawyers seeking to build their practices should recognize that they are longer-term investments and may be more time consuming (and more lonely) to prepare than networking activities. Another way to achieve recognition along these lines, however, is to make oneself available to the press for inquiries or commentary on trends in areas of legal expertise. One colleague of mine is fond of telling a story about how he phoned a reporter after reading an article about a trade dress case, and how the reporter subsequently called on him when writing additional stories in the field. A general counsel saw him quoted in one such article, interviewed him, and hired him to handle a significant piece of litigation after that. Obviously this was a combination of leveraging resources and luck, but is also a variation on the time-honored technique of getting one's name known through speaking and writing.

Marketing and Time Management

In client development, intentions are great, but results matter. Most women lawyers with whom I have talked over the years express frustration about not having enough time to market. For women raising children, the family demands can tug at and overshadow the demands of marketing effectively to develop a practice. The solution I can offer is to master time management and make marketing both a priority and a habit.

Thirteen years ago, when my youngest son was still a baby, my twin sons were in preschool, and I was a junior partner in a large firm, I determined that I had to take rainmaking seriously so I could control my own fate to a much greater degree. The demands at home and at work (both the litigation work and the rainmaking challenge) were staggering. I followed the advice of many time management experts, which can be summed up as follows: stay true to your values and goals, prioritize, delegate, and develop good, time-efficient habits. Because rainmaking was a goal to satisfy my value of control over my future success, it became a priority. I followed the time management experts' suggestion that new habits can be developed in twenty-one days, and I decided to try to incorporate at least one marketing activity daily, even if it was only to set a lunch date with a lead or a referral source. Women lawyers who want to be rainmakers should seriously consider calendaring fifteen minutes a day to plan or execute some aspect of a marketing plan. Results will surely follow from this consistency of activity. It may just give them that competitive edge, just as my entrepreneur client's goal to get that 1 percent lead gave him success.

Suggestions for Further Reading

Following are some suggestions for further reading on rainmaking and marketing issues:

◆ Ida Abbott, Ida Abbott Consulting, *Management Solutions* (Issue 7, Summer 2004); **www.idaabbott.com**, *Lawyers' Professional Development Plan: Guidelines, Baseline, Goal Categories, and Action*

- Harry Beckwith, *Selling the Invisible: A Field Guide to Modern Marketing* (Warner Books, 1997)
- Harry Beckwith, *The Invisible Touch: The Four Keys to Modern Marketing* (Warner Books, 2000)
- Jeffrey J. Fox, *How to Become a Marketing Superstar: Unexpected Rules That Ring the Cash Register* (Hyperion, 2003)
- Jeffrey J. Fox, *How to Become a Rainmaker: The People Who Get and Keep Customers* (Hyperion, 2000)
- Ford Harding, *Creating Rainmakers: How to Turn Professionals into Client Developers* (Adams Media, 1998)
- Theda C. Snyder, *Women Rainmakers' Best Marketing Tips*, Second Edition (ABA, 2003)

Newsletters, Brochures, and Other Marketing Tools

45

David M. Freedman

Introduction

I know a lawyer on the East Coast who established his solo practice quite nicely with a letterhead and a business card. He is active in various associations and organizations, so he gets out and meets people, and he promotes his services on the strength of his personality and his ability to articulate the compelling "features and benefits" of his services. His is a highly personalized approach to marketing: he is a good listener, and can focus on an individual's particular legal problem or challenge and persuade that person that he can help resolve it. Only after two years did he decide to start publishing a modest but informative quarterly newsletter, and then develop a simple Web site, so he could grow his practice in new directions.

Another lawyer, this one in the Midwest, started her solo practice part-time, intending to work no more than twenty hours a week. She had a letterhead and a business card and a one-page Web site. Her practice mushroomed, partly because her field is hot and partly because she cultivated the right referral sources, and also because she is knowledgeable and articulate. Now she works thirty hours a week and farms out some work to another lawyer. She finally decided she needed a brochure, which she developed over several months.

Brochures, newsletters, and Web sites certainly have their place in promoting solo practices. But you should not rely upon them to the exclusion of what I call primary marketing strategies:

- Having face-to-face contact with prospective clients and referral sources
- Establishing a high profile in your area of expertise (by writing articles and speaking at conferences, for example)
- Developing excellent communication skills, so that you can explain complex legal subjects in crystal-clear terms that your clients understand
- Maintaining high professional standards in the work that you do

As a rule, a fancy brochure, four-color newsletter, and whiz-bang interactive Web site can't carry the burden of promoting your practice without those primary marketing activities.

Promo Priorities

If you reach the point where you need promotional literature to help your practice grow, you need a plan and a budget. The disadvantage of being a small firm is that you do not have marketing expertise on staff (aside, perhaps, from a receptionist or nephew who knows a little desktop publishing) and your budget is, shall we say, limited. But you have three big advantages over larger firms. As the sole decision maker:

1. You don't have to form a committee and meet to approve every stage of the creative process.
2. You don't have to take several or dozens of opinions into account at every step.
3. You don't wind up watering down the message to assuage everyone's concerns about sounding too colorful, confident, or bold, until all the personality, style, and charm are blanched out of the literature, which then reads like every other firm's materials. ("We are a client-centric firm. . . . We don't just meet your expectations, we exceed them . . . by consistently providing the highest-quality legal representation.")

In other words, you not only have the opportunity to put your personality and style and charm into your promotional literature, but you *must*. This is true because you are selling yourself rather than a firm or an entity, like Trump Hotels and Casino Resorts sells Donald Trump. You can't differentiate yourself from other lawyers on the basis of vast resources or deep support staff, so you must differentiate yourself on the basis of your personal attributes.

With those advantages and limitations—as well as the personality-style-charm mandate—in mind, you can choose the promotional materials that best meet your marketing needs. (By the way, if you have no personality, style, or charm, you should be a building contractor, not a lawyer.) For this purpose, I will discuss three categories of promotional literature: brochures, educational literature, and periodicals. Note that a Web site can fall into one or more of those categories, depending upon how you use it.

Brochures

The primary purpose of a brochure is to introduce your practice to prospective clients, referral sources, the public, and, in some cases, the media. You can offer a brochure to people who inquire about your services, and distribute it to people who may have never heard of you.

A brochure should feature all the following information:

- Your name, firm name, and contact information
- A brief bio, perhaps with a head-and-shoulders photo
- The kinds of clients you serve
- The area(s) of the law in which you practice
- The attributes that differentiate you from other practices in the same field

One suggestion on the structure of the information in your brochure: Think about how a reader will search for information, and organize it accordingly. The *wrong* way to do it is to first list your practice areas, and then describe each area, including the clients you represent in that area. Readers do not want to scan all the practice areas to see whether you can represent them in this area, in that area, and in the other area. The *right* way to do it is to first list client groups, and then describe the services you offer to each client group. That way, the reader can find the group into which he or she fits, and no more scanning is required. You may believe your brochure is supposed to be about you, but it's not—it's about the client.

Similarly, when you write your bio, remember that readers want to know whether you are qualified and capable of solving their problems. Your practical experience, your evidence of success, and perhaps your license to practice in their jurisdiction help answer that question. In most cases, they are not initially interested in where you got your law degree or of which civic organizations you are an officer. You can offer a more comprehensive bio online, on a separate handout, or both—and you can update those cheaply and often.

When in doubt about how much to say in your brochure, be concise. After you give someone the brochure, follow up with a phone call or an in-person meeting and elaborate. Use your brochure as a foot in the door, not as a plunge into the room.

Flex Brochures

If you practice in more than one area, or if your brochure contains information that needs to be updated often, you should consider producing a flexible brochure instead of a fixed, permanent one. A flexible brochure lets you send slightly different information to different audiences, and revise the entire package from time to time.

One type of flex brochure consists of a folder in which you can enclose different inserts for different purposes. The folder itself features boilerplate information that you want everyone to see. Then you can prepare an insert for each client group or practice area, for example.

Another type of flex brochure is stored as an electronic template, and you can customize the content each time you need to produce it. Then you can print it on special paper stock. You can even have brochure "shells" printed in bulk quantities, and then print your customized content on those. That way, you can incorporate color and other graphic elements that can't be produced efficiently or in high quality on your own printer.

YourFirm.com

If you have a Web site, resist the temptation to simply dump the content from your printed brochure onto the Internet. In most cases, you should reformat the content, because people "consume" information differently online than in print. See more about Web sites in Chapter 47.

Educational Literature

You can claim in your brochure that you are an eminent authority in a particular practice area, but how do you prove it? One way is by distributing educational literature such as pamphlets, answers to frequently asked questions (FAQs), and backgrounders.

Unlike periodical literature, educational materials are handed out as needed, usually in response to a question or to reinforce advice or instructions that you give clients verbally. For promotional purposes, when you meet with a new client, you can also provide educational literature that relates to that client's specific industry or legal issue. Educational materials are also handy public relations tools when the press is looking for information about a certain issue in the news, if it's within your area of expertise.

Pamphlets

Pamphlets tend to be professionally designed and produced, whereas FAQs and backgrounders should be less formal, but tasteful. You can write your own pamphlets or use "canned" literature with your firm's imprint.

Composing your own gives you the opportunity to coordinate the design (and writing style) with your letterhead, brochure, and other materials. You know your clientele, and you can provide originally written information that is tailored precisely to their needs and issues. And you avoid the possibility that clients receive the same canned pamphlet from other firms, too. On the other hand, canned pamphlets save you time and, if you purchase bulk quantities, design and printing expense. A wide variety of literature is available from pamphlet publishers.

FAQs and Backgrounders

When you create these informal materials, you should focus upon authoritativeness, accuracy, readability, and educational value rather than impressive design. You can store the content electronically and print the materials as needed, or at least print a master and make photocopies as needed. In most cases, you can print or copy these on your letterhead or plain paper—lightly colored paper is fine, but don't use dark or bold colors, as this makes the text hard to read and makes the documents look too much like grocery store flyers.

An FAQ sheet should thoroughly answer a single question that clients ask, well, frequently. FAQs typically range in length from half a page to two pages (front and back of one sheet). At the end of the explanatory text, refer to further sources of information, such as books, articles, videotapes, and Web sites. And try to make those further sources available in your office.

Backgrounders are more comprehensive—typically three or four pages and sometimes longer—and typically a bit more sophisticated than FAQs.

Educational pieces are usually printed, but you can also make them available online as PDF downloads or rich-text files. The key is to make it ultraconvenient for clients to obtain them. All literature should bear your name and contact information.

Periodicals

Brochures and pamphlets can help create a good first impression for prospective clients and referral sources, but then you need to remind them from time to time that you are the lawyer to call—stay in their face, as it were. You can do this by distributing periodical literature such as newsletters, alerts, clippings, reprints, or a combination thereof.

Like pamphlets, periodicals must be largely informative rather than pro-motional in their editorial concept. If you publish information that is useful, that helps readers improve their bottom lines or stay out of trouble, they will remember you as a reliable source of valuable advice and information. They'll save it for future reference. They might even photocopy it and disseminate it to their colleagues, customers, and suppliers. Then you multiply your exposure in the marketplace.

If you want to distribute promotional literature—such as announcements of new practice areas, new Web site features, or additional staff—do that as a separate enclosure or separate mailing altogether, unless you can keep the information to no more than 15 percent of your newsletter space. If your periodical literature is too promotional and self-serving, readers won't take it seriously, and they certainly won't save it or pass it along to others.

Newsletters

Publishing a newsletter is a big commitment. Once you begin, you must follow through, or you'll appear unable to fulfill your promises. Before you begin, make a list of articles that might be included throughout the first full year of publication. (You can substitute more timely articles when the need or opportunity arises.) Estimate the time and expense involved in writing, producing, and distributing the newsletter. Then double your estimates.

To save time, you can do one of the following:

1. Hire a writer or a custom newsletter developer to produce the publication under your guidance.
2. Buy rights to articles prepared specifically for this purpose.
3. Distribute canned newsletters, which are available for various practice niches. Some content providers let you revise the articles for your clientele. These days, almost all canned content (individual articles and entire newsletters) are available in plain text and HTML formats, so that you can edit them, print them, and post them to your Web site. Some include graphics in JPG, TIF, and other formats. (For a list of quality content providers, visit **www.nwsltr.com/content-sources.shtml**).

That raises the question: In which format(s) should you publish your newsletter? Your first choice is between print and electronic. If you choose the latter, you must then choose among several formats. The two tables below provide rough guidelines, but the best way to proceed is to ask your clients what format they prefer. A word of advice: Some of the best newsletters (most useful to readers) are the simplest, printed in plain text on a firm's letterhead, with perhaps a (nongratuitous) chart or table. Don't assume anyone will read your newsletter just because it's a visual work of art.

TABLE 1: PRINT VERSUS ELECTRONIC NEWSLETTERS

Format	Advantages	Disadvantages
Printed	Easier to read. More convenient (doesn't require printing out). Allows greatest control over image quality, so makes best impression visually.	Generally more expensive to produce and distribute. Takes more time to distribute, so not appropriate for urgent or timely news.
Electronic	Lower production and distribution costs. Fast distribution, so best for urgent or timely news. Can use hypertext or embedded links. E-mail delivery makes reader response more likely. Readers can forward to others more easily (viral distribution).	Eyes get tired viewing materials on screen, so readers tend to scan, not read. Many readers print out in black and white to read, and lose color graphics. PDFs are not as clear as printed or photocopied letters. Must compete with spam. Can't limit distribution (Web site is everywhere).

For more tips on publishing client newsletters, I recommend the following sources:

♦ *Successful Client Newsletters*, by Milton W. Zwicker (ABA, 1998)
♦ *Newsletter Strategy Session*, a Web site with "everything for publishers of client newsletters" (**www.nwsltr.com**)

Alerts, Clips, and Reprints

A much easier and less time-consuming way to stay in touch with your clientele is to distribute alerts, clippings, and/or reprints.

An alert is like a newsletter, often with just one article, that you publish only when you have something newsworthy to tell readers—such as a new law, regulation, policy, decision, or other legal development that affects your clientele.

Instead of composing an alert, you could clip articles from news media and send photocopies to your clientele. If you are the author of an article that appears in the media, even better—distribute reprints. If you are interviewed on television or radio, transcribe the interview, edit it for clarity, and distribute the transcript. In the case of clippings and reprints, always enclose a cover letter giving a synopsis (no more than two to four sentences) and an analysis of how the story affects your readers specifically (a paragraph or

TABLE 2: ELECTRONIC NEWSLETTER FORMATS

Newsletter format	Software required to read/view	Main advantages	Disadvantages
Plain text e-mail message	Any e-mail client software (almost everyone)	Extremely fast, easy to compose and send. Everyone can read it. Ideal for urgent messages.	Cannot include color, vary fonts, or use basic formatting such as bold, italic, tables, or bullets.
Microsoft Word attachment to e-mail message	E-mail client and Microsoft Word software	Can use color, fonts, basic formatting and layout, and maybe even logo. Looks like newsletter, not e-mail message.	Readers will read attachment only if they trust you (and have Microsoft Word).
HTML e-mail message	HTML e-mail software	Can use photos, graphics, sophisticated design elements, and embedded links. Looks like Web page. Allows tracking and reporting (click-through rates).	Ten percent of readers don't have HTML-based e-mail systems. Must have open Internet connection to see images. Requires specialized skills to code in HTML.
Web site content	Web browser	Same as HTML e-mail message, plus it may be viewed by anyone in the world. Can link to archives.	Must remind reader to visit Web site. Printout not as readable as plain text, or attachment or PDF.
PDF	Adobe Reader	Broadest design possibilities. Easy to convert other formats to PDF with Adobe Acrobat and other software.	Can take long time to download; some e-mail programs won't accept huge PDF attachments.

two). The synopsis and analysis are for the benefit of those people who don't have time, or are not inclined, to read the enclosed piece.

In some cases, unless the fair-use doctrine of copyright law applies, you may need to obtain permission from the copyright owner to reproduce and distribute a published article.

If you distribute alerts, clippings, and/or reprints, try to do so on a somewhat regular basis, for maximum exposure and promotional value.

Editorial Guidelines

Educational and periodical literature should generally cover very narrow topics, so they can be thorough and detailed. A short piece that covers a broad topic is necessarily superficial—in other words, worthless. If you find that you don't have space to include examples, anecdotes, or cases in the article, the topic is probably too broad. Remember, the purpose of this literature is to showcase your expertise and authoritativeness, which you can do only by covering a topic in some depth and detail.

If you use real anecdotes and cases, you must get permission from the parties involved or disguise their identities. Hypothetical examples are safer from a privacy standpoint, but real cases (real people) are more compelling.

If you compose your own literature, always display the standard copyright notice (for example, © *2004 American Bar Association*). And hire a professional proofreader—errors of spelling, punctuation, grammar, and style may seem trivial to you, but they jump out at readers and scream, "Unprofessional!"

Finally, on any educational or periodical literature you produce (as well as a Web site), you need the not-legal-advice disclaimer: "This material is provided as information and is not intended as legal advice. For advice on specific legal matters, please call me."

Design Guidelines

In addition to imparting useful information, you want to present a professional-looking image. For that purpose, you should hire a talented graphic designer. Don't try to do everything yourself, and don't hire a novice. It may seem unfair, but amateurish graphics telegraph amateurish legal services.

Here's an important tip if you use canned pamphlets and newsletters: for goodness sake, hire a graphic designer to create and position your imprint on the pamphlet. I've seen beautifully produced pamphlets tragically degraded by amateurish graphics and poorly written promotional copy imprinted by the firms that distribute them. Don't underestimate the importance of creating a sterling first impression with professional-looking graphics.

Your printed brochure or newsletter should fit neatly into a standard-size envelope. You'd be surprised at how many graphic designers get carried away with the art form and forget about such practical considerations.

You Are a Brilliant Lawyer, Not a Marketing Expert

If you feel you need help deciding what kinds of promotional materials to produce and distribute, hire a smart marketing consultant or public relations firm to analyze your objectives, study your market, and formulate an integrated marketing plan. It costs money for that kind of planning, but, in the long run, it can pay off big-time. You might even decide that your best investment would be to take a class in networking or public speaking—the more personal, face-time marketing strategies—and scale back the impersonal words-on-page strategies.

Yellow Pages Advertising **46**

Kerry Randall

Yellow Pages advertising can play the major role in successfully marketing a small practice. In fact, many small practices rely nearly exclusively upon the Yellow Pages for client generation. Why? For many law firms, Yellow Pages advertising has proven itself to be the highest return-on-investment advertising vehicle. It is a great starting place for investing limited marketing dollars.

As you approach Yellow Pages advertising, keep in mind, as with all consumer-directed advertising, that the "best" products are not the best sellers—the *best-marketed* products are the best sellers. In the Yellow Pages, the best lawyers do not get the most calls; *the best ads get the most calls.*

Twenty Rules for Yellow Pages Advertising

This chapter outlines twenty essential rules for successfully navigating the Yellow Pages highway. Stick to the rules, and you will be on your way to building a Yellow Pages ad that will grab attention, hold attention, and, most importantly, get potential clients to call. (For a thorough discussion of Yellow Pages advertising, see my book, *Effective Yellow Pages Advertising for Lawyers; The Complete Guide to Creating Winning Ads,* published by the ABA.)

Remember: as a lawyer-advertiser, you are responsible for what appears in all your advertisements. Before you advertise, you must familiarize yourself with the rules of professional conduct set forth by any state in which you intend to advertise. The

ABA maintains a Web site that tracks state rules, updates, and changes: **www.abanet.org/legalservices/clientdevelopment/adrules.html**. Also, for a thorough understanding of ethics in lawyer advertising, see *Marketing and Legal Ethics: The Boundaries of Promoting Legal Services*, published by the ABA.

Rule One

Successful Yellow Pages ads are successful because they contain six key elements. In the past fifteen years, I've worked with thousands of Yellow Pages directories and many, many thousands of ads. By far, most of these ads are mediocre, at best. (That is good news for you.) Most Yellow Pages ads lack the key elements that make print ads successful. Be sure your ad contains all six elements:

1. Strong headlines that command attention and engage readers
2. A laser-sharp focus; a willingness to ignore most readers
3. Arresting, eye-captivating illustrations or photographs
4. Clearly identifiable differences (from competitive advertisers)
5. Relevant copy (text) that covers less than 50 percent of the ad space
6. Professional-looking, clutter-free layouts

Rule Two

The function of advertising is not *to sell.* The function of advertising is to *inspire* people to buy your products or services. The result of effective advertising is that when people buy the stuff they want or need, they buy your stuff. Powerful Yellow Pages advertising communicates that you are the best choice for where to buy (or from whom to buy). Powerful advertising establishes a desire to buy what you have to sell.

The most effective way to get people to buy your services is to stop selling your services and start communicating that you understand, and can satisfy, potential customers' needs (solve their problems) better than anybody else.

Rule Three

Consumers buy things because they are different. To get people to respond to your Yellow Pages ad, you must clearly communicate those things about your practice that are unique. Special services, experience, fields of expertise, types of law practiced, credentials, and location can set you apart.

Rule Four

Don't copy other advertisers. Both professional writer/designers and amateur advertisers look at their competitors' advertisements. Professional content developers look at competitors' ads so they can market over, around, and under them. They look for what is missing in those ads. They look for niches. They look for weaknesses.

Amateur advertisers look at competing ads so they can get ideas. What they end up doing is copying. However, readers—potential customers—respond to the things in ads that cause the advertiser to stand apart. Nothing sets your ad apart when you put everything in your ad that you found in your competitors' ads.

Rule Five

People don't buy things; people buy solutions to problems. For example, people do not buy shampoo; they buy clean hair. They pay for shampoo.

When you want your advertising to work powerfully, you must know what—precisely what—your customers truly want. You must dig beneath the surface.

Rule Six

Know the competition and the customer. You must know the following before you design and place your ad:

◆ Precisely *who* your competitors are
◆ *What* your competitors are marketing
◆ *How* your competitors are marketing
◆ *Who* your potential customers are
◆ *What* they are looking for
◆ *Where* they live and shop
◆ *Why* they are looking in the Yellow Pages

You can complete the research on your competitors easily and accurately in less than fifteen minutes with your Yellow Pages directory. Look at your competitors' advertising to see which features and copy points they list. You want to discover the following:

◆ *Who* they are
◆ *What* they are selling
◆ *How* they are selling
◆ *What* they are leaving out

As you look at these ads, put yourself in a customer's frame of mind. Only by knowing what your potential customers want can you see competitive ads the way they see them. (And, there is no other way to see competitive ads that is of any use to you.)

Pay special attention to all the ads that will come before your ad; your potential customers see these ads before they see yours. How well are your competitors meeting the wants and needs of your potential customers?

Rule Seven

Successful ads are targeted. Successful ads do not try to sell everything to everybody. Only amateur advertisers design their ads to reach a broad audience. The result is that their ads don't reach any audience powerfully. People needing representation for personal injury do not want to hire lawyers who can also represent them for divorce, bankruptcy, real estate litigation, probate, and criminal matters . . . unless they have serious brain injuries.

Rule Eight

Use the Define/Identify/Create/Speak Model to build your ad.

- ◆ *Define* the audience you are going to attract.
- ◆ *Identify* a need or a want this audience has that other advertisers have not reached through marketing.
- ◆ *Create* a unique place in the market. How do you do the better job of providing solutions to your potential customers' problems?
- ◆ *Speak* directly to the target audience in your ad and *only* to that target audience.

Rule Nine

The more you focus upon the customer's wants and needs in your advertising, the more new clients your advertising will generate. Forget about all that stuff that makes you unique. The only thing that matters to your potential customers is how you can do the better job of providing solutions to their problems.

Rule Ten

Yellow Pages readers seldom read text-heavy ads. Text-heavy ads are those with more than 50 percent of their space covered with text. Every word in your ad either helps or hurts your chances of generating a new client. Make certain every word speaks to your targeted readers' wants and needs. Look at every word from the perspective of your well-defined target audience, and then eliminate every word that does not inspire that reader to call you.

Rule Eleven

Buyer-focused headlines grab readers' attention and guarantee that ads get read. Which kinds of headlines work best?

- ◆ Headlines that provide solutions to readers' problems (or suggest to readers that if they continue reading they will find solutions to their problems)
- ◆ Headlines that communicate key buying points
- ◆ Headlines that jump off the page and grab readers' attention

If the headline of an ad is the name of a firm—"David L. Johnson, Attorney at Law"—the ad does not have a headline; it has a name at the top. Think of it this way: the headline of your ad is the ad for your ad.

Rule Twelve

Consider, and then reconsider, using your photograph. Many lawyers place photographs of themselves or their staff members in their ads. Is this good? Does it generate more telephone calls from the types of customers with whom you want to work?

Generally, a photograph of the lawyer(s) and/or staff is effective at setting a practice apart in a Yellow Pages ad only if:

◆ You (or your staff) are an ethnic minority
◆ You are a female lawyer
◆ You appear to be especially trustworthy or experienced

Rule Thirteen

Select your ad designer carefully. Talented designers communicate messages that go beyond text. Way beyond text. A masterful designer will create a spirit—*a feeling*—within the ad's design that communicates far, far more than words alone.

Though the Yellow Pages publisher does not charge extra to design ads, you are not required to have your ad designed by the publisher. Do you want your ad designed by the same team that designs all the other ads in the phone book? Consider using a graphic design studio or a specialized Yellow Pages design studio.

Rule Fourteen

Leave out of your ad any information that does not motivate potential customers to call. Any information in a Yellow Pages advertisement that does not drive potential customers to their telephones to call you drives them away. Drive-away content includes fax numbers, URLs, zip codes, and e-mail addresses.

The only job your Yellow Pages ad has is to bring customers to you. Any text in your ad with a purpose other than bringing customers to you can, and will, drive customers away. Read your text carefully.

Rule Fifteen

Don't trust the information contained in any survey or research document that was clearly designed to get you to buy ads, or spend more money on your advertising. Look at any survey a salesperson gives to you as a survey carefully designed to produce favorable results. Surveys designed to "discover the facts" are never used as marketing tools.

Rule Sixteen

It is far more productive to take a winning position in a single directory than to make many appearances in multiple directories.

Rule Seventeen

The most productive position for Yellow Pages advertising is in the front third of the heading. Contrary to popular misconception, all other things being equal, the first advertisement in the heading gets no more calls than other advertisements in the front third. Good ads get many more calls than "first" ads.

Rule Eighteen

In-column ads in Specialty Guides (by field of practice) can provide an excellent return on investment. In-column ads are not display ads. In-column ads are the ads within the columns constrained by the width of the column. They vary in height from one-half inch to four or five inches. Unlike display ads, in-column ads are listed alphabetically. (Larger in-column ads are not placed in front of smaller in-column ads.)

The cost for advertising in the guides can be relatively inexpensive (the ads are generally smaller), so you might be able to be the dominant advertiser in the guide without paying a fortune. However, Specialty Guides do not always offer good value. Consumers turn to the guide sections only when they cannot find what they are looking for in the main "Attorneys" heading.

As a general rule, in the guides, you are better off matching the size of the largest competing ad (unless that ad is really bad). Second-place advertisers do not get calls. In the guides, more than anywhere else, larger sizes generate visibility and readership.

Rule Nineteen

Color is a high-margin product for Yellow Pages publishers. Sales representatives tend to oversell its value. Generally, investments in larger, closer-to-the-front-of-the-heading ads provide better return on investment than the same dollars spent on color. Although color often gets more attention, color does not necessarily generate more phone calls, or more revenue.

Every time you decide how to spend your limited marketing dollars, evaluate from the perspective of return on investment: where can you find the greatest return on your investment?

Rule Twenty

Yellow Pages advertising is not for everybody. Placement in the first third of the advertisements is an important element to Yellow Pages success. If you cannot afford the price of first-third placement, consider investing your marketing dollars elsewhere.

Often, lawyers feel they *must* advertise in the Yellow Pages. They cannot afford much, but they reason, "There are a lot of potential customers looking through the Yellow Pages—I should have an ad there!" Without much of a budget to work with, they buy a small ad in the back third of a heading with seventy advertisers. Though it might feel good to be doing something, such placement simply does not work. As an advertiser, you must ask yourself, "Why would somebody turn past thirty or forty other advertisers to get to my ad? What wasn't in the other ads that readers might still be looking for?"

Marketing Legal Services on the Internet—Positioning and Branding on the Web

47

Larry Bodine

Now is the time for your law firm to get serious about its Web site. This is because Web sites do bring in business, clients really do check you and your firm online, and the Web is the most efficient way to market your practice.

Consider this:

- A 2003 survey of law firms conducted by TouchPoint Metrics of San Rafael, California, found that 73 percent of the firms generated new clients whose *first awareness of their firms was the firms' Web sites.*
- More than two-thirds of your potential clients expect to find your firm online, according to the 2003 Pew Internet and American Life Project.
- According to Jupiter Research, 63 percent of Americans use Internet research services online.
- The average amount of time online increased nearly 20 percent from 2000 to 2002, according to the 2003 UCLA Internet Project.
- Internet access spans every age range and, in some age ranges, approaches 100 percent.
- Internet usage among those over sixty-five years of age increased 17 percent from 2000 to 2002, according to the 2003 UCLA Internet Project.

- In 2002, more than 71 percent of Americans used the Internet, according to the 2003 UCLA Internet Project.

Clients Are Online, Too

Online marketing is more important than ever. According to Steve Noel, Director of Production for FindLaw.com, the nation's number-one law-related Web site:

- Corporate counsel spend over half their time during the week working at computers.
- Over 50 percent of corporate counsel visit Internet portals at least once a day.
- Over 35 percent of corporate counsel use free Internet sites as their first legal research destinations.

According to 2003 statistics released by the ABA Legal Technology Resource Center, 95 percent of all law firms with 50 or more lawyers have Web sites. The laggards are smaller firms: only 29 percent of sole practitioners have Web sites, and only 56 percent of law firms with two to nine lawyers have Web sites.

Some Web sites are executed perfectly. Law firms realize that most general counsel and corporate executives will study a law firm's Web site before retaining the firm. But does every law firm apply this knowledge? Not very likely.

Many law firms have done just the opposite. They've put up Web sites that spool out yards of text obscuring what the firm does. They've launched distracting graphics to slow down the visitors. They've put up Web sites that get in the way of their marketing missions.

According to User Interface Engineering, Inc., the truth is that visitors cannot find the information they seek on Web sites about 60 percent of the time; Web sites are losing repeat visits from 40 percent of users, who do not return because their first visits were negative experiences.

This is a shame, because Web sites are so efficient. They are available around the clock, unlike the rest of your marketing materials. They don't involve printing or postage costs, unlike printed newsletters. You can measure how many people looked at your Web site, unlike regular advertising. A good Web site is the best marketing investment your law firm can make.

What Clients Seek

The best clients are repeat customers, and therefore businesses make the best clients. Corporate executives and in-house counsel look for three things when they visit a law firm Web site:

1. Experience with a particular industry.
2. Representative clients.
3. Success stories.

The problem is that most Web sites are firm-centric. The typical law firm Web site shows the law firm talking about itself—listing its practice descriptions, giving a firm history, or displaying a glowing self-description. This isn't what visitors want, and the site should be built around what clients want to see.

One of the most important points of information that a law firm can put on its Web site is a list of industries it serves. Industry experience is one of the first things corporate executives and in-house counsel look for. They want to know if the lawyers are familiar with the trends affecting their businesses, and smart law firms put this information right up front. Think about it: when your firm is choosing among vendors, you inquire about whether the vendors have experience with the legal profession and can list other law firms as references. Corporations vet law firms in the same fashion.

A link to "Industries Served" should be on the home page. Don't hide it on the back pages, because industry representation is a key selling point. This takes advantage of the way clients and prospective clients think. Clients see themselves as being part of an industry. They do not view themselves as clients of a practice group. They also see their cases as business problems, not legal matters.

Examples of firms large and small that describe their industry experience effectively include the following:

- Miller Faucher & Cafferty, an 18-lawyer plaintiff class-action law firm in Chicago, **www.millerfaucher.com**, lists an even dozen industries in which it has experience.
- Reed Smith, **www.reedsmith.com**, emphasizes the financial services, health care, and technology industries. Each industry-focus page lists statistics, clients, publicity, and case examples.
- Stoel Rives, a firm with 375 lawyers and offices in Oregon, Washington, and elsewhere lists 18 industries it serves, from agriculture to winery management, at **www.stoel.com**.
- Kennedy Covington, with 165 lawyers in Charlotte and the Carolinas, lists 13 industries served at **www.kennedycovington.com**.
- Miller Nash, at **www.millernash.com**, a 50-lawyer firm with offices in Seattle, Portland, and Vancouver, serves 33 industries ranging from affordable housing to wholesalers.
- Womble Carlyle, with 470 lawyers based in Winston-Salem, and eight additional offices, has 12 industry groups ranging from bio-alliance to telecommunications listed at **www.wcsr.com**.

◆ Holland and Hart, at **www.hollandhart.com**, lists eight industries: broadband communications; construction and design; energy and electricity; health care; mining; oil and gas; skiing; and telecommunications.

An easy method to follow is to start with the firm's list of representative clients (or list of top 50 clients). Label each company according to the industry in which it is best known. You don't need to be precise in naming the industry, and you can use the categories found in the annual Fortune 500 listing or the *Wall Street Journal*'s regular reports on stocks. Once you've got all the clients labeled, sort them into industry categories and put the list on your Web site. You won't regret it.

Client List

In the old days, it was commonplace for firms to list representative clients in their directory listings. Somehow, this idea was never transferred to the Web, which is too bad. Perhaps it's because law firms fear that their competitors would poach their client lists, or that their clients would object for some reason. Whatever the reason, it is a marketing mistake to omit a list of representative clients on your Web site.

Buchanan Ingersoll, a Pittsburgh law firm, got the idea right. It lists 150 clients sorted into 17 industries at **www.bipc.com**. Equaling this is the Web site of a Denver law firm, Rothgerber Johnson & Lyons, which lists more than 100 clients online and sorts them according to areas of its practice, at **www.rothgerber.com**. Other examples include the following:

◆ Glenn H. Youngling, a sole practitioner serving homeowner associations, lists an incredible 87 clients on his Web site, at **www.youngling law.com/cid/assocclients.shtml**.

◆ Arnall, Golden, Gregory has a list of 30 clients at **www.agg.com**.

◆ Moore & VanAllen lists 65 clients at **www.mvalaw.com**.

◆ Drinker, Biddle & Reath lists 49 clients at **www.dbr.com**.

Success Stories

Law firm Web sites should showcase trial results and successful transactions that the firms accomplished for clients. They should be business stories, written in a journalistic style and described from the client's point of view. This is very effective marketing. For a good example of how this is done, see Client Successes on the Ballard Spahr Web site, at **www.ballardspahr.com**, where a visitor can find short stories about client work. These summaries can be expanded into detailed stories with photos. Additional law firms that list their clients include the following:

- Miller Faucher & Cafferty, with eighteen lawyers, lists more than two dozen success stories, each listing links to all the lawyers who worked on the cases.
- Manning Fulton, a thirty-two-lawyer firm in Raleigh, lists Client Stories as depicted in its advertising campaign featuring clients, including Carolantic Realty, Container Systems, Inc., Craig Davis Properties, Fonville Morisey, General Parts/CarQuest, Highwoods Properties, and Jordan Lumber and Supply at **www.mfslaw.com**.
- Sonsini Goodrich & Rosati has a client list by industry, client testimonials, and case studies at **www.wsgr.com**.
- The Law Offices of Ann Rankin, a homeowner association firm, lists numerous clients, situations, and results online at **www.annrankin.com/HOAcases.htm**.
- The Miller Law Firm, a homeowner association law firm in Newport Beach, lists verdicts and settlements online at **www.construction defects.com**.

Where Will Visitors Go?

Just as you don't need to clean out the garage when company comes for dinner, you don't need to rewrite every page of the site each month. Law firms should focus most of their attention upon the most frequently-visited pages of their Web sites. The identity of those pages can be found in the monthly Web site traffic reports that your Web host should provide.

In my consulting practice, I have reviewed dozens of law firm Web sites and traffic reports. Though no two sites are the same, I have discerned some patterns in where visitors go. The three top destinations ordinarily are these:

- Home page
- Lawyer bios
- Recruiting

All the other parts of the site—newsletters, events, press releases, articles, and practice descriptions—fall farther down the list.

Home Page

This page is the firm's face to the world, and is online twenty-four hours a day. The home page is the firm's only chance to make a good first impression, to interest visitors in staying on the site, and to entice them to return. This page should look professionally designed, not homemade. It should have fewer than ten well-chosen links; most law firms make the mistake of presenting too many options. And the entire home page should fit on one screen, with the resolution set at 1024 x 768 pixels. Visitors are unlikely to scroll down a home page to find more information.

If you have an old-style Web page that uses frames, now is the time to change it. Two years ago, framesets were widely adopted by law firms, but they create three important problems for Web sites. First, they confuse search engines and prevent them from indexing your site. Second, they make it difficult to bookmark or send a link to a page to a colleague, because the link will go to the home page frame, not the particular page you were viewing. Finally, Web sites in frames don't print properly; the displayed content breaks apart, and some pages won't print at all.

Lawyer Bios

Remember that clients hire lawyers, not law firms, so pay special attention to the lawyer bios. It makes a difference how you present yourself—in person and online. Lawyers usually make sure that they have a businesslike appearance, that their stationery reflects their firms, and that their business cards include all key contact information. Lawyers should also devote the same attention to online bios.

The human face of the law firm makes a difference in attracting new business. Your Web bio is your initial introduction to visitors, and, unlike random social contacts, you have total control over what you present in your online bio. Exercise this control so that your bio contains the following key items:

- *The Essentials*: Include a recent color photo, a list of the industries you represent, and representative clients.
- *Business Memberships*: It is important to list your board memberships and trade association memberships (but *not* law organizations; see note below).
- *Articles Available on the Web Site*: Provide links to any articles you wrote that you list on the firm's site. Visitors expect your Web site to be interactive; if the article isn't available on the Web site, it's much less impressive.

Here are some items that are considered boilerplate, and not particularly important in a lawyer's bio:

- *Law School Attended*: This may interest opposing lawyers who are profiling you, but it is not especially interesting to clients. They are not familiar with the comparative reputations of law schools, and consider lawyers' school records to be ancient history.

- ◆ *Bar Association Memberships*: This information is too "inside law" for clients to care about. They can't distinguish between a mandatory and voluntary bar, and it doesn't matter to them, anyway. Clients view bar memberships as lawyers talking among themselves.
- ◆ *Anything Old*: Don't clog your online bio with a collection of speeches, memberships, and articles you presented more than two years ago. A Web site is supposed to inform visitors about what you're doing right now, not archive what happened a long time ago.

Recruiting

Some law firms put too much emphasis on this page, and create jazzy, hip recruiting sections that diverge wildly from the "main site." This is a mistake, because students will see the staid "main site" and simply remember the difference. Some firms put too little emphasis on the recruiting page, leaving off the name of a contact person or the recruiting schedule. The firms that get it just right include their NALP forms, discuss what it's like to work at their firms, and describe their summer programs.

The point to remember is that a law firm should emphasize the areas that visitors seek most. Ask not what your law firm wants to say about itself; ask instead what your visitors want to find on your Web site.

Best Practices in Web Marketing

1. Start Writing a Blog

America became familiar with blogs, which is short for Web logs, during the Gulf War, when readers would go online to follow the experiences recorded in blogs of participants at the front. A blog is an online diary, which displays the writer's entries in chronological order. There are 9 million blogs as of May 2005, but only a paltry 750 lawyer blogs.

Blogs are the perfect platform for lawyers who always wanted to be newspaper columnists, or who want to publish short capsules of thought without needing to write full-blown articles. You simply jot down your thoughts or observations and publish them instantly to the Web. The beauty of blogging software is that it requires no knowledge of HTML—you simply type text in an online box and click "publish." What's more, blogging is free. Just go to **www.blogger.com** and register to establish an account; you can be blogging within minutes. I created the Professional Marketing Blog that you can find at **http://blog.LarryBodine.com.**

Your readers can find your blog by searching for you in Google. Web search engines are always looking for new material, and thus blogs come to the top of many online searches. Some of the better-known legal blogs are written by Howard Bashman, head of Buchanan Ingersoll's appellate practice. He writes a blog on appellate law that gets 50,000 page views a month, including by appellate court judges. Bashman once spotted an error in an opinion and the judge read his blog and corrected the opinion the same day. Another well-known blogger is Ernest Svenson, the tech partner at Gordon Arata in New Orleans. His blog got more than 100,000 page views in its first year, and is quoted in MSNC, the *ABA Journal*, and numerous other publications. Among the blogs I like to follow are those of Andy Havens, and Jerry Lawson, president of NetLawTools, at **www.netlawblog.com**.

2. Optimize Your Web Site for Search Engines

It's no good having a Web site if no one can find it. You need to tune up your site with elements that Google, Yahoo!, and other search vehicles seek.

Nothing beats hot, fresh content. Search engines primarily look for frequently updated information. Web sites are supposed to be showcases for new information, not archives of past newsletters and old events, so you should update your site often. Take a look at your Web traffic statistics to see how many referrals you're getting from search engines now; if Google and Yahoo! are not the top two referral sources, you need to put some new content online.

Also take note in your traffic logs of the terms that people are using to find your site. Take the most frequently used terms and make sure they appear in the material you put online. You should also add this information in your invisible metatags on the home page, and, importantly, in the title tags. The information in these tags is not displayed to visitors, but it is directly sought by search engines.

Several things can deflect search engines and send their roving "spiders" away, so eliminate these offensive items from your Web site. Topping the list are Flash animation, JavaScript, and frames; they provide nothing for search engines to index, and they'll lower your search engine rankings. Instead, put a lot of text on your Web site—this is the fodder the hungry spiders want.

"Link popularity" helps raise you in the rankings, too. This refers to the number of other sites that have links to your site; search engines consider these as votes for your site's popularity. You can tell how many sites link to your site by going to **www.alltheweb.com**, typing your URL in the search box, and checking the results. The more links, the better. The way to boost your link popularity is by putting your content on other people's Web sites. Do this by writing articles for other Web sites, freely granting reprints, and getting involved with newspaper Web sites.

3. Follow Web site Usability Norms on the Web

Your Web site should use a layout that visitors expect to see. Many law firms experiment with cluttered, busy, or unconventional layouts. They succeed in looking different, but they make the Web site difficult to use.

According to Web site usability principles, your site should mimic the layouts of popular corporate sites that viewers visit frequently. This way, they will be accustomed to the layout of your site from the moment they arrive. Do the following to achieve the optimal layout for your Web site:

- ◆ *Logo Placement*: Put your logo or firm name in the top left corner. This is where people start reading a book or newspaper, and where they start reading on your Web site.
- ◆ *Navigation Choices*: Offer a set of navigation choices down the left side and across the top of the page. These choices should be "persistent"; that is, they should also appear in the same place on all succeeding pages of the site.
- ◆ *Content*: Make sure the rest of the page—the lower right part—is full of content. This is where you should put news items, newsletter stories, and client successes.

4. Let Visitors Sign Up to Get an E-Newsletter on Your Web Site

Some sophisticated sites, like that of Hale and Dorr at **www.haledorr.com**, allow readers to pick from more than thirty-five newsletters with the ease of checking a box in the sign-up form. The approach has met with great success for firms like Baker & McKenzie, which distributes its Global E-Law Alert to more than 30,000 readers.

A few years ago, I started my own e-letter, the LawMarketing Newsletter, and have built the recipient list to 4,500 names. Twice a month, I send my newsletter via e-mail message to readers all over the world and use it to promote new articles on the PM Forum Web site (**www.PMForumNA.org**), Webinars that I present, my consulting practice, and advertising messages. It's a one-to-one, personal communication with each reader.

Sending e-mail newsletters is a tactic that many law firms have adopted. For starters, many firms have print newsletters, and it's easy to "re-purpose" them for electronic distribution. The beauty of e-mail newsletters is that they do not entail any printing or postage costs; they are inexpensive to create and distribute. If you send e-mail newsletters, be sure to note that readers may "freely redistribute the newsletter in whole," which will widen your audience.

E-mail newsletters also allow you to collect information about who is visiting your Web site. I recommend that home pages for law firm Web sites include links to newsletter sign-up pages. A link should lead to a sign-up form, which requests the reader's name, title, company, mailing address, e-mail address, and phone number. Ideally, this information will be saved in a database, which can be used to distribute the newsletter.

5. Send the E-Newsletter in HMTL Format

HTML newsletters are like sending readers a Web site—all the firm's graphics, color, and branding are preserved in the newsletter. Sophisticated firms like

Benesch, Friedlander, Coplan & Aronoff in Cleveland make sure the newsletter looks exactly like the firm's Web site and includes links to the site.

The hidden beauty of HTML newsletters is that they are trackable. Whenever a reader opens the e-mail message or clicks on one of the links in the newsletter, it leaves an electronic marker that can be counted. This way you know exactly how many people actually read the newsletter and which items they prefer.

HTML newsletters are for small, as well as large, law firms. Lorne MacLean, one of western Canada's most experienced family law lawyers, wanted to upgrade his clientele. As part of an overall marketing campaign, he put a newsletter sign-up page on his Web site, at **www.bcfamilylaw.ca**. The HTML newsletter was created by eLawMarketing.com at **www.elawmarketing .com**. MacLean touched a nerve—it turns out a lot of people are interested in family law issues. Readers get a newsletter with links to articles such as, "Family Trusts—How to Attack or Defend Them in Divorce Proceedings," which are displayed on his Web site. The campaign increased his profitability by 200 percent, won a national marketing award, and gave him enough new business to hire two associates.

6. Avoid Content Mistakes

Certain things appear on many law firm Web sites, mainly because the firms want to put them there, but not because visitors want to read them. Again, turn to your Web traffic reports and see what people are reading. Among the things that clients and potential clients **don't care** about and don't want to read are the following:

◆ *Welcome from the Managing Partner.* This is regarded as "happy talk" that adds nothing to a site visit. It contains the firm's mission, the high principles to which the firm adheres, and a lot of other material no one cares about. It's a holdover from the early days of the Web (way back in 1996) when people thought it was necessary to explain what was being viewed.

◆ *Firm History:* Typically this is illustrated with sepia-toned photos of Model T cars and views of Main Street before it was paved. The firm history starts with Lawyer A, a white male who was probably the commander of the local fort. One day he met Lawyer B, who represented the general store, and they founded the law firm. Lo, these many years later, the firm is still here. All law firm histories are the same, and few visitors want to read them.

◆ *Links Page:* Another holdover from the early days of the Web are the pages that link to other sites. This is a mistake, because all it does it take traffic away from your site. Further, it assumes visitors will use the law firm site to conduct research. This is usually not the case, because visitors use travel and chamber of commerce sites to learn about the locale and go to Westlaw and Lexis for legal research.

7. Become a Content Provider for AvantGo

AvantGo is a medium that allows users of personal digital assistants (PDAs) or Web-enabled telephones to see your Web content. For readers, AvantGo is a free service that allows them to read the *New York Times*, Yahoo!, and Web sites like the LawMarketing Portal on their handheld devices.

I've been an AvantGo channel provider for several years and use it as a fast-growing way to reach high-tech readers. For example, in January 2001, I had only 348 AvantGo subscribers, which grew to 882 in January 2002, and is 2,360 as of May 2005.

The content is a stripped-down version of what a firm currently presents on a Web site, deleting the graphics, links, and a lot of the formatting. This makes viewing easier on the small screen and low-bandwidth connection speeds of handheld devices. Subscribers sign up by visiting **www.avantgo.com** and downloading software to make the channel viewable.

AvantGo has the largest mobile audience, with eight million registered users worldwide. An AvantGo channel can be used for direct marketing, client relationship management, or e-commerce. Companies like GM, American Airlines, and Microsoft provide content channels. Among the law firms is Alschuler Grossman Stein & Kahan, a one-hundred-lawyer firm in Santa Monica, which created its AvantGo channel in 2000. "We want our content to be available to anyone, in any way they want to find us," said Andrea Hodges, the firm's director of marketing. "We do a lot of litigation and transactions that are Internet-related," she said.

Worst Practices in Web Marketing

Many law firm Web sites don't follow the rules of Web site usability. Ignoring marketing rules, many law firm sites don't display the things that clients want to see. Poorly done law firm Web sites never result in new business.

The 2003 TouchPoint Metrics Report identified "worst practices" committed online by law firms. I've added a few of my own to this "parade of horribles"—take careful note and make certain you avoid these mistakes on your Web site.

1. No Indication That the Site Is Operated by a Law Firm

TouchPoint Metrics thoroughly studied the Web sites of thirty leading law firms and, in July 2003, released a report, "Best Practice in Legal Marketing: Effective Use of Web Sites." According to TouchPoint's president, Hank Brigman, "The firm's Web site is a key tool that can either help or hinder a prospect's progress as they make decisions about their relationship with your firm." The worst practice his researchers found was a lack of identification on the home page that the site belonged to a law firm. If buyers can't tell what kind of store they are in, they are unlikely to buy anything.

2. No Articles or White Papers

TouchPoint Metrics interviewed the marketing executives at the firms whose Web sites they studied. The marketers reported that articles and white papers written by their firms' lawyers helped generate Web site traffic that resulted in new clients. Obviously, then, any failure to have the catalyst that makes customers buy is a major flaw on a law firm Web site.

3. No Connection with Firm's Other Marketing Efforts

TouchPoint Metrics found that a firm's Web site offers an excellent opportunity to brand and position the firm. The addition of tag lines, coupled with content that describes the firm's unique selling proposition, is another area of opportunity. Having a "stand-alone" Web site that does not relate to printed marketing collateral or carry the firm's marketing message is a missed opportunity.

4. Saying You Are a Full-Service Firm

Let's be honest here—there are probably only a hundred law firms in the United States that are truly full-service firms that can handle every matter companies or individuals throw at them. Yet many firms claim to be "full-service" firms, and it hurts them, because, in my opinion, buyers of legal services interpret the phrase to mean "all-purpose firm." What clients really want are lawyers who are **experts** at solving the clients' particular problems. Accordingly, it's better to describe the aspects of your firm that make it unique, not what it does in general.

5. Displaying a Cheap-Looking Site

Examples include sites with a lot of clip art, and those with homemade looks and navigation systems. TouchPoint Metrics found that the average cost of a Web site redesign was $21,500 for a small firm, $33,000 for a midsize firm, and $111,667 for a large firm. This is a lot of money. But, remember, your Web site is a very public presence that runs 24/7/365. Don't use it as a place to save money.

6. Having a Client Develop Your Site

In my experience, this is always a big mistake. A partner may think he or she is doing the client a favor by giving the client a project, or that the law firm will save money in the process. This rarely turns out to be the case. Instead, both parties eventually find themselves in an uncomfortable situation where the law firm is not happy with the client's work. I've seen cases where the law firm had to fire the developer, and lost a client in the process. My recommendation is to bid out the development work, and choose a Web supplier who has no entanglements with the firm.

7. Hiring a Web Developer with No Experience with the Legal Profession

It really is true: law firms are different from other businesses. Law firms are not at all like most wild-and-wooly ventures that want to go online. Lawyers must abide by mandatory ethics provisions and use many precise terms of art. Law firms generally are risk-averse, precedent-driven, and uncomfortable with marketing (which is not taught in law school). They make decisions based upon consensus, not by order of a CEO. Lawyers have unique personalities—they are typically smart, uncomfortable with graphics concepts, and happy with miles of text. These are not the personality traits that add up to successful experiences for uninitiated Web developers.

8. Using Generic Content

By this I mean boilerplate like "We pursue traditions of excellence," or "We adhere to the highest ethical standards," or "We hire the brightest students from the best law schools." The TouchPoint Metrics report charitably refers to this meaningless blather as "broadly descriptive content." Law firms should display their industry experience, list of representative clients, and matter-specific success stories. According to the report, "There is a key opportunity for firms to present matter-specific content, especially articles and white papers."

9. Displaying a Confusing Layout

Examples of this mistake include using yards of text, too many graphics, Flash or other animated graphics, elements that require a software download, and words that are themselves graphics. All these mistakes violate the rules of usability, which hold that visitors should be able to find what they want on a Web site without needing a set of instructions on how to use it.

10. Having No Extranet

Extranets are a "hot topic," according to the TouchPoint Metrics report, which states that "they present an online opportunity for law firms to enhance client services. Failure to offer clients a password-protected extranet is a missed chance to deepen relationships with clients." The report also states that when asked about their wish lists for Web sites, fifteen of seventeen marketing executives without extranets said they wanted to add this service.

Homework: How to Get Found Online

Let me conclude by giving you three items of homework for getting found on the Web. It involves the number-one search engine on the Web: Google. You are being Googled by your colleagues, employees, and competitors. More importantly, your clients and prospective clients are Googling you to confirm their decisions to retain you. They will certainly Google you before they call or ask for your brochure.

Google handles 200 million searches of the Web each day, a staggering one-third of the estimated daily total. More people are going online to find law firms. So you have to ask yourself: What will clients and prospective clients find when they Google me? Let's analyze this, step by step.

Google Yourself

Go to **www.Google.com** and type your own name in the search box. The worst thing that can happen is that you turn up nothing. This means you are invisible on the Web. Nowadays, many people use the Web instead of phone books to find phone numbers and addresses, so to be missing on the Web is a truly notable absence.

The best thing you can hope for is that a Google search finds substantive articles you've written for other Web sites. With good luck, there will be a link leading to one of your public appearances or an announcement of a seminar where you are a panelist. Ideally, the top link will lead to your biography, listing your extensive legal experience, examples of matters successfully handled, and well-known clients you have represented.

I Googled myself and found my Web page for my consulting practice, as well as several articles I've written for other Web sites. This was good. Amusingly, I also found a retired gentleman with exactly the same name as me living in Hays, Kansas. He's got a Web site about the town and its service organizations. It's surprising what you'll find on the Web.

The point is that you should start writing articles for Web sites and publications that have an online presence, so that searchers can find you. For starters, put your articles, speeches, and public appearances on your own firm's Web site. Then offer the material for publication on someone else's Web site. Editors of trade, industry, and association Web sites are often hunting for fresh content and may have opportunities to publish you online.

You should also beef up your bio on the Web. Make it easy for people to reach you by including all your contact information, including your land address, e-mail address, phone number, and a nice color photo. Surprisingly, some lawyer bios omit this key information. Your address and phone number may be somewhere on the firm's site, but make sure they appear in your bio.

Google Your Firm

Let's act as if you were a client or curious prospect, and Google your firm. If you have a Web site and you type the exact name of your firm, chances are it will be the top item in the roster of choices. This, of course, assumes that the Googler already knows your firm name, remembers how to spell it, and is looking for it in the first place.

So let's make the test more realistic, and not use the name of your firm. Why don't we type in "lawyer," an industry like "manufacturing," and a city like "Chicago." Does your firm appear in the first ten links? If not, you're going to be pretty hard to find.

What you *will* find is a list of firms that have put a lot of content on their sites and updated it frequently. "Search engines are now looking for Web pages with good content," writes Dr. Ralph F. Wilson in his newsletter, *Dr. EBiz.* "Make sure your important keywords appear in the title tag, headings, hyperlinked words, and your body text, especially in the first sentence or paragraph."

You might argue that it's "not fair" to Google a firm based upon an industry and a city. Thinking like a lawyer, you might feel it is more appropriate to search by area of law. After all, most law firms are organized by practice area. But remember, that's not the way clients think: they see themselves as members of industries, and they view their matters as business problems.

Google Your Competition

Now let's conduct some competitive intelligence: Google a competing law firm. Search for it the same way we did before—type in the exact name and see what happens. Does the firm come to the top of the list? Next, type in a few terms that the firm is known for—such as the names of its well-known lawyers or the clients it represents. Does this make its Web site pop to the top?

"Link popularity (the number of incoming links to your site) makes a lot of difference, too, especially with Google," Dr. Wilson notes. In other words, the more other sites link to your firm's site, the better. This alone is an incentive to put your articles on other Web sites, especially if there is a link back to your site.

More people are checking up on others by Googling them. Get yourself ready for when others Google you.

The Ins and Outs of Blogs   **48**

Richard P. Klau

In the early days of the Web, to admit to a personal Web site was to invite any number of groans. Personal Web pages were the antithesis of the Shoeless Joe mantra, "If you build it, they will come." People built them, and if everyone else knew what was good for them, they stayed away. In droves.

That has all changed, thanks to a relatively new concept called a Web log. In truth, Web logs (also known as blogs) have been around in one form or another since the late 1990s. But thanks to a veritable explosion of easy-to-use, inexpensive applications, Web logs have gone mainstream. Professional Web sites, no longer groan-inducing vanity presses, are now legitimate. Rather remarkably, blogs are proving to be excellent marketing vehicles for lawyers at large and small firms alike.

What distinguishes blogs from traditional Web sites? A few characteristics are common to most:

- Frequently updated content
- Chronologically organized posts
- Posts containing links to news items, other blogs, or Web sites of interest, along with comments about the linked item

Successful blogs focus upon particular topics or subjects and are updated frequently (at least several times a week, if not daily). Most blogs are run by individuals and often espouse the opinions of the authors. The advantage is that readers get a feel for a blog owner's point of view—and often form stronger bonds with that individual than they would with a more "corporate" site, where the company message trumps that of particular individuals.

A challenge in maintaining any Web site is adding content with as little effort as possible. Although tools like Microsoft FrontPage made the design of Web sites easier, they did not make the addition of new content simple. The result? Sites looked good, but nevertheless required effort and experience with HTML programming on the part of the site owner to keep the site current, which, in turn, resulted in stale sites that did not get updated nearly often enough. Blogs simplify this. Blogs are designed to publish content to the Web effortlessly, so the only thing you need to worry about is what to say. Everything else—formatting, uploading of the content, and linking of all the items—is taken care of by the particular application.

Before you get concerned that this sounds like it's adding yet another task to your already full schedule, don't worry. The whole goal of Web log software is to make updating your Web site as simple as sending an e-mail message. In fact, if you can make just one salient observation about your area of practice each day, you have the makings of an all-star "blogger."

What's a Web Log?

The terms Web log and blog refer to any Web site produced using Web log software. As noted above, Web logs are typically characterized by frequently updated content, links to other sites, and mostly short observations about a variety of topics. Unlike structured Web sites, which have certain formats and are often designed to be navigated from beginning to end, Web logs are akin to journals, where authors write their thoughts. As a result, Web logs are ordered by date, category (many Web log applications let you categorize your posts), or both.

Web logs that generate a fair amount of traffic often have a focus, such as appellate law, litigation techniques, or intellectual property law. At the same time, a key advantage to Web logs is that they let authors have individual voices—it is not unusual for even the most focused Web log to cover tangential topics simply because the author found them interesting.

Web Logs as Marketing Vehicles

There is nothing about a Web log that makes it an inherently effective marketing tool. Much of the early press about Web strategies centered on the philosophy that "content is king"—but only now does that mantra hold true. Whereas countless hours can be spent overdesigning firm Web sites (with predictable results: sizzle and no substance, which fails to encourage repeat visitors), Web logs emphasize substance almost to the exclusion of style. Many Web logs are text-only endeavors, and even those that do incorporate graphics do so sparingly and retain a heavy emphasis upon text.

The effectiveness of Web logs as marketing vehicles stems from (1) the popularity Web logs enjoy with the leading search engine, Google, (2) the cross-linking nature of many Web logs, which drives traffic from one to another, and (3) the inherently personal nature of many Web logs, which encourages unique personalities to shine through in text, something that visitors like.

For a sole practitioner looking to establish a presence on the Internet, it's often nearly impossible to rise above the noise level and become "findable." Not only do larger firms have more resources at their disposal to focus upon their online marketing efforts, they've likely been at it longer than most solos. Web logs break through that barrier almost overnight, giving even individual voices the ability to be instant experts on key issues—establishing them as authoritative on topics that people searching on Google care about.

There are two ways to establish visibility at Google: you can pay to sponsor keyword searches (your ad will show up in a box to the right of search results) or you can be considered by Google to be the most relevant page for the term the searcher entered. Assuming that as a sole practitioner you're operating on a limited budget, we'll assume that the first option isn't an option, at least for the short term. Fortunately, that's okay. If you can make just a few interesting observations about a particular topic each week, you can create a Web log. And Google absolutely *adores* Web logs.

Google

Although Google keeps its search algorithm proprietary, several things are known about how it ranks pages for search results (items are placed in approximate order of importance):

1. *Your Site's Page Rank: Each Web site in Google's index has a numerical rank, on a scale of one to ten. The higher your Page Rank, the more authoritative Google considers you (and the more influential links from your site are).*
2. *Inbound Links*: The more links to a particular page, the more "votes" that page has.
3. *Link Titles*: The words others use to link to a page tells Google about the words that might be most important on that page, thereby helping it establish the relative importance of those terms in a search result.
4. *Text on the Page*: Google searches text for keywords.

Although Google doesn't publicize how it arrives at a Page Rank score for a Web site, it appears to be primarily a calculation of the currency of a site (how often it updates) and links from other sites (taking into account the Page Rank of those sites—the higher a Page Rank, the more that link counts). You can see your site's Page Rank by installing the Google Toolbar (**http://tool bar.google.com**) for Internet Explorer and visiting your site with the toolbar enabled. You will see a visual indicator that, if you position your mouse over the graphic, will give you the numerical score. Compare your Page Rank with those of your competitors. Then look at some Web logs. In many cases, Web logs enjoy Page Ranks two to three times higher than "traditional" Web sites.

How to Become an Expert

Simply put, the best way to get Google to give your pages high rank in search results is to have many other sites link to your pages using the same term. If one hundred sites link to your mesothelioma Web log with the words "mesothelioma news," then you will almost certainly be the number-one search result for "mesothelioma news."

How can Web logs help address this? Web logs encourage linkable content. Each post becomes a separate Web page, and others who maintain other Web logs and see something they want to pass along to their readers can link to that individual page. Google interprets that link as a "vote" in favor of that page—the more votes, the more important Google decides the linked page is.

These conversations are the hallmark of the Web log community. Conversations develop about an item originally spotted on Web log A, Web log B links to Web log A and adds its own commentary, and then Web log C links to both A and B and adds even more information. Each link is a vote—and the more links you get, the more important your comments are considered. (As an aside, you may have heard that some have tried to take advantage of Google's system by influencing Google's rankings. It started as a prank: Someone got all his friends to link to his pal Andy's Web site using the words "talentless hack" as the link title; Google ultimately decided that the authority on talentless hacks must be this guy, Andy. More recently, it's been used politically: Opponents of presidential candidate John Kerry linked by the dozens to his campaign's Web site using the term "waffles"—making Kerry's site the number-one result for "waffles." Not to be outdone, Bush opponents around the world linked to a humorous fake error page using the words "weapons of mass destruction." Now when you search Google for "weapons of mass destruction," you get a cleverly worded error page that tweaks President Bush's WMD claims. This is known as "Google-bombing" when done in a concentrated fashion to appropriate a search term.)

No matter how compelling your law firm Web site may be, there are probably not many inbound links to your content from other sites. That is not a criticism of your site, but a reflection of the fact that even the most dynamically updated site is geared more for casual visitors than for people who maintain their own Web sites. As a result, though Google will index content at your Web site, it will view the content as being of relatively low importance, given the number of inbound links. Jerry Lawson, author of the ABA publication, *The Complete Internet Handbook for Lawyers*, compared the inbound links at several large-firm Web sites with those of a single lawyer, Ernest Svenson (publisher of the popular Web log, "Ernie the Attorney," at **www.erniethe attorney.net**). Inbound links to Svenson's site were as much as ten times higher than those of many other sites. In particular, Svenson's blog is ranked higher on search terms than Skadden Arp's site. The result of this is that searches for terms on Svenson's site will often appear more frequently in the top ten than similar searches for terms at Skadden's site.

If you view your Web log as a public relations campaign, one way you would measure the effectiveness of the campaign would be to evaluate the reach of the Web log. Though any given Web log might have just a handful of regular readers (most individual-lawyer Web logs have several dozen to several hundred regular readers), its reach expands geometrically as a result of Google's distribution. If the Web log covers popular, current topics, its author can expect hundreds of additional visitors *per day* simply by writing about issues in his or her area of expertise. Multiplied across numerous individuals in a law firm, the effect could be dramatic.

Any individual seeking to establish expertise in a particular area will find no better way to do so than by using a blog. Google will update its index of your site each day: type something in your blog today, and anyone searching for that topic at Google tomorrow will see your blog. In many cases, it will be one of the top-ten search results. The more focused your area of interest, the more likely Google will steer more visitors your way. (Incidentally, these tips are equally applicable if you choose to maintain your Web site manually instead of using a Web log application. The advantages of using a Web log application are ease of use and speed of publication.)

Your Web Log

How to Get Started with a Blog

Web log applications come in two flavors: those you install (either on your own PC or on your Web server) and those you "rent."

- *Installed Software—Movable Type*: Of the current crop of software available to install on your own machine, the most popular candidate is called Movable Type (**www.movabletype.com**). Movable Type runs on a Web server, and installation and configuration takes some advanced understanding of Web software.

Movable Type was formerly free to use, but with the release of version 3.0, it has a variable pricing model based upon the number of Web logs and the number of authors. If you are a relatively skilled user (meaning you understand FTP, can edit configuration files, and have a basic grasp of Web-based databases like mySQL), then Movable Type is a great choice for you. It is a very powerful application, giving you the ability not only to manage your Web log, but also to manage the "static" portions of your site. (Erik Heels, a Massachusetts patent lawyer, manages his entire Web site from within Movable Type.)

◆ *Rented Software—TypePad*: Made by the same company that makes Movable Type, TypePad is a hosted service that you pay for each month. (Prices start at $5 per month and include hosting.) TypePad is extremely user-friendly, and was designed with beginners in mind. That said, it's found considerable uptake among power users, as it sports some of the same extensibility of Movable Type and has some innovative features of its own.

◆ *Free Software—Blogger*: In 2003, Google bought a small San Francisco company called Pyra Labs; Pyra had created a Web site called Blogger, the site widely credited with increasing the popularity of Web logs among nontechnical users. Recently upgraded, Blogger is an extremely user-friendly application that works well for those looking for basic Web log functionality. Blogger is free to use, making it a terrific option for those on a tight budget.

Whatever Web log application you use, you should have the option to publish your blog to a domain name owned by the Web log application company or at your own domain. (TypePad blogs are often hosted at http://your-Weblogname.typepad.com; Blogger blogs are often hosted at http://yourWeblogname.blogspot.com.) Whatever you do, you should absolutely *not* publish at a domain not under your control. Not only is there a marketing advantage to reinforcing your domain name with your Web log, but, as a professional, you should not put yourself at the mercy of a company that may decide to change its business model (or go out of business altogether). For consistency's sake, publish your Web log at your domain. That way, should you need to change Web log applications for any reason, you can continue publishing at the same location instead of needing to switch domain names, as well as applications.

What to Say on Your Blog

Knowing that you want to *start* a Web log does not answer questions about what to *say* on the Web log. There is no magic or single method for maintaining a Web log; posts can be brief, include long commentary, or simply point to an interesting link somewhere else. Focus upon your area of interest and write about that. Spend some time following other Web logs to get a sense of their styles; after a while, you will find a format that feels comfortable for you. Following are some examples of Web logs that cover a range of styles:

- *Ernie the Attorney*: Author Ernest Svenson is a technology partner at Gordon Arata McCollam Duplantis & Eagan, a midsize New Orleans law firm. He writes primarily about law practice, law technology, and a variety of technology-related issues (**www.ernietheattorney.net**).
- *Bag & Baggage*: Maintained by Reed Smith appellate lawyer Denise Howell, this Web log focuses upon a wide range of legal and technology issues, with occasional forays into many other topics (**www.bag andbaggage.com**).
- *SCOTUS Blog*: A blog maintained by the D.C. law firm of Goldstein & Howe, this focuses exclusively upon each Supreme Court term and the cases heard, and has some of the most current and detailed information about the Court (**www.goldsteinhowe.com/blog**).
- *Overlawyered*: Walter Olson (who frequently appears on National Public Radio, *Crossfire*, *MacNeil-Lehrer*, and other media outlets and programs) chronicles the litigiousness of American society on this Web log, often with witty comments about unnecessary litigation. This is a good example of an expert's commentary coupled with a very personal point of view (**www.overlawyered.com**).
- *How Appealing*: One of the most popular legal Web logs, How Appealing is maintained by sole practitioner Howard Bashman. Focusing entirely upon appellate case law, Bashman provides in-depth commentary as only an expert could (**www.appellateblog.com**). Interestingly, Bashman's blog became so popular that it is now published by *Legal Affairs* magazine.
- *The Trademark Blog*: Maintained by New York City patent lawyer Martin Schwimmer, The Trademark Blog is a fantastic resource for anyone interested in trademark law. Frequently updated with news of trademark disputes, new decisions published on trademark-related issues, and trends for trademark owners, The Trademark Blog is a fantastic example of how a blog can instantly cement its author as an expert in a particular area of law (**http://trademark.blog.us**).
- *Professional Marketing Blog*: This blog is operated by Larry Bodine, a Chicago marketer and the Regional Director of PM Forum, an organization of law marketers. Larry reports from the conferences he attends, reports news in the marketing field, and offers opinions on what works in promoting a professional practice (**http://blog.LarryBodine.com**).

Publicizing Your Blog

Once you start your Web log, you must let people know about it. Start by telling other bloggers about your site. If you read some blogs today, send the site owners e-mail messages and let them know about your site. If they are interested, they will tell their readers and include links to your site. Several people—most notably Denise Howell (**www.bagandbaggage.com**) and Ernest Svenson (**www.ernietheattorney.net**)—maintain large directories of fellow lawyers who keep Web logs. Getting included in their directories is a good way to announce to the broader community that you have a site. Another good tactic for attracting readers is, oddly enough, to link to other sites whose focus mirrors your own. Because most bloggers monitor traffic to *their* sites, they will see the incoming links from your site. And they will often return the favor by sending readers your way.

Linking to Other Sites—Keeping a "Blogroll"

You will notice that many Web logs link to other sites, both in the content of the posts to the blog and in the site margins. The links in the margins—popularly referred to as blogrolls—offer your visitors a chance to see which other sites you find interesting or informative. It is also a way to reward other bloggers for keeping good sites by sending traffic their way.

If you know a little HTML, you can always maintain the list of links yourself; if you do not, you can use a third-party system like BlogRolling (**www.blogrolling.com**) to keep track of sites you think are worth mentioning. BlogRolling includes nice features such as noting when sites on your list update, so visitors to your site can get a visual indication that there is new content at the sites you think are worth visiting.

To find sites worth linking to, consider visiting a few of the largest directories of law blogs, also known as blawgs:

- Denise and Ernie's directories, already mentioned above (**www.ernietheattorney.net and www. bagandbaggage.com**)
- Detod, a company with a terrific directory of blawgs (**http://blawgs.detod.com**)
- Daily Whirl, a collection of posts from more than one hundred blawgs, updated throughout the day (**www.dailywhirl.com**)
- The Blawg Ring, a list of blawgs that link to each other and allow visitors to navigate from one to the next (**www.geocities.com/blawgring**)

Final Tips for Getting the Most out of Your Web Log

- *Make It Interactive*: Fans of the book, *The Cluetrain Manifesto*, by Rick Levine, Christopher Locke, Doc Searls, and David Weinberger, published by Perseus Books in December 1999, will remember that marketing is a conversation. To take advantage of a Web log as a marketing tool, you should encourage conversation on the site. Let readers leave comments, and engage your readers in dialogue. (The book is available online for free: **www.cluetrainmanifesto.com**. Incidentally, all four coauthors maintain their own Web logs.)

◆ *Change the Content Regularly*: If you fail to update the site, readers will notice and Google will ultimately ignore you. The value of a blog is directly related to the currency of its posts.

◆ *Reciprocate When Someone Links to You*: It is standard practice among bloggers to reciprocate when someone links to them. Not only does this acknowledge a favor of someone steering traffic to you, it can genuinely aid readers of your site. If someone linked to you, presumably it is because you said something the reader found interesting. Chances are good that the reader focuses upon similar issues and may have content that is interesting to your other readers.

◆ *Track Your Readership*: Though your Web hosting provider might keep track of statistics, those statistics may be either too difficult to read or too cumbersome to access. Consider using a free service like SiteMeter (**www.sitemeter.com**) to let you track visitors in real time.

Good Ethics = Good Business | 49

William E. Hornsby, Jr.

When students study ethics or professional responsibility in law school, they may find the rules remote or abstract. However, when practitioners come face-to-face with dilemmas, they know those rules are words to live by. Failure to comply with the ethics rules can lead to suspension from practice or, in the most egregious situations, revocation of the lawyer's law license. Even an allegation of impropriety can be embarrassing and result in a loss of business.

This chapter examines some of the ethics rules that govern the conduct of lawyers, with a focus upon those that apply to client development. After a brief overview, the chapter discusses ethics rules that govern fee sharing, marketing, responsibility for the acts of others, and the use of technology. The chapter concludes with a look at some of the resources that are available when you have further questions about ethical conduct.

Please note that this material is not comprehensive. It is not designed to substitute for your responsibility to read, understand, and follow the rules of your jurisdiction. The goals here are to alert you to some of your obligations, analyze common areas of concern, and encourage you to embrace sound ethical decision making on your road to a successful practice.

Overview

Before examining some of the specific rules, you need to keep in mind the basics about legal ethics. When you were in law school, you probably studied the ABA Model Rules of Professional Conduct. The first thing to remember is that those Model Rules may not be in place where you practice. The ethics rules are adopted on a state-by-state basis. They are usually drafted by the state bar, which then petitions the state's highest court to adopt them. Although the bars seriously consider the ABA Model Rules, and most states have adopted most of their provisions, hardly any state has adopted all of them verbatim. The point is you must follow the rules of the jurisdictions where you are admitted and not the ABA Model Rules.

Second, it is important to realize that the rules are dynamic. They change from time to time. From 1997 to 2002, the ABA reexamined its Model Rules through an initiative known as Ethics 2000. As a result of a great deal of discussion and debate, the ABA amended many of its rules in 2002. Since then, it has encouraged the states to adopt those changes. A few states did so quickly, but others are more deliberate. The process of states reviewing, accepting, or rejecting provisions of the Ethics 2000 changes will take several years. In the meantime, states will adopt changes to their ethics rules for other reasons. Rules governing aspects of marketing are amended by the states frequently. Make sure you follow current rules.

As we examine the specific rules governing marketing, keep in mind that these rules have broad application. We commonly refer to the "advertising rules," but, in fact, the ethics rules cover advertising, solicitation, marketing, and even the law firm's name. And, as we will see, the rules can be very particular.

Sharing Fees

The state ethics rules address the division of fees between lawyers who are not affiliated with each other, as well as the limitations on fee sharing with nonlawyers and paying someone to recommend the lawyer's services.

Lawyers in solo and small-firm practices frequently refer cases to other lawyers and/or receive referrals from their colleagues, even though they have no formal affiliation. The ethics rules set permissible parameters for when fees are divided among the lawyers who make and receive referrals.

In an earlier version of the ABA Model Rules, known as the Model Code of Professional Responsibility, fees could be shared between lawyers who were not in the same law firm only if:

1. the client consented to the division,
2. the total fee was reasonable, and
3. the division was made "in proportion to the services performed." In other words, a lawyer could be compensated only for the extent of his or her services, but not for the referral.

A few states, such as Nebraska and Iowa, continue to have this restriction.

The vast majority of states have adopted Model Rule 1.5(e), which includes a very significant change to the previous rule. Though it continues to require that the client agree to the arrangement and that the total fee is reasonable, the rule no longer requires the division to be in proportion to the services provided by each lawyer. In lieu of a division based upon the percentage of work done by each lawyer, the more recent rule requires only that each lawyer continue to be responsible for the representation. In other words, lawyers may divide fair fees as they agree, if they trust each other enough to maintain responsibility for the case.

Ethics rules also prohibit lawyers from sharing fees with nonlawyers and from giving anyone anything of value for recommending the lawyer's services. As with many rules, there are some narrow exceptions to these prohibitions. For example, under ABA Model Rule 5.4, which is in effect in most states, a lawyer may include nonlawyer employees in compensation or retirement plans, even if the plans are based upon profit sharing.

Model Rule 7.2 is designed to prevent ambulance chasing, as it prohibits a lawyer from giving anyone anything of value for recommending the lawyer's services. Exceptions to the rule do permit lawyers to pay the reasonable costs of advertisements and the usual charges of legal service plans or not-for-profit or approved lawyer referral services. Nearly every state has a similar prohibition, but the wording of the exceptions varies from one jurisdiction to another. For example, in many states, a lawyer may pay the usual charges of a nonprofit referral service, but not of a for-profit service. Also, a few jurisdictions have concluded that the rule should not be read as an absolute bar against giving *anything* of value. Arizona, for example, has concluded that lawyers may give gifts of de minimus value, which it deems to be those worth less than $100.

Check for the specific language of the rules in your state that govern fee sharing. If you practice in a state that has adopted the format of the ABA Model Rules, take a look at Rules 1.5, 5.4, and 7.2.

Marketing

Although the state ethics rules governing legal services marketing vary considerably, the single common denominator is the prohibition against false and misleading communications. It should seem simple enough for a lawyer to avoid false advertising, but the breadth of the ethics rules is far greater than it may seem. Nearly all states have adopted the Model Rule standard for "false or misleading communications" before the changes made by the ABA in 2002. This version of Model Rule 7.1 included four types of communications that were deemed false or misleading.

First, a lawyer may not communicate in a way that is a "material misrepresentation" of the facts or law. This is a relatively easy standard that basically tells us not to lie. Here are a couple examples: If a lawyer has never tried a case, but shows a television commercial with the lawyer arguing in front of a jury, the ad is false and a material misrepresentation. If a lawyer earned a J.D. from a local law school, later attended a weekend seminar at Harvard, and then advertised that he or she was "Harvard-Trained," the representation would be misleading and a violation of this rule.

The second prohibition disallows a lawyer from "omitting a fact necessary to make a statement considered as a whole not materially misleading." If a lawyer advertises a contingency-fee case by stating "no recovery—no fee," and says nothing about court costs, but then charges the client for court costs, the ad is a violation of this rule. Clients are often not aware that fees and costs are different, and would expect from this ad that there was no financial obligation. It would also be a violation to include support staff on the firm's letterhead without some designation making it clear they are not lawyers.

The third prong of former Model Rule 7.1 prohibits communications that create unjustified expectations by a potential client. This rule is predicated upon the assumption that every legal matter is unique. Therefore, clients should not base their decisions about hiring a lawyer upon the outcomes of prior cases. To lead a potential client to believe that his or her case will be successful because the lawyer was able to achieve success for other clients creates this unjustified expectation. This rule limits the lawyer's use of testimonials. If the content of a testimonial goes to the outcome of a prior case, it is likely to create an unjustified expectation and be impermissible. On the other hand, a testimonial about the level of service or relationship with the lawyer is likely to be acceptable in most states.

The fourth prong of the false and misleading standard is one that prohibits the comparison of a lawyer's services to that of another lawyer unless the comparison is "factually substantiated." You can say your firm is the largest, but not the best. The rule requires lawyers to avoid marketing superlatives, such as "the best and the brightest," "top notch," or "experts." The rule encourages lawyers to present their credentials in ways that encourage the potential client to draw that conclusion, while it prohibits puffery.

As a result of Ethics 2000, ABA Model Rule 7.1 now relegates the third and fourth prongs to the comments of the rule and prohibits communications that would lead a reasonable person to form an unjustified expectation or conclude a comparison can be substantiated when it cannot be. In states where this provision is adopted, lawyers will have a little more latitude in their advertisements. Note that many states, however, have added items to the list of prohibited communications that are deemed false or misleading.

Housekeeping Rules

In addition to prohibiting false or misleading communications, the state rules include what may be called "housekeeping" rules. Under the older version of Model Rule 7.2, lawyers were required to retain copies of their ads and to list the name of a lawyer in the firm who was responsible for the content of the ad. The current version of Model Rule 7.2 omits the retention requirement and amends the obligation to list the name of a lawyer and allows the firm to substitute the name of the firm itself.

Most state rules have additional housekeeping provisions. For example, some require lawyers to submit copies of their ads for filing or screening. Some limit the use of dramatizations. Some states require lawyers to include specific disclaimers on their ads. The application of disclaimers can be a little tricky. Some disclaimers are required only under certain circumstances. For example, in Texas, if not all members of a firm are certified as specialists in a field of practice and the firm advertises that field, the firm must include a disclaimer that not all members of the firm are certified specialists. If the firm does not advertise that field, however, the disclaimer would not be required. Other states have disclaimers that must be included if the firm advertises costs. In a few states, rules require the lawyer to include disclaimers in all ads except those that limit copy to specified information. This is an example of a "safe harbor" provision. Be sure to check your state rules for disclaimer requirements and read through all the provisions to see if you qualify under a safe harbor.

Lawyers are frequently unclear about their rights and obligations when it comes to direct contact with prospective clients or solicitation. Sometimes lawyers believe that all types of solicitation are unethical. However, though states ban some forms of direct contact, other forms are permissible and common. States have a constitutional right to ban in-person solicitation and frequently do so for most, but not all, prospective clients. Under Model Rule 7.3, a lawyer may not solicit in person, through live telephone conversations, or through real-time electronic contacts, such as chat rooms, unless the prospective client is another lawyer, a close friend, a family member, or someone with whom the lawyer has a prior professional relationship, such as a prior client. Many states do not permit lawyers to solicit other lawyers or close friends, however.

The Supreme Court has held that the state ban on in-person solicitation is constitutionally permissible because people in need of lawyers are often emotionally upset and lawyers are trained in the art of persuasion. As a result, the rule protects people against overreaching by lawyers seeking business. On the other hand, the Court has concluded that states may not ban lawyers from sending mailings to potential clients. In this situation, people can simply disregard the information.

Mailed Solicitations

Lawyers who send mailed solicitations are required to follow the state rules. First, note that the content of the mailed information must comply with the prohibitions against false and misleading communications. Second, states have labeling requirements. According to ABA Model Rule 7.3, mailings sent to those known to be in need of legal services must be labeled as "Advertising Material" on the envelope. This informs a potential client that the information is nothing more than an ad, which may be disregarded. Virtually all states require some form of this notice. Some states require more elaborate language in the labeling. Some specify a required type size and color. Some states require letters to be submitted to a state authority for filing or screening. About twelve states require lawyers to refrain from sending direct mail for personal injury or wrongful death representation for a designated period, usually thirty days, after the event that gives rise to the need for the legal services. In other words, a lawyer must wait a month until he or she can send letters to accident victims in those states.

Finally, most states include ethics rules that give direction on the use of the firm's name and letterhead. Firm names must not be false or misleading. For example, a sole practitioner, with no associates, must avoid practicing under a title that includes his or her name "and Associates" or similar designations that imply the lawyer has a greater capacity that he or she does. Firms must also avoid names that imply they are connected with a government, charitable, or public entity. "The Social Security Group," "The University Law Firm," or "Municipal Division Lawyers" would be examples of firm names that violate this rule. Lawyers must avoid stating or implying that they are affiliated when, in fact, they are not; lawyers who share office space must be particularly careful about their actions in connection with this rule. Again, this gives a misleading impression that the lawyer has a greater capacity than that which is available.

Acts of Others

Solos and small-firm practitioners are likely to outsource some of their client development endeavors. For example, in their efforts to obtain new business, these practitioners list in directories, join legal service plans, and hire copy editors for press releases. The directory publisher, plan administrator, and copy editor act as the lawyer's agents in these situations. The lawyer is then responsible for making sure their actions comply with ethical rules. Put another way, if *you* cannot say you are an expert in your field (because it would violate the pre-2001 Model Rule 7.1 or Model Rule 7.4), you cannot hire someone to issue a press release that says you are an expert. Likewise, you cannot participate in an online for-profit referral service that requires you to pay for cases in those states with ethics rules prohibiting the payment of anything of value for recommending your services.

Keep in mind that the ethics rules apply only to lawyers, and not to those entities that provide services to lawyers. If a directory fails to include a required disclaimer, no disciplinary action is taken against its publisher. But the lawyer can be charged with a failure to comply with the rules. Likewise, there are no consequences for the public relations company, the marketing consultant, or the Web site designer. Only the lawyer is subject to discipline for his or her actions, but the lawyer is also subject to discipline for the actions of any and all of his or her agents.

Use of Technology

Whether it's the commonly used e-mail systems, Web sites, or chat rooms, or the more complex aspects of metadata and search engine optimization, the introduction of online technologies into the practice of law has complicated our understanding of ethical compliance. For the most part, the ethics rules have not been promulgated with the current technological capacities in mind. Nevertheless, those rules govern all aspects of a lawyer's conduct.

Ethics opinions from a number of states have given us fundamental direction. The opinions consistently indicate that lawyers may use technology for client communication and marketing as long as they use it in ways that are consistent with the ethics rules. In other words, it's ethical to use technology as long as the way you use technology is ethical. That may seem like circular logic, but it's good advice. Consider the case of the first lawyer to spam, Laurence Canter.

Canter sent thousands of e-mail messages to people, through listserves and user groups, seeking clients for his immigration practice. He was licensed and disciplined for his actions in Tennessee. Of course, there was no ethics rule prohibiting a lawyer from spamming. In fact, a Supreme Court case clearly established that lawyers could send unsolicited mail to potential clients. However, Canter failed to label his e-mail messages as "advertising material," failed to submit a copy of the message to the state, and referred to himself as an "immigration lawyer," all of which were violations of the Tennessee ethics rules at that time. For these offenses, Canter was suspended for one year. (The sanction was probably greater than it would have been if Canter had defended and offered mitigating evidence, but he did not.)

A few technology issues have been specifically addressed, either by ethics opinions or rule changes. Some state ethics opinions have concluded that lawyers do not need to use their names in domain names, but the content of those domain names must comply with the rules. So, for example, if a lawyer were to create unjustified expectations by stating, "I win cases," a domain name of "www.iwincases.com" would be inappropriate. As mentioned above, sole practitioners must be cautious about overstating their capacities and adding "and Associates" to their names. Similarly, a solo without associates may mislead potential clients with a domain name like "www.janedoeandassociates.com."

Another technology issue addressed by a few states and, recently, by the ABA, involves solicitation through chat rooms. The dynamics of real-time electronic communications are considered more similar to the often unacceptable in-person solicitation, as compared with the acceptable mailed communications. Therefore, solicitations in real-time platforms have been deemed unethical in some jurisdictions.

Many other technology issues have not been specifically addressed. Issues such as the content of links, the use of metadata, and efforts for search engine optimization are not yet on the radar screens of most policy makers. Lawyers should seek their best real-world analogies when making decisions about the application of ethical rules to their conduct in these uncharted areas.

Resources

Although this chapter has tried to anticipate and provide direction on many of the issues that are important to solos and small-firm practitioners, it has only scratched the surface of potential dilemmas. Fortunately, lawyers have several resources that provide additional guidance:

- ◆ See **www.abanet.org/adrules** for links to the rules of professional conduct on client development for each state.
- ◆ Many states staff ethics hotlines, where lawyers can pose questions and get quick replies. See your state bar or disciplinary agency for more information.
- ◆ States and some local bars have procedures for lawyers to submit questions for written ethics opinions.
- ◆ The most authoritative source on legal ethics is the *ABA/BNA Lawyers' Manual on Professional Conduct*, available at **www.bna.com/products/ lit/mopc.htm**.
- ◆ Finally, a lawyer who is considering a novel or substantial marketing venture should not overlook the benefits of engaging another lawyer who specializes in professional responsibility. Large firms generally have lawyers among the ranks who provide this type of counsel. Solos and small-firm practitioners may benefit from preventive consultations. Many ethics experts belong to the Association of Professional Responsibility Lawyers (APRL) (**www.aprl.net**).

Selected Resources
for Part V

from the ABA Law Practice
Management Section

Effective Yellow Pages Advertising for Lawyers: The Complete Guide to Creating Winning Ads, by Kerry Randall, 2002.

How to Start and Build a Law Practice, Fifth Edition, by Jay G Foonberg, 2004.

Law Practice, bimonthly publication of the ABA Law Practice Management Section.

The Lawyer's Guide to Marketing on the Internet, Second Edition, by Gregory H. Siskind, Deborah McMurray, and Richard P. Klau, 2002.

The Lawyer's Guide to Marketing Your Practice, Second Edition, edited by James A. Durham and Deborah McMurray, 2003.

Marketing and Legal Ethics: The Boundaries of Promoting Legal Services, Third Edition, by William E. Hornsby, Jr., 2000.

Marketing Success Stories: Conversations with Leading Lawyers, Second Edition, by Hollis Hatfield Weishar and Joyce K. Smiley, 2004.

Through the Client's Eyes: New Approaches to Get Clients to Hire You Again and Again, Second Edition, by Henry W. Ewalt, 2002.

Women Rainmakers' Best Marketing Tips, Second Edition, by Theda C. Snyder, 2003.

Quality-of-Life Manual

The authors in Part VI offer real-life advice for real-life situations often faced by solos. Some of the information concerns serious, health-related issues—learning to combat loneliness and isolation, to cope with stress, and to deal with alcohol and drug problems.

Other chapters cover important practical matters such as how to sell your practice, how to merge with other lawyers or law firms, and how to plan for your disability or retirement.

The authors contributing to Part VI are much like experienced pilots—they have encountered everything from engine problems to rough weather but have landed safely. You will definitely benefit from their experiences.

Being Solo Does Not Mean Being Lonely

50

Carolyn Elefant

Oddly enough, my days of being lonely as a lawyer ended when I started my solo practice.

When I worked for others, I derived neither pleasure nor emotional satisfaction from my relationships with my colleagues. During my experience as a government lawyer and then as a law firm associate, my social contacts were narrowly circumscribed and ranged from simply superficial to downright uncomfortable. So-called watercooler chats and lunches with my immediate peers consisted of dull chitchat. No one ever talked about the things that draw people closer—like commiserating about a memo that had been ripped to shreds by a supervisor or sharing feelings of terror about an upcoming hearing—for fear of appearing incompetent or less than perfect. My relationships with supervisors and law firm partners fared no better; the stratified office hierarchy discouraged me (and others on my level) from initiating lunch dates with my superiors—not that I would have anyway, as every social encounter with them made me feel as if I was on an extended job interview.

After having been immersed in this kind of stunted social environment for five years, I actually looked forward to the solitude of solo practice. But, after a couple months squirreled away as a recluse in my basement office, I found myself craving social contact. Only now, liberated from the structures of an office, I found that I could expand my circle of colleagues and friends from my professional life to include a wider, more diverse, friendlier, and more supportive group than was ever possible in my office days. My circle of friends and colleagues now includes lawyers who practice in a variety of fields, as well as people who aren't lawyers, and reflects a broad range of age, gender, ethnicity, and location. To gather this new group of friends and colleagues, I had to break many of the long-ingrained rules about socializing, and also had to develop new ways to pursue friendships. Following is a discussion of what I did as a solo to lose the loneliness and gain the sense of connection that had eluded me most when I was working for others.

Forgetting the Old Rules

When working for an organization or even socializing in law school, it's our nature to gravitate toward those in our age group, professional level, or practice area—a propensity that artificially limits the scope of our social contacts. But solo lawyers, regardless of their ages or practice areas, function as partners and entrepreneurs always looking for ways to improve their businesses and expertise. Suddenly, the range of social possibilities magically expands—a twenty-five-year-old solo just out of law school now holds business partnership in common with the senior partner at the largest law firm in the city; a lawyer running his or her own firm now shares the same interest in running a business as accountants, engineers, and nonlegal personnel with whom he or she may have worked in the past but never identified as potential social contacts. Breaking the confines of the tight social circles impressed upon our profession holds the greatest promise for meeting others as a solo.

That's certainly been true of my experience as a solo. A couple weeks after I started my solo law practice, I invited a partner at a large firm to lunch so we could discuss an appellate matter where our clients shared mutual interests. Whereas just a few weeks earlier, as a law firm associate, I would have been nervous and self-conscious about making a good impression, now, as the proprietor of my own shop, I could discuss matters and express opinions with the newfound authority that my position conveyed. Since that day, I've asked other people my senior to lunch—including some of the partners with whom I dreaded socializing at my old firm. I've learned a great deal of substance from these colleagues and, as time has passed, I've discovered they have interesting lives outside of the law.

I've also learned that most lawyers, no matter their level of expertise, are eager to share their knowledge with those less experienced. Lawyers typically welcome calls from others who have substantive practice questions or who seek advice on where to find the best stationery or restaurants. I won't say that all lawyers are like this; phone calls and e-mail messages asking for assistance or extending invitations to lunch may yield some curt, "I'm sorry, can't help you" replies—believe me, I've had more than my share of those. It's just a matter of persisting beyond those few to find the majority of lawyers truly eager to pass on knowledge.

One way to ensure a positive interaction is to ask a colleague for an introduction to another lawyer you want to meet. Even a busy lawyer will make time for your call knowing it was suggested by a mutual contact. Also, many lawyers may not have time for lunch—and when you are starting your practice, you might not have the funds to foot the bill regularly. But you can offer to stop by a lawyer's office to chat, or meet for breakfast or a midday coffee break. A personal face-to-face encounter generally stimulates more productive discussion than a phone call, and also goes further toward satisfying the craving for contact.

Before long, other lawyers will start calling you for advice—and in fealty to those who helped in the past, you have an obligation to pay it forward. There's nothing I enjoy more than meeting with someone who is considering a solo practice or just started one. As much advice as I pass along, I find I always come away with new ideas of how to do things. And, of course, I have the privilege of sharing in the excitement of the launch of a new venture, which always rejuvenates my interest in my own practice.

Reaching Outside the Law

Some of the most enjoyable contacts I've made as a sole practitioner have been with the nonlegal professionals and personnel with whom I work. As an energy regulatory lawyer, I frequently team with engineers, inventors, and project developers; some are clients and others are consultants. I enjoy sharing my legal knowledge and learning about their respective areas of expertise. Consequently, I join trade association meetings and attend lunches for professional societies where I can meet nonlegal professionals. Of course, attending these functions makes for good client development, but it also allows solos to expand their circles of friends and colleagues beyond lawyers.

And there's no reason to limit contacts to professionals of that type. It's also good to talk with support staff and inquire politely about how they're doing. Not only does this improve the working environment, but support staff can also provide a source of work if they're comfortable enough with a lawyer to bring a case to his or her attention. And for lawyers who work at home, this kind of day-to-day interaction takes on even more importance. They may not have full-time secretaries, but likely work with per-diem paralegals, messengers, or even regular express-delivery persons or copy-shop contacts. If you are one of these lawyers, strike up conversations and soon you'll feel as though you have your own office community. Moreover, the mere recognition that these scattered people are part of a team that is your practice makes you feel that you're part of an entity bigger than yourself—which goes a long way toward combating feelings of isolation.

Joining Groups

One way to meet a whole bunch of new people all at once is to take advantage of bar association activities in your area. Generally speaking, the smaller local groups tend to be more collegial, not to mention less expensive, than the larger ones. If time and budget are considerations, and the local groups offer activities of interest to you (which is not always the case for me as an energy regulatory practitioner), then you might want to target your efforts there. Attending lunches and events will certainly help you make connections but really, the best way to get to know people and increase interactions is to assume a leadership role. Personally, though I often don't have the patience (or, as a part-time solo, the time) for endless committee meetings, I have found that I can bypass this kind of bureaucracy if I'm simply willing to take the lead on arranging a function. Here, too, is another chance to interact with others— you may need to contact potential speakers, finalize plans with committee members, greet attendees (standing at the doorway to shake hands as people enter is a low-key and sociable way to collect new business cards), and engage in any follow-up activities. So don't be shy about ruffling feathers—dive right in with your ideas and the elbow grease to carry them out. Soon, you may find yourself moving up in an organization, which means you're visible to other people who'll want to get in touch with you.

You can also become active in your community and meet others at the same time. Montgomery County, Maryland, where I live, has about sixty citizens committees that deal with issues ranging from education to energy and air quality (my expertise). I've been on a county committee for seven years now; the monthly meetings give me a chance to interact with others and, at the same time, to use my expertise to better my community.

Getting Out of the House or Office

Sometimes, sitting alone in a basement office or holed up in a corner office in an anonymous suite can make even the most reclusive solo feel cut off from civilization. The solution is not to crawl deeper into the hole, but simply to get out to a place where other people are.

You don't always need to attend a structured event—like a lunch or bar activity—to meet others. Often, the best encounters happen spontaneously and informally. When I handled court-appointed criminal work, I'd always make it a point to arrive at the lawyers' lounge an hour before any cases were called, just to chat and joke with the other lawyers. I rarely saw any of those lawyers outside the courthouse, but not every interaction has to end in lunch or a longstanding friendship. In many ways, the lawyers' lounge was like a neighborhood bar—a place to hang around and socialize simply for the sake of doing just that.

Solos can also go to other places to work, just for a change of scenery and to feel more connected. I cherish my trips to the Library of Congress and local law school libraries, where working alongside students and scholars makes me feel connected. These days, you can even take your laptop or Blackberry to the local coffee shop, just for a change of scenery.

Online Possibilities

One final option for finding camaraderie and support as a solo—and one that did not exist ten years ago when I started my practice—is the Internet. Many state and local bar associations, as well as "specialty bars" such as American of Trial Lawyers of America (ATLA) and others, offer listserves where members can exchange jokes and advice. Recently, the two-hundred-member Missouri solo and small-firm listserve kicked in several hundred dollars to help a colleague who'd been appointed by the court to prosecute an appeal in Missouri's highest court. The solo could not afford to pay for photocopying charges or the trip to argue the case, so the group came to the rescue with voluntary donations and offers to help review the brief.

Perhaps the largest and most well known of the lot is the ABA's seven-year-old listserve, Solosez (**www.solosez.org**). With membership hovering around one thousand lawyers from all over the country, the list generates a heap of mail daily; really, the only way to manage it is to segregate it in a separate mailbox.

If listserves like Solosez or the Missouri bar list existed only as online activities, they'd play a limited role in a solo's social life. But what's best about these lists is that their members have brought them to life. The D.C. and Baltimore Solosez contingents have monthly lunches, and the Boston group has added one, as well. And solos traveling to other cities can always find a comrade or two to meet for drinks or meals. When my family spent the summer in Birmingham a few years ago, I had lunch with a combined group from the Birmingham "Solosezzers" and the Birmingham bar's small-practice group. On a recent trip to Boston, I met fifteen solos for tapas and sangria at a local restaurant. Before going solo, I always dreaded the stuffy alumni lunches that I attended, where no one carried a business card or cracked a smile. And, at those lunches, there were even speakers to break the awkward silences. At these solo lunches, there's no planned entertainment—yet introductions and conversations flow freely. Though many of us never met previously, we wind up chatting like old friends.

Another online hobby that's brought me introductions to others is my Web log, **www.MyShingle.com**, a site I run for solos, small-firm lawyers, and those who dream of starting firms. There are probably another three hundred lawyers who operate Web logs (blogs) on topics as varied as ethics, appellate law, employment, legal technology, and even what it's like to be a new bankruptcy associate at a law firm. The group of lawyers who blog is still small and nascent enough that its members share a sense of camaraderie as they pioneer on this Internet frontier. We often write each other notes or highlight posts or news tips. In fact, when I saw that a fellow blogger was slated to give a talk at a library in D.C., I went to see him in person—and what do you know, he invited me to serve as a copresenter! Since then, we made another presentation to the Maryland State Bar Association and we keep each other up to date on our blogs.

Final Thoughts

If you think about it, loneliness is a state of mind. You can, as I did, feel lonely in a work environment though surrounded by others with whom you ought to share some commonality, if only you could scratch below the thick facade. Or, you can strike out as a solo and build a community of colleagues and friends who give support and sustenance against isolation and the frequent pressures of legal practice. That's the path I chose, and the greatest surprise I discovered was that as a solo, I wasn't alone anymore.

Tips and Resources That Helped Me

Following are some of the resources that helped me make contacts and break free from the spell of isolation that can plague solos:

- ◆ *Solosez Listserve*: This ABA listserve is open to ABA members and nonmembers alike, at no cost. List membership hovers around one thousand, and though not all members participate, there's still heavy volume. In addition to serving as a great resource for practice tips and substantive advice, the list offers several opportunities to socialize. Many solos in some of the larger cities hold monthly solosez lunches, and when solos travel to different cities, they often can get together with others on the list. There's also an annual group swearing-in to the U.S. Supreme Court, so lawyers can get admitted to the Court along with a group of solo colleagues. To sign up for the list, visit **www.solosez.org**.

♦ *Bar Associations*: Find the bar associations in your area and try to select membership based upon the group's cost and activities. In some locations, the county or city bars may prove most active, while in other locations, the state bar may be preferable. Most bars have sections, and that's where the real opportunities lie for getting active in planning events.

♦ *Local Groups and Meetings*: Read your local newspapers and local business journals. You may learn about meetings that might not be advertised in larger newspapers. In addition, many counties have citizens committees or ethics advisory boards, most of which are eager to have the assistance of lawyers.

Dealing with Stress **51**

George W. Kaufman

Introduction

Welcome. You and I are about to share a quiet time together pursuing ideas around elements that make a balanced life. Let me put all confessions up front. I cannot tell you what makes a balanced life for you, nor can I tell you whether a balanced life, even if we could define it, is one that you should pursue.

What I can share with you are the critical elements that have made a balanced life for me and what many friends, struggling for balance in their own lives, have explored in searching for answers. These elements did not appear out of whole cloth. Nor were they even considered until my own life was out of balance and the consequences of that imbalance started to appear. Most of my knowledge has come from mistakes, rather than triumphs. Triumphs have taught me that success and happiness are not synonymous. I used to think they were, until I found myself reaching goals I had set (partner, financial security, clients), but still not being happy. Triumphs didn't motivate me to change—mistakes did.

On these pages I have woven together a distillation of many ideas for you to sample. I urge you to consider only those that resonate with your own experience. I am not an advocate for change. Rather, I am a proponent of exploration. I want your experience of being a sole practitioner—whether you currently are one, or you are contemplating that alternative—to be fulfilling.

Changes that we make—and even those we consider—are explored when we are attracted to an alternative or repelled from our present circumstances. In either event, we bring ourselves to each new situation. John Kabat-Zinn, a former MIT professor, wrote a book entitled, *Wherever You Go, There You Are.* What the title suggests, and what I have found in my own experience, is that we cannot deny that our own personality, attitudes, approach, and style affect where we've been and will affect wherever we go. As we understand more about ourselves, we reduce the likelihood of disappointment in choices we make and increase the likelihood of achieving happiness.

In the succeeding pages I will share with you an overview of the elements that constitute balance for me, the stresses that unfold when life feels out of balance, and some tools I use to keep stress within manageable limits and balance within bounds. To do that, I will suggest a few exercises designed to give you some self-awareness tools and some questions and thoughts for you to consider about long-term purpose and satisfaction.

Let's start.

Stress

A stressor is anything that throws the body out of balance. It can be a physical event (such as an impending accident), an event we anticipate happening (an upcoming date before a judge), or a perceived danger (footsteps in the alley).

Our body responds to stressors in many ways, all designed genetically to help us survive the perceived threat. The list of bodily changes is really quite remarkable. Extra adrenaline is released into our bodies. Blood flow to our extremities and organs decreases to minimize bleeding. At the same time, chemicals enter the blood stream to enhance clotting. All these changes improve the body's ability to fight or flee from danger. While most dangers in the short history of mankind were external, today a significant number of stressors live in our heads, triggered just by our thoughts. Because our bodies can't distinguish between the two, they react the same way, whether the danger is external or thought created.

The two kinds of stressors we experience have different consequences. When the first danger—the external threat—is over, the body returns to its normal state and the changes that occurred are reversed. In the second kind of perceived danger—court dates, trial deadlines, unhappy clients, or dissatisfied partners—the threat never goes away. Work manages to produce an inexhaustible supply of changing stressors, keeping the body in a state of constant vigilance. And as long as the threat remains, the body stays vigilant.

The first kind of stress is called acute, and is actually a life-enhancing system. The second kind of stress is called chronic, and over time results in many deleterious consequences to our bodies. To name just a few:

- Weakened immune systems, making us more vulnerable to disease, and to the consequences of disease
- Greater likelihood of depression, insomnia, and memory loss
- Elevated blood pressure and a more rapid wearing out of our cardio-vascular systems
- Increased rate of miscarriages and greater likelihood of impotence

Stress does more than attack our bodies. It changes who we are. The data collected on lawyers are revealing—and disheartening. We suffer from alcohol and substance abuse at twice the national rate. Lawyers are four times more likely to be depressed than the average population, and suicide and suicide attempts for lawyers have climbed to alarming levels.

The invasion of stress is endemic to our profession. It is also endemic to the culture of our times. We may proceed as though we are victims with few options, but, in fact, our stresses reflect the consequences of choices we have made.

In the next section, I offer some thoughts on how we become entrained in particular behaviors, unaware of the powers and patterns that mold our lives, and some approaches for dealing with behaviors and actions that limit our options.

Influences

Stress can originate for many reasons and take many forms. I will look at four of them and offer suggestions for modifying—and perhaps even transforming—old habits and "stuck" behavior.

Not Doing What You Love

When I ask practitioners why they chose to become lawyers, two answers predominate, and both answers are disturbing. A common reason cited is that "my parents wanted me to be a lawyer." A second explanation given is that "all other options were worse." All occupations have high and low points. But when the low points appear, it would be comforting if the dream that brought us to our profession had been grounded in service or mentorship rather than parental satisfaction or a Hobson's choice.

We needn't be discouraged because in our twenties our reasons for choosing law were superficial. Once we started to practice, a different reality began. We were in daily contact with other lawyers, resolving real issues, addressing clients with real needs (or demands), and seeing how law theory actually worked in the marketplace. We may find our current experiences positive and affirming, whatever the initial reasons that thrust us toward the law. Or we may feel captured by a process that is draining us of all vitality. We need to think about what sustains us in our current practices, and what changes we should consider that will enhance our lives in the law.

Educator Parker Palmer begins his small and elegant book, *Let Your Life Speak,* with a poem by William Stafford, one line of which states as follows:

Ask me whether what I have done is my life.

He goes on to ask whether the life he is living is the life that wants to live in him. When there is a disparity between what we do and what we want to be doing, the common responses are tension, anger, depression, sadness, and surrender.

We each need to find a corner in life that's inviolate, dedicated and protected from the demands of work. In this small corner we find an oasis, that source of replenishment that alchemically converts numbness into hope.

Not Being Successful at What You Do

There are many reasons why success may elude us professionally. Timing and luck are certainly two factors to be acknowledged, even if unalterable. But other possibilities exist over which we may have some influence, and I want to offer them to you.

First, we may have gifts we don't fully recognize, and so there is a tendency to undervalue our accomplishments instead of playing to our strengths. Conversely, we have limited talents in other areas that we rail against instead of accept. For example, it's common to berate ourselves when we don't act effectively, even when the actions required are contrary to our natures. Worse, we often generalize our limitations and let that attitude damage the parts of ourselves that are productive and healthy.

Here's one way to check whether we are maximizing our gifts—or are testing our limitations—in our practices. At the end of this chapter is a list of skills and talents that are common to the needs of our profession. Some of us are better at some of these skills and worse at others. Take a moment and turn to that exercise. Next to each skill category rate yourself on a scale from 1 to 5, with 1 being the least successful and 5 being the most. Then return to this page for the next instruction.

If you've finished the prior instruction, look at the column next to your completed ratings. List on the same 1 to 5 scale the importance of the listed skills in your practice, with 1 being not important at all, and 5 being extremely important. When you are finished, take a look at two areas: those places where the disparity is the greatest, and where the compatibility is strongest.

If most of your practice reflects a disparity (for example, my writing skills are a 2 but in the demands of the job I rate it as a 5), that's a source of constant tension. If the skills are learnable, you may decide to put energy in that direction. However, on a long-term basis, it would be more productive to steer your practice to your strengths. The more your work can reflect your talents, the more you can eliminate some of the root causes of your stress. You have a chance to reshape your practice to match your professional comfort zone.

Not Living Your Values

What do we care about? What do we believe? What matters most? All these questions dance around the values by which we would like to live.

When I use the term "values," I mean human qualities we admire or practice. The ones most deeply ingrained in us get reflected through our behavior. Other values represent how we would *like* to live in the world, even when our performance falls woefully short of our intentions.

I have listed at the end of this chapter (yes—another exercise!) sixty values I believe are important. The list is incomplete. If there are values important to you that don't appear, substitute freely. Circle ten that matter most, and then list those ten in priority of most important to least important.

The order you just created says much about you. But it doesn't say whether in your daily behavior these values are visible. To help consider that point, create three circles, one inside the other, with you at the epicenter. In the first circle, list those values that get most of your time and energy each day. In the second circle, list those values you care about deeply, but practice only occasionally. In the third circle, list the remaining values; they are still important to you, but on a day-to-day basis, they have little influence on your behavior. The areas of greatest personal tension should be places where the values highest on your priority list fell into the second and third circles. Conversely, the first circle may be filled with your lowest-rated values.

Values serve us best in times of adversity. But if we're not practicing our values in tranquil times, we will be unprepared to fall back on our core values precisely when we need to draw upon them. If the values we care about most deeply are only marginally practiced by us, we are either doomed to lives we don't respect or we need to adjust our behavior to better reflect our beliefs.

There are three stages to incorporating values into our daily lives:

1. *Selection*: If we want to change our behavior, we need to select values that support the behavior change we want to make.
2. *Adoption*: When we adopt a value, it hovers constantly in our consciousness. We appreciate its inclusion and would feel empty at its omission.
3. *Reflection*: To reflect a value means to allow it to be seen in the world through our behavior. The intensity by which the reflection is practiced says much about us and about the depth of our commitment to that value.

In *The Teachings of Don Juan* by Carlos Castaneda, the main character advises his acolyte to look closely at every path. However, he admonishes Don Juan that if the path doesn't have a heart, it's of no use. By asking whether a path has heart, we are really asking ourselves whether the values we pick represent the best company we can take with us on our life journeys.

Not Hearing Your Own Voice

Carl Jung said that *nothing has a stronger influence on children than the unlived lives of their parents*. From our earliest memories, parents, teachers, counselors, aunts, uncles, and mentors all provided advice on our behavior. The strongest voices soon became internalized as we absorbed their beliefs, their admonitions, and their demands. For most of us, our parents were the dominant voices in a cacophony of messages. Jung suggests that the messages of our parents are driven by the complexity of their own lives. Most often, their strongest beliefs are based upon a scarcity approach (unfulfilled expectations) rather than an abundance approach (sufficiency).

Some have accepted their childhood training in its entirety, not challenging assumptions or motives. Others have rejected anything that smacks of family influence—often taking polar positions just to claim independence. Neither the formula of inclusion nor the stance of exclusion gives much consideration to exploring, experimenting, and finally adopting our own life values. Initially, that would require filtering through our experiences and deciding on principle, not origin.

As adults, we have bosses, clients, peers, partners, and family members shouting for our attention. Those messages often translate into "shoulds" and "oughts" of behavior. These competing voices can be so loud that our own voices drown or shrivel, leaving us uncertain about whether decisions we make serve our own agendas or the agendas of others. Garrison Keillor, in one of his monologues, reminisces that he never has to speak to his mother again, because there is a permanent tape of her inside his head. And, in a poignant moment, he realizes that her voice will be inside his head not until she dies, but until he dies. Most of us aren't even aware of the power of these voices to color our decisions, guide our behavior, and influence our values. We need to find ways of quieting those voices so we can leave space for our own to be heard.

If you are searching for where your voice stops and those of others take over, I suggest you consider any decision of moment you recently made, or are now considering. Then ask yourself these questions:

- What family member or close relation, living or dead, would be pleased if I decided in a particular way?
- What values are being supported by this decision?

◆ What family member or close relation, living or dead, would be displeased if I decided the opposite way?

◆ What values are being rejected by this decision?

The fact that some might agree or disagree with your decision doesn't invalidate either your process or your history. But your decision can be deeply revealing when you recognize those influences from your past that would be your ally or your opponent as you weigh a particular choice.

Addressing Stress

Stress is not the kind of challenge you can permanently fix or completely cure. Because we are constantly participating in situations that feed stress, the best we can expect to create is a process for managing the stress that seeps into our lives every day. Modest amounts of stress serve as adrenaline, boosting our attention and energizing our actions. When stress becomes excessive, it becomes harmful.

There are two avenues of management. The first addresses those times when stress levels are inordinately high. Like steam emanating from a pressure cooker, we need to find immediate ways to tone down anxiety. The second avenue contains a series of practices we can make into daily routines. Those practices are designed to keep stress levels from getting to acute stages.

Stress ratchets up when our lives are out of balance. By "out of balance" I mean—for lawyers—extreme emphasis on mind over body and spirit. Lawyers have a heady profession and culture. We are constantly called upon to use our minds in the service of our practices. Whether it is for analyzing, speaking, writing, or planning, our minds are constantly at work. Though it may once have been difficult to see the connection between our minds and our physical health, it is now commonly accepted that our minds affect our physical health. Most teaching hospitals, for example, currently offer some form of integrative medicine that combines modalities of both Eastern and Western medical approaches.

The concept that a balanced person is one who honors all three components—mind, body, and spirit—reflects a life approach that twenty years ago was considered relevant only by fringe elements of society. Today, whole industries survive on toning, exercising, or strengthening the body, teaching movement and flow, and advising about nutrition, fasting, and purification.

In the following sections, I address the challenges that stress presents by talking about ways that attention to mind, body, and spirit can profoundly mitigate stress.

Attending to the Body
Breathing
We can physically relax our bodies through simple exercises involving the breath. You might think that because we've been doing it for so long, we know how to breathe. We do know how to inhale and expel air, but we don't practice breathing in a way that enhances relaxation. Just remember our childhood behavior when we were angry—we held our breath.

To use your breath as a relaxation tool, start by placing one hand on your chest and the other on your diaphragm. Take some breaths and watch the movement of your hands. Chances are, the hand on the chest moves more than the hand on the diaphragm. Breathing from the upper lungs is shallow breathing, which is not conducive to relaxing. Practice breathing in a way that the hand on your diaphragm moves instead of the hand on your chest.

Find a space to lie down or lean back. This opens your stomach area and gives the diaphragm more room to expand. Also, practice breathing more slowly. If you are alone, hold your in-breath for a few seconds, and then let it out with an audible sigh. Just making that sound releases tension. You can do this practice effectively in just two minutes. Of course, you should stop if it ever feels difficult, painful, or problematic. This tool is particularly effective in stressful moments, but can be incorporated into your daily routine several times a day.

Muscle Relaxation
The ability to relax muscles allows us to reduce the tensions our bodies carry. You can either find guided relaxation exercises that progressively relax different parts of your body, or you can make a self-generated trip through your body, starting with your face and working down progressively to your neck, shoulders, arms and hands, chest and lungs, stomach, and, finally, hips, legs, and feet.

Relaxation works by first tensing the muscle you want to relax. Hold that tension for about five seconds (less if there is any tendency to cramp). Also, learn to modulate the degree of tension you introduce. After five seconds, relax the muscle, breathe out, and say the word "relax" to yourself. Repeat the relaxation component two times. Here is an example of how the relaxation process works on your face:

- ◆ Furrow your brow, then relax your brow
- ◆ Shut your eyes tightly, then relax them
- ◆ Flare your nostrils, then relax your nostrils
- ◆ Open your mouth until it feels stretched, then relax it
- ◆ Press your tongue against the top/bottom of your mouth, then relax it
- ◆ Clench your jaw, and relax it

The entire process could be done in as little as ten minutes, or, more luxuriously, in twenty. When finished, stay in that completed state for about five minutes. Note your breathing and the feelings in your body. Tension should be substantially reduced.

Exercise and Healthy Eating

As a society, our diets lean heavily toward fast foods, high caloric intake, excess sugar, and overdoses of salt. We ignore our bodies but expect them to be responsive to our needs. When illness strikes, often our first thought is that we have been let down rather than forewarned.

It is important to honor the body that serves you. Appropriate exercise and healthy eating are not difficult to accomplish. Both are easily available. But to effect change, you must first prioritize your needs so appropriate exercise and healthy eating are recognized as necessities and not luxuries. Necessities must be honored, while luxuries can be postponed (often indefinitely).

Exercise gets you away from the constant churning of your mind, offering short windows of freedom. It improves your cardiovascular system and overall health. You can pursue exercise with machines and weights, or through yoga, t'ai chi, swimming, or walking. Taking time to exercise is not only a life-extending personal commitment, it is a choice that places your needs above those that are work-related.

Healthy eating stops the huge swings in your body that are the consequences of too much sugar, too many refined carbohydrates, too much alcohol, and too many artificial ingredients. Healthy eating involves more than the food you eat. It includes the following, as well:

- ◆ Whether you eat on the run or take time for meals
- ◆ Whether you eat with some regularity or often skip meals
- ◆ Whether your food is ingested or inhaled

When we are aware of how and what we eat, we are mindful of the external world and our own interiority. By being conscious of the eating process, we are focused upon the task before us and not just ingesting food as fuel.

Attending to the Mind
Meditation

There are scores of books and programs that provide instruction on the use of meditation as a stress-reduction tool. Unlike golf or tennis as aids to "getting away," meditation requires no equipment, no partner, and no opponent, and can be accomplished in just twenty minutes. A resource list at the end of this chapter provides a few of the many books that provide basic meditation instruction.

What I want to emphasize is the function of meditation. It forces us to pay attention to silence. Most folks I know are uncomfortable with silence and rush to fill any perceived vacuum. Yet until the chatter dies away, we don't know what other thoughts want to bubble up. By practicing meditation, we create space that is free of external distractions.

As lawyers, we seem to live our lives with the fast-forward switch permanently engaged. Meditation moves that switch from automatic to manual, and then from manual to neutral. Through meditation, we become more conscious—more present—during each moment of our lives. In response to a comment from a stress-reduction student of Jon Kabat-Zinn that she now understood that the purpose of meditation is to live *for* the moment, he responded that she was close. "The purpose," suggested Jon, "is to live *in* the moment."

From my childhood, I remember a silo-shaped ride at the nearby amusement park. Riders flattened themselves against a wall, waiting for the machine to swirl around faster and faster. At a certain speed, centrifugal force took over, and you felt pinned to the sides of the barrel. The floor lowered a foot, but you were glued in place, unable to move. When we practice law in the fast-forward mode, we are stuck against the walls of work, unable to move. Meditation slows the speed of the moving silo and puts the floor back under our feet.

You can practice meditation before or after work, or even during a break in your workday. The number of minutes devoted to this endeavor is less important than the commitment to enter such a practice on a regular basis. Over time, your practice will deepen, and the relaxation benefits will pay larger dividends.

Journal Writing

Lawyers are effective writers, but work within sharply defined parameters. We can be analytic, probing, argumentative, and, in our best moments, persuasive. We write about "the other"—the history, the relevant precedents, the weaknesses in our opponent's position, and the strengths in ours. But rarely do we think of writing for our own well-being. Though it certainly would be expansive to have a secret career as a novelist or essayist (as a limited number of lawyers do), I'm referring to journaling—the act of privately writing in a personal notebook, done daily, and focused upon yourself.

Journal writing is an interior journey, offering an opportunity to be in touch with neglected parts of who you are, and a chance for those neglected parts to find their own voice through these writings. You can write about memories, friends, birthdays (yours or those you love), loss, career, dreams, curiosity, illness, or grace, and that scratches only a limited number of starting places out of an infinite number of opportunities. Journal writing can achieve the following:

- Diffuse anger and release stress
- Clarify issues and help develop solutions
- Heal grief
- Provide insight into your own life
- Allow you to engage in absolute truth telling

Where to start? In addition to suggestions offered in the resources at the end of this chapter, you can begin a journal with reflections of the day. What went well—or badly—and what role did you play in the outcome? What made you laugh or cry? What was painful and what was pleasant?

All these topics allow us time to pay attention to emotions that remain bottled up or had no time to be expressed. Where do they go? Unfortunately, most of those emotions get stuffed down and reappear as weariness or stress until they are so overwhelming that the body reacts with physical illness or mental breakdowns. By bringing these emotions to consciousness through writing, we create opportunities for release and fresh insights about ourselves.

Attending to the Spirit

Napoleon Bonaparte once said:

> *There are only two forces in the world; the sword and the spirit. In the long run, the sword will always be conquered by the spirit.*

When we use the word "spirit," we have a tendency to equate that term with religion. Although spirit can be found within that structure, it can also be found in nature, in community, in service, in purpose, and in a myriad of other places where the best of who we are finds its fullest expression.

How do we find meaning in our work that is sustaining, rather than draining? It is by far the most profound question facing all of us today, and I approach the subject with great caution. My own journey is an ongoing work in progress. On this path, I am more a fellow traveler than guide, and my thoughts have developed from personal trials that led me to individual errors, and individual errors that constantly lead me to new discoveries.

In this section, I look at spirituality through two lenses: higher purpose and open heart.

Higher Purpose

If there is a spiritual dimension to who we are, it follows that the qualities of spirit have the potential to be part of all we do—whether we are working, playing, or being in solitude.

Too few lawyers are inspired by their work. Our efforts seem more like an endurance contest than an alignment with our goals. Negativity leaks onto colleagues, clients, and, occasionally, even family.

When I first practiced in the 1960s, people had passion about their work. Law was a calling rather than an invasion of time and space. We could speculate on the factors that allowed such a sea change in attitude to predominate. But it is more appropriate to speculate on ways to recapture what had once been an operative norm.

Models exist. The Center for Contemplative Society has held several retreats for practitioners, students, and academics, teaching mindfulness and meditation. In Vermont, the International Alliance of Holistic Lawyers has now been serving lawyers for over a decade. And in Dallas, Texas, a lawyer friend has introduced a form of collaborative law to the world of domestic relations and divorce, and created forums where that methodology has been passed on to scores of other lawyers. I am limited by space—not by number of examples—in offering other models.

Earlier in this chapter I referred to William Stafford's poem, *Ask Me*. In analyzing the poem's question, "*Ask me whether what I have done is my life,*" the educator Parker Palmer rephrases the question to ask whether "the life I am living is . . . the same as the life that wants to live in me." Both questions confront our vocational decisions directly. Imbedded in those thoughts is the nugget of gold that asks how my life wants to find expression. The answer does not lie in imposing my will, taming my vocation, and producing a successful practice. Rather, there is a listening required that invites all parts of me to the conversation. What are my gifts? My values? My highest truths? Are they in my work, or could I transform the work I do so they appear? As Parker offers, "Vocation does not mean a goal that I pursue. It means a calling that I hear."

Mindfulness is a critical part of connecting with higher purpose. Viktor Frankl, in his book, *Man's Search for Meaning*, talks about his experiences as a doctor in concentration camps during World War II. He noted that some prisoners survived inhuman conditions, while others perished. He was confined in four such camps and lost almost his entire family. Frankl found that prisoners who could hold onto a life purpose were more likely to survive camp conditions. Out of that experience came the founding of logotherapy, his own form of psychology. Its theme is that each person needs to search for meaning in his or her own life, and then to actualize that meaning in the world.

Mindfulness addresses levels of our awareness. We spend too much of our lives on automatic pilot, numbing what would feel painful or foreign to our natures. As we become numb around the negative aspects of what we do, our tolerance for that kind of behavior grows.

We make sacrifices for what we hope will ultimately be rewarding, and rationalize the sacrifices we make as temporary compromises. Unfortunately, over time, we find that the sacrifices we make cannot be undone and the benefits we seek may have been overrated. Those sacrifices are self-justified by powerful forces within us—drivers—that direct our behavior. Some of the drivers familiar to me are rooted in fear, greed, competition, and responsibility, but each of us has individual demons that demand attention.

Many of the drivers I accepted led a direct path to success, when my definition of success was partnership, security, and money. But what I, and many of my colleagues, soon discovered was that success and happiness are not the same. That truth is often hidden as we struggle for success. But once reached, we discover that happiness may still elude our grasp. Only then do we begin to address the absences in our lives and begin the search for what is still missing.

Making changes in your practice involves choices, and those choices may require that present lifestyles and perceived needs be reexamined. The benefits that money buys come with a cost—and that cost needs to be examined carefully and either accepted or modified.

In India, there is a story of a merchant who marveled at an Indian ascetic for all that he had renounced in his Spartan life. The Yogi disagreed, telling the merchant that his renunciation was far greater, explaining, "I have only given up the finite for the Infinite, but you have surrendered the Infinite for the finite."

Open Heart

I think of spirit and heart as intimately connected. When I couldn't find any spirit in the law work I did, I found that I was practicing with a closed heart. My schooling had trained me to master facts and ignore feelings, to probe for weaknesses and not see whole pictures, and to dominate rather than collaborate. I adopted the value system before me and tried to compromise my own values into accepting new paradigms. That clash caused stress and began to alter who I was and what I valued. Eventually I found ways to work within the law that left intact what mattered most to me—but I had to see the dichotomy before I could wrestle with it.

Those challenges are not limited to our profession or even to our times. In the search for the Holy Grail through the Parcival myth, we find Parcival on a quest. He has been told that as soon as he finds the Holy Grail, he is to ask the question, "What ails thee brother?"—an inquiry grounded in compassion. And still, when he stumbles onto the Grail early in his quest, he fails to ask the question he has been taught. The lessons from his youth—and the voices from his childhood—prevail. His childhood training involved lessons that told him not to ask questions when in the company of strangers. On the second day, when he resolves nevertheless to ask the question, the Grail, the castle, and his opportunity have vanished. Parcival sets out on his quest again. After many years, when he spies the Grail once more, he has no hesitation in posing the question he has carried with him on his whole journey.

As one commentator offered, the victory over the quest is a triumph for spontaneity of the heart over the timidity that leads to an unimaginative life. The qualities of an open heart are learned less in a lifetime than over one. The journey gives us endless opportunities to choose or to shrink back. But once we adopt a course of action, it is hard to veer off. For many of us, our ultimate dreams may not be realized for many years. We may be forced to compromise our actions for necessities and responsibilities. There is no timetable. But an open-ended plan is better than no plan at all.

We may target five-year horizons or those that stretch to ten. Our yard-sticks may be putting kids through college, creating retirement funds, or ac-quiring vacation homes. Whatever the conditions that must be factored into an action plan, there are interim steps we can take that lead to a balanced life that honors mind, body, and spirit.

Mindfulness and balance leave room for what wants to live in us. To know what you ache for is a first step in reframing your relationship to work and enlivening your zest for life. If it is creativity you crave, you may find op-portunities within work or outside it. If you yearn for fellowship, community can be discovered in many of the relationships you already have forged. One friend I know joined a Big Brother program so his entire life wouldn't be sub-sumed at work. Nine years later, his "little" brother is now a permanent part of my friend's life and the young man's life has been affected forever by the in-tervention of a high-quality mentor.

E.L. Doctorow once commented about the art of writing with a simile that covers much more than writing:

> *Writing a novel is like driving a car at night. You can see only as far as your headlights, but you can make the whole trip that way.*

The places that a more balanced life will take you are a mystery that will slowly unfold over time. The mere decision to undertake that exploration will influence current choices, and current choices will expand the options avail-able to you.

Resources

Mindfulness

- ◆ Herbert Benson, M.D., *The Relaxation Response* (Avon Books, 1976)
- ◆ Lorin Roche, Ph.D., *Meditation Made Easy* (Harper, 1998)
- ◆ Shunryyu Suzuki, *Zen Mind, Beginner Mind* (Weatherhill, 1970)

Journal Writing
- Julia Cameron, *The Artist's Way* (Putnam Publishing Group, 1992)
- Lois Guarino, *Writing Your Authentic Self* (Dell Publishing, 1999)

Stress Reduction
- Amiram Elwork, Ph.D., *Stress Management for Lawyers* (The Vorkell Group, 1977)
- George Kaufman, *The Lawyer's Guide to Balancing Life and Work* (ABA, 1999)
- Robert Sapolsky, *Why Zebras Don't Get Ulcers* (W.H. Freeman and Company, 1998)

Exercise 1: Skills and Talents

Subject	*Personal Skill/Talent Level 1–5*	*Application Level 1–5*	
Writing			
Organization			
Creativity			
Teacher/training			
Administration			
Mentoring			
Sales (client getting)			
People skills			
Productivity			
Speaking			
Negotiating			
Analysis			
Decisiveness			
Finance/Business			
Initiative			
Leadership			
Management			
Perspective			
Research			
Service			
Other			

Exercise 2: Values

Love	Freedom	Security	Play
Power	Comfort	Competence	Exercise
Growth	Joy	Creativity	Vegging Out
Acceptance	Support	Warmth	Pride
Gratefulness	Honesty	Balance	Romance
Justice	Serenity	Humility	Frivolity
Trust	Fulfillment	Success	Spontaneity
Intimacy	Adventure	Passion	Perfection
Health	Service	Achievement	Appreciation
Humor	Harmony	Winning	Conscientiousness
Focus	Kindness	Appreciation	Wealth
Integrity	Desire	Presence	Aggressiveness
Honor	Family	Change	Tenacity
Beauty	Truthfulness	Understanding	Practicality
Expediency	Inquiry	Compassion	Loyalty

1. _____
2. _____
3. _____
4. _____
5. _____
6. _____
7. _____
8. _____
9. _____
10. _____

Lawyer Assistance Programs

52

Robert Blaine Holt

As professionals and as leaders in our communities, we are all concerned about the health of all our citizens and we must take responsibility for ending discrimination against people seeking to recover from substance use disorders. Addiction is not a moral failing; it is a disease, and a significant public health problem.

Alfred P. Carlton, Jr., a past president of the ABA, in his testimony to the 2002 Join Together project of Boston University School of Public Health*

Lawyers have always had to deal with the consequences of clients' use of alcohol and other drugs or mental and emotional problems. Experience teaches that when clients have such problems, their legal troubles multiply. They develop family problems, get arrested more often, and usually have trouble at work. People routinely seek advice from their lawyers and confide about how their drinking problems ruin their lives.

When it is the lawyer who suffers from the impairment, it is an altogether different story. When a lawyer has problems stemming from the same issues, it is often seen as such a moral failing that the lawyer is hesitant to admit openly to the problem and ask for help. The words of former ABA president Alfred P. Carlton,

---

*Join Together, founded in 1991 by a grant from The Robert Wood Johnson Foundation to the Boston University School of Public Health, supports community-based efforts to reduce substance abuse and gun violence. All references, quotes, and comments are provided with express permission.

quoted above, ring true for lawyers and other professionals: "Addiction is not a moral failing; it is a disease, and a significant public health issue."

Carlton was speaking to a project of Boston University's School of Public Health. That group later issued a comprehensive report addressing some of the barriers confronting people seeking treatment: "Over 30 percent cited lack of insurance, the cost of treatment, or the scarcity of treatment programs; almost 20 percent said they feared being fired or facing discrimination at work; and almost 40 percent said they were very or fairly concerned that other people would find out about their problem." (ABA Commission on Lawyer Assistance Programs.)

Since 1994, I have been involved with a professional organization called Colorado Lawyer's Health Program (CLHP). The organization was one of the first "broad stroke" lawyer-assistance programs; starting in the early 1980s, CLHP incorporated as a stand-alone, not-for-profit organization in 1993. During the past ten years, I have served as a panel member, a board member, and, until funding was reduced, as the part-time executive director of the organization. During my ten-year association with the organization, I have had the pleasure of meeting a wide variety of courageous practitioners, judges, and other professionals.

One surprising fact became clear over time as I worked with CLHP: a disproportional number of lawyers who sought assistance were in solo practice or small firms. Another surprising fact was the number of ways in which these lawyers were impaired. I confess that the breadth of situations causing impairment to practice was far greater than I could have imagined. Much to my amazement, the issues ranged from "traditional" chemical or alcohol dependence to obsessive-compulsive disorder, Alzheimer's disease, gambling addictions, and sexual addictions.

The ABA Commission on Lawyer Assistance Programs, under the tireless direction of Donna Spilis, has recognized and addressed the unspoken demons of the profession since 1986. The Commission emphasizes that while approximately 10 percent of the American population has substance abuse problems, 15 to 18 percent of lawyers and judges may suffer those problems. The Commission notes: "Because many lawyers and judges are overachievers who carry an enormous workload, the tendency to 'escape' from daily problems through the use of drugs and alcohol is prevalent in the legal community. Also, the daily pressures placed on these men and women can lead to inordinate amounts of stress and mental illness." Most would agree that the quest for the extra billable hours or the absolutely satisfied client or judge may greatly increase pressures on the most talented practitioner; what is not as clear is why these activities appear to exacerbate dependency in sole practitioners at a disproportionate rate.

Dr. Talbott of the Talbott Recovery Campus in Atlanta (**www.talbott campus.com**) has identified six critical elements unique to lawyers' and judges' characteristics and perceptions that greatly influence the recovery process:

1. *Superior Intellectual and Verbal Skills:* The downside of these skills is that they permit deflection of unwanted feedback, and inhibit strong emotional bonding with peers and the recovery process.
2. *Ability to Notice Differences between Persons and Circumstances:* This inhibits lawyers' abilities to see themselves as similar to other addicted persons, and promotes feelings of uniqueness.
3. *Reluctance to Acknowledge Even Minor Personal Shortcomings:* This characteristic promotes minimization of consequences, and inhibits emotional honesty.
4. *Preference for Concise, Logical Reasoning:* Though perhaps helpful in work settings, this attribute inhibits open expression of emotions, and promotes an academic "textbook" approach to recovery.
5. *Professional Demeanor.* Lawyers are prone to challenging the credentials of treatment staff, and often believe they need a treatment peer group comprising those of similar educational and socioeconomic backgrounds.
6. *Need for Continuing Care:* Lawyers need affiliation with recovering professionals, and ongoing support and advocacy from treating facilities.

Despite the insight of Dr. Talbott's analysis, it fails to differentiate between large-firm practitioners and small-firm or sole practitioners. In testimony before the Join Together Policy Panel, Betty Ford, a former First Lady and champion of recovery, noted:

> As a recovering woman, I have personally suffered the scorn of others who are confused, bitter and misled about addiction. I still today sometimes get the reaction of how could a nice person like me be an alcoholic. It is hard not to take it personally when I read public opinion polls of both professionals and the general public who believe addiction to be a moral weakness rather than a disease. How could people still believe this in the year 2002?

Certainly stigma plays a role in seeking treatment, but it does not explain the disparity between types of lawyers or judges. Despite reading statistics, reports, and guides from a myriad of sources, I found it difficult to assess exactly why a sole practitioner would be more prone to addiction or mental illness. As a neophyte in the Lawyer Assistance Program administration, I believed the vulnerability of the sole practitioner seemed to be fueled by some intangible element that makes solo practice "different."

While serving as a director of CLHP, I was invited to attend a facilitated peer assistance meeting for "allied" professionals outside the Denver metropolitan area. At that meeting, I was impressed with the number of medical professionals who shared their recovery history; many had felony convictions. This was a significant and distinctive difference from the lawyers' groups with which I was familiar. Though many problems had been exposed by misdemeanor offenses, a felony conviction meant expulsion from the profession. Upon reflection, I realized that two factors contributed to the divergence of experience between professions: availability of controlled substances, and the federal accountability of the substances. With the Food and Drug Administration providing a "supervisory" role, the medical practitioners were "nudged" into treatment when audits revealed their "secrets." Lawyers police themselves.

On the flight back to Denver, I mulled over the possibility of merging professions in peer assistance programs. One recurring difference that haunts lawyer peer support is the divisive nature of the substance being abused: merging addiction to alcohol with addiction to illicit substances often leads to heated debate and discussion among lawyers. A former federal agent who attended peer support meetings blamed much of her abuse of alcohol on the fact that it was the only "escape" that was *legal and available*. As I mentally reconciled the experiences, I came to realize *opportunity and availability* are salient features of addictive behavior and, of course, this factor is accentuated in the solo or small-firm practice.

Sole practitioners operate in a vacuum of isolation. They are responsible for the legal woes of clients, and supervision is minimal or nonexistent. When Dr. Talbott's characteristics are factored in, this unsupervised opportunity makes the solo or small-practice lawyer particularly vulnerable to becoming compulsive in seeking and using alcohol or other drugs. Often the behavior problem can be hidden—he's in court; she's preparing a brief; that solo is attending a seminar. All are routine "lawyer activities," and all provide a plethora of excuses for behavior that would require accounting, if not validation, in a larger law practice or more translucent workplace environment.

It is beyond the scope of this chapter to offer an extensive list of resources available for lawyers struggling with personal difficulties. However, I will note that almost every bar association in the United States and Canada has recognized the problem, adopted assistance programs to address situations of crisis, and pioneered educational elements to affect the legal community prophylactically and maintain healthy recovery habits. Most have recognized the extreme sensitivity and confidentiality required to prevent addiction and foster healthy and confidential recovery programs.

It should also be noted that almost all bar associations maintain confidential lawyer assistance programs. These programs are readily accessible by phone or the Internet. Links to most lawyer assistance programs and other valuable resources can be found on the Web site of the ABA Commission on Lawyer Assistance Programs: **www.abanet.org/legalservices/colap**.

Purchase or Sale of a Solo Practice: The Financial Issues

53

Edward Poll

There are now close to forty states that permit the sale of a law practice, and more jurisdictions are considering rule changes to follow suit. Unlike earlier times, when lawyers who were leaving the practice of law simply closed their office doors and walked away, sellers of law practices can now link with potential buyers and complete economic transactions that benefit both parties. And selling lawyers can finally take something with them for all the years of effort in building a valued reputation from the delivery of high-quality legal services. The question is: What is the value of a law practice?

Valuation

Valuation is a prophecy of the future based upon facts presently at hand. It is an evaluation that permits the buyer of a law practice to attain an acceptable rate of return on the assets purchased. Because the seller usually wants to obtain the highest value possible for the practice, each asset, including intangible assets,[1] must be specifically identified and valued. Conversely, the buyer typically wants to buy only tangible assets and thereby obtain the practice for the lowest possible price.

What are the assets of a law practice that can be identified and transferred? The property[2] to be valued and that may be transferred include the following items:

- Cash
- Furniture
- Fixtures
- Equipment (such as computers and photocopy machines)
- Supplies
- Law library
- Real property (where the office is located) and location value (proximity to the court, business center, or client population base)
- Leasehold interests
- Telephone number (especially if long-standing)
- Proprietary computer software
- Accounts receivable (less cost of collection)
- Costs advanced on behalf of the client
- Work in progress, which is partially completed, but not yet billed as a receivable[3]
- Work completed but not yet billed as a receivable
- Goodwill[4] of the practitioner/going concern[5] value:
  - Immediate use of tangible assets
  - Trained and assembled work force
  - Case files, qualified client/prospect list[6]

Factors Affecting Value

Assets and "going concern" values may be affected, on a "macro" level, by the general economic characteristics and conditions affecting the business of the law practice. These include the following:

- Prevailing general economic conditions, both on the national level and the local level
- Trends in the industry/profession
- Size and complexity of the practice
- Barriers to entry, such as technology (the cost of purchasing hardware and software used by the profession, generally, to be competitive) and education requirements
- Profitability
- Expected growth in the profession

On a "micro" level, the nature of the asset to be valued also determines which method of valuation will be used. For example, the cost or book-value method may be used for tangible assets such as furniture and equipment; fair market value may also be used to value fixed assets. On the other hand, the excess-earnings method may be used to value goodwill. The discounted future cash-flow method of valuation may be used to value the entire law practice, with the fixed assets necessary to produce that cash flow included.

Determining Value

Although it may be a common desire to seek a "simple," guaranteed method to determine the value of a practice for all purposes, this is impossible. However, there are several methods that can be described relatively easily, even if their applications are more difficult. In the broadest sense, there are three methods of valuing a business: cost, market, and income.

Cost or Book-Value Method

In the context of a professional practice, the cost approach may result in valuing only the physical or tangible assets, such as furniture, fixtures, library, and equipment. The historical cost less accumulated depreciation equals "book value." The resulting value would be relatively small. Except for tangible assets, the cost approach is not used for most valuation purposes concerning a law practice.

Fair Market Value Method

The "marketplace" concept is easy to grasp. It was expressed in an early California land case as follows: Fair market value is "the highest price estimated in terms of money which the land would bring if exposed for sale in the open market, with reasonable time allowed in which to find a purchaser buying with knowledge of all the uses and purposes to which it was adopted and for which it was capable."[7] Obtaining the "fair market value" requires searching for the sale of comparable assets. In the real estate field, a buyer (or seller) obtains the records of sales from the county recorder's office, reviews the nature of those properties, and then makes a subjective evaluation regarding the similarity of those properties with the property to be valued. By comparing the property in question with similar properties that have sold in the open market, a reasonable evaluation of the fair market value of the property can be made.

When valuing "rolling stock," such as cars and trucks, the Kelly Blue Book values would be a first step in determining the present fair market value of a particular vehicle. Other assets have similar source materials for determining fair market value. The essence of the procedure, however, is to learn the sale price of assets of a similar nature (comparables), which are being purchased and sold by other, independent persons who are not under compulsion to buy or sell.

The use of this market approach to value an entire law practice is currently developing, and over time will be as readily available as the valuation of other businesses.

Income or Cash-Flow Method
Rule-of-Thumb Approach

The somewhat simplistic rule-of-thumb approach to valuing a professional practice can be used to value intangible assets. It basically asks this question: After valuing the physical, or identifiable, assets, what is the stream of income worth to a prospective buyer?

The rule-of-thumb approach is uncomplicated and direct: multiply one year's gross revenue by a multiplier; the result will be the value of the stream of income.[8]

The gross revenue should be averaged over the last five years to even out any peculiar ups or downs in the revenue stream. This average year's gross revenue is then multiplied by a factor. The factor, or the multiplier, varies with the industry and even with the geographic location. Some accounting firms, for example, are valued at 1.0 to 1.5 times (100 to 150 percent) annual gross receipts. Medical practices are frequently valued at .4 to 1.0 times (40 to 100 percent) gross receipts.

A standard has not yet developed for the sale of law practices. However, based upon the figures used in accounting and medicine, it would appear that the multiplier for the rule-of-thumb method should be in the same range for law practices.

Whether the multiplier is in the lower or the higher level of the range depends primarily upon how much repeat business is expected, the nature of the law practice, the number of clients, and the transferability of client relationships.[9] If there is a great deal of repeat business and client loyalty can be transferred, the multiplier will be higher. If, however, a portion of the clients will not stay with the practice because of the close personal relationship between client and lawyer, this factor must be considered, and the multiplier will be lower.

Excess-Earnings Approach

A popular method of valuing law practices in family law cases has been the "excess-earnings" method. This method is a conservative approach. It is, in essence, a "no change" model. It appraises a practice based only upon what the practice has generated, with no attention to future prospects, up or down. It has, therefore, been acceptable in marital dissolution proceedings where projections are considered to be in violation of the standard that post-separation earnings are "separate property,"[10] and where speculation about future events is inadmissible evidence. "Excess earnings" has been defined as

> earnings over and above a normal return for similar services or intangible assets primarily attributable to exclusive control over an economic resource. In a business setting, this resource may be the location of the business or an established reputation for quality service. In a professional practice, the economic resource may be the personality or unique talent of the professional. For an employee, excess earnings may result from education, personality, special talent, business acquaintances, and other qualifications that confer advantage, differential treatment, and a relatively greater number of future employment options.[11]

Over the last fifteen years, family law courts have struggled with the concept of dividing intangible assets, particularly goodwill, between a professional spouse who could not sell his or her professional practice and a non-professional spouse who could not acquire or otherwise be directly involved in the professional practice because of the lack of the appropriate license.

The courts have constructed a variety of ruses to overcome the apparent inequity of not dividing something of obvious value. One such ruse was the establishment of the "goodwill"[12] doctrine. This idea ran into several logical barriers. One barrier was that the goodwill of a sole practitioner could not be transferred; the practice was not saleable. Thus, the goodwill was personal to the professional practitioner. If that were true, then the family benefited during all the years of marriage by the increased earnings of the professional. This would result in greater assets subject to division having been accumulated during the marriage and higher earnings from which to grant spousal support in the future. How, then, could the "goodwill" also be divided? It would be "double dipping."

To meet these challenges, and others, different definitions resulted, all of which were designed to overcome the logical inconsistencies between the definition, or its application, and economic reality. Recognizing the logical difficulty with the concept of goodwill as applied to family law, the courts developed the principle of "excess earnings."

Goodwill is conceived to be a differential advantage. It results from the ability to overcome competition by reason of personal skill, reputation, location, special talent, or other qualifications. "This differential advantage gives rise to earnings in excess of a normal return on assets including labor and services provided. The existence of goodwill, whether personal or commercial, results in excess earnings."[13] One commentator maintains that the professional-goodwill doctrine is broad enough to include "excess earnings" of an employee,[14] and that these excess earnings are subject to division by the family law court.

The excess-earnings method recognizes the economic reality that there is something special about the law practice that develops earnings above the norm and, if that special something can be transferred to someone else, it is something of value that can be sold. If there is nothing of special value, then there is nothing of value to be sold because the buyer could increase his or her business as much, if not more, by hiring a lawyer as an employee. In other words, there are no excess earnings in the particular law practice being valued.

The excess-earnings method seeks to measure the "investment value" of a law practice, not the fair market value. Where law practices cannot be sold, fair market value cannot be determined. An investment approach under these circumstances is the next best alternative, according to some domestic relations courts.

Excess earnings can be calculated as follows:[15]

1. Ascertain the earnings of the law firm (or lawyer, if a sole practitioner). Review the previous five years to obtain an average figure. Remove any unusually high contingency fees, so the earnings average is not distorted.
2. Fix the amount by which the law practice exceeds what an employee of comparable qualifications would earn.[16] (Compare education, training, skill, and effort by way of number of hours worked, for example.)[17]
3. Compute a fair return on investment in physical assets used in the practice.
4. The amount by which the five-year average earnings of the practice, less the fair return on physical assets, exceeds the figure for fair compensation of a comparable lawyer is the amount of excess earnings.
5. The excess-earnings amount is then capitalized to determine the value of the law practice. The "cap rate"[18] is a function of the risk of retaining the clientele, the stability of the earnings of the law practice during the time period chosen, the competitiveness of the practice, as well as other factors. The choice of "cap rate" is subjective.

To get the total value of the law practice, add the valuation obtained by calculating the excess earnings to the net tangible and other assets (total assets revalued to their present in-place value less liabilities). This would be the total value of the professional law practice.

Discounted Future Cash-Flow Approach

Discounted future cash flow is the present value of a future stream of income. This is a far more sophisticated method of valuation than generally used, especially in the sale of a law practice. The advantage of this approach, however, is to place a current or present value on the cash that is expected to be received in the future. When someone is buying an asset, the asset is generally an economically depreciating asset or an investment. An economically depreciating asset is one that will disappear over time as it is used in the business. The "disappearance" can be by its actual use in the business (supplies consumed in the practice or technological obsolescence of computers), or by lowering in value because of age (such as with cars). If the purchase doesn't fall into one of these categories, it is generally an investment, as with the purchase of real estate—or a law practice. If the purchase is an investment, the buyer generally expects to receive a return that will not only pay back the amount expended for the purchase, but also a return equal to or greater than the percentage that the buyer would have received if the money for the purchase were placed in the bank.

This refined method is used for valuing other professional practices. If, in fact, "cash is king" in today's world, then this approach is closer to economic reality and a more realistic valuation approach. It certainly is more realistic than the excess-earnings method of valuation. This method can be used in appraising law practices for sale as time passes and the need for greater sophistication increases.

How Much?

The question every selling lawyer wants answered is, "How much can I get for my practice?" At this point, "valuation" issues are out the door and the "bottom line" question is asked.

The price to be paid may be estimated by reference to financial data and certain marketplace guidelines, such as those described above. But no amount of analysis will determine the precise price a willing buyer and a willing seller will accept. That figure is subject to many different factors, including terms of payment, geography, nature of the practice, history of client retention by the selling firm, and size of the practice. But, whatever the price, a key issue for the buyer is whether the buyer will retain the practice being sold. To assure the buyer, an earn-out or payout based upon collections may be created. This will assure the buyer that payments will be made only for designated revenues received. The selling lawyer then has an incentive to help the buying lawyer in his or her efforts to keep the clients of the practice.

Outside Resources

Who should do the negotiating? Would you negotiate the purchase or sale of your own residence? Probably not. Traditionally, buyers and sellers of real es-

tate act through agents, or real estate brokers. Would you negotiate the purchase of a new car? Probably. What is the difference? One is the size of the
transaction. Another difference is the personal stake in the outcome. If you
can't buy the car you want because the seller is obstinate, you'll walk away,
not having your ego bruised. But, if you can't get the house you want, your vision of the future and your stature in the community is somehow affected. To
reduce the possibility of this happening, you might retain an independent
third party to help. Another difference is that sellers often talk themselves out
of a transaction after the deal has been negotiated, but before the papers have
been finalized. To reduce the chances of this occurrence, third-party experts
are engaged. The following are outside resources that may be able to help in
the sale of a law practice:

- *Law Firm Management Consultants*: They will know the ins and outs of
  the law firm in question. With a broad base of knowledge, they know
  the legal landscape and have credibility on both sides of the negotiating table. A consultant who represents the buyer can create a strategy
  for growth and a plan for exiting the practice. A consultant who represents the seller can create the prospectus, do the search for potential law firm buyers, develop the marketing, and do the negotiating.

- *Business Opportunities Brokers*: In some jurisdictions, the state licenses these brokers by way of real estate licenses. Business opportunities brokers are becoming more interested and involved in law
  practice sales. They generally want to standardize (and "commodi-
  tize") the field as they have done with medical and other professions.
  One organization is currently attempting to create national listings of
  law firms available for sale.

- *Accountants*: Some accountants, with law firms as clients, are attempting to interject themselves into sale-of-practice deals. Accountants are
  good at understanding the numbers, although they might not understand all the nuances of the legal profession.

- *Valuation Experts*: A valuation expert can be used for creating the initial valuation of the practice, especially in establishing a starting
  benchmark. However, valuation experts may not be so useful in negotiating actual price.

- *Psychologists*: A psychologist can help the participants understand the
  process of negotiating and the various ways of reaching a closed deal.

- *Lawyers*: An independent and objective lawyer should be used to document the deal (draft the contract). Neither the buyer nor the seller
  should draft the agreement. There is a question about whether the independent lawyer should also be the one doing the valuation or the
  negotiation during the process.

- *Marketing Consultants*: A marketing consultant can prepare the sale prospectus and develop the marketing strategy to sell the practice.
- *Executive Search Consultants*: Executive search consultants are frequently involved in the joining of two large firms, but not so frequently used in small-firm sales. Unfortunately, neither their bias nor their experience will generally permit them to ask for goodwill, a major component in any true law practice sale.

In addition to negotiating, there is the problem of getting the word out or learning about potential law firm sales. Business opportunities brokers, law firm management consultants, accountants, marketing consultants, valuation firms, and appraisers are excellent resources to help spread the word that a lawyer is looking to buy or sell a law firm practice. Another source, not yet used for this purpose, but not to be discounted, is the Internet and law-related bulletin boards. In the future, electronic means of spreading the word may be the most effective and least expensive method of communicating this information.

Will It Fly?

Is every practice saleable? Maybe not. Some practices are so small and so personal in nature that without a continuing involvement of the first lawyer, a second lawyer would not succeed in keeping the clients. However, even the smallest and most personal practices are likely to be saleable for the right price and under the right terms. If the buying lawyer was assured that he or she would receive that which was negotiated—a law practice of a certain volume of revenue or a certain client base that remained with the buying lawyer for a designated period of time—a sale would be highly likely even for the smallest firm.

Endnotes

1. An intangible asset may be defined as property whose value is not predicated upon its inherent physical characteristics. Intangible assets include, but are not limited to, leasehold interests, trademarks, trade names, patents, contracts, customer/client relationships, and goodwill. Because intangible assets are typically not recorded on financial records of a company/law practice, identification of these assets may be difficult.
2. *See, e.g., In re* Marriage of Lopez, 113 Cal. Rptr. 58, 38 Cal. App. 3d 93, 110 (Ct. App. 1974) (discussion of what trial court in dissolution of marriage proceeding looked for in determining value of law practice).

3. Contingency-fee agreements represent a unique asset in a law practice. This asset is a work in progress that cannot be billed or collected until the entire matter is successfully concluded. Valuing contingent-fee files may be done on one of several bases. One can wait until the conclusion of the matter and then estimate the amount of time expended on the file before and after the date of valuation. The appropriate percentage of the total fee would then be attributed to the value for work spent on the file before the date of valuation. Alternatively, one can reconstruct all the hours spent on the file before the date of valuation and assign an hourly rate to the hours spent. Another approach is to ascertain the costs advanced on a contingent-fee file, considering them to be an investment in that matter. Then, a designated return on these advanced costs would be used as the basis for determining the value of the file.

4. The court in In re *Marriage of Lopez*, 113 Cal. Rptr. 58, 38 Cal. App. 3d 93, 110 (Ct. App. 1974), was concerned with "goodwill of the practitioner in his law business as a going concern. . . ." Other commentators have made the distinction between a "going concern" value and a "goodwill" factor. In the case of the sale of a law practice, the going concern and/or goodwill factor(s) may be discounted to some degree by the perceived loss of clients resulting from the absence of the selling lawyer.

5. "Going concern value is defined as the additional element of value which attaches to [the assembled assets] by reason of [their] existence as an integral part of a going concern." *See* Margulis, *Appropriate Standards of Value and Their Use in Allocations of Purchase Price 590–91* (citing VGS Corp. v. Comm., 68 T.C. 563 (1977)). The theory, stated simply, is that the whole is greater than the sum of its parts, even in the absence of goodwill.

6. At worst, one can make the analogy, for purposes of valuing a list of clients, to a preselected and qualified mailing list. At best, the buyer will maintain an ongoing, attorney-client relationship and increase his or her practice as a result of the purchase.

7. *See* Sacramento R.R. Co. v. Heilborn, 156 Cal. 408, 409 (1909). Although *Heilborn* discussed land, the same concept and definition applies regardless of the asset being valued. *See also* Internal Rev. Reg. § 20.2031-1(b) (1986), 1986 Internal Revenue Code, as amended.

8. Some rule-of-thumb multipliers result in a value for intangibles; others result in total value, including all tangible assets. A multiple of 1.0 gross income or higher is generally for all assets.

9. *See, e.g., In re* Hull, 712 P.2d 1317 (Mont. 1986).

10. This is a logical inconsistency, because goodwill is predicated upon the future patronage of past clients.
11. *See* Harper, *Excess Earnings: Redefining the Professional Goodwill Doctrine,* 17 Pac. L.J. 165, 176 (1985) [hereinafter Harper].
12. The traditional definition of goodwill is the expectation of continued public patronage. *See, e.g.,* Cal. Bus. & Prof. Code § 14100. Goodwill connotes above-average success and profitability.
13. *See* Harper, *supra* note 11, at 176.
14. *Id.*
15. *See, e.g.,* Dugan v. Dugan, 457 A.2d 1 (N.J. 1983); *see also* Hunt v. Hunt, 698 P.2d 1168 (Alaska 1985); *In re* Kapusta, 491 N.E.2d 48 (Ill. App. Ct. 1986); Nelson v. Nelson, 411 N.W.2d 868 (Minn. Ct. App. 1987).
16. Use local, not national, statistics to reflect local conditions accurately. Certain organizations regularly conduct surveys for information on compensation and related matters. Examples include Daniel J. Cantor & Co., Altman & Weil, Inc. (for example, 1994 Survey of Law Firm Economics), Dun & Bradstreet, Survey of Small Businesses, Almanac of Business Ratios, and local bar associations, among others.
17. One criticism of this method is that one must first deduct the fair compensation to get excess earnings. The more valuable the person's contribution, the higher will be the compensation entitlement or replacement cost. Thus, no excess earnings result. And, one cannot use average earnings because the efforts of this practitioner are exceptional. One must compare actual to actual, not theoretical.
18. The following example illustrates the effect that different capitalization rates have when applied to the same excess earnings. Different rates are applied based upon the assessment of risk: $50,000 $50,000 $50,000 Excess Earning Multiplier Value: x3 x5 x8 $150,000 $250,000 $400,000.

Glossary:
Selected Terms of Valuation

Edward Poll

1. Account payable: A debt incurred as a result of a current purchase of supplies or other goods and services used by the purchaser. The debt is to be paid sometime in the future, usually thirty days.
2. Balance sheet: One of three financial statements currently prepared for business enterprises. The balance sheet lists the assets and liabilities of the enterprise as of a date certain. The formula expressed by accountants is: Assets equals the sum of Liabilities and Equity (A = L + E).
3. Aged accounts receivable: The accounts receivable listed in one column by alphabet or category spread across by month of creation. The accounts receivable will become more difficult to collect as time passes.
4. Book value: The historical cost value less accumulated depreciation. Accelerated depreciation for tax purposes may also cause an even lower book value. One is also permitted to write off equipment purchases up to $10,000 per year. Some assets, if expensed as noted, may never appear on the balance sheet. Care must be taken to separate tax return treatment and financial statement (or book) treatment. Appropriate accounting rules need to be reviewed for interpretation of any given question.
5. Capitalization rate: The "cap rate" is the projected cost of capital. A conservative approach is to use a relatively high figure, indicating that there is substantial risk and the investor should be entitled to a comparable rate of return for the risk involved.
6. Cash Flow Statement: One of three financial statements prepared for a business enterprise. Arguably, this is the single most important financial statement used by a business. This statement reflects the actual cash received, not revenue billed, and expenses paid, not debt incurred.
7. Discounted cash flow: The present value of a stream of cash in the future.
8. Fair market value: The price a willing buyer would pay and a willing seller would accept, each with adequate time, neither being under any compulsion to buy or sell, and each with reasonable knowledge of all relevant facts.

9. Going concern value: As distinguished from goodwill, is the increased value of the assembled assets due to their existence as an integral part of an ongoing business.

10. Goodwill: The expectation of continued public patronage in the future. The economist's definition is the present value of future earnings.

11. Income statement: Also known as Profit and Loss Statement. This financial statement, one of the three normally used by business enterprises, reflects the revenues and expenses of a business enterprise over a period of time, usually one month, a quarter (three months), or a year (annual).

12. In place value: The present condition of the asset plus delivery and installation costs.

13. Liquidation value: The value based on a "forced" sale with little or no time to properly advertise the availability of the property or asset for sale.

14. Market comparables: Factors used to make comparison of similar assets. The factors used for comparison include such data as sales; net income; book value; earnings before interest and taxes; cash flow.

15. Net accounts receivable: The gross accounts receivable, aged, less cost of collection. Statements outstanding in excess of six (6) months may be considered uncollectible and turned over to an outside service for collection. Statements outstanding for twelve (12) months would be deemed uncollectible and not included in the accounts receivable.

16. Net Worth: Net worth, also known as equity, is defined by accountants as Assets minus Liabilities (E = A − L).

17. Normal value: The value in the long run under conditions of perfect competition.

18. Replacement value: The cost to replace an asset, new, delivered and installed.

Purchase or Sale of a Solo Practice: The Ethical Issues

54

Demetrios Dimitriou

Introduction

The disposition or acquisition of a sole practitioner's or law firm's practice can be of interest to other lawyers and firms under various circumstances. The most obvious situations in which practices are sold or purchased are involuntary dispositions caused by death or disability of sole practitioners, or voluntary sales of existing practices due to firm dissolution, lawyer retirement, or lawyer relocation.

As more lawyers find the partnership track in large firms unattractive or unattainable, and as larger firms downsize, the market for existing sole and small-firm practices is growing at an increasing rate. Thus, what may have initially been of interest only to sole practitioners, their estates, and others who were beginning practices is now of growing interest to seasoned lawyers or practice groups who wish to practice in smaller settings or become sole practitioners.

Acquisitions and dispositions of solo practices involve ethical issues of interest to both purchasers and sellers, because they affect the ultimate value of the assets subject to the transactions.

In most states, before adoption of Rule 1.17 of the ABA Model Rules of Professional Conduct in 1990, it was impermissible for a lawyer, or law firm, to sell or purchase a law practice, including its goodwill. As states adopt Model Rule 1.17 (Sale of Law Practice), or modified versions of the rule, more lawyers and firms will engage in the purchase and sale of law practices and eclectic areas of law practices.

Historically, the goodwill of a practice could not be sold. The theory was that clients were not chattel and therefore could not be sold. The underlying value of most practices, however, is goodwill; that is, the expectation of continuing client patronage, which can hopefully be transferred to purchasing lawyers. Thus, until the advent of Model Rule 1.17, partners could obtain the economic benefits attributable to goodwill, but sole practitioners could not. It has always been possible for lawyers to sell the physical assets of law practices, including substantive systems, to other lawyers.

Each jurisdiction's applicable rules must be reviewed to discern the extent to which they are consistent with Model Rule 1.17 and with the following discussions regarding the sale and purchase of law practices, areas of practice, and goodwill.

In those jurisdictions that have adopted Model Rule 1.17, any lawyer, law firm, or estate of a deceased lawyer can sell or buy all the assets of a practice, or area of practice, including related goodwill, provided requirements of the rule are followed (see Appendix B). These requirements can materially affect the marketability of a practice being sold. For example, under the rule, a purchaser cannot pick and choose either cases or clients. Essentially, the purchaser takes all—or substantially all—of the practice, even though the clients are always free to seek any lawyers to handle their matters. Even with the detailed provisions of the rule, there are several problem areas that should be considered. Various issues regarding the sale and purchase of a practice, often overlooked by both seller and purchaser as they concentrate upon negotiation of price and terms, could be of great significance, and are discussed in the following sections.

Client Communications

Has the seller maintained adequate contact with clients, active as well as inactive? A purchaser is always interested in determining how many clients can be successfully transferred, and will rely upon the ability of the seller, or the seller's estate, to provide material assistance in such a transfer. The greater the probability of successful transfer of clients, both old and current, the higher the goodwill value of the practice. Some specific concerns regarding this issue follow.

Continued Representation of Existing Clients

Will problems arise if the purchaser decides to discontinue representing an existing client, or wants to be substituted in, or out, as the "attorney of record" in a pending court or administrative proceeding? If the client does not cooperate or cannot be located, then a problem exists. The purchaser may not be getting the bargained-for consideration. Also, the seller, or seller's estate, would continue to be responsible for any case or matter in which a formal substitution of lawyers was required and not accomplished, or in which there was an uncompleted engagement and the client had not responded to the notice of sale. The purchaser and seller must remember the need to comply with the formal procedures to effect substitutions or withdrawals in pending matters as outlined in the applicable jurisdiction's counterpart to Model Rule 1.16 (Declining or Terminating Representation).

Notice to Clients

Model Rule 1.17 requires that written notice of the sale be given to all clients, sets forth what the notice must contain, and gives clients ninety days within which to respond. Although the purchaser, after notice of the sale has been given to clients, can begin to act on behalf of those clients who have not responded within the ninety days, does the purchasing lawyer *want* to act and thus accept the responsibility for those clients? Does the responsibility automatically shift to the purchasing lawyer at the end of the ninety-day period? The rule is silent on these matters. What about the rule's requirement that essentially the entire practice, or area of practice, be sold as a unit? Does that mean that after the ninety days pass, all clients who did not (1) affirmatively opt not to follow the purchaser, (2) ask for their files, or (3) retain other counsel automatically become the purchaser's clients? Again, no clear answer can be found in the rule. The agreement between the seller and purchaser should address this issue, as it may be that client responsibility continues to rest with the seller until the purchaser begins to act or assumes responsibility. The new rule does provide that if the client fails to take action, or does not otherwise object within ninety days of receipt of the notice, it is to be presumed that the client has consented to the purchaser continuing as counsel. What can the purchasing lawyer do if he or she does not want this presumption to apply? The rule is silent.

A Caveat

The client file should follow the client. Should the purchaser accept custody of client files for those clients who fail to cooperate or cannot be located? Prudence dictates not.

Notice to Clients of a Deceased Lawyer

The client notice issue is exacerbated for the estate of a deceased lawyer. The estate of the lawyer may well continue to be exposed to client damage claims for injury or loss that occurred because matters were not properly handled after the lawyer's demise. (See Model Rule 1.3, Diligence.) The deceased lawyer's estate may have an obligation to act prudently to protect client interests in connection with pending matters until the clients obtain other counsel, accept the purchaser as their lawyer, or instruct the estate to return the matters to the clients for their handling. Although reasonable attempts by the estate to give actual notice to clients is helpful, the responsibility to look after client matters and take steps to minimize loss to clients would seem to continue as an estate obligation.

Additional Ethical Considerations

Other ethical concerns include protecting client interests and confidences, both before and after the sale of the practice. Confidential client communications may have been included in file notes, client documents, or memoranda found in both active and closed files. Also not to be forgotten are unearned fees, trust funds, other assets held by the seller and belonging to clients, and possible conflicts of interest that may exist with the purchaser's existing client base.

Protecting Client Interests

In addition to the need for withdrawal or substitution of counsel for clients involved in litigation, consideration must be given to all other clients to see that their matters are handled in ways that do not prejudice them. Do not overlook the need to return client fees advanced and yet unearned, trust funds belonging to clients that are not transferred to the purchasing lawyer, client files, and other papers or documents belonging to clients.

Client Confidences

The seller must exercise care not to disclose any confidential client information to prospective purchasers. (See Model Rule 1.6, Confidentiality of Information.) This includes care in allowing others to review files. Absent prior client approval, random file reviews or access to files not purged of confidential information should not be permitted. Information about types of cases and income derived, as long as not identified with specific clients, is permissible. The names and addresses of clients may be given to prospective purchasers, except in those unusual situations where the disclosure of a client's identity would disclose a client confidence. Even if the seller is the executor of an estate, this issue continues as a concern because if a client is damaged by disclosure of a confidence protected by the privilege, the estate may be liable.

Client Files and Funds

What is to be done with client files? To the extent that a client affirmatively agrees to remain with the purchaser, the answer is simple—or is it? Give the file to the purchaser; but should the seller get a receipt? If so, should it come from the lawyer or the client? What about a dispute regarding the file's contents? Do you inventory the file? Choose your level of risk taking and decide.

The practical answer probably includes a certain amount of risk taking in this area of exposure. There is also the vexing problem of closed client files held by the seller that do not involve "pending" matters and may contain confidential client information and materials. (See Model Rule 1.6, Confidentiality of Information.) Existing closed files should not be transferred to the purchaser, absent client or former client approval, unless the files have been reviewed to be sure that no confidential information or any items of value to the client are contained in those files. Damages suffered by the client as a result of such oversight would probably rest with the seller. (Model Rule 1.15, Safekeeping Property.)

Client trust funds and property held in trust must be returned to the client unless the client directs otherwise. To the extent the selling lawyer was acting as a bailee in connection with property belonging to the client, absent client acquiescence to the transfer or other disposition of the property, bailee liability to the client continues.

Conflicts with Purchasing Lawyer's Existing Clients

An additional problem that is not addressed in Model Rule 1.17 is the interaction of conflict-of-interest rules with the sale (Model Rule 1.7, Conflict of Interest: Current Clients; Model Rule 1.8, Conflict of Interest: Current Clients: Specific Rules; Model Rule 1.9, Duties to Former Clients; Model Rule 1.10, Imputation of Conflicts of Interest: General Rule; and Model Rule 1.12, Former Judge, Arbitrator, Mediator or Other Third-Party Neutral).

The purchaser needs to be cognizant of this issue and either attempt to screen before the purchase or do so immediately after the purchase to identify all conflict matters or issues and take appropriate action. If there is a conflict, the seller may have an obligation to reimburse the client for any additional expense the client may incur as a result of having to find a new lawyer and bring him or her "up to speed," as the conflict with the purchaser was caused by the sale. The risk of the existence of a client conflict when reviewing the selling lawyer's list of current and former clients with the parallel client lists of the purchaser will largely depend upon overlapping areas of practice and geographic areas of activity. Nevertheless, a conflicts check is necessary in all cases except when the purchaser has yet to enter practice. The cost to the purchaser of failing to do so can be the loss of a most favored client. See, for example, *Picker International Inc. v. Varian Associates, Inc.,* 670 F. Supp. 1363 (N.D. Ohio 1987) and *Truck Insurance Exchange v. Fireman's Fund Insurance Co.,* 8 Cal. Rptr. 2d 228, 6 Cal. App. 4th 1050 (Ct. App. 1992). Even more serious is the possibility of the loss of fees earned or disgorgement of fees received. See In re *Eric Alden Lewis, Debtor, Law Offices of Nicholas A. Franke v. Marcy J.K. Tiffany, U.S. Trustee,* 113 F.3d 1040 (9th Cir. 1997); In re *Joseph Basham and Mary Basham, Debtors; Michael Byrne and Terry Byrne, Debtors; Tom Hale, Appellant v. United States Trustee,* 208 B.R. 926 (B.A.P. 9th Cir. 1997); and *Goldstein v. Lees,* 120 Cal. Rptr. 253, 46 Cal. App. 3d 614 (Ct. App. 1975).

Estates and Ethical Rules

In those instances where the seller's estate is making the sale, ethical rules still must be considered. Although the ethical rules do not control the activities of the estate representative, the client may have a claim against the estate itself for any loss or injury suffered by disclosure of client confidences, failure to return client papers and other assets (including cash and documents of value) to the client, or breach of other ethical rules.

Using the seller's staff members may be helpful and efficient, as they are knowledgeable about client files and matters, and presumably subject to the same ethical rules that governed the lawyer in connection with confidential information. Thus, the staff members, unlike the estate representative or surviving spouse, should be able to review files and return to the client any confidential information and materials, as well as property held by the decedent as bailee.

Another problem to be considered is the inadvertent missing of deadlines or statutes of limitations, and similar concerns. The best interests of both the estate and the client might require that staff members or others review files to protect against the inadvertent failure to act in connection with such matters, even at the risk of an unintended breach of client confidences. The damages to the client might be less than if the file were not reviewed at all.

A Caveat

Remember, the seller has an ethical responsibility to comply with Model Rule 1.16 (Declining or Terminating Representation), which requires the lawyer, upon termination of the attorney-client relationship, to deliver client papers and property (see Appendix B). The answer probably depends upon the context within which the demand by the client for his or her "file" takes place. For instance, is trial imminent? Are there alternative sources for the information reasonably available to the client? Court and ethics opinions concerning the composition of "client papers" and the "client file" address these and similar questions. The underlying rationale is that if failure to give a paper or document to the client would cause reasonably foreseeable prejudice to the client, then it should be given to the client.

There is useful information concerning client papers and client files in the *Restatement (Third) of the Law Governing Lawyers* § 46, and the reporter's note. Also providing some guidance is the State Bar of California Standing Committee on Professional Responsibility and Conduct, Formal Opinion 2001-157. An extensive discussion on the topic can be found in the *Law Library Journal*, volume 93 (Winter 2001), published by the American Association of Law Libraries.

Presumably the estate's obligation to the client would be the same, not as an ethical duty, but for purposes of mitigating damages or injury suffered by the client due to failure to notify the tribunal of the death, to deliver client papers and property, and to refund unearned fees.

Purchaser's Competency

What is the exposure to the seller (or his or her estate) if the purchaser is not competent to handle particular cases or matters? (See Model Rule 1.1, Competence.) Although the seller or seller's estate is not a guarantor, there may be a responsibility to undertake a reasonable investigation of the purchaser's competency.

The purchaser needs to be concerned, as well. What if the purchaser is not competent to handle certain matters? Can the sale proceed? Model Rule 1.17 requires that the practice be sold as an entity. Can the purchaser refer to others those matters the purchaser is not competent to handle or does not wish to handle? Would this be considered a "resale" and violate the rule, particularly if the purchaser were paid a referral fee? If the purchaser associated with appropriate counsel, with client consent, perhaps these concerns would be addressed.

Seller's Representations about Purchaser

Has the seller or seller's estate made any representations about the quality or qualifications of the purchaser? Each should be concerned about representations made to clients and former clients about the qualifications or expertise of the purchaser. These representations may expose the seller to damages if the representations are misleading or untrue. The seller also should be mindful of the limitations set forth in the applicable jurisdiction's advertising rules.

Purchaser's Discovery of Seller's Errors

More vexing issues for the purchaser are the following: Does the purchaser have any duty to the acquired clients to disclose evidence of incompetence or malpractice if found in the files? What are the purchaser's responsibilities if violations of Model Rules 1.2 (Scope of Representation and Allocation of Authority between Client and Lawyer), 3.1 (Meritorious Claims and Contentions), 3.2 (Expediting Litigation), 3.3 (Candor toward the Tribunal), 3.4 (Fairness to Opposing Party and Counsel), or other rules are found to exist as a result of the selling lawyer's activities or advice? Will any of the above issues involve the purchaser in litigation, even if ultimately no purchaser liability is found? These are easy questions to ask, but the answers are much more difficult to come by. The issues represent a risk exposure for the purchaser. The purchaser may have a professional responsibility to disclose any of the above matters and advise the client concerning the client's rights. In many cases, it might be prudent to have the client seek independent legal advice.

Limiting Liability by Contract

Lawyers must not overlook the fact that they cannot limit their liability to a client, nor settle a claim or potential claim for such liability to a client, without informing the client, in writing, of his or her right to seek independent legal advice. (See Appendix B, Model Rule 1.8(h), Conflict of Interest: Current Clients: Specific Rules.) Therefore, a hold-harmless agreement with a client, absent another lawyer's independent review, would violate this rule. An indemnity agreement between the purchaser and seller (or seller's estate) relating to past or future malpractice issues may be helpful. Also, the purchasing lawyer may be able to enter an agreement with clients to arbitrate disputes that may arise during the representation, including fee and malpractice claims, depending upon the jurisdiction's rules. Useful information on arbitration questions can be found in the *Restatement (Third) of the Law Governing Lawyers* §§ 42, 54 (fee disputes and malpractice claims).

Covenant Not to Compete

Can the sale of a law practice include a covenant not to compete? The answer may now be yes. Model Rule 1.17(a) provides that in the sale of the practice, the seller is required to cease practicing within a certain geographical area or jurisdiction. Also see *Howard v. Babcock,* 6 Cal. 4th 409 (1993).

Fee Issues

Model Rule 1.17(d) addresses the fee question. Essentially, it provides that fees charged cannot be increased by reason of the sale. Must, or should, the purchaser enter new fee agreements with each client? Does Model Rule 1.5

(Fees) require new fee agreements with clients? If the purchaser intends to change a fee agreement with a client, assuming it would not violate Rule 1.17, compliance with Rule 1.5 would be necessary. (See Appendix B).

Economic and Other Considerations

Obviously, there are many factors to consider in deciding whether to sell or purchase a law practice. In addition to those already discussed, there are basic economic considerations that must be addressed, such as transference of title, evaluation and treatment of accounts receivable, verification of funds held in trust, analysis of outstanding debts and lease provisions, and determination of the adequacy of staff to be retained.

Does the purchase make economic sense? Is there insurance available, at reasonable cost, to cover the various risks? Is the quality of the practice being purchased acceptable, not only from an economic perspective, but also in terms of its clients? Is the seller's reputation in the community appropriate for the purchaser? What are the risks of client attrition? When can the purchaser contact the seller's clients? (See Appendix B, Model Rule 7.3, Direct Contact with Prospective Clients.) If there is a commission being paid to a broker, or a finder's fee, does this violate the jurisdiction's fee-splitting or advertising rules? (See Appendix B, Model Rule 5.4, Professional Independence of a Lawyer, and Model Rule 7.2, Advertising.) These are just a few of the many additional concerns involved in the sale of a practice.

Establishing Value and Purchase Price

After considering all the issues discussed above, how do you place a value on the practice and set a purchase price? Arriving at a fair purchase price for a law practice is more art than science. There are many methods for setting value. Some are based upon an average of several years' gross annual income. This figure is then adjusted by the economic factors discussed above to arrive at the purchase price. Variations on this formula include lengthening or shortening the time period used to calculate average gross income. Calculating a value for goodwill is the least precise element and the most difficult to establish.

The other aspect of the sale to be agreed upon is the method of payment of the purchase price. It is unusual for the purchaser to pay the entire purchase price in a lump sum up front. Payment is usually made over time, and the length of time and number of payments can affect the purchase price.

Occasionally, the purchase price is based upon the amount of income earned from the seller's client base. Usually, a certain percentage (similar to a referral fee) is paid to the seller as the fees are earned. The length of time over which payment is made is an item to be negotiated as part of the overall purchase and sale agreement. The length of time is typically two to five years, depending upon the type of practice involved. One needs to be aware of local ethical rules that may differ from Model Rule 5.4(a)(2), which permits fee sharing when there is a purchase of a practice from a deceased, disabled, or disappeared lawyer (see Appendix B). The Model Rules do not appear to allow payment of referral fees if the seller is simply retiring or continuing to practice in a different location.

Expanding Through Merger—and the Sequel

55

Joel P. Bennett

Real-Life Experience

One of the problems of being a sole practitioner or a two-lawyer firm, especially in a large metropolitan area, is the difficulty in competing with larger firms for corporate and institutional clients, such as labor unions. In addition to having a difficult time supporting the increased overhead of associates and legal assistants with only one or two partners, it is also difficult to avoid the stereotype of not being able to provide high-quality (high-power) work for corporate and institutional clients. In short, sole practitioners and small firms sometimes suffer from a negative image.

Merger Exploration

The lawyers mentioned in this chapter, each of whom has either a small number of such clients or none (but seeks some), decided to explore expanding their capabilities through merger of existing practices. We arrived at this decision by various routes. One of us was spurred to make a decision when he noticed a three-lawyer firm on his floor moving out after merging with a two-lawyer firm. Another of us had always thought about merger as the best and fastest means of achieving growth. A third was concerned with economies of scale and reducing overhead. We began meeting on a monthly basis. Soon it became apparent to all concerned that we needed to meet more frequently if real progress was to be made.

The beginning group consisted of five lawyers—three sole practitioners and two lawyers practicing together in partnership. As we began meeting, it became clear that we all knew other lawyers whom we thought would be worthy members of our group. We grew somewhat precipitately, up to ten members, plus one member who would have been of counsel. We soon realized that the group was too large. No one wanted to ask anyone to leave, so we waited until the group worked itself by attrition down to seven members. During this time, without knowing it, we were engaged in an educational process. We discussed the various areas of practice in which we currently worked, the new areas that interested us, and the kinds of work we were not interested in doing at all. We soon found that we needed to keep minutes of our meetings, so we could keep track of our discussions, activities, and objectives.

We determined that we needed to indicate the assets we would be bringing to the prospective firm in addition to our own abilities and clients. We exchanged lists of personnel currently in our employ, equipment and library materials we presently had, and equipment desired.

One of the most important topics—and one that took a great deal of time to resolve—was income distribution. After much discussion and some hesitation on the part of each of us (because we had never apportioned income before), we agreed upon a formula based upon the Hale and Dorr method, as set forth by the late Reginald Heber Smith in a monograph entitled, *Law Office Organization*, published by the ABA Law Practice Management Section. The basic way in which we agreed to apply this formula was that after expenses were paid, the profit would be split, with 35 percent going to the person originating the business and 65 percent to those doing the work on the matter, divided pro rata by hours spent. We felt the large percentage ascribed to the originating partner was justified, because of the great emphasis we placed upon growth. We wanted to encourage as much new business as possible, for we felt we could always process the work.

Another important topic discussed was whether we would have a draw from the beginning or live off savings if we had no profits the first few months. It was eventually decided that we would not have a draw until we made the first quarterly distribution of profits. We felt we would only be making loans to ourselves by having to capitalize the firm enough to afford partners' draws from day one.

When, by mutual agreement, we felt that discussions and intentions were serious, we realized that a budget was a must. Our budget was revised many times as we refined and honed our projections. Revisions were necessitated both by changes in the number of persons in the group and by changes in our thinking on various line items.

Another difficult decision was whether to commence business as a partnership or as a professional corporation. There was substantial variation in the gross incomes and profit margins among those in the group. For some, incorporation was essential to defer income, while for others, no appreciable benefit was to be derived from it. On the whole, however, we decided to let the tax planner and accountant working with us decide that question after all the other major issues had been resolved.

The nature of the practice of law in the District of Columbia metropolitan area required consideration of multiple offices. The group consisted of lawyers licensed to practice in the District of Columbia, Maryland, and Virginia. We soon realized that multiple offices would be too expensive initially and would detract from the synergism and camaraderie we were trying to develop for the firm. Because the majority of our clients were located in the District of Columbia, we decided upon a headquarters office in downtown Washington, with offices in Maryland and Virginia that would be used, and paid for, only as and when needed. This was an important decision, as office space is up to one-third more expensive in Washington than in surrounding suburbs. We felt the added cost of a downtown office was justified, as we were striving for—and wanted to present—a high-quality image. We also decided to take more space than we needed initially and to sublease the excess to facilitate expansion as we grew.

Decisions about the proper debt/equity ratio for capitalizing start-up costs and the first few months of operating expenses followed much discussion among ourselves and with our accountant. We eventually chose to fund the venture on a 50/50 debt/equity basis.

As we got to know one another better and tackled the more involved questions, we realized that more frequent meetings were essential. We doubled the number of our monthly conferences. About this time, we decided to exchange personal financial statements and profit-and-loss statements. The former was necessary to ensure that participants had resources if additional capital were needed in the event business expectations were not met.

Other issues resolved included the firm's minimum hourly rate, if any (based upon our projected budget and partner profit expectations), and the charge, if any, for an initial consultation. We also discussed the form of management for the firm—whether there would be one managing partner or a management committee. Another difficult decision involved the firm name—the number of individual names to be shown, whose names would be shown, and the order of the names. After protracted discussion, a decision was reached by secret-ballot vote: the three partners' names would be listed in alphabetical order.

Because some of us did a significant amount of contingent-fee personal injury work, dealing with these cases financially was a problem. Those lawyers already in partnerships (where all fees are divided equally) were accustomed to receiving income from hourly work performed by their partners even when their contingent-fee cases were not bringing in income. We discussed the possibility of having hours spent on contingent-fee cases compensated at a preset reduced hourly rate, to be reconciled when the fee, if any, was realized. This led to consideration of how to compensate partners for time spent on firm administration. We decided that it was essential to good firm management and partner harmony for managing partners to be compensated for their time. It was also decided that with our income distribution formula, it would probably be necessary to use a data-processing service bureau or an in-house data-processing system to keep time and financial records.

As we came closer to making our decision to join or not to join, a list of tasks to be accomplished and items to be considered before or after the commitment date was drawn up. They included the following:

- Partnership or professional corporation
- Bylaws/articles
- Finding space
- Designing space
- Decorating space
- Personnel/office manual
- Partners' manual
- Retainer/per-diem fees
- Personal injury compensation regarding fees
- Final budget
- Financing
- Stationery/announcements
- Telephone system
- Photocopier
- Library
- Insurance
- Retirement/profit sharing
- Filing system
- Office forms
- Equipment
- Docket control
- ADP (Accountant's Data Processing) system for billing, timekeeping, client accounts, and general ledger
- Substantive-form file
- Firm brochure

As our negotiations progressed, certain pros and cons from different members of the group emerged. Generally, the pros took the position that merger would achieve the following:

- Provide additional backup to other lawyers
- Decrease pro-rata overhead over the long run
- Generate better-quality business referrals to and from partners
- Increase income through referrals to and from partners
- Attract better-quality corporate, administrative, and institutional clients
- Increase the ability to hire associates and legal assistants and generate income from their work
- Reduce the nonlawyer support staff/lawyer ratio, easing the burden of paperwork

The cons that developed included the following:

- Loss of some independence related to working hours, spending decisions, and personnel decisions
- Substantial start-up expenses and moving expenses
- Losing advantages of our present space, which for some of us included extensive libraries, expansive conference rooms, a more sophisticated photocopy machine, and better kitchen facilities than our resources would allow in our new space

Given the spread of net income among those in the discussion group, one sticking point was retirement and profit-sharing plans. We discussed the possibility of having one or more lawyers form a professional corporation within the partnership. This would allow such persons to defer more income without requiring the other partners to do so. We consulted our tax counsel and accountant about this.

After several meetings, we had more or less agreed upon an income distribution formula, but the sticking point became how to divide the expenses. Due to a fairly wide disparity of incomes and overhead percentages, we were unable to reach an agreement about whether to divide operating expenses equally or pro rata, based upon generation and source of income. We could not resolve the dispute of whether operating expenses varied directly with income received. We attempted to reach a compromise to split some expenses equally and vary others by income received by partner, but we were unable to agree upon such a formula.

We decided to table our discussions for approximately one year to allow observation of the participants' financial results. We had learned a great deal from our discussion group, and we hoped to continue it in the immediate future. Perhaps by that time our operating results would be closer so that we could resolve the expense-allocation problem. Even if we could not, we all felt that the experience was a worthwhile one.

Merger

Finally, after four years as a sole practitioner, I merged with two other lawyers to form a three-lawyer firm. Soon we had a fourth partner, two "of counsel," an associate, and a staff of eight nonlawyers. Therefore, at this juncture, it is useful to look back on the experience and offer whatever insight was gained from it. From the benefit of our experience, a number of revisions to our partnership agreement were appropriate.

Insights and Recommendations

Items that were not covered in our partnership agreement, but which should have been, included the form of management to be utilized by the firm. Was management to be by consensus of the partners or by a managing partner? What authority would the managing partner have without consulting the other partners? What compensation would the managing partner receive for time spent on management? Who would decide the compensation?

Another issue not addressed was the capital balance of the partners. Would the partners be allowed to carry a negative partnership account? If so, for how long? Would a partner be able to obtain additional draws if his or her partnership account was below a certain figure? Should each partner be required to maintain a certain positive balance in the partnership account? How often should accounts be reconciled?

We found that our original income formula (75 percent to the partners doing the work, 15 percent to the originating partner(s), and 10 percent to a fund to be distributed as agreed among the partners) was too cumbersome to use. We revised that formula to provide that 85 percent of cash received was to be allocated to the partner(s) doing the work, while 15 percent was to go to the partner who originated the matter. This worked without any problems in terms of determining origination. As for income distribution under our partnership agreement, we never had occasion to deviate from the 85/15 percent profit allocation for matters that produced unusually large profits for the partnership. The formula worked in all cases.

One matter that ought to receive clear and thorough attention by solos before merging into a firm is the firm's decision-making process—what items must be decided by a unanimous vote of the partnership and what items should be decided by a majority? This is especially true for expenditures. The obvious benefit of having majority rule is that decisions are made more quickly and efficiently, and the firm is not paralyzed by one dissenter. However, if you are the dissenter, it is likely that you will become alienated from your partners if they are always united against your wishes. It is beneficial to develop guidelines regarding expenditures and economic philosophy in advance, preferably in writing, to avoid this possible polarization. We learned that it is important to try to reach consensus on all important decisions.

Reviewing our partnership agreement, it was clear that some provisions were superfluous. For example, the paragraph on vacations (one month per year per partner) never served any purpose. Given our income distribution formula, partners took as much or as little vacation as they liked.

Although my professional corporation maintained separate books from the partnership, we did not maintain separate employees. All the employees were employees of the partnership, with the exception of myself.

The arrangement worked reasonably well for everyone. What every sole practitioner must keep in mind is that going into a partnership is somewhat like getting married. You must be able to compromise, and you must realize that you will be giving up some independence and the ability to have everything your own way for the benefits of shared resources, intrafirm referrals, and the other benefits of a partnership.

Sole practitioners and very small firms can band together and expand their existing practices. In a large metropolitan area such as ours, true "general practitioners" are rare among younger lawyers. A major benefit of a merger is being able to have a "general practice" composed of specialists. For example, our four partners practiced in the following areas: employment discrimination, government personnel law, general civil litigation, torts, labor law, probate, commercial law, landlord-tenant law, domestic relations, and oil and gas tax shelters. One "of counsel" added substantial expertise in antitrust and trade regulation.

Some more traditional lawyers heard about our income and expense formula and characterized our firm as a space-sharing arrangement. That was not so. We believed our formula encouraged productivity, economy, and intrafirm referrals. There was little or no danger of any one partner feeling he was carrying another.

In summary, a sole practitioner who feels he or she has "plateaued" in terms of income and/or quality of practice can expand by merging with other solos or small firms. Based upon my experience, the economic benefits outweighed the sacrifices.

Sequel

Later, my former partners announced that they had decided to move when our lease was up. Such a move would entail substantial expenses for a new phone system and other items. By that time, I had a growing concern about our overhead, so I decided to withdraw from the partnership and resume solo practice.

This proved to be the right decision for me. I sent announcements outlining my areas of practice—employment law, civil service law, general civil practice, and personal injury law. This resulted in a great many referrals from other lawyers.

I was also able to obtain better control of my overhead and did not have to compromise concerning office procedures. My subsequent years of solo practice have been rewarding, financially and otherwise. Though there are times when I miss the intrafirm referrals, consultation, and greater resources, flying solo clearly suits me better now than being in a partnership.

Solo Practice and Disability

56

Richard M. Howland

I graduated from Amherst College in 1961 and started the next week at Merrill Lynch as a junior trainee. The Berlin Wall went up, and so did my draft number. Rather than getting drafted, I enlisted in the navy. Four years later I was back in New York, driving a taxi and attending Columbia Law School.

This is the story of my life, and about how my eventual disability affected my life and my law practice. My story could be your story. The question I would like you to consider is simply this: If this becomes your story, are you prepared to protect yourself, your family, and your employees?

Before you can protect yourself adequately, you need information. Information about planning for disability is readily available. Today we have access to far more information, especially online, than we can possibly digest. We can read books and articles by other lawyers and benefit from their advice and counsel. We can seek advice directly from lawyers and professionals who make it their business to help people prepare for the worst life has to offer. An insurance advisor and an accountant are worth their weight in gold. If you consult these experts early in your career, before crisis strikes, and consider their advice before making decisions, you may be able to minimize the effect of an injury or illness that may befall you years later. These professionals can help to evaluate the financial and tax consequences of various disability insurance plans and other financial products.

When I first started practicing law I was young and, like most young people, was convinced that I was immortal and indestructible. I soon learned otherwise.

After I returned from nearly four years in the U.S. Navy and after I passed the Massachusetts bar exam, I went to work as an associate in a large law firm in Boston. I didn't know it at the time, but I was a serious alcoholic. Everyone else knew, but not me. In 1970 I woke up to my alcoholism and spent a long twenty-eight days in recovery. I have not taken a drink since May 25, 1970, and won't today. But my story isn't really about that.

I then spent two years knocking around Boston law firms, fully expecting my law career to be short-lived and thinking I would end up as a house painter or truck driver. My self-esteem was in the tank, but things improved when I was hired by a university in Amherst to be the lawyer for its students. Actually, I was an independent contractor, which meant I had to take care of my own taxes, health care, and other expenses, just as if I were in private practice. I liked being on my own and living in the town where I had grown up. I was feeling good. I got back in good physical shape. I joined Kiwanis, a service organization for professionals and business people.

In Kiwanis, I met a member—let's call him "Herb"—who was a certified public accountant and an instructor at a local college. He did some work for small businesses on the side, and we began talking about the law as a business. My lack of knowledge about taxes, banking, insurance, and the like must have surprised Herb, but he took me under his wing and offered advice freely. At his urging, I got malpractice insurance in case a client sued me, liability insurance in case somebody slipped and fell on my property, health insurance to pay medical bills, and, perhaps most importantly, disability insurance in case I couldn't work.

Business was good at the university. My office was flooded with students (about forty per day) who had all the usual student problems: bad housing, low income, too many bills, and problems related to love, marriage, divorce, and children. I helped these young people with problems stemming from drugs and alcohol and resulting run-ins with the criminal justice system. I worked full-time and was still able to dabble in real estate and do some private legal work on the side on my own time. Eventually I developed an interest in poverty law. My confidence and self-esteem were both on the upswing. I didn't have many thoughts of truck driving or house painting anymore.

I met my wife, married, bought a new house, and started a practice full-time in a downtown office. I handled mainly personal injury cases, but also did some family law and medical malpractice work. Herb continued to help me with my finances, including making sure that the disability insurance premiums got paid every month. Life was good.

Eventually, we bought a large house and were able to take regular vacations.

By 1979, my wife and I had two athletic daughters. When my older daughter took up figure skating a couple years later, I hauled out the old hockey skates to show her everything I had learned about skating in my youth. By the time the lesson was over, my knee had swollen to the point that I had to go to the local hospital emergency room. I saw an orthopedist, who diagnosed a torn ligament and some cartilage damage.

The doctor fixed my knee as best he could, but the state of surgery, particularly arthroscopic surgery, was fairly primitive in those days. I lived with the pain and lack of mobility for a few years, but eventually decided to submit to a fairly exotic surgery, one that required me to spend a long time in a cast afterward. To make matters worse, I developed a staph infection in the hospital that caused me a lot of pain and required me to take a lot of pain medication.

My knee never really got back to normal, but things got much worse a few years later. In 1992, I was president of the Amherst Chamber of Commerce and went to Japan as part of a sister-city delegation. During the visit, I found that it was becoming hard to walk and I began falling a lot. When I returned home, I fell getting off the plane. I stumbled regularly and when I didn't improve, I sought advice from several doctors.

Eventually, the doctors decided that my problem was with my back and I reluctantly agreed to undergo a six-hour surgery. After surgery, I found myself permanently disabled at the age of fifty-three, with only a slight chance of returning to my law practice—at least of returning to my previous level of practice. Some of my clients couldn't wait for my recovery and took their files to other lawyers. I laid off most of my staff and downsized my office.

Thanks to Herb's wise counsel, I had not one, but two disability insurance policies. One paid for my lost income, as well as part of my office expenses. The other—the original policy that I bought in 1970—would provide me with tax-free income for the next twenty-five years. I had a lot of expenses, too, with two daughters in high school.

In what was probably not the best of timing, my wife moved out the same day I was discharged from the hospital, leaving me to care for our two daughters (or, more accurately, leaving my daughters to care for me). With my older daughter driving me to court, I eventually returned to work at a reduced level. My stamina was not improving and I found that walking with canes and crutches was causing my pain to get worse.

In time, my stamina waned and my pain worsened and I found myself needing drugs that affected my ability to practice law. In 1998, after thirty years of practice, I filed a disability claim with my insurance company (and with the Social Security Administration) and began receiving benefits.

Since then, I have been able to send my two daughters to college, something that would have been impossible without the disability insurance policy.

Although I don't practice law anymore, I did become certified as a schoolteacher after my disability. I work as a substitute teacher eight days a month, which works well, as I am limited in both how much money I can earn and how much work my body can tolerate. In my spare time, I like to travel and I also work as a referee for soccer, track, and swimming.

That is my story. It may never be your story, but your story may eventually be similar. You cannot plan how you are, or will be, disabled. You cannot anticipate that whatever you experience will cause the same degree of disability in someone else. Keeping that in mind, my advice to you is as follows:

1. *Plan for the worst.* If you plan for the worst, then even the worst won't be as bad to handle. Preparation is essential for the well-being of everyone who depends upon you and cares for you.

2. *Remember that your life can remain productive.* Many people bounce back from injury or illness, no matter how serious it is at first. After a while, almost everyone is able to return to work and lead a productive life. Even those who can't return to work can still lead productive and satisfying lives.

3. *Find a lawyer who can take over your practice.* We should all have backup lawyers to cover for our vacations, if for no other reason. For your backup lawyer, select someone you respect and trust completely. Your backup should be familiar with your practice field, should be free of conflicts involving your clients, and should reside nearby. The duties of a backup lawyer can include any of the following, depending upon the need:

   ◆ Take possession of the office and especially the files, without reading the files.

   ◆ Review mail, and leave it aside when not requiring some action due to time.

   ◆ If action is required, notify the party, court, and/or opposing counsel of the situation and seek an agreement for an extension.

   ◆ Make notes of all actions taken for the absent lawyer.

   ◆ If a client wants his or her file, obtain a receipt and letter from the client explaining, or at least making, the request. Ascertain that the account is paid to date or make secure arrangements for payment.

   ◆ If an appearance in court is required, notify the court of the reason and file only a limited appearance.

   ◆ Review all the files, select those where there is a conflict (with the backup lawyer), flag or otherwise note them, set them aside, and provide for an alternate lawyer to make the review. Many state and local bar associations provide programs and institutional organizations that can handle these tasks.

When I Die . . .

57

Ross A. Sussman

This chapter is dedicated to my friends and colleagues who are sole practitioners. We jealously guard our independence, as well as our right to work or not work as we see fit. We may not have the facilities or security of large firms, but we have the independence of doing what we want, when we want, and if we want.

When anyone dies—a client, a friend, or a lawyer colleague—there are many things that have to be taken care of. Unfortunately, most of the basic information dies with the person. Therefore, my suggestion is to write a letter to your primary survivor (such as your spouse), spelling out the things that will have to be done, who should do them, and other pointers on settling your estate.

But leaving the letter isn't enough. You must discuss this information with your designee. Both of you must make good notes and an outline of things to be done. The best procedure is to discuss what will have to be done, show your designee where the documents and information are located, and introduce him or her to your advisors. Then, write a letter, and, most important, discuss it with your designee. The first time may be the hardest, but it is the most important. Annually, you and your designee should update the letter. Perhaps he or she will have additional questions. Or perhaps things will have changed in your practice, business, or financial affairs. Any changes should be reviewed in the letter.

I've tried to touch on many things your designee should know, and I've covered other points that we as lawyers should consider. Following is my personal example for a letter.

Dear Evy,

When I die, there will be many things to do. But before I explain them, let me thank you for your love, support, and encouragement. We've had a good life together and, after I'm gone, I want to make the details as easy as possible for you. That's why I like to meet with you each year to review and update this letter.

This is a summary of the things we discussed. Although there are many items, they can be divided into sections because not everything has to be done at once.

For Immediate Attention

Funeral

I would like you to spend as little money as possible for the casket and funeral. But before the body is given to the undertaker, you should ask the doctor if my eyes or any organs could be used to help another person or to further medical research. If that's possible, then I wholeheartedly approve your decision for organ donation.

Services

As we discussed, I would like our Rabbi to present the eulogy, if possible. Throughout the years, we have exchanged correspondence and notes, and discussed many topics that would give him good background information about me.

Our Wills and Trusts

Copies of these documents are in the "Estate Planning" notebook on the bottom shelf of the bookcase in our home office. The originals are in the vault under "Sussman." Basically, our wills give our property to each other, either outright or in trust, and there are special trust provisions for certain children.

For Consideration in Fifteen Days

Insurance

The bottom shelf of the bookcase in our home office also holds a black notebook labeled "Insurance Notebook." Section I contains a summary of my life insurance. Claim forms are in Section II, so immediate application can be made for the policy proceeds. The other sections of the Insurance Notebook contain summaries and actual policies for our home, cars, and personal property. Section VII has the business policies.

Home Mortgage

Our home mortgage interest rate could be significantly lower than current mortgage rates. Therefore, do not be in a hurry to pay off the mortgage. Rather, consider investing any excess cash, and then make the mortgage payments each month.

American Bar Association

I've been active in the Law Practice Management Section of the American Bar Association. I suggest you call the staff liaison to let him or her know of my death. Also, you should inform the director of publications because I have been spending a good deal of my effort working in that area. You should ask the staff liaison to contact the current chairperson of the Law Practice Management Section. Those three people will have a good idea of the projects I'm involved in, so someone can take them over. I've tried to keep each project file updated by memos or notes. The ABA files can be returned to the staff liaison or whoever can make best use of them.

Financial

In addition to the insurance money, there will be money from the law practice, social security, and other investments. I suggest you sit down with our accountant to discuss your entire financial/income situation. I've made a rough draft of the income you might expect, and that's in Section V of the Insurance Notebook.

For Consideration in Thirty Days

Advisors

You should first select a lawyer and investment advisor to help you with estate administration and financial affairs. My suggestion for a lawyer is my associate, Gina. She would work closely with our legal assistant and handle things in a simple, straightforward manner. Talk to her first and see how you feel, and then make your decision. And be sure to discuss fees so there will be no surprises.

Financial Information

Next to the Insurance Notebook is a black notebook labeled "RAS Financial Information." This is a listing of our assets, bank balances, asset ownership, and other financial data that will be useful. I have tried to keep it updated. By way of summary, a personal and business financial statement is included in the first section of the notebook. A draft of the Federal Estate Tax Return (Form 706) is in the third section of the notebook.

Personal Property

Attached to our wills are lists specifying items of personal property we would like to give to other people. In Section V of the RAS Financial Information notebook is a list of special items of personal property I own. These are significant objects, generally artwork or other items of special value, with comments about them, when and where they were purchased, my reason for buying them, the significance of the items, values and who could furnish up-to-date valuations, and, sometimes, who the item should be given to.

Other than the items specified on the lists, you and the children should decide who should get what. If some book, postcard, item of jewelry, or artwork appeals to one child, then he or she should have it. In fact, if you and they can't agree, I would suggest a "round-robin" selection. That is, you all take turns choosing an object until all the objects are chosen.

If the boys want any of my clothing, that's great, but the decision is up to them. If you want some of my favorite ties to make a skirt, vest, or something else, that is just fine with me. The rest should be donated to a charity resale shop.

Safe-Deposit Box

Although I do not have a safe-deposit box, any "valuable papers" are kept in the vault.

Office Lease

The lease runs until August 31, 2008. However, the lease is cancelable if I should become disabled for six months or upon my death. This is not a decision you must make immediately. However, it is something for you to discuss with Gina. Because Gina is my associate, she implicitly has the right to complete the work on my files.

Accounts Receivable

Each month a detailed list of accounts receivable is prepared. You should meet with Gina to decide what should be done to collect the unpaid accounts. We have tried to keep on top of them each month, but we are not always successful.

Law Cases

Gina is quite familiar with almost all the cases in the office. I suggest the attached letter be sent to all clients with pending matters. Another attached letter is to be sent to clients with closed matters.

Books, Furniture, and Other Office Equipment

If Gina will continue with my cases, then I suggest you ask her to purchase my furniture, computers, office equipment, library, and other personal business property.

Old Files

Although we eliminated most of the old files, there still are many boxes of old files in the garage. To start with, you and Gina should refer to the most recent edition of the *Law Office Policy and Procedures Manual for Solos and Small Firms* (ABA, 2005), written by my friend, Demetrios Dimitriou. Then decide how to dispose of these files. Each file should be checked to see if it contains any valuable documents. It is best to have one of our secretaries or law clerks do that (after proper instruction, of course). If there are original court papers in the files, they could be filed with the clerk of the court. However, I would not recommend paying the filing fees to open a new file. Instead, it might be wise to use the last attached letter and return the papers to the client. And when the papers are mailed to the client, it's a good idea to have the words "Address Change Requested" typed on the envelope. That way, you will receive notification from the post office of the client's new address for your records. If the file pertains to a minor, then I suggest you keep it for seven years after the person reaches his or her eighteenth birthday.

Client Index

We maintain a detailed client index on our computer system. When a file is destroyed, that fact is noted on the index, including the date of destruction and who authorized it.

Pending Files

This was covered in an earlier paragraph. However, because of our increased specialization and selectivity in accepting cases, there shouldn't be very many, if any, cases that have to be referred to other lawyers. Gina has a list of other lawyers who specialize in various areas. So, if she thinks a referral is appropriate, she may want to refer the client to those other specialized lawyers, or she may want to use them as consultants to help her complete the pending matters. But that should be done only with client authorization.

Investments and Banker

As you know, my investments consist largely of art objects, rather than the traditional stocks, bonds, or real estate. We also have a money-market fund at Associated Bank. Our banker and account representative is Mary Carlson. Gina knows her and deals with her frequently for various clients. I suggest you meet with her and listen to her recommendations. You should listen to her advice, but don't take it blindly; use your own internal judgment. Whatever the investments are, they must be something you are comfortable with and can live with from day to day.

For Consideration Within Sixty Days

Book and Photography Collections

Throughout the years, I have accumulated private-press books. Like etchings and lithographs, these are produced in limited editions, generally hand-printed on specially made paper and bound by hand. The invoices for the books, and sometimes special articles about the book, are usually kept inside the front cover of each book. In addition, I have correspondence and ephemera from the press in a file folder organized alphabetically by the publisher/press. Right now, this information is in the top drawer of my black file cabinet. If you wonder what the value of the books may be, you should check the book catalogs we regularly receive, and contact Daile Kaplan at Swann Galleries (an auction house in New York City). Daile can advise you concerning my photography collection.

For Consideration After Six Months

Malpractice Insurance

Under Tab 10 of the Insurance Notebook, you will find the current malpractice policy. In the old business files, you will find the old malpractice policies filed under MLM—that's the malpractice insurance carrier sponsored by the Minnesota Bar Association. These policies should be retained, literally, forever. If any claims are made against my estate for improper handling of cases, you should immediately contact MLM. In fact, you should send MLM a copy of the papers by registered mail, return-receipt requested, so you have proof of filing the claim. My estate can purchase a one-time policy to cover any future malpractice claims that may be made. There is a reasonable premium charge for this coverage, and I would recommend that you do it.

Bar Memorial

Each year around May, the Hennepin County Bar Association has a memorial service for the lawyers who died during the past year. You will be invited to it. Whether you and the children attend is up to you.

Forever

Remarriage

Should you consider remarriage, and I hope you do, you should absolutely, definitely, and positively have an antenuptial agreement. This agreement spells out the rights you and your prospective spouse have in the assets you own. Each of you must have your own lawyer. The agreement will not be valid if you use the same lawyer, or two lawyers from the same office. Even though you may be marrying for love, there are certain financial matters that must be taken care of. After all, we have worked during our marriage to accumulate the things we have, and I am sure you want many of them to go to the children.

Finally, thank you for everything, and I shall miss you.

Love and kisses and lots of hugs—
Ross

This letter covers the basic points, advisors, and what to do. Your letter, of course, should cover your own particular situation. Other topics you might want to consider are estates for which you are executor, trusts for which you are trustee, and so on.

The important thing, though, is to discuss these things periodically with your spouse or other designee. We carry a lot of information in our heads—and when we're gone, it's gone, too. So put it in writing and review it now. It's a good project for you and your family. If not now, when?

Exhibit 1

Sample Letter to Clients with Pending Matters

I. M. Client
123 Main Street
Happy Valley, Minnesota 55333

Dear Client:

At your last meeting with Ross, you discussed your estate plan and decided upon the terms of your will and trusts. He was to draft the documents for your review.

I am sorry to report that Ross died unexpectedly last Thursday after a massive heart attack. I have been Ross's associate for several years, and together we worked extensively in the estate planning areas. If you would like, I would be glad to complete your will and trusts. Just call me, and we will discuss what remains to be done. We can personally meet before the documents are drafted, and there will be no charge for this meeting. Or, if you would like to discuss these things by phone, please call me. If I don't hear from you within two weeks, I will call you.

If you would like another lawyer to complete your will and trusts, please let me know, and I will transfer your file to him or her.

We, too, are sad. Ross was such a joy to have around. We shall miss his smile and jokes and goldfish in the watercooler.

Sincerely,

Gina Associate

Exhibit 2

Sample Letter to Clients with Closed Files

I. M. Client
123 Main Street
Happy Valley, Minnesota 55333

Dear Client:

As you may know, Ross died last Thursday after a massive heart attack.
We are now in the process of closing the office. I will continue doing work on the "active" files. However, because your file is not active, we would like to know what to do with it. You have several choices:

1. You can pick up your file or ask us to mail it to you.
2. We can destroy it.
3. We can transfer it to another lawyer for you.

We would like to know what you would like us to do. Just circle number 1, 2, or 3 on the enclosed copy of this letter and mail it to us. We shall do what you want. However, if we don't hear from you within thirty days, we will assume you want this file destroyed, and we will do so, accordingly.

Meanwhile, if you have any questions, please call.

Sincerely,

Gina Associate

Exhibit 3

Sample Letter to Clients for Whom We Have Valuable Documents

I. M. Client
123 Main Street
Happy Valley, Minnesota 55333

Dear Client:

I am sorry to report that Ross died unexpectedly last Thursday after a massive heart attack.

As you may know, I have been Ross's associate for several years, and together we worked extensively in the estate planning areas. Recently, I reviewed the documents in our vault and found the following documents for you, which we are enclosing with this letter:

◆ Original Will, dated May 10, 1995
◆ Original Power of Attorney, dated May 10, 1995
◆ Original Living Will, dated May 10, 1995

Let me suggest that you review these documents to make sure they are still what you want. If you would like to make some changes or have any questions, I would be happy to help you.

We, too, are sad. Ross was such a joy to have around. We shall miss his smile and jokes and goldfish in the watercooler.

Sincerely,

Gina Associate
Enclosures

Selected Resources
for Part VI

*from the ABA Law Practice
Management Section*

How to Start and Build a Law Practice, Fifth Edition, by Jay G
   Foonberg, 2004.
Law Practice, bimonthly publication of the ABA Law Practice
   Management Section.
*The Lawyer's Guide to Balancing Life and Work: Taking the Stress
   Out of Success,* by George W. Kaufman, 1999.
*The Successful Lawyer: Powerful Strategies for Transforming Your
   Practice,* by Gerald A. Riskin (available as a book, audio CD,
   or combination package), 2005.
Telecommuting for Lawyers, by Nicole Belson Goluboff, 1998
Women-at-Law: Lessons Learned Along the Pathways to Success,
   by Phyllis Horn Epstein, 2004.

Appendix A

CHECKLIST FOR STARTING A LAW PRACTICE

This checklist is designed simply as a guideline to provoke thought when considering starting a law practice.
It is not meant to be all inclusive.

I. PLANNING/BUDGETING
- ❑ Do self-assessment about starting a practice
  - ❑ Tolerance for Risk
  - ❑ Managerial Skills
  - ❑ Marketing Skills
  - ❑ Confidence Level in Legal Skills
- ❑ Write a Business and Marketing Plan
  - ❑ Projection of gross receipts
  - ❑ Projection of overhead and expenses
  - ❑ Projection of net receipts
  - ❑ Cash flow projections
    - ❑ Projection of hours worked
  - ❑ Marketable experience
  - ❑ Setting fees to make a profit
    - ❑ Written fee agreements

II. MARKETING PLAN/PRACTICE DEVELOPMENT
- ❑ Potential Client Base
- ❑ Advertising
  - ❑ Yellow Page ad
  - ❑ Website

❏ TV, radio, billboard
❏ Office signage
❏ Sign up for Lawyer Referral Service
❏ Sign up for free Lawyer Search service on MOBAR website
❏ Firm brochure
❏ Client newsletter
❏ Join civic organizations
❏ Produce community seminars
❏ Announcements
❏ Speak at CLE programs

III. FORMS OF PRACTICE

❏ Considerations in Selecting Form of Practice
  ❏ taxation
  ❏ liability
  ❏ succession/dissolution
❏ Solo Practice
❏ Partnership
❏ Professional Corporation
  ❏ Articles of Incorporation
  ❏ shareholders, officers, chief operating officer
  ❏ Statement of Good Standing from Clerk of Supreme Court
❏ Limited Liability Company
  ❏ Articles of Organization
  ❏ members
❏ Limited Liability Partnership
❏ Consult with CPA
❏ Specialized/General Practice
❏ Partnership Agreement in writing
  ❏ Capital/equity from partners
  ❏ Withdrawal/retirement issues
  ❏ Compensation and profit distribution
  ❏ Each partner's role in the practice
    ❏ Managing Partner
    ❏ Rainmaker
    ❏ Others

IV. OFFICE SPACE/LOCATION CONSIDERATIONS

❏ Office Building
  ❏ Image, upscale, informal
  ❏ Square footage
  ❏ ADA considerations

❑ Parking
❑ Services, janitorial
❑ Expansion Opportunities
❑ Renovation Needs
❑ Location
❑ Office sharing
❑ Renting, leasing
❑ Purchasing/buy into a law practice
❑ Working from home

V. ACCOUNTING NEEDS

❑ Consult with CPA
  ❑ set up accounting procedures
    ❑ Chart of accounts
    ❑ Profit and loss statements
    ❑ Balance sheets
    ❑ Cash Flow Statement
  ❑ quarterly and annual tax returns
  ❑ payroll services
  ❑ bank and trust accounting systems/reconciliation procedures
  ❑ software compatible with accountant

VI. START UP COSTS/CREDIT SOURCES

❑ Highly suggested that enough cash or a line of credit be available to cover start-up costs and at least the first 6 months to one year of operating expenses plus personal living expenses.
❑ Sources of credit
  ❑ Local bank/Credit Union
    ❑ personal, business loan
    ❑ home equity, home refinance
    ❑ line-of-credit to be drawn upon as needed
    ❑ lease, equipment loans
    ❑ family loans/private investor loans
  ❑ Personal savings

VII. BANK ACCOUNTS

❑ Trust account (separate account)
  ❑ IOLTA account, if applicable
❑ Business operating account for expenses/payroll
❑ Short term savings
❑ Safety deposit box
❑ Firm credit card

❑ Investments
❑ Checks, deposit slips, endorsement stamp
❑ Set up account to accept credit cards
❑ Retirement plan

VIII. TECHNOLOGY
❑ Software
  ❑ Word processing
  ❑ Time and billing/accounting
  ❑ Calendaring and docketing
  ❑ Conflicts checking
  ❑ Case Management
  ❑ Document assembly
  ❑ Office Suite Software
    ❑ Word processing
    ❑ E-mail
    ❑ Spreadsheet
    ❑ Presentation Software (such as PowerPoint)
    ❑ Others
  ❑ Virus protection for computers
  ❑ Voice Recognition
  ❑ Other specialized or practice specific software
❑ Hardware
  ❑ Computers
    ❑ Operating system
    ❑ Back-up system
    ❑ Lease or purchase
  ❑ Printers
  ❑ Network/Firewall
  ❑ Scanners
  ❑ CD-ROM
  ❑ Laptop Computer
  ❑ Personal Digital Assistant (PDA)

IX. OFFICE EQUIPMENT/SERVICES/SUPPLIES
❑ Fax Machine
❑ Photocopier
❑ Scanner
❑ Shredder
❑ Dictation equipment/Voice Recognition Software
❑ Internet Service Provider

- ❏ Email address
- ❏ High speed Internet access or DSL line
- ❏ Telephone System
    - ❏ Equipment/answering machine
    - ❏ Voice mail/manual message system
    - ❏ Answering service
    - ❏ Local and long distance carrier
    - ❏ Conference calling
    - ❏ Music on hold
    - ❏ Cell phone/service
    - ❏ Pager
- ❏ Postage scale/mail equipment
    - ❏ Establish UPS and Fed Ex accounts
- ❏ Office furniture for lawyer(s), staff, reception area, file cabinets, conference, room furniture, carpeting and area rugs, book shelves, art work/office decorating needs
- ❏ Office supplies, paper, envelopes, pens, staplers, file folders, etc.
- ❏ Business cards, announcements
- ❏ Order public information brochures from the Bar for clients

X. LIBRARY/LEGAL RESEARCH
- ❏ Online legal research provider
- ❏ Purchase new or used law books
- ❏ Local law library
- ❏ Law school library
- ❏ Courts library
- ❏ Internet research
- ❏ CD-ROM
- ❏ CLE Deskbooks

XI. OFFICE SYSTEMS/PROCEDURES
- ❏ Develop office manual/operating procedures manual
    - ❏ Standard procedures/policies for practice
    - ❏ Personnel issues/benefits
- ❏ Docketing, calendaring, tickler system
    - ❏ Computer (dual-system is highly recommended)
    - ❏ Manual
- ❏ File organization
    - ❏ Alpha/numeric
    - ❏ Centralized/decentralized
    - ❏ Opening file procedures

- ❏ Closing file procedures/retention/storage/destruction
- ❏ Document maintenance
  - ❏ Offsite—safety deposit box
  - ❏ Computer backup
  - ❏ Fireproof files
- ❏ Forms used in practice
  - ❏ Client interview form
  - ❏ Engagement/non-engagement letters
  - ❏ Written fee agreements
  - ❏ Practice specific checklists
  - ❏ Billing Statement Form
  - ❏ General client correspondence, notices, etc.
  - ❏ Client survey form after conclusion of representation
- ❏ Client billing procedures
  - ❏ Regular monthly statements even if no amount due
  - ❏ Detailed billing statement
  - ❏ Expense billing
  - ❏ Costs to be billed
    - ❏ legal assistant time/paralegal time
    - ❏ telephone expenses
    - ❏ duplicating expenses
    - ❏ computerized legal research
    - ❏ mailing costs
    - ❏ others
  - ❏ Collection policy
  - ❏ Credit cards for payment
- ❏ Client Relations Policy
  - ❏ Setting appointments, introducing staff
  - ❏ Returning phone calls, e-mail messages
  - ❏ Client intake form/survey at conclusion of representation
  - ❏ Keeping clients informed
    - ❏ Send copies of work, documents
  - ❏ Communicating Fees
    - ❏ Clear discussion about fees
    - ❏ Written fee agreements/engagement letters
- ❏ Accounting Procedures
  - ❏ Bank account reconciliation
  - ❏ Cash Flow Statement
  - ❏ Accounts Receivables/Payables
    - ❏ aging review
  - ❏ Expense Approval System
  - ❏ Counter signature requirement on checks
  - ❏ Others

XII. INSURANCE PROTECTION
- ❑ Professional liability
- ❑ Workers' Compensation
- ❑ Health Plan
- ❑ Car Insurance for business use
- ❑ Property (liability, wind, fire, earthquake, etc.)
- ❑ Loss of valuable documents
- ❑ Life
- ❑ Disability
- ❑ Business Interruption

XIII. PERSONNEL
- ❑ Legal Assistant/Paralegal
  - ❑ Full-time
  - ❑ Part-time
  - ❑ Temporary
  - ❑ Hours, flex-time
  - ❑ Sharing personnel with other professionals
  - ❑ Training
- ❑ Employee benefits
  - ❑ Vacation, holidays
  - ❑ Sick leave
  - ❑ Overtime policy
  - ❑ Medical insurance
  - ❑ Retirement Plan
  - ❑ Others
- ❑ Secure I-9 forms, W-4 forms, confidentiality agreement, employment applications, etc

XIV. MISCELLANEOUS
- ❑ Call your bar's Law Practice Management Information Center for assistance
  - ❑ Lending library
- ❑ Register fictitious name (if applicable)
- ❑ Obtain city or county business licenses or permits
- ❑ Order Post Office Box (if needed)
- ❑ Build a forms file
- ❑ Become a notary or have someone on staff or close by that is available
- ❑ Develop a disaster plan for your office, files, computer, etc.
- ❑ Develop a plan for your illness, incapacity or death.
- ❑ Consider attending The Missouri Bar's Solo and Small Firm Conference held annually in June.

- ❑ Join a Solo and Small Firm Committee or Section and email listserv for access to a network of other solo and small firm lawyers.
- ❑ Change address with your bar
- ❑ Call your bar's Ethics Counsel with prospective ethical questions.
- ❑ Join local bar association
- ❑ _____
- ❑ _____
- ❑ _____
- ❑ _____
- ❑ _____
- ❑ _____
- ❑ _____
- ❑ _____
- ❑ _____
- ❑ _____
- ❑ _____
- ❑ _____

Appendix B

This Appendix contains the ABA Model Rules of Professional Conduct that are prominently discussed in this book. Although the ethics rules as whole apply with equal force to solos as they do to law firm lawyers, the Model Rules cited here are discussed in greater depth in one or more chapters. We have included the Comments to these Model Rules, because the Comments help to clarify and appreciate the meaning of the Rules themselves.

As noted in the text, readers will want to look at rules of professional conduct for the jurisdiction(s) where they are licensed. Many states have adopted provisions that differ from the Model Rules, adopted by the ABA House of Delegates. Specifically, the Model Rules reproduced here include amendments adopted as part of the Ethics 2000 review process, which have not been adopted by all jurisdictions at the time this book went to press. In some states, case law or statutory enactments may supplement the responsibilities articulated in the rules of professional conduct.

For additional information on the Model Rules, go to **http://abanet.org/cpr**, or to **http://ababooks.org**, for information on how to purchase the print version of the Model Rules of Professional Conduct or the more expansive *Annotated Model Rules of Professional Conduct*, to subscribe to the *ABA/BN Manual of Professional Conduct*, and to join the ABA Center for Professional Responsibility.

ABA Model Rules of Professional Conduct reprinted from Model Rules of Professional Conduct, 2004 Edition, *published by the Center for Professional Responsibility, American Bar Association, 2004. Reprinted with permission. Copies of ABA* Model Rules of Professional Conduct 2004 *are available from Service Center, American Bar Association, 321 N. Clark Street, Chicago, IL 60610, 1-800-285-2221.*

RULE 1.4 COMMUNICATION

(a) A lawyer shall:
  (1) promptly inform the client of any decision or circumstance with re-
      spect to which the client's informed consent, as defined in Rule
      1.0(e), is required by these Rules;
  (2) reasonably consult with the client about the means by which the
      client's objectives are to be accomplished;
  (3) keep the client reasonably informed about the status of the matter;
  (4) promptly comply with reasonable requests for information; and
  (5) consult with the client about any relevant limitation on the lawyer's
      conduct when the lawyer knows that the client expects assistance
      not permitted by the Rules of Professional Conduct or other law.
(b) A lawyer shall explain a matter to the extent reasonably necessary to
    permit the client to make informed decisions regarding the represen-
    tation.

Comment

[1] Reasonable communication between the lawyer and the client is necessary for the client effectively to participate in the representation.

Communicating with Client

[2] If these Rules require that a particular decision about the representation
be made by the client, paragraph (a)(1) requires that the lawyer promptly
consult with and secure the client's consent prior to taking action unless prior
discussions with the client have resolved what action the client wants the
lawyer to take. For example, a lawyer who receives from opposing counsel an
offer of settlement in a civil controversy or a proffered plea bargain in a criminal case must promptly inform the client of its substance unless the client
has previously indicated that the proposal will be acceptable or unacceptable
or has authorized the lawyer to accept or to reject the offer. See Rule 1.2(a).

[3] Paragraph (a)(2) requires the lawyer to reasonably consult with the
client about the means to be used to accomplish the client's objectives. In
some situations—depending on both the importance of the action under consideration and the feasibility of consulting with the client—this duty will require consultation prior to taking action. In other circumstances, such as during a trial when an immediate decision must be made, the exigency of the
situation may require the lawyer to act without prior consultation. In such
cases the lawyer must nonetheless act reasonably to inform the client of actions the lawyer has taken on the client's behalf. Additionally, paragraph
(a)(3) requires that the lawyer keep the client reasonably informed about the

status of the matter, such as significant developments affecting the timing or the substance of the representation.

[4] A lawyer's regular communication with clients will minimize the occasions on which a client will need to request information concerning the representation. When a client makes a reasonable request for information, however, paragraph (a)(4) requires prompt compliance with the request, or if a prompt response is not feasible, that the lawyer, or a member of the lawyer's staff, acknowledge receipt of the request and advise the client when a response may be expected. Client telephone calls should be promptly returned or acknowledged.

Explaining Matters

[5] The client should have sufficient information to participate intelligently in decisions concerning the objectives of the representation and the means by which they are to be pursued, to the extent the client is willing and able to do so. Adequacy of communication depends in part on the kind of advice or assistance that is involved. For example, when there is time to explain a proposal made in a negotiation, the lawyer should review all important provisions with the client before proceeding to an agreement. In litigation a lawyer should explain the general strategy and prospects of success and ordinarily should consult the client on tactics that are likely to result in significant expense or to injure or coerce others. On the other hand, a lawyer ordinarily will not be expected to describe trial or negotiation strategy in detail. The guiding principle is that the lawyer should fulfill reasonable client expectations for information consistent with the duty to act in the client's best interests, and the client's overall requirements as to the character of representation. In certain circumstances, such as when a lawyer asks a client to consent to a representation affected by a conflict of interest, the client must give informed consent, as defined in Rule 1.0(e).

[6] Ordinarily, the information to be provided is that appropriate for a client who is a comprehending and responsible adult. However, fully informing the client according to this standard may be impracticable, for example, where the client is a child or suffers from diminished capacity. See Rule 1.14. When the client is an organization or group, it is often impossible or inappropriate to inform every one of its members about its legal affairs; ordinarily, the lawyer should address communications to the appropriate officials of the organization. See Rule 1.13. Where many routine matters are involved, a system of limited or occasional reporting may be arranged with the client.

Withholding Information

[7] In some circumstances, a lawyer may be justified in delaying transmission of information when the client would be likely to react imprudently to an immediate communication. Thus, a lawyer might withhold a psychiatric diagno-

sis of a client when the examining psychiatrist indicates that disclosure would harm the client. A lawyer may not withhold information to serve the lawyer's own interest or convenience or the interests or convenience of another person. Rules or court orders governing litigation may provide that information supplied to a lawyer may not be disclosed to the client. Rule 3.4(c) directs compliance with such rules or orders.

RULE 1.5 FEES

(a) A lawyer shall not make an agreement for, charge, or collect an unreasonable fee or an unreasonable amount for expenses. The factors to be considered in determining the reasonableness of a fee include the following:

    (1) the time and labor required, the novelty and difficulty of the questions involved, and the skill requisite to perform the legal service properly;

    (2) the likelihood, if apparent to the client, that the acceptance of the particular employment will preclude other employment by the lawyer;

    (3) the fee customarily charged in the locality for similar legal services;

    (4) the amount involved and the results obtained;

    (5) the time limitations imposed by the client or by the circumstances;

    (6) the nature and length of the professional relationship with the client;

    (7) the experience, reputation, and ability of the lawyer or lawyers performing the services; and

    (8) whether the fee is fixed or contingent.

(b) The scope of the representation and the basis or rate of the fee and expenses for which the client will be responsible shall be communicated to the client, preferably in writing, before or within a reasonable time after commencing the representation, except when the lawyer will charge a regularly represented client on the same basis or rate. Any changes in the basis or rate of the fee or expenses shall also be communicated to the client.

(c) A fee may be contingent on the outcome of the matter for which the service is rendered, except in a matter in which a contingent fee is prohibited by paragraph (d) or other law. A contingent fee agreement shall be in a writing signed by the client and shall state the method by which the fee is to be determined, including the percentage or percentages that shall accrue to the lawyer in the event of settlement, trial or appeal; litigation and other expenses to be deducted from the recovery; and whether such expenses are to be deducted before or after the contingent fee is calculated. The agreement must clearly notify the client of any expenses for which the client will be liable whether or not the client is the prevailing party. Upon conclusion of a contingent fee matter, the lawyer shall provide the client with a written statement stating the outcome of the matter and, if there is a recovery, showing the remittance to the client and the method of its determination.

(d) A lawyer shall not enter into an arrangement for, charge, or collect:

    (1) any fee in a domestic relations matter, the payment or amount of which is contingent upon the securing of a divorce or upon the amount of alimony or support, or property settlement in lieu thereof; or

    (2) a contingent fee for representing a defendant in a criminal case.

(e) A division of a fee between lawyers who are not in the same firm may be made only if:

    (1) the division is in proportion to the services performed by each lawyer or each lawyer assumes joint responsibility for the representation;

    (2) the client agrees to the arrangement, including the share each lawyer will receive, and the agreement is confirmed in writing; and

    (3) the total fee is reasonable.

Comment

Reasonableness of Fee and Expenses

[1] Paragraph (a) requires that lawyers charge fees that are reasonable under the circumstances. The factors specified in (1) through (8) are not exclusive. Nor will each factor be relevant in each instance. Paragraph (a) also requires that expenses for which the client will be charged must be reasonable. A lawyer may seek reimbursement for the cost of services performed in-house, such as copying, or for other expenses incurred in-house, such as telephone charges, either by charging a reasonable amount to which the client has agreed in advance or by charging an amount that reasonably reflects the cost incurred by the lawyer.

Basis or Rate of Fee

[2] When the lawyer has regularly represented a client, they ordinarily will have evolved an understanding concerning the basis or rate of the fee and the expenses for which the client will be responsible. In a new client-lawyer relationship, however, an understanding as to fees and expenses must be promptly established. Generally, it is desirable to furnish the client with at least a simple memorandum or copy of the lawyer's customary fee arrangements that states the general nature of the legal services to be provided, the

basis, rate or total amount of the fee and whether and to what extent the client will be responsible for any costs, expenses or disbursements in the course of the representation. A written statement concerning the terms of the engagement reduces the possibility of misunderstanding.

[3] Contingent fees, like any other fees, are subject to the reasonableness standard of paragraph (a) of this Rule. In determining whether a particular contingent fee is reasonable, or whether it is reasonable to charge any form of contingent fee, a lawyer must consider the factors that are relevant under the circumstances. Applicable law may impose limitations on contingent fees, such as a ceiling on the percentage allowable, or may require a lawyer to offer clients an alternative basis for the fee. Applicable law also may apply to situations other than a contingent fee, for example, government regulations regarding fees in certain tax matters.

Terms of Payment

[4] A lawyer may require advance payment of a fee, but is obliged to return any unearned portion. See Rule 1.16(d). A lawyer may accept property in payment for services, such as an ownership interest in an enterprise, providing this does not involve acquisition of a proprietary interest in the cause of action or subject matter of the litigation contrary to Rule 1.8 (i). However, a fee paid in property instead of money may be subject to the requirements of Rule 1.8(a) because such fees often have the essential qualities of a business transaction with the client.

[5] An agreement may not be made whose terms might induce the lawyer improperly to curtail services for the client or perform them in a way contrary to the client's interest. For example, a lawyer should not enter into an agreement whereby services are to be provided only up to a stated amount when it is foreseeable that more extensive services probably will be required, unless the situation is adequately explained to the client. Otherwise, the client might have to bargain for further assistance in the midst of a proceeding or transaction. However, it is proper to define the extent of services in light of the client's ability to pay. A lawyer should not exploit a fee arrangement based primarily on hourly charges by using wasteful procedures.

Prohibited Contingent Fees

[6] Paragraph (d) prohibits a lawyer from charging a contingent fee in a domestic relations matter when payment is contingent upon the securing of a divorce or upon the amount of alimony or support or property settlement to be obtained. This provision does not preclude a contract for a contingent fee for legal representation in connection with the recovery of post-judgment balances due under support, alimony or other financial orders because such contracts do not implicate the same policy concerns.

Division of Fee

[7] A division of fee is a single billing to a client covering the fee of two or more lawyers who are not in the same firm. A division of fee facilitates association of more than one lawyer in a matter in which neither alone could serve the client as well, and most often is used when the fee is contingent and the division is between a referring lawyer and a trial specialist. Paragraph (e) permits the lawyers to divide a fee either on the basis of the proportion of services they render or if each lawyer assumes responsibility for the representation as a whole. In addition, the client must agree to the arrangement, including the share that each lawyer is to receive, and the agreement must be confirmed in writing. Contingent fee agreements must be in a writing signed by the client and must otherwise comply with paragraph (c) of this Rule. Joint responsibility for the representation entails financial and ethical responsibility for the representation as if the lawyers were associated in a partnership. A lawyer should only refer a matter to a lawyer whom the referring lawyer reasonably believes is competent to handle the matter. See Rule 1.1.

[8] Paragraph (e) does not prohibit or regulate division of fees to be received in the future for work done when lawyers were previously associated in a law firm.

Disputes over Fees

[9] If a procedure has been established for resolution of fee disputes, such as an arbitration or mediation procedure established by the bar, the lawyer must comply with the procedure when it is mandatory, and, even when it is voluntary, the lawyer should conscientiously consider submitting to it. Law may prescribe a procedure for determining a lawyer's fee, for example, in representation of an executor or administrator, a class or a person entitled to a reasonable fee as part of the measure of damages. The lawyer entitled to such a fee and a lawyer representing another party concerned with the fee should comply with the prescribed procedure.

RULE 1.8 CONFLICT OF INTEREST: CURRENT CLIENTS: SPECIFIC RULES

(a) **A lawyer shall not enter into a business transaction with a client or knowingly acquire an ownership, possessory, security or other pecuniary interest adverse to a client unless:**

    (1) **the transaction and terms on which the lawyer acquires the interest are fair and reasonable to the client and are fully disclosed and transmitted in writing in a manner that can be reasonably understood by the client;**

(2) the client is advised in writing of the desirability of seeking and is given a reasonable opportunity to seek the advice of independent legal counsel on the transaction; and

(3) the client gives informed consent, in a writing signed by the client, to the essential terms of the transaction and the lawyer's role in the transaction, including whether the lawyer is representing the client in the transaction.

(b) A lawyer shall not use information relating to representation of a client to the disadvantage of the client unless the client gives informed consent, except as permitted or required by these Rules.

(c) A lawyer shall not solicit any substantial gift from a client, including a testamentary gift, or prepare on behalf of a client an instrument giving the lawyer or a person related to the lawyer any substantial gift unless the lawyer or other recipient of the gift is related to the client. For purposes of this paragraph, related persons include a spouse, child, grandchild, parent, grandparent or other relative or individual with whom the lawyer or the client maintains a close, familial relationship.

(d) Prior to the conclusion of representation of a client, a lawyer shall not make or negotiate an agreement giving the lawyer literary or media rights to a portrayal or account based in substantial part on information relating to the representation.

(e) A lawyer shall not provide financial assistance to a client in connection with pending or contemplated litigation, except that:

(1) a lawyer may advance court costs and expenses of litigation, the repayment of which may be contingent on the outcome of the matter; and

(2) a lawyer representing an indigent client may pay court costs and expenses of litigation on behalf of the client.

(f) A lawyer shall not accept compensation for representing a client from one other than the client unless:

(1) the client gives informed consent;

(2) there is no interference with the lawyer's independence of professional judgment or with the client-lawyer relationship; and

(3) information relating to representation of a client is protected as required by Rule 1.6.

(g) A lawyer who represents two or more clients shall not participate in making an aggregate settlement of the claims of or against the clients, or in a criminal case an aggregated agreement as to guilty or nolo contendere pleas, unless each client gives informed consent, in a writing signed by the client. The lawyer's disclosure shall include the existence and nature of all the claims or pleas involved and of the participation of each person in the settlement.

(h) A lawyer shall not:
  (1) make an agreement prospectively limiting the lawyer's liability to a client for malpractice unless the client is independently represented in making the agreement; or
  (2) settle a claim or potential claim for such liability with an unrepresented client or former client unless that person is advised in writing of the desirability of seeking and is given a reasonable opportunity to seek the advice of independent legal counsel in connection therewith.
(i) A lawyer shall not acquire a proprietary interest in the cause of action or subject matter of litigation the lawyer is conducting for a client, except that the lawyer may:
  (1) acquire a lien authorized by law to secure the lawyer's fee or expenses; and
  (2) contract with a client for a reasonable contingent fee in a civil case.
(j) A lawyer shall not have sexual relations with a client unless a consensual sexual relationship existed between them when the client-lawyer relationship commenced.
(k) While lawyers are associated in a firm, a prohibition in the foregoing paragraphs (a) through (i) that applies to any one of them shall apply to all of them.

Comment

Business Transactions Between Client and Lawyer

[1] A lawyer's legal skill and training, together with the relationship of trust and confidence between lawyer and client, create the possibility of over-reaching when the lawyer participates in a business, property or financial transaction with a client, for example, a loan or sales transaction or a lawyer investment on behalf of a client. The requirements of paragraph (a) must be met even when the transaction is not closely related to the subject matter of the representation, as when a lawyer drafting a will for a client learns that the client needs money for unrelated expenses and offers to make a loan to the client. The Rule applies to lawyers engaged in the sale of goods or services related to the practice of law, for example, the sale of title insurance or investment services to existing clients of the lawyer's legal practice. See Rule 5.7. It also applies to lawyers purchasing property from estates they represent. It does not apply to ordinary fee arrangements between client and lawyer, which are governed by Rule 1.5, although its requirements must be met when the lawyer accepts an interest in the client's business or other nonmonetary property as payment of all or part of a fee. In addition, the Rule does not apply

to standard commercial transactions between the lawyer and the client for products or services that the client generally markets to others, for example, banking or brokerage services, medical services, products manufactured or distributed by the client, and utilities' services. In such transactions, the lawyer has no advantage in dealing with the client, and the restrictions in paragraph (a) are unnecessary and impracticable.

[2] Paragraph (a)(1) requires that the transaction itself be fair to the client and that its essential terms be communicated to the client, in writing, in a manner that can be reasonably understood. Paragraph (a)(2) requires that the client also be advised, in writing, of the desirability of seeking the advice of independent legal counsel. It also requires that the client be given a reasonable opportunity to obtain such advice. Paragraph (a)(3) requires that the lawyer obtain the client's informed consent, in a writing signed by the client, both to the essential terms of the transaction and to the lawyer's role. When necessary, the lawyer should discuss both the material risks of the proposed transaction, including any risk presented by the lawyer's involvement, and the existence of reasonably available alternatives and should explain why the advice of independent legal counsel is desirable. See Rule 1.0(e) (definition of informed consent).

[3] The risk to a client is greatest when the client expects the lawyer to represent the client in the transaction itself or when the lawyer's financial interest otherwise poses a significant risk that the lawyer's representation of the client will be materially limited by the lawyer's financial interest in the transaction. Here the lawyer's role requires that the lawyer must comply, not only with the requirements of paragraph (a), but also with the requirements of Rule 1.7. Under that Rule, the lawyer must disclose the risks associated with the lawyer's dual role as both legal adviser and participant in the transaction, such as the risk that the lawyer will structure the transaction or give legal advice in a way that favors the lawyer's interests at the expense of the client. Moreover, the lawyer must obtain the client's informed consent. In some cases, the lawyer's interest may be such that Rule 1.7 will preclude the lawyer from seeking the client's consent to the transaction.

[4] If the client is independently represented in the transaction, paragraph (a)(2) of this Rule is inapplicable, and the paragraph (a)(1) requirement for full disclosure is satisfied either by a written disclosure by the lawyer involved in the transaction or by the client's independent counsel. The fact that the client was independently represented in the transaction is relevant in determining whether the agreement was fair and reasonable to the client as paragraph (a)(1) further requires.

Use of Information Related to Representation

[5] Use of information relating to the representation to the disadvantage of the client violates the lawyer's duty of loyalty. Paragraph (b) applies when the

information is used to benefit either the lawyer or a third person, such as another client or business associate of the lawyer. For example, if a lawyer learns that a client intends to purchase and develop several parcels of land, the lawyer may not use that information to purchase one of the parcels in competition with the client or to recommend that another client make such a purchase. The Rule does not prohibit uses that do not disadvantage the client. For example, a lawyer who learns a government agency's interpretation of trade legislation during the representation of one client may properly use that information to benefit other clients. Paragraph (b) prohibits disadvantageous use of client information unless the client gives informed consent, except as permitted or required by these Rules. See Rules 1.2(d), 1.6, 1.9(c), 3.3, 4.1(b), 8.1 and 8.3.

Gifts to Lawyers

[6] A lawyer may accept a gift from a client, if the transaction meets general standards of fairness. For example, a simple gift such as a present given at a holiday or as a token of appreciation is permitted. If a client offers the lawyer a more substantial gift, paragraph (c) does not prohibit the lawyer from accepting it, although such a gift may be voidable by the client under the doctrine of undue influence, which treats client gifts as presumptively fraudulent. In any event, due to concerns about overreaching and imposition on clients, a lawyer may not suggest that a substantial gift be made to the lawyer or for the lawyer's benefit, except where the lawyer is related to the client as set forth in paragraph (c).

[7] If effectuation of a substantial gift requires preparing a legal instrument such as a will or conveyance the client should have the detached advice that another lawyer can provide. The sole exception to this Rule is where the client is a relative of the donee.

[8] This Rule does not prohibit a lawyer from seeking to have the lawyer or a partner or associate of the lawyer named as executor of the client's estate or to another potentially lucrative fiduciary position. Nevertheless, such appointments will be subject to the general conflict of interest provision in Rule 1.7 when there is a significant risk that the lawyer's interest in obtaining the appointment will materially limit the lawyer's independent professional judgment in advising the client concerning the choice of an executor or other fiduciary. In obtaining the client's informed consent to the conflict, the lawyer should advise the client concerning the nature and extent of the lawyer's financial interest in the appointment, as well as the availability of alternative candidates for the position.

Literary Rights

[9] An agreement by which a lawyer acquires literary or media rights concerning the conduct of the representation creates a conflict between the in-

terests of the client and the personal interests of the lawyer. Measures suitable in the representation of the client may detract from the publication value of an account of the representation. Paragraph (d) does not prohibit a lawyer representing a client in a transaction concerning literary property from agreeing that the lawyer's fee shall consist of a share in ownership in the property, if the arrangement conforms to Rule 1.5 and paragraphs (a) and (i).

Financial Assistance

[10] Lawyers may not subsidize lawsuits or administrative proceedings brought on behalf of their clients, including making or guaranteeing loans to their clients for living expenses, because to do so would encourage clients to pursue lawsuits that might not otherwise be brought and because such assistance gives lawyers too great a financial stake in the litigation. These dangers do not warrant a prohibition on a lawyer lending a client court costs and litigation expenses, including the expenses of medical examination and the costs of obtaining and presenting evidence, because these advances are virtually indistinguishable from contingent fees and help ensure access to the courts. Similarly, an exception allowing lawyers representing indigent clients to pay court costs and litigation expenses regardless of whether these funds will be repaid is warranted.

Person Paying for a Lawyer's Services

[11] Lawyers are frequently asked to represent a client under circumstances in which a third person will compensate the lawyer, in whole or in part. The third person might be a relative or friend, an indemnitor (such as a liability insurance company) or a co-client (such as a corporation sued along with one or more of its employees). Because third-party payers frequently have interests that differ from those of the client, including interests in minimizing the amount spent on the representation and in learning how the representation is progressing, lawyers are prohibited from accepting or continuing such representations unless the lawyer determines that there will be no interference with the lawyer's independent professional judgment and there is informed consent from the client. See also Rule 5.4(c) (prohibiting interference with a lawyer's professional judgment by one who recommends, employs or pays the lawyer to render legal services for another).

[12] Sometimes, it will be sufficient for the lawyer to obtain the client's informed consent regarding the fact of the payment and the identity of the third-party payer. If, however, the fee arrangement creates a conflict of interest for the lawyer, then the lawyer must comply with Rule. 1.7. The lawyer must also conform to the requirements of Rule 1.6 concerning confidentiality. Under Rule 1.7(a), a conflict of interest exists if there is significant risk that the lawyer's representation of the client will be materially limited by the lawyer's own interest in the fee arrangement or by the lawyer's responsibilities to the

third-party payer (for example, when the third-party payer is a co-client). Under Rule 1.7(b), the lawyer may accept or continue the representation with the informed consent of each affected client, unless the conflict is nonconsentable under that paragraph. Under Rule 1.7(b), the informed consent must be confirmed in writing.

Aggregate Settlements

[13] Differences in willingness to make or accept an offer of settlement are among the risks of common representation of multiple clients by a single lawyer. Under Rule 1.7, this is one of the risks that should be discussed before undertaking the representation, as part of the process of obtaining the clients' informed consent. In addition, Rule 1.2(a) protects each client's right to have the final say in deciding whether to accept or reject an offer of settlement and in deciding whether to enter a guilty or nolo contendere plea in a criminal case. The rule stated in this paragraph is a corollary of both these Rules and provides that, before any settlement offer or plea bargain is made or accepted on behalf of multiple clients, the lawyer must inform each of them about all the material terms of the settlement, including what the other clients will receive or pay if the settlement or plea offer is accepted. See also Rule 1.0(e) (definition of informed consent). Lawyers representing a class of plaintiffs or defendants, or those proceeding derivatively, may not have a full client-lawyer relationship with each member of the class; nevertheless, such lawyers must comply with applicable rules regulating notification of class members and other procedural requirements designed to ensure adequate protection of the entire class.

Limiting Liability and Settling Malpractice Claims

[14] Agreements prospectively limiting a lawyer's liability for malpractice are prohibited unless the client is independently represented in making the agreement because they are likely to undermine competent and diligent representation. Also, many clients are unable to evaluate the desirability of making such an agreement before a dispute has arisen, particularly if they are then represented by the lawyer seeking the agreement. This paragraph does not, however, prohibit a lawyer from entering into an agreement with the client to arbitrate legal malpractice claims, provided such agreements are enforceable and the client is fully informed of the scope and effect of the agreement. Nor does this paragraph limit the ability of lawyers to practice in the form of a limited-liability entity, where permitted by law, provided that each lawyer remains personally liable to the client for his or her own conduct and the firm complies with any conditions required by law, such as provisions requiring client notification or maintenance of adequate liability insurance. Nor does it prohibit an agreement in accordance with Rule 1.2 that defines the scope of the representation, although a definition of scope that makes the obligations of representation illusory will amount to an attempt to limit liability.

[15] Agreements settling a claim or a potential claim for malpractice are not prohibited by this Rule. Nevertheless, in view of the danger that a lawyer will take unfair advantage of an unrepresented client or former client, the lawyer must first advise such a person in writing of the appropriateness of independent representation in connection with such a settlement. In addition, the lawyer must give the client or former client a reasonable opportunity to find and consult independent counsel.

Acquiring Proprietary Interest in Litigation

[16] Paragraph (i) states the traditional general rule that lawyers are prohibited from acquiring a proprietary interest in litigation. Like paragraph (e), the general rule has its basis in common law champerty and maintenance and is designed to avoid giving the lawyer too great an interest in the representation. In addition, when the lawyer acquires an ownership interest in the subject of the representation, it will be more difficult for a client to discharge the lawyer if the client so desires. The Rule is subject to specific exceptions developed in decisional law and continued in these Rules. The exception for certain advances of the costs of litigation is set forth in paragraph (e). In addition, paragraph (i) sets forth exceptions for liens authorized by law to secure the lawyer's fees or expenses and contracts for reasonable contingent fees. The law of each jurisdiction determines which liens are authorized by law. These may include liens granted by statute, liens originating in common law and liens acquired by contract with the client. When a lawyer acquires by contract a security interest in property other than that recovered through the lawyer's efforts in the litigation, such an acquisition is a business or financial transaction with a client and is governed by the requirements of paragraph (a). Contracts for contingent fees in civil cases are governed by Rule 1.5.

Client-Lawyer Sexual Relationships

[17] The relationship between lawyer and client is a fiduciary one in which the lawyer occupies the highest position of trust and confidence. The relationship is almost always unequal; thus, a sexual relationship between lawyer and client can involve unfair exploitation of the lawyer's fiduciary role, in violation of the lawyer's basic ethical obligation not to use the trust of the client to the client's disadvantage. In addition, such a relationship presents a significant danger that, because of the lawyer's emotional involvement, the lawyer will be unable to represent the client without impairment of the exercise of independent professional judgment. Moreover, a blurred line between the professional and personal relationships may make it difficult to predict to what extent client confidences will be protected by the attorney-client evidentiary privilege, since client confidences are protected by privilege only when they are imparted in the context of the client-lawyer relationship. Because of the

significant danger of harm to client interests and because the client's own emotional involvement renders it unlikely that the client could give adequate informed consent, this Rule prohibits the lawyer from having sexual relations with a client regardless of whether the relationship is consensual and regardless of the absence of prejudice to the client.

[18] Sexual relationships that predate the client-lawyer relationship are not prohibited. Issues relating to the exploitation of the fiduciary relationship and client dependency are diminished when the sexual relationship existed prior to the commencement of the client-lawyer relationship. However, before proceeding with the representation in these circumstances, the lawyer should consider whether the lawyer's ability to represent the client will be materially limited by the relationship. See Rule 1.7(a)(2).

[19] When the client is an organization, paragraph (j) of this Rule prohibits a lawyer for the organization (whether inside counsel or outside counsel) from having a sexual relationship with a constituent of the organization who supervises, directs or regularly consults with that lawyer concerning the organization's legal matters.

Imputation of Prohibitions

[20] Under paragraph (k), a prohibition on conduct by an individual lawyer in paragraphs (a) through (i) also applies to all lawyers associated in a firm with the personally prohibited lawyer. For example, one lawyer in a firm may not enter into a business transaction with a client of another member of the firm without complying with paragraph (a), even if the first lawyer is not personally involved in the representation of the client. The prohibition set forth in paragraph (j) is personal and is not applied to associated lawyers.

RULE 1.15 SAFEKEEPING PROPERTY

(a) **A lawyer shall hold property of clients or third persons that is in a lawyer's possession in connection with a representation separate from the lawyer's own property. Funds shall be kept in a separate account maintained in the state where the lawyer's office is situated, or elsewhere with the consent of the client or third person. Other property shall be identified as such and appropriately safeguarded. Complete records of such account funds and other property shall be kept by the lawyer and shall be preserved for a period of [five years] after termination of the representation.**

(b) **A lawyer may deposit the lawyer's own funds in a client trust account for the sole purpose of paying bank service charges on that account, but only in an amount necessary for that purpose.**

(c) A lawyer shall deposit into a client trust account legal fees and expenses that have been paid in advance, to be withdrawn by the lawyer only as fees are earned or expenses incurred.

(d) Upon receiving funds or other property in which a client or third person has an interest, a lawyer shall promptly notify the client or third person. Except as stated in this rule or otherwise permitted by law or by agreement with the client, a lawyer shall promptly deliver to the client or third person any funds or other property that the client or third person is entitled to receive and, upon request by the client or third person, shall promptly render a full accounting regarding such property.

(e) When in the course of representation a lawyer is in possession of property in which two or more persons (one of whom may be the lawyer) claim interests, the property shall be kept separate by the lawyer until the dispute is resolved. The lawyer shall promptly distribute all portions of the property as to which the interests are not in dispute.

Comment

[1] A lawyer should hold property of others with the care required of a professional fiduciary. Securities should be kept in a safe deposit box, except when some other form of safekeeping is warranted by special circumstances. All property that is the property of clients or third persons, including prospective clients, must be kept separate from the lawyer's business and personal property and, if monies, in one or more trust accounts. Separate trust accounts may be warranted when administering estate monies or acting in similar fiduciary capacities. A lawyer should maintain on a current basis books and records in accordance with generally accepted accounting practice and comply with any recordkeeping rules established by law or court order. See, e.g., ABA Model Financial Recordkeeping Rule.

[2] While normally it is impermissible to commingle the lawyer's own funds with client funds, paragraph (b) provides that it is permissible when necessary to pay bank service charges on that account. Accurate records must be kept regarding which part of the funds are the lawyer's.

[3] Lawyers often receive funds from which the lawyer's fee will be paid. The lawyer is not required to remit to the client funds that the lawyer reasonably believes represent fees owed. However, a lawyer may not hold funds to coerce a client into accepting the lawyer's contention. The disputed portion of the funds must be kept in a trust account and the lawyer should suggest means for prompt resolution of the dispute, such as arbitration. The undisputed portion of the funds shall be promptly distributed.

[4] Paragraph (e) also recognizes that third parties may have lawful claims against specific funds or other property in a lawyer's custody, such as a client's creditor who has a lien on funds recovered in a personal injury action. A lawyer may have a duty under applicable law to protect such third-party claims against wrongful interference by the client. In such cases, when the third-party claim is not frivolous under applicable law, the lawyer must refuse to surrender the property to the client until the claims are resolved. A lawyer should not unilaterally assume to arbitrate a dispute between the client and the third party, but, when there are substantial grounds for dispute as to the person entitled to the funds, the lawyer may file an action to have a court resolve the dispute.

[5] The obligations of a lawyer under this Rule are independent of those arising from activity other than rendering legal services. For example, a lawyer who serves only as an escrow agent is governed by the applicable law relating to fiduciaries even though the lawyer does not render legal services in the transaction and is not governed by this Rule.

[6] A lawyers' fund for client protection provides a means through the collective efforts of the bar to reimburse persons who have lost money or property as a result of dishonest conduct of a lawyer. Where such a fund has been established, a lawyer must participate where it is mandatory, and, even when it is voluntary, the lawyer should participate.

RULE 1.16 DECLINING OR TERMINATING REPRESENTATION

(a) Except as stated in paragraph (c), a lawyer shall not represent a client or, where representation has commenced, shall withdraw from the representation of a client if:
  (1) the representation will result in violation of the rules of professional conduct or other law;
  (2) the lawyer's physical or mental condition materially impairs the lawyer's ability to represent the client; or
  (3) the lawyer is discharged.
(b) Except as stated in paragraph (c), a lawyer may withdraw from representing a client if:
  (1) withdrawal can be accomplished without material adverse effect on the interests of the client;
  (2) the client persists in a course of action involving the lawyer's services that the lawyer reasonably believes is criminal or fraudulent;
  (3) the client has used the lawyer's services to perpetrate a crime or fraud;

(4) the client insists upon taking action that the lawyer considers repugnant or with which the lawyer has a fundamental disagreement;

(5) the client fails substantially to fulfill an obligation to the lawyer regarding the lawyer's services and has been given reasonable warning that the lawyer will withdraw unless the obligation is fulfilled;

(6) the representation will result in an unreasonable financial burden on the lawyer or has been rendered unreasonably difficult by the client; or

(7) other good cause for withdrawal exists.

(c) A lawyer must comply with applicable law requiring notice to or permission of a tribunal when terminating a representation. When ordered to do so by a tribunal, a lawyer shall continue representation notwithstanding good cause for terminating the representation.

(d) Upon termination of representation, a lawyer shall take steps to the extent reasonably practicable to protect a client's interests, such as giving reasonable notice to the client, allowing time for employment of other counsel, surrendering papers and property to which the client is entitled and refunding any advance payment of fee or expense that has not been earned or incurred. The lawyer may retain papers relating to the client to the extent permitted by other law.

Comment

[1] A lawyer should not accept representation in a matter unless it can be performed competently, promptly, without improper conflict of interest and to completion. Ordinarily, a representation in a matter is completed when the agreed-upon assistance has been concluded. See Rules 1.2(c) and 6.5. See also Rule 1.3, Comment [4].

Mandatory Withdrawal

[2] A lawyer ordinarily must decline or withdraw from representation if the client demands that the lawyer engage in conduct that is illegal or violates the Rules of Professional Conduct or other law. The lawyer is not obliged to decline or withdraw simply because the client suggests such a course of conduct; a client may make such a suggestion in the hope that a lawyer will not be constrained by a professional obligation.

[3] When a lawyer has been appointed to represent a client, withdrawal ordinarily requires approval of the appointing authority. See also Rule 6.2. Similarly, court approval or notice to the court is often required by applicable law before a lawyer withdraws from pending litigation. Difficulty may be encountered if withdrawal is based on the client's demand that the lawyer engage in unprofessional conduct. The court may request an explanation for the

withdrawal, while the lawyer may be bound to keep confidential the facts that would constitute such an explanation. The lawyer's statement that professional considerations require termination of the representation ordinarily should be accepted as sufficient. Lawyers should be mindful of their obligations to both clients and the court under Rules 1.6 and 3.3.

Discharge

[4] A client has a right to discharge a lawyer at any time, with or without cause, subject to liability for payment for the lawyer's services. Where future dispute about the withdrawal may be anticipated, it may be advisable to prepare a written statement reciting the circumstances.

[5] Whether a client can discharge appointed counsel may depend on applicable law. A client seeking to do so should be given a full explanation of the consequences. These consequences may include a decision by the appointing authority that appointment of successor counsel is unjustified, thus requiring self-representation by the client.

[6] If the client has severely diminished capacity, the client may lack the legal capacity to discharge the lawyer, and in any event the discharge may be seriously adverse to the client's interests. The lawyer should make special effort to help the client consider the consequences and may take reasonably necessary protective action as provided in Rule 1.14.

Optional Withdrawal

[7] A lawyer may withdraw from representation in some circumstances. The lawyer has the option to withdraw if it can be accomplished without material adverse effect on the client's interests. Withdrawal is also justified if the client persists in a course of action that the lawyer reasonably believes is criminal or fraudulent, for a lawyer is not required to be associated with such conduct even if the lawyer does not further it. Withdrawal is also permitted if the lawyer's services were misused in the past even if that would materially prejudice the client. The lawyer may also withdraw where the client insists on taking action that the lawyer considers repugnant or with which the lawyer has a fundamental disagreement.

[8] A lawyer may withdraw if the client refuses to abide by the terms of an agreement relating to the representation, such as an agreement concerning fees or court costs or an agreement limiting the objectives of the representation.

Assisting the Client upon Withdrawal

[9] Even if the lawyer has been unfairly discharged by the client, a lawyer must take all reasonable steps to mitigate the consequences to the client. The lawyer may retain papers as security for a fee only to the extent permitted by law. See Rule 1.15.

RULE 1.17 SALE OF LAW PRACTICE

A lawyer or a law firm may sell or purchase a law practice, or an area of law practice, including good will, if the following conditions are satisfied:

(a) The seller ceases to engage in the private practice of law, or in the area of practice that has been sold, [in the geographic area] [in the jurisdiction] (a jurisdiction may elect either version) in which the practice has been conducted;

(b) The entire practice, or the entire area of practice, is sold to one or more lawyers or law firms;

(c) The seller gives written notice to each of the seller's clients regarding:
   (1) the proposed sale;
   (2) the client's right to retain other counsel or to take possession of the file; and
   (3) the fact that the client's consent to the transfer of the client's files will be presumed if the client does not take any action or does not otherwise object within ninety (90) days of receipt of the notice.

If a client cannot be given notice, the representation of that client may be transferred to the purchaser only upon entry of an order so authorizing by a court having jurisdiction. The seller may disclose to the court in camera information relating to the representation only to the extent necessary to obtain an order authorizing the transfer of a file.

(d) The fees charged clients shall not be increased by reason of the sale.

Comment

[1] The practice of law is a profession, not merely a business. Clients are not commodities that can be purchased and sold at will. Pursuant to this Rule, when a lawyer or an entire firm ceases to practice, or ceases to practice in an area of law, and other lawyers or firms take over the representation, the selling lawyer or firm may obtain compensation for the reasonable value of the practice as may withdrawing partners of law firms. See Rules 5.4 and 5.6.

Termination of Practice by the Seller

[2] The requirement that all of the private practice, or all of an area of practice, be sold is satisfied if the seller in good faith makes the entire practice, or the area of practice, available for sale to the purchasers. The fact that a number of the seller's clients decide not to be represented by the purchasers but take their matters elsewhere, therefore, does not result in a violation. Return to private practice as a result of an unanticipated change in circumstances

does not necessarily result in a violation. For example, a lawyer who has sold the practice to accept an appointment to judicial office does not violate the requirement that the sale be attendant to cessation of practice if the lawyer later resumes private practice upon being defeated in a contested or a retention election for the office or resigns from a judiciary position.

[3] The requirement that the seller cease to engage in the private practice of law does not prohibit employment as a lawyer on the staff of a public agency or a legal services entity that provides legal services to the poor, or as in-house counsel to a business.

[4] The Rule permits a sale of an entire practice attendant upon retirement from the private practice of law within the jurisdiction. Its provisions, therefore, accommodate the lawyer who sells the practice on the occasion of moving to another state. Some states are so large that a move from one locale therein to another is tantamount to leaving the jurisdiction in which the lawyer has engaged in the practice of law. To also accommodate lawyers so situated, states may permit the sale of the practice when the lawyer leaves the geographical area rather than the jurisdiction. The alternative desired should be indicated by selecting one of the two provided for in Rule 1.17(a).

[5] This Rule also permits a lawyer or law firm to sell an area of practice. If an area of practice is sold and the lawyer remains in the active practice of law, the lawyer must cease accepting any matters in the area of practice that has been sold, either as counsel or co-counsel or by assuming joint responsibility for a matter in connection with the division of a fee with another lawyer as would otherwise be permitted by Rule 1.5(e). For example, a lawyer with a substantial number of estate planning matters and a substantial number of probate administration cases may sell the estate planning portion of the practice but remain in the practice of law by concentrating on probate administration; however, that practitioner may not thereafter accept any estate planning matters. Although a lawyer who leaves a jurisdiction or geographical area typically would sell the entire practice, this Rule permits the lawyer to limit the sale to one or more areas of the practice, thereby preserving the lawyer's right to continue practice in the areas of the practice that were not sold.

Sale of Entire Practice or Entire Area of Practice

[6] The Rule requires that the seller's entire practice, or an entire area of practice, be sold. The prohibition against sale of less than an entire practice area protects those clients whose matters are less lucrative and who might find it difficult to secure other counsel if a sale could be limited to substantial fee-generating matters. The purchasers are required to undertake all client matters in the practice or practice area, subject to client consent. This requirement is satisfied, however, even if a purchaser is unable to undertake a particular client matter because of a conflict of interest.

Client Confidences, Consent and Notice

[7] Negotiations between seller and prospective purchaser prior to disclosure of information relating to a specific representation of an identifiable client no more violate the confidentiality provisions of Model Rule 1.6 than do preliminary discussions concerning the possible association of another lawyer or mergers between firms, with respect to which client consent is not required. Providing the purchaser access to client-specific information relating to the representation and to the file, however, requires client consent. The Rule provides that before such information can be disclosed by the seller to the purchaser the client must be given actual written notice of the contemplated sale, including the identity of the purchaser, and must be told that the decision to consent or make other arrangements must be made within 90 days. If nothing is heard from the client within that time, consent to the sale is presumed.

[8] A lawyer or law firm ceasing to practice cannot be required to remain in practice because some clients cannot be given actual notice of the proposed purchase. Since these clients cannot themselves consent to the purchase or direct any other disposition of their files, the Rule requires an order from a court having jurisdiction authorizing their transfer or other disposition. The Court can be expected to determine whether reasonable efforts to locate the client have been exhausted, and whether the absent client's legitimate interests will be served by authorizing the transfer of the file so that the purchaser may continue the representation. Preservation of client confidences requires that the petition for a court order be considered in camera. (A procedure by which such an order can be obtained needs to be established in jurisdictions in which it presently does not exist).

[9] All elements of client autonomy, including the client's absolute right to discharge a lawyer and transfer the representation to another, survive the sale of the practice or area of practice.

Fee Arrangements Between Client and Purchaser

[10] The sale may not be financed by increases in fees charged the clients of the practice. Existing arrangements between the seller and the client as to fees and the scope of the work must be honored by the purchaser.

Other Applicable Ethical Standards

[11] Lawyers participating in the sale of a law practice or a practice area are subject to the ethical standards applicable to involving another lawyer in the representation of a client. These include, for example, the seller's obligation to exercise competence in identifying a purchaser qualified to assume the practice and the purchaser's obligation to undertake the representation competently (see Rule 1.1); the obligation to avoid disqualifying conflicts, and to secure the client's informed consent for those conflicts that can be agreed to

(see Rule 1.7 regarding conflicts and Rule 1.0(e) for the definition of informed consent); and the obligation to protect information relating to the representation (see Rules 1.6 and 1.9).

[12] If approval of the substitution of the purchasing lawyer for the selling lawyer is required by the rules of any tribunal in which a matter is pending, such approval must be obtained before the matter can be included in the sale (see Rule 1.16).

Applicability of the Rule

[13] This Rule applies to the sale of a law practice of a deceased, disabled or disappeared lawyer. Thus, the seller may be represented by a non-lawyer representative not subject to these Rules. Since, however, no lawyer may participate in a sale of a law practice which does not conform to the requirements of this Rule, the representatives of the seller as well as the purchasing lawyer can be expected to see to it that they are met.

[14] Admission to or retirement from a law partnership or professional association, retirement plans and similar arrangements, and a sale of tangible assets of a law practice, do not constitute a sale or purchase governed by this Rule.

[15] This Rule does not apply to the transfers of legal representation between lawyers when such transfers are unrelated to the sale of a practice or an area of practice.

RULE 1.18 DUTIES TO PROSPECTIVE CLIENT

(a) A person who discusses with a lawyer the possibility of forming a client-lawyer relationship with respect to a matter is a prospective client.

(b) Even when no client-lawyer relationship ensues, a lawyer who has had discussions with a prospective client shall not use or reveal information learned in the consultation, except as Rule 1.9 would permit with respect to information of a former client.

(c) A lawyer subject to paragraph (b) shall not represent a client with interests materially adverse to those of a prospective client in the same or a substantially related matter if the lawyer received information from the prospective client that could be significantly harmful to that person in the matter, except as provided in paragraph (d). If a lawyer is disqualified from representation under this paragraph, no lawyer in a firm with which that lawyer is associated may knowingly undertake or continue representation in such a matter, except as provided in paragraph (d).

(d) When the lawyer has received disqualifying information as defined in paragraph (c), representation is permissible if:

(1) **both the affected client and the prospective client have given informed consent, confirmed in writing, or:**

(2) **the lawyer who received the information took reasonable measures to avoid exposure to more disqualifying information than was reasonably necessary to determine whether to represent the prospective client; and**

    (i) **the disqualified lawyer is timely screened from any participation in the matter and is apportioned no part of the fee therefrom; and**

    (ii) **written notice is promptly given to the prospective client.**

Comment

[1] Prospective clients, like clients, may disclose information to a lawyer, place documents or other property in the lawyer's custody, or rely on the lawyer's advice. A lawyer's discussions with a prospective client usually are limited in time and depth and leave both the prospective client and the lawyer free (and sometimes required) to proceed no further. Hence, prospective clients should receive some but not all of the protection afforded clients.

[2] Not all persons who communicate information to a lawyer are entitled to protection under this Rule. A person who communicates information unilaterally to a lawyer, without any reasonable expectation that the lawyer is willing to discuss the possibility of forming a client-lawyer relationship, is not a "prospective client" within the meaning of paragraph (a).

[3] It is often necessary for a prospective client to reveal information to the lawyer during an initial consultation prior to the decision about formation of a client-lawyer relationship. The lawyer often must learn such information to determine whether there is a conflict of interest with an existing client and whether the matter is one that the lawyer is willing to undertake. Paragraph (b) prohibits the lawyer from using or revealing that information, except as permitted by Rule 1.9, even if the client or lawyer decides not to proceed with the representation. The duty exists regardless of how brief the initial conference may be.

[4] In order to avoid acquiring disqualifying information from a prospective client, a lawyer considering whether or not to undertake a new matter should limit the initial interview to only such information as reasonably appears necessary for that purpose. Where the information indicates that a conflict of interest or other reason for non-representation exists, the lawyer should so inform the prospective client or decline the representation. If the prospective client wishes to retain the lawyer, and if consent is possible under Rule 1.7, then consent from all affected present or former clients must be obtained before accepting the representation.

[5] A lawyer may condition conversations with a prospective client on the person's informed consent that no information disclosed during the consultation will prohibit the lawyer from representing a different client in the matter. See Rule 1.0(e) for the definition of informed consent. If the agreement expressly so provides, the prospective client may also consent to the lawyer's subsequent use of information received from the prospective client.

[6] Even in the absence of an agreement, under paragraph (c), the lawyer is not prohibited from representing a client with interests adverse to those of the prospective client in the same or a substantially related matter unless the lawyer has received from the prospective client information that could be significantly harmful if used in the matter.

[7] Under paragraph (c), the prohibition in this Rule is imputed to other lawyers as provided in Rule 1.10, but, under paragraph (d)(1), imputation may be avoided if the lawyer obtains the informed consent, confirmed in writing, of both the prospective and affected clients. In the alternative, imputation may be avoided if the conditions of paragraph (d)(2) are met and all disqualified lawyers are timely screened and written notice is promptly given to the prospective client. See Rule 1.0(k) (requirements for screening procedures). Paragraph (d)(2)(i) does not prohibit the screened lawyer from receiving a salary or partnership share established by prior independent agreement, but that lawyer may not receive compensation directly related to the matter in which the lawyer is disqualified.

[8] Notice, including a general description of the subject matter about which the lawyer was consulted, and of the screening procedures employed, generally should be given as soon as practicable after the need for screening becomes apparent.

[9] For the duty of competence of a lawyer who gives assistance on the merits of a matter to a prospective client, see Rule 1.1. For a lawyer's duties when a prospective client entrusts valuables or papers to the lawyer's care, see Rule 1.15.

RULE 5.3 RESPONSIBILITIES REGARDING NONLAWYER ASSISTANTS

With respect to a nonlawyer employed or retained by or associated with a lawyer:

(a) a partner, and a lawyer who individually or together with other lawyers possesses comparable managerial authority in a law firm shall make reasonable efforts to ensure that the firm has in effect measures giving reasonable assurance that the person's conduct is compatible with the professional obligations of the lawyer;

(b) a lawyer having direct supervisory authority over the nonlawyer shall make reasonable efforts to ensure that the person's conduct is compatible with the professional obligations of the lawyer; and

(c) a lawyer shall be responsible for conduct of such a person that would be a violation of the Rules of Professional Conduct if engaged in by a lawyer if:

(1) the lawyer orders or, with the knowledge of the specific conduct, ratifies the conduct involved; or

(2) the lawyer is a partner or has comparable managerial authority in the law firm in which the person is employed, or has direct supervisory authority over the person, and knows of the conduct at a time when its consequences can be avoided or mitigated but fails to take reasonable remedial action.

Comment

[1] Lawyers generally employ assistants in their practice, including secretaries, investigators, law student interns, and paraprofessionals. Such assistants, whether employees or independent contractors, act for the lawyer in rendition of the lawyer's professional services. A lawyer must give such assistants appropriate instruction and supervision concerning the ethical aspects of their employment, particularly regarding the obligation not to disclose information relating to representation of the client, and should be responsible for their work product. The measures employed in supervising nonlawyers should take account of the fact that they do not have legal training and are not subject to professional discipline.

[2] Paragraph (a) requires lawyers with managerial authority within a law firm to make reasonable efforts to establish internal policies and procedures designed to provide reasonable assurance that nonlawyers in the firm will act in a way compatible with the Rules of Professional Conduct. See Comment [1] to Rule 5.1. Paragraph (b) applies to lawyers who have supervisory authority over the work of a nonlawyer. Paragraph (c) specifies the circumstances in which a lawyer is responsible for conduct of a nonlawyer that would be a violation of the Rules of Professional Conduct if engaged in by a lawyer.

RULE 5.4 PROFESSIONAL INDEPENDENCE OF A LAWYER

(a) A lawyer or law firm shall not share legal fees with a nonlawyer, except that:

(1) an agreement by a lawyer with the lawyer's firm, partner, or associate may provide for the payment of money, over a reasonable period of time after the lawyer's death, to the lawyer's estate or to one or more specified persons;

(2) a lawyer who purchases the practice of a deceased, disabled, or disappeared lawyer may, pursuant to the provisions of Rule 1.17, pay to the estate or other representative of that lawyer the agreed-upon purchase price;

(3) a lawyer or law firm may include nonlawyer employees in a compensation or retirement plan, even though the plan is based in whole or in part on a profit-sharing arrangement; and

(4) a lawyer may share court-awarded legal fees with a nonprofit organization that employed, retained or recommended employment of the lawyer in the matter.

(b) A lawyer shall not form a partnership with a nonlawyer if any of the activities of the partnership consist of the practice of law.

(c) A lawyer shall not permit a person who recommends, employs, or pays the lawyer to render legal services for another to direct or regulate the lawyer's professional judgment in rendering such legal services.

(d) A lawyer shall not practice with or in the form of a professional corporation or association authorized to practice law for a profit, if:

(1) a nonlawyer owns any interest therein, except that a fiduciary representative of the estate of a lawyer may hold the stock or interest of the lawyer for a reasonable time during administration;

(2) a nonlawyer is a corporate director or officer thereof or occupies the position of similar responsibility in any form of association other than a corporation; or

(3) a nonlawyer has the right to direct or control the professional judgment of a lawyer.

Comment

[1] The provisions of this Rule express traditional limitations on sharing fees. These limitations are to protect the lawyer's professional independence of judgment. Where someone other than the client pays the lawyer's fee or salary, or recommends employment of the lawyer, that arrangement does not modify the lawyer's obligation to the client. As stated in paragraph (c), such arrangements should not interfere with the lawyer's professional judgment.

[2] This Rule also expresses traditional limitations on permitting a third party to direct or regulate the lawyer's professional judgment in rendering legal services to another. See also Rule 1.8(f) (lawyer may accept compensa-

tion from a third party as long as there is no interference with the lawyer's independent professional judgment and the client gives informed consent).

RULE 5.5 UNAUTHORIZED PRACTICE OF LAW; MULTIJURISDICTIONAL PRACTICE OF LAW

(a) A lawyer shall not practice law in a jurisdiction in violation of the regulation of the legal profession in that jurisdiction, or assist another in doing so.

(b) A lawyer who is not admitted to practice in this jurisdiction shall not:

    (1) except as authorized by these Rules or other law, establish an office or other systematic and continuous presence in this jurisdiction for the practice of law; or

    (2) hold out to the public or otherwise represent that the lawyer is admitted to practice law in this jurisdiction.

(c) A lawyer admitted in another United States jurisdiction, and not disbarred or suspended from practice in any jurisdiction, may provide legal services on a temporary basis in this jurisdiction that:

    (1) are undertaken in association with a lawyer who is admitted to practice in this jurisdiction and who actively participates in the matter;

    (2) are in or reasonably related to a pending or potential proceeding before a tribunal in this or another jurisdiction, if the lawyer, or a person the lawyer is assisting, is authorized by law or order to appear in such proceeding or reasonably expects to be so authorized;

    (3) are in or reasonably related to a pending or potential arbitration, mediation, or other alternative dispute resolution proceeding in this or another jurisdiction, if the services arise out of or are reasonably related to the lawyer's practice in a jurisdiction in which the lawyer is admitted to practice and are not services for which the forum requires pro hac vice admission; or

    (4) are not within paragraphs (c)(2) or (c)(3) and arise out of or are reasonably related to the lawyer's practice in a jurisdiction in which the lawyer is admitted to practice.

(d) A lawyer admitted in another United States jurisdiction, and not disbarred or suspended from practice in any jurisdiction, may provide legal services in this jurisdiction that:

    (1) are provided to the lawyer's employer or its organizational affiliates and are not services for which the forum requires pro hac vice admission; or

    (2) are services that the lawyer is authorized to provide by federal law or other law of this jurisdiction.

Comment

[1] A lawyer may practice law only in a jurisdiction in which the lawyer is authorized to practice. A lawyer may be admitted to practice law in a jurisdiction on a regular basis or may be authorized by court rule or order or by law to practice for a limited purpose or on a restricted basis. Paragraph (a) applies to unauthorized practice of law by a lawyer, whether through the lawyer's direct action or by the lawyer assisting another person.

[2] The definition of the practice of law is established by law and varies from one jurisdiction to another. Whatever the definition, limiting the practice of law to members of the bar protects the public against rendition of legal services by unqualified persons. This Rule does not prohibit a lawyer from employing the services of paraprofessionals and delegating functions to them, so long as the lawyer supervises the delegated work and retains responsibility for their work. See Rule 5.3.

[3] A lawyer may provide professional advice and instruction to nonlawyers whose employment requires knowledge of the law; for example, claims adjusters, employees of financial or commercial institutions, social workers, accountants and persons employed in government agencies. Lawyers also may assist independent nonlawyers, such as paraprofessionals, who are authorized by the law of a jurisdiction to provide particular law-related services. In addition, a lawyer may counsel nonlawyers who wish to proceed pro se.

[4] Other than as authorized by law or this Rule, a lawyer who is not admitted to practice generally in this jurisdiction violates paragraph (b) if the lawyer establishes an office or other systematic and continuous presence in this jurisdiction for the practice of law. Presence may be systematic and continuous even if the lawyer is not physically present here. Such a lawyer must not hold out to the public or otherwise represent that the lawyer is admitted to practice law in this jurisdiction. See also Rules 7.1(a) and 7.5(b).

[5] There are occasions in which a lawyer admitted to practice in another United States jurisdiction, and not disbarred or suspended from practice in any jurisdiction, may provide legal services on a temporary basis in this jurisdiction under circumstances that do not create an unreasonable risk to the interests of their clients, the public or the courts. Paragraph (c) identifies four such circumstances. The fact that conduct is not so identified does not imply that the conduct is or is not authorized. With the exception of paragraphs (d)(1) and (d)(2), this Rule does not authorize a lawyer to establish an office or other systematic and continuous presence in this jurisdiction without being admitted to practice generally here.

[6] There is no single test to determine whether a lawyer's services are provided on a "temporary basis" in this jurisdiction, and may therefore be

permissible under paragraph (c). Services may be "temporary" even though the lawyer provides services in this jurisdiction on a recurring basis, or for an extended period of time, as when the lawyer is representing a client in a single lengthy negotiation or litigation.

[7] Paragraphs (c) and (d) apply to lawyers who are admitted to practice law in any United States jurisdiction, which includes the District of Columbia and any state, territory or commonwealth of the United States. The word "admitted" in paragraph (c) contemplates that the lawyer is authorized to practice in the jurisdiction in which the lawyer is admitted and excludes a lawyer who while technically admitted is not authorized to practice, because, for example, the lawyer is on inactive status.

[8] Paragraph (c)(1) recognizes that the interests of clients and the public are protected if a lawyer admitted only in another jurisdiction associates with a lawyer licensed to practice in this jurisdiction. For this paragraph to apply, however, the lawyer admitted to practice in this jurisdiction must actively participate in and share responsibility for the representation of the client.

[9] Lawyers not admitted to practice generally in a jurisdiction may be authorized by law or order of a tribunal or an administrative agency to appear before the tribunal or agency. This authority may be granted pursuant to formal rules governing admission pro hac vice or pursuant to informal practice of the tribunal or agency. Under paragraph (c)(2), a lawyer does not violate this Rule when the lawyer appears before a tribunal or agency pursuant to such authority. To the extent that a court rule or other law of this jurisdiction requires a lawyer who is not admitted to practice in this jurisdiction to obtain admission pro hac vice before appearing before a tribunal or administrative agency, this Rule requires the lawyer to obtain that authority.

[10] Paragraph (c)(2) also provides that a lawyer rendering services in this jurisdiction on a temporary basis does not violate this Rule when the lawyer engages in conduct in anticipation of a proceeding or hearing in a jurisdiction in which the lawyer is authorized to practice law or in which the lawyer reasonably expects to be admitted pro hac vice. Examples of such conduct include meetings with the client, interviews of potential witnesses, and the review of documents. Similarly, a lawyer admitted only in another jurisdiction may engage in conduct temporarily in this jurisdiction in connection with pending litigation in another jurisdiction in which the lawyer is or reasonably expects to be authorized to appear, including taking depositions in this jurisdiction.

[11] When a lawyer has been or reasonably expects to be admitted to appear before a court or administrative agency, paragraph (c)(2) also permits conduct by lawyers who are associated with that lawyer in the matter, but who do not expect to appear before the court or administrative agency. For

example, subordinate lawyers may conduct research, review documents, and attend meetings with witnesses in support of the lawyer responsible for the litigation.

[12] Paragraph (c)(3) permits a lawyer admitted to practice law in another jurisdiction to perform services on a temporary basis in this jurisdiction if those services are in or reasonably related to a pending or potential arbitration, mediation, or other alternative dispute resolution proceeding in this or another jurisdiction, if the services arise out of or are reasonably related to the lawyer's practice in a jurisdiction in which the lawyer is admitted to practice. The lawyer, however, must obtain admission pro hac vice in the case of a court-annexed arbitration or mediation or otherwise if court rules or law so require.

[13] Paragraph (c)(4) permits a lawyer admitted in another jurisdiction to provide certain legal services on a temporary basis in this jurisdiction that arise out of or are reasonably related to the lawyer's practice in a jurisdiction in which the lawyer is admitted but are not within paragraphs (c)(2) or (c)(3). These services include both legal services and services that nonlawyers may perform but that are considered the practice of law when performed by lawyers.

[14] Paragraphs (c)(3) and (c)(4) require that the services arise out of or be reasonably related to the lawyer's practice in a jurisdiction in which the lawyer is admitted. A variety of factors evidence such a relationship. The lawyer's client may have been previously represented by the lawyer, or may be resident in or have substantial contacts with the jurisdiction in which the lawyer is admitted. The matter, although involving other jurisdictions, may have a significant connection with that jurisdiction. In other cases, significant aspects of the lawyer's work might be conducted in that jurisdiction or a significant aspect of the matter may involve the law of that jurisdiction. The necessary relationship might arise when the client's activities or the legal issues involve multiple jurisdictions, such as when the officers of a multinational corporation survey potential business sites and seek the services of their lawyer in assessing the relative merits of each. In addition, the services may draw on the lawyer's recognized expertise developed through the regular practice of law on behalf of clients in matters involving a particular body of federal, nationally-uniform, foreign, or international law.

[15] Paragraph (d) identifies two circumstances in which a lawyer who is admitted to practice in another United States jurisdiction, and is not disbarred or suspended from practice in any jurisdiction, may establish an office or other systematic and continuous presence in this jurisdiction for the practice of law as well as provide legal services on a temporary basis. Except as provided in paragraphs (d)(1) and (d)(2), a lawyer who is admitted to practice law in another jurisdiction and who establishes an office or other sys-

tematic or continuous presence in this jurisdiction must become admitted to practice law generally in this jurisdiction.

[16] Paragraph (d)(1) applies to a lawyer who is employed by a client to provide legal services to the client or its organizational affiliates, i.e., entities that control, are controlled by, or are under common control with the employer. This paragraph does not authorize the provision of personal legal services to the employer's officers or employees. The paragraph applies to in-house corporate lawyers, government lawyers and others who are employed to render legal services to the employer. The lawyer's ability to represent the employer outside the jurisdiction in which the lawyer is licensed generally serves the interests of the employer and does not create an unreasonable risk to the client and others because the employer is well situated to assess the lawyer's qualifications and the quality of the lawyer's work.

[17] If an employed lawyer establishes an office or other systematic presence in this jurisdiction for the purpose of rendering legal services to the employer, the lawyer may be subject to registration or other requirements, including assessments for client protection funds and mandatory continuing legal education.

[18] Paragraph (d)(2) recognizes that a lawyer may provide legal services in a jurisdiction in which the lawyer is not licensed when authorized to do so by federal or other law, which includes statute, court rule, executive regulation or judicial precedent.

[19] A lawyer who practices law in this jurisdiction pursuant to paragraphs (c) or (d) or otherwise is subject to the disciplinary authority of this jurisdiction. See Rule 8.5(a).

[20] In some circumstances, a lawyer who practices law in this jurisdiction pursuant to paragraphs (c) or (d) may have to inform the client that the lawyer is not licensed to practice law in this jurisdiction. For example, that may be required when the representation occurs primarily in this jurisdiction and requires knowledge of the law of this jurisdiction. See Rule 1.4(b).

[21] Paragraphs (c) and (d) do not authorize communications advertising legal services to prospective clients in this jurisdiction by lawyers who are admitted to practice in other jurisdictions. Whether and how lawyers may communicate the availability of their services to prospective clients in this jurisdiction is governed by Rules 7.1 to 7.5.

RULE 5.6 RESTRICTIONS ON RIGHT TO PRACTICE

A lawyer shall not participate in offering or making:

(a) a partnership, shareholders, operating, employment, or other similar type of agreement that restricts the right of a lawyer to practice after

termination of the relationship, except an agreement concerning benefits upon retirement; or

(b) an agreement in which a restriction on the lawyer's right to practice is
part of the settlement of a client controversy.

Comment

[1] An agreement restricting the right of lawyers to practice after leaving a
firm not only limits their professional autonomy but also limits the freedom of
clients to choose a lawyer. Paragraph (a) prohibits such agreements except
for restrictions incident to provisions concerning retirement benefits for service with the firm.

[2] Paragraph (b) prohibits a lawyer from agreeing not to represent other
persons in connection with settling a claim on behalf of a client.

[3] This Rule does not apply to prohibit restrictions that may be included
in the terms of the sale of a law practice pursuant to Rule 1.17.

RULE 7.1 COMMUNICATIONS CONCERNING A LAWYER'S SERVICES

A lawyer shall not make a false or misleading communication about the
lawyer or the lawyer's services. A communication is false or misleading if it
contains a material misrepresentation of fact or law, or omits a fact necessary
to make the statement considered as a whole not materially misleading.

Comment

[1] This Rule governs all communications about a lawyer's services, including
advertising permitted by Rule 7.2. Whatever means are used to make known a
lawyer's services, statements about them must be truthful.

[2] Truthful statements that are misleading are also prohibited by this
Rule. A truthful statement is misleading if it omits a fact necessary to make the
lawyer's communication considered as a whole not materially misleading. A
truthful statement is also misleading if there is a substantial likelihood that it
will lead a reasonable person to formulate a specific conclusion about the
lawyer or the lawyer's services for which there is no reasonable factual foundation.

[3] An advertisement that truthfully reports a lawyer's achievements on
behalf of clients or former clients may be misleading if presented so as to lead
a reasonable person to form an unjustified expectation that the same results

could be obtained for other clients in similar matters without reference to the specific factual and legal circumstances of each client's case. Similarly, an unsubstantiated comparison of the lawyer's services or fees with the services or fees of other lawyers may be misleading if presented with such specificity as would lead a reasonable person to conclude that the comparison can be substantiated. The inclusion of an appropriate disclaimer or qualifying language may preclude a finding that a statement is likely to create unjustified expectations or otherwise mislead a prospective client.

[4] See also Rule 8.4(e) for the prohibition against stating or implying an ability to influence improperly a government agency or official or to achieve results by means that violate the Rules of Professional Conduct or other law.

RULE 7.2 ADVERTISING

(a) **Subject to the requirements of Rules 7.1 and 7.3, a lawyer may advertise services through written, recorded or electronic communication, including public media.**
(b) **A lawyer shall not give anything of value to a person for recommending the lawyer's services except that a lawyer may**
   (1) **pay the reasonable costs of advertisements or communications permitted by this Rule;**
   (2) **pay the usual charges of a legal service plan or a not-for-profit or qualified lawyer referral service. A qualified lawyer referral service is a lawyer referral service that has been approved by an appropriate regulatory authority;**
   (3) **pay for a law practice in accordance with Rule 1.17; and**
   (4) **refer clients to another lawyer or a nonlawyer professional pursuant to an agreement not otherwise prohibited under these Rules that provides for the other person to refer clients or customers to the lawyer, if**
      (i) **the reciprocal referral agreement is not exclusive, and**
      (ii) **the client is informed of the existence and nature of the agreement.**
(c) **Any communication made pursuant to this rule shall include the name and office address of at least one lawyer or law firm responsible for its content.**

Comment

[1] To assist the public in obtaining legal services, lawyers should be allowed to make known their services not only through reputation but also through or-

ganized information campaigns in the form of advertising. Advertising involves an active quest for clients, contrary to the tradition that a lawyer should not seek clientele. However, the public's need to know about legal services can be fulfilled in part through advertising. This need is particularly acute in the case of persons of moderate means who have not made extensive use of legal services. The interest in expanding public information about legal services ought to prevail over considerations of tradition. Nevertheless, advertising by lawyers entails the risk of practices that are misleading or over-reaching.

[2] This Rule permits public dissemination of information concerning a lawyer's name or firm name, address and telephone number; the kinds of services the lawyer will undertake; the basis on which the lawyer's fees are determined, including prices for specific services and payment and credit arrangements; a lawyer's foreign language ability; names of references and, with their consent, names of clients regularly represented; and other information that might invite the attention of those seeking legal assistance.

[3] Questions of effectiveness and taste in advertising are matters of speculation and subjective judgment. Some jurisdictions have had extensive prohibitions against television advertising, against advertising going beyond specified facts about a lawyer, or against "undignified" advertising. Television is now one of the most powerful media for getting information to the public, particularly persons of low and moderate income; prohibiting television advertising, therefore, would impede the flow of information about legal services to many sectors of the public. Limiting the information that may be advertised has a similar effect and assumes that the bar can accurately forecast the kind of information that the public would regard as relevant. Similarly, electronic media, such as the Internet, can be an important source of information about legal services, and lawful communication by electronic mail is permitted by this Rule. But see Rule 7.3(a) for the prohibition against the solicitation of a prospective client through a real-time electronic exchange that is not initiated by the prospective client.

[4] Neither this Rule nor Rule 7.3 prohibits communications authorized by law, such as notice to members of a class in class action litigation.

Paying Others to Recommend a Lawyer

[5] Lawyers are not permitted to pay others for channeling professional work. Paragraph (b)(1), however, allows a lawyer to pay for advertising and communications permitted by this Rule, including the costs of print directory listings, on-line directory listings, newspaper ads, television and radio airtime, domain-name registrations, sponsorship fees, banner ads, and group advertising. A lawyer may compensate employees, agents and vendors who are engaged to provide marketing or client-development services, such as publicists, public-relations personnel, business-development staff and website

designers. See Rule 5.3 for the duties of lawyers and law firms with respect to the conduct of nonlawyers who prepare marketing materials for them.

[6] A lawyer may pay the usual charges of a legal service plan or a not-for-profit or qualified lawyer referral service. A legal service plan is a prepaid or group legal service plan or a similar delivery system that assists prospective clients to secure legal representation. A lawyer referral service, on the other hand, is any organization that holds itself out to the public as a lawyer referral service. Such referral services are understood by laypersons to be consumer-oriented organizations that provide unbiased referrals to lawyers with appropriate experience in the subject matter of the representation and afford other client protections, such as complaint procedures or malpractice insurance requirements. Consequently, this Rule only permits a lawyer to pay the usual charges of a not-for-profit or qualified lawyer referral service. A qualified lawyer referral service is one that is approved by an appropriate regulatory authority as affording adequate protections for prospective clients. See, e.g., the American Bar Association's Model Supreme Court Rules Governing Lawyer Referral Services and Model Lawyer Referral and Information Service Quality Assurance Act (requiring that organizations that are identified as lawyer referral services (i) permit the participation of all lawyers who are licensed and eligible to practice in the jurisdiction and who meet reasonable objective eligibility requirements as may be established by the referral service for the protection of prospective clients; (ii) require each participating lawyer to carry reasonably adequate malpractice insurance; (iii) act reasonably to assess client satisfaction and address client complaints; and (iv) do not refer prospective clients to lawyers who own, operate or are employed by the referral service.)

[7] A lawyer who accepts assignments or referrals from a legal service plan or referrals from a lawyer referral service must act reasonably to assure that the activities of the plan or service are compatible with the lawyer's professional obligations. See Rule 5.3. Legal service plans and lawyer referral services may communicate with prospective clients, but such communication must be in conformity with these Rules. Thus, advertising must not be false or misleading, as would be the case if the communications of a group advertising program or a group legal services plan would mislead prospective clients to think that it was a lawyer referral service sponsored by a state agency or bar association. Nor could the lawyer allow in-person, telephonic, or real-time contacts that would violate Rule 7.3.

[8] A lawyer also may agree to refer clients to another lawyer or a non-lawyer professional, in return for the undertaking of that person to refer clients or customers to the lawyer. Such reciprocal referral arrangements must not interfere with the lawyer's professional judgment as to making referrals or as to providing substantive legal services. See Rules 2.1 and 5.4(c).

Except as provided in Rule 1.5(e), a lawyer who receives referrals from a lawyer or nonlawyer professional must not pay anything solely for the referral, but the lawyer does not violate paragraph (b) of this Rule by agreeing to refer clients to the other lawyer or nonlawyer professional, so long as the reciprocal referral agreement is not exclusive and the client is informed of the referral agreement. Conflicts of interest created by such arrangements are governed by Rule 1.7. Reciprocal referral agreements should not be of indefinite duration and should be reviewed periodically to determine whether they comply with these Rules. This Rule does not restrict referrals or divisions of revenues or net income among lawyers within firms comprised of multiple entities.

RULE 7.3 DIRECT CONTACT WITH PROSPECTIVE CLIENTS

(a) A lawyer shall not by in-person, live telephone or real-time electronic contact solicit professional employment from a prospective client when a significant motive for the lawyer's doing so is the lawyer's pecuniary gain, unless the person contacted:
   (1) is a lawyer; or
   (2) has a family, close personal, or prior professional relationship with the lawyer.

(b) A lawyer shall not solicit professional employment from a prospective client by written, recorded or electronic communication or by in-person, telephone or real-time electronic contact even when not otherwise prohibited by paragraph (a), if:
   (1) the prospective client has made known to the lawyer a desire not to be solicited by the lawyer; or
   (2) the solicitation involves coercion, duress or harassment.

(c) Every written, recorded or electronic communication from a lawyer soliciting professional employment from a prospective client known to be in need of legal services in a particular matter shall include the words "Advertising Material" on the outside envelope, if any, and at the beginning and ending of any recorded or electronic communication, unless the recipient of the communication is a person specified in paragraphs (a)(1) or (a)(2).

(d) Notwithstanding the prohibitions in paragraph (a), a lawyer may participate with a prepaid or group legal service plan operated by an organization not owned or directed by the lawyer that uses in-person or telephone contact to solicit memberships or subscriptions for the plan from persons who are not known to need legal services in a particular matter covered by the plan.

Comment

[1] There is a potential for abuse inherent in direct in-person, live telephone or real-time electronic contact by a lawyer with a prospective client known to need legal services. These forms of contact between a lawyer and a prospective client subject the layperson to the private importuning of the trained advocate in a direct interpersonal encounter. The prospective client, who may already feel overwhelmed by the circumstances giving rise to the need for legal services, may find it difficult fully to evaluate all available alternatives with reasoned judgment and appropriate self-interest in the face of the lawyer's presence and insistence upon being retained immediately. The situation is fraught with the possibility of undue influence, intimidation, and overreaching.

[2] This potential for abuse inherent in direct in-person, live telephone or real-time electronic solicitation of prospective clients justifies its prohibition, particularly since lawyer advertising and written and recorded communication permitted under Rule 7.2 offer alternative means of conveying necessary information to those who may be in need of legal services. Advertising and written and recorded communications which may be mailed or autodialed make it possible for a prospective client to be informed about the need for legal services, and about the qualifications of available lawyers and law firms, without subjecting the prospective client to direct in-person, telephone or real-time electronic persuasion that may overwhelm the client's judgment.

[3] The use of general advertising and written, recorded or electronic communications to transmit information from lawyer to prospective client, rather than direct in-person, live telephone or real-time electronic contact, will help to assure that the information flows cleanly as well as freely. The contents of advertisements and communications permitted under Rule 7.2 can be permanently recorded so that they cannot be disputed and may be shared with others who know the lawyer. This potential for informal review is itself likely to help guard against statements and claims that might constitute false and misleading communications, in violation of Rule 7.1. The contents of direct in-person, live telephone or real-time electronic conversations between a lawyer and a prospective client can be disputed and may not be subject to third-party scrutiny. Consequently, they are much more likely to approach (and occasionally cross) the dividing line between accurate representations and those that are false and misleading.

[4] There is far less likelihood that a lawyer would engage in abusive practices against an individual who is a former client, or with whom the lawyer has close personal or family relationship, or in situations in which the lawyer is motivated by considerations other than the lawyer's pecuniary gain.

Nor is there a serious potential for abuse when the person contacted is a lawyer. Consequently, the general prohibition in Rule 7.3(a) and the requirements of Rule 7.3(c) are not applicable in those situations. Also, paragraph (a) is not intended to prohibit a lawyer from participating in constitutionally protected activities of public or charitable legal-service organizations or bona fide political, social, civic, fraternal, employee or trade organizations whose purposes include providing or recommending legal services to its members or beneficiaries.

[5] But even permitted forms of solicitation can be abused. Thus, any solicitation which contains information which is false or misleading within the meaning of Rule 7.1, which involves coercion, duress or harassment within the meaning of Rule 7.3(b)(2), or which involves contact with a prospective client who has made known to the lawyer a desire not to be solicited by the lawyer within the meaning of Rule 7.3(b)(1) is prohibited. Moreover, if after sending a letter or other communication to a client as permitted by Rule 7.2 the lawyer receives no response, any further effort to communicate with the prospective client may violate the provisions of Rule 7.3(b).

[6] This Rule is not intended to prohibit a lawyer from contacting representatives of organizations or groups that may be interested in establishing a group or prepaid legal plan for their members, insureds, beneficiaries or other third parties for the purpose of informing such entities of the availability of and details concerning the plan or arrangement which the lawyer or lawyer's firm is willing to offer. This form of communication is not directed to a prospective client. Rather, it is usually addressed to an individual acting in a fiduciary capacity seeking a supplier of legal services for others who may, if they choose, become prospective clients of the lawyer. Under these circumstances, the activity which the lawyer undertakes in communicating with such representatives and the type of information transmitted to the individual are functionally similar to and serve the same purpose as advertising permitted under Rule 7.2.

[7] The requirement in Rule 7.3(c) that certain communications be marked "Advertising Material" does not apply to communications sent in response to requests of potential clients or their spokespersons or sponsors. General announcements by lawyers, including changes in personnel or office location, do not constitute communications soliciting professional employment from a client known to be in need of legal services within the meaning of this Rule.

[8] Paragraph (d) of this Rule permits a lawyer to participate with an organization which uses personal contact to solicit members for its group or prepaid legal service plan, provided that the personal contact is not undertaken by any lawyer who would be a provider of legal services through the plan. The organization must not be owned by or directed (whether as man-

ager or otherwise) by any lawyer or law firm that participates in the plan. For example, paragraph (d) would not permit a lawyer to create an organization controlled directly or indirectly by the lawyer and use the organization for the in-person or telephone solicitation of legal employment of the lawyer through memberships in the plan or otherwise. The communication permitted by these organizations also must not be directed to a person known to need legal services in a particular matter, but is to be designed to inform potential plan members generally of another means of affordable legal services. Lawyers who participate in a legal service plan must reasonably assure that the plan sponsors are in compliance with Rules 7.1, 7.2 and 7.3(b). See 8.4(a).

RULE 7.4 COMMUNICATION OF FIELDS OF PRACTICE AND SPECIALIZATION

(a) **A lawyer may communicate the fact that the lawyer does or does not practice in particular fields of law.**

(b) **A lawyer admitted to engage in patent practice before the United States Patent and Trademark Office may use the designation "Patent Attorney" or a substantially similar designation.**

(c) **A lawyer engaged in Admiralty practice may use the designation "Admiralty," "Proctor in Admiralty" or a substantially similar designation.**

(d) **A lawyer shall not state or imply that a lawyer is certified as a specialist in a particular field of law, unless:**

 (1) **the lawyer has been certified as a specialist by an organization that has been approved by an appropriate state authority or that has been accredited by the American Bar Association; and**

 (2) **the name of the certifying organization is clearly identified in the communication.**

Comment

[1] Paragraph (a) of this Rule permits a lawyer to indicate areas of practice in communications about the lawyer's services. If a lawyer practices only in certain fields, or will not accept matters except in a specified field or fields, the lawyer is permitted to so indicate. A lawyer is generally permitted to state that the lawyer is a "specialist," practices a "specialty," or "specializes in" particular fields, but such communications are subject to the "false and misleading" standard applied in Rule 7.1 to communications concerning a lawyer's services.

[2] Paragraph (b) recognizes the long-established policy of the Patent and Trademark Office for the designation of lawyers practicing before the Office. Paragraph (c) recognizes that designation of Admiralty practice has a long historical tradition associated with maritime commerce and the federal courts.

[3] Paragraph (d) permits a lawyer to state that the lawyer is certified as a specialist in a field of law if such certification is granted by an organization approved by an appropriate state authority or accredited by the American Bar Association or another organization, such as a state bar association, that has been approved by the state authority to accredit organizations that certify lawyers as specialists. Certification signifies that an objective entity has recognized an advanced degree of knowledge and experience in the specialty area greater than is suggested by general licensure to practice law. Certifying organizations may be expected to apply standards of experience, knowledge and proficiency to insure that a lawyer's recognition as a specialist is meaningful and reliable. In order to insure that consumers can obtain access to useful information about an organization granting certification, the name of the certifying organization must be included in any communication regarding the certification.

About the Editor

K. William Gibson is a lawyer and arbitrator/mediator in Portland, Oregon. For the past fifteen years, he has handled personal injury cases exclusively. He was admitted to the Oregon State Bar in 1979. Mr. Gibson is a Past Chair of the ABA Law Practice Management Section, and presently serves as Chair of the Editorial Board of *Law Practice*  magazine. He also serves on the ABA Standing Committee on Publishing Oversight.

Mr. Gibson is the founder of De Novo Systems Inc., a Vancouver, Washington, software company that publishes De Novo CaseMgr, a case management system for lawyers.

About the Contributors

Edna R.S. Alvarez is retired. She practiced in Los Angeles as a sole practitioner for twenty years, specializing in sophisticated estate planning and estate administration matters. Ms. Alvarez lectured and wrote extensively on estate planning and law practice management. She was a member of the American College of Trust and Estate Counsel. She served on many boards, including the California State Board of Accountancy, the Los Angeles County Bar Association Board of Trustees, and the ABA Law Practice Management Council. Ms. Alvarez was the founder of the Law Practice Management Institute for Solo and Small Practices.

Joel P. Bennett is a sole practitioner in Washington, D.C., where he concentrates on employment law and civil litigation. Before starting his own law practice in 1976, he clerked for a federal district judge in Chicago, worked for the Federal Trade Commission in Washington, and was associated with a small firm in Washington. He is a past chair of the ABA Law Practice Management Section, and cofounder and first chair of the Law Practice Management Section of the District of Columbia Bar. He also served as president of the voluntary Bar Association of the District of Columbia. Mr. Bennett has written many articles and several books, including *How to Start and Build a Law Practice in the District of Columbia*, published by the Bar Association of the District of Columbia. He was the editor of *Flying Solo*, Second Edition.

David J. Bilinsky is the practice management advisor and staff lawyer for the Law Society of British Columbia. He is a Fellow of the College of Law Practice Management, a member of the National Executive for the Law Practice Management and Technology Section for the Canadian Bar Association, the founder and current chair of the Pacific Legal Technology Conference, and a member of the Technology for Lawyers Conference Advisory Board. He is also past chair of the ABA TECHSHOW®. Mr. Bilinsky combines his law, math/computer science, and MBA degrees to focus upon practice management issues emphasizing strategic planning, finance, productivity, and career satisfaction. He is an international lecturer in legal technology and has contributed to several books, including *Barristers & Solicitors in Practice* (Butterworths), *Flying Solo*, Third Edition (ABA), *Law Office Procedures Manual for Solos and Small Firms*, Second Edition (ABA), *Managing Your Law Firm* (CLE-BC), and *Annual Review of Law and Practice* (CLE-BC). He wrote *Amicus Attorney in One Hour for Lawyers* (ABA). He is a contributing author and past member of the editorial advisory board for *Law Technology News* and for *Law Practice* magazine, has written for many other publications, including *Law Office Computing*, *GP-Solo*, and *The National Magazine*, and is a regular columnist for several law association publications.

Larry Bodine is the regional director for North America of the PM Forum, a global association of 3,000 marketers in the law, accounting, consulting, and professional services fields. He is also a marketing and Web site consultant, and has conducted Web site audits for law firms throughout North America. (See **www.LarryBodine.com**.) He can be reached at 630-942-0977 and **lbodine@lawmarketing.com**.

Gisela B. Bradley is director of the Law Office Management Program of the State Bar of Texas. She managed law firms of various sizes for fifteen years, and also owned and managed Management Support Services, Inc. She served on the ABA Law Practice Management Section's special task force on law office management, and also served as vice chair of the Section's Practice Management Advisors' Committee. She is a frequent author and speaker; her publications include *Start-Up Kit for a Small Law Practice* and *Planning to Conquer the Real World of Private Practice* (a practical preparation course for law students). She also developed The Law Office Management Institute, a twelve-month, comprehensive management-training course for lawyers.

Barry L. Brickner is a sole practitioner in Bingham Farms, Michigan. He has been active in the ABA Law Practice Management Section for many years. He has written and edited several articles for Section newsletters, and has spoken about solo practice and law office technology for the ABA, state and local bar organizations, and the Institute for Continuing Legal Education. When he is not practicing law and engaging in bar activities, Mr. Brickner is a city councilman in his hometown of Farmington Hills, Michigan.

Joan R. Bullock is a professor at the Florida A&M University College of Law where she teaches Accounting for Lawyers, Business Organizations, Contracts, Law Office Management, Professional Responsibility, Sales, and Secured Transactions. Prior to her tenure at Florida A&M, Ms. Bullock's academic career also included several years at the University of Toledo College of Law and at Georgia State University College of Law. In addition to her teaching career, she has practiced before the United States Tax Court and has assisted many start-up enterprises, including law firms, with legal, accounting, tax, and general business expertise. Prior to teaching, Ms. Bullock worked as a certified public accountant for the Detroit office of Coopers & Lybrand. There, she practiced in the areas of corporate tax, mergers and acquisitions, and valuation services.

James A. Calloway currently serves as the director of the Oklahoma Bar Association Management Assistance Program. He is an active member of the ABA Law Practice Management Section and the ABA General Practice, Solo and Small Firm Section, where he serves as technology chair. He coauthored *Winning Alternatives to the Billable Hour*, Second Edition (ABA), and has been a featured speaker at several ABA annual meeting programs and the ABA TECHSHOW, as well as other legal technology and legal management conferences. He served as chair of the ABA TECHSHOW in 2005. His articles have been published in *Lawyers Weekly USA*, *Law Practice*, *GPSolo*, and the *Oklahoma Bar Association Journal*.

M. Joe Crosthwait, Jr. is a past president of the Oklahoma Bar Association. He is also a past chair of the ABA Standing Committee on Solo and Small Firm Practitioners; a Fellow of the American Bar Foundation; and a member of the ABA House of Delegates. Mr. Crosthwait was also a member of the Executive Council of the National Conference of Bar Presidents (2001–2004). He also served four years as the president of the Oklahoma City University School of Law Alumni Association. He is currently a member of the ABA Committee on Research into the Future of the Profession (frequently referred to as the Futures Committee). Mr. Crosthwait was also a recipient of the ABA Small Firm Merit Award in 1999.

Demetrios Dimitriou is a San Francisco sole practitioner with a statewide practice acting as counsel to lawyers who are starting, moving, selling, or terminating their practices. He has served on several ethics and practice committees, including service as chair of the Bar Association of San Francisco's Ethics Committee and its Law Practice Management Executive Committee, and chair of a task force on multidisciplinary practice and professionalism, ethics, and competency. Mr. Dimitriou acts as an ethics expert witness, and as counsel to individual lawyers and law firms concerning documentation, attorneys' fees, professional liability, ethics, and internal practice management. He also provides estate planning and general business advice for professionals. Mr. Dimitriou is the author of *Law Office Procedures Manual for Solos and Small Firms*, Third Edition (2005, ABA). He lectures nationally and has written extensively on ethics and law practice management issues, including ethical rules for fees, engagement agreements, and conflicts.

Diane L. Drain graduated from the University of Arizona Law School in 1985. In 1990, she left large-firm practice and established one of the first woman-owned "boutique" firms, marketed as a "referral firm" focusing on real property and bankruptcy. Ms. Drain practices primarily in the areas of creditor and debtor bankruptcy, commercial real estate and development, work-out, foreclosure, and trustee sales. She also established a consulting service to assist lawyers in law office organization, administration, computerization, client development, and staff education. Ms. Drain has served as a faculty member in numerous county, state, and professional seminars regarding office management skills, bankruptcy, and trustee sale/foreclosure actions; she also teaches basic bankruptcy, real property, and legal theory classes at a local professional school. She is a member of the Arizona State Bar Board of Governors and several professional organizations.

Carolyn Elefant is the principal lawyer in her own firm, Law Offices of Carolyn Elefant, and is Of Counsel to the Law Offices of Scott Hempling, a national energy practice. She is also the creator of **www.myshingle.com**, a Web site that serves solo and small-firm lawyers as well as those who yearn to start their own practices. Ms. Elefant holds a BA from Brandeis University and a JD from Cornell Law School.

Diane M. Ellis, MBA, CEAP, has more than twenty years experience in law office management and consulting. She is a frequent speaker and author on issues related to management and technology. She is President of Ellis Management Consulting in Springfield, Missouri, which assists lawyers, particularly those in solo or small firm practices, in making their practices more efficient and satisfying. Before relocating to Missouri, Diane served for ten years as Director of the State Bar of Arizona's Law Office Management Assistance Program. For the last three years of her tenure with the State Bar of Arizona, she also served as Director of the Member Assistance Program. Diane holds a Master of Business Administration degree in Management from Western International University in Phoenix, Arizona, and is a Certified Employee Assistance Professional. She expects to receive a doctorate in Clinical Psychology in October 2007 from Forest Institute of Professional Psychology in Springfield, Missouri.

Daniel B. Evans practices in the areas of estate planning, estate and trust administration, and related tax planning for closely held businesses. He also serves as a consultant to Leimberg & LeClair, Inc., in Bryn Mawr, Pennsylvania, to develop and improve software for lawyers and estate planners. Mr. Evans has written and spoken extensively on estate planning and legal technology. He is on the editorial board and serves as articles editor for *Law Practice* magazine, published by the ABA. He is currently serving as the Probate-Technology editor of *Probate and Property* magazine, also published by the ABA, and is a member of the Office Technology Committee of the Probate Section of the Philadelphia Bar. Mr. Evans is the author of *Wills, Trusts, and Technology: An Estate Lawyer's Guide to Automation*, Second Edition (ABA), *How to Build and Manage an Estates Pracrice* (ABA), and coauthor of *The New Book of Trusts* (Leimberg Associates, Inc.).

Storm Evans is an independent consultant offering automation and management services to small law firms in southeastern Pennsylvania and neighboring states. Her primary goal is to help firms become more effective through better use of computers, support staff, and internal procedures. A graduate of East Texas State University, Ms. Evans has been assisting lawyers in the practice of law since 1976. She was an information systems manager at Fulbright & Jaworski in Houston, was an in-house consultant for Squire, Sanders & Dempsey in Cleveland, and now focuses upon assisting small law firms.

Ms. Evans has been active in the ABA Law Practice Management Section since 1983. She has been on the faculty of many of the ABA's technology programs and has presented continuing legal education programs to bar associations and the Association of Legal Administrators throughout the United States and Canada. She writes the "Product Watch" column for *Law Practice* magazine and serves on its editorial board, is a frequent contributor to other legal publications, and is the author of *Time Matters for Lawyers in One Hour* (ABA).

Mindy G. Farber is a Phi Beta Kappa, summa cum laude graduate of The Johns Hopkins University and a Root-Tilden Scholar graduate of New York University School of Law. She has served as a commissioner on her county's Office of Human Rights and Women's Commission, is a legal advisor to the American Association of University Women and the National Organization for Women, and is a board member of the Center for Labor and Employment Law, for which she lectures annually to federal judges on employment law. Ms. Farber has served on the executive committee of her local bar association, was president of the Women's Bar Association, and was active in the ABA Law Practice Management Section. She is the author of *How to Build and Manage an Employment Law Practice* (ABA), as well as numerous articles on employment law for books and journals, and has also freelanced for the *New York Times* and *Washington Post*.

Jay G Foonberg is a longtime practicing lawyer whose books and articles on law practice management and marketing have been purchased and used by hundreds of thousands of lawyers. He is author of the ABA bestseller *How to Start & Build a Law Firm Practice*, Fifth Edition. Mr. Foonberg is the chair and an executive committee member of the State Bar of California Senior Lawyers and a council member of the ABA Senior Lawyers Division. His advice on representing seniors is based upon his own experiences in his practice as well as the experiences of lawyers throughout the world that he has heard in the many programs and seminars he has led. His seminars on retirement, elder law practice, and teaching computer and e-mail skills to seniors, as well as his practice in helping seniors and their families when there has been financial abuse, also provide much of the "nuts and bolts" and hands-on guidance needed by lawyers new to the field and by those who want a refresher course on the basics of representing seniors. Parts of Mr. Foonberg's writing in this book will be used in his forthcoming work, *Workbook for Closing or Selling a Law Practice*, and in the forthcoming third edition of *How to Get and Keep Good Clients*. All of Mr. Foonberg's works are available from the ABA.

David M. Freedman is a Chicago-based writer, editor, and publishing consultant who specializes in the fields of law, business management, and personal finance (**www.dmfreedman.com**). He is the founder and director of Newsletter Strategy Session (**www.nwsltr.com**), a Web site for publishers of client newsletters. He is also president of Eminent Publishing Company (**www.empub.com**). Mr. Freedman's articles on law firm marketing have appeared in *Law Practice* magazine (ABA), *Strategies* magazine (LMA), and the LawMarketing Portal (**www.lawmarketing.com**).

William D. Henslee is an associate professor of law at Florida A&M University College of Law and a member of the founding faculty, and previously taught at Pepperdine University School of Law. Before joining the faculty at Pepperdine, he represented clients in the music business and was a principal in the firm of Henslee & Weisberger. In addition, he established American Pride Publishing, a music publishing company. He has been a certified contract advisor for the National Football League Players Association since 1994 and has been certified by the Canadian Football League Players Association since 1998. In 1994, Professor Henslee returned to school to further his knowledge of the entertainment business, and in 1996 was awarded an MFA from the University of California at Los Angeles Graduate School of Theatre, Film, and Television. Professor Henslee is currently a member of the ABA Law Practice Management Section's Council and Publishing Board, and is chair of the Section's Education Board. He is also the editor and a contributing writer for the ABA Career Series publications. Professor Henslee is coauthor of three textbooks: *Entertainment Law: Cases and Materials on Film, Television, and Music* (2004), *Cases and Materials in Theater Law* (2004), and *Travel Law* (1997). He is coauthor of *Nonlegal Careers for Lawyers*, Fourth Edition (ABA) and author of *Entertainment Law Careers*, Second Edition.

Robert Blaine Holt is a private practitioner with a unique background in a wide variety of appellate, civil, and administrative arenas. He worked as a briefing lawyer for the criminal jurisdiction arm of the bifurcated Texas Supreme Court, and served as a research and senior staff attorney for the Dallas Court of Appeals. After leaving the public sector for private practice in Texas, Mr. Holt was recognized as America's premier legal authority on the then-emerging topic of AIDS/HIV law. Recognizing the impact the future pandemic could present, he appeared regularly on the *CBS Evening News*, the *McNeill-Leher News Hour*, and other national media outlets. He gave a series of presentations for the University of Florida's Center for Employment Relations and Law, and lectured at various venues regarding the enormity of the legal implications presented by the virus. Mr. Holt later participated in complex criminal appeals in the Colorado public defender system, and also developed a demand and following for interstate transactional association with lawyers trying to reconcile the property systems of Texas and Colorado. Mr. Holt has been an active member of various bar associations and programs, and is a contributor to *Marketing Success Stories*, Second Edition (ABA).

William E. Hornsby, Jr. has served as staff counsel at the ABA since 1988. He has worked with the Standing Committee on Professionalism, the Standing Committee on the Delivery of Legal Services, and the Commission on Advertising. Mr. Hornsby has written and lectured extensively on issues of client development, technology, and ethics. His articles have appeared in the *Georgetown Journal of Legal Ethics*, the *University of Richmond Law Review*, and the *Arizona State University Law Review*. He contributed to *The Lawyer's Guide to Marketing Your Practice*, Second Edition, and authored *Marketing and Legal Ethics*, Third Edition, both published by the ABA. He serves as a chair of the Illinois Attorney Registration and Disciplinary Commission Hearing Panel and is an adjunct faculty member of John Marshall Law School, where he teaches the nation's only course on the professional responsibilities of a technology-based law practice.

Richard M. Howland graduated from Columbia School of Law in 1968 after serving in the U.S. Navy in the Far East. Living most of his life in Amherst, Massachusetts, he was a general practice lawyer there, with a concentration in litigation. He started substitute teaching after retiring in 1998, and works in inner-city Springfield high schools as much as possible. A sports fan, he referees soccer, swimming, diving, and track, and is a master USATF referee for track and field. Mr. Howland travels as much as possible, is an avid gardener and reader, and is hopelessly curious about everything.

Nancy Byerly Jones is a practicing lawyer and certified mediator, and also serves as president of Nancy Byerly Jones & Associates, Inc., a law office management consulting and mediation service firm located in Banner Elk, North Carolina. Her law practice focuses upon preventative law, risk management, and alternative resolutions to litigation. Her primary practice areas include domestic relations, juvenile law, contracts, and equine law. Her consulting firm services include mediation, strategic planning, retreat facilitation, leadership development, employee motivation and training, and career coaching. Ms. Jones is a graduate of the University of North Carolina School of Law, where she was awarded the Henry B. Brandis scholarship. Ms. Jones has served as an adjunct professor of law at Campbell University School of Law, an advisory member of the North Carolina State Bar Ethics Committee, management counsel for the North Carolina State Bar and executive director of its Lawyers' Management Assistance Program, vice president/risk manager of Lawyers Mutual of North Carolina, a member of the ABA Law Practice Management Section's Council, and charter chair of the U.S. and Canadian Practice Management Advisors Task Force. In the High Country area, she serves as board chair of the local legal aid program. Ms. Jones is a nationally recognized speaker and a widely published author on law office management and related topics. She authored *Easy Self-Audits for the Busy Law Office* (ABA), and writes a monthly column for *Lawyer's Weekly USA*. She can be reached at **nancy@nbjlegal.com**.

Thomas E. Kane is a former practicing lawyer and in-house marketer with more than seventeen years of legal marketing experience. He formed Kane Consulting Inc. to assist small firms and sole practitioners with legal marketing. He adheres to the philosophy that small law firms and sole practitioners can be just as effective at marketing their law firms as larger firms. Based in Sarasota, Florida, he can be reached at (941) 376-3366 and **tkane@kanecon sultinginc.com**.

George W. Kaufman is a lawyer and businessperson who has practiced law as an associate, partner, and counsel for more than thirty-five years. He recently served as counsel to the national law firm of Arnold & Porter and as president of a consulting business created by that firm. He has been involved with the Omega Institute for Holistic Studies—the largest retreat and holistic study center in the country—for more than fifteen years. He served as a director of Omega for five years and as chair for three. Since 1994, Mr. Kaufman has delivered programs and lectures on balancing personal life and work responsibilities. His audiences have included lawyers, bar associations, and other groups. Although he continues to practice law part-time, most of his work is now focused upon writing and lecturing. He lives with his wife, Helen, in Saugerties, New York.

Dennis Kennedy is a well-known legal technology expert and computer lawyer in St. Louis, Missouri (**dmk@denniskennedy.com**). He is a member of the ABA Law Practice Management Section's Council, Webzine Board, and TECHSHOW Board. A frequent author and speaker, he was named the 2001 TechnoLawyer of the Year by TechnoLawyer.com for his role in promoting the use of technology in the practice of law. His blog (**www.denniskennedy.com/blog/**) and Web page, Legal Technology Central (**www.denniskennedy.com/legaltechcentral.htm**), are highly regarded resources on technology law and legal technology topics. He is also a cofounder of the Blawg Channel (**www.blawgchannel.com**).

Neal A. Kennedy is an attorney with over eighteen years of experience representing individuals and businesses in a wide range of legal and financial matters. Mr. Kennedy earned his B.B.A. degree, in Finance, from the University of Texas in 1984, and his J.D. degree from Southern Methodist University in 1987. From 1987 until 1998, Mr. Kennedy practiced financial and business law with national law firms based in Houston, New York, Atlanta and Dallas, where he represented a wide range of individual and corporate clients in the real estate, financial, high-tech, oil and gas, publishing, and retail industries. In 1998, Mr. Kennedy left his national law firm practice to open a small town law office in Marble Falls, Texas, serving the legal needs of individuals and businesses throughout the Texas Hill Country. Mr. Kennedy's areas of practice include real estate transactions, business and estate planning, and commercial and real estate litigation.

Rick Klau is VP, Business Development for FeedBurner, a Chicago-based Internet company. A graduate of the University of Richmond School of Law, Rick is a columnist for the ABA's *Law Practice* magazine, coauthor of *The Lawyer's Guide to Marketing on the Internet*, Second Edition (ABA, 2002), and a frequent speaker at technology and marketing conferences around the country. He maintains a weblog about law, technology, and business strategy at **www.rklau.com/tins/**.

Jerry Lawson is a practicing lawyer in Washington, D.C. He is the author of *The Complete Internet Handbook for Lawyers* (ABA) and scores of articles on lawyer use of technology. He operates several Web sites, including Netlawblog (**www.netlawblog.com**) and Fedlawyerguy (**www.fedlawyerguy.org**). He moderates two team Web sites: eLawyering.org (**www.elawyering.org**) and the Interagency Ethics Counsel Journal (**www.iecjournal.org**).

Susan G. Manch is a principal in the consulting firm of Shannon & Manch, LLP, where her practice focuses upon the design, development, review, and implementation of lawyer management systems for law firms, corporations, the federal government, and other legal employers. She has trained lawyers and legal administrators in mentoring, management, communication, leadership, and strategic planning. A regular contributor to major legal publications, Ms. Manch is also a frequent speaker for law firms and organizations such as the ABA, the National Association for Law Placement, and the Women's Bar Association. She is the author of *Partner & Practice Group Acquisition: A Primer on Management & Administrative Practices* (National Association for Law Placement, 2004) and coauthor of *Recruiting Lawyers: How to Hire the Best Talent* (ABA).

David L. Masters is a small-firm, small-town general practitioner in western Colorado, whose practice focuses upon transactions and litigation. He writes and speaks frequently on the use of information technology in the practice of law. Outside the practice of law, he loves to climb mountains. Mr. Masters is the author of *The Lawyer's Guide to Adobe Acrobat*, Second Edition (ABA), as well as a new chapter on electronic briefs for the *Colorado Appellate Practice Guide 5d, Continuing Legal Education in Colorado, Inc.* (publication scheduled for January 2005). He attended the University of Montana School of Law and obtained his JD in 1986. His professional affiliations include the ABA (Law Practice Management Section and General Practice, Solo, and Small Firm Section), the Colorado Bar Association, *The Colorado Lawyer* board of editors (1999–2004), West Publishing CD-ROM advisory board (1995), the National Institute for Trial Advocacy, Rocky Mountain Region, faculty (2001–present), and Mesa State College, Montrose Campus, adjunct faculty (1992–present).

Paul McLaughlin spent the first fifteen years of his career as a solo/small-firm lawyer in Ontario and Alberta. During that time he practiced in eight different settings, including two solo start-ups. He then became a practice management advisor and was able to offer the benefit of his experience to other lawyers in transition. He is the author of *Welcome to Reality: A New Lawyer's Guide to Success*, as well as numerous articles. He has presented at seminars and conferences throughout Canada and the United States, as well as in China, Ukraine, and Palestine. After thirteen years with the Law Society of Alberta, Mr.

McLaughlin returned to private practice in 2004 when he and his son, Andrew, established Turning Point Law, a wills and estates/professional responsibility boutique (**www.turningpointlaw.ca**). He continues to offer career coaching and transition counseling. He can be reached at **pmclaughlin@turningpoint law.ca**.

Gary A. Munneke is a professor of law at Pace University School of Law, in White Plains, New York, where he teaches courses in law practice management, torts, and professional responsibility. He currently serves as a delegate to the ABA House of Delegates, after previously serving as chair of the ABA Law Practice Management Section. He is the author of numerous books and articles about current issues in the legal profession including *The Essential Formbook: Comprehensive Management Tools for Lawyers, Volumes I–IV* (ABA). A 1973 graduate of the University of Texas School of Law, Professor Munneke is a member of the Texas and Pennsylvania bars, and is a Fellow of the American Bar Foundation and the College of Law Practice Management.

Linda Oligschlaeger is the membership services director at the Missour Bar. Ms. Oligschlaeger assists Missouri Bar members with law practice management needs by providing telephone consultations, information, and educational opportunities. She is responsible for the development and oversight of the Missouri Bar's award-winning Solo and Small Firm Conference. She is also the administrator of the Missouri Bar's Fee Dispute Resolution and Complaint Resolution Programs. Additionally, she oversees the development and operation of MoVar Net, a statewide subscription service for Missouri lawyers. Ms. Oligschlaeger develops member benefits and services programs for the Missouri Bar, and she was responsible for the development of the Missouri Bar's Mentoring Program. Ms. Oligschlaeger received her bachelor's degree in business administration from Columbia College, where she graduated with honors.

Terri Olson is the owner of Olson Legal Consulting, a Tallahassee-based firm specializing in management and technology assistance for law firms. She also founded and directed the Law Practice Management Program of the Georgia bar and worked as an analyst for the Law Office Management Assistance Program of the Florida bar. She is the author of numerous articles on law office accounting, organization, general management, and technology issues, as well as a frequent speaker on these topics. She can be contacted at **olsonlegal@ comcast.net**.

Theodore P. Orenstein graduated from the University of Texas School of Law in 1967. After spending two years in the U.S. Army, he began practicing law in Massachusetts in 1970. He has always had a general practice, but also began specializing in matrimonial law in 1978. He was chair of the Massachusetts Bar

Association Young Lawyers Section and its Law Practice Section, as well as a member of the Massachusetts Bar Association Board of Delegates and Executive Committee. He also served on the Council of the ABA Law Practice Management Section, the Council of the Massachusetts Bar Association Family Law Section, and the Board of Managers of the Massachusetts Chapter of the American Academy of Matrimonial Lawyers. He was appointed by the Supreme Judicial Court of Massachusetts to its Advisory Committee on Legal Education, and by Lawyers Alert to its Board of Experts. Mr. Orenstein has published articles in a number of legal periodicals and has lectured extensively throughout the United States. In 1974, he created the "How to Start and Run a Successful Law Practice" course for the Massachusetts Bar Association, and he taught it for twenty-four years. In 1978, he created "The Traveling Workshop of Law Practice Management," and with it traveled to county and local bar associations, introducing the concepts of itemized billing, timekeeping, the use of paralegals, and other facets of law practice management to small-firm lawyers throughout Massachusetts.

James J. Orlow received a BS with honors from the University of Pennsylvania in 1956, and JD from Harvard University in 1959. He is a member of the Philadelphia Bar Association, having served as chair of the Committee on Specialization in 1976. He also served as chair of the American Bar Association's Committee on Immigration and Nationality, Section of Administrative Law, from 1970–1973, and as chair of the Committee on Competence for the ABA Law Practice Management Section from 1982–1984. He was president of the American Immigration Lawyers Association from 1974–1975, and has served as its director since 1975.

Catherine Pennington Paunov is a lawyer, technology consultant, and former law librarian. Her firm, Pennington Consulting, provides services to law firms, corporate law departments, law schools, and businesses. She has been active in the ABA Law Practice Management Section since passing the bar in 1981. She has served on its Council and as chair of its Library Committee. She also authored a book and edited two others for the Section.

J. R. Phelps has served the members of The Florida Bar as director of the Law Office Management Assistance Service for the past twenty-five years. He was the first practice advisor in the United States affiliated with a bar association. As a practice management advisor, Mr. Phelps assists individuals and law firms in improving performance skills competency through individualized education, coaching, and consulting. He is an active member of the ABA Law Practice Management Section and a Fellow of the College of Law Practice Management.

Daniel E. Pinnington received a joint LLB/JD degree from the Universities of Windsor and Detroit in 1991. He practiced for seven years in the litigation department of a Niagara Falls law firm, and also held the position of manager of information systems at his firm. He is currently director of practicePRO at the Lawyers' Professional Indemnity Company (LawPRO), the malpractice carrier for 20,000 Ontario lawyers. PracticePRO provides lawyers with tools and resources for avoiding malpractice claims. He is well known in legal technology circles, and writes articles on risk management and technology issues for various publications. Mr. Pinnington is a regular presenter at continuing legal education programs and conferences. He actively participates in a variety of law-related organizations, including the Ontario Bar Association, where he has served as chair of the Technology Committee, executive for the Solo, Small Firm and General Practice Section, and chair of the Law Practice Management Section. He is currently chair of the Canadian Bar Association Law Practice Management and Technology Section, and is active in the ABA Law Practice Management Section, serving as a coeditor of the *Law Practice Today* Webzine and as an ABA TECHSHOW board member.

Edward Poll is a nationally recognized lawyer coach and law firm management consultant, helping lawyers increase revenues and improve profitability. He is an author, workshop leader, and keynote speaker. Mr. Poll focuses upon law firm management, financial analysis and cash-flow improvement, and practice development. He is the author of several books, including *Collecting Your Fee: Getting Paid from Intake to Invoice* (ABA), *Attorney and Law Firm Guide to the Business of Law*, Second Edition (ABA), *Secrets of the Business of Law: Successful Practices to Increase Your Profits!*, and *The Profitable Law Office Handbook: Attorney's Guide to Successful Business Planning*. He is also the creator and publisher of the monthly series Law Practice Management Review: The Audio Magazine for Busy Attorneys (see **www.lawbiz.com** and **www.lawbizblog.com**).

Kerry Randall is the founder of the marketing firm *the lawyer marketing guy* (**www.lawyermarketingguy.com**). He is the author of *Effective Yellow Pages Advertising for Lawyers* (ABA). With nearly thirty years of marketing experience, he has created thousands of Yellow Pages ads, direct-mail campaigns, print ads, billboards, and television commercials for lawyers. His marketing clients have also included more than one hundred companies listed in the Fortune 500.

Linda J. Ravdin is a shareholder in Pasternak & Fidis, P.C., a thirteen-lawyer firm in Bethesda, Maryland. She is a member of the Maryland, District of Columbia, and Virginia bars, and practices divorce and family law exclusively. Previously, for twenty-eight years, she practiced as a solo or in her own small firm. She graduated from George Washington University Law School in 1974. Ms. Ravdin has been an active member of the ABA Law Practice Management Section since 1986, and has participated in planning or as a speaker in many continuing legal education programs for the Section. She is a past chair of the Law Practice Management Publishing Board, and is a Fellow of the College of Law Practice Management.

Mark A. Robertson is a partner in the law firm of Robertson & Williams in Oklahoma City. His practice focuses upon representing businesses and the families who own them, and corporate and securities law. Mr. Robertson is currently chair of the ABA Law Practice Management Section, and a Fellow of the College of Law Practice Management. He is a frequent lecturer on small and midsize law firm marketing and management issues, and has written on law firm management topics in various national, state, and local bar association publications. He is the coauthor of *Winning Alternatives to the Billable Hour*, Second Edition (ABA).

RJon Robins practices with the bankruptcy and creditors' rights group at Kluger, Peretz, Kaplan & Berlin in Miami, where he focuses upon helping the owners and shareholders of private and publicly traded companies restructure and otherwise preserve their equity. At the time Mr. Robins made his original contribution to *Flying Solo*, he was a practice management advisor with The Florida Bar's Law Office Management Assistance Service, and had the unique opportunity to work with hundreds of lawyers in the development and execution of their marketing and overall business plans, including law firm start-up issues. Mr. Robins began his legal career as a sole practitioner, helping the owners of businesses protect and enhance their equity ownership positions. Before he could accomplish this, however, he had to address many of the issues addressed in his chapter in this book.

Diana M. Savit practices civil litigation, emphasizing resolving business disputes. She also handles employment and educational issues. She is admitted to practice in Maryland and the District of Columbia. She earned her J.D. with honors from George Washington University Law School in 1976 and was one of the first women to earn a BA (cum laude) from Princeton University, in 1973.

After graduating from law school, Ms. Savit worked for the U.S. Customs Service as a general attorney and for the Office of the Corporation Counsel, D.C., as a trial lawyer. She entered private practice in 1985. Although never a solo practitioner, her status as the only litigator in a larger firm for most of her private practice career graphically taught her the perils and pleasures of going it alone.

Ms. Savit currently practices law in Bethesda, Maryland, with her husband, Marvin Szymkowicz, at Bowytz Savit Szymkowicz, LLP. They have three children, none of whom plans to be a lawyer.

Jon S. Schultz is a professor of law at the University of Houston, a law library expert, and a registered builder. A former senior associate dean for information technology and for libraries at the University of Houston Law Center, he served as chair of the committee to develop the ABA's standards for law school libraries. A prolific author, he has joined Suzette S. Schultz to produce the forthcoming edition of *The Complete Guide to Designing Your Law Office* for the ABA. As a consultant, Professor Schultz provides advice on buildings and disaster planning to law firm, court, and academic libraries.

Suzette S. Schultz is president of Interior Space Design, Inc. (ISD), a firm specializing in law firm design throughout the United States and abroad. Her credits include personally designing more than four million square feet of law firm space, as well as a broad portfolio of corporate executive offices. An honors graduate of the University of Houston, she consults on all aspects of law firm building, including work letter negotiation, design of facilities, and project management. ISD's offices are located on Galveston Island, Texas.

Carol A. Seelig uses her twenty years of private practice experience to help lawyers improve the efficiency of their offices and enhance the skills they need to increase their client bases. She is a member of the ABA Practice Management Advisors Committee, a contributing editor to several ABA publications on law practice management, and a member of the ABA Law Practice Management Section's Publishing Board. In addition, she teaches "How to Start a New Business" at New York University School of Continuing Professional Education. When in private practice, Ms. Seelig focused upon hedge funds, derivative financial products, and other financial services regulatory issues. She graduated cum laude from Suffolk University Law School, and is a member of four bars: Illinois, Maine, Minnesota, and New York.

Marcia Pennington Shannon is a principal in the consulting firm of Shannon & Manch, LLP, which specializes in lawyer management issues, including mentoring, recruiting, coaching, and career transition counseling. Ms. Shannon is the former assistant director of career services at Georgetown University Law Center. She holds degrees from Emory University and the University of Cincinnati. She is a member of the ABA Law Practice Management Section, the International Coach Federation, and the National Career Development Association. In addition to coauthoring the ABA book, *Recruiting Lawyers*, she also writes the award-winning "Managing" column for *Law Practice* magazine.

Lynda C. Shely, of The Shely Firm, PC, provides ethics and risk management advice to lawyers and serves as an expert witness on professional responsibility and fee issues. Before opening her own firm, she was the director of lawyer ethics for the State Bar of Arizona for ten years, where she provided ethics advice, presented continuing legal education ethics courses, and served as counsel to the Ethics Committee, Fee Arbitration Program, Client Protection Fund Board, Unauthorized Practice of Law Department, and Peer Review Committee. She is a past chair and member of the ABA Standing Committee on Client Protection, a member of the ABA Standing Committee on Professionalism, and a Fellow of the American Bar Foundation. She served as a member of the State Bar of Arizona's Ethical Rules Review Group that proposed the 2003 revisions to the ethical rules. She currently serves on the state bar's Professionalism Task Force and UPL Advisory Opinion Committee. Ms. Shely received her JD degree from The Catholic University, and was previously an intellectual property associate with Morgan, Lewis & Bockius in Washington, D.C.

Jerry R. Sullenberger is a Practice Management Advisor with The Florida Bar's Law Office Management Assistance Service (LOMAS). Mr. Sullenberger has over twenty-four years of experience as a law firm administrator, corporate manager, technical consultant and trainer. He assists attorneys with all aspects of office and practice management in law firms, corporate legal departments and government law offices. Before joining LOMAS, Mr. Sullenberger was president of On Point Training, Inc., a computer consulting and training company. He is a Certified Technical Trainer, Microsoft Certified System Engineer and a Certified Novell Engineer. Mr. Sullenberger worked as a legal administrator in Florida for more than seven years. In addition, he was an operations manager in a Fortune 500 corporation and a general manager in a smaller organization, after more than twelve years as an active-duty Army officer. He has a BSJm degree from the University of Florida.

Ross A. Sussman, who used to telecommute from a sailboat on Lake Michigan, is now starting his practice all over again because he has been mentoring a very bright lawyer who has blossomed into his associate. He has been practicing estate and business planning law in Minneapolis, Minnesota, for quite some time. Mr. Sussman and his wife enjoy European traveling and almost have a second home in Portugal. He has four grandchildren and the requisite number of children to produce the same. He is now working on "When I Die, Part II," and hopes to equal Rambo in the number of sequels.

Natalie R. Thornwell is the director of the State Bar of Georgia Law Practice Management Program, which provides extensive practice management and technology consulting to bar members. Ms. Thornwell attended law school at the University of Miami and Georgia State University. She is an adjunct professor at John Marshall Law School, teaching law office management. She actively participates in the ABA Law Practice Management Section, where she is a member of the Practice Management Advisors Committee. She has served on the publishing board of the Law Practice Management Section and the ABA TECHSHOW board. She is also on the editorial board of the General Practice, Solo and Small Firm Section's *GPSolo Technology and Practice Guide*. Ms. Thornwell holds membership in the National Bar Association, the National Association of Legal Administrators, and the National Association of Bar Executives. She is a certified consultant and trainer for ABACUS, Amicus Attorney, PCLaw, Practice Master, TABS3, TimeMatters, BillingMatters, and Timeslips software applications. Ms. Thornwell is a frequent writer and presenter on practice management and legal technology topics. She resides in Atlanta, Georgia, with her daughter, Roschelle Jasmyn, and her fiancé, Charles.

Reid F. Trautz is the director of the District of Columbia Bar Lawyer Practice Assistance Program. He provides confidential practice management information and business consulting services to lawyers, to help them enhance their practices and the delivery of legal services to their clients. Before creating the D.C. bar program, Mr. Trautz practiced law for nine years with a five-lawyer firm in Alexandria, Virginia. He is a nationally known speaker on practice management issues, including attorney-client communications, marketing and client development, law office technology, financial management, risk management, and starting a law practice. He is the author of numerous practice management articles and publications, including "The Fine Art of Getting Paid" (ABA, 2002), "Ten Financial Mistakes Small Firms Make" (ABA, 2003), and "Managing the Risks of Solo Practice" (ABA, 2003). He is also active in the ABA, currently serving as chair of the Law Practice Management Section Publishing Board. He is a member of the District of Columbia, Minnesota, and Virginia bars.

Gilda R. Turitz has been practicing commercial litigation since 1980 in San Francisco, California. She concentrates her practice in complex commercial transactional matters and alternative dispute resolution, serving as a neutral mediator, early neutral evaluator, and arbitrator in litigation matters. She coheads the litigation department of the twenty-five-lawyer firm, Sideman & Bancroft, LLP, and was named a "Super Lawyer" in Northern California for 2004. Before joining the firm in 1998, Ms. Turitz was the head of litigation at the San Francisco office of Graham & James, LLP. She was cochair of the ABA Law Practice Management Section's Women Rainmakers group from 1992 through 1996, and was awarded the Golden Hammer Award for her efforts in shattering the glass ceiling. Ms. Turitz has also been active in local bar associations, and frequently lectures and writes on rainmaking, mentoring, and work-life balance issues. She has served on several boards of directors of nonprofit organizations, including those involved in civil rights and promotion of women professionals.

Index

The Lawyer's Guide to Marketing Your Practice, Second Edition
Edited by James A. Durham and Deborah McMurray
This book is packed with practical ideas, innovative strategies, useful checklists, and sample marketing and action plans to help you implement a successful, multi-faceted, and profit-enhancing marketing plan for your firm. Organized into four sections, this illuminating resource covers: Developing Your Approach; Enhancing Your Image; Implementing Marketing Strategies; and Maintaining Your Program. Appendix materials include an instructive primer on market research to inform you on research methodologies that support the marketing of legal services. The accompanying CD-ROM contains a wealth of checklists, plans, and other sample reports, questionnaires, and templates—all designed to make implementing your marketing strategy as easy as possible!

Through the Client's Eyes: New Approaches to Get Clients to Hire You Again and Again, Second Edition
By Henry W. Ewalt
This edition covers every aspect of the lawyer-client relationship, giving sound advice and fresh ideas on how to develop and maintain excellent client relationships. Author and seasoned practitioner Henry Ewalt shares tips on building relationships and trust, uncovering some unlikely ways to make connections in addition to traditional methods. Marketing techniques including brochures, newsletters, client dinners, and sporting events are discussed. Other topics that are covered include client intake, client meetings, follow-up, dissemination of news, fee setting and collection, and other client issues.

The Lawyer's Guide to Creating Persuasive Computer Presentations, Second Edition
By Ann Brenden and John Goodhue
This book explains the advantages of computer presentation resources, how to use them, what they can do, and the legal issues involved in their use. You'll learn how to use computer presentations in the courtroom, during opening statements, direct examination, cross examination, closing arguments, appellate arguments and more. This revised second edition has been updated to include new chapters on hardware and software that is currently being used for digital displays, and all-new sections that walk the reader through beginning skills, and some advanced PowerPoint® techniques. Also included is a CD-ROM containing on-screen tutorials illustrating techniques such as animating text, insertion and configuration of text and images, and a full sample PowerPoint final argument complete with audio, and much more.

The Lawyer's Guide to Strategic Planning: Defining, Setting, and Achieving Your Firm's Goals
By Thomas C. Grella and Michael L. Hudkins
This practice-building resource can be your guide to planning dynamic strategic plans and implementing them at your firm. You'll learn about the strategic planning process and how to establish goals in key planning areas such as law firm governance, competition, opening a new office, financial management, technology, marketing and competitive intelligence, client development and retention, and more. The accompanying CD-ROM contains a wealth of sample plans, policies, and statements, as well as numerous questionnaires. If you're serious about improving the way your firm works, increasing productivity, making better decisions, and setting your firm on the right course, this book is the resource you need.

Collecting Your Fee: Getting Paid from Intake to Invoice
By Edward Poll
This practical and user-friendly guide provides you with proven strategies and sound advice that will make the process of collecting your fees simpler, easier, and more effective! This handy resource provides you with the framework around which to structure your collection efforts. You'll learn how you can streamline your billing and collection process by hiring the appropriate staff and drafting a bill that the client is motivated to pay. In addition, you'll benefit from the strategies to use when the client fails to pay the bill on time and what you need to do to get paid when all else fails. Also included is a CD-ROM with sample forms, letters, agreements, and more for you to customize to your own practice needs.

Marketing Success Stories: Conversations with Leading Lawyers
Edited by Hollis Hatfield Weishar and Joyce K. Smiley
This practice-building resource is an insightful collection of anecdotes on successful and creative marketing techniques used by lawyers and marketing professionals in a variety of practice settings. These stories of marketing strategies that paid off will inspire you to greater heights. You'll gain an inside look at how successful lawyers market themselves, their practice specialties and their firms. In addition to dozens of first-hand accounts of success stories from practitioners, you'll find advice from in-house counsel and others who give candid feedback on how strategic marketing influences their decision to hire a specific firm. Learn how to make new contacts, gain more repeat business, increase your visibility within the community, and learn many other action steps with this worthwhile addition to your law firm's marketing library.

30-Day Risk-Free Order Form
Call Today! 1-800-285-2221
Monday–Friday, 7:30 AM – 5:30 PM, Central Time

Qty	Title	LPM Price	Regular Price	Total
_____	Collecting Your Fee: Getting Paid From Intake to Invoice (5110490)	$ 69.95	$ 79.95	$_____
_____	The Essential Formbook, Volume I (5110424V1)	169.95	199.95	$_____
_____	The Essential Formbook, Volume II (5110424V2)	169.95	199.95	$_____
_____	The Essential Formbook, Volume III (5110424V3)	169.95	199.95	$_____
_____	The Essential Formbook, Volume IV (5110424V4)	169.95	199.95	$_____
_____	How to Start and Build a Law Practice, Platinum Fifth Edition (5110508)	57.95	69.95	$_____
_____	Law Office Procedures Manual for Solos and Small Firms, Third Edition (5110522)	69.95	79.95	$_____
_____	The Lawyer's Guide to Creating Persuasive Computer Presentations, Second Edition (5110530)	79.95	99.95	$_____
_____	The Lawyer's Guide to Fact Finding on the Internet, Second Edition (5110497)	69.95	79.95	$_____
_____	The Lawyer's Guide to Marketing Your Practice, Second Edition (5110500)	79.95	89.95	$_____
_____	The Lawyer's Guide to Marketing on the Internet, Second Edition (5110484)	69.95	79.95	$_____
_____	The Lawyer's Guide to Strategic Planning (5110520)	59.95	79.95	$_____
_____	Marketing Success Stories, Second Edition (5110511)	64.95	74.95	$_____
_____	Through the Client's Eyes, Second Edition (5110480)	69.95	79.95	$_____
_____	Winning Alternatives to the Billable Hour, Second Edition (5110483)	129.95	149.95	$_____

*Postage and Handling	
$10.00 to $24.99	$5.95
$25.00 to $49.99	$9.95
$50.00 to $99.99	$12.95
$100.00 to $349.99	$17.95
$350 to $499.99	$24.95

**Tax
DC residents add 5.75%
IL residents add 8.75%
MD residents add 5%

*Postage and Handling $_____
**Tax $_____
TOTAL $_____

PAYMENT

❏ Check enclosed (to the ABA)

❏ Visa ❏ MasterCard ❏ American Express

_____
Account Number   Exp. Date   Signature

Name _____ Firm _____
Address _____
City _____ State _____ Zip _____
Phone Number _____ E-Mail Address _____

Note: E-Mail address is required if ordering the
The Lawyer's Guide to Fact Finding on the Internet
E-mail Newsletter (5110498)

Guarantee

If—for any reason—you are not satisfied with your purchase, you may
return it within 30 days of receipt for a complete refund of the price of the
book(s). No questions asked!

Mail: ABA Publication Orders, P.O. Box 10892, Chicago, Illinois 60610-0892
♦ **Phone: 1-800-285-2221** ♦ **FAX: 312-988-5568**

E-Mail: abasvcctr@abanet.org ♦ **Internet: http://www.lawpractice.org/catalog**